The Stirling / South Caro[lina]

General Editors: Douglas S. Mack and Gillian Hughes

Reviews

Chastity, carnality, carnage and carnivorousness are among his favourite subjects, and dance together in his writings to the music of a divided life. [...] The later eighteenth century was a time when [Scotland] had taken to producing writers and thinkers of world consequence. One of these–though long disregarded as such, long unimaginable as such–was Hogg.

(Karl Miller, *TLS*)

Simple congratulations are in order at the outset, to the editors and publisher of these first three handsome volumes of the projected *Collected Works* of James Hogg. It has taken a long time for Hogg to be recognised as one of the most notable Scottish writers, and it can fairly be said that the process of getting him into full and clear focus is still far from complete. That process is immeasurably helped by the provision of proper and unbowdlerised texts (in many cases for the first time), and in this the ongoing *Collected Works* will be a milestone. [...] There can be little doubt that in the prose and verse of these three volumes we have an author of unique interest, force, and originality.

(Edwin Morgan, *Scottish Literary Journal*)

Edinburgh University Press are also to be praised for the elegant presentation of the books. It is wonderful that at last we are going to have a collected edition of this important author without bowdlerisation or linguistic interference. [...] The stories [of *Tales of the Wars of Montrose*] are certainly entertaining and their history is described by the editor Gillian Hughes who has also provided notes, a glossary, an introduction, and guidance on the historical period. These books of Hogg have been wonderfully presented and edited. Hogg's own idiosyncratic style has been left untouched.

(Iain Crichton Smith, *Studies in Scottish Literature*)

A quiet revolution in Scottish literary studies has been going on over the past 10 years. The Stirling/South Carolina research edition of the collected works of James Hogg has been steadily forcing a reassessment of one of our best-known but least-read authors. **(James Robertson, *The Herald*)**

Reviews of the Stirling / South Carolina Edition
(on *The Queen's Wake*)

[Hogg in *The Queen's Wake*] found himself able to create and inhabit a variety of voices, and to load these voices with all kinds of social, political and historical significance. Published in 1813, it successfully re-launched Hogg's literary career. [...] It extends our understanding of the complexity of Hogg as man and writer, and broadens our view of the diversity of literary voices in an age which was, undoubtedly, a golden one for Scottish letters.

(James Robertson, *The Herald*)

The decision to reprint the two editions of the poem [*The Queen's Wake*] is fully justified. As the introduction notes, it reflects a recent acceptance of the 'irreducible plurality of texts' (p. lxxviii, quoting Paul Werstine) which manifested itself, for example, in the Oxford Shakespeare's 1986 'landmark decision to publish two versions of *King Lear*' (p. lxxviii). Not only does it give us two interestingly different forms of the poem, 'Hogg's edgy and challenging original version [...] and his carefully revised and polished final version' (p. lxxviii), but it also allows us to assess the poem against the two quite different contexts in which it first appeared: in early 1813, pre-Waterloo, and then reworked in post-Waterloo days in 1819. Furthermore, we have both the poem as Hogg originally conceived it, in a form hitherto only available to the small group of readers who have access to a copy of the first edition, and also in the form which provided the basis for almost all the editions (including the widely disseminated *Poetical Works* published in 1838–40) which were read from the later part of Hogg's life through to the early twentieth century at the time when its reputation was so high. [...] The introduction is a model of what an introduction should be, elucidating the text for modern readers but enabling us to understand what it might have meant to its early readers as well. [...] The introduction is followed by O'Halloran's excellent essay [...] which further extends our understanding of the poem.

(Graham Tulloch, *Studies in Hogg and his World*)

JAMES HOGG

The Queen's Wake
A Legendary Tale

Edited by
Douglas S. Mack

With an Essay on the Illustrations by Meiko O'Halloran
a Glossary by Janette Currie
and a Chronology by Gillian Hughes

EDINBURGH UNIVERSITY PRESS
2005

© Edinburgh University Press, 2005

Edinburgh University Press
22 George Square
Edinburgh
EH8 9LF

Typeset at the University of Stirling
Printed and bound in England by MPG Books Ltd, Bodmin, Cornwall

ISBN 0 7486 2088 5

The publisher acknowledges support from

 Scottish
Arts Council

towards the publication of this volume

Hogg Rediscovered
A New Edition of a Major Writer

This book forms part of a series of paperback reprints of selected volumes from the Stirling / South Carolina Research Edition of the Collected Works of James Hogg (S/SC Edition). Published by Edinburgh University Press, the S/SC Edition (when completed) will run to some thirty-four volumes. The existence of this large-scale international scholarly project is a confirmation of the current consensus that James Hogg (1770–1835) is one of Scotland's major writers.

The high regard in which Hogg is now held is a comparatively recent development. In his own lifetime, he was regarded as one of the leading writers of the day, but the nature of his fame was influenced by the fact that, as a young man, he had been a self-educated shepherd. The second edition (1813) of his long poem *The Queen's Wake* contains an 'Advertisement' which begins as follows.

> The Publisher having been favoured with letters from gentlemen in various parts of the United Kingdom respecting the Author of the *Queen's Wake*, and most of them expressing doubts of his being a Scotch Shepherd; he takes this opportunity of assuring the Public, that *The Queen's Wake* is really and truly the production of *James Hogg*, a common shepherd, bred among the mountains of Ettrick Forest, who went to service when only seven years of age; and since that period has never received any education whatever.

This 'Advertisement' is redolent of a class prejudice also reflected in the various early reviews of *The Private Memoirs and Confessions of a Justified Sinner*, the book by which Hogg is now best known. This novel appeared anonymously in 1824, but many of the early reviews identify Hogg as the author, and see the *Justified Sinner* as presenting 'an incongruous mixture of the strongest powers with the strongest absurdities'. The Scotch Shepherd was regarded as a man of powerful and original talent, but it was felt that his lack of education caused his work to be marred by frequent failures in discretion, in expression, and in knowledge of the world. Worst of all was Hogg's lack of what was called 'delicacy', a failing which caused him to deal in his writings with subjects (such as prostitution) that were felt to be unsuitable for mention in polite literature. Hogg was regarded by these reviewers, and by his contemporaries in general, as a man of undoubted genius, but his genius was felt to be seriously flawed.

A posthumous collected edition of Hogg was published in the late 1830s. As was perhaps natural in all the circumstances, the publishers (Blackie & Son of Glasgow) took pains to smooth away what they took to be the rough edges of Hogg's writing, and to remove his numerous 'indelicacies'. This process was taken even further in the 1860s, when the Rev. Thomas Thomson prepared a revised edition of Hogg's *Works* for publication by Blackie. These Blackie editions present a bland and lifeless version of Hogg's writings. It was in this version that Hogg was read by the Victorians, and, unsurprisingly, he came to be regarded as a minor figure, of no great importance or interest. Indeed, by the first half of the twentieth century Hogg's reputation had dwindled to such an extent that he was widely dismissed as a vain, talent-free, and oafish peasant.

Nevertheless, the latter part of the twentieth century saw a substantial revival of Hogg's reputation. This revival was sparked by the republication in 1947 of an unbowdlerised edition of the *Justified Sinner*, with an enthusiastic Introduction by André Gide. During the second half of the twentieth century Hogg's rehabilitation continued, thanks to the republication of some of his texts in new editions. This process entered a new phase when the first three volumes of the S/SC Edition appeared in 1995, and the S/SC Edition as it proceeds is revealing a hitherto unsuspected range and depth in Hogg's achievement. It is no longer possible to regard him as a one-book wonder.

Some of the books that are being published in the S/SC Edition had been out of print for more than a century and a half, while others, still less fortunate, had never been published at all in their original, unbowdlerised condition. Hogg is now being revealed as a major writer whose true stature was not recognised in his own lifetime because his social origins led to his being smothered in genteel condescension; and whose true stature has not been recognised since, because of a lack of adequate editions. The poet Douglas Dunn wrote of Hogg in the *Glasgow Herald* in September 1988: 'I can't help but think that in almost any other country of Europe a complete, modern edition of a comparable author would have been available long ago'. The Stirling / South Carolina Research Edition of James Hogg, from which the present paperback is reprinted, seeks to fill the gap identified by Douglas Dunn.

Douglas S. Mack

General Editors' Acknowledgements

We are grateful for the support of the University of Stirling and the University of South Carolina, and for assistance from the Association for Scottish Literary Studies and the James Hogg Society. We also record with gratitude the fact that the substantial contributions of Dr Gillian Hughes and Dr Janette Currie to the present volume (see Volume Editor's Acknowledgements) were made possible by a major research grant awarded by the United Kingdom's Arts and Humanities Research Board to the Stirling/South Carolina Edition of James Hogg.

Volume Editor's Acknowledgements

My interest in *The Queen's Wake* began forty years ago, in the early 1960s, and this edition is the fruit of an interest that has continued unabated ever since. The debts incurred in a long-term project of this kind are numerous and complex, but I should like to give particular thanks to my colleague Gillian Hughes, who has been an extremely helpful General Editor for this volume, which she has strengthened in numerous ways, not least through her AHRB-funded work on her forthcoming edition of Hogg's letters. Particular thanks are also due to Meiko O'Halloran for assistance of various kinds, and especially for her valuable essay on the illustrations to *The Queen's Wake*; and to Janette Currie, whose numerous contributions to the volume have included the preparation of the Glossary. Additionally, I have been indebted for help and advice of various kinds to many people, among whom especial thanks are due to J. H. Alexander, Peter Garside, Suzanne Gilbert, Richard Jackson, and Wilma Mack. As with previous volumes, Patrick Scott and his team of helpers at the University of South Carolina have made a most valuable contribution, in particular with the tracing of reviews, and with collations.

Gordon Willis and Helen Beardsley of Stirling University LIbrary have once again been most helpful and efficient, and particular thanks are also due to Mike Kelly of the Fales Library & Special Collections, New York University; to William H. Loos of the Grosvenor Rare Book Room of the Buffalo & Erie County Public Library; and to Vera Ryhazlo of the Bodleian Library, Oxford University.

I am grateful to the Fales Library & Special Collections, New York University for permission to quote from manuscript material in their

viii

collections. Similar thanks are due to the John Murray Archive; to the Buffalo & Erie County Public Library, Buffalo, New York; and (once again) to the Trustees of the National Library of Scotland. I am also grateful to the Bodleian Library and to Stirling University Library for permission to reproduce illustrations from books held in their collections.

Douglas S. Mack
University of Stirling

Contents

The Queen's Wake (1813)

The Queen's Wake (1819)

Introduction

1. Contexts: Hogg and his World in 1812–13

In the 1821 version of 'Memoir of the Author's Life', Hogg gives a revealing account of his feelings when the first edition of *The Queen's Wake* was published in late January 1813. He writes:

> As I said, nobody had seen the work; and, on the day after it was published, I came up to Edinburgh as anxious as a man could be. I walked sometimes about the streets, and read the title of my book on the booksellers' windows, yet I durst not go into any of the shops. I was like a man between death and life, waiting for the sentence of the jury. The first encouragement that I got, was from my countryman, Mr William Dunlop, spirit merchant, who, on observing me going sauntering up the plainstones of the High Street, came over from the Cross, arm in arm with another gentleman, a stranger to me. I remember his salutation, word for word; and singular as it was, it had a strong impression; for I knew that Mr Dunlop had a great deal of rough common sense.
>
> "Ye useless poetical b—h that ye're!" said he, "what hae ye been doing a' this time?"–"What doing, Willie! what do you mean?"–"D—n your stupid head, ye hae been pestering us wi' fourpenny papers an' daft shilly-shally sangs, an' bletherin' an' speakin' i' the forum, an' yet had stuff in ye to produce a thing like this."–"Ay, Willie," said I; "have you seen my new beuk?"–"Ay; that I have, man; and it has lickit me out o' a night's sleep. Ye hae hit the right nail on the head now. Yon's the very thing, sir."–"I'm very glad to hear you say sae, Willie; but what do ye ken about poems?"–"Never ye mind how I ken; I gi'e you my word for it, yon's the thing that will do. If ye hadna made a fool o' yoursel' afore, man, yon wad hae sold better than ever a book sold. Od, wha wad hae thought there was as muckle in that sheep's-head o' yours! d—d stupid poetical b—h that ye're!" And with that he went away, laughing and miscalling me over his shoulder.
>
> This address gave me a little confidence, and I faced my acquaintances one by one; and every thing that I heard was laudatory. The first report of any work that goes abroad, be it

good or bad, spreads like fire set to a hill of heather in a warm spring day, and no one knows where it will stop. From that day forward every one has spoken well of the work; and every review praised its general features, save the Eclectic, which, in the number for 1813, tried to hold it up to ridicule and contempt.[1]

The Queen's Wake was a project of crucial importance for its author, who in January 1813 was much in need of a success to retrieve his fortunes. Born in 1770, Hogg had grown up in the remote and mountainous sheep-farming district of Ettrick Forest in the Scottish Borders, where his family on his mother's side were noted bearers of the district's rich oral tradition. His father, a tenant-farmer and sheep-dealer, became bankrupt around 1776, and the family's resulting destitution brought Hogg's formal education to a very early end. The rest of his childhood was spent in poverty and real hardship, earning his keep on various local farms by herding cows. The 1807 version of the 'Memoir of the Author's Life' gives a picture of his formative years as a cow-herd that is both vivid and surprisingly lacking in bitterness.

Thus terminated my education: – After this I was never another day at any school whatever; and was again, that very spring, sent away to my old occupation of herding cows. This employment, the worst and lowest known in our country, I was engaged in for several years under sundry masters, till at length I got into the more honourable one of herding sheep. [...] From some of my masters I received very hard usage; in particular, while with one shepherd, I was often nearly exhausted by hunger and fatigue. All this while, I neither read nor wrote, nor had I access to any books, saving the Bible. I was greatly taken with our version of the Psalms of David, learned the most of them by heart, and have a great partiality for them unto this day. Every little pittance that I earned of wages, was carried directly to my parents, who supplied me with what cloaths I had. These were often scarcely worthy of the appellation; in particular, I remember of being exceedingly scarce of shirts. Time after time I had but two; which grew often so bad, that I was obliged to quit wearing them altogether; for, when I put them on, they hung down in long tatters as far as my heels. At these times I certainly made a very grotesque figure; for, on quitting the shirt, I could never induce my breeches to keep up to their proper sphere. When fourteen years of age, I saved five shillings of my wages, with which I bought an old violin. This occupied all my leisure hours, and hath been my favourite amusement ever since.[2]

This musical young Scottish sansculotte eventually got access to books in his late teens when working as a shepherd in Ettrick Forest, and from that point onwards he read voraciously. Strongly enthusiastic about literature, he began to gain a local reputation in Ettrick as a poet and song-writer.

When Walter Scott was collecting traditional ballads for his *Minstrelsy of the Scottish Border* (1802–03), Hogg was able to provide him with several texts from the repertoire of members of his mother's family. Through this connection a friendship developed between Scott and Hogg, and in February 1807, thanks to Scott's encouragement, the leading Edinburgh publisher Archibald Constable brought out *The Mountain Bard*, a collection of modern ballads and songs by Hogg. Scott was a lawyer and the son of a lawyer, a man of the professions rather than an aristocrat. Nevertheless, he moved comfortably in aristocratic circles. For example, he was for many years on warmly friendly terms with Charles William Henry Scott, fourth Duke of Buccleuch, and this friendship lasted until the duke's death in 1819. Furthermore, Scott was destined to become a baronet himself, after a campaign in which various people (notably William Adam of Blair Adam) lobbied energetically on his behalf.[3] The offer of the baronetcy was made in 1818 by the Prince Regent (later George IV), and in due course Scott became Sir Walter Scott of Abbotsford.

The friendship between Scott and Hogg was sincere on both sides, but the two men tended to see that friendship in different ways. From the beginning Scott was aware of the social gulf between the gentleman and the farm labourer, and saw their relationship as that of patron and client. Hogg, for his part, was animated by more democratic and egalitarian principles: while he enthusiastically admired Scott's writings and was grateful for Scott's interest and patronage, he nevertheless aspired to a friendship in which the two men could meet on equal terms, as brother poets.[4]

It is clear from many passages in Hogg's writings that recognition as a poet was deeply important to him. In particular, he yearned to be seen as a worthy successor to that other Scottish poet and farm labourer, Robert Burns (1759–96). In his 'Memoir of the Author's Life', Hogg writes:

I remember in the year 1812, the year before the publication of the "Queen's Wake," that I told my friend, the Rev. James

Nicol, that I had an inward consciousness that I should yet live to be compared with Burns; and though I might never equal him in some things, I thought I might excel him in others. He reprobated the idea, and thought the assumption so audacious, that he told it as a bitter jest against me in a party that same evening. But the rest seeing me mortified, there was not one joined in the laugh against me, and Mr. John Grieve replied in these words, which I will never forget, "After what he has done, there is no man can say *what* he may do."[5]

John Grieve, a friend of Hogg's Ettrick youth and an enthusiast about poetry, had established himself by the early 1810s as a prosperous Edinburgh hatter. We shall hear of him again in the story of the development of *The Queen's Wake*.

When *The Mountain Bard* was published in 1807 it achieved a modest commercial success, and the proceeds helped to fund an attempt by Hogg to establish himself as a farmer in Dumfriesshire in south-west Scotland. Perhaps a desire to model himself on Burns played a part in Hogg's choice of Dumfriesshire for this venture: Burns had been a Dumfriesshire farmer (at Ellisland) from 1788 until 1791, before moving to Dumfries itself in his final years (1791–96) to work as an exciseman.

Hogg lived in Dumfriesshire, first as a hired shepherd and later as a farmer, from 1805 until 1809. During these years he made various lasting friendships, for example with the stonemason poet Allan Cunningham (1784–1842), who as a boy had walked in Burns's funeral procession in 1796. Furthermore, in his book-length *Memoir of Burns*, Hogg records that in 1804, during his own Dumfriesshire years, he 'was accustomed to sit in the seat next to' Burns's widow 'in the old church of Dumfries'. Hogg also remarks 'I think Mrs Burns had been pretty', and continues:

> though always a brunette, she was then smartly dressed, had fine eyes, and looked very well. She had several wooers at that time, according to report. Some seven or eight years afterwards, I had a chance of a few weeks of intimate and daily acquaintance with her in Edinburgh, and scarcely ever met a woman, either high or low, who improved as much on acquaintance. She had a great deal of good sense and good nature.[6]

This later acquaintance with Mrs Burns took place when she was staying with Hogg's future brother-in-law James Gray, who had been a close friend of Burns when the poet lived in Dumfries.

Unfortunately, Hogg's Dumfriesshire farming project did not thrive. He got into escalating financial difficulties, his behaviour became increasingly reckless, and in the autumn of 1809 he absconded, leaving unpaid debts behind him. In addition (and here it is perhaps possible to sense again the influence of Burns as a role model) he left behind a pregnant lover (Margaret Beattie), and an illegitimate daughter, Catherine Hogg, the child of Catherine Henderson.[7]

Returning to Ettrick after his Dumfriesshire fiasco, Hogg found that he was regarded as disgraced, and unemployable in his old occupation as a shepherd. By now about forty years old, he set out for Edinburgh in February 1810 to attempt to establish himself there as a professional writer. *The Forest Minstrel*, a collection of songs by himself and by some of his friends, was published by Archibald Constable in August 1810, but this attempt to repeat the success of *The Mountain Bard* made little impact: William Dunlop's verdict of 'daft shilly-shally sangs' (see the quotation from Hogg's 'Memoir of the Author's Life' at the beginning of this Introduction) was not untypical. Hogg's next project was *The Spy*, a fourpenny weekly periodical that made its first appearance on 1 September 1810, and ran until 24 August 1811. At this stage of his life Hogg also played a prominent part in 'The Forum', an Edinburgh debating society that attracted large paying audiences to its regular public meetings.[8]

In the early 1810s Edinburgh was an intellectual and literary centre of world importance. For example, the *Edinburgh Review*, the Whig periodical edited by Francis Jeffrey and published by Archibald Constable, was at the height of its influence and prestige. Similarly, the huge popularity of *The Lady of the Lake* (1810) had served to enhance Scott's already great fame as a poet. Through his friendship with Scott, Hogg had links with the world of the literary superstars of Edinburgh's intellectual and social elite. However, the failed Dumfriesshire farmer's life in the early 1810s was centred on a different Edinburgh, an Edinburgh with which he was in lively contact through *The Spy* and the Forum. Susan Manning discusses this other Edinburgh in a review of Gillian Hughes's Stirling / South Carolina edition of *The Spy*:

> It was surely a good decision to present the work entire, including not only Hogg's contributions but those of John Ballantyne, James Gray and his wife Mary, Thomas Gillespie, John Black and others. The editor's meticulous notes not only supply attributions of authorship for every article, based on collated annotations from the range of surviving copies, but a

series of invaluable 'Notes on Contributors' which (perhaps better than anything else currently available) gives a sense of Hogg's immediate literary milieu. This is of considerable interest both for the information that enables us to reconstruct the conditions of *The Spy*'s original production and because it fleshes out a fascinating, dense alternative if not counter culture flourishing in early nineteenth-century Edinburgh. This is not a world of lairds, lawyers and aristocrats, the visible face of Scotland's official literary landscape in the Regency period, where Scott, Jeffrey, Mackenzie and Wilson were the legislators and Hogg would always, as an outsider, be an easy target. Here instead are professionals: printers, schoolteachers, physicians, working farmers. And also women, not only as subjects of adoration or satire, but also as authors, contributors in their own right to social debate. *The Spy* stands at an interestingly oblique angle to the 'official' milieu that it not-quite-completely claims to represent to itself. [...] *The Spy* is not only an adumbration of Hogg's mature themes; it is a treasure trove of voice, of genre, and of social information which should have an essential place in any cultural history of Scotland.[9]

The alternative Edinburgh world of *The Spy* and the Forum included talented people of progressive, and even radical, views. For example, one of Hogg's Forum friends was Dr Andrew Duncan (1744–1824), who had visited Robert Fergusson (1750–74) in Edinburgh's City Bedlam during that remarkable poet's last days. Shocked by this experience, Dr Duncan began to campaign for the reform of the treatment of the mentally ill in the city, and his efforts eventually bore fruit with the opening of the new Edinburgh Asylum in 1813.[10] Likewise, one of the notable contributors to *The Spy* was Hogg's friend and future brother-in-law James Gray (1770–1830), who in the early 1810s was classics master of the Edinburgh High School. In his *Memoir of Burns*, Hogg records that 'Mr Gray, the friend of Burns, was master of the High-school of Dumfries all the time that Burns was there, saw much of him, and was greatly attached to him'. Hogg also records that Gray was 'a violent democrate', who often spoke with enthusiasm about Burns's '*glorious* political principles'.[11] Gray's progressive and passionately-held views are clearly visible in his contributions to *The Spy*, for example when he engages in a forceful attack on the slave trade in the number for 10 November 1810.[12]

Burns's circle in Dumfries was notably radical. In a review article that discusses the 2001 Canongate *Complete Poems and Songs of Robert Burns* edited by Andrew Noble and Patrick Scott Hogg, Robert Crawford writes as follows about the significance of this period of Burns's life:

> The other reason that the *Canongate Burns* is so important is the thoroughgoing way it argues the case for Burns as a radical Scottish republican. As the editors contend, this interpretation depends less on the newly collected pieces than on a careful reading of those poems which are already part of Burns's canon. Though Kinsley's remains the best text of those works, Noble and Hogg show how the conservative Kinsley went out of his way to play down Burns's political radicalism. Burns, after all, was a man whose friends in Dumfries included William Maxwell, who had been a member of the guard at the execution of the French King and Queen, was execrated by a dagger-wielding Burke in the House of Commons, and was branded Britain's most dangerous Jacobin by London's *Sun* newspaper.[13]

Recent research, notably that of Gillian Hughes, has greatly deepened our understanding of the circles in which Hogg moved in the early 1810s, and it is now clear that the political views of some members of these circles had a distinctly radical tinge. This research has provided a new insight that has been, in some ways, a surprising one. *Blackwood's Edinburgh Magazine* was a leading Tory periodical, and the strong (albeit troubled) links Hogg forged with *Blackwood's* in his later years are well known. These links, together with Hogg's valued (albeit troubled) friendships with leading Tories such as Walter Scott and John Wilson, have given strength to the straightforward traditional view that Hogg was himself a Tory. No doubt, in some senses and in some ways, he was. For example, it is clear that he placed a high value on the traditional culture of his native Ettrick community, and he does not seem to have rejoiced in change for the sake of change. Such attitudes emerge, for example, in Hogg's short story 'On the Separate Existence of the Soul' (1831), in which the young Laird of Gillian Brae sets about to reform his newly-inherited estate. However, as Hogg's narrator puts it,

> every earthly thing, good or evil, wears to an end. CHANGE! CHANGE! is legibly engraven on every earthly object, that he who runs may read. The good old laird died, and then indeed there *was* a change on the estate of Gillian Brae! The small farmers were all turned adrift; down went their houses, and

up went granaries, barns, and thrashing-mills. Marshes were to drain, hedges to raise, manures to frame, and a hundred grand new plans of aggrandisement all going on at once.

Hogg writes: 'The small farmers were all turned adrift'. Clearly there is a hint here of the traumatic evictions of the Highland Clearances of the 1810s and 1820s and of the parallel upheavals that Edward J. Cowan has aptly described as the 'Lowland clearances',[14] but in writing these words Hogg's thoughts must also have turned to the traumas of his childhood, when his own family were 'turned adrift' following his father's bankruptcy. At all events, in Hogg's story, the narrator's sympathies seem to lie not with the modernising young laird but with the old shepherd Robin Robson, who

> steadily upheld the propriety of keeping by old-established customs, and of improving these leisurely and prudently; but deprecated all rash theories of throwing the experience of ages aside as useless and unprofitable lumber, as if the world were void of common sense and discernment, till it brought forth the present generation, the most enlightened of whom, in his own estimation, was the young laird of Gillian Brae.[15]

Clearly, a turn of mind that is broadly conservative can be sensed lying behind 'On the Separate Existence of the Soul', and it would be difficult to see the older Hogg, who wrote this story in the 1830s, as an out-and-out political revolutionary. In this context it may be worth remembering that Wordsworth's political views had become much more conservative by the 1830s than they had been during that writer's radical youth in the 1790s. Nevertheless, it would be difficult to see Hogg at any stage of his career as anything other than a man of strongly-held egalitarian views. Such views emerge (for example) in the opening pages of another Hogg text of the 1830s, his manuscript 'Anecdotes of Sir W. Scott':

> The only blemish or perhaps I should say foible that I ever discerned in my illustrious friend's character was a too high devotion for titled rank. This in him was mixed with an enthusiasm which I cannot describe amounting in some cases almost to adoration if not servility. This was to me the strangest disposition imaginable! For me who never could learn to discern any distinction in ranks save what was constituted by talents or moral worth. [...]
>
> However to return to our amiable Baronet's aristocratic feelings I shall give a few instances of these. Although of course

he acknowledged Buccleuch as the head and chief of the whole Clan of Scott yet he always acknowledged Harden as his immediate chief or chieftain of that particular and most powerful sept of Scotts. And Sir Walter was wont often to relate how he and his father before him and his grandfather before that always kept their Christmass with Harden in acknowledgement of their vassallage. This he used to tell with a degree of exultation which I thought must has [sic] been astounding to every one who heard it as if his illustrious name did not throw a blaze of glory on the house of Harden even a hundred times more than the descent from that hardy and valiant house could through [sic] upon him. It was no matter what people thought no body could eradicate those feelings from his mind.[16]

In short, recent research has shown that Hogg, as well as being in the 1820s a prominent member of the group of Tory writers associated with *Blackwood's Edinburgh Magazine*, was also a man who, when he was writing *The Queen's Wake* in the early 1810s, operated on terms of relaxed and comfortable friendship with the much more radical group associated with *The Spy*. The traditional and easy pigeonhole of '*Blackwood's* Tory' can no longer be safely regarded as an adequate account of the full range and complexity of Hogg's political sympathies.

At all events, *The Spy* ceased publication in August 1811. It had always been a precarious venture by a literary outsider, but its ultimate failure, however predictable, must have been a grievous disappointment for Hogg: it must have seemed as if his attempt to become an Edinburgh man of letters was going the same way as his attempt to become a Dumfriesshire farmer. Nevertheless, Hogg continued to be active in the affairs of the Forum after the demise of *The Spy*, and it appears from his 'Memoir of the Author's Life' that around this period he reviewed John Wilson's *Isle of Palms* (1812) and various other poems 'in a Scottish Review then going on in Edinburgh'.[17] As David Groves has shown, the 'Scottish Review' in question was probably a little-known periodical

published by the bookseller Peter Hill, and printed by D. Schaw and Son, Lawnmarket. It began its precarious life in March 1811 as *The Edinburgh Quarterly Magazine and Review*. In the subsequent issues of June, September, and December, the title was reversed to read *The Edinburgh Quarterly Review and Magazine*. The long number for March 1812 is entitled *The Edinburgh Quarterly Review*, and has 'vol. II' on the title page.

Evidently the next number appeared in September 1812, under the new banner of *Scotish* [*sic*] *Review*, and with 'vol. II' on the title page.[18]

David Groves points out that the March 1812 number of this periodical contains a lengthy article (presumably by Hogg) on Wilson's *The Isle of Palms*. Furthermore the March 1812 number also indicates that Hogg's next major literary effort, *The Queen's Wake*, was beginning to take shape, as it announces that 'Mr. Hogg the "Etterick Shepherd," is preparing for publication a Legendary Tale called the "Queen's Wake," in ten cantos'. In its September 1812 number, this periodical (by now called *The Scotish Review*) informs its readers that 'Mr. Hogg the Etterick Shepherd, has made considerable progress with his Queen's Wake, in ten cantos;—it will be published in the spring'.[19]

As is well known, 1812 was a momentous year for Europe, a year in which the Napoleonic Wars began to move towards their final phase. During the earlier part of the year, the French Emperor had been in a strong position, but Napoleon's cause received a setback when Wellington's victory over the French at Salamanca opened the way for the Allies to enter Madrid on 12 August 1812. In late October the tide of the Peninsular War temporarily turned again when lack of success in besieging Burgos forced Wellington to begin a retreat to Portugal under heavy pressure from the French. However, still more momentous events were taking place further north. Napoleon's invasion of Russia began in June 1812, and his appallingly costly victory at the Battle of Borodino on 7 September 1812 seemed to open the way for a conquest of Russia that would have still further strengthened the French Emperor's dominance of Europe. However, by the time Hogg's poem was published in late January 1813, retreat from Moscow in the depths of the Russian winter had devastated Napoleon's army, thus preparing the way for the French Emperor's defeat and exile to Elba in 1814.

In the first decade of the nineteenth century there had been recurring and lively fears that Napoleon was about to lead an invasion of Britain. Unsurprisingly in these circumstances, in 1812 there was a long-standing tendency in Scotland, as in other parts of Britain, to demonise Napoleon as the nation's enemy, as a man about to bring the devastations and atrocities of war to a peaceful country. Nevertheless, in some circles in Britain there was a willingness to sympathise with Napoleon as a ruler who could be seen as the heir of the egalitarian principles of the French Revolution. Napoleon's willingness to clear the path to advancement for talented people from all classes of society had distinct and obvious attractions for those who disliked the restrictions and injustices imposed by the rigid class structures of early-nineteenth-century Britain. An incident that is revealing in this context took place in the west of Scotland in 1815, when thousands of 'democrats' celebrated Napoleon's return to France from exile in Elba by gathering at Drumclog, scene of a memorable victory by Scottish Covenanters who had taken up arms in 1679 to assert the rights and freedoms of the people against the claims of what they regarded as despotic royal authority.[20]

Like most working-class Lowland Scots of his generation, Hogg had an inherited and instinctive sympathy with the Covenanters. It is therefore not particularly surprising to find that (like Burns, Wordsworth, and many others) he seems to have been in sympathy with the principles and aims of the French Revolution of 1789, especially in the Revolution's early years. John MacQueen has argued persuasively that such feelings can be glimpsed in Hogg's account, in 'Storms' (1819), of a 'literary society' of young Ettrick shepherds that had been active in the early 1790s. Hogg was a member of this society, and MacQueen (after pointing to the links, at that time, between freemasonry and radical politics) writes as follows about the account in 'Storms' of a meeting of Hogg's 'literary society' in January 1794, at the time of a great snow-storm:

> In the Scotland of 1794, a more or less secret meeting of young agricultural labourers probably included several freemasons in its number; equally probably, the agenda included the forbidden subject of radical politics and the need for reform, if not revolution. Hogg had himself prepared a "flaming bombastical essay" for the meeting, and had his "tongue trained to many wise and profound remarks". The phrases are vague, but in 1819 (the year of Peterloo) when the article was first published, it was probably wiser to be no more specific.[21]

Revolutionary change was very much in the air during the months leading up to the meeting of these young agricultural labourers in Ettrick in January 1794. In France in September 1792 the National Convention took forward the revolutionary project by abolishing the monarchy and establishing a republic. In the period that followed, internal opposition to the new republican regime was broken by the Reign of Terror. Among very many other victims of the guillotine, Louis XVI was executed in January 1793, and his widow, Marie Antoinette, was executed in October 1793. As 1793 advanced, the French revolutionary government was raising an army of more than 1,000,000 men, an army that was to win major victories over France's external enemies during the spring and summer of 1794. In January 1794 the foundations of Europe's old order were manifestly being shaken—but, as we shall see, the British elite was ready, willing, and able to mount a ferocious and effective defence of the status quo.

In 1793 and 1794, Hogg and Scott were both in their early twenties. In his monumental nine-volume *Life of Napoleon Buonaparte*, published in 1827, a much older Scott looks back to 1793–94 and describes the response in Britain to what he calls the French government's invitation

> to the subjects of other states, to imitate the example of the Republic, cast away the rubbish of their old institutions, dethrone their Kings, demolish their nobility, divide the lands of the church and the aristocracy among the lower classes, and arise a free and regenerated people. In Britain as elsewhere, these doctrines carried a fascinating sound; for Britain as well as France had men of parts, who thought themselves neglected,—men of merit, who conceived themselves oppressed,—experimentalists, who would willingly put the laws in their revolutionary crucible,—and men desirous of novelties in the church and in the state, either from the eagerness of restless curiosity, or the hopes of bettering by the change. Above all, Britain had a far too ample mass of poverty and ignorance, subject always to be acted upon by the hope of license.[22]

Scott was not an admirer of what he regarded as the mob rule of democracy. He goes on discuss pro-revolutionary 'affiliated societies' that were formed all over Britain in the early 1790s:

> The persons who composed these societies had, generally speaking, little pretension to rank or influence; and though they contained some men of considerable parts, there was a deficiency of anything like weight or respectability in their meetings. Their consequence lay chiefly in the numbers who were likely to be influenced by their arguments; and these were extraordinarily great, especially in large towns, and in the manufacturing districts. (II, 209)

The agricultural labourers who made up Hogg's 'literary society' certainly had 'little pretension to rank or influence', but they formed part of a movement that caused real alarm among the British ruling

elite. John Barrell has written as follows of the London Correspond-
ing Society, which 'was founded early in 1792 by a group of trades-
men who met in a pub off the Strand':

> From 1793 to at least the end of 1795, the Society was the co-
> ordinator of the numerous popular reform societies scattered
> throughout the country, which together constituted the first
> nationwide popular political movement in Britain.[23]

In the spring of 1794 the leaders of the London Corresponding So-
ciety were arrested and charged with high treason. By the end of the
year they had been acquitted, but the outcome was less favourable
for those accused in the Scottish sedition trials of August 1793, in
which, as Liam McIlvanney puts it in his book *Burns the Radical*,
'savage' punishments were 'handed down by the coarse and gloat-
ing Lord Braxfield'. McIlvanney continues:

> For Thomas Muir's trial, the jury was drawn from members
> of an Edinburgh loyalist club. Muir got fourteen years' trans-
> portation—an unheard-of tariff for the crime of sedition—and
> William Fysshe Palmer, a Unitarian minister from Dundee,
> got seven.[24]

In his account of such matters in his *Life of Napoleon*, Scott records
that the British aristocracy made common cause against the pro-
revolutionary 'affiliated societies' in the early 1790s, and

> by the weight of influence, character, and fortune, soon ob-
> tained a superiority, which made it dangerous, or at least in-
> convenient, to many, whose situations in society rendered
> them in some degree dependent upon the favour of the aris-
> tocracy, to dissent violently from their opinions. (II, 209–10)

Very many people were subjected to pressure of this kind. For ex-
ample, Robert Burns faced the real possibility of destitution in the
winter of 1792–93, because his job as an exciseman came under
threat when (to quote Liam McIlvanney) he 'was denounced to the
authorities as a republican, and the Excise Board launched an en-
quiry into his political conduct'.[25]

All this tends to suggest that, in the early 1790s, Hogg was a fiery
and radical young agricultural labourer in sympathy with the French
Revolution, at a time when such views were not only widespread in
Britain, but were also seen by a nervous British elite as potentially
very dangerous. However, enthusiastic sympathy with the revolu-
tionary principles of liberty, equality, and fraternity did not neces-

sarily involve unquestioning and sustained support for every action of France's post-Revolution governments. Responding to being denounced as a republican, Burns wrote as follows on 5 January 1793 to his friend Robert Graham of Fintry, a Commissioner of the Scottish Excise Board:

> As to France, I was her enthusiastic votary in the beginning of the business.—When she came to shew her old avidity for conquest, in annexing Savoy, &c. to her dominions, & invading the rights of Holland, I altered my sentiments.[26]

In *Burns the Radical* Liam McIlvanney has argued cogently that, while Burns's instincts were in sympathy with revolutionary France, 'uncritical Francophilia' was not 'a precondition of genuine radicalism'. McIlvanney continues: 'There is no reason why Burns, as a British radical, should feel obliged to defend the annexation of Savoy or for that matter the September Massacres'.[27] For Hogg as for Burns, early sympathy with the French Revolution did not necessarily lead to 'uncritical Francophilia' as subsequent events unfolded. *The Queen's Wake* was written in 1812, two decades on from the widespread radical pro-French enthusiasms of the early 1790s, and it is clear that by 1812 Hogg's views were not as pro-French as they appear to have been in the heady days of January 1794.

This change in attitude can of course be explained readily enough: it is not unusual to be less fiery and more prudent in one's early forties than one had been in one's early twenties. However, if Hogg had changed in the period between the early 1790s and the early 1810s, so too had France. In the Brumaire coup of November 1799 Napoleon complicated his credentials as a hero of the Revolution by seizing personal power as First Consul, and in the opening years of the nineteenth century Napoleonic France was actively preparing to invade Britain. At this point Hogg wrote 'Donald M'Donald', a rousing war-song that caught a mood within Britain of popular defiance of a man described in the original version of Hogg's song as 'the proud CONSUL'.[28] Napoleon declared himself Emperor of France in 1804, a move that still further complicated his claims to be regarded as a hero of the Revolution, and 'Kilmeny' in *The Queen's Wake* contains passages that suggest that by 1812 Hogg had come to regard the French Emperor as a man whose ambitions had generated large-scale wars that had imposed truly appalling suffering and loss of life on the population of Europe. Nevertheless, *The Queen's Wake* was a product of the somewhat radical alternative Edinburgh that had generated *The Spy*, and the Hogg of 1812 remained a man

of strongly egalitarian and democratic instincts. In thinking about
the context in which Hogg wrote *The Queen's Wake* in 1812, it can be
helpful and illuminating to remember the shaping influence of his
sansculotte childhood, and to remember his roots in the radical as-
pirations of the early 1790s, when his 'literary society' held its 'more
or less secret meeting of young agricultural labourers'. It would be
extremely interesting to read the 'flaming bombastical essay' Hogg
prepared for that meeting, but unfortunately (and perhaps
unsurprisingly) the essay does not appear to have survived.

2. The First Version of *The Queen's Wake*: Bards, Harps, and the 1812–13 Context

> But while we sing God Save the KING
> We'll ne'er forget THE PEOPLE!
> Burns, 'The Dumfries Volunteers'

When a bankrupt and discredited James Hogg arrived in Edinburgh
in February 1810 seeking to establish himself as a professional writer,
he received much-needed encouragement and financial support from
his old Ettrick friend John Grieve. It appears that Grieve also gave
Hogg valuable encouragement after the failure of *The Spy*. In his
'Memoir of the Author's Life' Hogg writes:

> During the time that the Forum was going on the poetry of
> Mr. Walter Scott and Lord Byron was exciting general atten-
> tion. I had published some pieces in "The Spy" that Grieve
> thought exceedingly good; and nothing would serve him but
> that I should take the field once more as a poet, and try my
> fate with others. I promised; and having some ballads or met-
> rical tales by me, which I did not like to lose, I planned the
> "Queen's Wake," in order that I might take these all in, and
> had it ready in a few months after it was first proposed.[29]

In the early 1810s huge sales were achieved by Scott's *The Lady of
the Lake* (published in 1810) and Byron's *Childe Harold's Pilgrimage*,
the first two cantos of which appeared in 1812. If he were to emu-
late the success of these book-length narrative poems, Hogg would
have to produce a book-length narrative poem of his own. What he
had to hand, however, were short 'ballads or metrical tales'. His
solution to this problem was as simple as it was successful: his book-
length poem would be about a poetic competition (a 'wake') held by
the bards of Scotland in Edinburgh's royal palace of Holyroodhouse

to welcome Mary, Queen of Scots on her return to her native land from France in 1561. *The Queen's Wake* tells the story of this imagined competition, and also gives the 'ballads or metrical tales' sung by some of the competing bards. Two of these ('Macgregor' and 'King Edward's Dream') had appeared in *The Spy*, but the remainder of the first edition of *The Queen's Wake* consists of previously unpublished work.

Clearly, Hogg's poem reflects the narrative pattern of Chaucer's *Canterbury Tales*. There may also be a debt to the feast in Canto Sixth of Scott's *Lay of the Last Minstrel* (1805), in which songs are sung by minstrels representing the south, the north, and the debatable land. At all events, *The Queen's Wake* consists of a series of separate tales contained within a larger narrative in which the narrators of these tales appear as characters, and are described in detail. Hogg took to this narrative pattern like a duck to water. Writing about *The Spy*, Susan Manning has commented on Hogg's 'extraordinarily economical capacity to inhabit instantly-recognisable voices from across the social spectrum'.[30] This ability to inhabit a wide variety of voices can perhaps be linked to the unusually wide range of Hogg's political and religious sympathies. At all events, it enables him in *The Queen's Wake* to present a series of very different verse narratives, each of which has an appropriate and tellingly-described narrator. Interestingly, some of Hogg's friends can be readily recognised in the descriptions of the bards of the wake: for example, the Fourteenth Bard is a portrait of John Grieve, the Fifteenth Bard is a portrait of James Gray, and the Sixteenth Bard is a portrait of Allan Cunningham.[31]

In *The Queen's Wake*, the prize for which the bards of Scotland compete is a magnificent harp, to be presented by the Queen. The harp (and in particular the Eolian harp, which produces a musical sound when the wind passes over its strings) was a powerful symbol of poetic inspiration for the Romantics, and the prize harp of Hogg's poem should be seen in that context. Furthermore, in the second half of the eighteenth century texts like Thomas Gray's 'The Bard' (1757) and James Macpherson's *Poems of Ossian* (1760–65) had helped to focus attention on the traditional figure of the harp-playing bard, and in her seminal book *Bardic Nationalism: The Romantic Novel and the British Empire* (Princeton University Press, 1997), Katie Trumpener demonstrates that the bard at this period came to symbolise the indigenous oral culture of the Celtic parts of the British Isles—Ireland, Wales, and Scotland. Trumpener argues that traditional Celtic oral culture was dismissed as backward and primitive by some influential figures such as Dr Samuel Johnson, who prided themselves on basing their view of the past, not on the unsubstantiated stories handed down by bardic oral tradition, but on the eighteenth-century Enlightenment's methods of rational investigation of the evidence. But, as Trumpener puts it, in the late eighteenth and early nineteenth centuries the 'famous indifference' of people like Johnson to Celtic bardic oral culture

> catalyzes literary counterrepresentations and the articulation of an oppositional nationalist aesthetics. Responding in particular to Enlightenment dismissals of Gaelic oral traditions, Irish and Scottish antiquaries reconceive national history and literary history under the sign of the bard. According to their theories, bardic performance binds the nation together across time and across social divides; it reanimates a national landscape made desolate first by conquest and then by modernization, infusing it with historical memory. A figure both of the traditional aristocratic culture that preceded English occupation and of continued national resistance to that occupation, the bard symbolizes the central role of literature in defining national identity.[32]

Seen in this context, the bardic contest of *The Queen's Wake* emerges as an attempt to explore, to recover, and to reanimate a Scottish national identity that had been obscured and complicated, for Hogg's generation, by the 1707 Union with England. However, Hogg's poem adds an interesting extra ingredient to the situation described by Katie Trumpener. Thinking of the Irish and Welsh as well as the Scottish contexts, Trumpener sees the bard as a figure 'of the traditional aristocratic culture that preceded English occupation'. In *The Queen's Wake*, however, Hogg gives his own particular spin to this question by envisaging rival aristocratic and non-aristocratic versions of the traditional bardic culture of pre-Union Scotland.

These rival versions of the bardic tradition are symbolised by the two prize harps of Hogg's poem, and by the bards who win these prizes. The major prize harp of *The Queen's Wake* is awarded at the end of the poem to Gardyn, a long-descended and aristocratic Highland bard. Gardyn is described in Night the First as 'no man of mean degree', and we are also told that his eye 'glowed with native dignity' (*1813*, ll. 276, 270). Furthermore,

> Upon his harp, of wonderous frame,
> Was carved his lineage and his name.
> (*1813*, ll. 277–78)

However, after Gardyn's victory the Queen also presents a less ornate harp as a consolation prize to the Bard of Ettrick—that is to say, to the bard who represents Hogg himself within the poem. When introduced in Night the Second, this bard 'excited merriment around':

> For such a simple air and mien
> Before a court had never been.
> A clown he was, bred in the wild,
> And late from native moors exiled,
> In hopes his mellow mountain strain
> High favour from the great would gain.
> Poor wight! he never weened how hard
> For poverty to earn regard! (*1813*, ll. 245–52)

Nevertheless, the court's 'merriment' begins to change when he starts his song:

> Then first was noted in his eye,
> A gleam of native energy. (*1813*, ll. 305–06)

The Bard of Ettrick (like Hogg himself, we are given to understand) turns out to be the embodiment of an ancient oral popular culture that speaks in and through those eloquent and powerful songs of the people, the traditional oral ballads of the Scottish Borders.

The Queen's Wake, it begins to appear, revolves around a contest in which the aristocratic version of Scottish bardic culture symbolised by the prize harp won by Gardyn is challenged by the non-elite version of that culture symbolised by the prize harp won by the Bard of Ettrick. In describing the two prize harps of his poem, Hogg draws on a book published by Archibald Constable in 1807, John Gunn's *An Historical Enquiry Respecting the Performance on the Harp in the Highlands of Scotland*. The titlepage of Gunn's book promises 'An account of a very ancient Caledonian Harp, and of the Harp of Queen Mary', both of which had been kept for many years by the Robertson family 'in the house of Lude, in the Highlands of Perthshire'. The two harps described by Gunn are now (2004) preserved and exhibited in the National Museum of Scotland, in Edinburgh.

The aristocratic 'Harp of Queen Mary', the prototype of the harp won by Gardyn in Hogg's poem, is described by Gunn as follows:

QUEEN MARY, in a hunting excursion in the highlands of Perthshire, had taken with her the Harp, of which the engraving, Plate III., is an exact representation, and had made a present of it to Miss Beatrix Gardyn, daughter of Mr Gardyn of Banchory, whose family is now represented by Mr Garden of Troup.[33]

It appears that Queen Mary's harp came into the possession of the Robertsons of Lude when one of Beatrix Gardyn's 'female descendants' married into that family. Gunn goes on to describe this harp's original rich ornamentation in gold and jewels, all of which, according to a letter to Gunn from General Robertson of Lude, had been looted in the rebellion of 1745, 'either by the persons to whose care the Harp had been at that time confided; or, as these people asserted, had been taken away by the soldiery during the existence of these troubles'.[34]

So much for the harp that in *The Queen's Wake* represents the aristocratic version of the pre-Union Scottish bardic tradition. Let us now turn to the harp of the people, the prototype of the non-aristocratic harp won by the Bard of Ettrick in Hogg's poem. The House of Lude's 'Caledonian Harp' is described by Gunn as follows:

> The oldest of the two Harps, which I have called the CALEDO-NIAN HARP, was brought from Argyleshire about the year 1460, by a Lady of the family of Lamont, to the House of Lude, upon her marriage into the family of Robertson of Lude, where it has ever since remained. The workmanship of this Harp is very good; and the instrument being evidently intended for durability and great strength, it is constructed on a simple plan, without any affectation of ornament, but the work is perfectly smooth, and well finished.[35]

Clearly, the harp awarded to the Bard of Ettrick has its own kind of simple but substantial worth. Gunn goes on to stress the antiquity of the House of Lude's Caledonian Harp, and its rootedness in the culture of Highland Scotland:

> It exhibits, however, several marks and proofs of its having suffered considerable violence, and of its having, at different periods, received very severe blows, which it is much more likely to have received in traversing different parts of the Highlands, and Western Islands, both by land and sea, than in having been constantly in the possession of a single family; so that these marks indicate, not very equivocally, its having been, in all probability for several centuries, the Harp of a succession of Highland Bards, before it came into the possession of the family of Lamont.[36]

There is something of a puzzle here. In *The Queen's Wake*, the poetry of the Bard of Ettrick grows out of the ancient oral culture of the Scottish Borders, the popular culture that produced the traditional ballads that had been collected by Scott for *Minstrelsy of the Scottish Border* (1802–03). No doubt this is a kind of poetry that is in some ways ideally suited to the simple, well-made, unostentatious, robust, and ancient Caledonian Harp–but why is this very Highland harp given to the Bard of Ettrick, a man deeply rooted in the distinctly non-Highland culture of the Borders? The answer, as we shall see, seems to be connected with Hogg's strong sense of sympathetic solidarity with the sufferings of the people of the Highlands, and not least with their sufferings during the Highland Clearances.

Hogg travelled frequently in the Highlands: indeed, by the early 1810s he had known the Highlands at first hand for around twenty years, and he had published accounts of two of his Highland journeys in *The Scots Magazine*.[37] In Hogg's day, attitudes towards the Highlands and towards Highlanders were coloured by memories of the Jacobite rising of 1745–46. Scottish support for that rising was not confined to the Highlands, but the rising began and ended in the Highlands, and the Jacobite cause was strongly linked to Highland culture in the popular mind. As a Presbyterian and as an admirer of the Covenanters, Hogg was not naturally in sympathy with the Jacobite cause. Nevertheless, as can be seen (for example) in *The Three Perils of Woman* (1823), he empathised deeply with the terrible sufferings of the Highland people in the aftermath of the failure of the Jacobite rising of 1745–46, seeing in this a foreshadowing of the traumatic evictions of the Highland Clearances, evictions which began in the latter part of the eighteenth century and continued into Hogg's own day and beyond.[38]

Sympathy with the Highland people also emerges in Hogg's *Jacobite Relics*, his two-volume collection of traditional Jacobite songs (1819 and 1821). Murray Pittock writes in the Introduction to the Stirling / South Carolina Edition of the second series of *Jacobite Relics*:

> Hogg may well have seen the clear-cut Scots and established airs of many of the Scottish Jacobite songs as signs of their status as a popular voice, the literature of the people. Hogg was in other places in his work loyal to that voice, employing it (e.g. in *Confessions*) as a choric commentator on the follies of fanaticism and urban rationalism alike. The Jacobite song represented a political tradition disliked alike by Hume and Smith, Wodrow and Peden. It was not Hogg's own tradition, but he saw it as kin, certainly insofar as it represented the suffering

of ordinary people (and of course the metaphors of domesticity and patriot poverty were heavily used by the Jacobites). In such a case, Hogg was unlikely to censor the Jacobite voice into unequivocally polite sentiment to satisfy the demands of a social and literary elite concerning whom his own feelings were decidedly equivocal.[39]

It begins to appear, then, that the Caledonian Harp, the harp of the Bard of Ettrick in *The Queen's Wake*, has the status of 'a popular voice, the literature of the people'. This harp speaks for and from *all* the non-elite people of Scotland, both Highland and Lowland. Like the Ettrick farmer Wat Laidlaw in Hogg's novel *The Brownie of Bodsbeck* (1818), the Ettrick Shepherd empathises with the people in their sufferings. As Wat puts it in praising the brave, humane, and compassionate conduct of his daughter Kate in a time of civil war, it is right and proper to be on 'the side o' human nature; the suffering and the humble side'.[40]

If the Caledonian harp speaks for and from the people, it (like Gardyn's aristocratic prize) can also be seen as a national symbol of Scotland. This aspect of the harp emerges, for example, in the traditional Jacobite song 'King William's March', which Hogg prints as Song XIV in the first series of his *Jacobite Relics*. Murray Pittock writes of this song:

> As Hogg suggests, likely (from internal evidence) to be a song of 1690. The linkage of the 'piper' and the 'auld harper' with the 'true king' in the last stanza is a revealing one, which should be borne in mind when interpreting the thematic importance of musical instruments in the Jacobite song more generally. The harp and the pipes were national symbols of Scotland, as the harp was of Ireland, and they carry with them a freight of symbolic nationhood.[41]

Furthermore, it seems that the harp could be present in the background on occasions when people of Jacobin sympathies drew on Jacobite sources. Pittock comments on 'The Sow's Tail to Geordie', Song LV in the first series of *Jacobite Relics*:

> Hogg implies that this song has been long in the oral tradition. The song quoted in Hogg's note once again exemplifies the use of the harper as a symbol for the patriot Scot. [...] W. H. Langhorne records that this song was one of those sung by the Rev. Mr Troup of Muchalls during his confinement in Stonehaven Jail in 1746 [Rev. W. H. Langhorne, *Reminiscences* (Edinburgh, 1893), p. 12]. Henry Meikle records that it had

an afterlife in the period of the French Revolution (cf. the Jacobin / Jacobite political identity of some of Burns' writing– Burns uses this air at Kinsley 468) [Henry W. Meikle, *Scotland and the French Revolution* (Glasgow: James Maclehose, 1912), p. 147]. In April 1794, during a staging of Alexander Fyfe's *The Royal Martyr* in Scotland, radicals called for 'Ca ira', 'God save the People' and 'The Sow's Tail to Geordie'.[42]

Commenting on 'My Laddie', Song LXIX in the first series of *Jacobite Relics*, Murray Pittock writes that 'In Ireland in the 1790s the motto of the United Irishmen was "It [the harp] is new strung and shall be heard"'.[43] The United Irishmen were radical supporters of the French Revolution, and their new-strung harp, symbol of the Irish people, played a tune deeply out of sympathy with the worldview of the British establishment of the day.

The annual *The Musical Bijou* for 1829 contained 'The Harp of Ossian', a subversive little song by Hogg which deplores the silencing of the 'Old harp of the Highlands', the voice of the old, indigenous Scottish culture.[44] 'The Harp of Ossian' presents a colonised Scotland, in which English cultural norms have replaced the native tradition, and in which the Gaelic and Scots languages are being replaced by English: Scotland's 'sons condescend from new models to borrow', and 'voices of strangers prevail'. With this context in mind, one can see why, during the bardic contest of *The Queen's Wake*, Gardyn's eyes glow with '*native* dignity', while the Bard of Ettrick's eyes show a gleam of '*native* energy' (emphasis added). *The Queen's Wake* can be understood as an attempt to contest the situation described by Katie Trumpener in *Bardic Nationalism*, a situation in which 'the voices of strangers prevail'. Ultimately, Hogg's poem approaches this task by seeking to give voice to the insights, the culture, and the concerns of the marginalised non-elite people of Scotland. In the words of the radical United Irishmen, the harp in Hogg's poem 'is new strung and shall be heard'.

Famously, James Macpherson had already attempted to re-string the harp of Ossian. Macpherson had been born in the Highland district of Badenoch in 1736, in the territory of his uncle, the clan chief Ewan Macpherson of Cluny. He was therefore a child of an impressionable age during the Jacobite rising of 1745–46, the rising by which Queen Mary's great-great-great-grandson Prince Charles Edward ('Bonnie Prince Charlie') tried to regain the British throne for the deposed Stuarts. Macpherson of Cluny and his followers were prominent in Prince Charles's Jacobite army, and the young James would have shared in the triumphant hopes of his relatives in

1745. However, he also had to share the experience of seeing things fall apart after their catastrophic defeat at Culloden in 1746. In her Introduction to an edition of Macpherson's *Poems of Ossian* published in 1996 by the Edinburgh University Press, Fiona Stafford has summed up James Macpherson's personal experience of the aftermath of Culloden:

> With defeat came disgrace for Clan Macpherson, as Cluny Castle was razed and much of the local community destroyed by the violence of the victorious army. [...] Between the ages of ten and eighteen, James Macpherson thus lived through scenes of appalling violence, and saw his home and family under the constant threat of further oppression. During this period, a series of measures were implemented to crush the distinctive Highland way of life, and render the region safe for ever. After 1746, the tartan plaid was banned, and no Highlander allowed to carry arms or play the bagpipes. The estates of prominent rebel chiefs (including Cluny) were forfeited to the Crown, while the ancient systems of wardholding and heritable jurisdiction were abolished. Such measures were a more Draconian development from the earlier, relatively peaceful, attempts to open communications and transport networks in the Highlands, and to encourage the use of English rather than Gaelic. But it is in the context of systematic cultural destruction that Macpherson's efforts to collect old heroic poetry can be seen; they were, at least in part, an attempt to repair some of the damage to the Highlands sustained in the wake of the Jacobite Risings.[45]

James Macpherson undoubtedly hoped to find fame and fortune through his *Ossian* poems, but, in the new situation created by the triumph of the forces of the modern post-Union British state at Culloden, he also seems to have been motivated by a desire to re-vivify the poetry of an ancient and aristocratic Highland culture. 'Young Kennedy', the Ossianic poem contributed by Gardyn to Queen Mary's wake, can be seen as a tribute by Hogg to Macpherson. However, *The Queen's Wake* seeks to re-string not only the ornate aristocratic harp of Queen Mary, but also the stronger, simpler, and more ancient Caledonian harp, the harp of the Scottish people. And, even although the Queen awards victory to Gardyn in the contest, it may well be felt that the subliminal message of *The Queen's Wake* is that the 'native energy' of the people's poet is ultimately even more valuable than the 'native dignity' of the aristocratic Gardyn.

3. The First Version of *The Queen's Wake*:
The Pattern of the Bardic Contest

In the first version of *The Queen's Wake*, the poem's overall narrative
pattern is shaped by the nature of the wake as a poetic *contest*. Thus
Night the First opens with 'Malcolm of Lorn', the song of the Italian
Rizzio, the 'gaudy minstrel of the south' (*1813*, l. 10) who is the
Queen's favourite. Rizzio's 'fervid, flowery lay' (*1813*, l. 30) is im-
mediately contrasted with the sterner native fare offered by 'Young
Kennedy', the song of the Ossianic and aristocratic Highlander
Gardyn ('no man of mean degree') (*1813*, l. 276). In spite of this
opening skirmish, however, it turns out that the main contest of *The
Queen's Wake* will not lie between Scottish and non-Scottish poetry.
Instead, the contest will lie between rival aristocratic and popular
strands within the Scottish poetic tradition. In Night the First the
songs of the first two bards are immediately followed by 'The Witch
of Fife', which is sung by the Eighth Bard: 'The rest who sung that
night are lost' (*1813*, l. 592). Unlike Gardyn, the aristocratic High-
lander who eventually wins the Harp of Queen Mary, the Eighth
Bard is a Lowlander, a man of the people who holds 'worldly pomp
in high derision' (*1813*, l. 615). The Eighth Bard, it would appear,
has something in common with so-called 'peasant poets' such as
Robert Burns and James Hogg, and in Night the First he is the rep-
resentative of the long-established demotic Scottish tradition sym-
bolised in *The Queen's Wake* by the Caledonian Harp, the consolation
prize eventually won by the Bard of Ettrick.

The contest between these rival strands in Scottish poetry takes
centre stage in Night the Second, as songs from the Ossianic / aristo-
cratic Highland tradition ('Glen-Avin' and 'Macgregor') alternate
with two very different songs sung by demotic Lowlanders ('Old
David' and 'Earl Walter'). Night the Second then concludes with
'Kilmeny', which draws on aspects of *both* strands of the native tradi-
tion: thus its bard, Drummond, is presented both as an aristocrat
and as a shepherd.

The contest continues in the climactic Night the Third of the *Wake*,
in which pride of place is given to Hogg's own Lowland / demotic
tradition. This emphasis provides an affirmation of the world of *The
Spy*, the world from which the first version of *The Queen's Wake*
emerged. Of the four songs of Night the Third, the first three are
sung by bards who can be recognised as portraits of three of Hogg's
key friends from that period: John Grieve, James Gray, and Allan

Cunningham. Night the Third then concludes with 'The Abbot M'Kinnon', the song in which the Bard of Mull makes a final contribution from the Highland / Ossianic tradition.

An additional perspective on the narrative pattern generated by the bardic contest of the first version of *The Queen's Wake* is provided by a famous passage in Hogg's *Familiar Anecdotes of Sir Walter Scott*, which records a conversation about a projected review by Scott of Hogg's epic poem *Queen Hynde* (1824), which Scott admired:

> But seeing I suppose that the poem did not take so well as he had anticipated he never accomplished his kind intent. I asked him the following year why he had not fulfilled his promise to me.
>
> "Why the truth is Hogg" said he "that I began the thing and took a number of notes marking extracts but I found that to give a proper view of your poetical progress and character I was under the necessity of beginning with the ballads and following through THE WAKE and all the rest and upon the whole I felt that we were so much of the same school that if I had said of you as I wished to say I would have been thought by the world to be applauding myself."
>
> I cannot aver that these were Sir Walter's very words but they were precisely to that purport. But I like other dissapointed men not being half quite satisfied with the answer said "Dear Sir Walter ye can never suppose that I belang to your school o' chivalry? Ye are the king o' that school but I'm the king o' the mountain an' fairy school which is a far higher ane nor yours."[46]

It seems clear that the poetic contest of *The Queen's Wake* connects with Hogg's view of the relative merits of Scott's 'school of chivalry' and his own ballad-based 'mountain an' fairy school'. For example, we learn in Night the Second (*1813*, ll. 711–12) that 'the Bard of Ettrick' (the Hogg-figure of *The Queen's Wake*) 'once had dared, at flatterer's call, | To tune his harp in Branxholm hall'. This sets up an implied comparison between the bard of Ettrick and the minstrel of Scott's long narrative poem *The Lay of the Last Minstrel* (1805).

Much of the action of the *Lay* takes place in Branxholm (or, as Scott calls it, Branksome) Castle: Scott explains in his Notes that 'Branxholm is the proper name of the barony; but Branksome has been adopted as suitable to the pronunciation, and more proper for poetry'.[47] At all events, Scott records that Branxholm came into the possession of the aristocratic Scotts of Buccleuch in the days of Scotland's James I (1395–1437), and 'continued to be the principal seat of the Buccleuch family, while security was any object in the choice of a mansion' (*Lay*, pp. 197, 199). In the *Lay*, the stirring deeds of the Scotts of Buccleuch at Branxholm are recounted by a minstrel who is presented as being the last representative of the Border minstrels who had produced the old ballads Scott had collected for his *Minstrelsy of the Scottish Border* (1802–03): 'The last of all the Bards was he, | Who sung of Border chivalry' (*Lay*, p. 3).

Scott presents the life of a minstrel of old in positive terms:

> courted and caressed,
> High placed in hall, a welcome guest,
> He poured, to lord and lady gay,
> The unpremeditated lay.   (*Lay*, p. 4)

We learn that the Last Minstrel had himself enjoyed favour when Charles II visited Holyrood after the Restoration. Times have changed, however, and the Last Minstrel is now living out his days in the final years of the seventeenth century, 'A wandering harper, scorned and poor' (*Lay*, p. 4). Nevertheless, he is given a welcome at Newark (the new headquarters of the Buccleuch family) by Anne, Duchess of Buccleuch and Monmouth, just as his predecessors had been welcomed by the Duchess's predecessors at Branxholm. This picture is elegantly completed by the thought that Walter Scott (a kinsman of the Scotts of Buccleuch) is singing 'of Border chivalry' as he re-creates the lay of the Last Minstrel as an offering to his friend the Countess of Dalkeith, wife of the Duke of Buccleuch's heir, and herself a future Duchess of Buccleuch.[48] This is all very aristocratic, as is confirmed by a description of the lay sung by the Last Minstrel of Scott's poem: 'It was not framed for village churles, | But for high dames and mighty earls' (*Lay*, p. 7).

Clearly, in presenting the Last Minstrel's lay to a modern poetry-reading audience Scott is reviving an old minstrelsy, and he is thus to some extent echoing Macpherson's project in his *Ossian* texts. Equally clearly, Hogg is engaged in a broadly similar project in *The Queen's Wake*. But Hogg's Bard of Ettrick is a very different kind of harper from both Scott's Last Minstrel and Macpherson's Ossian. Indeed, in *The Queen's Wake* Hogg seems to go out of his way to assert that the old oral ballads of the Borders are poems of the people, poems that belong to 'village churles' rather than 'high dames and mighty earls'—and are none the worse for that. In short, the 1813 version of *The Queen's Wake* debates with Scott's *Lay of the Last Minstrel* by asserting its own demotic understanding of the old ballad tradition of the minstrelsy of the Scottish Border. Scott's Last Minstrel is in his natural habitat when he sings to the Duchess at Branxholm, but it will be remembered that Hogg's Bard of Ettrick only 'once had dared, at flatterer's call, | To tune his harp in Branxholm hall'.

An article in *The Spy* for 12 January 1811 offers an insight into the ways in which the traditional oral ballads operated among the people Scott calls 'village churles'. This article was published anonymously, but there is some evidence to suggest that it was by Hogg himself. The relevant passage reads as follows:[49]

The greatest mental delight I ever experienced, has been in listening to the *goodwife*, sitting at her wheel, singing these old warlike, or rural songs. I have seen the ruddy maiden turn round, ashamed of her tenderness, and wipe away the dropping tear that melted from her soft beaming eye, for the fall of Gil Morice, or Graham and Bewick. I have seen the brown healthy boys, all clad in blue drugget, sitting around the blazing *ingle*, each with his mouth open, and his eyes fixed on the dame, swallowing her inchanting strains with the utmost avidity. How I have seen their eyes kindle and glow, when they heard the feats of Old Maitland's three Sons, Robin Hood and the Three Giants, or the battle of Chevy-Chace! and instead of being wearied by the length of them, they would beg as a particular favour to hear some favourite parts a second time. I have even heard some of them cry, because she refused to begin and sing one of them all over again.

The view expressed here of the nature of the traditional oral ballads connects powerfully with the kind of poetry advocated by Wordsworth in the 1802 Preface to *Lyrical Ballads*. Wordsworth writes:

Low and rustic life was generally chosen, because in that condition, the essential passions of the heart find a better soil in which they can attain their maturity, are less under restraint, and speak a plainer and more emphatic language; because in that condition of life our elementary feelings co-exist in a state of greater simplicity, and, consequently, may be more accurately contemplated, and more forcibly communicated; because the manners of rural life germinate from those elementary feelings; and, from the necessary character of rural occupations, are more easily comprehended; and are more durable; and lastly, because in that condition the passions of men are incorporated with the beautiful and permanent forms of nature.[50]

Reading this, Hogg must have felt that, while the circumstances of his upbringing were noticeably different from those of a university-educated gentleman-poet, they nevertheless brought him some advantages as he sought to re-tune the harp of Ettrick's old oral ballads, in his capacity as successor to Robert Burns as a national bard who could speak on behalf of the people of Scotland.

4. The First Version of *The Queen's Wake:* Mary, Queen of Scots and the 1561 Context

Orthodox, orthodox,
Wha believe in John Knox
Burns, 'The Kirk's Alarm'

We have seen that momentous events took place during the months when *The Queen's Wake* was being written, printed, and published– events such as the Battle of Salamanca and Napoleon's retreat from Moscow. These events form one of the contexts in which it is helpful to see Hogg's poem, but another significant context is provided by 1561, the year in which *The Queen's Wake* is set. This was the year in which the young Mary, Queen of Scots (1542–87) returned to Scotland from France, where she had lived since 1548.

In 1561 as in 1812–13, France was involved in a struggle with England for European dominance, and Scotland's future hung in the balance. Mary, Queen of Scots, daughter of James V, King of Scots, had close ties with both the English and the French royal families. She had a royal English grandmother in Margaret Tudor, sister of England's Henry VIII and wife of Scotland's James IV. However, her own mother (Mary of Guise) was French, and pre-Reformation Scotland had a long-standing alliance with France against England. It was for this reason that Mary, Queen of Scots was educated at the French court, where in due course she married the heir to the French throne, thus cementing still further the ties between France and Scotland. The return of the young Queen to Scotland in 1561 took place because her husband, François II, died approximately a year after inheriting the French throne from his father, Henri II.

France and the other Catholic powers of Europe regarded Mary, Queen of Scots (the granddaughter, it will be remembered, of Margaret Tudor) as the rightful Queen of England. Indeed Mary's son James VI was to inherit the English throne (as James I) in 1603, after the death of Queen Elizabeth of England. Elizabeth had been crowned as Queen of England in 1559, but this Protestant daughter of Henry VIII was the child of a marriage to Anne Boleyn undertaken after her father's divorce from Catherine of Arragon. Catholics regarded this divorce as invalid, and therefore regarded Elizabeth as an illegitimate child. In consequence, Mary's claim to the English throne made her an important figure in the ongoing power struggle between France and Elizabethan England. The first readers of *The Queen's Wake* would of course be alert to potential parallels between this power struggle and the then current conflict between post-Revolutionary Napoleonic France and Regency Britain. Hogg's notably sympathetic portrait of the 'French' Mary has some relevance in this context.

A complicated and difficult situation awaited Mary on her return to Scotland in 1561. In 1560 the Scottish parliament had passed the legislation that brought in the Scottish Reformation by cutting the ties between the Scottish church and Rome. Mary thus found herself the Catholic Queen of what had only very recently become a Protestant country, a country in which the great Calvinist preacher John Knox had emerged as an influential and powerful figure. In reading *The Queen's Wake*, it can be illuminating to keep in mind that the Scotland of Hogg's generation formed part of the new British state that had been established as recently as 1707 by the Union between England and Scotland. As Linda Colley and others have shown,[51] the 'Britain' of the eighteenth and early nineteenth centuries found its role and its identity as an emphatically Protestant state. 'Britain' aspired to be a bastion of modernity, freedom, and moderation against what it took to be the medieval superstitions of Catholicism, and against what it regarded as the arbitrary despotism exemplified not only by the deposed Stuarts and their Jacobite supporters, but also by both pre-Revolutionary and post-Revolutionary France. In the eighteenth and early nineteenth centuries, Mary, Queen of Scots had her British defenders. Nevertheless, in the pro-Protestant and anti-French climate of mainstream British opinion of the time, she tended to be viewed with hostility, partly because of her links with France, partly because she was a Catholic, and partly because she was one of the allegedly despotic Stuart monarchs.

The vehemence of this hostility is plainly visible in an incident that took place in the Palace of Holyroodhouse in the aftermath of Bonnie Prince Charlie's Jacobite rising of 1745–46. This incident involved the well-known series of paintings of the 110 legendary and real Scottish monarchs from Fergus I to Charles II, a series produced by Jacob de Wet in the 1680s for the Great Gallery at Holyrood in celebration of the dynastic claims of the Stuarts. In the current (2003) official guidebook to Holyrood, Ian Gow writes:

> The paintings are said to have been 'slashed by the sabres' of English troops quartered in the palace after the 1745 Rebellion and archaeological evidence during conservation has confirmed this. Especial violence was reserved for the portrait of Mary, Queen of Scots. By 1826 they had been 'repaired; and after having been removed from their hanging frames, fixed in the panels of the wainscoting'—but a number still hung loose in the window-embrasures at the end of the nineteenth century.[52]

This offers a telling insight—although perhaps it would have been more accurate to speak of 'British' rather than 'English' troops. Rather than a conflict between Scotland and England, the rising of 1745–46 was a conflict between supporters of the currently reigning Hanoverian monarchs, and Jacobites who sought to restore the deposed Stuarts. When the troops of the Hanoverian British government slashed Queen Mary's portrait with their sabres, they were in effect striking blows for Protestant Britain against a Catholic Stuart queen.

Mary is likewise treated unsympathetically in Thomas McCrie's influential and widely read *Life of John Knox*. Published in Edinburgh in 1811, with a revised second edition appearing in 1813, McCrie's book (like the first version of *The Queen's Wake*) is a product of the Edinburgh of the early 1810s.[53] Queen Mary's return from France 'on the 19th of August 1561' is described by McCrie as follows:

> The reception which she met with on her first arrival in Scotland was flattering; but an occurrence that took place soon after, damped the joy which had been expressed, and prognosticated future jealousies and confusion. Resolved to give her subjects an early proof of her firm determination to adhere to the Roman Catholic worship, Mary directed preparations to be made for the celebration of a solemn mass in the chapel of Holyroodhouse, on the first Sabbath after her arrival. This service had not been celebrated in Scotland since the conclusion of the civil war, and was prohibited under certain penalties by an act of the late parliament. And so great was the horror with which the protestants viewed its restoration, and the alarm which they felt at finding it countenanced by their Queen, that the first rumour of the design excited

violent murmurs, which would have burst into an open tumult, had not some of the leading men among the protestants interfered, and exerted their authority to repress the zeal of the multitude.

McCrie is anxious to defend Mary's Protestant opponents against charges of 'intolerance', so he points out that they 'were actuated by a strong abhorrence of popish idolatry, a feeling which is fully justified by the spirit and the precepts of Christianity', and he goes on to write of their fears that the land would again be 'defiled' by the revival of the 'impure rites' of the Catholic mass. To clinch his argument, McCrie appeals to that bastion of Protestantism, the British constitution:

> After all, it is surely unnecessary to apologize, for the restrictions which our ancestors were desirous of imposing on Queen Mary, to those who approve of the present constitution of Britain, according to which every papist is excluded from succeeding to the throne, and the reigning monarch, by setting up mass in his chapel, would virtually forfeit his crown. Is popery more dangerous now than it was two hundred and fifty years ago?[54]

Astonishingly, in the opening years of the twenty-first century 'the present constitution of Britain' still dictates that 'every papist is excluded from succeeding to the throne', as McCrie puts it. However, in the early 1810s this requirement was no mere anachronistic survival, and McCrie was reflecting a major element in the mainstream British opinion of the time when he wrote that 'the reigning monarch, by setting up mass in his chapel, would virtually forfeit his crown'. As we shall see, however, in *The Queen's Wake* Hogg chooses to go against the grain of some of the rooted assumptions and prejudices of the Britain of his day, as he paints an unexpectedly sympathetic picture both of Mary and of pre-Reformation Catholic Scotland.

According to the Enlightenment-based consensus of the Scottish intellectual elite of Hogg's period, human society was making progress from a state of ignorant and superstitious barbarity into a state of rational and civilised enlightenment. The 'literati' of the Scottish Enlightenment, in holding this view, tended to see the Reformation as a welcome movement away from medieval Catholic superstition towards a more modern and more rational form of religion offered by Protestantism. For such people, a belief in Progress made it natural to suppose that only well-educated, enlightened, and highly civilised gentlemen like themselves were in a position to make sound judgements on important matters. Hogg, being a member of a class dismissed by the literati as superstitious peasants, was not wholly comfortable with such assumptions, and his writings often tease the literati by raising the possibility that there might be something of merit in an old, pre-Enlightenment world-view. This process can be seen, for example, in Hogg's most famous novel. 'The Editor's Narrative' in *The Private Memoirs and Confessions of a Justified Sinner* (1824) sets out to tell the story of Robert Wringhim's life as it might be told by an enlightened member of the Edinburgh intellectual establishment of the 1820s. As the novel proceeds, however, the Editor and his narrative are increasingly subverted, not least by a series of choric comments associated with the people and with oral tradition. Here as elsewhere, the Ettrick Shepherd teases and disturbs his enlightened and gentlemanly readers with the possibility that (contrary to their confident assumptions) they might not have all the answers; that they might, indeed, have much to learn from prostitutes, servant-girls, and other persons who live pre-modern lives on or beyond the margins of modern society. A notable example of such a person is the poor 'hind' (that is to say, farm servant) who offers much-needed shelter to Robert towards the end of the novel.[55]

It is in this spirit of teasingly questioning the assumptions of the literati that *The Queen's Wake* sets out to valorise the world of the old pre-1560 Scotland, a world which the literati regarded as being tainted with the superstition and credulity of medieval Catholicism. Hogg's sympathy with the old pre-1560 world emerges strongly in 'Kilmeny' and 'The Witch of Fife', two of the poems from *The Queen's Wake*. In the first edition, these two poems, and only these two, are written in what Hogg called his 'ancient stile'. That is to say, they are written in a language that seeks to evoke the Middle Scots of pre-Reformation poets like Dunbar and Henryson. Peter Garside has written as follows about Hogg's 'ancient stile' as it appears in the poems of *A Queer Book* (1832):

> Its extended linguistic range and spontaneous rhythmic effects allowed an escape from the stereotypical English lyricism of the journals, as well too from an increasingly tired-looking form of Anglo-Scots ballad which had proliferated in the wake of Scott's *Minstrelsy of the Scottish Border* (1802–03). Hogg also found freedom to mix different genres, combining pathos with dark humour, physical and spiritual levels of experience, the supernatural and the satirical, sometimes creating a kind of 'magic realism' not dissimilar to that now seen in postmodern

fiction. Through word play, allegory, and the camouflage provided by 'antiquity', he could also be more daring in sexual terms than in any other contemporary public mode, and so discovered a means of circumventing, if only for brief moments, the incipient prudishness of the later 1820s.[56]

In the first edition of *The Queen's Wake*, the use of the 'ancient stile' in 'Kilmeny' and 'The Witch of Fife' emphasises that these two poems (sung to the beautiful young Catholic Queen in 1561) speak out of the old, pre-1560 world of medieval, Catholic Scotland. Appropriately enough, 'Kilmeny' operates in territory akin to that explored in medieval poems like the Gawain-poet's *Pearl* and *Purity*, and can be read as an evocation of medieval hymns to the Blessed Virgin. 'The Witch of Fife', equally appropriately, proves to be a riotous and exuberant evocation of medieval witchcraft and diablerie. The following extract provides an example of Hogg's mock-medieval 'ancient stile', as it appears in Night the Second, in 'Kilmeny':

> In yond grein wudde there is a waike,
> And in that waike there is a wene,
>   And in that wene there is a maike,
> That nouther hes flesch, blude, nor bene;
> And dune in yond greinwudde he walkis his lene.

> In that greine wene Kilmeny lay,
> Her bosom happit with flouris gay;
> But the ayre was soft, and the silens deipe,
> And bonny Kilmeny fell sunde asleipe.
> Scho kend ne mair, nor openit her ee,
> Till wekit by the hymis of ane farr cuntrye.
>   (*1813*, ll. 1398–408)

This passage echoes lines from the traditional ballad 'Erlinton', and as it happens Hogg had a hand in the transmission of the A-version of 'Erlinton' in Francis James Child's *English and Scottish Popular Ballads*. Child takes his A-version from Scott's *Minstrelsy of the Scottish Border* (1802–03), and for this ballad in the *Minstrelsy* Scott had drawn on material supplied by Hogg from the oral tradition of Ettrick. The relevant lines from 'Erlinton' appear in Child as follows:

> 'But in my bower there is a wake,
>   An at the wake there is a wane;
> But I'll come to the green-wood the morn,
>   Whar blooms the brier, by mornin dawn.'

In 'Erlinton', a young woman is imprisoned in a bower by her father, and a watch is set over her; but she escapes to join her lover in the greenwood. These ideas are adopted and adjusted in 'Kilmeny'. The heroine of Hogg's poem is a young woman who is 'pure as pure culde be', a 'sinless virgin' watched over by a 'meike and reverent' spirit (Night the Second *1813*, ll. 1350, 1421, 1416). Kilmeny goes to a *waike* in the greenwood, and in Hogg's poem *waike* appears to mean 'a district to watch over', or 'a walk'.[57] The watcher is an unearthly creature (a *maike*), whose dwelling or *wene* appears to be a magical place, a greenwood bower of enchantment. From this wene Kilmeny is spirited away to a mysterious land whose ravishing and opulent beauty seems to combine features of Heaven, Fairyland, and Eden. Seven years later Kilmeny returns briefly to this world, bringing a heavenly serenity and glory with her.

> But quhairevir her pecefu form appeirit,
> The wylde besties of the hill war cheirit;
> The ouf playit lythely runde the feilde,
> The lordlye byson lowit and kneilit;
> The dun deire wooit with manyr bland,
> And courit aneath her lille hand. [...]
> The ouf and the kydd their raike began,
> And the tod, and the lam, and the leurit ran;
> The hauke and the herne attour them hung,
> And the merl and the maives forehooit their yung;
> And all in ane pecefu ryng war hurlit:
> It was lyke ane eve in a sinlesse worild!
> (*1813*, ll. 1608–33)

This passage seems to echo Book IV of Milton's *Paradise Lost*, in which Satan, on arriving in Eden, finds Adam and Eve surrounded by the animal creation of an as yet unfallen world:[58]

> About them frisking played
> All beasts of th' earth, since wild, and of all chase
> In wood or wilderness, forest or den;
> Sporting the lion ramped, and in his paw
> Dandled the kid; bears, tigers, ounces, pards,
> Gambolled before them; th' unwieldy elephant,
> To make them mirth, used all his might, and wreathed
> His lithe proboscis.   (Book IV, ll. 340–47)

'Kilmeny' also contains an echo of the episode in Books XI and XII of *Paradise Lost* in which the Archangel Michael takes Adam to the highest hill in Paradise, and shows him a vision of the future course of human history. In Hogg's poem, the spirits take Kilmeny 'to ane mountyn greine' (1813, l. 1494), and show her a vision of the future, in which she sees the troubles which Mary, Queen of Scots had to encounter after 1561, including her conflicts with the 'gruff untowyrd gysart' Knox, and her death in exile in England (1813, ll. 1518–39). Kilmeny's vision then takes in the sufferings of the Covenanters in the religious wars of seventeenth-century Scotland, before concluding with images of the Napoleonic Wars (1813, ll. 1540–73). Here again The Queen's Wake is alive to parallels and links between the world of 1561 and the world of 1813.

After describing Adam's vision of the future, Milton's poem ends with the expulsion of Adam and Eve from Paradise:

> They, looking back, all the eastern side beheld
> Of Paradise, so late their happy seat,
> Waved over by that flaming brand, the gate
> With dreadful faces thronged and fiery arms:
> Some natural tears they dropped, but wiped them soon;
> The world was all before them, where to choose
> Their place of rest, and Providence their guide:
> They, hand in hand, with wandering steps and slow,
> Through Eden took their solitary way.
>   (Book XII, ll. 641–49)

'Kilmeny' ends with these lines:

> It walsna her heme, and scho culdna remayne;
> Scho left this worild of sorrow and paine,
> And returnit to the land of thochte againe.
>   (1813, ll. 1642–44)

Clearly, 'Kilmeny' is a poem about loss: about Paradise lost, indeed. In Hogg's poem, Kilmeny in her greenwood waike calls to mind Queen Mary at her wake, and in The Queen's Wake the 'sinless virgin' Kilmeny unites with a Queen Mary who is still young and still hopeful, not yet overwhelmed by the misfortunes of her later years. In this way Hogg's poem contrives to offer a most unexpected glimpse, from the post-Enlightenment and Protestant Scotland of the early nineteenth century, of the nature of the Blessed Virgin Mary, a most highly favoured lady, full of grace, and Queen of Heaven.[59] There are, perhaps, qualities in 'Kilmeny' that connect both with the visionary mysticism of William Blake and with the voluptuous medievalism of the pre-Raphaelites.

Thomas Crawford once suggested, in effect, that Hogg might be described as Blake with a sense of humour.[60] This sense of humour is strongly present in 'The Witch of Fife', the other 'ancient stile' poem in the first edition of *The Queen's Wake*. In 'The Witch of Fife', the witch's husband overhears her magic word, and uses it to fly through the night sky after her to a riotous revel in the Bishop of Carlisle's wine-cellar. The old man, very drunk, is left behind by the witches when morning comes, and he is caught in the cellars 'by five rough Englishmen' (Night the First *1813*, l. 865). In the first edition the old man is condemned to death by his captors, and burnt at the stake. The poem then ends in a tone of mock-moralising similar to the conclusion of Burns's 'Tam o' Shanter':

> Let never ane auld man after this
> To lawless greide inclyne;
> Let never an auld man after this
> Rin post to the diel for wyne. (*1813*, ll. 889–92)

The poetic competition in *The Queen's Wake* lasts for three nights. 'The Witch of Fife' concludes the first night, and 'Kilmeny' concludes the second night. This prominent placing helps the two 'ancient stile' poems to stand out as a matched but contrasting pair of medieval images, as a poem of Heaven and a poem of Hell, as a holy statue and a gargoyle from the old pre-1560 world distrusted by Scott and the other heirs of the Scottish Enlightenment, but valued by Hogg. Significantly, the pattern of 'medieval' poems that can be clearly discerned in the first edition of *The Queen's Wake* is completed by 'The Abbot M'Kinnon', the poem that concludes the third and final night of the wake. Unlike 'Kilmeny' and 'The Witch of Fife', 'The Abbot M'Kinnon' does not seek to articulate the world-view of medieval Catholicism. Rather, it is a narrative, set on the holy island of Iona, about the collapse of the old medieval Scottish Catholic church.

In 563 St Columba and a few companions went from Ireland to Iona, and the monastic community they founded played a key role in establishing Christianity in Scotland. More than nine hundred years later, John Mackinnon, who died around 1499, was the last Abbot of Iona.[61] In the sixty or so years between Mackinnon's death and the Reformation, the Abbey was administered by successive Bishops of the Isles, and in this period the Abbey Church of Iona became in effect the Cathedral of the Isles. The communal life of the Abbey ceased in the years following 1560, and its buildings gradually fell into ruin. In this state they were famously visited and pondered over in 1773 by Dr Samuel Johnson, who in *A Journey to the Western Islands of Scotland* (1775) eloquently deplored the neglect that had caused their decay. The Abbey remained ruinous until the twentieth century, when the Abbey Church was restored by the Iona Cathedral Trustees and the associated monastic buildings were restored by the religious society known as the Iona Community.[62]

In Hogg's poem, the Abbot M'Kinnon is a deeply corrupt man who, in 'his visioned sleep', is called to account by the spirit of Saint Columba, 'the saint of the isle' (Night the Third *1813*, ll. 1747, 1727). The Abbot duly gets his comeuppance, through supernatural agency, on the nearby small island of Staffa. This island is the location of the spectacular natural phenomenon known as Fingal's Cave, and Staffa was one of Scotland's most prized tourist attractions in the nineteenth century. Staffa's famous grandeur makes it an appropriate location for the dramatic events through which Hogg's poem enacts the collapse of the medieval church through the weight of its own corruption.

For the Scottish intellectual establishment of Hogg's generation, the collapse of the medieval Catholic church at the time of the Reformation represented the march of progress, the banishing of corruption and superstition through the arrival of a purer and more rational form of religion. 'The Abbot M'Kinnon' significantly modifies this interpretation of events, however, by presenting the corruption as a departure from a pre-existing medieval Catholic purity represented by Columba. In 'The Abbot M'Kinnon', value lies not so much with the new Reformed and Enlightened world that will follow the last Abbot and will allow Iona Abbey to fall into ruin, but rather with an old early-medieval Catholic world, the world of St Columba, St Patrick, and the Book of Kells, the world whose legacy the last Abbot of Iona has betrayed. Likewise, medieval Catholicism is celebrated in 'Kilmeny' and 'The Witch of Fife'.

In *The Rise of the Historical Novel*, John MacQueen points out that Hogg's novel *The Three Perils of Man* (1822) gives a sympathetic treatment to religious themes from medieval romance. MacQueen writes: 'It is curious that Hogg's sympathies, normally so much for the Protestant Reformation and the Covenanters, should extend in this way to the Catholic Middle Ages'.[63] This puzzle (akin in a way to the surprising range of Hogg's political sympathies) is perhaps best understood in the context of Hogg's willingness to question some of the assumptions of the Enlightenment—for example, Enlightenment assumptions about the backwardness and worthlessness of superstitious peasants. Something of this can be glimpsed in Hogg's ac-

count, in his *Highland Journeys*, of his visit in 1803 to Loch Maree in
the company of Mr Mackenzie of Auchnasheen:

> we landed on St Mary's Isle, and I had the superstition to go
> and drink of the holy well, so renowned in that country, among
> the vulgar and superstitious like me, for the cure of insanity
> in all its stages, and so well authenticated are the facts, the
> most stubborn of all proofs, that even people of the most po-
> lite and modern ways of thinking are obliged to allow of its
> efficacy in some instances: but as mine was only an attack of
> poetical hydrophobia, inclining my tendency to knight-errantry,
> which, however ridiculous to some, I take a pleasure in; I
> omitted, however, the appendage of the ceremony, which in
> all probability is the most necessary and efficacious branch of
> it; namely, that of being plunged over head and ears three
> times in the lake.
>
> But though I write thus lightly to you of the subject, I ac-
> knowledge that I felt a kind of awe on my mind on wandering
> over the burying ground, and ruins of the Virgins chapel, held
> in such veneration by the devout, though illiterate fathers of
> the present generation: this I mentioned to Mr. Mackenzie,
> who assured me that had I visited it before the wood was cut
> down, such was the effect, that it was impossible not to be
> struck with a religious awe.[64]

Such attitudes appear to have encouraged Hogg to celebrate the life
and insights of a pre-Enlightenment Catholic world in the book-length
poem with which he hoped to emulate the successes of Scott and
Byron.

5. Publication and Reception of the First Version: The First and Second Editions (1813)

Clearly, Hogg had to find a publisher for *The Queen's Wake*. As was
natural, his first approach was made to Archibald Constable, who
had brought out *The Mountain Bard* in 1807, and who had also pub-
lished *The Forest Minstrel* in 1810. Hogg wrote as follows to Consta-
ble on 24 September 1812:

> Having now compleated the Queen's Wake I must settle about
> the publication for I am desirous that it should appear in Jan[r].
> or Feb[r] next. Of course as your right I give you the first offer

of it. [...] Geo. Goldie requests a share of it that shall be as you please. I will expect an answer with your conveniency.[65]

In 1807, Constable had paid the substantial sum of 1,000 guineas for the rights of Scott's *Marmion*, a book-length poem that was published with great success in 1808. Constable, that is to say, had every reason to wish to stay on good terms with Scott in 1807, and this no doubt played a part in his willingness to publish *The Mountain Bard* in that year, at Scott's suggestion. In 1808, however, serious tensions developed between the Whig Constable and the Tory Scott, partly because *Marmion* received a notably hostile review by Francis Jeffrey in Constable's Whig-supporting *Edinburgh Review*, and partly because of Scott's irritation at the *Edinburgh Review*'s opposition to Britain's involvement in the Peninsular War. These tensions helped to generate a quarrel between Scott and Constable, and at the beginning of 1809 Scott set up a new publishing house, John Ballantyne & Co., as a rival to Constable's firm. Scott's hugely successful poem *The Lady of the Lake* was published by the new firm in 1810, and there was to be no reconciliation between Scott and Constable until 1813, by which time John Ballantyne & Co. was in serious financial difficulties, and Constable came to the rescue in order to regain his highly profitable position as Scott's publisher. In 1810, therefore, Constable had no particular reason to feel that he owed Scott a favour, but he nevertheless published *The Forest Minstrel* in that year, partly as a favour to Hogg, and partly because *The Mountain Bard* had turned out to be a successful book. *The Forest Minstrel* failed to repeat the success of *The Mountain Bard*, however, and in September 1812 Constable was not particularly enthused by the prospect of publishing *The Queen's Wake*. George Goldie, a young Edinburgh publisher known to Hogg through the Forum, offered more favourable terms than Constable, and duly became the publisher, in partnership with the London firm of Longman, Hurst, Rees, Orme, and Brown.[66]

The first edition of *The Queen's Wake* was advertised as 'this day is published' in the *Edinburgh Evening Courant* of 30 January 1813. Prior to its launch Hogg's poem did not seem to be a particularly promising proposition. Its publisher was inexperienced and lacked capital, and in recent years its author had failed to find lasting success either as a Dumfriesshire farmer or as an Edinburgh journalist. Nevertheless, when *The Queen's Wake* appeared many people shared the enthusiasm attributed to William Dunlop in the passage from 'Memoir of the Author's Life' quoted at the beginning of the present Introduction. Finding that he had an unexpected success on his hands,

George Goldie enterprisingly took steps to generate further publicity by bringing out a 'second edition', which was advertised as 'this day is published' in the *Edinburgh Evening Courant* of 14 June 1813. This 'second' edition (again published in partnership with the London firm of Longman) in fact consisted of the remaining copies of the first edition, reissued with replacement pages at the beginning and end of the book. The replacement pages contain new material, some of it designed to highlight the extraordinary fact that this remarkable new poem was the work of a largely self-taught former farm labourer. For example, the new material includes laudatory 'Stanzas Addressed to The Ettrick Shepherd on the publication of The Queen's Wake'. An earlier version of this poem by the Suffolk poet and merchant Bernard Barton had been published in the *Edinburgh Evening Courant* for 29 April 1813.[67] Goldie's second edition also includes an 'Advertisement' (reprinted in the present edition's Appendix) in which the publisher is at pains to assure his readers that '*The Queen's Wake* is really and truly the production of *James Hogg*, a common Shepherd'. Hogg also took the opportunity to slip in a few short additional notes at the end of the poem. These new notes replaced the final few notes of the first edition, and were carried forward into the third and subsequent editions. Nevertheless, the second edition is essentially a repackaging, for publicity purposes, of the remaining copies of the first edition.

Reviews of *The Queen's Wake* began to appear soon after the publication of the first edition in January 1813, and many of them focus on Hogg's status as a poet of the people. A prompt review in the *Edinburgh Star* newspaper for 5 February 1813 praises the 'genius, taste, and skill' exhibited in *The Queen's Wake*, as well as the 'versatility of talent' of the author. Summing up, this reviewer writes:

> when it is recollected, that the author is a simple shepherd, who at the age of twenty could neither read nor write, perhaps even yet cannot boast of the benefits of polite learning, we trust it will be an additional inducement to the public to bestow their patronage upon a work, which, independently of all personal consideration, deserves to be treasured and admired. ([p. 3])

Likewise, the number of the *Scots Magazine* for February 1813 remarks that 'Mr Hogg seems at present to hold, in this country, the first rank among men of self-taught genius', and this review goes on to say that *The Queen's Wake* contains 'ballads, upon those subjects which have always been favourite with the national peasantry, the tenderness and vicissitudes of love, and the exploits of supernatural agency'.[68]

By May 1813 a favourable response to Hogg's poem began to emerge in England. The *Monthly Magazine* for that month includes a letter to the Editor (p. 501) in which the miscellaneous writer Capell Lofft (1751–1824) gives particularly warm praise to *The Queen's Wake*. In 1813 Lofft was a friend of Bernard Barton, and at an earlier stage of his career he had been involved in the arrangements for the publication of *The Farmer's Boy* by the shoemaker-poet Robert Bloomfield (1800). Lofft's letter to the *Monthly Magazine* of May 1813 comments on the new book by the Scottish shepherd-poet:

> Greater ease and spirit, a sweeter, richer, more animated and easy flow of versification, more clearness of language, more beauty of imagery, more grandeur, fervor, pathos, and occasionally more vivid and aweful sublimity, can hardly be found.

In the same month the *Theatrical Inquisitor* carried a notably enthusiastic review of *The Queen's Wake*. This review asserts that, while Scott

> still remains without a rival in the forcible delineation of character, in the rapid creation of incident and scenery, in the distinctness and beauty of local description, and in occasional loftiness of thought; he must share with the Ettrick Shepherd the honors of natural and unaffected sentiment, of simple, lively, and impressive narration, of graceful and natural expression, and of flowing and harmonious verse. In one respect Mr. Hogg is decidedly superior; his humour is natural and original; he never offends by abortive attempts at badinage or merriment; and in the only example of his comic powers that the volume contains, he is decidedly successful.[69]

This reviewer sees 'imperfections' in Hogg's poem that 'are the result of those personal disadvantages under which he has been doomed to labour' (p. 219), but one of the poems of the *Wake* is seen as being particularly impressive: 'We are not sure that in the whole compass of modern poetry there is any thing superior in elegance, pathos, and simplicity, to the ballad entitled, *Mary Scott*' (p. 222). Furthermore, the review in the *Theatrical Inquisitor* remarks that 'Mr. Hogg is always consistent with himself; his language and versification bear the most perfect accordance with the character he calls into action, the events that he relates, and the scenery that surrounds him' (p. 225).

Another favourable review appeared in the June 1813 number of the *British Critic*: 'The whole forms a most pleasing volume, which all lovers of simple, unembellished poetry, will read with delight'.[70] The *Eclectic Review* of June 1813 was more hostile, believing that 'the public begin to have enough of ghosts and goblins, of spirits of the storm, and ladies of the glen, and wraiths, and second-seers, and wee wee men'.[71] These 'gothic beings' had once been credible to 'a people residing in a gloomy climate, and picturesque country, and besides under the dominion of monks and superstitious terrors' (p. 647), but (thanks to the efforts of poets and commentators) the mysteries of 'ghosts and brownies, and vampires, and grim-white women are grown as familiar as cats and dogs that sleep upon the parlour rug' (p. 648). It will be remembered that, in the passage from his 'Memoir' quoted at the beginning of this Introduction, Hogg says that in 1813 the *Eclectic* tried to hold up *The Queen's Wake* 'to ridicule and contempt'. However, even this hostile reviewer takes the view that 'The Witch of Fife' is 'very entertaining', while 'some parts' of 'Kilmeny' are said to be 'very beautiful' (p. 651).

A long and detailed early review of *The Queen's Wake* in the *Scotish [sic] Review* takes the usual view of Hogg's background: 'From his situation in life, and very defective education, or rather total want of education, a certain vulgarity of conception was necessarily entailed upon him'.[72] According to this reviewer, vulgarity had been a marked feature of *The Mountain Bard*. All is now changed, however:

> No person, we will venture to say, who has formed his opinion of the Ettrick shepherd from "The Mountain Bard," can have the faintest anticipation of the treasure he is to meet with in "The Queen's Wake." Instead of that vulgarity which once so justly gave offence, he will meet with a delicacy of sentiment and expression which would do honour to the most skilful master in the art of numbers; that imagination which seemed shackled down by local habits, he will behold soaring into the furthest regions of human thought; and, throughout the whole, he will perceive the most indubitable marks of a great, original, and truly poetic mind. (p. 109)

The appearance of the first edition of *The Queen's Wake* was a life-changing event for Hogg. In the autumn of 1809 he had been disgraced and unemployable as a shepherd in his native Ettrick, but the dazzling success of *The Queen's Wake* converted him into a famous author, and new friendships and new horizons began to open up. The unemployable ex-shepherd soon found himself on friendly terms with such people as Lord Byron and William Wordsworth. Now he could with justice feel that he was being taken seriously as a poet. His inward consciousness that he would live to be compared with Burns was no longer an aspiration to be automatically dismissed as outrageously and absurdly audacious. Hogg had arrived.

6. Revising *The Queen's Wake*: The Third and Fourth Editions (1814)

The third edition of *The Queen's Wake* was published by Goldie in Edinburgh and by Henry Colburn in London: there is evidence that Goldie had been dissatisfied with the efforts made on behalf of Hogg's poem by the London firm of Longman, with whom he had published the first and second editions.[73] At all events, the third edition was advertised as 'this day is published' in the *Edinburgh Evening Courant* for 14 July 1814, and it retains the new material that had been inserted at the beginning and end of the second edition. Unlike the second edition, however, the third edition was an entirely new printing, and thus offered Hogg an opportunity to make corrections and revisions at any point of his choosing in his poem. *The Queen's Wake* had proved itself to be a valuable commercial property, and this prompted major players in Edinburgh's literary world to sit up, take notice, and offer Hogg advice about how his poem could be enhanced. No doubt flattered by the attention, Hogg took at least some of the advice, and as a result the third edition contains significant changes in a few particular areas of the text.

For example, the ending of 'The Witch of Fife' was completely changed at Scott's suggestion, as Hogg explains in his *Familiar Anecdotes of Sir Walter Scott*:

> I was indebted to him for the most happy and splendid piece of humorous ballad poetry which I ever wrote. He said to me one day after dinner "It was but very lately Mr Hogg that I was drawn by our friend Kirkpatrick Sharpe to note the merits of your ballad The Witch of Fife. There never was such a thing written for genuine and ludicrous humour but why in the name of wonder did you suffer the gude auld man to be burnt skin and bone by the English at Carlisle (for in the first and second editions that was the issue). I never saw a piece of such bad taste in all my life. What had the poor old carl done to deserve such a fate? Only taken a drappy o' drink too much at another man's expense which you and I have done often. It is a *finale* which I cannot bear and you *must* bring of[f] the old

man by some means or other no matter how extravagant or ridiculous in such a ballad as yon but by all means bring off the fine old fellow for the present termination of the ballad is one which I cannot brook." I went home and certainly brought off the old man with flying colours which is by far the best part of the ballad.[74]

Hogg here writes generously about Scott's suggestion for changing the ending of 'The Witch of Fife', and it is certainly true that this poem works well with the revised ending published in the third and subsequent editions. However, the original version of the first two editions also works well in the context of *The Queen's Wake* as a whole, a context in which the exuberant satanic diablerie of 'The Witch of Fife' forms a significant contrast with the heavenly serenity and purity of 'Kilmeny'.

The third edition of *The Queen's Wake* also makes changes to a passage in the 'Conclusion' in which Scott appears in the guise of 'Walter the abbot'. The passage in question relates to an incident that seems to have taken place in 1804. In *Anecdotes of Sir W. Scott*, Hogg mentions that Scott at that time

engaged me to Lord Porchester as his chief shepherd to have a riding horse, house and small farm free of rent, and £20 over and above, but with this strick proviso that "I was to put my poetical talent under lock and key for ever" I copy the very words. Of course I spurned at the idea and refused to implement the bargain. I think my friend the present Lord Porchester would have been sorry to have put me under the same restrictions. This is the circumstance alluded to in The Queen's Wake as a reflection on Walter the Abbot.[75]

We shall return to the 'reflection on Walter the Abbot', but first let us consider the event of 1804 that provoked the 'reflection'. By 1804, Hogg was already a published poet: various pieces had appeared in the *Scots Magazine*, and his slim volume of *Scottish Pastorals* had been published in 1801. Furthermore, Scott's *Minstrelsy of the Scottish Border* (1802–03) had contained several items obtained from Ettrick oral tradition through Hogg's good offices. It would appear that in 1804 a well-intentioned and grateful Scott, having obtained a plum shepherding job for his ballad-collecting protégé, was anxious to ensure that Hogg would focus on his day job and forget his literary ambitions. This attitude clearly grew out of a genuine and practical concern for Hogg's well-being, but it is also compatible with the reservations about the activities of lower-class poets expressed in

an anonymous article (generally attributed to Scott) that appeared
in the first volume of the *Edinburgh Annual Register*. This volume (pub-
lished in 1810) relates to the events of 1808. The article in question
is entitled 'Of the Living Poets of Great Britain', and in it Hogg is
mentioned as an example of

> the poets who daily spring up among the lees of the people,
> and find admirers to patronize them because they write "won-
> derfully well *considering*." This is, abstractedly, one of the most
> absurd claims to distinction possible. We do not suppose any
> living poet, Southey for instance, or Campbell, would gain
> much credit for making a pair of shoes, although they might
> be very well made *considering*. [...] Yet let a weaver, a shoe-
> maker, or a tailor, produce a copy of verses, and he shall find
> those to extol him above the best poets of the time, and to
> silence all objection and criticism, by referring, as an apology,
> to that which should have withheld him from the attempt,–his
> ignorance and his want of education.

Scott goes on to make the point that the exceptional case of Burns
shows that 'a poet in the noblest sense of the word' may arise 'from
the lower ranks of society'. Nevertheless, Scott deplores the danger
of 'turning the brain of an useful peasant or artizan', a danger that
he believes arises when members of 'a class of subaltern literati'
seduce 'honest ploughmen from their teams, mechanics from their
shopboards, and milk maids from their pails, to enlist them in the
precarious service of Apollo'. Scott continues:

> We wish we could consider this folly as disinterested in pro-
> portion to its absurdity; but such patrons make a stalkinghorse
> of the *protegé*, tagging the poetry of the *paysan parvenu* with
> their own more worthless *dicta* and commentaries, assuming
> the airs of a Mæcenas at a cheap rate, and, under pretence of
> doing justice to obscure merit, intruding upon the public their
> own contemptible personages in the character of its master of
> ceremonies. It was thus that Mr. Capel Lofft contrived to ride
> forward into public notice on the shoulders of poor
> BLOOMFIELD [...].

Placing the shoemaker-poet Bloomfield 'at a distance incalculably
beneath the Ayrshire ploughman', Scott goes on to deplore the fact
that the success of Burns

> had the effect of exciting general emulation among all of his
> class in Scotland who were able to tag a rhyme. The quantity

of Scottish verses with which we were inundated was abso-
lutely overwhelming. Poets began to chirp in every corner
like grasshoppers in a sunshine day. The steep rocks poured
down poetical goatherds, and the bowels of the earth vomited
forth rhyming colliers; but of all the herd we can only distin-
guish James Hogg, the Selkirkshire shepherd, as having at all
merited the public attention; and there cleaves to his poetry a
vulgarity of conception and expression which we greatly ques-
tion his ever being able to overcome. In other respects his
talents, though less noticed, are at least equal to those of Mr.
Bloomfield.[76]

Scott's line of argument here seems to be that the pursuit of poetical
excellence is an activity most appropriately undertaken by a gentle-
man: just as the proverbial cobbler should stick to his last, so a shep-
herd should stick to his sheep-fold. Scott's article appeared in 1810,
and Hogg responded angrily to it in the number of *The Spy* for 24
August 1811.[77] It may well be that this dispute lends energy to the
contest in the 1813 version of *The Queen's Wake* between the poets of
the Harp of Queen Mary and the poets of the Caledonian Harp, but
at all events significant consequences were to follow from the Ettrick
Shepherd's refusal to put his poetical talent under lock and key for
ever in order to devote himself to Lord Porchester's sheep.

During 1804, the year of the Porchester offer, Hogg lost his sav-
ings in an abortive attempt to set himself up as a sheep-farmer in the
Hebrides. He then spent the winter of 1804–05 working on poems
for *The Mountain Bard*, which was eventually published in 1807.
During 1805 Hogg found employment (which lasted until 1807) as
a shepherd working for a Mr Harkness in Dumfriesshire. While
working for Mr Harkness Hogg was sought out by another work-
ing-class enthusiast for poetry, the young Allan Cunningham, later
to become the famous 'stonemason poet'. In his 'Reminiscences of
Former Days' in *Altrive Tales* Hogg writes of being approached by
two strangers 'as I was herding my master's ewes on the great hill of
Queensberry'. The younger was 'the very model of Burns, and ex-
actly such a man'. Hogg continues:

> The eldest came up and addressed me frankly, asking me if
> I was Mr. Harkness's shepherd, and if my name was James
> Hogg? to both of which queries I answered cautiously in the
> affirmative, for I was afraid they were come to look after me
> with an accusation regarding some of the lasses. The younger
> stood at a respectful distance, as if I had been the Duke of

Queensberry, instead of a ragged servant lad herding sheep. The other seized my hand, and said, "Well, then, sir, I am glad to see you. There is not a man in Scotland whose hand I am prouder to hold."

I could not say a single word in answer to this address; but when he called me SIR, I looked down at my bare feet and ragged coat, to remind the man whom he was addressing. But he continued: "My name is James Cunningham, a name unknown to you, though yours is not entirely so to me; and this is my younger brother Allan, the greatest admirer that you have on earth, and himself a young aspiring poet of some promise. You will be so kind as excuse this intrusion of ours on your solitude, for, in truth, I could get no peace either night or day with Allan, till I consented to come and see you."

[...] Young as he was, I had heard of [Allan's] name, although slightly, and, I think, seen one or two of his juvenile pieces. Of an elder brother of his, Thomas Mouncey, I had, previous to that, conceived a very high idea, and I always marvel how he could possibly put his poetical vein under lock and key, as he did all at once; for he certainly then bade fair to be the first of Scottish bards.

I had a small bothy upon the hill, in which I took my breakfast and dinner on wet days, and rested myself. It was so small, that we had to walk in on all-fours; and when we were in, we could not get up our heads any way, but in a sitting posture. It was exactly my own length, and, on the one side, I had a bed of rushes, which served likewise as a seat; on this we all three sat down, and there we spent the whole afternoon,—and, I am sure, a happier group of three never met on the hill of Queensberry. [...] Thus began at that bothy in the wilderness a friendship, and a mutual attachment between two aspiring Scottish peasants, over which the shadow of a cloud has never yet passed.[78]

Hogg would undoubtedly have been more comfortable (although not necessarily more happy) if he had accepted Scott's advice, put his poetical talent under lock and key for ever, and accepted Lord Porchester's offer—and this provides a context for the evident and strong feelings that lie behind the mention of the incident of Scott and Lord Porchester in the 'Conclusion' of *The Queen's Wake*. In the first edition, the 'Conclusion' tells how ('blest be the day') Scott, in the guise of 'Walter the abbot', found the neglected ancient

harp of Scottish Border minstrelsy, re-tuned it, and made it play
again to glorious effect: 'Then poured the numbers bold and free, |
The simple magic melody' (*1813*, ll. 309, 314–15). Hogg's voice
then continues (*1813*, ll. 326–45):

> Blest be his generous heart for ay!
> He told me where the relic lay;
> Pointed my way with ready will,
> Afar on Ettrick's wildest hill;
> Watched my first notes with curious eye,
> And wondered at my minstrelsy:
> He little weened, a parent's tongue
> Such strains had o'er my cradle sung.
>
> But when, to native feelings true,
> I struck upon a chord was new;
> When by myself I 'gan to play
> He tried to wile my harp away.
> Just when her notes began with skill,
> To sound beneath the southern hill,
> And twine around my bosom's core,
> How could we part for evermore?
> 'Twas kindness all, I cannot blame,
> For bootless is the minstrel flame;
> But sure, a bard might well have known
> Another's feelings by his own!

In the first edition's 'Conclusion', Hogg makes high claims for
Scott's poetry. However, he arguably makes even higher claims for
his own poetry, which is presented as being more firmly rooted
than Scott's in the culture of the people: being 'to native feelings
true', Hogg's poetry is able to strike a new chord. Clearly, he does
not aspire to be a mere disciple of Scott, humbly following in his
master's footsteps. Instead, he sees himself as an alternative, a rival,
to Scott. And the rivalry has a certain edge. Perhaps a hint of para-
noia can be detected in these lines in their implied suggestion that
Scott's wish to put Hogg's poetical talent under lock and key for
ever may have sprung from a devious desire to silence a rival: 'When
by myself I 'gan to play | He tried to wile my harp away'. Clearly,
such a view would be unfair to Scott. Nevertheless, a trace of para-
noia on Hogg's part would perhaps be understandable, in all the
circumstances. However that may be, the third and subsequent edi-
tions of *The Queen's Wake* tone down the paranoia by replacing the

first four lines of the second verse paragraph quoted above. The new version reads:

> O could the bard I loved so long,
> Reprove my fond aspiring song!
> Or could his tongue of candour say,
> That I should throw my harp away!

Even in this later, softened version, however, there is an acute sense that an aspiring poet has felt betrayed by a fellow poet's lack of imaginative sympathy.

Hogg's reaction to this incident doubtless derived its emotional intensity precisely because of his hero-worship of Scott as a pre-eminent writer. Indeed, as he brings *Anecdotes of Sir W. Scott* to a close, Hogg writes:

> But to put an end to these trivial anecdotes for trivial they are were they not about so extraordinary a man. The greatest man in the world while he lived and must long be remembered as such now that he is gone What are kings or emperors compared with Sir Walter Scott? Dust and Sand! The most part of their names regarded with detestation. But here is a name that next to that of William Shakespere's will descend with rapt admiration to all the ages of futurity. And is it not a proud boast for an old shepherd that he could call this man FRIEND and could associate with him every day and every hour that he chose?[79]

Clearly, for Hogg, a great poet like Scott was much more deserving of respect than his widely-detested contemporaries, Britain's King George IV, and Napoleon Bonaparte, Emperor of France. But there is an assertive edge to Hogg's declaration, as well as genuine and affectionate respect for Scott. If talent as a writer rather than social standing is what really counts in the end, then the great social gulf between the baronet and the shepherd withers into insignificance. There is a suggestion here, not too far below the surface, that the Author of *The Queen's Wake* is entitled to look anyone in the eye, as he successfully re-tunes the ancient Caledonian harp, the harp of the people. Even in their revised and toned-down version, the lines in *The Queen's Wake* to 'Walter the abbot' draw a raw emotional energy from Hogg's desire to be accepted as Burns's successor as the poet who gives voice to the experiences and insights of the non-elite people of Scotland.

Significant revisions were also made to 'Kilmeny' for the third edition of *The Queen's Wake*. Peter Garside has shown that, in the 1820s, the publisher William Blackwood tended to be distinctly uneasy about Hogg's 'ancient stile', and took steps to remove it from the poems published in *A Queer Book* in 1832.[80] Blackwood's motive for this is evident: the 'ancient stile' poems would be easier to read, and therefore more marketable, if they were re-presented in more modern and more familiar language. A similar motivation would appear to lie behind the major revision of 'Kilmeny' undertaken for the third edition of *The Queen's Wake*. It is not known whether Hogg undertook this revision on his own initiative or at the suggestion of others, but at all events, in the third and subsequent editions, 'Kilmeny' is translated into a conventional modern literary Scots little different from standard English. We have already quoted the concluding lines of 'Kilmeny' as they appear in the first edition:

> It walsna her heme, and scho culdna remayne;
> Scho left this worild of sorrow and paine,
> And returnit to the land of thochte againe.

In the third edition these lines become:

> It wasna her hame, and she couldna remain;
> She left this world of sorrow and pain,
> And returned to the land of thought again.[81]

The removal of Hogg's 'ancient stile' tends to make 'Kilmeny' prettier and more easily accessible, but it also tends to make the poem less hard-edged and unsettling. Above all, this change involves the loss of the original version's medieval feel, the loss of its attempt to locate value in the old pre-1560 Scotland. In short, it appears that significant changes were made to 'Kilmeny' and 'The Witch of Fife' for the third edition of *The Queen's Wake*, with a view to making these poems more accessible and more acceptable to the reading public of the mid-1810s. However, these changes tend to obscure a coherent and somewhat subversive aspect of the narrative structure of the original version.

7. The Publication and Reception of the Third and Fourth Editions of *The Queen's Wake*

Arrangements for the publication of the third edition of *The Queen's Wake* in July 1814 did not prove to be straightforward, because

George Goldie was in financial difficulties. We have already seen that Scott's publishing firm John Ballantyne & Co. was in deep financial trouble in 1813, and the Ballantyne firm's difficulties (like Goldie's) owed a good deal to the general British financial crisis of 1812–14. The current progress of the Napoleonic Wars was a significant factor in this crisis. After their disastrous retreat from Moscow during the winter of 1812–13, Napoleon's forces were gradually ground down by the large armies of an extensive coalition which included Russia, Austria, and Prussia. Britain played a major but costly role in financing this massive war effort. However, the stresses and strains involved produced a reward in April 1814 when the armies of the allies entered Paris. Following this, a defeated Napoleon was exiled to the island of Elba.

The undercapitalised publishing business of George Goldie was no more immune than John Ballantyne & Co. to the financial pressures of 1812–14, and it appears that rumours began to circulate in 1813 that Goldie was about to be declared bankrupt. Indeed, many members of the Edinburgh book trade were in severe difficulties in 1813. In his *Sir Walter Scott: The Great Unknown*, Edgar Johnson writes:

> Under the war strain, business conditions grew steadily worse; booksellers were failing and banks refusing loans. Clarke of St. Andrew Street, Walker of Hunter Square, and numbers of smaller houses had all gone under, leaving masses of dishonored bills.[82]

In this climate, and aware of Goldie's financial fragility, Hogg wished to place the third edition of *The Queen's Wake* with the long-established and apparently financially stable Archibald Constable. This was a natural reaction, but Goldie (equally naturally) wished to remain the publisher of this notably successful poem, as he fought for his financial life. At all events, in the 'Memoir of the Author's Life' Hogg tells us that, alarmed by the rumours of Goldie's impending bankruptcy, he offered the third edition of *The Queen's Wake* to Constable. Hogg continues:

> We closed a bargain at once, and the book was sent to Mr. [James] Ballantyne to print. But after a part was thrown off, Goldie got notice of the transaction, and was neither to hold nor bind, pretending that he had been exceedingly ill used. He waited on Mr. Constable one hour, and corresponded with him the next, till he induced him to give up the bargain. It was in vain that I remonstrated, affirming that the work was my

own, and I would give it to whom I pleased. I had no one to take my part, and I was browbeat out of it—Goldie alleging that I had no reason to complain, as he now entered precisely into Constable's terms, and had run all the risk of the former editions. I durst not say that he was going to break, and never pay me; so I was obliged to suffer the edition to be printed off in Goldie's name.[83]

The third edition of *The Queen's Wake* was duly published under Goldie's imprint, and made its appearance on 14 July 1814 in an Edinburgh that was still rejoicing in the recent fall of Paris and the apparent ending of the Napoleonic Wars. George Goldie's financial difficulties remained real and pressing, however, and within three weeks of the publication of the third edition the Author of *The Queen's Wake* was complaining to his fellow poet Lord Byron about Goldie's failure to honour his financial obligations.[84] In the event Goldie struggled on for a few weeks more, but he was declared bankrupt in early September 1814. Sales of the third edition appear to have been going very well until this benign process was abruptly halted by Goldie's bankruptcy. Clearly, Hogg had to try to get the remaining copies of the third edition released for sale as soon as possible, before the current tide of interest in his poem ebbed away. Accordingly, on 28 October 1814 he wrote as follows to the up-and-coming Tory Edinburgh publisher William Blackwood, who had been appointed as one of Goldie's trustees:

> I request that one half of the copies be instantly given up to me for circulation in which case I will give up all claims upon the estate for that edition and grant security to the trustees to the full amount of one half of the paper and printing.[85]

This was Hogg's first business contact with Blackwood. It was to lead to a long, mutually advantageous, but often acrimonious working relationship between the two men.

In his 'Memoir of the Author's Life' Hogg records that Goldie's trustees treated him generously with regard to the third edition of *The Queen's Wake*. They agreed that he should have:

> the whole of the remaining copies, 490 in number, charging me only with the expenses of printing, &c. These, to my agreeable astonishment, amounted only to two shillings and tenpence halfpenny per volume. The work sold at twelve shillings, so that a good reversion appeared to be mine. Mr. Blackwood sold the copies for me on commission, and ultimately paid me more than double of what I was to have received from Goldie.

For this I was indebted to the consideration and kindness of the trustees.[86]

At this period Blackwood was becoming a significant publisher in his own right, but he was also John Ballantyne's successor as the Scottish agent of the leading London publisher, John Murray of Albemarle Street. Just as Blackwood sold Murray's books in Edinburgh, so Murray sold Blackwood's books in London, and in a letter to Murray of 25 November 1814, Blackwood discusses entries for Murray's catalogue:

> You might also insert Hogg's Queen's Wake, 8vo sells at 12/ He is to get upwards of 500 copies from Goldie's Trustees and print a new title page calling it the fourth edition with your name and mine.[87]

On 11 December 1814 Blackwood wrote again to Murray, saying that three hundred copies of *The Queen's Wake* were now on their way to London by ship. Working with round figures, he adds 'I have only 100 left of the Q. Wake as there were only 400 in Goldie's stock'.[88] The fourth edition of *The Queen's Wake* duly appeared a few days later, being described as 'just published' in the *Edinburgh Evening Courant* for 15 December 1814.

The importance of making copies of *The Queen's Wake* once again available for sale was underlined by the appearance of a long and favourable review of the third edition of the poem in the November 1814 number of the *Edinburgh Review*. In this review, Francis Jeffrey provides a memorable portrait of Hogg at this stage of his career:

> In the mean time, it must be agreeable to his readers to know, that they are engaged with the work of an author who has in reality all that devotion and enthusiasm for his calling which is so often pretended to disguise the less noble motives which sometimes lead to its adoption; and who, we verily believe, would rather starve upon poetry, than accept of ease and affluence on condition of renouncing it. Delighting still more in the pursuit itself, than in the glory to which he no doubt thinks it is to conduct him, he is resolute, we are persuaded, to serve the Muses, even without the appropriate wages of fame—and will not be induced to abandon them by the want of that success which he will at all events believe he has deserved. It ought also be recorded to his honour, that he has uniformly sought this success by the fairest and most manly means; and that neither poverty nor ambition has been able to produce in

him the slightest degree of obsequiousness towards the pos-
sessors of glory or power; or even to subdue him in a certain
disposition to bid defiance to critics, and to hold poets and
patrons equally cheap and familiar; and to think that they can
in general give no more honour than they receive from his
acquaintance. These traits we think are unusual in men whom
talents have raised out of a humble condition in society—espe-
cially where they are unaccompanied, as in the present in-
stance, either with any inherent insolence of character, or any
irregularities, in private life; and therefore we have thought it
right to notice them. But at all events, the merit of the volume
before us is such, as to entitle it to our notice; and as the au-
thor has fairly fought his way to that distinction, we are not
disposed to withhold from him either the additional notoriety
which it may still be in our power to bestow, or the admoni-
tions which may enable him still further to improve a talent
that has already surprised us so much by its improvement.[89]

Jeffrey goes on to praise the connecting narrative of *The Queen's
Wake* as 'a fiction not without elegance or ingenuity' (p. 161). He
asserts that Hogg 'gives occasional indications of bad taste in assort-
ing harsh and homely pictures with others that are elegant and im-
pressive', but nevertheless this poet's 'great merit' is 'an occasional
exaltation of fancy that brings him now and then to the borders of a
very high species of poetry' (p. 162). Jeffrey singles out 'Kilmeny'
and 'The Abbot M'Kinnon' for special praise. He describes
'Kilmeny' as a 'singular composition; upon the strength of which
alone we should feel ourselves completely justified, in assuring the
author, that no doubt can be entertained that he is a poet—in the
highest acceptation of the name' (p. 168).

Unsurprisingly, Hogg was much buoyed up by such a positive
response to his poem in a periodical as influential (and as exacting
in its standards) as the *Edinburgh Review*. Some signs of a reaction
against Hogg can be traced in other reviews of 1814 and 1815, how-
ever. For example, a certain irritation at the current fashion for Scot-
tish poetry can be seen in the distinctly unsympathetic account of
The Queen's Wake to be found in *The Monthly Review* for December
1814:

Mary, Queen of Scots, is supposed to hold her court at
Holyrood House; and for a period of three nights to be kept
awake (which we consider as quite miraculous if she listened,
but quite natural if she was merely disturbed) by the succes-

sive songs, of all sorts and sizes, of *seventeen* Scotish [*sic*] minstrels![90]

This reviewer, not mincing his words, declares that *The Queen's Wake* exhibits 'the violation of every principle and rule of poetry' (p. 435). The *New Universal Magazine*, in its number for April 1815, is disposed to be a little more charitable. This review ends as follows:

> Mr. Hogg has certainly produced a volume indicative of no ordinary degree of poetical talent; but we should be happy to see that talent cultivated and applied to topics less wild, improbable and absurd than those which he selects from evident predilection.[91]

However, *La Belle Assemblée* in its number for October 1815 comes closer to articulating the general consensus about *The Queen's Wake* when it comments: 'the fiction introduced is elegant, and marks an inventive genius'.[92]

Of all the reviews of Hogg's poem in 1814 and 1815, by far the most influential was Jeffrey's in the November 1814 number of the *Edinburgh Review*. The weight carried by this review can be sensed, for example, in the newspaper *The Champion* for 15 January 1815, which declares, under the heading 'Mr. Hogg the Poet':

> We extract the following passages from a criticism in the last number of the Edinburgh Review, on the *Queen's Wake* of this writer, whose works are not yet sufficiently known. We think the extracts from the poetry will plead powerfully with our readers to know more of him.

When *The Queen's Wake* first found its way into the bookshops early in 1813 it had not seemed a particularly promising candidate for fame, but by the early months of 1815 Jeffrey's influential seal of approval was ensuring its status as one of the recognised British literary landmarks of the age. Hogg's poem was also finding readers in North America. An edition was published in Baltimore by Coale and Maxwell in 1815, another edition appeared in Philadelphia in the same year, and still another edition was published in New York by A. T. Goodrich in 1818.[93] At the beginning of the 1810s Hogg had been a discredited and unemployable shepherd, but by the middle of the decade he had transformed himself through *The Queen's Wake* into an admired and internationally-known poet. As a result, from 1815 onwards Hogg's new books regularly and proudly use their titlepages to proclaim themselves to be the work of that notable and respected figure, 'The Author of *The Queen's Wake*'.

8. The Delayed Publication of the Fifth and Sixth Editions (1819)

When the fourth edition of *The Queen's Wake* was published in December 1814 Hogg's poem was already an established success. Furthermore, it had recently received a valuable boost from the *Edinburgh Review*, and Hogg seemed to have secured a place alongside Scott and Byron as one of the leading British poets of the 1810s. The fourth edition of *The Queen's Wake*, representing the remnant of the bankrupt Goldie's third edition, was in the capable and enterprising hands of William Blackwood and John Murray, and the reasonable expectation was that a fifth edition would soon be required. In the event, a fifth edition was indeed published by Blackwood and Murray. However, its publication was delayed until 1819, and when it did eventually appear it was not a resounding success. In short, in the middle and late 1810s Hogg's career as a poet lost momentum.

What, then, lay behind this unexpected and disappointing development? A clue is provided by the fate of *Mador of the Moor*, one of the long narrative poems with which Hogg tried to follow up the success of *The Queen's Wake*. It appears that *Mador* 'was begun, and in a very short time completed'[94] while Hogg was on a visit to the Highlands in the summer of 1813, a few months after the publication of the first edition of *The Queen's Wake*. As James Barcus has argued, the name 'Mador' suggests 'made o'er' or 'made over', and *Mador of the Moor* is in effect a makeover of *The Lady of the Lake* (1810), the greatest popular success among Scott's long poems.[95] Hogg's poem, like Scott's, tells how a deer-hunt in the Highlands leads an incognito King of Scots into an adventure involving a young woman. Scott's Lady of the Lake is a young Lowland aristocrat living in exile in the Highlands, and her relationship with the incognito king is a chaste one. In contrast, Hogg's Ila Moore is a Highland girl of low social standing who is made pregnant by the incognito king of her poem. However, Ila's inherent resourcefulness and strength of character suggest that a peasant girl pregnant out of wedlock can be a person much more worthy of respect than *Mador*'s frequently absurd aristocrats: even the king cuts a comic and discreditable figure at some points. Hogg offered this poem to Archibald Constable in February 1814, but his offer was not accepted:[96] perhaps Constable felt that the reading public was not quite ready for a heroine like Ila. (Much later in the nineteenth century Hardy was to have severe problems with regard to *Tess of the D'Urbervilles*.) At all events Hogg had to wait until 1816 before his poem was eventually published by William Blackwood.

Mador of the Moor is a wonderfully readable poem, but its challengingly egalitarian narrative did not match the taste and prejudices of the most powerful players in the literary marketplace of the 1810s. In that marketplace *The Queen's Wake* had been an intriguing novelty, being (as George Goldie had pointed out in the second edition) an attractive and interesting poem by (of all delightfully improbable things!) 'a common shepherd'. However, on closer acquaintance the common shepherd began to seem less appealing, and even a little alarming. Although the fellow undoubtedly possessed a good deal of unrefined raw talent, he was all too clearly an uppity boor who did not know his place, and who had wildly inappropriate ambitions for a man of his lowly station. During the 1810s he even started work on an epic poem, *Queen Hynde*. Apparently this farm labourer imagined he could emulate Homer and Milton!

The middle and late 1810s were not a propitious time for Hogg's attempt to offer the British poetry-reading public a series of challengingly egalitarian texts. The French Revolution's ideals of liberty, equality, and fraternity had led directly to the long struggle of the Napoleonic Wars, and in 1814 military defeat for Napoleon and the fall of Paris had sparked off wild rejoicing in Regency Britain, not least in Edinburgh. However, supporters of the British political status quo were deeply alarmed early in 1815 when Napoleon's return to France from exile in Elba caused the overthrow of the recently-restored Bourbon monarchy, and set in motion the heady events of the Hundred Days. During the Hundred Days the egalitarian genie seemed to be out of its bottle once more, and acute fears of revolutionary social unrest were to continue to haunt the British elite even after the decisive allied victory over Napoleon at Waterloo in June 1815. For example, 1819 saw the infamous Peterloo Massacre, in which a peaceful Radical political meeting in Manchester was violently dispersed by cavalry. In times like these many of the British gentry class, when they turned to poetry, were not likely to be particularly sympathetic to a radically egalitarian voice of the kind to be heard in texts like *Mador of the Moor*. This was the context in which the popularity of the Author of *The Queen's Wake* faltered.

Nevertheless, Hogg was naturally anxious to maintain the momentum of his poetic career after the publication of the fourth edition of *The Queen's Wake* in December 1814, and he wrote to William Blackwood on 6 October 1815 to suggest the publication of a three-volume 'edition of all my poetry'.[97] Blackwood's dampening response

is dated 9 October 1815, and declares the projected collected edition
to be

> entirly [*sic*] out of the question at present, as there are so many
> on hand both of the queens wake and the pilgrims. Of the
> former Mr Murray has 80 Copies & I have upwards of 120. I
> am not so certain of the quantity of the pilgrims, but I suppose
> there are about 400 copies remaining.[98]

Blackwood here mentions *Pilgrims of the Sun* (1814),[99] another of the
poems with which Hogg tried to follow up the success of *The Queen's
Wake*. The slow sales of *Pilgrims of the Sun* and the fourth edition of
The Queen's Wake inevitably meant that the preparation of a fifth edi-
tion of *The Queen's Wake* was not seen as a matter of urgency during
1815 and 1816. Indeed, the dampened enthusiasm for Hogg's po-
etry meant that when plans for a new edition of *The Queen's Wake*
finally began to move towards fruition, this project was not an en-
tirely straightforward commercial venture. Blackwood wrote to
Murray on 28 May 1817, saying that Hogg

> has laid aside for the present his intention of a pocket edition of
> the Queen's Wake. We found it would make too thick a vol-
> ume for the foolscap size, and that therefore it would be better
> to print another edition as formerly in Octavo which can be got
> ready for next winter. In the mean time Mr Scott and some of
> his friends, in order to raise a sum of money to make the poor
> Shepherd comfortable, have projected a 4to [quarto] edition
> with a few plates to be published by subscription.[100]

In publication 'by subscription', subscribers were obtained for a
proposed book in advance of publication. When, early in his ca-
reer, Scott was able to sell the copyright of *Minstrelsy of the Scottish
Border* for £500, he rejoiced in having been able to avoid publica-
tion by subscription: 'it is asking the public to become bound to pay
for what they have not seen, & carries with it if not the reality at least
the appearance of personal solicitation & personal obligation'.[101] How-
ever, if Scott felt that publication by subscription was not the most
desirable route for a gentleman to take, he nevertheless saw it as a
suitable way for a gentleman to help a dependent author such as
Hogg. Scott's efforts to help Hogg were genuinely admirable in their
own way, and it was with a view to giving Hogg real and much-
needed help that Scott tried in 1817 to drum up subscribers for the
projected quarto edition of *The Queen's Wake*. Scott wrote on this matter
to Lord Montagu on 8 June 1817 (but unfortunately could not resist

one of the pig puns on Hogg's name that gave much amusement to
the Shepherd's gentlemanly friends):

> MY DEAR LORD,—I am honourd with your letter and will not
> fail to take care that the Shepherd profits by your kind inten-
> tions and those of Lady Montagu. This is a scheme which I
> did not devise for I fear it will end in disappointment but for
> which I have done and will do all I possibly can. There is an
> old saying of the seamens every man is not born to be a boat-
> swain and I think I have heard of men born under a six penny
> planet and doomd never to be worth a groat. I fear something
> of this vile sixpenny influence has gleamd in at the cottage
> window when poor Hogg first came squeaking into this world.
> [...] But no one has loose guineas now to give to poor poets
> and I greatly doubt the scheme succeeding unless it is more
> strongly patronized than almost can be expected. In Bookselling
> matters an author must either be the conjuror who commands
> the devil or the witch who serves him and few are those whose
> situation is sufficiently independent to enable them to assume
> the higher character.[102]

Scott's efforts to assist the proposed subscription edition of *The
Queen's Wake* extended to drafting advertising material (reprinted in
the present edition's Appendix). However, subscriptions came in
slowly in spite of these exertions, as Hogg explains in a letter of 14
December 1817 to his friend and literary confidante Eliza Izett:

> The Queen's Wake will not I fear be published this year as
> the subscriptions have come in but very slow and the work is
> expensive. We do not yet know of many above 200 and would
> like to have about 1000 before putting to press.[103]

By January 1818 Hogg's discussions with Scott and others led to a
change of plan. The proposed two-guinea quarto subscription edi-
tion 'with a few plates' was not attracting subscribers in sufficient
numbers, so it was decided to scale down to a royal octavo with
only one plate, costing one guinea rather than two.[104] Murray wrote
to Hogg about this on 24 January 1818:

> With regard to the projected quarto edition of 'The Queen's
> Wake,' I am not sorry that it is at an end; for you will gain
> more, I think, by one in royal octavo. But I really think that
> you ought to print a thousand in demy octavo to sell for 9*s.*,
> and throw off no more in the larger size than you are confi-
> dent of obtaining subscribers for—[105]

Murray here outlines what in the event actually took place: the publication of a subscription edition (the 'fifth') printed on large 'royal' sheets, and a trade edition (the 'sixth') printed from the same type but on smaller 'demy' sheets. However, progress in obtaining subscriptions remained slow,[106] and the fifth and sixth editions of *The Queen's Wake* did not appear until the summer of 1819.[107]

The publishing double act of Blackwood in Edinburgh and Murray in London had seemed to be ideally placed to give a fair wind to *The Queen's Wake* and Hogg's other writings. Strains began to appear between Blackwood and Murray, however, and—unfortunately for *The Queen's Wake*—by December 1819 their working relationship had come to an acrimonious end. Peter Garside has pointed out that 'On a visit to London late in June 1818, Robert Cadell scarcely needed to prompt Murray's outbursts of rage against his associate ("M. says that the disgust he feels at the fellows presence is extreme—his look his laugh his impudence ...")'.[108] Murray and Blackwood were different kinds of Tory. While Murray leaned towards the aristocratic, Blackwood's focus was more commercial—and in the London publisher's attitude towards his Edinburgh associate one senses a whiff of the disdain with which the long-descended owner of a country estate might regard a self-made garage proprietor.

Blackwood was happy enough to publish demotic and anti-aristocratic texts by Hogg such as *Mador of the Moor* (1816) and the novel *The Brownie of Bodsbeck* (1818). Murray was less happy to have his name on these titlepages, however. Peter Garside writes:

> Arguably the most up-market publisher in London, insofar as Murray dealt in fiction it was only with most unexceptionable titles such as Jane Austen's *Emma* (1816). In 1819 he was also to bring out Thomas Hope's *Anastasius*, the first three-decker novel to sell at a guinea-and-a-half—shortly to become a set price for elegant fiction. With the Hon. Mr Listlesses of the day increasingly on the look-out for the 'aristocratical' in literature, it is not unfeasible that Murray and [his literary adviser] Gifford at least half-publicly rejected the 'vulgar' and (in its depiction of Claverhouse) anti-aristocratical novel that, not fully invited, had found its way from the wharf to their salon.[109]

The novel in question is *The Brownie of Bodsbeck*, and, as Garside shows, sales of *The Brownie* faltered badly after a strong start.

Following his acrimonious break with Murray in December 1819, Blackwood attempted to persuade Hogg to make Cadell & Davies his London publisher, rather than Murray. Hogg declined, however, and *The Queen's Wake* remained in Murray's hands. Garside writes:

> Moving to Cadell & Davies could only improve the prospect of sales, Blackwood assured Hogg: 'He [Murray] has never done justice to any of your Books, and now he will be less disposed than ever'. Even then, Hogg wrote to ask Murray to keep the *Brownie* and *Queen's Wake*: 'I would much rather, not only from affection, but interest, that you should continue to dispose of them'. From this point he wrote into a vacuum, with only the odd letter from clerks in return. Over-impressed by the 'friendship' he had met with earlier from Murray, and perhaps victim to a touch of snobbery on his own part, Hogg I suspect never fully understood the extent to which he had been dropped.[110]

9. Revising *The Queen's Wake* for the Fifth Edition (1819)

We have seen that in 1813 Hogg inserted some new Notes at the end of the second edition of *The Queen's Wake*, and that in 1814 he made further local revisions for the third edition. The fourth edition was a re-issue of the third, so the next opportunity to revise the poem was provided by the fifth edition, which made its appearance in 1819. The fifth edition could be produced on a more opulent scale than the previous editions because it was published by subscription, and Hogg responded to this situation by preparing a carefully revised text of his most famous poem. This was to prove to be his last revision of *The Queen's Wake*, and the fifth edition can therefore be regarded as an expression of Hogg's final intentions for his poem.

In preparing copy for the printer of the fifth edition Hogg marked his revisions on a set of the sheets that had been printed for the third edition of 1814, and this enabled him to ensure that his newly-revised text would incorporate the earlier alterations made for the second and third editions. The printer's copy that Hogg prepared in this way is preserved in the National Library of Scotland as MS 20440, and this document shows him focusing with care on some of the smaller details of the presentation of his text: for example, he systematically changes the 'royal wake' of the earlier editions to 'Royal Wake'. Such changes duly made their way into the fifth edition. Hogg also made detailed changes in the wording of his text.

For example, in the 'Introduction' he adds a new couplet to the discussion of the song ('O lady dear') that catches the rapt attention of the Queen:

> These words prophetic seemed to be,
> Foreboding wo and misery.   (*1819*, ll. 269–70)

This addition makes it harder for the reader to miss the sense, already strongly suggested by the 'Introduction', that the glamour and promise generated by Mary's return home will not prove to be lasting. A few lines later the first four editions read 'To view the lands and city round,' (*1813*, l. 272). Hogg revises this in NLS MS 20440, and accordingly it becomes in the fifth edition: 'To view the city's ample round,' (*1819*, l. 274). Such fine-tunings of the words of the text are scattered through *The Queen's Wake*, and are recorded in the Editor's Notes of the present edition.

A more substantial revision comes in 'Mary Scott', the Fourteenth Bard's song. Hogg's reasons for making this change emerge in a letter he wrote on 8 March 1818 to William Napier of Thirlestane in Ettrick Forest, who had served as a Captain in the Royal Navy during the Napoleonic Wars, and who became 8th Baron Napier in 1822. Hogg writes:

> Hon^d sir
>
> I was sorry I missed you the other day as I happened just to be engaged with you. In revising the Queen's Wake for this new and splendid edition which Mr. Scott has set on foot I came to an odious reflection on some one of your ancestors which had quite escaped my memory. I instantly reccollected that I had written it in the plenitude of poetic wrath for which perhaps I had as little reason as ever one of the irritable tribe of rhymsters had for anger since the world began. But that which overpowered me most of all was the thought of your manly generosity that had scorned to take the least notice of the thing but had used me always as a friend and associate though I deserved to have been kicked for it. Of course the moment that my eye came on it I blotted it out, but in its place I could not refrain having a joke upon you for though I regard you as a most noble fellow I cannot help thinking there is something peculiar in your character.[111]

In the original 1813 version 'Francis, Lord of Thirlestane' ('To all the gallant name a soil') hides ignominiously during a fight between the Scotts and the Pringles (Night the Third, ll. 704–07). This connects with Captain William Napier's father, Francis, 7th Baron Napier, who was 'Lord of Thirlestane' in 1813. Hogg had quarrelled with the 7th Baron in 1801 in connection with a dispute about a radical Kelso newspaper (see Editor's Notes 125, ll. 704–07). However, the 1819 version of this passage (Night the Third, ll. 708–35) is substantially revised: Captain William Napier had used his powers as landowner to prevent Hogg from keeping a sailing-boat on St Mary's Loch, and a jocular revenge is now exacted (see Editor's Notes 321–22, ll. 708–35). In the 1819 version 'Red Will of Thirlestane' fights valiantly, but is driven back, and has to fight 'within his feudal lake':

> Wild looked he round from side to side;
> No friendly skiff was there that day!
> For why? the knight in bootless pride,
> Had driven them from the wave away.
>
> Sore did he rue the stern decree!
> Red rolled the billow from the west;
> And fishes swam indignantly
> Deep o'er the hero's boardly breast.   (ll. 716–23)

For the fifth edition Hogg also expanded the descriptions of three of the bards, converting them into readily recognisable portraits of prominent literary figures in the Edinburgh of the late 1810s. In section 3 of the present Introduction (pp. xxxiv–xxxviii), we saw that the first version of *The Queen's Wake* has a clear narrative pattern involving a contest between bards representing an aristocratic Highland tradition of Scottish poetry, and bards representing a more popular Lowland tradition. However, the fifth edition's three extended portraits change the nature of the bards concerned, and Hogg's 1819 changes tend to obscure the narrative pattern of the first version of *The Queen's Wake*. For example, in the original version of Hogg's poem the Eighth Bard, the Bard of Fife, is very much a man of the people. However, in 1819 he becomes much more gentlemanly when he is transformed into a portrait of William Tennant (1784–1848), author of *Anster Fair* (1812). Tennant was a noted linguist as well as a poet: indeed, in 1834 he became Professor of Hebrew at St Andrews.

The nature of the Ninth Bard is also transformed in the fifth edition. In the original 1813 version of *The Queen's Wake* this bard takes his appropriate place in the narrative pattern of the poem as the epitome of the aristocratic Highlander. However, in the 1819 version he is converted into a portrait of that famous Lowlander John Wilson, the 'Christopher North' of *Blackwood's Edinburgh Magazine*. Likewise, the Eleventh Bard of 1813, as a man of the people, fits neatly into the narrative pattern of the first version of *The Queen's Wake* : 'plain his garb, and plain his lay' (*1813*, Night the Second, l. 1003). However, in 1819 he becomes a portrait of the *Blackwood's* writer Thomas Hamilton, and his social class is transformed: 'A captain in the wars was he, | And sprung of noble pedigree' (*1819*, Night the Second, ll. 1021–22).

In short, Hogg's 1819 expansions of the descriptions of the Eighth, Ninth, and Eleventh Bards are interesting and valuable: one would be sorry not to have these fresh and telling portraits, each of which is attached to a song that is in some way appropriate to the person concerned. However, the fifth edition's descriptions of these bards do change their nature, and this tends to obscure the carefully constructed narrative pattern which, in the first version of *The Queen's Wake*, shapes the poem's contest between the bards of the aristocratic / Highland tradition and the bards of the demotic / Lowland tradition.

Through its narrative pattern and in other ways, *The Queen's Wake* of 1813 is willing and eager to assert that the old popular tradition of Border balladry has been successfully revived in the early nineteenth century, and is currently in a state of rude health under the auspices of one James Hogg (Ettrick Shepherd, Mountain Bard, Forest Minstrel, and Bard of Ettrick). In 1819 the focus is subtly different, however, and the fifth edition's revised *Queen's Wake* clearly flows from a careful and creative attempt by Hogg to re-present his most famous poem to advantage, in a way compatible with its reputation as one of the most notable products of the vibrant literary world of Regency Britain.

It should be stressed that Hogg's achievement in the fifth edition rests not only with his textual revisions, but also, as Meiko O'Halloran shows in her essay below, with his efforts to enhance and focus the impact of his poem through the inclusion of appropriate illustrations. In this aspect of his re-presenting of *The Queen's Wake* in 1819 Hogg anticipated the fruitful bringing together of poetry and illustrations that contributed greatly to the popularity of the annuals and gift-books that came into fashion in the 1820s. Handsomely produced and copiously illustrated, the annuals were compilations of new short texts by various hands, and these publications paid significant fees to secure contributions from famous names. As Jerome McGann has pointed out, for a substantial part of the nineteenth century the annuals were 'a dominating influence on imaginative writing that exploited relatively brief forms (like lyric and short story)'.[112] Hogg's project was a fraction ahead of its time, however: the conditions in which the annuals flourished only came into being after 1819, the year in which the American Jacob Perkins patented his method of printing illustrations from steel printing plates—a method that made it possible for the first time to produce high-quality book illustrations cheaply and in large numbers. The copper plates that had previously been used could print only a limited number of copies before having to be expensively refurbished. Steel plates, on the other hand, could print many thousands of copies without loss of quality.[113] Perhaps Hogg's illustrated edition of *The Queen's Wake* would have achieved the popularity it deserved if it had been published (annuals-style) at an affordable cost, with several high-quality illustrations printed from examples of Perkins's newly-patented steel plates.

10. *The Queen's Wake* after 1819

By the early 1820s the most heady days of Hogg's career as a poet were already over: he had been unable to recapture the acclaim with which *The Queen's Wake* had initially been received. The Author of *The Queen's Wake* was no longer generally seen as someone to be mentioned alongside Scott and Byron, but he was still a figure of sufficient substance for Archibald Constable to be willing to publish a four-volume edition of his *Poetical Works* in 1822. In recognition of its fame, *The Queen's Wake* is given pride of place, and occupies the first volume. It is clear that Hogg was aware of potential textual pitfalls during the preparation of the *Poetical Works*, and in a letter of 8 February 1822 he urges Constable to 'be sure to take either the *fifth* or *sixth edition* of the Wake for sake of the late additions'.[114] The revised text of the fifth edition was now established as the standard version of *The Queen's Wake*, and this was the version that would normally be reprinted throughout the nineteenth century.

In 1825 continuing American interest in Hogg's poetry was confirmed when Constable's 1822 edition of the *Poetical Works* was reprinted in two volumes by D. Mallory of New York, and *The Queen's Wake* was printed in its entirety in *The British Poets of the Nineteenth Century*, [ed. by J. W. Lake], (Paris: Baudry, 1828; also Francfort O. M.: Brönner, 1828). In a letter of 20 October 1830 Hogg urged Blackwood to consider a new edition: 'I think there should likewise be a cabinet edition of The Queen's Wake for the *buodoir* [*sic*] but perhaps Ackerman or some of these ornamental chaps would be the best hand for that'.[115] 'Ackerman' is Rudolph Ackermann (1764–1834), who had pioneered British annuals with *Forget Me Not [...] for 1823* (published November 1822).[116] In line with his ideas for the fifth edition, Hogg clearly continued to see *The Queen's Wake* as a poem that could be enhanced by appropriate illustrations.

Nothing came of Hogg's suggestion in his letter to Blackwood of 20 October 1830, but the possibility of an illustrated subscription edition of *The Queen's Wake* was again mooted in 1831 and 1832. In her essay in the present volume on 'Hogg, Mary Queen of Scots, and the Illustrations to *The Queen's Wake*', Meiko O'Halloran gives an account of these discussions and the very interesting possibilities for illustration raised in them. Her essay goes on to discuss later publications involving illustrations of *The Queen's Wake*.

After Hogg's death in 1835, Blackie & Son of Glasgow brought out a six-volume edition of his *Tales and Sketches* (1837), and a five-volume edition of his *Poetical Works* (1838–40). These editions are incomplete and in places bowdlerised, but they provided the basis for most of the subsequent nineteenth-century editions of Hogg's writings, including the Rev. Thomas Thomson's well-known two-volume edition of *The Works of The Ettrick Shepherd*, published by Blackie in 1865.

Hogg's reputation gradually declined as the nineteenth century advanced, but *The Queen's Wake* continued to be admired, and separate editions of this poem continued to be produced. For example, a 'People's Edition' appeared in 1841, and there were also editions by Orr (1841); by Nelson (1842, 1844, 1845); by Chambers (1867, 1872); and by Ogle (1871). Furthermore, a volume of selections from *The Queen's Wake* was published in the 'Blackie's School Classics' series in 1880.[117] Interestingly, the 'People's Edition' (Edinburgh: Chambers, 1841–'price eightpence') returns to the text of the second edition of Hogg's poem.

In the middle years of the twentieth century *The Queen's Wake* was out of print and seldom read. Interest in Hogg revived in the later decades of the century, however, and extracts from *The Queen's Wake* were included in selections of Hogg's poetry edited by Douglas Mack (Oxford: Clarendon Press, 1970) and by David Groves (Edinburgh: Scottish Academic Press, 1986). The present edition represents an advance on these two late-twentieth-century publications, in that it makes *The Queen's Wake* readily available once more as a complete poem.

11. The Present Edition

In 1813 Hogg inserted some new Notes at the end of George Goldie's second edition of *The Queen's Wake*. More revisions followed in the third edition of 1814, and still further revisions appeared in the fifth edition of 1819, which also incorporated the revisions made for the second and third editions. The revisions for the third and fifth editions were substantial, and tend to obscure a coherent and somewhat subversive strand in the overall structural pattern of the original version of Hogg's poem. In this situation, how should a modern edition of *The Queen's Wake* proceed?

Following Scott's death in 1832, Hogg produced two manuscript versions of his anecdotes of his friend. The manuscript of the first version (*Anecdotes of Sir W. Scott*) is now in the Alexander Turnbull Library in New Zealand, while the manuscript of the second version (*Familiar Anecdotes of Sir Walter Scott*) is now in the Pierpont Morgan Library, New York. In her edition of Hogg's *Anecdotes of Scott* (Stirling / South Carolina Edition, 1999) Jill Rubenstein edited both versions, and J. H. Alexander has subsequently produced a brilliant analysis of the differences between the two versions. Alexander concludes his analysis as follows:

> What we see in the re-working of *Anecdotes* into *Familiar Anecdotes* is an example of what we are now familiar with in literary history. An author returns to a text without properly reading himself into it, without fully entering into it imaginatively: he attempts to make it tidier and wiser, but in the process he deprives it of a good deal of its essential life. The most celebrated example in Hogg's period is of course *The Prelude*. In Wordsworth's case the successive revisions spanned decades, but there are parallels in some of Scott's proof corrections to Hogg's evident problems in re-entering a text fully only a matter of weeks after the initial composition. There is of course new material in *Familiar Anecdotes* to be appreciated, and there are many incidental enhancements to be savoured, but for the real Hoggian and Romantic daring and excitement we must go to New Zealand rather than the United States.[118]

Likewise, there are many enhancements to be savoured in the final version of Hogg's most famous poem, and real loss would be involved if these enhancements were to fall out of view. Nevertheless, there is a clear case for saying that 'the real Hoggian and Romantic daring and excitement' of *The Queen's Wake* is most fully to be encountered in the first version of 1813.

In this situation, how should a modern edition of this poem proceed? During the 1810s *The Queen's Wake* was published in four significantly different authorial versions, and each of these versions reflects the author's concerns and circumstances at the time when it was prepared. In this, *The Queen's Wake* is similar to such texts as Frances Burney's *Camilla*, Samuel Taylor Coleridge's 'The Rime of the Ancient Mariner', Wordsworth's *The Prelude*, and Mary Shelley's *Frankenstein*, all of which underwent substantial authorial revision after their first appearance in print. Traditionally, in such cases editors tended to produce a text designed to reflect the author's final intentions. However, a new consensus has now emerged, reflecting what Paul Werstine has described as 'the recent shift in editorial culture from the New Bibliographers' concern with establishing authorial final intentions for a work, to a recognition of the irreducible plurality of texts'.[119] The landmark decision to publish two versions of *King Lear* in the Oxford Shakespeare (1986) was a decisive moment in this 'recent shift in editorial culture'. According to the editors of the Oxford Shakespeare, one of the versions of *Lear* represents the play as Shakespeare originally wrote it, while the other represents the play as he subsequently substantially revised it. Post-1986, it now seems natural and desirable that there are (for example) popular editions of both the 1818 and the 1831 versions of *Frankenstein* in current circulation.

We have seen that the first, second, third, and fifth editions of *The Queen's Wake* represent four distinct authorial versions of the poem. It has not been thought practical to print all four versions in the present edition of Hogg's poem. However, the versions of the second and third editions can reasonably be regarded as stages in the evolution of Hogg's final version, because (as we have seen) the fifth edition incorporates the changes made for the second and third editions. The present volume therefore offers both Hogg's edgy and challenging original version of *The Queen's Wake* (from the first edition), and his carefully revised and polished final version (from the fifth edition). The illustrations in the fifth edition are included, as they form an integral part of the final version of Hogg's poem. The Editor's Notes in the present volume point out readings in the final version that derive from the second edition, as well as readings that derive from the third edition, and readings that derive from revisions made for the fifth edition.

In short, the Stirling / South Carolina edition of *The Queen's Wake* sets out to give readers access to complete texts of both the first version and the final version of Hogg's poem, and it also sets out to lay bare the processes by which the first version evolved into the final version. It follows the practice of the Oxford Shakespeare with regard to *King Lear* by printing its two versions consecutively, rather than in parallel. In reading a parallel text edition, it is difficult to prevent the eye from straying to the facing page in order to make detailed comparisons. One therefore tends to focus on the similarities and differences between the two parallel versions, rather than focusing on the life and flow and structure of each of them. Hogg's first and final versions of *The Queen's Wake* are (in their different ways) rich, powerful, and enjoyable poems. They ought not to be experienced as a dry exercise in textual comparison. Each deserves to be experienced in its own right as a complete and living poem, and the present edition seeks to allow each of them to be experienced in that way.

Notes

1   Hogg, 'Memoir of the Life of James Hogg', in *The Mountain Bard*, 3rd edn (Edinburgh: Oliver & Boyd, 1821), pp. xli–xliii. An expanded and revised version, entitled 'Memoir of the Author's Life', appeared in Hogg's *Altrive Tales* (London: Cochrane, 1832), and the 1832 version of this passage is reprinted in the relevant volume of the Stirling / South Carolina Research Edition of the Collected Works of James Hogg (hereafter S/SC Edition). See Hogg, *Altrive Tales*, ed. by Gillian Hughes (S/SC, 2003), p. 30.

2   Hogg, *The Mountain Bard* (Edinburgh: Constable; London, Murray, 1807) pp. iv–vi; for the 1832 version, see *Altrive Tales*, ed. Hughes, pp. 13–14. When Hogg mentions 'our version of the Psalms of David' he has in mind the Church of Scotland's metrical version, much used in church services and in the regular family worship usual at that period.

3   See Peter Garside, 'Patriotism and Patronage: New Light on Scott's Baronetcy', *MLR*, 77 (1982), 16–28.

4   For discussions of the Scott / Hogg relationship see Robin W. MacLachlan, 'Scott and Hogg: Friendship and Literary Influence', in *Scott and his Influence*, ed. by J. H. Alexander and David Hewitt (Aberdeen: ASLS, 1983), pp. 331–40; and Ian Duncan, 'Shadows of the Potentate: Scott in Hogg's Fiction', *Studies in Hogg and his World*, 4 (1993), 12–25.

5   See Hogg, *Altrive Tales*, ed. Hughes, p. 18.

6   Hogg, 'Memoir of Burns', in *The Works of Robert Burns*, ed. by the Ettrick Shepherd and William Motherwell, 5 vols (Glasgow: Archibald Fullarton, 1834–36), V, 1–263 (p. 246).

7   See Gillian Hughes, 'James Hogg and the "Bastard Brood" ', *Studies in Hogg and his World*, 11 (2000), 56–68 (pp. 56–62).

8   For further details see Gillian Hughes, 'James Hogg and the Forum', *Studies in Hogg and his World*, 1 (1990), 57–70.

9 Susan Manning's review appears in *Studies in Hogg and his World*, 11 (2000), 134–37 (pp. 135, 137).

10 See Allan Beveridge, 'James Hogg and Abnormal Psychology: Some Background Notes', *Studies in Hogg and his World*, 2 (1991), 91–94 (pp. 91–92).

11 Hogg, 'Memoir of Burns', pp. 153, 152.

12 See Hogg, *The Spy*, ed. by Gillian Hughes (S/SC, 2000), pp. 115–16. Further information about James Gray's radicalism can be found in Peter Jackson, 'William Wordsworth, James Gray, and the *Letter to a Friend of Robert Burns*: Some Unpublished Correspondence', *Notes and Queries*, n.s. 50 (2003), 293–97.

13 Robert Crawford, 'Bard of Friendly Fire', *London Review of Books*, 25 July 2002, 16–18 (p. 17). James Kinsley's three-volume edition of Burns was published by the Oxford University Press in 1968.

14 See Edward J. Cowan, 'From the Southern Uplands to Southern Ontario: Nineteenth-Century Emigration from the Scottish Borders', in *Scottish Emigration and Scottish Society: Proceedings of the Scottish Historical Studies Seminar, University of Strathclyde, 1990–91*, ed. by T. M. Devine (Edinburgh: John Donald, 1992), pp. 61–83 (p. 63).

15 'On the Separate Existence of the Soul', in Hogg, *Selected Stories and Sketches*, ed. by Douglas S. Mack (Edinburgh: Scottish Academic Press, 1982), pp. 180–95 (pp. 182, 181). The story was first published in the December 1831 number of *Fraser's Magazine*.

16 See Hogg, *Anecdotes of Scott*, ed. by Jill Rubenstein (S/SC, 1999), pp. 3–4.

17 See Hogg, *Altrive Tales*, ed. Hughes, p. 32.

18 See David Groves, 'Four Unrecorded Book Reviews by the Ettrick Shepherd, 1811–1812', *Studies in Scottish Literature*, 25 (1990), 23–48 (p. 24). Groves records (p. 24) that only one set of this periodical is known to exist, and that it is:

> bound in two volumes at the National Library of Scotland. Unluckily, this set ends with the first issue of *Scotish Review*, and it seems that later copies of the magazine (which became *The Scottish Review* in 1814), have completely disappeared. The only evidence for its continued existence comes from the *Analectic Magazine* of Philadelphia, which regularly reprinted articles from the *Scotish Review* and then *The Scottish Review* until 1815.

19 See Groves, 'Four Unrecorded Book Reviews by the Ettrick Shepherd, 1811–1812', p. 24.

20 See David Stevenson, *The Covenanters: The National Covenant and Scotland* (Edinburgh: Saltire Society, 1988), pp. 76–77.

21 John MacQueen, *The Rise of the Historical Novel* (Edinburgh: Scottish Academic Press, 1989), pp. 207–08. For 'Storms' see Hogg, *The Shepherd's Calendar*, ed. by Douglas S. Mack (S/SC, 1995), pp. 1–21 (p. 5).

22 Scott, *The Life of Napoleon Buonaparte, Emperor of the French*, 9 vols (Edinburgh: Cadell; London: Longman, 1827), II, 208–09. Subsequent references are to this edition, and are given in the text.

23 John Barrell, 'Divided we Grow', *London Review of Books*, 5 June 2003, pp. 8–11 (p. 8).

24 Liam McIlvanney, *Burns the Radical: Poetry and Politics in Late Eighteenth-Century Scotland* (East Linton: Tuckwell Press, 2002), p. 212.

25 McIlvanney, p. 205.

26 *The Letters of Robert Burns*, ed. by J. De Lancy Ferguson, 2nd edn, rev. by G. Ross Roy, 2 vols (Oxford: Clarendon Press, 1985) II, 174: see also McIlvanney, pp. 206–07.

27 McIlvanney, p. 208.

28 The original version of this song is reprinted in Hogg, *Anecdotes of Scott*, ed. Rubenstein, pp. 80–81.

29 Hogg, *Altrive Tales*, ed. Hughes, p. 28.

30 See Susan Manning's review of Gillian Hughes's S/SC edition of *The Spy*, in *Studies in Hogg and his World*, 11 (2000), 134–37 (p. 134).

31 Hogg provided manuscript notes in a surviving copy of the fifth edition (1819) of *The Queen's Wake*, in order to indicate which modern poets are portrayed in the descriptions of the competitors of the wake: see Alan Grant, 'A Presentation Copy of *The Queen's Wake*', *Newsletter of the James Hogg Society*, 8 (1989), 21–22. Whenever the present Introduction identifies a description of a Bard of *The Queen's Wake* as a portrait of a literary figure of Hogg's day, this identification is based on Hogg's annotation of the copy described by Alan Grant.

32 Katie Trumpener, *Bardic Nationalism: The Romantic Novel and the British Empire* (Princeton: Princeton University Press, 1997), p. xii.

33 John Gunn, *An Historical Enquiry Respecting the Performance on the Harp in the Highlands of Scotland; from the Earliest Times, until it was Discontinued, about the Year 1734* (Edinburgh: Constable, 1807), p. 13 and footnote on p. 78. In at least some copies (e.g., the copy of the Bodleian Library, Oxford) Queen Mary's harp is depicted in the second rather than the third plate.

34 Gunn, p. 14.

35 Gunn, pp. 1–2.

36 Gunn, p. 4.

37 See 'The Unpublished Conclusion of James Hogg's 1802 Highland Journey', edited and with annotations by H. B. de Groot, *Studies in Hogg and his World*, 6 (1995), 55–66 (pp. 60–61).

38 See the 'Historical and Geographical Note' in the paperback edition of Hogg, *The Three Perils of Woman*, ed. by Antony Hasler and Douglas S. Mack (Edinburgh: Edinburgh University Press, 2002), 417–37 (pp. 427–34). Because of Hogg's willingness to identify with Highlanders in spite of cultural differences, the 'devastations of the Highlands' in 1746 are summed up in *The Three Perils of Woman* (p. 407) by the sufferings of the Lowlander Sally Niven, a woman of Hogg's own cultural background.

39 Hogg, *The Jacobite Relics of Scotland Second Series*, ed. by Murray G. H. Pittock (S/SC, 2003), p. xviii.

40 Hogg, *The Brownie of Bodsbeck*, ed. by Douglas S. Mack (Edinburgh: Scottish Academic Press, 1976), p. 163.

41 Hogg, *The Jacobite Relics of Scotland [First Series]*, ed. by Murray G. H. Pittock (S/SC, 2002), p. 433.

42 Hogg, *Jacobite Relics [First Series]*, ed. Pittock, p. 454.

43 Hogg, *Jacobite Relics [First Series]*, ed. Pittock, p. 459.

44 'The Harp of Ossian' appears at pp. 2–7 of the *Musical Bijou* for 1829, and it also appears in Hogg's *Songs by the Ettrick Shepherd: Now First Collected* (Edinburgh: Blackwood; London: Cadell, 1831), pp. 75–76.

45 James Macpherson, *The Poems of Ossian and Related Works*, ed. by Howard Gaskell with an Introduction by Fiona Stafford (Edinburgh: Edinburgh University Press, 1996), pp. ix–x.

46 Hogg, *Anecdotes of Scott*, ed. Rubenstein, pp. 60–61, 8–9. See also the note on 74, ll. 711–12 in the present edition.

47 Walter Scott, *The Lay of the Last Minstrel* (London: Longman; Edinburgh: Constable, 1805), p. 197. Subsequent page references are to this edition, and are given in the text.

48 See John Sutherland, *The Life of Walter Scott: A Critical Biography* (Oxford: Blackwell, 1995), pp. 98–99.

49 'On the Folly of Playing at Cards and the Decay of our Ancient Amusements', in Hogg, *The Spy*, ed. Hughes, 204–08 (p. 207). In her edition of *The Spy* Gillian Hughes comments: 'Author: Unknown–the NLS, St Andrews, and Guelph marked copies suppose this anonymous paper to be Scott's, though it is not characteristic of his style and in his *Anecdotes*, p. 19, Hogg states that Scott's only contribution to *The Spy* was a letter enclosing two poems by John Leyden' (p. 599). However, in the forthcoming first volume of her S/SC edition of Hogg's *Letters*, Gillian Hughes records the new information that Hogg claimed authorship of this article when writing about *The Spy* to Bernard Barton: see Hogg's letter to Barton of 5 July [1813] and the relevant editorial notes. Perhaps, when he came to attribute this noticeably un-Scott-like article to Scott in the three marked copies of *The Spy*, Hogg was indulging in some playful mischief-making.

50 *The Oxford Authors: William Wordsworth*, ed. by Stephen Gill (Oxford: Oxford University Press, 1984), p. 597.

51 See Linda Colley, *Britons: Forging the Nation 1707–1837* (New Haven: Yale University Press, 1992).

52 Ian Gow, *The Palace of Holyroodhouse: Official Guidebook* (London: Royal Collection Enterprises, 2002), p. 49.

53 Hogg's familiarity with McCrie's *Life of John Knox* is confirmed by his letter to Blackwood of 10 January 1820 (NLS, MS 4005, fols 148–49).

54 The first edition of Thomas McCrie, *The Life of John Knox* was published in Edinburgh in 1811 by John Ogle and William Blackwood. The quotations here are taken from the revised two-volume second edition (Edinburgh: John Ogle and William Blackwood, 1813), II, 21, 24, 25, 29.

55 See Hogg, *The Private Memoirs and Confessions of a Justified Sinner*, ed. by P. D. Garside (S/SC, 2001), p. 162.

56 Hogg, *A Queer Book*, ed. by P. D. Garside, (S/SC, 1995), pp. xv–xvi.

57 This interpretation is based on the helpful discussion of this passage by James Logie Robertson ('Hugh Haliburton') in his *Furth in Field* (London: Unwin, 1894), pp. 111–15. For Hogg's part in the transmission of Child's A-version of 'Erlinton', see *The English and Scottish Popular Ballads*, ed. by Francis James Child, 5 vols (Boston: Houghton Mifflin, 1882–98; repr. New York: Folklore Press, 1957), I, 106–11; and Edith C. Batho, *The Ettrick Shepherd* (Cambridge: Cambridge University Press, 1927), p. 19.

58 In these passages, the ultimate source for both Hogg and Milton would appear to be Isaiah 11. 6–9 and Isaiah 65. 17–18, 25: see James Hogg, *Selected Poems*, ed. by Douglas S. Mack (Oxford: Clarendon Press, 1970), p. xxv.

59 See also Douglas S. Mack, 'Hogg and the Blessed Virgin Mary', *Studies in Hogg and his World*, 3 (1992), 68–75.

60 See Thomas Crawford, 'James Hogg: The Play of Region and Nation', in *The History of Scottish Literature: Volume 3, Nineteenth Century*, ed. by Douglas Gifford, general editor Cairns Craig (Aberdeen: Aberdeen University Press, 1988), pp. 89–106 (p. 103).

61 Abbot John Mackinnon's tomb in Iona Abbey and his place in the ecclesiastical history of Iona are discussed in *Iona Abbey: A Short Tour* (Glasgow: The Iona Community, [*c.* 1997]), p. 9.

62 See E. Mairi MacArthur, *Columba's Island: Iona from Past to Present* (Edinburgh: Edinburgh University Press, 1995), pp. 44, 83–92, 148–62.

63 MacQueen, *The Rise of the Historical Novel*, p. 229.

64 Hogg, 'A Journey through the Western Highlands and Islands of Scotland, on the months of May, June, July, and August. A.D. 1803', in Stirling University Library, MS 25 box 1(2), notebook 1 fol. 11 – notebook 3 fol. 4 (notebook 2 fol. 26). A corner of the leaf on which the passage quoted appears is now missing, and the resulting gaps in the text have been supplied from the (generally somewhat inaccurate) transcription made available in 1888, when this text was first published: see Hogg, *A Tour in the Highlands in 1803* (Paisley: Alexander Gardner, 1888), pp. 84–85. See also the *Scottish Review*, 12 (July 1888), 1–66. In the final sentence of the passage quoted, Hogg's manuscript reads 'not [*end of line*] not to be struck'. H. B. de Groot is editing Hogg's *Highland Journeys* for the S/SC Edition.

65 NLS, MS 7200, fol. 202.

66 See Sutherland, *The Life of Walter Scott*, pp. 120–27, 135–40; and Hogg, *Altrive Tales*, ed. Hughes, pp. 29–30.

67 In the *Edinburgh Evening Courant*, the poem appears in a somewhat different version as 'To James Hogg, The Ettrick Shepherd, by a Gentleman of Suffolk': for further information see the first volume of Gillian Hughes's forthcoming S/SC edition of Hogg's *Letters* (letters to Barton of 14 May, 7 June, and 5 July 1813, and editorial commentary).

68 *Scots Magazine*, 75 (February 1813), 126–31 (pp. 126, 127).

69 Letter by Capell Lofft in the *Monthly Magazine*, 35 (May 1813), 501; and review in the *Theatrical Inquisitor*, 2 (May 1813), 218–25 (pp. 218–19). Subsequent page references to this review are given in the text. I am grateful to Gillian Hughes for drawing my attention to Lofft's letter in the *Monthly Magazine*.

70 *British Critic*, 41 (June 1813), 639–40 (p. 640).

71 *Eclectic Review*, 9 (June 1813), 647–53 (p. 647). Subsequent page references to this review are given in the text.

72 Reprinted in Philadelphia in the *Analectic Magazine*, n.s. 3 (February 1814), 104–25 (p. 108). It appears that no copy of the relevant number of *The Scotish Review* has survived: see Groves, 'Four Unrecorded Book Reviews by the Ettrick Shepherd, 1811–1812', p. 24.

73 See the first volume of Gillian Hughes's forthcoming S/SC edition of Hogg's

Letters (letter to Walter Scott of 3 April 1813 and editorial commentary).

74   Hogg, *Anecdotes of Scott*, ed. Rubenstein, p. 65.

75   Hogg, *Anecdotes of Scott*, ed. Rubenstein, p. 8. In annotating this passage, Jill Rubenstein quotes Scott's opinion of the younger Lord Porchester: 'a young man who lies on the carpet and looks poetical and dandyish–fine lad too'. In a letter to Scott of 3 April 1813 (NLS, MS 3884, fols 122–23) Hogg writes 'I can never however get quit of the idea that you wished to discourage me from ever touching the harp more'.

76   Scott's article is reprinted in Kenneth Curry's *Sir Walter Scott's Edinburgh Annual Register* (Knoxville: University of Tennessee Press, 1977), pp. 60–99 (pp. 94–96).

77   See *The Spy*, ed. Hughes, pp. 517, 628. See also Hogg, *Anecdotes of Scott*, ed. Rubenstein, pp. 20–21, 101; and Hogg, *Memoir of the Author's Life; and, Familiar Anecdotes of Sir Walter Scott*, ed. by Douglas S. Mack (Edinburgh: Scottish Academic Press, 1972), pp. 103–05.

78   Hogg, *Altrive Tales*, ed. Hughes, pp. 69–70.

79   Hogg, *Anecdotes of Scott*, ed. Rubenstein, p. 29.

80   See Hogg, *A Queer Book*, ed. Garside, p. xv.

81   Hogg, *The Queen's Wake*, 3rd edn (Edinburgh: Goldie; London: Colburn, 1814), p. 188.

82   Edgar Johnson, *Sir Walter Scott: The Great Unknown*, 2 vols (London: Hamish Hamilton, 1970), I, 412.

83   Hogg, *Altrive Tales*, ed. Hughes, p. 31. Hogg's account in his 'Memoir' of his dealings with Goldie over *The Queen's Wake* was strenuously disputed by Goldie in a pamphlet entitled *A Letter to a Friend* ([Edinburgh], [1821]); 2nd edn (Edinburgh: Douglas, 1832): see *Altrive Tales*, ed. Hughes, pp. 230–31. In seeking to defend his own reputation as a man of business, Goldie sets out to discredit Hogg's 'Memoir', and his tone in his pamphlet is more notable for vigour than for quiet understatement. In the 1821 version of his 'Memoir' Hogg gives an account of a conversation he had with William Dunlop on the day after the publication of *The Queen's Wake*, and this passage from the 'Memoir' is quoted at the beginning of the present Introduction. In his pamphlet, Goldie describes this passage as:

> a story which wears such an appearance of low and vulgar blackguardism, that it is hard to believe it possible to have happened but between persons of the most abandoned habits. I particularly allude to the words put into this gentleman's [i.e., Dunlop's] mouth. If any thing like this interview ever happened, no man who had any regard to decency or decorum himself, or valued these qualities in others, would, on any account, have defiled his pages with a detestable and revolting slang, equally offensive to pure religion and sound morals, and calculated even to degrade the nymphs of Billingsgate, or the pick-pockets of St Giles's. (Quoted from 2nd edn, pp. 11–12.)

84   See *Byron's Letters and Journals*, ed. by Leslie A. Marchand, 12 vols (London: Murray, 1973–82), IV, 151.

85   NLS, MS 4001, fols 207–08.

86   Hogg, *Altrive Tales*, ed. Hughes, p. 32.

87   John Murray Archive, Blackwood Box 2.

88 John Murray Archive, Blackwood Box 2.
89 Review by Francis Jeffrey, *Edinburgh Review*, 24 (November 1814), 157–74 (pp. 160–61).
90 *Monthly Review*, 75 (December 1814), 435–37 (p. 435). Subsequent page references to this review are given in the text.
91 *New Universal Magazine*, 2 (April 1815), 282–88 (p. 288).
92 *La Belle Assemblée*, 12 (October 1815), 176–78 (p. 176).
93 See Stephanie Anderson-Currie, *Preliminary Census of Early Hogg Editions in North American Libraries*, South Carolina Working Papers in Scottish Bibliography, 3 (Columbia, SC: University of South Carolina, 1993), p. 10.
94 James Hogg, *Altrive Tales*, ed. Hughes, pp. 35, 34. In the 'Memoir' Hogg writes that *Mador* was begun in the summer of 1814, but his letters suggest that 1813 was in fact the year: see Hogg's letter to Alexander Bald of 14 November 1813 (NLS, Acc. 9953), and *Altrive Tales*, ed. Hughes, p. 234.
95 See the Introduction of James Barcus's forthcoming S/SC edition of *Mador of the Moor*.
96 See Hogg's letter to Archibald Constable of 1 February 1814 (NLS, MS 7200, fols 207–08).
97 Transcript in the Hogg Letters Project papers, University of Stirling.
98 Transcript in the Hogg Letters Project papers, University of Stirling.
99 The book was published by Blackwood and Murray. It has 1815 on its titlepage, but is announced as 'this day published' in the *Edinburgh Evening Courant* for 15 December 1814.
100 John Murray Archive, Blackwood Box 3.
101 *The Letters of Sir Walter Scott*, ed. by H. J. C. Grierson, 12 vols (London: Constable, 1932–37) I, 163.
102 *The Letters of Sir Walter Scott*, IV, 460–61.
103 Beinecke Rare Book and Manuscript Library, Yale University: James Hogg Collection, GEN MSS 61, Box 1, Folder 38.
104 See Hogg's letter to Blackwood of 5 January 1818 (NLS, MS 4003, fols 84–85), and Hogg's letter to Murray of 15 January 1818 (Murray Archive, Box 37).
105 Samuel Smiles, *A Publisher and his Friends: Memoir and Correspondence of the Late John Murray*, 2 vols (London: Murray, 1891), II, 4: original in John Murray Archive, Box 37.
106 See Hogg's letter to Murray of 4 June 1818 (Murray Archive, Box 37).
107 Gillian Hughes has traced newspaper advertisements that establish a summer 1819 date for the publication of the fifth and sixth editions of *The Queen's Wake*.
108 Peter Garside, 'Three Perils in Publishing: Hogg and the Popular Novel', *Studies in Hogg and his World*, 2 (1991), 45–63 (p. 54).
109 Garside, 'Three Perils in Publishing', pp. 53–54: Garside discusses sales of *The Brownie* at pp. 52–55.
110 Garside, 'Three Perils in Publishing', p. 54. Because of the breakdown in the working relationship between Blackwood and Murray, Hogg had difficulty in obtaining money due to him from his publishers for *The Brownie of Bodsbeck* and the sixth edition of *The Queen's Wake*: see Peter Garside, 'James Hogg's Fifty Pounds', *Studies in Hogg and his World*, 1 (1990), 128–32.

111 NLS, MS 786, fols 55–56.

112 Quoted from 'Example D' in Jerome McGann, 'The Rationale of HyperText',
http://jefferson.village.virginia.edu/public/jjm2f/rationale.html (accessed 19
May 2001).

113 See Iain Bain, 'Gift Book and Annual Illustrations: Some Notes on their
Production', in Frederick W. Faxon, *Literary Annuals and Gift Books: A Bibliography 1823–1903* (Pinner: Private Libraries Association, 1973), [19]–[25].

114 NLS, MS 7200, fols 213–14. However, the text of *The Queen's Wake* in the
1822 *Poetical Works* introduces a few changes to the 1819 text (fifth and
sixth editions). Some of these changes are clearly errors, as for example
when 1819's 'Ross's rude impervious bound' (Night the Third, l. 1711,
referring to the Ross of Mull) becomes 'Rosa's rude impervious bound).
Other changes seem to derive from an urge to introduce perceived corrections, typical of the work of early-nineteenth-century printers. For example
at Night the Third ll. 234–35, the 1819 reading is 'And many a daughter
lain awake, | When parents trowed them sleeping sound'. In 1822 this
becomes 'And many a daughter lain awake, | When parents trowed her
sleeping sound'. All in all, the 1822 variants tend to suggest activity by the
printer rather than authorial revision. One possible exception comes at
Night the Third l. 1006, when 'there shall the power of thy nations' (1819)
becomes 'there the dread power of thy nations' (1822).

115 NLS, MS 4027, fols 198–99.

116 See Eleanore Jamieson, 'The Binding Styles of the Gift Books and Annuals', in Frederick W. Faxon, *Literary Annuals and Gift Books: A Bibliography
1823–1903* (Pinner: Private Libraries Association, 1973), [7]–[17] (p. [7]).

117 See Edith C. Batho, *The Ettrick Shepherd* (Cambridge: Cambridge University Press, 1927), p. 193. See also *The British Library General Catalogue* and *The
National Union Catalog*.

118 J. H. Alexander, '*Anecdotes* to *Familiar Anecdotes*', *Studies in Hogg and his World*,
13 (2002), 5–15 (p. 14).

119 Werstine makes these comments in a review of *The First Quarto of King
Richard III*, ed. by Peter Davidson (Cambridge: Cambridge University Press,
1996): see *Yearbook of English Studies*, 29 (1999), 295–96 (p. 295).

Hogg, Mary, Queen of Scots, and the Illustrations to *The Queen's Wake*

Meiko O'Halloran

The fifth edition of *The Queen's Wake*, which was published by subscription in June 1819, after Hogg had achieved fame and success as author, reflects a distinct historical moment from that of the first edition of January 1813. First suggested by William Blackwood, the subscription edition presented Hogg with a unique opportunity to offer readers a small run of elegant and ornate illustrated copies of the poem which had made his name. The three images Hogg chose to accompany the text contribute significantly towards creating a special new experience of his poem for readers, heightening our perception and strengthening our appreciation of the compelling ideas and convictions about national identity and poetry which he expresses. By examining the illustrations in the context of Hogg's preparations for the subscription edition and their strikingly evocative appearance in the poem, we can appreciate more fully their crucial role in developing our awareness of a Scottish poetic tradition, and indicating the author's sense of his place within, and in relation to, that tradition.

The Subscription Edition of 1819

As early as 1817 plans were made for a more costly and attractive edition of Hogg's by now very famous poem. His friends undertook to promote the project, and on 24 May 1817 Walter Scott drew up a prospectus for an illustrated two-guinea edition of *The Queen's Wake*, to be published by William Blackwood. The subscription edition was, Scott explained, principally intended to benefit the author, who had seen little profit from previous editions of his work. Despite the poem's wide acclaim and circulation, the volatile climate for publishing meant that it had proved 'less advantageous to the authors fortune than to his reputation'. Inviting prospective subscribers of the new edition to rectify 'the great stain upon our age [...] the neglect of one self-elevated genius whose circumstances were not greatly different from those of M^r. Hogg', namely the neglect of Robert Burns, Scott emphasised the national character of the enterprise.[1]

The proposed volume would celebrate a work of native genius, handsomely 'ornamented with engravings from designs by Scottish artists'. Hogg was perhaps planning to solicit illustrations from his friends in the Edinburgh Dilettanti Society, among whom were Alexander Nasmyth (1758–1840), William Nicholson (1781–1844), and William Allan (1782–1850).[2]

Unfortunately, the prospectus of May 1817, which was hoped to attract a thousand subscriptions, succeeded in drawing only two hundred by the end of the year. Plans for the projected edition were therefore curtailed early in 1818, while Hogg was staying with Scott at Abbotsford. Hogg wrote to Blackwood on 5 January communicating Scott's approval of their new idea for a royal octavo subscription edition.[3] Scott's revised prospectus noted carefully that although the plan for a two-guinea illustrated edition had 'met with liberal encouragement from the public', it had been discovered that the considerable expense of producing engravings would reduce the author's profit. He described the new plan:

> The frontispiece representing (from the Witch of Fife) a dance of Scottish witches with the fairies of Lapland is therefore the only embellishment proposed. It is the gift of an amateur friendly to that genius of which he himself professes no common share the traits of whose pencil are marked by a mingled wildness gaiety and humour happily adapted to a subject so singular.
>
> In consequence of dropping the idea of other embellishments the Subscription price of the work is reduced from two to one guinea which the friends of the author trust may extend the subscription more widely.[4]

The projected two-guinea illustrated edition was thus abandoned in favour of a less ornate volume, to be prefaced with a single design by the Dumfriesshire-born antiquary and artist Charles Kirkpatrick Sharpe (1781–1851), illustrating 'The Witch of Fife', one of the best-loved songs in *The Queen's Wake*.

The importance of the two other plates which appeared in the final edition is suggested by Hogg's secretive efforts to obtain them. Once details of the one-guinea subscription edition were circulated and preparations for printing were under way, he set about applying to Archibald Constable and Charles Kirkpatrick Sharpe to acquire another two plates privately. Responding to a letter from Constable earlier that month, Hogg wrote on 30 October, thanking him warmly for generously allowing him use of a plate of Queen

Mary's harp which had appeared in John Gunn's *Historical Enquiry Respecting the Performance of the Harp in the Highlands of Scotland*, published by Constable in 1807. There were to be 550 copies of the subscription edition in royal octavo, and having requested that Constable arrange for the necessary impressions of the plate to be made on his behalf, Hogg added, 'and I think it is best never to let my publishers know of it till the plate appear'.[5] He made similarly covert negotiations with Sharpe, to whom he wrote on 24 November, when printing of the poem was at an advanced stage:

> The large edition of the Queen's Wake is [...] in the press and well advanced–will be ready about the beginning of the year, and I must depend on your friendship to get me the *witches* etched by Lizars and the portrait of Queen Mary properly engraved for the frontispiece. It is useless to say any thing about it to the publishers only I wish it could be ready by the time the work is ready for delivery your own superintendance [*sic*] of the engravings is all that is necessary and pray make it a lovely likeness of my darling queen.[6]

In addition to preparing his own sketch, Sharpe therefore supervised the engraving of an image of Mary, Queen of Scots. These careful preparations reveal Hogg's keenness to determine the presentation of this special edition of his hugely successful work himself. He clearly placed great importance on the inclusion of the portrait of Queen Mary and the image of her harp, and the two plates were added to the edition only towards the final stages, preventing possible objections from Blackwood and John Murray, his Edinburgh and London publishers.

Five hundred and fifty copies of the fifth edition of *The Queen's Wake* carrying the three illustrative plates Hogg had selected and arranged were published and distributed to subscribers in June 1819. By studying the portrait of Mary, the illustration of the Witches in Lapland, and the image of the Queen Mary harp more closely it becomes evident that the illustrations individually and collectively inform and shape our reading of the poem in several important ways.

I. Mary, Queen of Scots

The frontispiece is a very elegant portrait of the young Mary, Queen of Scots, in which she is shown head and shoulders, facing half-left, looking young and beautiful, with a gentle expression. She is handsomely dressed and bejewelled, and wears a small hat with a feather.

The inscription 'Marie Queen of Scots, Sketched by Sir John Medina from a Picture in Royal Cabinet at Versailles' emphasises Mary's French background at the time of her return to Scotland in August 1561. Educated from childhood to become Queen of France, Mary Stuart had worn the French crown for little over a year before she was widowed by the death of her young husband, François II, in December 1560. She was only eighteen when she returned to Scotland. The artist, Sir John de Medina (1659–1710), was a Spanish-Flemish painter and a leading portraitist in Edinburgh during the 1690s and early 1700s. He had quickly established himself as 'the Kneller of the North', was much in demand amongst the Scottish aristocracy, and became the last man knighted in Scotland before the Treaty of Union in 1707. He was reputed to have made and sold a number of copies of portraits of Mary Stuart, presumably supplying a keen contemporary market.[7] It is not clear on whose picture Medina's sketch is based, but Hogg perhaps saw this sketch in Edinburgh during the 1810s or heard about it, perhaps from Sharpe, while he was planning the subscription edition. In this attractive image of Mary he found the ideal frontispiece for his poem about a poetry competition hosted by the young queen. His specific request that William Home Lizars (1788–1859) execute the etching of the portrait together with the sketch of the witches suggests that he wanted sophisticated and first-rate craftsmanship in their reproduction. He must surely have been aware that Lizars was the leading Edinburgh etcher of the day.[8]

The image of Mary Stuart supports Hogg's portrayal of the eighteen-year-old Mary in *The Queen's Wake* as a charming and gracious young sovereign, and a generous and sensitive patroness, presented on the point of leading a new era in the life of the Scottish nation. This can be contrasted with more hostile contemporary portrayals of Mary at later stages of her reign, when questions of her adultery with Lord Bothwell, involvement in the murder of her second husband, Lord Darnley, and alleged authorship of the incriminating Casket Letters were dominant. Mary's dramatic life story and enigmatic character naturally made her an especially intriguing and compelling figure for Romantic writers, artists, and historians. In the 1780s artists such as Gavin Hamilton (1723–98) and Alexander Runciman (1736–85) chose to represent the abdication of Mary, Queen of Scots in painting. The Royal Academy exhibition of 1791 included no less than three scenes from her life by David Allan (1744–96), *The Murder of Rizzio*, *The Abdication of Mary Queen of Scots*, and *Queen Mary Hears the Warrant for her Execution*, and William Allan's later depiction of *Mary Queen of Scots Admonished by Knox on the Day that her Intended Marriage to Darnley was made Public* (exhibited in 1823) inspired a host of imitators. Of greater consequence than the sensational human drama of her story, however, was its continuing political resonance. In the mid eighteenth century a huge Marian controversy had raged over the uncertain authenticity of the Casket Letters Mary allegedly wrote to Bothwell, which appeared to reveal the queen's adulterous passion and her willing complicity in Darnley's murder.[9] At the heart of this debate were intense concerns about the powerful political passions which Mary's story excited. In the 1750s, as Karen O'Brien remarks, Mary 'steadily grew into a potent symbol of a Stuart, independent Scotland lost after the Union and Hanoverian succession'.[10] It was in this context that William Robertson's (1721–93) *History of Scotland During the Reigns of Queen Mary and James VI* (1759) first appeared, offering a sentimental portrayal of Mary as a beautiful tragic heroine, in startling contrast to David Hume's presentation of her as a stubborn and rather foolish woman in the Tudor volumes of his *History of England* (1754–62). O'Brien demonstrates that it was precisely Robertson's masterly use of the rhetoric of sentiment in his literary treatment of Mary which succeeded in uniting his Scottish and English readers in sympathy for the helpless queen, while simultaneously 'eras[ing] Mary as a political symbol' and diffusing her potency and significance through 'carefully contained nostalgia'.[11] In this way Robertson skilfully combined his sympathy for Mary with his Enlightenment patriotism, putting the independent Catholic Scotland Mary and her descendants represented firmly in the past and indicating that Scotland's future lay with Protestant England.

There was another revival of interest in Mary, Queen of Scots in the late 1810s and 1820s, and Hogg and his associates undoubtedly assimilated and contributed to a large body of inherited and contemporary Marian discourse. Sharpe, who had a well-known Jacobite ancestor and had been raised on Jacobite tradition from his infancy, shared Hogg's admiration for Mary. During the summer of 1817, the year before he provided the sketch of 'The Witch of Fife' for Hogg's subscription edition, he corresponded with George Chalmers (1742–1825), an antiquarian and leading champion of Mary Stuart, who wanted to consult him about the biography of Mary he was preparing at this time, particularly with regard to pictures of her. In a separate but simultaneous correspondence with Scott, Sharpe mentions that he had recently been promised the loan of two portraits by Sir John Medina (of David Wilkinson and his wife Jean Straiton) and was planning to copy both pictures.[12] The portrait of Mary sketched by Medina is not among the plates in Chalmers's biography of Mary, but given Sharpe's extensive knowledge about representations of the queen, his admiration of Medina's work, and his own contribution of an illustration to *The Queen's Wake*, it seems likely that he may have drawn Hogg's attention to the sketch. Chalmers's substantial two-volume *Life of Mary Queen of Scots* reworked and considerably expanded unfinished manuscript material by William Robertson, originally intended for the historian's own projected biography of Mary, which remained unfinished at his death. It appeared in December 1818, a few months before the publication of Hogg's subscription edition of *The Queen's Wake*, to which Chalmers subscribed.[13]

Hogg, like Chalmers and Sharpe, was genuinely sympathetic to Mary. He was working on the first volume of his *Jacobite Relics* (1819) alongside his preparation of *The Queen's Wake* subscription edition, and he had a strong interest of his own in Jacobitism.[14] His representation of the young queen is predominantly loyal and generous. But he was also making the most of the contemporary interest in the Stuarts, and taking the opportunity to express concerns about the future of Scottish poetry. His portrayal of Mary in *The Queen's Wake* draws upon a Robertsonian sympathy for her as a beautiful, gentle, and essentially impressionable heroine. Crucially, however, his presentation of Mary, particularly in the subscription edition, seeks to restore her as a powerful national symbol.

Mary's love of poetry is the central aspect of her character in Hogg's poem and the reason for the wake. While Hogg's poetic portrayal of her did not change between the first and fifth editions of *The Queen's Wake*, the inclusion of the portrait in the fifth edition draws attention to Mary's presence and role in a far more striking way. Nearly all the reviewers of early editions of *The Queen's Wake* had commented on Hogg's clever use of a poetry competition as the plausible occasion or framing device for bringing together a group of poems in varying styles, and showcasing his gift for assuming different voices. In these reviews Mary is taken for granted simply as part of this narrative framework and regarded as a convenient and suitably pleasing figurehead for the wake. The portrait at the beginning of the fifth edition serves to foreground Mary's presence much more suggestively. Instead of appearing as a token figurehead, she is celebrated as promising with her patronage and interest in Scottish song the continuity of a national poetic tradition; her reign potentially heralding an exciting new age in the history of Scottish

verse. At a time when the Elizabethan era was being widely eulo-
gised by Hazlitt and others as representing a 'Golden Age' in litera-
ture, *The Queen's Wake* effectively presents readers with an alterna-
tive Stuart tradition to rival that of Elizabeth.

The portrait corresponds with the description of Mary on page
29 (pp. 211–12 in the present edition), as indicated in the top right
corner of the etching. When considered in relation to the portrait,
Hogg's laudatory description of the queen carries interesting new
overtones. What might at first appear to be a piece of generic poetic
flattery may have more specific and profound national implications.

> Oft the rapt bard had thought alone,
> Of charms by mankind never known,
> Of virgins, pure as opening day,
> Or bosom of the flower of May :
> Oft dreamed of beings free from stain,
> Of maidens of the emerald main,
> Of fairy dames in grove at even,
> Of angels in the walks of heaven :
> But, nor in earth, the sea, nor sky,
> In fairy dream, nor fancy's eye,
> Vision his soul had ever seen
> Like MARY STUART, Scotland's Queen.
>   (Introduction, *1819*, ll. 491–502)

Mary Stuart is presented here as the culmination of all Hogg's vir-
gin heroines, including the pure Kilmeny of the Thirteenth Bard's
song and Mary Lee of *Pilgrims of the Sun* (1815). Given the enormous
lasting controversy over Mary Stuart's alleged adultery with Bothwell
and the fact that virginity was far from being a trait with which she
was usually associated, the description is especially curious. The
accompanying portrait engraved by Lizars seems to invite us to con-
sider this emphasis on virginity further. As Mary inclines to her
right, our eyes are drawn to a prominent cross in the background,
reminding us of her Catholicism. A smaller cross appears on top of
the crown beside it, and we see the cross again in the pendant worn
around her neck. These visual reminders of her religious faith, to-
gether with the emphasis on sexual purity in the description, have
the combined effect of linking Mary Stuart with the Virgin Mary.
Douglas Mack has drawn attention to the importance of the Blessed
Virgin Mary in the Pre-Reformation worlds of 'Kilmeny' and *Pil-
grims of the Sun*.[15] In the Introduction to *The Queen's Wake*, Hogg's
flattering lines associate Mary with the Virgin Mary and Catholic

faith, but also appear to direct us implicitly to a comparison of Mary, Queen of Scots and England's virgin queen, Elizabeth, thereby drawing attention to the rival English and Scottish traditions.

In *The Queen's Wake*, the mood of excitement and promise surrounding the young Mary at the outset of her reign is complicated by the reader's awareness that Mary Stuart's was one of the last Scottish courts. The accession of Mary's son James VI to the English throne, and the Union of the Crowns in 1603, saw the royal court remove to London as its political and cultural centre. Mary's legacy in terms of a Scottish court tradition was therefore short-lived. An acute sense of this lost potential emerges throughout *The Queen's Wake*, and is underscored particularly in the first of Hogg's notes to the poem, annotating the following passage:

> Those Wakes, now played by minstrels poor,
> At midnight's darkest, chillest hour,
> Those humble Wakes, now scorned by all,
> Were first begun in courtly hall,
> When royal MARY, blithe of mood,
> Kept holiday at Holyrood.
> (Introduction, *1819*, ll. 85–90)

In his note, Hogg develops his comparison of old and modern wakes, contrasting the celebrations of poetry and song in the 1561 historical setting of the Wake and the Ettrick Shepherd's present day both in England and Scotland. Where once the activities of the English wake were merely by 'habit or study directed', Hogg finds that the 'wake' had been easily integrated into English culture and now signifies 'many fairs and festivals of long standing'. The proud native tradition of Scotland, on the other hand, 'which was always the land of music and of song', and where 'music and song were the principal, often the only, amusements of the Wake', has fallen low and the wake is almost obsolete. 'In Scotland,' he writes, 'the term is not used to distinguish any thing either subsistent or relative, save those serenades played by itinerant and nameless minstrels in the streets and squares of Edinburgh, which are inhabited by the great and wealthy, after midnight, about the time of the Christmas holidays'. He goes on to compare the high privileges enjoyed by minstrels in the reign of the Stuarts with the total obscurity of modern performers of the wake, who 'seem to be despised'.[16] The frontispiece image of Queen Mary helps to foreground such expressions of anxiety about the future of Scottish poetry in the text and editorial apparatus of the poem. Mary is clearly being presented as the head of a

Scottish court tradition, which, as the image of her harp later poignantly reminds us, has long ended. Hogg thereby aligns himself with the vital moment of cultural potential in Mary's reign, while also placing himself at the centre of an important Border inheritance. The illustration of 'The Witch of Fife' which appeared at the centre of the subscription edition serves to affirm and extend his claims.

II. The Witch of Fife

Originally intended as the frontispiece and sole illustration of the one-guinea subscription edition outlined by Scott in January 1818, Sharpe's illustration of a scene from 'The Witch of Fife', the Eighth Bard's song, became the second image in the eventual subscription edition. The double-page plate (also etched by Lizars) appears between pages 76 and 77 (see p. 237 in the present edition).[17] Like Hogg and Scott, Sharpe had a long-standing interest in fairy lore and ballad tradition. His contribution of ballads to the third volume of Scott's *Minstrelsy of the Scottish Border* included two imitations of his own, and as Scott observed, he also possessed an artistic genius for 'mingled wildness gaiety and humour', which was particularly suited to Hogg's poetry. Sharpe's correspondence with Hogg reveals an amicable collaboration between artist and poet. Although the request for an illustration had come from Hogg, it was Sharpe who selected the passage his sketch illustrates, and Hogg approved a preliminary sketch before the final version was produced.[18]

'The Witch of Fife' had immediately attracted wide admiration among critics and readers, and was by this time extremely popular, as was 'Kilmeny'. It was therefore an ideal choice for an illustration, and became the only song in the subscription edition which had a commissioned picture to go with it. The corresponding passage in the poem (again indicated in the top left corner of the etching) has the Witch of Fife relating her nocturnal adventures to her husband:

'And quhan we cam to the Lapland lone,
  The fairies war all in array;
For all the genii of the north
  War keepyng their holeday.

'The warlock men and the weird wemyng,
  And the fays of the wood and the steep,
And the phantom hunteris all war there,
  And the mermaidis of the deep.

'And they washit us all with the witch-water,
    Distillit fra the moorland dew,
Quhill our beauty blumit like the Lapland rose,
    That wylde in the foreste grew.'–
                    (Night the First, *1819*, ll. 751–62)

Her husband replies:

"Ye lee, ye lee, ye ill womyne,
    Se loud as I heir ye lee !
For the warst-faurd wyfe on the shoris of Fyfe
    Is cumlye comparet wi' thee."–
                    (Night the First, *1819*, ll. 763–66)

An odd medley of characters is crammed into the picture. At the top
left the phantom hunters arrive, blowing their horns, while a lone
mermaid in the foreground responds, blowing through a shell, held
up with a webbed hand. The small dog floating in the water beside
her is one of a number of strange animals featured in the scene.
Above the mermaid's head, a hunting dog hungrily eyes a pair of
aggressive-looking cats which are scratching at a book of music, while
the old man beside them sits cradling what appears to be a docile
pet reptile. Looking over the shoulder of the central figure, a myste-
rious wide-eyed hybrid creature appears, its features so unnatural
and its tunic strangely human that it might be the mask-like disguise
of a child or elf.

Commanding the centre of the composition, a remarkably serene-
looking woman sits, playing a long-necked lute and looking at us
coyly. The lute and her flirtatious expression, combined with her
open-collared low-cut dress and revealing state of dishabille, sug-
gest the sexual immorality of the scene. This presumably is the Witch
of Fife, who would naturally consider herself as holding a central
place in these revels and want to be shown to advantage, her beauty
blooming 'like the Lapland rose' in complacent defiance of her hus-
band's irritable remark that she makes the ugly wives of Fife look
handsome. As the only figure engaging our eye contact, she invites
us into the scene which Hogg's poem presents her describing. Just
as she takes centre stage as the protagonist-narrator within the Eighth
Bard's song, so Sharpe's picture presents us with what the Witch of
Fife wants us to see, as she herself describes it. But Sharpe also
appears to have enjoyed creatively elaborating the scene. Where
Queen Mary appears in tasteful and refined splendour, the Witch of
Fife comically presents us with a less subtle brand of charm and

humour. Her extravagant dress and flaunting posture, the huge feathers in her head-dress, and her majestic air all contribute to create the impression that she sees herself holding pride of place in an unorthodox alternative court of her own. Warlock men and weird women congregate in the background. Behind her a sinister pair appear poised to sacrifice a baby as part of a spell, while the talons of the warlock next to them loom ominously over the heads of his gossiping companions, as if he too is casting a spell. A group in the foreground on the right are occupied with bathing. Two female fairies ply one of the men with witch-water to improve his appearance, while his ugly companion eagerly awaits his turn, and another peers into a mirror to admire the after effects.

Sharpe's distinctly parodic picture is, like Hogg's poem, very enjoyably grotesque. The illustration stands in contrast to later stylised Victorian images of fairies as pretty, dainty, and delicate beings. These fairies are physically substantial rather than ephemeral and fragile, and the facial expression of the taller of the two is somewhat ambiguous. Sharpe's enigmatic figures are very much in keeping with Hogg's depictions of fairies. 'Old David', the song performed by the Ettrick Bard, for example, relates a battle fought by Old David and his sons against a ruthless band of supposed fairies who have taken a young woman captive. Similarly, 'Mary Burnet', a story in *The Shepherd's Calendar* (1829), tells of a young woman who is spirited away following the unhallowed momentary wish of her frustrated fiancé, and drowned. 'A fairy, an evil spirit, or changeling of some sort' temporarily appears in her place, and years later her unhappy lover appears to be lured to his destruction by fairies purporting to be his lost Mary.[19] In this way, Hogg's fairies are shown to have their sinister and malicious side, but at the same time, both Hogg's and Sharpe's treatments of supernatural beings convey a powerful sense of attraction and evoke a strong feeling of intimacy. We are literally at home with the witches and fairies in this picture, and able to observe the details of the scene through the protagonist-narrator drawing us in. As the poet figure here, the Witch of Fife can to some extent be regarded as a parodic representative of Hogg himself. The picture in effect contributes to Hogg's statement of his literary identity, supporting and consolidating his claim to the title of 'king o' the mountain an' fairy school', and celebrating his special ability to invite us into a secret domain of Border folklore and legend.[20]

III. Queen Mary's Harp

The image with which we are left at the end of the poem is a beautiful engraving of Queen Mary's harp, the prize for which the bards at the wake have been contending. The picture of the harp appears alongside the passage in which the Highlander, Gardyn, the Ossianic warrior bard, is reported to have won the competition:

> Queen Mary's harp on high that hung,
> And every tone responsive rung,
> With gems and gold that dazzling shone,
> That harp is to the Highlands gone,
> Gardyn is crowned with garlands gay,
> And bears the envied prize away.
> Long, long that harp, the hills among,
> Resounded Ossian's warrior song;
> Waked slumbering lyres from every tree
> Adown the banks of Don and Dee,
> At length was borne, by beauteous bride,
> To woo the airs on Garry side.
>
> When full two hundred years had fled,
> And all the northern bards were dead,
> That costly harp, of wonderous mould,
> Defaced of all its gems and gold,
> With that which Gardyn erst did play,
> Back to Dunedin found its way.
> (Conclusion, *1819*, ll. 177–94)

We see the harp in the engraving in its reduced state, stripped of its costly decorations over the years, though it is still very beautiful. Hogg was particularly pleased that Constable allowed him use of this plate, which had originally appeared in Gunn's *Historical Enquiry* as one of three images drawn and engraved by Daniel Somerville. Gunn's treatise appears to have been an important source for *The Queen's Wake*. Commissioned by the Highland Society in 1805, it focused on tracing the histories and describing the present condition of two harps: the Queen Mary harp and the Caledonian harp.[21] In Gunn's work, as in Hogg's poem, Mary appears in the role of a generous young patroness. Gunn relates the story of a royal visit paid by Mary and her party to the family of a young lady called Beatrix Gardyn in Perthshire in 1563, during which there was a grand Ossianic-style hunting expedition, followed by a feast at which

Beatrix played for the queen and was presented by Mary with a harp as a gift in recognition of her musical talent.[22]

Gunn says little about the symbolism of the markings burnt into the wood of the harp, but he stresses its Celtic origins, Scottish workmanship, and history.[23] The queen's portrait and the arms of Scotland originally appeared in gold in front of the upper arm of the instrument, and 'in the circular space near the upper end of the fore arm, was placed a jewel of considerable value, and on the opposite side, in a similar circular space, was fixed another precious stone; of all which it was despoiled in the rebellion 1745'.[24] In Somerville's engraving, we see a number of Celtic crosses and decorative patterns running in diagonal lines on the main body of the harp, and lots of intricate designs along its fore arm. Drawings of these details from the Queen Mary harp can be studied more closely in *Tree of Strings* (Midlothian, 1992).[25] As Keith Sanger and Alison Kinnaird explain, the details reveal carved images of several mythical beasts–at the top a lion (usually associated with the Resurrection), and a griffin (often used as a symbol of Christ the Conqueror); at the base of the fore pillar a two-footed dragon (perhaps representing Evil conquered), and a group composed of a unicorn trampling on a wingless dragon or serpent and feeding it with a fish (suggestive of Christ overcoming Satan with his perfect truth). The lion and unicorn group are visible in the engraving which Hogg used. Sanger and Kinnaird go on to observe that the strength and purity of the unicorn made it a potent symbol of Christ, and 'the belief that though it was extremely wild and fierce, it could be captured by a virgin of spotless character, made it easily linked with the Incarnation of Christ through the Virgin Mary'.[26] Smaller Celtic crosses are worked into the leafy designs on the instrument. The carvings on the harp thus coincide harmoniously with some of the themes emphasised in Hogg's poetic description of Mary and the portrait by Medina which he selected. Collectively, the beautifully crafted details also indicate the religious purpose for which the harp was made, and the great national significance of the prize.

Appearing as it does at the end of *The Queen's Wake*, the image of the Queen Mary harp in its forlorn condition comments on the lack of appreciation for Scottish poets in Hogg's day, and serves as a powerful visual reminder of the need to cultivate and patronise indigenous talent to ensure its continuity. In the passage after this, Hogg re-directs attention to another harp–the Caledonian or Lamont harp which he himself (as Ettrick Bard) receives from Queen Mary, 'framed by wizard of the wild'. An engraving of this harp, also by

Somerville, appears in Gunn's treatise as the companion engraving to the Queen Mary harp. Taller and larger than the Queen Mary harp, the Caledonian harp is much sturdier, with a simpler frame, and more metalwork. Sanger and Kinnaird comment: 'the strong, simple lines of the harp, and the lack of carved decoration, suggest that it may have been the "working instrument" of a professional harper, rather than a ceremonial or aristocrat's instrument'.[27] Gunn also remarks on a structural feature of this harp which allowed 'the voice of the performer to extend more freely, in all directions, to his audience'. More specifically, he identifies it as part of a long-standing Bardic tradition. It exhibits, he writes, 'several marks and proofs of its having suffered considerable violence', indicative of its having changed hands repeatedly and been 'in all probability for several centuries, the Harp of a succession of Highland Bards'.[28] In his poetic appropriation of the Caledonian harp, Hogg also intimates that although much less ornate and ceremonial, it is musically far more interesting and significantly enduring. Hogg's decision to use the picture of the Queen Mary harp as the final image in his poem serves as a call to continue the national celebration of Scottish verse. His poetic treatment of the Caledonian harp, the Ettrick bard's prize, as he concludes *The Queen's Wake*, simultaneously draws attention to the existence of another, more enduring Scottish poetic tradition, of which he was part.

The Second Subscription for *The Queen's Wake*

A second subscription edition of *The Queen's Wake* appears to have been proposed in 1831. Arrangements towards this were being made early the following year, when, in the spring of 1832, at the age of sixty-one, Hogg was plunged into dire financial circumstances by the sudden bankruptcy of James Cochrane, the publisher of his *Altrive Tales* (1832). Hogg's severe financial straits made a second subscription edition of *The Queen's Wake* an urgent priority, and John Murray with one or two others undertook to produce a one-guinea edition to raise money on his behalf. Hogg had been hoping to attract subscribers with a volume resembling the exquisitely illustrated literary annuals which were becoming fashionable commodities in the late 1820s and early 1830s. On 9 February 1832 he wrote to John Gibson Lockhart, mentioning his receipt of a generous subscription from an eager friend, and urging that efforts towards the subscription edition continue:

Drawn and Engraved by Daniel Somerville 1807.

THE CALEDONIAN HARP.

It should be a work something like The Keepsake with fewer
ornaments yet so as to make it a drawing-room book. If Mar-
tin would paint bonny Kilmeny first wakening in the land of
thought or the sinking of the Abbot M,kinnon's ship I know
some others who would do one for me *con amore*.[29]

The Northumbrian-born artist John Martin (1789–1854) regularly
contributed illustrations to annuals such as *The Keepsake*, *Literary Sou-
venir*, and *The Amulet*. The first indication of Hogg's interest in Mar-
tin's work came when, in the *Blackwood's* 'Noctes Ambrosianae' of
January 1827, John Wilson had the Ettrick Shepherd recommend
him as 'the greatest painter o' them a',' with 'a maist magnificent
imagination', before going on to discuss his print of *Alexander and
Diogenes* in the most recent *Literary Souvenir*, to which Hogg had also
contributed.[30] Hogg continued to admire Martin's work through the
annuals, and was delighted to meet him during his London visit
between January and March 1832. The diaries of Serjeant Ralph
Thomas describe a splendid evening held in Hogg's honour at Mar-
tin's house, at which Mrs Burns and Captain Burns (youngest son
of the poet), Allan Cunningham, Thomas Pringle (editor of *Friend-
ship's Offering*), and many other literary friends and publishers gath-
ered, and Hogg delighted everyone by singing songs with such en-
ergy that Thomas took him to be 'fifty-three, very strong and healthy,
the heartiest old cock I ever met'.[31] It was perhaps on one such occa-
sion that Hogg expressed his hope that Martin would make 'Kilmeny'
the subject of an illustration. He also met a number of other artists
during his stay in London, widening his existing circle of artist friends
and acquaintances, and increasing his choice of possible illustrators.

Hogg received the devastating news of Cochrane's bankruptcy
soon after his return to Scotland.[32] Notices appeared in *The Atlas*
and *Literary Gazette* of 10 and 16 June, relating news of the publish-
er's failure and Hogg's ensuing pecuniary distress. *The Atlas* reminded
readers of the poverty and hardship with which Hogg had struggled
from his childhood, and which 'his talents and his manly spirit' had
successfully overcome, while the *Literary Gazette* called on 'the hun-
dreds of high rank and great wealth, who enjoyed the Shepherd's
original and entertaining society whilst in the metropolis, to help
him in the hour when all his humour and hilarity must be turned to
grief'.[33] Announcing that Murray had undertaken a second subscrip-
tion edition of *The Queen's Wake* to cost a guinea a copy, for which the
prospectus had been issued, the newspaper writers warmly urged
the public to support Hogg in his hour of need. On 21 June Lockhart
was able to report that the Literary Fund had boosted subscriptions

by putting their names down for forty copies.[34] Hogg must also have been encouraged to receive £100 from Murray's son soon afterwards, with news that the subscription list was expected to increase further.[35]

The political agitation surrounding the 1832 Reform Bill made this a devastating period for the publishing and bookselling trade, however, and Hogg was one of many writers who suffered as a result.[36] Scott, who had been with Byron one of the most spectacularly successful authors of the age, died in September after a severe and prolonged illness, having worked himself to death. Given the severe conditions of the literary marketplace, it is perhaps unsurprising that, in the event, support for the second *Queen's Wake* subscription edition fell short of requirement. Hogg urged Lockhart desperately in October, 'There *must* at all events be a drawing-room copy of The Queen's Wake and for the honour of some who have been so liberal I will likewise publish all the names and the number of copies'. He received a further£61–5 subscription money in September 1833, but the hoped-for edition was never produced.[37]

John Martin's watercolour *Kilmeny* was exhibited at the Society of British Artists at Pall Mall in London at the end of March 1833. Hogg was unable to attend, but Martin wrote to him afterwards:

> I have at length in accordance with your desire and my own, made a drawing from your beautiful poem of "Kilmeny"; but I have not taken the passage you wished, for I was afraid to venture "the light of a sunless day" on canvass: indeed there are some subjects that appear distinctly in the 'mind's eye' of the poet, which are most difficult if not impossible, to delineate with the matter of fact pencil.–The passage I have taken, however, is one of the most charming to my taste, in the poem; it begins–
>
> > "They took her far to a mountain green,
> > To see what mortal had never seen;"
>
> & continues through the whole beautiful description to when
>
> > "Kilmeny sighed and seemed to grieve,
> > For she found her heart to that Land did cleave;"[38]

Hogg had evidently suggested that Martin represent the moment at which Kilmeny is welcomed into the heavenly land of spirits and led towards her baptism in 'the stream of life' (p. 291 in the present edition):

> They lifted Kilmeny, they led her away,
> And she walked in the light of a sunless day:
> The sky was a dome of crystal bright,
> The fountain of vision, and fountain of light:
> The emerald fields were of dazzling glow,
> And the flowers of everlasting blow.
>
> (Night the Second, *1819*, ll. 1487–92)

These are Kilmeny's last moments of ordinary humanity. Martin's choice was no less ambitious. He illustrated the passage after this, in which Kilmeny is taken to a mountain, seated 'high on a purple sward' and shown 'what mortal never had seen'. She is asked to survey 'the land of thought' of which she is now part and sees a panoramic succession of enchanting landscapes, reminiscent of earth yet perfect and eternal, 'little peaceful heavens in the bosom of earth' (see *1819*, Night the Second ll. 1530–59).

Martin was famed for compositions in which vast landscapes and apocalyptic scenery predominate, and diminutive human figures enhance the general impression of cosmic magnitude. On this occasion, however, his picture disappointed his daughter, Isabella, who was the model. He remarks good-humouredly, 'In consequence of the landscape being extensive I have been obliged to make the figures small, which has given great offence to my daughter Isabella, whose head had been well nigh turned by the high compliment you have paid her'. Hogg must have met the Martin children on his London visit and suggested that Isabella would make an exemplary model for *Kilmeny*. Isabella Mary Martin (1812–79), the painter's eldest daughter and favourite, was in 1832 the same age as Hogg's heroine, who is said to have for 'full twenty years [...] lived as free | As the spirits that sojourn this countrye'. She was also very beautiful and kind-natured, and became her father's lifelong assistant and companion.[39] 'I wish you could see the drawing and tell how you like it;' Martin wrote to Hogg, '–if you were rich enough to purchase it, & I rich enough to give it you I should have the greatest pleasure & I should like it much to be in your possession on immediate security'. But Martin was also struggling financially, and Hogg was never to see the picture.[40] Perhaps he saw another *Kilmeny* painting exhibited in 1833, at the Scottish Academy, the work of the Edinburgh-born artist Andrew Somerville (1804–34), who often painted subjects drawn from Border ballads.[41]

Later Illustrations of *The Queen's Wake*

The later nineteenth century saw numerous small intricate editions of *The Queen's Wake*. A fine example is *The Queen's Wake* volume from *The Poetical Works of the Ettrick Shepherd* (1838–40), reprinted by Blackie & Son in 1852. All five volumes of this collected edition have the image of the Queen Mary harp from the 1819 subscription edition embossed in gold on the cover and framed by an oval of ivy, with the inscription 'NATVRÆ DONVM' ('Gift of Nature') below. This was Hogg's personal motto, proclaimed on the Ettrick Bard's own harp in *The Queen's Wake*, where instead of his family arms we see '*Naturæ Donum* graved above'. The title page of *The Queen's Wake* carries a romanticised, intricately detailed picture of Fingal's Cave, depicting the monks in 'The Abbot M'Kinnon' arriving at Staffa, by the Edinburgh artist, David Octavius Hill (1802–70). Of the other Victorian editions of the poem, *The Works of the Ettrick Shepherd* in two volumes, also published by Blackie & Son in 1865, is the most notable for illustrations. The two engraved plates which accompany *The Queen's Wake* form an interesting contrast to the illustrations in the fifth edition.

The first, 'The Queen's Wake–Tenth Bard's Song, "A Fairy Band Came Riding On"' (II, 21), painted by Keeley Halswelle and engraved by Thomas Brown, shows the arrival of the fairies in 'Old David'. The overall emphasis is on ceremonial spectacle, with each rank of the fairy army taking a different form. Armed guards lead the way on prancing steeds. At the centre, dressed in pure white, with her head bowed, the human prisoner Ann of Raeburn appears in the habit of a medieval lady or princess. Three fairy knights can be glimpsed beneath the moon in the background, followed by a party of fairy lords and ladies. Two footmen with oversized heads and stocky bodies stride beside them, while in the foreground a rougher group of diminutive civilians are poised to tackle a frog which is crouched threateningly over one of their companions. A welcoming committee of miniature courtiers bow obsequiously to the approaching party, while a group of elves or fairies belonging to another order look on light-heartedly from their perch in the tree above–some playing musical instruments, and one comically suspended over the heads of the party, having slipped from his branch. Details such as the tiny infant-like figures sitting in the foliage on the lower right, and the small children hanging out of a hole in the tree to watch a young man leaning casually against the bark to address the coy female within, contribute to our impression of a whole fairy society.

THE QUEEN'S WAKE — TENTH BARD'S SONG.

"A FAIRY BAND CAML RIDING ON"

BLACKIE & SON GLASGOW EDINBURGH & LONDON

This charming procession aptly invites the kind of admiration Old David initially feels as he watches them—'a lovelier troop was never seen'—but they are by no means the troop of unruly robbers which the rest of Hogg's poem might lead us to expect. Unlike the peculiarly grotesque yet strangely appealing beings in Sharpe's rendering of 'The Witch of Fife', the figures represented here are part of an orderly, idealised, and sanitised supernatural—a Victorian reinvention. They are regimented and methodical rather than mysterious; quite unlike the ambiguous and unpredictable supernatural entities that Hogg and Sharpe created.

The second engraving, 'Queen Mary's Wake in Holyrood, The Thirteenth Bard' (II, 31), also by Halswelle, presents us with an image from within the narrative frame of the poem rather than an illustration of one of the songs from the wake. When considered alongside Sharpe's 'Witch of Fife', this portrayal of Mary at her wake reinforces the viewer's feeling that the Witch of Fife's heterogeneous *en plein air* gathering offers a lively alternative to the stiff formality of the royal court. Here, the young Queen of Scots is shown presiding over the poetry contest in a richly decorated medieval court, as the thirteenth bard presents himself to perform 'Kilmeny'. Mary inclines gracefully towards the bard, Drummond of Ern, as he bows 'with modest, yet majestic mien' at the foot of the dais on which she and her chief courtiers are assembled. The rigidly attentive postures of the courtiers, all turned towards him, their solemn expressions, and the fact that nearly all eyes are focused on the bard, intensify the austere feeling of the scene. The intimacy and familiarity of Sharpe's picture and the closeness of his composition are offset in Halswelle's by the greater spacing out of the figures and the intrinsic impression of dividedness conveyed.

Amidst the heightened atmosphere of tense anticipation, there are subtle suggestions of court intrigue. The forbidding figure of Knox stands sternly behind two of Mary's ladies, frowning in the direction of the queen, while a sharp-eyed man on the far right stares at the clergyman from the edge of the composition, and is in turn watched by his immediate companion. The sword of the man seated nearest us at the table is visibly turned towards us, and the Henry VIII-type figure standing behind him with his back to us is also armed. The rich tapestries and Stuart heraldry adorning the hall are suggestive of tradition and continuity, but the massive pillars upholding the structures of Holyrood belie the unstable foundations of the court within. The sumptuous fruit and decanters of wine on the table, and the vase beneath can be regarded as symbols of tran-

QUEEN MARY'S WAKE IN HOLYROOD.

THE THIRTEENTH BARD.

BLACKIE & SON GLASGOW EDINBURGH & LONDON

sience and fragility, subject either to decay or being shattered. The tray propped against the table can be likened to a mirror reflecting human vanity, and the cushion lying on the floor in the immediate foreground may perhaps indicate that despite the appearance of decorum things are out of place. Halswelle's illustration of Mary's wake firmly places it in the distant past. By comparison, the portrait of Mary which Hogg selected for the frontispiece of the subscription edition, seeks to represent her as a national figure of lasting significance for his present day–a reminder of lost potential, which might be turned to good for the future.

In the early twentieth century Jessie M. King's illustrations highlighted the enduring imaginative appeal of another story of loss in *The Queen's Wake*, 'Kilmeny'. *Kilmeny* appeared in October 1911 as one of a series of small booklets published by Constable and Foulis, which included poems by Coleridge, Robert Browning, Emerson, and Dante Gabriel Rossetti. Four tiny delicate watercolours illustrate first, the heroine being lulled asleep by spirits before she returns home, her appreciation of nature, her mother anxiously awaiting her return, and finally, Kilmeny elevated on a purple hill in the land of thought.[42] The scenes occur in a different sequence in the poem, with Kilmeny picking flowers in the wood and her mother's search for her related in the opening lines, and Kilmeny's vision of future ages taking place later, when she has been taken into the land of thought. King's illustrations are arranged not as a linear progression from earth to a celestial world, but in effect form a response to Hogg's suggestion at the end of the poem that the heavenly realm is Kilmeny's true home. In choosing to begin with Kilmeny falling asleep in the spirit world and end with her restoration there, with her earthly visit in between, the artist appears to suggest that Kilmeny's journey began in the heavenly realm and that she has been but a visitor to our 'world of sorrow and pain'.

This idea is supported by the detail in the illustrations. In 'They lulled Kilmeny sound asleep' the pale form of Kilmeny is seen in a white dress, asleep by a stream in a wood. At her head, a small female figure kneels in an attitude of prayer, a smaller child-like figure at her feet, with three other pale spirit forms gathered nearby. To the left, an elongated figure plays a lyre. The mood is mystical and religious, the spirits loosely reminiscent of the angel who appeared at the tomb of Christ. A halo of light is visible around Kilmeny's head in this and the next picture, as she stoops by a small tree in the woodland setting, 'And pu' the cress-flower round the spring'. 'But lang may her minny look o'er the wa',' has a female figure in a pink dress and white cap, with her back to us, looking anxiously into the distance. As Christ's death is traditionally depicted with a group of mourners which includes his mother Mary, so this image of Kilmeny's mother is a poignant reminder of the domestic aspect of human grief and anxiety that accompanies loss. The closing image, 'They seated her high on a purple sward', has Kilmeny in a long pale dress, her golden brown hair flowing over her shoulders and her head bathed in a halo of light, looking up wistfully from her mountain seat, with her hand slightly raised as if to touch her vision. In terms of style, King's illustrations clearly draw on a post Pre-Raphaelite aesthetic, and as a sequence they suggest parallels in Christian art–of Christ in the garden of Gethsemane, his death and resurrection, the mourning of the women at the tomb, and his enthronement in Heaven, which tend to emphasise Kilmeny as a figure of perfect heavenly purity, although King chooses to underplay her humanity. King's vaguely etherealised images for 'Kilmeny', as with Halswelle's 'Old David', are not as in tune with Hogg's interesting and varied representations of the human, supernatural, and otherworldly as Sharpe's vivid rendering of 'The Witch of Fife', but they nevertheless offer a different and interesting interpretation.

Collectively, the illustrations Hogg chose for the fifth edition of *The Queen's Wake* are particularly striking for the apt, attractive, and imaginative way in which they support Hogg's broad cultural idea of a Scottish Marian tradition to compete with that of the English Elizabethan, and his more specific claims for a thriving Border heritage. The images play a significant part in promoting the author as a poetic heir of both the Edinburgh court and Ettrick country, and representing indigenous talent as a main player in the broader Romantic canon. They not only complement his poem, but also work in a richly suggestive way to help create a new experience of it. In 1819 this pleasure was available only to the 550 readers who had supported Hogg by subscribing to the fifth edition. The original illustrations are restored to the text for the first time in this edition, and once more serve to foreground Hogg's commitment to and celebration of a national school of poetry, and his place among an enduring succession of bards–this time, it is hoped, for the enjoyment of a wider audience.

Notes

I would like to offer my warmest thanks to Gillian Hughes, Douglas Mack, and Fiona Stafford for their generous advice and numerous enlightening suggestions and comments during the preparation of this essay. I am indebted to Gillian Hughes for drawing my attention to much relevant manuscript material. My thanks also to Meg Duff at the Tate Library in London, Nicola Kalinsky at the Scottish National Portrait Gallery, and Michael J. Campbell of Campbell Fine Art for their very helpful responses to my enquiries, and Vera Ryhazlo at the Bodleian Library for her help with obtaining reproductions of the illustrations.

1   Prospectus of Subscription Edition of Queen's Wake drawn up by Walter Scott, in National Library of Scotland (hereafter NLS), MS 30921. (See also the present edition's 'Appendix: Advertisements for *The Queen's Wake*'.) I am grateful to the Trustees of the National Library of Scotland for permission to quote from manuscripts in their collection in the present essay. For Hogg and Burns, see Douglas S. Mack, 'Hogg as Poet: A Successor to Burns?', in *Love and Liberty: Robert Burns, a Bicentenary Celebration*, ed. by Kenneth Simpson (East Linton, East Lothian: Tuckwell Press, 1997), pp. 119–27.

2   For Hogg's interest in art and his involvement in the Dilettanti Society, see Gillian Hughes, 'Hogg and Fuseli's Satan', in James Hogg, *The Three Perils of Woman*, ed. by Antony Hasler and Douglas Mack (Edinburgh: Edinburgh University Press, 2002), pp. 409–16. I am very grateful to Dr Hughes for showing me a draft of her essay, 'Hogg, Art, and the Annuals', intended for the forthcoming *Literary Annuals* volume, edited by Janette Currie and Gillian Hughes, as part of the Stirling / South Carolina Research Edition of *The Collected Works of James Hogg*, published by Edinburgh University Press.

3   Hogg to William Blackwood, 5 January 1818 (NLS, MS 4003, fols 84–85).

4   Printed prospectus of subscription edition of *The Queen's Wake*, revised by Walter Scott (NLS, MS 4937, fol. 82).

5   Hogg to Archibald Constable, 30 October 1818 (NLS, MS 7200, fols 211–12).

6   Case Y 185. H6745, The Newberry Library, Chicago. The letter is in the Newberry Library's copy of *The Queen's Wake* subscription edition (Edinburgh, 1819). I am grateful to the Newberry Library for permission to quote from this manuscript.

7   See J. J. Foster, *Concerning the True Portraiture of Mary Queen of Scots* (Glasgow: Maclehose, 1904), pp. 44–45. Foster also mentions a portrait, which may have been the picture Medina worked from in his sketch: 'There is still, I believe, at Versailles a picture of Mary to the waist, looking to the spectator's left. She wears a large ruff, a lace-edged mantle, and a cap which is surmounted by a high crown; a crucifix hangs over several rows of pearls at her breast', p. 31. The portrait is no longer in the collection of the Château de Versailles.

8   The etching of 'Marie Queen of Scots' by Lizars (200 mm x 130 mm) used in *The Queen's Wake* is now in the collection of the Scottish National Portrait Gallery. I have been unable to discover any other reproductions of Medina's sketch, or the painting on which it was based.

9   See Laurence L. Bongie, 'The Eighteenth-Century Marian Controversy and an unpublished letter by David Hume', *Studies in Scottish Literature*, 1 (1963–64), 236–52.

10   Karen O'Brien, *Narratives of Enlightenment: Cosmopolitan Histories from Voltaire to Gibbon* (Cambridge: Cambridge University Press, 1997), p. 114.

11   See Karen O'Brien, 'Robertson's place in the development of eighteenth-century narrative history', in *William Robertson and the Expansion of Empire*, ed. by Stewart J. Brown (Cambridge: Cambridge University Press, 1997), pp. 74–91 (p. 87), and *Narratives of Enlightenment*, pp. 104–27 (p. 108).

12   See *Letters from and to Charles Kirkpatrick Sharpe, Esq.* ed. by Alexander Allardyce, with a memoir by the Rev. W. K. R. Bedford, 2 vols (Edinburgh: Blackwood, 1888), II, 155–57, 159–60.

13   'Subscription Copies of Hogg's Queen's Wake Ed5 to W. Blackwood', 21 April 1821 (NLS, MS 30002, fols 32–33).

14   See Douglas Mack's Introduction to the present volume, pp. xxx–xxxi, Murray Pittock, *Poetry and Jacobite Politics in Eighteenth-Century Britain and Ireland* (Cambridge: Cambridge University Press, 1994), and new editions of Hogg's *Jacobite Relics of Scotland [First Series]* and *Second Series*, ed. by Murray Pittock (S/SC, 2002 and 2003).

15   See Douglas S. Mack, 'Hogg and the Blessed Virgin Mary', *Studies in Hogg and his World*, 3 (1992), 68–75 and Introduction to the present volume, pp. xlii–xlv.

16   *The Queen's Wake*, 5th edn (Edinburgh: Blackwood; London: Murray, 1819), Note I, pp. 343–45. All subsequent page references are given in the text.

17   'The Witch of Fife' is also reproduced in *Etchings by Charles Kirkpatrick Sharpe* (Edinburgh: Blackwood, 1869), Item VII, listed on p. 143.

18   Charles Kirkpatrick Sharpe to Hogg, undated letter, a photocopy of which is held in the National Archives of Scotland, RH1/2/664.

19   *The Shepherd's Calendar*, ed. by Douglas S. Mack (S/SC, 1995), pp. 200–22. The story first appeared in the February 1828 number of *Blackwood's*, as part of 'The Shepherd's Calendar' series, 'Class IX. Fairies, Brownies, and Witches': see *Blackwood's* 23, 214–27 (p. 219).

20   James Hogg, *Familiar Anecdotes of Sir Walter Scott*, in *Anecdotes of Scott*, ed. by Jill Rubenstein (S/SC, 1999), p. 61.

21   For more on Gunn's *Historical Enquiry*, see the Introduction to the present volume, pp. xxviii–xxix. Both harps are now in the collection of the National Museum of Scotland.

22   Gunn, pp. 75–84.

23   Gunn, pp. 84–85.

24   Gunn, pp. 13–14.

25   Keith Sanger and Alison Kinnaird, *Tree of Strings, crann nan teud: A History of the Harp in Scotland* (Midlothian: Kinmor Music, 1992), p. 60. See especially chapter five.

26   Sanger and Kinnaird, p. 61.

27   Sanger and Kinnaird, p. 74.

28   Gunn, pp. 8, 4.

29   Hogg to John Gibson Lockhart, 9 February 1832, British Library, Add. MS 70949, fols 135–36. I would like to thank the British Library for permission to quote from this.

30   Thomas Balston, *John Martin 1789–1854, His Life and Works* (London: Duckworth, 1947), p. 69. The episode occurs in 'Noctes Ambrosianae',

Blackwood's, 21, 100–108 (p. 106). Balston also draws attention to the March 1827 'Noctes', in which Christopher North and the Shepherd admire a recent engraving of Martin's mezzotint *The Paphian Bower*, p. 75. See *Blackwood's*, 21, 344–60 (p. 352).

31 See the extract from Serjeant Ralph Thomas's diaries in Mary L. Pendered, *John Martin, Painter, His Life and Times* (London: Hurst & Blackett, 1923), pp. 177–78. Balston explains that the diaries have since been lost, p. 293, n.4.

32 For Hogg's relationship with Cochrane, see *Altrive Tales*, ed. by Gillian Hughes (S/SC, 2003), pp. xx–xxxiv.

33 *The Atlas*, 10 June 1832, p. 378, and *Literary Gazette*, 16 June 1832, p. 381.

34 Lockhart to Hogg, 21 June 1832, in a presentation copy of Lockhart's *The History of Matthew Wald* at the University of Otago Library. In a letter to William Laidlaw in March 1832, Lockhart mentions the possibility of the Highland Society patronising *The Queen's Wake* subscription edition similarly. See *The Life and Letters of John Gibson Lockhart*, ed. by Andrew Lang, 2 vols (London: Nimmo, 1897), II, 110–11.

35 John Murray III to Hogg, 26 June 1832 (John Murray Archive, Box 37).

36 See Gillian Hughes's Introduction to Hogg's *Altrive Tales* (S/SC, 2003), pp. xxi, xxix–xxx.

37 Hogg to Lockhart, 4 October 1832 (NLS, MS 924, no. 83). Lockhart to Hogg, 23 September 1833 (NLS, MS 2245, fols 232–33).

38 John Martin to Hogg, 29 May 1833 (NLS, MS 2245, fol. 222). For the lines Martin quotes, see Night the Second, *1819*, ll. 1530–31 and 1560–61.

39 For more on Isabella Martin, see Pendered who also includes a portrait of the young Isabella opposite p. 258.

40 Martin's *Kilmeny* was exhibited again in 1837 by the New Watercolour Society. It is now believed to be in a private collection. A small reproduction appears in a publication (now out of print) compiled by Michael J. Campbell and Adam Lowe, *John Martin* (Tokyo: Lampoon House, 1996), published in English with a Japanese translation by Kyoichi Tsuzuki, p. 5. *Kilmeny* also appears on the cover of the catalogue of *Agnew's 115th Annual Exhibition of Watercolours and Drawings* (29 February–31 March, 1988), but is miscatalogued within as *The Plains of Calypso* (item 75). It is executed in pencil, watercolour, gum arabic, and oil paint. The dimensions, 65.6 x 81.5 cm, are unusually large for a Martin watercolour.

41 The notice of the Scottish Academy exhibition in the *Edinburgh Evening Post* of 13 April 1833 described Somerville's painting: 'The landscape is all in a subdued tone, while a prophetic stillness glimmers in the sky. Kilmeny is simply attired, her bright blue eye gazing upwards, reflecting on the magic spell by which she had been recently bound'. The related passage describes Kilmeny's mysterious return home, beginning 'Kilmeny looked up with a lovely grace, | But nae smile was seen on Kilmeny's face;' to 'Kilmeny had been where the cock ne'er crew, | Where the rain never fell, and the wind never blew'.

42 *Kilmeny* by James Hogg, with Illustrations by Jessie M. King (Edinburgh: Constable; London: Foulis, October 1911), opposite pp. 8, 17, 20, 28. Larger reproductions of King's illustrations to 'Kilmeny' can be found in *The Songs of the Ettrick Shepherd* (London: Foulis, 1913).

Select Bibliography

Editions of *The Queen's Wake*

For details of earlier editions of *The Queen's Wake*, see the Introduction. The present edition is a paperback reprint of the hardback Stirling / South Carolina edition of *The Queen's Wake* (2004).

Collected Editions

The Stirling / South Carolina Research Edition of the Collected Works of James Hogg (Edinburgh: Edinburgh University Press, 1995–), now underway but not yet complete, is a modern scholarly edition. Previous editions which are useful but bowdlerised are *Tales and Sketches by the Ettrick Shepherd*, 6 vols (Glasgow: Blackie and Son, 1836–37), *The Poetical Works of the Ettrick Shepherd*, 5 vols (Glasgow: Blackie and Son, 1838–40), and *The Works of the Ettrick Shepherd*, ed. by Thomas Thomson, 2 vols (Glasgow: Blackie and Son, 1865).

Bibliography

Edith C. Batho's Bibliography in *The Ettrick Shepherd* (Cambridge: Cambridge University Press, 1927), is still useful, together with her supplementary 'Notes on the Bibliography of James Hogg, the Ettrick Shepherd', in *The Library*, 16 (1935–36), 309–26. Two more modern and reader-friendly bibliographies are Douglas S. Mack, *Hogg's Prose: An Annotated Listing* (Stirling: The James Hogg Society, 1985), and Gillian Hughes, *Hogg's Verse and Drama: A Chronological Listing* (Stirling: The James Hogg Society, 1990). Subsequent information about recently-discovered Hogg items may be gleaned from various articles in *The Bibliotheck* and *Studies in Hogg and his World*.

Biography

Karl Miller's perceptive and illuminating *Electric Shepherd: A Likeness of James Hogg* (London: Faber, 2003) contains much biographical information. Gillian Hughes is currently writing a full and detailed biography: her forthcoming *James Hogg: A Life* (Edinburgh University Press) will draw on her definitive three-volume edition of Hogg's *Collected Letters*, the first volume of which was published by Edinburgh University Press in 2004. Hogg's life up to 1825 is covered by Alan Lang Strout's *The Life and Letters of James Hogg, The Ettrick Shepherd Volume 1 (1770–1825)*, Texas Technological College Research Publications, 15 (Lubbock, Texas: Texas Technological College, 1946). Much valuable information may be obtained from Mrs M. G. Garden's memoir of her father, *Memorials of James Hogg, the Ettrick Shepherd* (London: Alexander Gardner, 1885), and from Mrs Norah Parr's account of Hogg's domestic life in *James Hogg at Home* (Dollar: Douglas S. Mack, 1980). Also useful are Sir George Douglas, *James Hogg*, Famous Scots Series (Edinburgh: Oliphant Anderson & Ferrier, 1899), and Henry Thew Stephenson's *The Ettrick Shepherd: A Biography*, Indiana University Studies, 54 (Bloomington, Indiana: Indiana University, 1922).

General Criticism

Edith C. Batho, *The Ettrick Shepherd* (Cambridge: Cambridge University Press, 1927)

Louis Simpson, *James Hogg: A Critical Study* (Edinburgh and London: Oliver & Boyd, 1962)

Douglas Gifford, *James Hogg* (Edinburgh: The Ramsay Head Press, 1976)

Nelson C. Smith, *James Hogg*, Twayne's English Authors Series (Boston: Twayne Publishers, 1980)

Thomas Crawford, 'James Hogg: The Play of Region and Nation', in *The History of Scottish Literature: Volume 3 Nineteenth Century*, ed. by Douglas Gifford (Aberdeen: Aberdeen University Press, 1988), pp. 89–105

David Groves, *James Hogg: The Growth of a Writer* (Edinburgh: Scottish Academic Press, 1988)

Silvia Mergenthal, *James Hogg: Selbstbild und Bild*, Publications of the Scottish Studies Centre of the Johannes Gutenberg Universität Mainz in Germersheim, 9 (Frankfurt-am-Main: Peter Lang, 1990)

Penny Fielding, *Writing and Orality: Nationality, Culture, and Nineteenth-Century Scottish Fiction* (Oxford: Clarendon Press, 1996)

Karl Miller, *Electric Shepherd: A Likeness of James Hogg* (London: Faber, 2003)

Criticism on *The Queen's Wake*

In addition to discussions in the books listed under 'General Criticism', the following articles contain material relevant to *The Queen's Wake*.

Douglas S. Mack, 'Hogg's "Kilmeny": An Interpretation', *Studies in Scottish Literature*, 4 (1966), 42–45

Douglas S. Mack, 'Hogg's Use of Scots in "Kilmeny"', *Studies in Scottish Literature*, 6 (1968), 123–26

J. R. Mair, 'A Note on Hogg's "Kilmeny"', *Scottish Literary News*, 3 (1973), 17–21

Alan Grant, 'A Presentation Copy of *The Queen's Wake*', *Newsletter of the James Hogg Society*, 8 (1989), 21–22

Barbara Bloedé, 'The Witchcraft Tradition in Hogg's Tales and Verse', *Studies in Hogg and his World*, 1 (1990), 91–102

Peter Garside, 'James Hogg's Fifty Pounds', *Studies in Hogg and his World*, 1 (1990), 128–32

Douglas S. Mack, 'Hogg and the Blessed Virgin Mary', *Studies in Hogg and his World*, 3 (1992), 68–75

Gioia Angeletti, 'Hogg's Debt to William Tennant: the Influence of *Anster Fair* on Hogg's Poetry', *Studies in Hogg and his World*, 6 (1995), 22–32

Suzanne Gilbert, 'Hogg's "Kilmeny" and the Ballad of Supernatural Abduction', *Studies in Hogg and his World*, 8 (1997), 42–55

Valentina Bold, 'The Mountain Bard: James Hogg and Macpherson's Ossian', *Studies in Hogg and his World*, 9 (1998), 32–44

Douglas S. Mack, 'James Hogg and his Publishers: *The Queen's Wake* and *Queen Hynde*', in *Authorship, Commerce and the Public: Scenes of Writing 1750–1850*, ed. by E. J. Clery, Caroline Franklin and Peter Garside (Basingstoke: Palgrave Macmillan, 2002), pp. 67–83

Robin W. MacLachlan, 'Hogg and the Art of Brand Management', *Studies in Hogg and his World*, 14 (2003), 5–15

Meiko O'Halloran, 'Hogg's Kaleidoscopic Art: Identity, Tradition, and Legitimacy in the Work of James Hogg' (unpublished D. Phil. thesis, University of Oxford, 2004)

Chronology of James Hogg

1770 On 9 December James Hogg is baptised in Ettrick Church, Selkirkshire, the date of his birth going unrecorded. His father, Robert Hogg (*c.*1729–1820), a former shepherd, was then tenant of Ettrickhall, a modest farm almost within sight of the church. His mother, Margaret Laidlaw (1730–1813), belonged to a local family noted for their athleticism and also for their stock of ballads and other traditional lore. Hogg's parents married in Ettrick on 27 May 1765, and had four sons, William (b.1767), James (b.1770), David (b.1773), and Robert (b.1776).

1775–76 Hogg attends the parish school kept by John Beattie for a few months before his formal education is abruptly terminated by his father's bankruptcy as a stock-farmer and sheep-dealer and the family's consequent destitution. Their possessions are sold by auction, but a compassionate neighbour, Walter Bryden of Crosslee, takes a lease of the farm of Ettrickhouse and places Robert Hogg there as his shepherd.

1776–85 Due to his family's poverty Hogg is employed as a farm servant throughout his childhood, beginning with the job of herding a few cows in the summer and progressing as his strength increases to general farmwork and acting as a shepherd's assistant. He learns the Metrical Psalms and other parts of the Bible, listens eagerly to the legends of his mother and her brother William (*c.*1735–1829), of itinerants who visit the parish, and of the old men he is engaged with on the lightest and least demanding farm-work.

1778 Death on 17 September of Hogg's maternal grandfather, William Laidlaw, 'the far-famed Will o' Phaup', a noted athlete and reputedly the last man in the district to have spoken with the fairies.

c. **1784** Having saved five shillings from his wages, at the age of fourteen Hogg purchases an old fiddle and teaches himself to play it at the end of his day's work.

1785 Hogg serves a year from Martinmas (11 November) with Mr Scott, the tenant-farmer of Singlee, at 'working with horses, threshing, &c.'

1786 Hogg serves eighteen months from Martinmas with Mr Laidlaw at Elibank, 'the most quiet and sequestered place in Scotland'.

1788 The father of Mr Laidlaw of Elibank, who farms at Willenslee, gives Hogg his first engagement as a shepherd from Whitsunday (15 May); here he stays for two years and begins to read while tending the ewes. His master's wife lends him newspapers and theological works, and he also reads Allan Ramsay's *The Gentle Shepherd* and William Hamilton of Gilbertfield's paraphrase of Blind Harry's *The Life and Adventures of William Wallace*.

1790 Hogg begins a ten-years' service from Whitsunday as shepherd to James Laidlaw of Blackhouse farm, whose kindness he later described as 'much more like that of a father than a master'. Hogg reads his master's books, as well as those of Mr Elder's Peebles circulating library, and begins to compose songs for the local lasses to sing. He makes a congenial and life-long friend in his master's eldest son, William Laidlaw (1779–1845), and with his elder brother William and a number of cousins forms a literary society of shepherds. Alexander Laidlaw, shepherd at Bowerhope in Yarrow, is also an intimate friend who shares Hogg's efforts at self-improvement. 'The Mistakes of a Night', a Scots poem, is published in the *Scots Magazine* for October 1794, and in 1797 Hogg first hears of Robert Burns (1759–96) when a half-daft man named Jock Scott recites 'Tam o' Shanter' to him on the hillside. Towards the end of this period Hogg composes plays and pastorals as well as songs. His journeying as a drover of sheep stimulates an interest in the Highlands of Scotland, and initiates a series of exploratory tours taken in the summer over a succession of years.

1800 At Whitsunday Hogg leaves Blackhouse to look after his ageing parents at Ettrickhouse. Going into Edinburgh in the autumn to sell sheep he decides to print his poems: his *Scottish Pastorals* is published early in the following year and receives favourable attention in the *Scots Magazine* for 1801. More popular still is his patriotic song of 'Donald Macdonald' also composed at about this time, in fear of a French invasion.

1802 Hogg is recruited by William Laidlaw in the spring as a ballad-collector for Scott's *Minstrelsy of the Scottish Border*, and meets Walter Scott himself (1771–1832) later in the year. He begins to contribute to the *Edinburgh Magazine*, and keeps a journal of his Highland Tour in July and August that is eventually published in the *Scots Magazine*.

1803 The lease of Ettrickhouse expires at Whitsunday and Hogg uses his savings to lease a Highland sheep farm, signing a five-year lease for Shelibost in Harris on 13 July, to begin from Whitsunday 1804. On his journey home he stops at Greenock where he meets the future novelist John Galt (1779–1839) and his friend James Park. He is now a regular contributor to the *Scots Magazine*, and also earns prizes from the Highland Society of Scotland for his essays on sheep.

1804 Hogg loses his money and fails to gain possession of Shelibost through a legal complication, retiring into England for the summer. On his return home he fails to find employment, but occupies himself in writing ballad-imitations for the collection published in 1807 as *The Mountain Bard*.

1805–1806 Hogg is engaged from Whitsunday 1805 as a shepherd at Mitchelslacks farm in Closeburn parish, Dumfriesshire: his master Mr Harkness belongs to a local family famous for their support of the Covenanters. He is visited on the hillside by the young Allan Cunningham (1784–1842), and becomes friendly with the whole talented Cunningham family. Around Halloween 1806 (31 October) he becomes the lover of Catherine Henderson. Towards the end of the year Hogg signs leases on two farms in Dumfriesshire, Corfardin and Locherben, to begin from Whitsunday 1807.

1807 *The Mountain Bard* is published by Archibald Constable (1774–1827) in Edinburgh in February. At Whitsunday Hogg moves to Corfardin farm in Tynron parish. *The Shepherd's Guide*, a sheep-farming and veterinary manual, is published in June. Hogg acknowledges paternity of Catherine Henderson's baby, born towards the end of the summer and baptised Catherine Hogg on 13 December.

1808–09 As a result of trips to Edinburgh Hogg becomes acquainted with James Gray (1770–1830), classics master of the Edinburgh High School and his future brother-in-law. He also meets a number of literary women, including Mary Peacock, Jessie Stuart, Mary Brunton, and Eliza Izett. After the death of his sheep in a storm Hogg moves to Locherben farm and tries to earn a living by grazing sheep for other farmers. His debts escalate, he becomes increasingly reckless, and around Whitsunday 1809 becomes the lover of Margaret Beattie. In the autumn Hogg absconds from Locherben and his creditors, returning to Ettrick where he is considered to be disgraced and unemployable.

1810 In February Hogg moves to Edinburgh in an attempt to pursue a career as a professional literary man. In Dumfries-shire Margaret Beattie's daughter is born on 13 March, and her birth is recorded retrospectively as Elizabeth Hogg in June, Hogg presumably having acknowledged paternity. Later that year Hogg meets his future wife, Margaret Phillips (1789–1870), while she is paying a visit to her brother-in-law James Gray in Edinburgh. He explores the cultural life of Edinburgh, and is supported by the generosity of an Ettrick friend, John Grieve (1781–1836), now a prosperous Edinburgh hatter. A song-collection entitled *The Forest Minstrel* is published in August. On 1 September the first number of Hogg's own weekly periodical *The Spy* appears, which in spite of its perceived improprieties, continues for a whole year.

1811–12 During the winter of 1810–11 Hogg becomes an active member of the Forum, a public debating society, eventually being appointed Secretary. This brings him into contact with John M'Diarmid (1792–1852), later to become a noted Scottish journalist, and the reforming mental health specialist Dr Andrew Duncan (1744–1828). With Grieve's encouragement Hogg takes rural lodgings at Deanhaugh on the outskirts of Edinburgh and plans a long narrative poem centred on a poetical contest at the court of Mary, Queen of Scots.

1813 Hogg becomes a literary celebrity in Edinburgh when *The Queen's Wake* is published at the end of January, and makes new friends in R. P. Gillies (1788–1858) and John Wilson (1785–1854), his correspondence widening to include Lord Byron (1788–1824) early the following year. Hogg's mother dies in the course of the summer. Hogg tries to interest Constable in a series of Scottish Rural Tales, and also takes advice from various literary friends on the suitability of his play, *The Hunting of Badlewe*, for the stage. In the autumn during his customary Highland Tour he is detained at Kinnaird House near Dunkeld by a cold and begins a poem in the Spenserian stanza, eventually to become *Mador of the Moor*.

1814 Hogg intervenes successfully to secure publication of the work of other writers such as R. P. Gillies, James Gray, and William Nicholson (1782–1849). George Goldie publishes *The Hunting of Badlewe* in April, as the Allies enter Paris and the end of the long war with France seems imminent. During the summer Hogg meets William Wordsworth (1770–1850) in Edinburgh, and visits him and other poets in an excursion to the Lake District. He proposes a poetical repository, and obtains several promises of contributions from important contemporary poets, though the project leads to a serious quarrel with Scott in the autumn. The bankruptcy of George Goldie halts sales of *The Queen's Wake*, but introduces Hogg to the publisher William Blackwood (1776–1834). Having offered Constable *Mador of the Moor* in February, Hogg is persuaded by James Park to publish *The Pilgrims of the Sun* first: the poem is brought out by John Murray (1778–1843) and William Blackwood in Edinburgh in December. Towards the end of the year Hogg and his young Edinburgh friends form the Right and Wrong Club which meets nightly and where heavy drinking takes place.

1815 Hogg begins the year with a serious illness, but at the end of January is better and learns that the Duke of Buccleuch has granted him the small farm of Eltrive Moss effectively rent-free for his lifetime. He takes possession at Whitsunday, but as the house there is barely habitable continues to spend much of his time in Edinburgh. He writes songs for the Scottish collector George Thomson (1757–1851). Scott's publication of a poem celebrating the ending of the Napoleonic Wars with the battle of Waterloo on 18 June prompts Hogg to write 'The Field of Waterloo'. Hogg also writes 'To the Ancient Banner of Buccleuch' for the local contest at football at Carterhaugh on 4 December.

1816 Hogg contributes songs to John Clarke-Whitfeld's *Twelve Vocal Melodies*, and plans a collected edition of his own poetry. *Mador of the Moor* is published in April. Despairing of the success of his poetical repository Hogg turns it into a collection of his own parodies, published in October as *The Poetic Mirror*. The volume is unusually successful, a second edition being published in December. The Edinburgh musician Alexander Campbell visits Hogg in Yarrow, enlisting his help with the song-collection *Albyn's Anthology* (1816–18). William Blackwood moves into Princes Street, signalling his intention to become one of Edinburgh's foremost publishers.

1817 Blackwood begins an *Edinburgh Monthly Magazine* in April, with Hogg's support, but with Thomas Pringle and James Cleghorn as editors it is a lacklustre publication and a breach between publisher and editors ensues. Hogg, holding by Blackwood, sends him a draft of the notorious 'Chaldee Manuscript', the scandal surrounding which ensures the success of the relaunched *Blackwood's Edinburgh Magazine*. Hogg's two-volume

Dramatic Tales are published in May. Hogg spends much of the summer at his farm of Altrive, writing songs for *Hebrew Melodies*, a Byron-inspired collection proposed by the composer W. E. Heather. In October George Thomson receives a proposal from the Highland Society of London for a collection of Jacobite Songs, a commission which he passes on to Hogg.

1818 *The Brownie of Bodsbeck; and Other Tales* is published by Blackwood in March, by which time Hogg is busily working on *Jacobite Relics*, his major preoccupation this year. A modern stone-built cottage is built at Altrive, the cost of which Hogg hopes to defray in part by a new one guinea subscription edition of *The Queen's Wake*, which is at press in October though publication did not occur until early the following year.

1819 On a visit to Edinburgh towards the end of February Hogg meets again with Margaret Phillips; his courtship of her becomes more intense, and he proposes marriage. Hogg's song-collection *A Border Garland* is published in May, and in August Hogg signs a contract with Oliver and Boyd for the publication of *Winter Evening Tales*, also working on a long Border Romance. The first volume of *Jacobite Relics* is published in December.

1820 During the spring Hogg is working on the second volume of his *Jacobite Relics* and also on a revised edition of *The Mountain Bard*, as well as planning his marriage to Margaret Phillips, which takes place on 28 April. His second work of fiction, *Winter Evening Tales,* is published at the end of April. Very little literary work is accomplished during the autumn: the Hoggs make their wedding visits in Dumfriesshire during September, and then on 24 October Hogg's old father dies at Altrive.

1821 The second volume of *Jacobite Relics* is published in February and a third (enlarged) edition of *The Mountain Bard* in March. The inclusion in the latter of an updated 'Memoir of the Author's Life' raises an immediate outcry. Hogg's son, James Robert Hogg, is born in Edinburgh on 18 March and baptised on the couple's first wedding anniversary. Serious long-term financial troubles begin for Hogg with the signing of a nine-year lease from Whitsunday of the large farm of Mount Benger in Yarrow, part of the estates of the Duke of Buccleuch—Hogg having insufficient capital for such an ambitious venture. In June Oliver and Boyd's refusal to publish Hogg's

Border Romance, *The Three Perils of Man*, leads to a breach with the firm. Hogg also breaks temporarily with Blackwood in August when a savage review of his 'Memoir of the Author's Life' appears in *Blackwood's Edinburgh Magazine*, and begins again to write for Constable's less lively *Edinburgh Magazine*. In September there is a measles epidemic in Yarrow, and Hogg becomes extremely ill with the disease. By the end of the year Hogg is negotiating with the Constable firm for an edition of his collected poems in four volumes.

1822 The first of the 'Noctes Ambrosianae' appears in the March issue of *Blackwood's Edinburgh Magazine*: Hogg is portrayed in this long-running series as the Shepherd, a 'boozing buffoon'. June sees the publication of Hogg's four-volume *Poetical Works* by Constable, and Longmans publish his novel *The Three Perils of Man*. There is great excitement in Edinburgh surrounding the visit of George IV to the city in August, and Hogg marks the occasion with the publication of his Scottish masque, *The Royal Jubilee*. A neighbouring landowner in Ettrick Forest, Captain Napier of Thirlestane, publishes *A Treatise on Practical Store-Farming* in October, with help from Hogg and his friend Alexander Laidlaw of Bowerhope. James Gray leaves Edinburgh to become Rector of Belfast Academy.

1823 In debt to William Blackwood Hogg sets about retrieving his finances with a series of tales for *Blackwood's Edinburgh Magazine* under the title of 'The Shepherd's Calendar'. His daughter Janet Phillips Hogg ('Jessie') is born on 23 April. That summer a suicide is exhumed in Yarrow, and Hogg writes an account for *Blackwood's*. *The Three Perils of Woman*, another novel, is published in August, and Hogg subsequently plans to publish an eight-volume collection of his Scottish tales.

1824 Hogg is working on his epic poem *Queen Hynde* during the spring when his attention is distracted by family troubles. His once prosperous father-in-law is in need of a home, so Hogg moves his own family to the old thatched farmhouse of Mount Benger leaving his new cottage at Altrive for the old couple. *The Private Memoirs and Confessions of a Justified Sinner*, written at Altrive during the preceding months, is published in June. Hogg contributes to the *Literary Souvenir* for 1825, this signalling the opening of a new and lucrative market for his work in Literary Annuals. In November a major conflagration destroys part of Edinburgh's Old Town. *Queen Hynde* is published early in December.

1825 Another daughter is born to the Hoggs on 18 January and named Margaret Laidlaw Hogg ('Maggie'). Hogg turns his attention to a new work of prose fiction, 'Lives of Eminent Men', the precursor of his *Tales of the Wars of Montrose*. In December John Gibson Lockhart (1794–1854), Scott's son-in-law and a leading light of *Blackwood's*, moves to London to take up the post of editor of the *Quarterly Review*, accompanied by Hogg's nephew and literary assistant Robert Hogg.

1826 Hogg is in arrears with his rent for Mount Benger at a time which sees the failure of the Constable publishing firm, involving Sir Walter Scott and also Hogg's friend John Aitken. By July Hogg himself is threatened with arrestment for debt, while the Edinburgh book trade is in a state of near-stagnation. James Gray is also in debt and leaves Belfast for India, leaving his two daughters, Janet and Mary, in the care of Hogg and his wife.

1827 Hogg's financial affairs are in crisis at the beginning of the year when the Buccleuch estate managers order him to pay his arrears of rent at Whitsunday or relinquish the Mount Benger farm. However, 'The Shepherd's Calendar' stories are appearing regularly in *Blackwood's Edinburgh Magazine* and Hogg is confident of earning a decent income by his pen as applications for contributions to Annuals and other periodicals increase. The death of his father-in-law Peter Phillips in May relieves him from the expense of supporting two households. Hogg founds the St Ronan's Border Club, the first sporting meeting of which takes place at Innerleithen in September. The year ends quietly for the Hoggs, who are both convalescent—Margaret from the birth of the couple's third daughter, Harriet Sidney Hogg, on 18 December, and Hogg from the lameness resulting from having been struck by a horse.

1828 Although a more productive year for Hogg than the last, with the publication of his *Select and Rare Scotish Melodies* in London in the autumn and the signing of a contract with Robert Purdie for a new edition of his *Border Garland*, the book-trade is still at a comparative standstill. Hogg's daughter Harriet is discovered to have a deformed foot that may render her lame. A new weekly periodical entitled the *Edinburgh Literary Journal* is started in Edinburgh by Hogg's young friend, Henry Glassford Bell (1803–74).

1829 Hogg continues to write songs and to make contributions to Annuals and other periodicals, while the spring sees the publication of *The Shepherd's Calendar* in book form. Hogg continues to relish shooting during the autumn months and the country sports of the St Ronan's Border Club.

1830 Hogg's lease of the Mount Benger farm is not renewed, and the family return to Altrive at Whitsunday. Inspired by the success of Scott's *magnum opus* edition of the Waverley Novels, Hogg pushes for the publication of his own tales in monthly numbers. Blackwood agrees to publish a small volume of Hogg's best songs, and Hogg finds a new outlet for his work with the foundation in February of *Fraser's Magazine*. Towards the end of September Hogg meets with Scott for the last time.

1831 *Songs by the Ettrick Shepherd* is published at the start of the year, and a companion volume of ballads, *A Queer Book*, is printed, though publication is held up by Blackwood, who argues that the political agitation surrounding the Reform Bill is hurtful to his trade. He is also increasingly reluctant to print Hogg's work in his magazine. Hogg's youngest child, Mary Gray Hogg, is born on 21 August. Early in December Hogg quarrels openly with Blackwood and resolves to start the publication of his collected prose tales in London. After a short stay in Edinburgh he departs by sea and arrives in London on the last day of the year.

1832 From January to March Hogg enjoys being a literary lion in London while he forwards the publication of his collected prose tales. Within a few weeks of his arrival he publishes a devotional manual for children entitled *A Father's New Year's Gift*, and also works on the first volume of his *Altrive Tales*, published in April after his return to Altrive. Blackwood, no doubt aware of Hogg's metropolitan celebrity, finally publishes *A Queer Book* in April too. The Glasgow publisher Archibald Fullarton offers Hogg a substantial fee for producing a new edition of the works of Robert Burns with a memoir of the poet. The financial failure of Hogg's London publisher, James Cochrane, stops the sale and production of *Altrive Tales* soon after the publication of the first (and only) volume. Sir Walter Scott dies on 21 September, and Hogg reflects on the subject of a Scott biography. In October Hogg is invited to contribute to a new cheap paper, *Chambers's Edinburgh Journal*.

1833 During a January visit to Edinburgh Hogg falls through the ice while out curling and a serious illness results. In February he tries to interest the numbers publisher Blackie and Son of Glasgow in a continuation of his collected prose tales. He tries

to mend the breach with Blackwood, who for his part is seri-
ously offended by Hogg's allusions to their financial dealings
in the 'Memoir' prefacing *Altrive Tales*. Hogg sends a collection
of anecdotes about Scott for publication in London but with-
draws them in deference to Lockhart as Scott's son-in-law,
forwarding a rewritten version to America in June for publi-
cation there. He offers Cochrane, now back in business as
a publisher, some tales about the wars of Montrose, and by
November has reached an agreement with Blackie and Son.
The young Duke of Buccleuch grants Hogg a 99-year lease
for the house at Altrive and a fragment of the land, a measure
designed to secure a vote for him in elections but which also
ensures a small financial provision for Hogg's young family
after his death.

1834 Hogg's nephew and literary assistant Robert Hogg dies of
consumption on 9 January, aged thirty-one. Hogg revises his
work on the edition of Burns, now with William Motherwell
as a co-editor. His *Lay Sermons* is published in April, and the
same month sees the publication of his *Familiar Anecdotes of Sir
Walter Scott* in America. When a pirated version comes out in
Glasgow in June Lockhart breaks off all friendly relations with
Hogg. The breach with William Blackwood is mended in May,
but Blackwood's death on 16 November loosens Hogg's con-
nection both with the publishing firm and *Blackwood's Edin-
burgh Magazine*.

1835 *Tales of the Wars of Montrose* is published in March. Hogg seems
healthy enough in June, when his wife and daughter, Harriet,
leave him at Altrive while paying a visit to Edinburgh. Even
in August he is well enough to go out shooting on the moors
as usual and to take what proves to be a last look at Blackhouse
and other scenes of his youth. Soon afterwards, however, his
normally excellent constitution begins to fail and by October
he is confined first to the house and then to his bed. He dies
on 21 November, and is buried among his relations in Ettrick
kirkyard a short distance from the place of his birth.

THE

QUEEN'S WAKE:

A

Legendary Poem.

BY

JAMES HOGG.

Be mine to read the visions old,
Which thy awakening Bards have told ;
And whilst they meet thy tranced view,
Hold each strange tale devoutly true.
                                    CÓLLINS.

EDINBURGH:

PRINTED BY ANDREW BALFOUR,

FOR GEORGE GOLDIE, 34. PRINCE'S STREET, EDINBURGH ;

AND

LONGMAN, HURST, REES, ORME, AND BROWN,
LONDON.

1813.

Introduction

Introduction

Now burst, ye Winter clouds that lower,
Fling from your folds the piercing shower;
Sing to the tower and leafless tree,
Ye cold winds of adversity;
Your blights, your chilling influence shed,   5
On wareless heart, and houseless head;
Your ruth or fury I disdain,
I've found my Mountain Lyre again.

Come to my heart, my only stay!
Companion of a happier day!   10
Thou gift of heaven! thou pledge of good!
Harp of the mountain and the wood!
I little thought, when first I tried
Thy notes by lone Saint Mary's side;
When in a deep untrodden den,   15
I found thee in the braken glen,
I little thought that idle toy
Should e'er become my only joy!

A maiden's youthful smiles had wove
Around my heart the toils of love,   20
When first thy magic wires I rung,
And on the breeze thy numbers flung.
The fervid tear played in mine eye;
I trembled, wept, and wondered why.
Sweet was the thrilling ecstasy: 25
I know not if 'twas love or thee.

Weened not my heart, when youth had flown,
Friendship would fade, or fortune frown;
When pleasure, love, and mirth were past,
That thou should'st prove my all at last!   30
Jeered by conceit and lordly pride,
I flung my soothing harp aside;
With wayward fortune strove a while;
Wrecked in a world of self and guile.

Again I sought the braken hill;   35
Again sat musing by the rill;
My wild sensations all were gone,
And only thou wert left alone.
Long hast thou in the moorland lain,
Now welcome to my heart again.   40

   The russet weed of mountain gray
No more shall round thy border play;
No more the brake-flowers, o'er thee piled,
Shall mar thy tones and measures wild.
Harp of the Forest, thou shalt be   45
Fair as the bud on forest tree!
Sweet be thy strains, as those that swell
In Ettrick's green and fairy dell;
Soft as the breeze of falling even,
And purer than the dews of heaven.   50

   Of minstrel honours, now no more;
Of bards, who sung in days of yore;
Of gallant chiefs, in courtly guise;
Of ladies' smiles; of ladies' eyes;
Of royal feasts and obsequies;   55
When Caledon, with look severe,
Saw Beauty's hand her sceptre bear,–
By cliff and haunted wild I'll sing,
Responsive to thy dulcet string.

   When wanes the circling year away,   60
When scarcely smiles the doubtful day,
Fair daughter of Dunedin, say,
Hast thou not heard, at midnight deep,
Soft music on thy slumbers creep?
At such a time, if careless thrown   65
Thy slender form on couch of down,
Hast thou not felt, to nature true,
The tear steal from thine eye so blue?
If then thy guiltless bosom strove
In blissful dreams of conscious love,   70
And even shrunk from proffer bland
Of lover's visionary hand,
On such ecstatic dream when brake

The music of the midnight wake,
Hast thou not weened thyself on high,   75
List'ning to angels' melody,
'Scaped from a world of cares away,
To dream of love and bliss for ay?

The dream dispelled, the music gone,
Hast thou not, sighing, all alone,   80
Proffered thy vows to heaven, and then
Blest the sweet wake, and slept again?

Then list, ye maidens, to my lay,
Though old the tale, and past the day;
Those wakes, now played by minstrels poor,   85
At midnight's darkest, chillest hour,
Those humble wakes, now scorned by all,
Were first begun in courtly hall,
When royal MARY, blithe of mood,
Kept holiday at Holyrood.   90

Scotland, involved in factious broils,
Groaned deep beneath her woes and toils,
And looked o'er meadow, dale, and lea,
For many a day her Queen to see;
Hoping that then her woes would cease,   95
And all her vallies smile in peace.
The Spring was past, the Summer gone;
Still vacant stood the Scottish throne:
But scarce had Autumn's mellow hand
Waved her rich banner o'er the land,   100
When rang the shouts, from tower and tree,
That Scotland's Queen was on the sea.
Swift spread the news o'er down and dale,
Swift as the lively Autumn gale;
Away, away, it echoed still,   105
O'er many a moor and Highland hill,
Till rang each glen and verdant plain,
From Cheviot to the northern main.

Each bard attuned the loyal lay,
And for Dunedin hied away;   110
Each harp was strung in woodland bower,

In praise of beauty's bonniest flower.
The chiefs forsook their ladies fair;
The priest his beads and books of prayer;
The farmer left his harvest day;   115
The shepherd all his flocks to stray;
The forester forsook the wood,
And hasted on to Holyrood.

    After a youth, by woes o'ercast,
After a thousand sorrows past,   120
The lovely Mary once again
Set foot upon her native plain;
Kneeled on the pier with modest grace,
And turned to heaven her beauteous face.
'Twas then the caps in air were blended,   125
A thousand thousand shouts ascended;
Shivered the breeze around the throng;
Gray barrier cliffs the peals prolong;
And every tongue gave thanks to heaven,
That Mary to their hopes was given.   130

    Her comely form and graceful mien,
Bespoke the Lady and the Queen;
The woes of one so fair and young,
Moved every heart and every tongue.
Driven from her home, a helpless child,   135
To brave the winds and billows wild;
An exile bred in realms afar,
Amid commotions, broils, and war.
In one short year her hopes all crossed,—
A parent, husband, kingdom lost!   140
And all ere eighteen years had shed
Their honours o'er her royal head.
For such a Queen, the Stuarts' heir,
A Queen so courteous, young, and fair,
Who would not every foe defy!   145
Who would not stand! who would not die!

    Light on her airy steed she sprung,
Around with golden tassels hung,
No chieftain there rode half so free,
Or half so light and gracefully.   150

How sweet to see her ringlets pale
Wide waving in the southland gale,
Which through the broom-wood blossoms flew,
To fan her cheeks of rosy hue!
Whene'er it heaved her bosom's screen,   155
What beauties in her form were seen!
And when her courser's mane it swung,
A thousand silver bells were rung.
A sight so fair, on Scottish plain,
A Scot shall never see again!   160

When Mary turned her wondering eyes
On rocks that seemed to prop the skies;
On palace, park, and battled pile;
On lake, on river, sea, and isle;
O'er woods and meadows bathed in dew,   165
To distant mountains wild and blue;
She thought the isle that gave her birth,
The sweetest, wildest land on earth.

Slowly she ambled on her way
Amid her lords and ladies gay.   170
Priest, abbot, layman, all were there,
And Presbyter with look severe.
There rode the lords of France and Spain,
Of England, Flanders, and Lorraine,
While serried thousands round them stood,   175
From shore of Leith to Holyrood.

Though Mary's heart was light as air
To find a home so wild and fair;
To see a gathered nation by,
And rays of joy from every eye;   180
Though frequent shouts the welkin broke,
Though courtiers bowed and ladies spoke,
An absent look they oft could trace
Deep settled on her comely face.
Was it the thought, that all alone   185
She must support a rocking throne?
That Caledonia's rugged land
Might scorn a Lady's weak command,
And the Red Lion's haughty eye
Scowl at a maiden's feet to lie?   190

No; 'twas the notes of Scottish song,
Soft pealing from the countless throng.
So mellowed came the distant swell,
That on her ravished ear it fell
Like dew of heaven, at evening close,   195
On forest flower or woodland rose.
For Mary's heart, to nature true,
The powers of song and music knew:
But all the choral measures bland,
Of anthems sung in southern land,   200
Appeared an useless pile of art,
Unfit to sway or melt the heart,
Compared with that which floated bye,–
Her simple native melody.

As she drew nigh the Abbey stile,   205
She halted, reined, and bent the while:
She heard the Caledonian lyre
Pour forth its notes of runic fire;
But scarcely caught the ravished Queen
The minstrel's song that flowed between;   210
Entranced upon the strain she hung,
'Twas thus the gray-haired minstrel sung.–

The Song

"O! Lady dear, fair is thy noon,
But man is like the inconstant moon:
Last night she smiled o'er lawn and lea;   215
That moon will change, and so will he.

"Thy time, dear Lady, 's a passing shower;
Thy beauty is but a fading flower:
Watch thy young bosom, and maiden eye,
For the shower must fall, and the flowret die."–   220

What ails my Queen? said good Argyle,
Why fades upon her cheek the smile?
Say, rears your steed too fierce and high?
Or sits your golden seat awry?–

Ah! no, my Lord! this noble steed,   225
Of Rouen's calm and generous breed,
Has borne me over hill and plain,
Swift as the dun-deer of the Seine.
But such a wild and simple lay,
Poured from the harp of minstrel gray,   230
My every sense away it stole,
And swayed a while my raptured soul.
O! say, my Lord, (for you must know
What strains along your vallies flow,
And all the hoards of Highland lore,)   235
Was ever song so sweet before?–

Replied the Earl, as round he flung,–
Feeble the strain that minstrel sung!
My royal Dame, if once you heard
The Scottish lay from Highland bard,   240
Then might you say, in raptures meet,
No song was ever half so sweet!

It nerves the arm of warrior wight
To deeds of more than mortal might;
'Twill make the maid, in all her charms,   245
Fall weeping in her lover's arms.
'Twill charm the mermaid from the deep;
Make mountain oaks to bend and weep;
Thrill every heart with horrors dire,
And shape the breeze to forms of fire.   250

When poured from greenwood-bower at even,
'Twill draw the spirits down from heaven;
And all the fays that haunt the wood,
To dance around in frantic mood,
And tune their mimic harps so boon   255
Beneath the cliff and midnight moon.
Ah! yes, my Queen! if once you heard
The Scottish lay from Highland bard,
Then might you say in raptures meet,
No song was ever half so sweet.–   260

Queen Mary lighted in the court;
Queen Mary joined the evening's sport;

Yet though at table all were seen,
To wonder at her air and mien;
Though courtiers fawned and ladies sung,   265
Still in her ear the accents rung,–
"*Watch thy young bosom and maiden eye,*
"*For the shower must fall and the flowret die.*"
And much she wished to prove ere long,
The wonderous powers of Scottish song.   270

When next to ride the Queen was bound,
To view the lands and city round,
On high amid the gathered crowd,
A herald thus proclaim'd aloud:–

"Peace, peace to Scotland's wasted vales,   275
To her dark heaths and Highland dales;
To her brave sons of warlike mood,
To all her daughters fair and good;
Peace o'er her ruined vales shall pour,
Like beam of heaven behind the shower.   280
Let every harp and echo ring;
Let maidens smile and poets sing;
For love and peace entwined shall sleep,
Calm as the moon-beam on the deep;
By waving wood and wandering rill,   285
On purple heath and Highland hill.

"The soul of warrior stern to charm,
And bigotry and rage disarm,
Our Queen commands, that every bard
Due honours have, and high regard.   290
If, to his song of rolling fire,
He join the Caledonian lyre,
And skill in legendary lore,
Still higher shall his honours soar.
For all the arts beneath the heaven,   295
That man has found, or God has given,
None draws the soul so sweet away,
As music's melting mystic lay;
Slight emblem of the bliss above,
It soothes the spirit all to love.   300

"To cherish this attractive art,
To lull the passions, mend the heart,
And break the moping zealot's chains,
Hear what our lovely Queen ordains.

"Each Caledonian bard must seek   305
Her courtly halls on Easter week,
That then the royal Wake may be
Cheered by their thrilling minstrelsy.
No ribaldry the Queen must hear,
No song unmeet for maiden's ear,   310
No jest, nor adulation bland,
But legends of our native land;
And he whom most the Court regards,
High be his honours and rewards.
Let every Scottish bard give ear,   315
Let every Scottish bard appear;
He then before the Court must stand,
In native garb, with harp in hand.
At home no minstrel dare to tarry:
High the behest.—God save Queen Mary!"   320

    Little recked they, that countless throng,
Of music's power or minstrel's song;
But crowding their young Queen around,
Whose stately courser pawed the ground,
Her beauty more their wonder swayed,   325
Than all the noisy herald said;
Judging the proffer all in sport,
An idle whim of idle Court.
But many a bard preferred his prayer;
For many a Scottish bard was there.   330
Quaked each fond heart with raptures strong,
Each thought upon his harp and song;
And turning home without delay,
Coned his wild strain by mountain gray.

    Each glen was sought for tales of old,   335
Of luckless love, of warrior bold,
Of ravished maid, or stolen child
By freakish fairy of the wild;
Of sheeted ghost, that had revealed

Dark deeds of guilt from man concealed;   340
Of boding dreams, of wandering spright,
Of dead-lights glimmering through the night.
Yea, every tale of ruth or weir,
Could waken pity, love, or fear,
Were decked anew, with anxious pain,   345
And sung to native airs again.

Alas! those lays of fire once more
Are wrecked 'mid heaps of mouldering lore!
And feeble he who dares presume
That heavenly wake-light to relume.   350
But, grieved the legendary lay
Should perish from our land for ay,
While sings the lark above the wold,
And all his flocks rest in the fold,
Fondly he strikes, beside the pen,   355
The harp of Yarrow's braken glen.

December came; his aspect stern
Glared deadly o'er the mountain cairn;
A polar sheet was round him flung,
And ice-spears at his girdle hung;   360
O'er frigid field, and drifted cone,
He strode undaunted and alone;
Or, throned amid the Grampians gray,
Kept thaws and suns of heaven at bay.

Not stern December's fierce controul   365
Could quench the flame of minstrel's soul:
Little recked they, our bards of old,
Of Autumn's showers, or Winter's cold.
Sound slept they on the nighted hill,
Lulled by the winds or babbling rill: 370
Curtained within the Winter cloud;
The heath their couch, the sky their shroud.
Yet their's the strains that touch the heart,
Bold, rapid, wild, and void of art.

Unlike the bards, whose milky lays   375
Delight in these degenerate days:
Their crystal spring, and heather brown,
Is changed to wine and couch of down;

Effeminate as lady gay,–
Such as the bard, so is his lay!   380

  But then was seen, from every vale,
Through drifting snows and rattling hail,
Each Caledonian minstrel true,
Dressed in his plaid and bonnet blue,
With harp across his shoulders slung,   385
And music murmuring round his tongue,
Forcing his way, in raptures high,
To Holyrood his skill to try.

  Ah! when at home the songs they raised,
When gaping rustics stood and gazed,   390
Each bard believed, with ready will,
Unmatched his song, unmatched his skill!
But when the royal halls appeared,
Each aspect changed, each bosom feared;
And when in court of Holyrood   395
Filed harps and bards around him stood,
His eye emitted cheerless ray,
His hope, his spirit sunk away:
There stood the minstrel, but his mind
Seemed left in native glen behind.   400

  Unknown to men of sordid heart,
What joys the poet's hopes impart;
Unknown, how his high soul is torn
By cold neglect, or canting scorn:
That meteor torch of mental light,   405
A breath can quench, or kindle bright.
Oft has that mind, which braved serene
The shafts of poverty and pain,
The Summer toil, the Winter blast,
Fallen victim to a frown at last.   410
Easy the boon he asks of thee;
O, spare his heart in courtesy!

  There rolled each bard his anxious eye,
Or strode his adversary bye.
No cause was there for names to scan,   415
Each minstrel's plaid bespoke his clan;
And the blunt Borderer's plain array,

The bonnet broad and blanket gray.
Bard sought of bard a look to steal;
Eyes measured each from head to heel.   420
Much wonder rose, that men so famed,
Men save with rapture never named,
Looked only so,–they could not tell,–
Like other men, and scarce so well.
Though keen the blast, and long the way,   425
When twilight closed that dubious day,
When round the table all were set,
Small heart had they to talk or eat;
Red look askance, blunt whisper low,
Awkward remark, uncourtly bow,   430
Were all that past in that bright throng,
That group of genuine sons of song.

One did the honours of the board,
Who seemed a courtier or a lord.
Strange his array and speech withal,   435
Gael deemed him southern–southern, Gael.
Courteous his mien, his accents weak,
Lady in manner as in make;
Yet round the board a whisper ran,
That that same gay and simpering man   440
A minstrel was of wonderous fame,
Who from a distant region came,
To bear the prize beyond the sea
To the green shores of Italy.

The wine was served, and, sooth to say,   445
Insensibly it stole away.
Thrice did they drain th' allotted store,
And wondering skinkers dun for more;
Which vanished swifter than the first,–
Little weened they the poets' thirst.   450

Still as that ruddy juice they drained,
The eyes were cleared, the speech regained;
And latent sparks of fancy glowed,
Till one abundant torrent flowed,
Of wit, of humour, social glee,   455
Wild music, mirth, and revelry.

Just when a jest had thrilled the crowd,
Just when the laugh was long and loud,
Entered a squire with summons smart;—
That was the knell that pierced the heart:— 460
"The Court awaits;"—he bowed—was gone,—
Our bards sat changed to busts of stone.
As ever ye heard the green-wood dell,
On morn of June one warbled swell,
If burst the thunder from on high, 465
How hushed the woodland melody!
Even so our bards sunk at the view
Of what they wished, and what they knew.

Their numbers given, the lots were cast,
To fix the names of first and last; 470
Then to the dazzling hall were led,
Poor minstrels less alive than dead.

There such a scene entranced the view,
As heart of poet never knew.
'Twas not the flash of golden gear, 475
Nor blaze of silver chandelier;
Not Scotland's chiefs of noble air,
Nor dazzling rows of ladies fair;
'Twas one enthroned the rest above,—
Sure 'twas the Queen of grace and love! 480
Taper the form, and fair the breast
Yon radiant golden zones invest,
Where the vexed rubies blench in death,
Beneath yon lips and balmy breath.
Coronal gems of every dye, 485
Look dim above yon beaming eye;
Yon cheeks outvie the dawning's glow,
Red shadowed on a wreath of snow.

Oft the rapt bard had thought alone,
Of charms by mankind never known; 490
Of virgins, pure as opening day,
Or bosom of the flower of May:
Oft dreamed of beings free from stain,
Of maidens of the emerald main,

Of fairy dames in grove at even,   495
Of angels in the walks of heaven:
But, nor in earth, the sea, nor sky,
In fairy dream, nor fancy's eye,
Vision his soul had ever seen
Like MARY STUART, Scotland's Queen.   500

The Queen's Wake

Night the First

The
Queen's Wake

HUSHED was the Court—the courtiers gazed—
Each eye was bent, each soul amazed,
To see that group of genuine worth,
Those far-famed Minstrels of the North.
So motley wild their garments seemed;   5
Their eyes, where tints of madness gleamed,
Fired with impatience every breast,
And expectation stood confest.

   Short was the pause; the stranger youth,
The gaudy minstrel of the south,   10
Whose glossy eye and lady form
Had never braved the northern storm,
Stepped lightly forth,—kneeled three times low,—
And then, with many a smile and bow,
Mounted the form amid the ring,   15
And rung his harp's responsive string.
Though true the chords, and mellow-toned,
Long, long he twisted, long he coned;
Well pleased to hear his name they knew;
"'Tis Rizzio!" round in whispers flew.   20

   Valet with Parma's knight he came,
An angler in the tides of fame;
And oft had tried, with anxious pain,
Respect of Scotland's Queen to gain.
Too well his eye, with searching art,   25
Perceived her fond, her wareless heart;
And though unskilled in Scottish song,
Her notice he had wooed so long;
With pain by night, and care by day,
He framed this fervid, flowery lay.—   30

Malcolm of Lorn

THE FIRST BARD'S SONG

I.

Came ye by Ora's verdant steep,
   That smiles the restless ocean over?
Heard ye a suffering maiden weep?
   Heard ye her name a faithful lover?
Saw ye an aged matron stand   35
O'er yon green grave above the strand,
Bent like the trunk of withered tree,
Or yon old thorn that sips the sea?
Fixed her dim eye, her face as pale
   As the mists that o'er her flew: 40
Her joy is fled like the flower of the vale,
   Her hope like the morning dew!
That matron was lately as proud of her stay,
As the mightiest monarch of sceptre or sway:
O list to the tale! 'tis a tale of soft sorrow,   45
Of Malcolm of Lorn, and young Ann of Glen-Ora.

II.

The sun is sweet at early morn,
   Just blushing from the ocean's bosom;
The rose that decks the woodland thorn
   Is fairest in its opening blossom.   50
Sweeter than opening rose in dew,
Than vernal flowers of richest hue,
Than fragrant birch or weeping willow,
Than red sun resting on the billow;
Sweeter than aught to mortals given   55
   The heart and soul to prove;
Sweeter than aught beneath the heaven,
   The joys of early love!
Never did maiden, and manly youth,
Love with such fervor, and love with such truth;   60
Or pleasures and virtues alternately borrow,
As Malcolm of Lorn, and fair Ann of Glen-Ora.

III.

The day is come, the dreaded day,
   Must part two loving hearts for ever;

The ship lies rocking in the bay,   65
   The boat comes rippling up the river:
O happy has the gloaming's eye
   In green Glen-Ora's bosom seen them!
But soon shall lands and nations lie,
   And angry oceans roll between them.   70
Yes, they must part, for ever part;
Chill falls the truth on either heart;
For honour, titles, wealth, and state,
In distant lands her sire await.
The maid must with her sire away,   75
   She cannot stay behind;
Straight to the south the pennons play,
   And steady is the wind.
Shall Malcolm relinquish the home of his youth,
And sail with his love to the lands of the south?   80
Ah, no! for his father is gone to the tomb:
One parent survives in her desolate home!
No child but her Malcolm to cheer her lone way:
Break not her fond heart, gentle Malcolm, O, stay!

IV.

The boat impatient leans ashore,   85
   Her prow sleeps on a sandy pillow;
The rower leans upon his oar,
   Already bent to brush the billow.
O! Malcolm, view yon melting eyes,
   With tears yon stainless roses steeping!   90
O! Malcolm, list thy mother's sighs;
   She's leaning o'er her staff and weeping!
Thy Anna's heart is bound to thine,
And must that gentle heart repine!
Quick from the shore the boat must fly;   95
Her soul is speaking through her eye:
Think of thy joys in Ora's shade;
   From Anna canst thou sever?
Think of the vows thou often hast made,
   To love the dear maiden for ever.   100
And canst thou forego such beauty and youth,
Such maiden honour and spotless truth?
Forbid it!—He yields; to the boat he draws nigh.
Haste Malcolm aboard, and revert not thine eye.

V.

That trembling voice, in murmurs weak,   105
    Comes not to blast the hopes before thee;
For pity, Malcolm, turn, and take
    A last farewell of her that bore thee.
She says no word to mar thy bliss;
A last embrace, a parting kiss,   110
Her love deserves;—then be thou gone;
A mother's joys are thine alone.
Friendship may fade, and fortune prove
    Deceitful to thy heart;
But never can a mother's love   115
    From her own offspring part.
That tender form, now bent and gray,
Shall quickly sink to her native clay;
Then who shall watch her parting breath,
And shed a tear o'er her couch of death?   120
Who follow the dust to its long long home,
And lay that head in an honoured tomb?

VI.

Oft hast thou, to her bosom prest,
    For many a day about been borne;
Oft hushed and cradled on her breast,   125
    And canst thou leave that breast forlorn?
O'er all thy ails her heart has bled;
Oft has she watched beside thy bed;
Oft prayed for thee in dell at even,
Beneath the pitying stars of Heaven.   130
Ah! Malcolm, ne'er was parent yet
    So tender, so benign!
Never was maid so loved, so sweet,
    Nor soul so rent as thine!
He looked to the boat,—slow she heaved from the
    shore;   135
He saw his loved Anna all speechless implore:
But, grasped by a cold and a trembling hand,
He clung to his parent, and sunk on the strand.

VII.

The boat across the tide flew fast,
    And left a silver curve behind;   140
Loud sung the sailor from the mast,

Spreading his sails before the wind.
The stately ship, adown the bay,
    A corslet framed of heaving snow,
And flurred on high the slender spray,   145
    Till rainbows gleamed around her prow.
How strained was Malcolm's watery eye,
Yon fleeting vision to descry!
But, ah! her lessening form so fair,
Soon vanished in the liquid air.   150
Away to Ora's headland steep
    The youth retired the while,
And saw th' unpitying vessel sweep
    Around yon Highland isle.
His heart and his mind with that vessel had gone;   155
His sorrow was deep, and despairing his moan,
When, lifting his eyes from the green heaving deep,
He prayed the Almighty his Anna to keep.

VIII.

High o'er the crested cliffs of Lorn
    The curlew coned her wild bravura;   160
The sun, in pall of purple borne,
    Was hastening down the steeps of Jura.
The glowing ocean heaved her breast,
    Her wandering lover's glances under;
And showed his radiant form, imprest   165
    Deep in a wavy world of wonder.
Not all the ocean's dyes at even,
Though varied as the bow of heaven;
The countless isles so dusky blue,
Nor medley of the gray curlew,   170
Could light on Malcolm's spirit shed;
    Their glory all was gone!
For his joy was fled, his hope was dead,
    And his heart forsaken and lone.
The sea-bird sought her roofless nest,   175
To warm her brood with her downy breast;
And near her home, on the margin dun,
A mother weeps o'er her duteous son.

IX.

One little boat alone is seen
    On all the lovely dappled main,   180

That softly sinks the waves between,
  Then vaults their heaving breasts again;
With snowy sail, and rower's sweep,
  Across the tide she seems to fly.
Why bears she on yon headland steep,   185
  Where neither house nor home is nigh?
Is that a vision from the deep
That springs ashore and scales the steep,
Nor ever stays its ardent haste
Till sunk upon young Malcolm's breast?   190
O! spare that breast so lowly laid,
  So fraught with deepest sorrow!
It is his own, his darling maid,
  Young Anna of Glen-Ora!–
"My Malcolm! part we ne'er again!   195
My father saw thy bosom's pain;
Pitied my grief from thee to sever;
Now I, and Glen-Ora, am thine for ever!"–

X.

That blaze of joy, through clouds of woe,
  Too fierce upon his heart did fall.   200
But ah! the shaft had left the bow,
  Which power of man could not recall!
No word of love could Malcolm speak;
  No raptured kiss his lips impart;
No tear bedewed his shivering cheek,   205
  To ease the grasp that held his heart.
His arms essayed one kind embrace–
  Will they enclose her? never! never!
A smile set softly on his face,
  But ah! the eye was set for ever!–   210
'Twas more than broken heart could brook!
How throbs that breast!–How glazed that look!
One shiver more!–All! all is o'er!–
As melts the wave on level shore;
As fades the dye of falling even,   215
Far on the silver verge of heaven;
As on thy ear, the minstrel's lay,–
So died the comely youth away."

The strain died soft in note of woe,
Nor breath nor whisper 'gan to flow   220
From courtly circle; all as still
As midnight on the lonely hill.
So well that foreign minstrel's strain
Had mimicked passion, woe, and pain;
Seemed even the chilly hand of death   225
Stealing away his mellow breath.
So sighed—so stopp'd—so died his lay,—
His spirit too seemed fled for ay.

'Tis true, the gay attentive throng
Admired, but loved not much, his song: 230
Admired his wonderous voice and skill,
His harp that thrilled or wept at will.
But that affected gaudy rhyme,
The querulous keys, and changing chime,
Scarce could the Highland chieftain brook: 235
Disdain seemed kindling in his look,
That song so vapid, artful, terse,
Should e'er compete with Scottish verse.

But she, the fairest of the fair,
Who sat enthroned in gilded chair,   240
Well skilled in foreign minstrelsy
And artful airs of Italy,
Listened his song, with raptures wild,
And on the happy minstrel smiled.
Soon did the wily stranger's eye   245
The notice most he wished espy,
Then poured his numbers bold and free,
Fired by the grace of majesty;
And when his last notes died away,
When sunk in well-feigned death he lay,   250
When round the crowd began to ring,
Thinking his spirit on the wing,—
First of the dames she came along,
Wept, sighed, and marvelled 'mid the throng.
And when they raised him, it was said   255
The beauteous Sovereign deigned her aid;
And in her hands, so soft and warm,
Upheld the minstrel's hand and arm.

Then oped his eye with rapture fired;
He smiled, and bowing oft, retired;   260
Pleased he so soon had realized,
What more than gold or fame he prized.

Next in the list was Gardyn's name:
No sooner called, than forth he came.
Stately he strode, nor bow made he,   265
Nor even a look of courtesy.
The simpering cringe, and fawning look,
Of him who late the lists forsook,
Roused his proud heart, and fired his eye,
That glowed with native dignity.   270

Full sixty years the bard had seen,
Yet still his manly form and mien,
His garb of ancient Caledon,
Where lines of silk and scarlet shone,
And golden garters 'neath his knee,   275
Announced no man of mean degree.

Upon his harp, of wonderous frame,
Was carved his lineage and his name.
There stood the cross that name above,
Fair emblem of almighty love;   280
Beneath rose an embossment proud,—
A rose beneath a thistle bowed.

Lightly upon the form he sprung,
And his bold harp impetuous rung.
Not one by one the chords he tried,   285
But brushed them o'er from side to side,
With either hand, so rapid, loud,
Shook were the halls of Holyrood.
Then in a mellow tone, and strong,
He poured this wild and dreadful song.—   290

𝔜𝔬𝔲𝔫𝔤 𝔎𝔢𝔫𝔫𝔢𝔡𝔶

THE SECOND BARD'S SONG

I.

When the gusts of October had rifled the thorn,
  Had dappled the woodland, and umbered the plain,
In den of the mountain was Kennedy born:
  There hushed by the tempest, baptized with the rain.
His cradle, a mat that swung light on the oak;   295
His couch, the sear mountain-fern, spread on the rock;
The white knobs of ice from the chilled nipple hung,
And loud winter-torrents his lullaby sung.

II.

Unheeded he shivered, unheeded he cried;
  Soon died on the breeze of the forest his moan.   300
To his wailings, the weary wood-echo replied;
  His watcher, the wondering redbreast alone.
Oft gazed his young eye on the whirl of the storm,
And all the wild shades that the desert deform;
From cleft in the correi, which thunders had riven,   305
It oped on the pale flitting billows of heaven.

III.

The nursling of misery, young Kennedy, learned
  His hunger, his thirst, and his passions to feed:
With pity for others his heart never yearned,—
  Their pain was his pleasure,—their sorrow his meed.   310
His eye was the eagle's, the twilight his hue;
His stature like pine of the hill where he grew;
His soul was the neal-fire, inhaled from his den,
And never knew fear, save for ghost of the glen.

IV.

His father a chief, for barbarity known,   315
  Proscribed, and by gallant Macdougal expelled;
Where rolls the dark Teith through the valley of Down,
  The conqueror's menial, he toiled in the field.
His master he loved not, obeyed with a scowl,
Scarce smothered his hate, and his rancour of soul;   320
When challenged, his eye and his colour would change,
His proud bosom nursing and planning revenge.

V.

Matilda, ah! woe that the wild rose's dye,
   Shed over thy maiden cheek, caused thee to rue!
O! why was the sphere of thy love-rolling eye,   325
   Inlaid with the diamond, and dipt in the dew!
Thy father's sole daughter; his hope, and his care;
The child of his age, and the child of his prayer;
And thine was the heart, that was gentle and kind,
And light as the feather, that sports in the wind.   330

VI.

To her home, from the Lowlands, Matilda returned;
   All fair was her form, and untainted her mind.
Young Kennedy saw her, his appetite burned
   As fierce as the moor-flame impelled by the wind.
Was it love? No; the ray his dark soul never knew,   335
That spark which eternity burns to renew.
'Twas the flash of desire, kindled fierce by revenge,
Which savages feel the brown desert that range.

VII.

Sweet woman! too well is thy tenderness known;
   Too often deep sorrow succeeds thy love smile;   340
Too oft, in a moment, thy peace overthrown,—
   Fair butt of delusion, of passion, and guile!
What heart will not bleed for Matilda so gay,
To art and to long perseverance a prey?
Why sings yon scared blackbird in sorrowful mood   345
Why blushes the daisy deep in the green-wood?

VIII.

Sweet woman! with virtue, thou'rt lofty, thou'rt free;
   Yield that, thou'rt a slave, and the mark of disdain:
No blossom of spring is beleaguered like thee,
   Though brushed by the lightning, the wind, and the rain. 350
Matilda is fallen! With tears in her eye,
She seeks her destroyer; but only can sigh.
Matilda is fallen, and sorrow her doom,—
The flower of the valley is nipt in the bloom!

IX.

Ah! Kennedy, vengeance hangs over thine head!   355
   Escape to thy native Glengary forlorn.

Why art thou at midnight away from thy bed?
  Why quakes thy big heart at the break of the morn?
Why chatters yon magpie on gable so loud?
Why flits yon light vision in gossamer shroud?   360
How came yon white doves from the window to fly,
And hover on weariless wing to the sky?

X.

Yon pie is the prophet of terror and death;
  O'er Abel's green arbour that omen was given.
Yon pale boding phantom, a messenger wraith;   365
  Yon doves, two fair angels commissioned of heaven.
The sun is in state, and the reapers in motion;
Why were they not called to their morning devotion?
Why slumbers Macdougal so long in his bed?
Ah! pale on his couch the old chieftain lies dead!   370

XI.

Though grateful the hope to the death-bed that flies,
  That lovers and friends o'er our ashes will weep;
The soul, when released from her lingering ties,
  In secret may see if their sorrows are deep.
Who wept for the worthy Macdougal?—Not one!   375
His darling Matilda, who, two months agone,
Would have mourned for her father in sorrow extreme,
Indulged in a painful delectable dream.

XII.

But, why do the matrons, while dressing the dead,
  Sit silent, and look as if something they knew?   380
Why gaze on the features? Why move they the head,
  And point at the bosom so dappled and blue?
Say, was there foul play?—Then, why sleeps the red thunder?
Ah! hold, for Suspicion stands silent with wonder.
The body's entomb'd, and the green turf laid over,—   385
Matilda is wed to her dark Highland lover.

XIII.

Yes, the new moon that stooped over green Aberfoyle,
  And shed her light dews on a father's new grave,
Beheld, in her wane, the gay wedding turmoil,
  And lighted the bride to her chamber at eve: 390
Blue, blue was the heaven; and, o'er the wide scene,

A vapoury silver veil floated serene,
A fairy perspective, that bore from the eye
Wood, mountain, and meadow, in distance to lie.

XIV.

The scene was so still, it was all like a vision;   395
    The lamp of the moon seemed as fading for ever.
'Twas awfully soft, without shade or elision;
    And nothing was heard, but the rush of the river.
But why won't the bride-maidens walk on the lea,
Nor lovers steal out to the sycamore tree?   400
Why turn to the hall with those looks of confusion?
There's nothing abroad!–'tis a dream!–a delusion!

XV.

But why do the horses snort over their food,
    And cling to the manger in seeming dismay?
What scares the old owlet afar to the wood?   405
    Why screams the blue heron, as hastening away?
Say, why is the dog hid so deep in his cover?
Each window barred up, and the curtain drawn over;
Each white maiden bosom still heaving so high,
And fix'd on another each fear-speaking eye?   410

XVI.

'Tis all an illusion! the lamp let us trim!
    Come, rouse thee, old minstrel, to strains of renown;
The old cup is empty, fill round to the brim,
    And drink the young pair to their chamber just gone.
Ha! why is the cup from the lip ta'en away?   415
Why fix'd every form like a statue of clay?
Say, whence is that noise and that horrible clamour?
Oh, heavens! it comes from the marriage bedchamber.

XVII.

O! haste thee Strath-Allan, Glen-Ogle, away,
    These outcries betoken wild horror and woe;   420
The dull ear of midnight is stunned with dismay;
    Glen-Ogle! Strath-Allan! fly swift as the roe.
Mid darkness and death, on eternity's brim,
You stood with Macdonald and Archbald the grim;
Then why do you hesitate? why do you stand   425
With claymore unsheathed, and red taper in hand?

XVIII.

The tumult is o'er; not a murmur nor groan;
    What footsteps so madly pace through the saloon?
'Tis Kennedy, naked and ghastly alone,
    Who hies him away by the light of the moon.   430
All prostrate and bleeding, Matilda they found,
The threshold her pillow, her couch the cold ground;
Her features distorted, her colour the clay,
Her feelings, her voice, and her reason away.

XIX.

Ere morn they returned; but how well had they never!   435
    They brought with them horror too deep to sustain;
Returned but to chasten, and vanish for ever,
    To harrow the bosom and fever the brain.
List, list to her tale, youth, levity, beauty;–
O! sweet is the path of devotion and duty!–   440
When pleasure smiles sweetest, dread danger and death,
And think of Matilda, the flower of the Teith.

XX.

The Bride's Tale

"I had just laid me down, but no word could I pray;
    I had pillowed my head, and drawn up the bed-cover;
I thought of the bed where my loved father lay,   445
    So damp and so cold, with the grass growing over.
I turned to my husband; but just as he spread
His arms to enfold me, we saw round the bed,
A ghastly refulgence as bright as day-noon,
Though shut was the chamber from eye of the moon.   450

XXI.

"Bestower of being! in pity, O! hide
    That sight from the eye of my spirit for ever;
That page from the volume of memory divide,
    Or memory and being eternally sever!
My father approached; our bed-curtains he drew;   455
Ah! well the gray locks and pale features I knew.
I saw his fixt eye-balls indignantly glow;
Yet still in that look there was pity and woe.

XXII.

"O! hide thee, my daughter, he eagerly cried;
　O haste from the bed of that parricide lover!　　　　　460
Embrace not thy husband, unfortunate bride,
　Thy red cup of misery already runs over.
He strangled thy father! thy guilt paved the way;
Thy heart yet is blameless, O fly while you may!
Thy portion of life must calamity leaven;　　　　　465
But fly while there's hope of forgiveness from heaven.

XXIII.

"And thou, fell destroyer of virtue and life!
　O! well may'st thou quake at thy terrible doom;
For body or soul, with barbarity rife,
　On earth is no refuge, in heaven no room.　　　　　470
Fly whither thou wilt, I will follow thee still,
To dens of the forest, or mists of the hill;
The task I'm assigned, which I'll never forego,
But chace thee from earth to thy dwelling below.

XXIV.

"The cave shall not cover, the cloud shall not hide thee;　　475
　At noon I will wither thy sight with my frown;
In gloom of the night, I will lay me beside thee,
　And pierce with this weapon thy bosom of stone.
Fast fled the despoiler with howlings most dire,
Fast followed the spirit with rapier of fire;–　　　　　480
Away, and away, through the silent saloon,
And away, and away, by the light of the moon.

XXV.

"To follow I tried, but sunk down at the door.
　Alas! from that trance that I ever awoke.
How wanders my mind! I shall see him no more,　　　　485
　Till God shall yon gates everlasting unlock.
My poor brow is open, 'tis burning with pain,
O kiss it, sweet vision! O kiss it again!
Now give me thine hand; I will fly! I will fly!
Away, on the morn's dappled wing, to the sky."　　　　490

XXVI.

The Conclusion

O! shepherd of Braco, look well to thy flock,
   The piles of Glen-Ardochy murmur and jar;
The rook and the raven converse from the rock,
   The beasts of the forest are howling afar.
Shrill pipes the goss-hawk his dire tidings to tell,   495
The gray mountain-falcon accords with his yell;
Aloft on bold pinion the eagle is borne,
To ring the alarm at the gates of the morn.

XXVII.

Ah! shepherd, thy kids wander safe in the wood,
   Thy lambs feed in peace on Ben-Ardochy's brow;   500
Then why is the hoary cliff sheeted with blood?
   And what the poor carcase lies mangled below?
Oh hie thee away to thy hut at the fountain,
And dig a lone grave on the top of yon mountain;
But fly it for ever when falls the gray gloaming,   505
For there a grim phantom still naked is roaming.

    Gardyn with stately step withdrew,
    While plaudits round the circle flew.

    Woe that the bard, whose thrilling song
    Has poured from age to age along,   510
    Should perish from the lists of fame,
    And lose his only boon, a name.
    Yet many a song of wonderous power,
    Well known in cot and green-wood bower,
    Wherever swells the shepherd's reed   515
    On Yarrow's banks and braes of Tweed;
    Yes, many a song of olden time,
    Of rude array, and air sublime,
    Though long on time's dark whirlpool tossed,
    The song is saved, the bard is lost.   520

    Yet have I weened, when these I sung
    On Ettrick banks, while mind was young;

When on the eve their strains I threw,
And youths and maidens round me drew;
Or chaunted in the lonely glen,   525
Far from the haunts and eyes of men;
Yes, I have weened, with fondest sigh,
The spirit of the bard was nigh;
Swung by the breeze on braken pile,
Or hovering o'er me with a smile.   530
Would Fancy still her dreams combine,
That spirit, too, might breath on mine;
Well pleased to see her songs the joy
Of that poor lonely shepherd boy.

    'Tis said, and I believe the tale,   535
That many rhymes which still prevail,
Of genuine ardour, bold and free,
Were ay admired, and ay will be,
Had never been, or shortly stood,
But for that Wake at Holyrood.   540
Certes that many a bard of name,
Who there appeared and strove for fame,
No record names, nor minstrel's tongue;
Not even are known the lays they sung.

    The fifth was from a western shore,   545
Where rolls the dark and sullen Orr.
Of peasant make, and doubtful mien,
Affecting airs of proud disdain;
Wide curled his raven locks and high,
Dark was his visage, dark his eye,   550
That glanced around on dames and men
Like falcons on the cliffs of Ken.
No one could read the character,
If *knave* or *genius* writ was there;
But all supposed, from mien and frame,   555
From Erin he an exile came.

    With hollow voice, and harp well strung,
"Fair Margaret" was the song he sung,
Well known to maid and matron gray,
Through all the glens of Galloway.   560
When first the bard his song began,

Of dreams and bodings hard to scan,
Listened the Court, with sidelong bend,
In wonder how the strain would end.
But long ere that, it grew so plain, 565
They scarce from hooting could refrain;
And when the minstrel ceased to sing,
A smothered hiss ran round the ring.
Red looked our bard around the form,
With eye of fire, and face of storm; 570
Sprung to his seat, with awkward leap,
And muttered curses dark and deep.

The sixth, too, from that country he,
Where heath-cocks bay o'er western Dee;
Where Summer spreads her purple screen 575
O'er moors, where greensward ne'er was seen;
Nor shade, o'er all the prospect stern,
Save crusted rock, or warrior's cairn.

Gentle his form, his manners meet,
His harp was soft, his voice was sweet; 580
He sung Lochryan's hapless maid,
In bloom of youth by love betrayed:
Turned from her lover's bower at last,
To brave the chilly midnight blast;
And bitterer far, the pangs to prove, 585
Of ruined fame, and slighted love;
A tender babe, her arms within,
Sobbing and "shivering at the chin."
No lady's cheek in Court was dry,
So softly poured the melody. 590

The eighth was from the Leven coast:
The rest who sung that night are lost.

Mounted the bard of Fife on high,
Bushy his beard, and wild his eye:
His haggard cheek was pale as clay, 595
And his thin locks were long and gray.
Some wizard of the wild he seemed,
Who through the scenes of life had dreamed,
Of spells that vital life benumb,

Of formless spirits wandering dumb,   600
Where aspins in the moon-beam quake,
By mouldering pile, or mountain lake.

He deemed that fays and spectres wan
Held converse with the thoughts of man;
In dreams their future fates foretold,   605
And spread the death-flame on the wold;
Or flagged at eve each restless wing,
In dells their vesper hymns to sing.

Such was our bard, such were his lays;
And long by green Benarty's base,   610
His wild wood notes, from ivy cave,
Had waked the dawning from the wave.
At evening fall, in lonesome dale,
He kept strange converse with the gale;
Held worldly pomp in high derision,   615
And wandered in a world of vision.

Of mountain ash his harp was framed,
The brazen chords all trembling flamed,
As in a rugged northern tongue,
This mad unearthly song he sung.   620

The Witch of Fife

THE EIGHTH BARD'S SONG

"Quhare haif ye been, ye ill womyne,
    These three lang nightis fra hame?
Quhat garris the sweit drap fra yer brow,
    Like clotis of the saut sea faem?

It fearis me muckil ye haif seen   625
    Quhat good man never knew;
It fearis me muckil ye haif been
    Quhare the gray cock never crew.

But the spell may crack, and the brydel breck,
    Then sherpe yer werde will be;   630

Ye had better sleipe in yer bed at hame,
  Wi yer deire littil bairnis and me."–

'Sit dune, sit dune, my leile auld man,
  Sit dune, and listin to me;
I'll gar the hayre stand on yer crown,   635
  And the cauld sweit blind yer e'e.

But tell nae wordis, my gude auld man,
  Tell never word again;
Or deire shall be yer courtisye,
  And driche and sair yer pain.   640

The first leet-night, quhan the new moon set,
  Quhan all was douffe and mirk,
We saddled ouir naigis wi the moon-fern leif,
  And rode fra Kilmerrin kirk.

Some horses ware of the brume-cow framit,   645
  And some of the greine bay tree;
But mine was made of ane humloke schaw,
  And a stout stallion was he.

We raide the tod doune on the hill,
  The martin on the law;   650
And we huntyd the hoolet out of brethe,
  And forcit him doune to fa'.–

"Quhat guid was that, ye ill womyn?
  Quhat guid was that to thee?
Ye wald better haif bein in yer bed at hame,   655
  Wi yer deire littil bairnis and me."–

'And ay we raide, and se merrily we raide,
  Throw the merkist gloffis of the night;
And we swam the floode, and we darnit the woode,
  Till we cam to the Lommond height.   660

And quhen we cam to the Lommond height,
  Se lythlye we lychtid doune;
And we drank fra the hornis that never grew,
  The beer that was never browin.

Than up there rase ane wee wee man, 665
  Franethe the moss-gray stane;
His fece was wan like the collifloure,
  For he nouthir had blude nor bane.

He set ane reid-pipe till his muthe,
  And he playit se bonnilye, 670
Till the grey curlew, and the black-cock, flew
  To listen his melodye.

It rang se sweet through the green Lommond,
  That the nycht-winde lowner blew;
And it soupit alang the Loch Leven, 675
  And wakinit the white sea-mew.

It rang se sweet through the grein Lommond,
  Se sweitly butt and se shill,
That the wezilis laup out of their mouldy holis,
  And dancit on the mydnycht hill. 680

The corby craw cam gledgin near,
  The ern gede veeryng bye;
And the troutis laup out of the Leven Louch,
  Charmit with the melodye.

And ay we dancit on the green Lommond, 685
  Till the dawn on the ocean grew:
Ne wonder I was a weary wycht
  Quhan I cam hame to you.'—

"Quhat guid, quhat guid, my weird weird wyfe,
  Quhat guid was that to thee? 690
Ye wald better haif bein in yer bed at hame,
  Wi yer deire littil bairnis and me."—

'The second nychte, quhan the new moon set,
  O'er the roaryng sea we flew;
The cockle-shell our trusty bark, 695
  Our sailis of the grein sea-rue.

And the bauld windis blew, and the fire flauchtis flew,
  And the sea ran to the skie;

And the thunner it growlit, and the sea dogs howlit,
  As we gaed scouryng bye.   700

And ay we mountit the sea green hillis,
  Quhill we brushit thro' the cludis of the hevin;
Than sousit dounright like the stern-shot light,
  Fra the liftis blue casement driven.

But our taickil stood, and our bark was good,   705
  And se pang was our pearily prowe;
Quhan we culdna speil the brow of the wavis,
  We needilit them throu belowe.

As fast as the hail, as fast as the gale,
  As fast as the midnycht leme,   710
We borit the breiste of the burstyng swale,
  Or fluffit i' the flotyng faem.

And quhan to the Norraway shore we wan,
  We muntyd our steedis of the wynd,
And we splashit the floode, and we darnit the woode, 715
  And we left the shouir behynde.

Fleet is the roe on the green Lommond,
  And swift is the couryng grew;
The rein deir dun can eithly run,
  Quhan the houndis and the hornis pursue.   720

But nowther the roe, nor the rein-deir dun,
  The hinde nor the couryng grew,
Culde fly owr muntaine, muir, and dale,
  As owr braw steedis they flew.

The dales war deep, and the Doffrinis steep,   725
  And we rase to the skyis ee-bree;
Quhite, quhite was ouir rode, that was never trode,
  Owr the snawis of eternity!

And quhan we cam to the Lapland lone
  The fairies war all in array,   730
For all the genii of the north
  War keepyng their holeday.

The warlock men and the weerd wemyng,
    And the fays of the wood and the steep,
And the phantom hunteris all war there,   735
    And the mermaidis of the deep.

And they washit us all with the witch-water,
    Distillit fra the moorland dew,
Quhill our beauty blumit like the Lapland rose,
    That wylde in the foreste grew.'–   740

"Ye lee, ye lee, ye ill womyne,
    Se loud as I heir ye lee!
For the warst-faurd wyfe on the shoris of Fyfe
    Is cumlye comparet wi thee."–

'Then the mer-maidis sang and the woodlandis rang,   745
    Se sweetly swellit the quire;
On every cliff a herpe they hang,
    On every tree a lyre.

And ay they sang, and the woodlandis rang,
    And we drank, and we drank se deep;   750
Then soft in the armis of the warlock men,
    We laid us dune to sleep.'–

"Away, away, ye ill womyne,
    An ill deide met ye dee!
Quhan ye hae pruvit se false to yer God,   755
    Ye can never pruve trew to me."–

'And there we lernit fra the fairy foke,
    And fra our master true,
The wordis that can beire us throu the air,
    And lokkis and baris undo.   760

Last nycht we met at Maisry's cot;
    Richt weil the wordis we knew;
And we set a foot on the black cruik-shell,
    And out at the lum we flew.

And we flew owr hill, and we flew owr dale,   765
    And we flew owr firth and sea,

Until we cam to merry Carlisle,
　　Quhar we lightit on the lea.

We gaed to the vault beyound the towir,
　　Quhar we enterit free as ayr;　　　　　770
And we drank, and we drank of the bishopis wine
　　Quhill we culde drynk ne mair.'—

"Gin that be trew, my gude auld wyfe,
　　Whilk thou hast tauld to me,
Betide my death, betide my lyfe,　　　　775
　　I'll beire thee companye.

Neist tyme ye gaung to merry Carlisle
　　To drynk of the blude-reid wine,
Beshrew my heart, I'll fly with thee,
　　If the diel shulde fly behynde."—　　780

'Ah! little do ye ken, my silly auld man,
　　The daingeris we maun dree;
Last nichte we drank of the bishopis wyne,
　　Quhill near near taen war we.

Afore we wan to the sandy ford,　　　　785
　　The gor-cockis nichering flew;
The lofty crest of Ettrick Pen
　　Was wavit about with blew,
And, flichtering throu the air, we fand
　　The chill chill mornyng dew.　　　　790

As we flew owr the hillis of Braid,
　　The sun rase fair and clear;
There gurly James, and his baronis braw,
　　War out to hunt the deere.

Their bowis they drew, their arrowis flew,　　795
　　And peircit the ayr with speede,
Quhill purpil fell the mornyng dew
　　With witch-blude rank and reide.

Littil do ye ken, my silly auld man,
　　The dangeris we maun dree;　　　　800

Ne wonder I am a weary wycht
 Quhan I come hame to thee.'–

"But tell me the *word*, my gude auld wyfe,
 Come tell it me speedilye;
For I lang to drink of the gude reide wyne, 805
 And to wyng the ayr with thee.

Yer hellish horse I wilna ryde,
 Nor sail the seas in the wynd;
But I can flee as well as thee,
 And I'll drynk quhill ye be blynd."– 810

'O fy! O fy! my leil auld man,
 That word I darena tell;
It wald turn this warld all upside down,
 And make it warse than hell.

For all the lasses in the land 815
 Wald munt the wynd and fly;
And the men wald doff their doublets syde,
 And after them wald ply.'–

But the auld gudeman was ane cunnyng auld man,
 And ane cunnyng auld man was he; 820
And he watchit, and he watchit for mony a night,
 The witches' flychte to see.

Ane nychte he darnit in Maisry's cot;
 The fearless haggs came in;
And he heard the word of awsome weird, 825
 And he saw their deedis of synn.

Then ane by ane, they said that word,
 As fast to the fire they drew;
Then set a foot on the black cruik-shell,
 And out at the lum they flew. 830

The auld gude-man cam fra his hole
 With feire and muckil dreide,
But yet he culdna think to rue,
 For the wyne came in his head.

He set his foot in the black cruik-shell,   835
   With ane fixit and ane wawlyng ee;
And he said the word that I darena say,
   And out at the lum flew he.

The witches skalit the moon-beam pale;
   Deep groanit the trembling wynde;   840
But they never wist till our auld gude-man
   Was hoveryng them behynde.

They flew to the vaultis of merry Carlisle,
   Quhair they enterit free as ayr;
And they drank and they drank of the byshopis wyne 845
   Quhill they culde drynk ne mair.

The auld gude-man he grew se crouse,
   He dancit on the mouldy ground,
And he sang the bonniest sangis of Fife,
   And he tuzzlit the kerlyngs round.   850

And ay he percit the tither butt,
   And he suckit, and he suckit se lang,
Quhill his een they closit, and his voice grew low,
   And his tongue wold hardly gang.

The kerlyngs drank of the bishopis wyne   855
   Quhill they scentit the mornyng wynde;
Then clove again the yeilding ayr,
   And left the auld man behynde.

And ay he slepit on the damp damp floor,
   He slepit and he snorit amain;   860
He never dremit he was far fra hame,
   Or that the auld wyvis war gane.

And ay he slepit on the damp damp floor
   Quhill past the mid-day highte,
Quhan wakenit by five rough Englishmen,   865
   That trailit him to the lychte.

"Now quha are ye, ye silly auld man,
   That sleepis se sound and se weil?

Or how gat ye into the bishopis vault
  Throu lokkis and barris of steel?"–   870

The auld gude-man he tryit to speak,
  But ane word he culdna fynde;
He tryit to think, but his head whirlit round,
  And ane thing he culdna mynde:–
"I cam fra Fyfe," the auld man cryit,   875
  "And I cam on the midnycht wynde."

They nickit the auld man, and they prickit the auld
      man,
  And they yerkit his limbis with twine,
Quhill the reid blude ran in his hose and shoon,
  But some cryit it was wyne.   880

They lickit the auld man, and they prickit the auld
      man,
  And they tyit him till ane stone;
And they set ane bele-fire him about,
  And they burnit him skin and bone.

Now wae be to the puir auld man   885
  That ever he saw the day!
And wae be to all the ill wemyng,
  That lead puir men astray!

Let never ane auld man after this
  To lawless greide inclyne;   890
Let never an auld man after this
  Rin post to the diel for wyne.

————————

When ceased the minstrel's crazy song,
His heedful glance embraced the throng,
And found the smile of free delight   895
Dimpling the cheeks of ladies bright.
Ah! never yet was bard unmoved,
When beauty smiled or birth approved!
For though his song he holds at nought—

"An idle strain! a passing thought!"– 900
Child of the soul! 'tis held more dear
Than aught by mortals valued here.

When Leven's bard the Court had viewed,
His eye, his vigour, was renewed.
No, not the evening's closing eye, 905
Veiled in the rainbow's deepest dye,
By summer breezes lulled to rest,
Cradled on Leven's silver breast,
Or slumbering on the distant sea,
Imparted sweeter ecstacy. 910

Nor even the angel of the night,
Kindling his holy sphere of light,
Afar upon the heaving deep,
To light a world of peaceful sleep,
Though in her beam night-spirits glanced, 915
And lovely fays in circles danced,
Or rank by rank rode lightly bye,
Was sweeter to our minstrel's eye.

Unheard the bird of morning crew;
Unheard the breeze of Ocean blew; 920
The night unweened had passed away,
And dawning ushered in the day.
The Queen's young maids, of cherub hue,
Aside the silken curtains drew,
And lo the Night, in still profound, 925
In fleece of heaven had clothed the ground;
And still her furs, so light and fair,
Floated along the morning air.
Low stooped the pine amid the wood,
And the tall cliffs of Salsbury stood 930
Like marble columns bent and riven,
Propping a pale and frowning heaven.

The Queen bent from her gilded chair,
And waved her hand with graceful air:–
"Break up the court, my lords; away, 935
And use the day as best you may,
In sleep, in love, or wassail cheer;

The day is dark, the evening near,
Say, will you grace my halls the while,
And in the dance the day beguile?   940
Break up the court, my lords; away,
And use the day as best you may.
Give order that my minstrels true
Have royal fare and honours due;
And warned by evening's bugle shrill,   945
We meet to judge their minstrel skill."—

Whether that royal wake gave birth
To days of sleep and nights of mirth,
Which kings and courtiers still approve,
Which sages blame, and ladies love,   950
Imports not;—but our courtly throng,
(That chapel wake being kept so long,)
Slept out the lowering short-lived days,
And heard by night their native lays,
Till fell the eve of Christmas good,   955
The dedication of the rood.

Ah me! at routs and revels gay,
Reproach of this unthrifty day,
Though none amongst the dames or men
Rank higher than a citizen,   960
In chair or chariot all are borne,
Closed from the piercing eye of morn;
But then, though dawning blasts were keen,
Scotland's high dames you might have seen,
Ere from the banquet hall they rose,   965
Shift their laced shoes and silken hose;
Their broidered kirtles round them throw,
And wade their way through wreaths of snow,
Leaning on Lord or lover's arm,
Cheerful and reckless of all harm.   970
Vanished those hardy times outright;
So is our ancient Scottish might.

Sweet be her home, admired her charms,
Bliss to her couch in lover's arms,
I bid in every minstrel's name,   975
I bid to every lovely dame,

That ever gave one hour away
To cheer the bard or list his lay!

To all who love the raptures high
Of Scottish song and minstrelsy,   980
Till next the night, in sable shroud,
Shall wrap the halls of Holyrood,
That rival minstrels' songs I borrow,—
I bid a hearty kind good-morrow.

END OF NIGHT THE FIRST

The Queen's Wake

Night the Second

The
Queen's Wake

SCARCE fled the dawning's dubious gray,
So transient was that dismal day.
The lurid vapours, dense and stern,
Unpierced save by the crusted cairn,
In ten-fold shroud the heavens deform; 5
While far within the moving storm,
Travelled the sun in lonely blue,
And noontide wore a twilight hue.

 The sprites that through the welkin wing,
That light and shade alternate bring, 10
That wrap the eve in dusky veil,
And weave the morning's purple rail;
From pendent clouds of deepest grain,
Shed that dull twilight o'er the main.
Each spire, each tower, and cliff sublime, 15
Were hooded in the wreathy rime;
And all, ere fell the murk of even,
Were lost within the folds of heaven.
It seemed as if the welkin's breast
Had bowed upon the world to rest; 20
As heaven and earth to close began,
And seal the destiny of man.

 The supper bell at Court had rung;
The mass was said, the vesper sung;
In true devotion's sweetest mood, 25
Beauty had kneeled before the rood;
But all was done in secret guise,
Close from the zealot's searching eyes.

 Then burst the bugle's lordly peal
Along the earth's incumbent veil; 30
Swam on the cloud and lingering shower,
To festive hall and lady's bower;

And found its way, with rapid boom,
To rocks far curtained in the gloom,
And waked their viewless bugle's strain,   35
That sung the softened notes again.

    Upsprung the maid from her love-dream;
The matron from her silken seam;
The abbot from his holy shrine;
The chiefs and warriors from their wine: 40
For ay the bugle seemed to say,
"The Wake's begun! away, away!"

    Fast poured they in, all fair and boon,
Till crowded was the grand saloon;
And scarce was left a little ring,   45
In which the rival bards might sing.

    First in the list that night to play,
Was Farquhar, from the hills of Spey:
A gay and comely youth was he,
And seemed of noble pedigree.   50
Well known to him Loch-Avin's shore,
And all the dens of dark Glen-More;
Where oft, amid his roving clan,
His shaft had pierced the ptarmigan;
And oft the dun-deer's velvet side   55
That winged shaft had ruthless dyed,
Had struck the heath-cock whirring high,
And brought the eagle from the sky.

    Amid those scenes the youth was bred,
Where Nature's eye is stern and dread;   60
Mid forests dark, and caverns wild,
And mountains above mountains piled,
Whose hoary summits, tempest-riven,
Uprear eternal snows to heaven.

    Aloof from battle's fierce alarms,   65
Prone his young mind to music's charms.
The cliffs and woods of dark Glen-More
He taught to chaunt in mystic lore;
For well he weened, by tarn and hill,

Kind viewless spirits wandered still;   70
And fondly trowed the groups to spy,
Listening his cliff-born melody.
On Leven's bard with scorn he looked,
His homely song he scarcely brooked;
But proudly mounting on the form,   75
Thus sung *The Spirit of the Storm.*

Glen-Avin

THE NINTH BARD'S SONG

Beyond the grizzly cliffs, which guard
   The infant rills of Highland Dee,
Where hunter's horn was never heard,
   Nor bugle of the forest bee;   80

Mid wastes that dern and dreary lie,
   One mountain rears his mighty form,
Disturbs the moon in passing bye,
   And smiles above the thunder storm.

There Avin spreads her ample deep,   85
   To mirror cliffs that brush the wain;
Whose frigid eyes eternal weep,
   In Summer suns and Autumn rain.

There matin hymn was never sung;
   Nor vesper, save the plover's wail;   90
But mountain eagles breed their young,
   And aerial spirits ride the gale.

An hoary sage once lingered there,
   Intent to prove some mystic scene;
Though cavern deep, and forest sere,   95
   Had whooped November's boisterous reign.

That noontide fell so stern and still,
   The breath of nature seemed away;
The distant sigh of mountain rill
   Alone disturbed that solemn day.   100

Oft had that seer, at break of morn,
　　Beheld the fahm glide o'er the fell;
And 'neath the new moon's silver horn,
　　The fairies dancing in the dell.

Had seen the spirits of the Glen,   105
　　In every form that Ossian knew;
And wailings heard for living men
　　Were never more the light to view.

But, ah! that dull forboding day,
　　He saw what mortal could not bear;   110
A sight that scared the erne away,
　　And drove the wild deer from his lair.

Firm in his magic ring he stood,
　　When, lo! aloft on gray Cairn-Gorm,
A form appeared that chilled his blood,—   115
　　The giant Spirit of the Storm.

His face was like the spectre wan,
　　Slow gliding from the midnight isle;
His stature, on the mighty plan
　　Of smoke-tower o'er the burning pile.   120

Red, red and grizzly were his eyes;
　　His cap the moon-cloud's silver gray;
His staff the writhed snake, that lies
　　Pale, bending o'er the milky way.

He cried, "Away, begone, begone!   125
　　Half-naked, hoary, feeble form!
How darest thou hold my realms alone,
　　And brave the Angel of the Storm?"—

"And who art thou," the seer replied,
　　"That bear'st destruction on thy brow?   130
Whose eye no mortal can abide?
　　Dread mountain Spirit! what art thou?"—

"Within this desert, dank and lone,
　　Since rolled the world a shoreless sea,

I've held my elemental throne,   135
   The terror of thy race and thee.

I wrap the sun of heaven in blood,
   Veiling his orient beams of light;
And hide the moon in sable shroud,
   Far in the alcove of the night.   140

I ride the red bolt's rapid wing,
   High on the sweeping whirlwind sail,
And list to hear my tempests sing
   Around Glen-Avin's ample wale.

These everlasting hills are riven;   145
   Their reverend heads are bald and gray;
The Greenland waves salute the heaven,
   And quench the burning stars with spray.

Who was it reared those whelming waves?
   Who scalped the brows of old Cairn-Gorm?   150
And scooped these ever-yawning caves?
   'Twas I, the Spirit of the Storm.

And hence shalt thou, for evermore,
   Be doomed to ride the blast with me;
To shriek, amid the tempest's roar,   155
   By fountain, ford, and forest tree."–

The wizard cowred him to the earth,
   And orisons of dread began:
"Hence, Spirit of infernal birth!
   Thou enemy of God and man!"   160

He waved his sceptre north away,
   The arctic ring was rift asunder;
And through the heaven, the startling bray
   Burst louder than the loudest thunder.

The feathery clouds, condensed and curled,   165
   In columns swept the quaking glen;
Destruction down the dale was hurled,
   O'er bleating flocks, and wondering men.

The Grampians groaned beneath the storm;
   New mountains o'er the correis lean'd;   170
Ben-Nevis shook his shaggy form,
   And wondered what his Sovereign mean'd.

Even far on Yarrow's fairy dale,
   The shepherd paused in dumb dismay;
And passing shrieks adown the vale,   175
   Lured many a pitying hind away.

The Lowthers felt the tyrant's wrath;
   Proud Hartfell quaked beneath his brand;
And Cheviot heard the cries of death,
   Guarding his loved Northumberland.   180

But, O! as fell that fateful night,
   What horrors Avin wilds deform,
And choke the ghastly lingering light!
   There whirled the vortex of the storm.

Ere morn the wind grew deadly still,   185
   And dawning in the air, updrew,
From many a shelve and shining hill,
   Her folding robe of fairy blue.

Then, what a smooth and wonderous scene
   Hung o'er Loch-Avin's lonely breast!   190
Not top of tallest pine was seen,
   On which the dazzled eye could rest.

But mitred cliff, and crested fell,
   In lucid curls her brows adorn,
Aloft the radiant crescents swell,   195
   All pure as robes by angels worn.

Sound sleeps our seer, far from the day,
   Beneath yon sleek and wreathed cone!
His spirit steals, unmissed, away,
   And dreams across the desert lone.   200

Sound sleeps our seer! the tempests rave,
   And cold sheets o'er his bosom fling;

The moldwarp digs his mossy grave;
    His requiem Avin eagles sing.

Why howls the fox above yon wreath,   205
    That mocks the blazing Summer sun?
Why croaks the sable bird of death,
    As hovering o'er yon desert dun?

When circling years have past away,
    And Summer blooms in Avin glen,   210
Why stands yon peasant in dismay,
    Still gazing o'er the bloated den?

Green grows the grass! the bones are white!
    Not bones of mountain stag they seem!
There hooted once the owl by night,   215
    Above the dead-light's lambent beam!

See yon lone cairn, so gray with age,
    Above the base of proud Cairn-Gorm:
There lies the dust of Avin's sage,
    Who raised the Spirit of the Storm.   220

Yet still at eve, or midnight drear,
    When Wintry winds begin to sweep,
When passing shrieks assail thine ear,
    Or murmurs by the mountain steep;

When from the dark and sedgy dells   225
    Came eldrich cries of wildered men,
Or wind-harp at thy window swells,—
    Beware the sprite of Avin Glen!

———————

    Young Farquhar ceased, and rising slow,
Doffed his plumed bonnet, wiped his brow,   230
And flushed with conscious dignity,
Cast o'er the crowd his falcon eye,
And found them all in silence deep,
As listening for the tempest's sweep.
So well his tale of Avin's seer   235

Suited the rigour of the year;
So high his strain, so bold his lyre,
So fraught with rays of Celtic fire,
They almost weened each hum that past
The spirit of the northern blast.   240

    The next was named,—the very sound
Excited merriment around.
But when the bard himself appeared,
The ladies smiled, the courtiers sneered;
For such a simple air and mien   245
Before a court had never been.
A clown he was, bred in the wild,
And late from native moors exiled,
In hopes his mellow mountain strain
High favour from the great would gain.   250
Poor wight! he never weened how hard
For poverty to earn regard!
Dejection o'er his visage ran,
His coat was bare, his colour wan,
His forest doublet darned and torn,   255
His shepherd plaid all rent and worn;
Yet dear the symbols to his eye,
Memorials of a time gone bye.

    The bard on Ettrick's mountains green
In Nature's bosom nursed had been,   260
And oft had marked in forest lone
Her beauties on her mountain throne;
Had seen her deck the wild-wood tree,
And star with snowy gems the lea;
In loveliest colours paint the plain,   265
And sow the moor with purple grain.
By golden mead and mountain sheer,
Had viewed the Ettrick waving clear,
Where shadowy flocks of purest snow
Seemed grazing in a world below.   270

    Instead of Ocean's billowy pride,
Where monsters play and navies ride,
Oft had he viewed, as morning rose,
The bosom of the lonely Lowes,

Plowed far by many a downy keel, 275
Of wild-duck and of vagrant teal.
Oft thrilled his heart at close of even,
To see the dappled vales of heaven,
With many a mountain, moor, and tree,
Asleep upon the Saint Mary. 280
The pilot swan majestic wind,
With all his cygnet fleet behind,
So softly sail, and swiftly row,
With sable oar and silken prow.
Instead of war's unhallowed form, 285
His eye had seen the thunder storm
Descend within the mountain's brim,
And shroud him in its chambers grim.
Then from its bowels burst amain
The sheeted flame and sounding rain, 290
And by the bolts in thunder borne,
The heaven's own breast and mountain torn.
The wild roe from the forest driven;
The oaks of ages peeled and riven;
Impending oceans whirl and boil, 295
Convulsed by Nature's grand turmoil.

Instead of arms or golden crest,
His harp with mimic flowers was drest:
Around, in graceful streamers, fell
The briar-rose and the heather bell; 300
And there his learning deep to prove,
Naturæ Donum graved above.
When o'er her mellow notes he ran,
And his wild mountain chaunt began;
Then first was noted in his eye, 305
A gleam of native energy.

Old David

THE TENTH BARD'S SONG

Old David rose ere it was day,
And climbed old Wonfell's wizard brae;
Looked round, with visage grim and sour,
O'er Ettrick woods and Eskdale-moor. 310

An outlaw from the south he came,
And Ludlow was his father's name;
His native land had used him ill,
And Scotland bore him no good will.

As fixed he stood, in sullen scorn,   315
Regardless of the streaks of morn,
Old David spied, on Wonfell cone,
A fairy band come riding on.
A lovelier troop was never seen;
Their steeds were white, their doublets green,   320
Their faces shone like opening morn,
And bloomed like roses on the thorn.
At every flowing mane was hung,
A silver bell that lightly rung;
That sound, borne on the breeze away,   325
Oft set the mountaineer to pray.

Old David crept close in the heath,
Scarce moved a limb, scarce drew a breath;
But as the tinkling sound came nigh,
Old David's heart beat wonderous high.   330
He thought of riding on the wind;
Of leaving hawk and hern behind;
Of sailing lightly o'er the sea,
In mussel shell, to Germany;
Of revel raids by dale and down;   335
Of lighting torches at the moon;
Or through the sounding spheres to sing,
Borne on the fiery meteor's wing;
Of dancing 'neath the moonlight sky;
Of sleeping in the dew-cup's eye.   340
And then he thought—O! dread to tell!—
Of tithes the fairies paid to hell!

David turned up a reverend eye,
And fixed it on the morning sky;
He knew a mighty one lived there,   345
That sometimes heard a warrior's prayer—
No word, save one, could David say:
Old David had not learned to pray.

Scarce will a Scotsman yet regard
What David saw, and what he heard.   350
He heard their horses snort and tread,
And every word the riders said;
While green portmanteaus, long and low,
Lay bended o'er each saddle bow.
A lovely maiden rode between,   355
Whom David judged the fairy Queen;
But strange! he heard her moans resound,
And saw her feet with fetters bound.

    Fast spur they on through bush and brake;
To Ettrick woods their course they take.   360
Old David followed still in view,
Till near the Lochilaw they drew;
There in a deep and wonderous dell,
Where wandering sun-beam never fell,
Where noon-tide breezes never blew   365
From flowers to drink the morning dew;
There, underneath the sylvan shade,
The fairies' spacious bower was made.
Its rampart was the tangling sloe,
The bending briar, and misletoe;   370
And o'er its roof, the crooked oak
Waved wildly from the frowning rock.

    This wonderous bower, this haunted dell,
The forest shepherd shunned as hell!
When sound of fairies' silver horn   375
Came on the evening breezes borne,
Homeward he fled, nor made a stand,
Thinking the spirits hard at hand.
But when he heard the eldrich swell
Of giggling laugh and bridle bell,   380
Or saw the riders troop along,
His orisons were loud and strong.
His household fare he yielded free
To this mysterious company,
The fairest maid his cot within   385
Resigned with awe and little din;
True he might weep, but nothing say,
For none durst say the fairies nay.

Old David hasted home that night,
A wondering and a wearied wight.   390
Seven sons he had, alert and keen,
Had all in Border battles been;
Had wielded brand, and bent the bow,
For those who sought their overthrow.
Their hearts were true, their arms were strong,   395
Their faulchions keen, their arrows long;
The race of fairies they denied,–
No fairies kept the English side.

Our yeomen on their armour threw,
Their brands of steel and bows of yew;   400
Long arrows at their backs they sling,
Fledged from the Snowdon eagle's wing,
And boun' away brisk as the wind,
The sire before, the sons behind.

That evening fell so sweetly still,   405
So mild on lonely moor and hill,
The little genii of the fell
Forsook the purple heather bell,
And all their dripping beds of dew,
In wind-flower, thyme, and violet blue;   410
Aloft their viewless looms they heave,
And dew-webs round the helmets weave.
The waning moon her lustre threw
Pale round her throne of softened blue;
Her circuit, round the southland sky,   415
Was languid, low, and quickly bye;
Leaning on cloud so faint and fair,
And cradled on the golden air;
Modest and pale as maiden bride,
She sunk upon the trembling tide.   420

What late in daylight proved a jest,
Was now the doubt of every breast.
That fairies *were*, was not disputed;
But *what* they were, was greatly doubted.
Each argument was guarded well,   425
With "if," and "should," and "who can tell."

"Sure He that made majestic man,
And framed the world's stupendous plan;
Who placed on high the steady pole,
And sowed the stars that round it roll;   430
And made that sky, so large and blue,—
Could surely make a fairy too."

The sooth to say, each valiant core
Knew feelings never felt before.
Oft had they darned the midnight brake,   435
Fearless of aught save bog and lake;
But now the nod of sapling fir,
The heath-cock's loud exulting whirr,
The cry of hern from sedgy pool,
Or airy bleeter's rolling howl,   440
Came fraught with more dismaying dread
Than warder's horn, or warrior's tread.

Just as the gloom of midnight fell,
They reached the fairies' lonely dell.
O heavens! that dell was dark as death!   445
Perhaps the pit-fall yawned beneath!
Perhaps that lane that winded low,
Led to a nether world of woe!
But stern necessity's controul,
Resistless sways the human soul.   450

The bows are bent, the tinders smoke
With fire by sword struck from the rock.
Old David held the torch before;
His right hand heaved a dread claymore,
Whose Rippon edge he meant to try   455
On the first fairy met his eye.
Above his head his brand was raised;
Above his head the taper blazed;
A sterner or a ghastlier sight,
Ne'er entered bower at dead of night.   460
Below each lifted arm was seen
The barbed point of arrow keen,
Which waited but the twang of bow
To fly like lightning on the foe.
Slow move they on, with steady eye,   465
Resolved to conquer or to die.

At length they spied a massive door,
Deep in a nook, unseen before;
And by it slept, on wicker chair,
A sprite of dreadful form and air.   470
His grizzly beard flowed round his throat,
Like shaggy hair of mountain goat;
His open jaws and visage grim,
His half-shut eye so deadly dim,
Made David's blood to's bosom rush,   475
And his gray hair his helmet brush.
He squared, and made his faulchion wheel
Around his back from head to heel;
Then rising, tiptoe struck amain,
Down fell the sleeper's head in twain;   480
And springing blood, in veil of smoke,
Whizzed high against the bending oak.

"By heaven!" said George, with jocund air,
"Father, if all the fairies there
Are of the same materials made,   485
Let them beware the Rippon blade!"
A ghastly smile was seen to play
O'er David's visage, stern and gray;
He hoped, and feared; but ne'er till then
Knew whether he fought with sprites or men.   490

The massy door they next unlock,
That oped to hall beneath the rock,
In which new wonders met the eye:
The room was ample, rude, and high,
The arches caverned, dark, and torn,   495
On Nature's rifted columns borne;
Of moulding rude the embrazure,
And all the wild entablature;
And far o'er roof and architrave,
The ivy's ringlets bend and wave.   500
In each abrupt recess was seen
A couch of heath and rushes green;
While every alcove's sombre hue,
Was gem'd with drops of midnight dew.

Why stand our heroes still as death,   505
Nor muscle move, nor heave a breath?

See how the sire his torch has lowered,
And bends recumbent o'er his sword!
The arcubalister has thrown
His threatening, thirsty arrows down!   510
Struck in one moment, all the band
Entranced like moveless statues stand!
Enchantment sure arrests the spear,
And stints the warrior's bold career!

    List, list, what mellow angel sound   515
Distils from yonder gloom profound!
'Tis not the note of gathering shell,
Of fairy horn, nor silver bell!
No, 'tis the lute's mellifluous swell,
Mixed with a maiden's voice so clear,   520
The flitting bats flock round to hear!

    So wildly o'er the vault it rung,
That song, if in the green-wood sung,
Would draw the fays of wood and plain
To kiss the lips that poured the strain.   525
The lofty pine would listening lean;
The wild birch wave her tresses green;
And larks, that rose the dawn to greet,
Drop lifeless at the singer's feet.
The air was old, the measure slow,   530
The words were plain, but words of woe.

    Soft died the strain; the warriors stand,
Nor rested lance, nor lifted brand,
But listening bend, in hopes again
To hear that sweetly plaintive strain.   535
'Tis gone! and each uplifts his eye,
As waked from dream of ecstacy.

    Why stoops young Owen's gilded crest?
Why heave those groans from Owen's breast?
While kinsmen's eyes in raptures speak,   540
Why steals the tear o'er Owen's cheek?
That melting song, that song of pain,
Was sung to Owen's favourite strain;
The words were new, but that sweet lay
Had Owen heard in happier day.   545

Fast press they on; in close-set row,
Winded the lab'rinth far and low,
Till, in the cave's extremest bound,
Arrayed in sea-green silk, they found
Five beauteous dames, all fair and young;   550
And she, who late so sweetly sung,
Sat leaning o'er a silver lute,
Pale with despair, with terror mute.

When back her auburn locks she threw,
And raised her eyes so lovely blue,   555
'Twas like the woodland rose in dew!
That look was soft as morning flower,
And mild as sun-beam through the shower.
Old David gazed, and weened the while,
He saw a suffering angel smile;   560
Weened he had heard a seraph sing,
And sounds of a celestial string.

But when young Owen met her view,
She shrieked, and to his bosom flew:
For, oft before, in Moodlaw bowers,   565
They two had past the evening hours.
She was the loveliest mountain maid,
That e'er by grove or riv'let strayed;
Old Raeburn's child, the fairest flower
That ever bloomed in Eskdale-moor.   570
'Twas she the Sire that morn had seen,
And judged to be the Fairy Queen;
'Twas she who framed the artless lay,
That stopped the warriors on their way.

Close to her lover's breast she clung,   575
And round his neck enraptured hung:–
"O, my dear Owen! haste and tell,
What caused thee dare this lonely dell,
And seek your maid, at midnight still,
Deep in the bowels of the hill?   580
Here in this dark and drear abode,
By all deserted but my God,
Must I have reft the life he gave,
Or lived in shame a villain's slave.

I was, at midnight's murkest hour,   585
Stole from my father's stately tower,
And never thought again to view
The sun or sky's ethereal blue;
But since the first of Border-men
Has found me in this dismal den,   590
I to his arms for shelter fly,
With him to live, or with him die."

How glowed brave Owen's manly face,
While in that lady's kind embrace!
Warm tears of joy his utterance staid;   595
"O, my loved Ann!" was all he said.
Though well they loved, her high estate
Caused Owen ay aloof to wait;
And watch her bower, beside the rill,
When twilight rocked the breezes still,   600
And waked the music of the grove
To hymn the vesper song of love.
There, underneath the green-wood bough,
Oft had they breathed the tender vow.

With Ann of Raeburn here they found   605
The flowers of all the Border round;
From whom the strangest tale they hear,
That e'er astounded warrior's ear.
'Twould make even Superstition blush,
And all her tales of spirits hush.   610

That night the spoilers ranged the vale,
By Dryhope towers, and Meggat-dale
Ah! little trowed the fraudful train,
They ne'er should see their wealth again!
Their lemans, and their mighty store,   615
For which they nightly toils had bore,
Full twenty Autumn moons and more!
They little deemed, when morning dawned,
To meet the deadly Rippon brand;
And only find, at their return,   620
In their loved cave an early urn.

Ill suits it simple bard to tell
Of bloody work that there befel.

He lists not deeds of death to sing,
Of splintered spear, and twanging string;   625
Of piercing arrow's purpled wing,
How faulchions flash, and helmets ring.
Not one of all that prowling band,
So long the terror of the land,
Not one escaped their deeds to tell;   630
All in the winding lab'rinth fell.
The spoil was from the cave conveyed,
Where in a heap the dead were laid:
The outer cave our yeomen fill,
And left them in the hollow hill.   635

But still that dell, and bourn beneath,
The forest shepherd dreads as death.
Not there at evening dares he stray,
Though love impatient points the way;
Though throbs his heart the maid to see,   640
That's waiting by the trysting tree.

Even the old Sire, so reverend gray,
Ere turns the scale of night and day,
Oft breathes the short and ardent prayer,
That heaven may guard his footsteps there!   645
His eyes, meantime, so dim with dread,
Scarce ken the turf his foot must tread.
For still 'tis told, and still believed,
That there the spirits were deceived,
And maidens from their grasp retrieved: 650
That this they still preserve in mind,
And watch, when sighs the midnight wind,
To wreck their rage on humankind.

Old David, for this doughty raid,
Was keeper of the forest made;   655
A trooper he of gallant fame,
And first of all the Laidlaw name.

E'er since, in Ettrick's glens so green,
Spirits, though there, are seldom seen;
And fears of elf, and fairy raid,   660
Have like a morning dream decayed.

The bare-foot maid, of rosy hue,
Dares from the heath-flower brush the dew,
To meet her love in moon-light still,
By flowery den or tinkling rill;   665
And well dares she till midnight stay,
Among the coils of fragrant hay.

True, some weak shepherds, gone astray,
As fell the dusk of Hallow-day,
Have heard the tinkling sound aloof,   670
And gentle tread of horse's hoof;
And flying swifter than the wind,
Left all their scattered flocks behind.

True, when the evening tales are told,
When winter nights are dark and cold,   675
The boy dares not to barn repair
Alone, to say his evening prayer.
Nor dare the maiden ope the door,
Unless her lover walk before;
Then well can counterfeit the fright,   680
If star-beam on the water light;
And to his breast in terror cling,
For such a dread and dangerous thing.

O, Ettrick! shelter of my youth!
Thou sweetest glen of all the south!   685
Thy fairy tales, and songs of yore,
Shall never fire my bosom more.
Thy winding glades, and mountains wild,
The scenes that pleased me when a child,
Each verdant vale, and flowery lea,   690
Still in my midnight dreams I see;
And waking oft, I sigh for thee.
Thy hapless bard, though forced to roam
Afar from thee without a home,
Still there his glowing breast shall turn,   695
Till thy green bosom fold his urn.
Then, underneath thy mountain stone,
Shall sleep unnoticed and unknown.

When ceased the shepherd's simple lay,
With careless mien he lounged away.   700
No bow he deigned, nor anxious looked
How the gay throng their minstrel brooked.
No doubt within his bosom grew,
That to his skill the prize was due.
Well might he hope, for while he sung,   705
Louder and louder plaudits rung;
And when he ceased his numbers wild,
Fair Royalty approved and smiled.
Long had the bard, with hopes elate,
Sung to the low, the gay, the great;   710
And once had dared, at flatterer's call,
To tune his harp in Branxholm hall;
But, nor his notes of soothing sound,
Nor zealous word of bard renowned,
Might those persuade, that worth could be   715
Inherent in such mean degree.
But when the smile of Sovereign fair
Attested genuine nature there,
Throbbed high with rapture every breast,
And all his merit stood confest.   720

Different the next the herald named;
Warrior he was, in battle maimed,
When Lennox, on the downs of Kyle,
O'erthrew Maconnel and Argyle.
Unable more the sword to wield   725
With dark Clan-Alpine in the field,
Or rouse the dun-deer from her den
With fierce Macfarlane and his men;
He strove to earn a minstrel name,
And fondly nursed the sacred flame.   730
Warm was his heart, and bold his strain,
Wild fancies in his moody brain
Gamboled, unbridled, and unbound,
Lured by a shade, decoyed by sound.

In tender age, when mind was free,   735
As standing by his nurse's knee,
He heard a tale, so passing strange,
Of injured spirit's cool revenge;

It chilled his heart with blasting dread,
Which never more that bosom fled. 740
When passion's flush had fled his eye,
And gray hairs told that youth was bye;
Still quaked his heart at bush or stone,
As wandering in the gloom alone.

Where foxes roam, and eagles rave, 745
And dark woods round Ben-Lomond wave,
Once on a night, a night of dread!
He held convention with the dead;
Brought warnings to the house of death,
And tidings from a world beneath. 750

Loud blew the blast—the evening came,
The way was long, the minstrel lame;
The mountain's side was dern with oak,
Darkened with pine, and ribbed with rock:
Blue billows round its base were driven, 755
Its top was steeped in waves of heaven.
The wood, the wind, the billow's moan,
All spoke in language of their own;
But too well to our minstrel known.
Wearied, bewildered, in amaze, 760
Hymning in heart the Virgin's praise,
A cross he framed, of birchen bough,
And 'neath that cross he laid him low;
Hid by the heath, and Highland plaid,
His old harp in his bosom laid. 765
O! when the winds that wandered by,
Sung on her breast their lullaby,
How thrilled the tones his bosom through,
And deeper, holier, poured his vow!

No sleep was his—he raised his eye, 770
To note if dangerous place was nigh.
There columned rocks, abrupt and rude,
Hung o'er his gateless solitude:
The muffled sloe, and tangling brier,
Precluded freak or entrance here; 775
But yonder oped a little path,
O'ershadowed, deep, and dark as death.

Trembling, he groped around his lair
For mountain ash, but none was there.
Teeming with forms, his terror grew;   780
Heedful he watched, for well he knew,
That in that dark and devious dell,
Some lingering ghost or sprite must dwell:
So as he trowed, so it befel.

The stars were wrapt in curtain gray,   785
The blast of midnight died away;
'Twas just the hour of solemn dread,
When walk the spirits of the dead.
Rustled the leaves with gentle motion,
Groaned his chilled soul in deep devotion.   790
The lake-fowl's wake was heard no more;
The wave forgot to brush the shore;
Hushed was the bleat, on moor and hill;
The wandering clouds of heaven stood still.

What heart could bear, what eye could meet,   795
The spirits in their lone retreat!
Rustled again the darksome dell;
Straight on the minstrel's vision fell,
A trembling and unwonted light,
That showed the phantoms to his sight.   800

Came first a slender female form,
Pale as the moon in Winter storm;
A babe of sweet simplicity
Clung to her breast as pale as she,
And ay she sung its lullaby.   805
That cradle-song of the phantom's child,
O! but it was soothing, holy, and wild!
But, O! that song can ill be sung,
By Lowland bard, or Lowland tongue.

The Spectre's Cradle-Song

Hush, my bonny babe! hush, and be still!   810
Thy mother's arms shall shield thee from ill.

Far have I borne thee, in sorrow and pain,
To drink the breeze of the world again.
The dew shall moisten thy brow so meek,
And the breeze of midnight fan thy cheek,   815
And soon shall we rest in the bow of the hill;
Hush, my bonny babe! hush, and be still!
For thee have I travailed, in weakness and woe,
The world above and the world below.
My heart was soft, and it fell in the snare;   820
Thy father was cruel, but thou wert fair.
I sinned, I sorrowed, I died for thee;
Smile, my bonny babe! smile on me!

See yon thick clouds of murky hue;
Yon star that peeps from its window blue;   825
Above yon clouds, that wander far,
Away, above yon little star,
There's a home of peace that shall soon be thine,
And there shalt thou see thy Father and mine.
The flowers of the world shall bud and decay,   830
The trees of the forest be weeded away;
But there shalt *thou* bloom for ever and ay.
The time will come, I shall follow thee;
But long, long hence, that time shall be!
Smile now, my bonny babe! smile on me!   835

Slow moved she on with dignity,
Nor bush, nor brake, nor rock, nor tree,
Her footsteps staid—o'er cliff so bold,
Where not the wren its foot could hold,
Stately she wandered, firm and free,   840
Singing her softened lullaby.

Three naked phantoms next came on;
They beckoned low, past, and were gone.
Then came a troop of sheeted dead,
With shade of chieftain at their head: 845
And with our bard, in brake forlorn,
Held converse till the break of morn.
Their ghostly rites, their looks, their mould,

Or words to man, he never told;
But much he learned of mystery,   850
Of that was past, and that should be.
Thenceforth he troubles oft divined,
And scarcely held his perfect mind;
Yet still the song, admired when young,
He loved, and that in Court he sung.   855

Macgregor

THE ELEVENTH BARD'S SONG

"Macgregor, Macgregor, remember our foemen;
The moon rises broad from the brow of Ben-Lomond;
The clans are impatient, and chide thy delay;
Arise! let us bound to Glen-Lyon away."–

  Stern scowled the Macgregor, then silent and sullen,   860
He turned his red eye to the braes of Strathfillan;
"Go, Malcolm, to sleep, let the clans be dismissed;
The Campbells this night for Macgregor must rest."–

  "Macgregor, Macgregor, our scouts have been flying,
Three days, round the hills of M'Nab and Glen-Lyon;   865
Of riding and running such tidings they bear,
We must meet them at home else they'll quickly be here."–

  "The Campbell may come, as his promises bind him,
And haughty M'Nab, with his giants behind him;
This night I am bound to relinquish the fray,   870
And do what it freezes my vitals to say.
Forgive me, dear brother, this horror of mind;
Thou knowest in the strife I was never behind,
Nor ever receded a foot from the van,
Or blenched at the ire or the prowess of man.   875
But I've sworn by the cross, by my God, and my all!
An oath which I cannot, and dare not recal;
Ere the shadows of midnight fall east from the pile,
To meet with a spirit this night in Glen-Gyle.

  Last night, in my chamber, all thoughtful and lone,   880
I called to remembrance some deeds I had done,

When entered a lady, with visage so wan,
And looks, such as never were fastened on man.
I knew her, O brother! I knew her too well!
Of that once fair dame such a tale I could tell, 885
As would thrill thy bold heart; but how long she remained,
So racked was my spirit, my bosom so pained,
I knew not—but ages seemed short to the while.
Though proffer the Highlands, nay, all the green isle,
With length of existence no man can enjoy, 890
The same to endure, the dread proffer I'd fly!
The thrice threatened pangs of last night to forego,
Macgregor would dive to the mansions below.
Despairing and mad, to futurity blind,
The present to shun, and some respite to find, 895
I swore, ere the shadow fell east from the pile,
To meet her alone by the brook of Glen-Gyle.

She told me, and turned my chilled heart to a stone,
The glory and name of Macgregor was gone:
That the pine, which for ages had shed a bright halo, 900
Afar on the mountains of Highland Glen-Falo,
Should wither and fall ere the turn of yon moon,
Smit through by the canker of hated Colquhoun:
That a feast on Macgregors each day should be common,
For years, to the eagles of Lennox and Lomond. 905

A parting embrace, in one moment, she gave:
Her breath was a furnace; her bosom the grave!
Then flitting elusive, she said, with a frown,
'The mighty Macgregor shall yet be my own!'—

"Macgregor, thy fancies are wild as the wind; 910
The dreams of the night have disordered thy mind.
Come, buckle thy panoply—march to the field,—
See, brother, how hacked are thy helmet and shield!
Aye, that was M'Nab, in the height of his pride,
When the lions of Dochart stood firm by his side. 915
This night the proud chief his presumption shall rue;
Rise, brother, these chinks in his heart-blood will glue:
Thy fantasies frightful shall flit on the wing,
When loud with thy bugle Glen-Lyon shall ring."—

Like glimpse of the moon through the storm of the night,
Macgregor's red eye shed one sparkle of light:
It faded—it darkened—he shuddered—he sighed,—
"No! not for the universe!" low he replied.

Away went Macgregor, but went not alone;
To watch the dread rendezvous, Malcolm has gone.   925
They oared the broad Lomond, so still and serene,
And deep in her bosom, how aweful the scene!
O'er mountains inverted the blue waters curled,
And rocked them on skies of a far nether world.

All silent they went, for the time was approaching;   930
The moon the blue zenith already was touching;
No foot was abroad on the forest or hill,
No sound but the lullaby sung by the rill:
Young Malcolm at distance, couched, trembling the while,—
Macgregor stood lone by the brook of Glen-Gyle.   935

Few minutes had passed, ere they spied on the stream,
A skiff sailing light, where a lady did seem;
Her sail was the web of the gossamer's loom,
The glow-worm her wakelight, the rainbow her boom;
A dim rayless beam was her prow and her mast,   940
Like wold-fire, at midnight, that glares on the waste.
Though rough was the river with rock and cascade,
No torrent, no rock, her velocity staid;
She wimpled the water to weather and lee,
And heaved as if borne on the waves of the sea.   945
Mute Nature was roused in the bounds of the glen;
The wild deer of Gairtney abandoned his den,
Fled panting away, over river and isle,
Nor once turned his eye to the brook of Glen-Gyle.

The fox fled in terror; the eagle awoke,   950
As slumbering he dozed in the shelve of the rock;
Astonished, to hide in the moon-beam he flew,
And screwed the night-heaven till lost in the blue.

Young Malcolm beheld the pale lady approach,
The chieftain salute her, and shrink from her touch.   955
He saw the Macgregor kneel down on the plain,

As begging for something he could not obtain;
She raised him indignant, derided his stay,
Then bore him on board, set her sail, and away.

   Though fast the red bark down the river did glide,   960
Yet faster ran Malcolm adown by its side;
"Macgregor! Macgregor!" he bitterly cried;
"Macgregor! Macgregor!" the echoes replied.
He struck at the lady, but, strange though it seem,
His sword only fell on the rocks and the stream;   965
But the groans from the boat, that ascended amain,
Were groans from a bosom in horror and pain.—
They reached the dark lake, and bore lightly away;
Macgregor is vanished for ever and ay!

      Abrupt as glance of morning sun,   970
The bard of Lomond's lay is done.
Loves not the swain, from path of dew,
At morn the golden orb to view,
Rise broad and yellow from the main,
While scarce a shadow lines the plain.   975
Well knows he then the gathering cloud
Shall all his noontide glories shroud.
Like smile of morn before the rain,
Appeared the minstrel's mounting strain.
As easy inexperienced hind,   980
Who sees not coming rains and wind,
The beacon of the dawning hour,
Nor notes the blink before the shower,
Astonished, mid his open grain,
Sees round him pour the sudden rain,—   985
So looked the still attentive throng,
When closed at once Macfarlane's song.

      Time was it,—when he 'gan to tell
Of spectre stern, and barge of hell;
Loud, and more loud, the minstrel sung;   990
Loud, and more loud, the chords he rung;
Wild grew his looks, for well he knew
The scene was dread, the tale was true!

And ere Loch Ketturine's wave was won,
Faultered his voice, his breath was done.   995
He raised his brown hand to his brow,
To veil his eye's enraptured glow;
Flung back his locks of silver gray,
Lifted his crutch, and limped away.

   The Bard of Clyde stepped next in view;   1000
Fair was his form, his harp was new;
His eyes were bright, his manner gay,
But plain his garb, and plain his lay.

Earl Walter

THE TWELFTH BARD'S SONG

"What makes Earl Walter pace the wood
  In the wan light of the moon?   1005
Why altered is Earl Walter's mood
  So strangely, and so soon?"–

"Ah! he is fallen to fight a knight
  Whom man could never tame,
To morrow, in his Sovereign's sight,   1010
  Or bear perpetual shame."–

"Go warn the Clyde, go warn the Ayr,
  Go warn them suddenly,
If none will fight for Earl Walter,
  Some one may fight for me."–   1015

"Now hold your tongue, my daughter dear,
  Now hold your tongue for shame,
For never shall my son Walter
  Disgrace his father's name.

Shall ladies tell, and minstrels sing,   1020
  How lord of Scottish blood
By proxy fought before his king?
  No, never! by the rood!"–

Earl Walter rose ere it was day,
   For battle made him boun';   1025
Earl Walter mounted his bonny gray,
   And rode to Stirling town.

Old Hamilton from the tower came down,
   "Go saddle a steed for me,
And I'll away to Stirling town,   1030
   This deadly bout to see.

Mine eye is dim, my locks are gray,
   My cheek is furred and wan;
Ah, me! but I have seen the day
   I feared no single man!   1035

Bring me my steed," said Hamilton;
   "Darcie his vaunts may rue;
Whoever slays my only son
   Must fight the father too.

Whoever fights my noble son   1040
   May foin the best he can;
Whoever braves Wat Hamilton,
   Shall know he braves a man."–

And there was riding in belt and brand,
   And running o'er holt and lea;   1045
For all the lords of fair Scotland
   Came there the fight to see.

And squire, and groom, and baron bold,
   Trooping in thousands came,
And many a hind, and warrior old,   1050
   And many a lovely dame.

When good Earl Walter rode the ring
   Upon his mettled gray,
There was none so ready as our good king
   To bid that Earl good day.   1055

For one so gallant and so young,
   Oh, many a heart beat high;

And no fair eye in all the throng,
    Nor rosy cheek was dry.

But up then spoke the king's daughter,   1060
    Fair Margaret was her name,—
"If we should lose brave Earl Walter,
    My sire is sore to blame.

Forbid the fight, my liege, I pray,
    Upon my bended knee."—   1065
"Daughter, I'm loth to say you nay;
    It cannot, must not be."—

"Proclaim it round," the princess cried,
    "Proclaim it suddenly;
If none will fight for Earl Walter,   1070
    Some one may fight for me.

In Douglas-dale I have a tower,
    With many a holm and hill,
I'll give them all, and ten times more,
    To him will Darcie kill."—   1075

But up then spoke old Hamilton,
    And doffed his bonnet blue;
In his sunk eye the tear-drop shone,
    And his gray locks o'er it flew:—

"Cease, cease, thou lovely royal maid,   1080
    Small cause hast thou for pain;
Wat Hamilton shall have no aid
    'Gainst lord of France or Spain.

I love my boy, but should he fly,
    Or other for him fight,   1085
Heaven grant that first his parent's eye
    May set in starless night!"—

Young Margaret blushed, her weeping staid,
    And quietly looked on:
Now Margaret was the fairest maid   1090
    On whom the day light shone.

Her eye was like the star of love,
   That blinks across the evening dun;
The locks that waved that eye above,
   Like light clouds curling round the sun.   1095

When Darcie entered in the ring,
   A shudder round the circle flew:
Like men who from a serpent spring,
   They startled at the view.

His look so fierce, his crest so high,   1100
   His belts and bands of gold,
And the glances of his charger's eye,
   Were dreadful to behold.

But when he saw Earl Walter's face,
   So rosy and so young,   1105
He frowned, and sneered with haughty grace,
   And round disdainful flung.

"What! dost thou turn my skill to sport,
   And break thy jests on me?
Thinkst thou I sought the Scottish court,   1110
   To play with boys like thee?

Fond youth, go home and learn to ride;
   For pity get thee gone;
Tilt with the girls and boys of Clyde,
   And boast of what thou'st done.   1115

If Darcie's spear but touch thy breast,
   It flies thy body through;
If Darcie's sword come o'er thy crest,
   It cleaves thy heart in two."—

"I came not here to vaunt, Darcie;   1120
   I came not here to scold;
It ill befits a knight like thee
   Such proud discourse to hold.

To-morrow boast, amid the rout,
   Of deeds which thou hast done;   1125

To-day beware thy saucy snout;
  Rude blusterer, come on!"–

Rip went the spurs in either steed,
  To different posts they sprung;
Quivered each spear o'er charger's head;   1130
  Forward each warrior hung.

The horn blew once–the horn blew twice–
  Oh! many a heart beat high!
'Twas silence all!–the horn blew thrice–
  Dazzled was every eye.   1135

Hast thou not seen, from heaven, in ire
  The eagle swift descend?
Hast thou not seen the sheeted fire
  The lowering darkness rend?

Not faster glides the eagle gray   1140
  Adown the yielding wind;
Not faster bears the bolt away,
  Leaving the storm behind;

Than flew the warriors on their way,
  With full suspended breath;   1145
Than flew the warriors on their way
  Across the field of death.

So fierce the shock, so loud the clang,
  The gleams of fire were seen;
The rocks and towers of Stirling rang,   1150
  And the red blood fell between.

Earl Walter's grey was borne aside,
  Lord Darcie's black held on.
"Oh! ever alack," fair Margaret cried,
  "The brave Earl Walter's gone!"   1155
"Oh! ever alack," the king replied,
  "That ever the deed was done!"

Earl Walter's broken corslet doffed,
  He turned with lightened eye;

His glancing spear he raised aloft,   1160
    And seemed to threat the sky.

Lord Darcie's spear, aimed at his breast,
    He parried dext'rously;
Then caught him rudely by the wrist,
    Saying, "warrior come with me!"   1165

Lord Darcie drew, Lord Darcie threw;
    But threw and drew in vain;
Lord Darcie drew, Lord Darcie threw,
    And spurred his black amain.

Down came Lord Darcie, casque and brand   1170
    Loud rattled on the clay;
Down came Earl Walter, hand in hand,
    And head to head they lay.

Lord Darcie's steed turned to his lord,
    And, trembling, stood behind;   1175
But off Earl Walter's dapple scoured
    Far fleeter than the wind;
Nor stop, nor stay, nor gate, nor ford,
    Could make her look behind.

O'er holt, o'er hill, o'er slope and slack,   1180
    She sought her native stall;
She liked not Darcie's doughty black,
    Nor Darcie's spear at all.

"Even go thy ways," Earl Walter cried,
    "Since better may not be;   1185
I'll trust my life with weapon tried,
    But never again with thee.

Rise up, Lord Darcie, sey thy brand,
    And fling thy mail away;
For foot to foot, and hand to hand,   1190
    We'll now decide the day."

So said, so done; their helms they flung,
    Their doublets linked and sheen;

And hawberk, armlet, cuirass, rung
  Promiscuous on the green.   1195

"Now, Darcie! now, thy dreaded name,
  That oft hast chilled a foe,
Thy hard-earned honours, and thy fame,
  Depend on every blow.

Sharp be thine eye, and firm thy hand;   1200
  Thy heart unmoved remain;
For never was the Scottish brand
  Upreared, and reared in vain."–

"Now do thy best, young Hamilton,
  Rewarded shalt thou be;   1205
Thy king, thy country, and thy kin,
  All, all depend on thee!

Thy father's heart yearns for his son,
  The ladies' cheeks grow wan;
Wat Hamilton! Wat Hamilton,   1210
  Now prove thyself a man!"–

What makes Lord Darcie shift and dance
  So fast around the plain?
What makes Lord Darcie strike and lance,
  As passion fired his brain?   1215

"Lay on, lay on," said Hamilton;
  "Thou bearest thee boist'rously;
If thou shouldst pelt till day be done,
  Thy weapon I defy."

What makes Lord Darcie shift and wear   1220
  So fast around the plain?
Why is Lord Darcie's hollands fair
  All stripped with crimson grain?–

The first blow that Earl Walter made
  He clove his bearded chin.   1225
"Beshrew thy heart," Lord Darcie said,
  "Ye sharply do begin!"

The next blow that Earl Walter made,
  Quite through the gare it ran.
"Now by my faith," Lord Darcie said,   1230
  "That's stricken like a man."

The third blow that Earl Walter made,
  It scooped his lordly side.
"Now, by my troth," Lord Darcie said,
  "Thy marks are ill to bide."   1235

Lord Darcie's sword he forced a-hight,
  And tripped him on the plain.
"O, ever alack," then cried the knight,
  "I ne'er shall rise again!"

When good Earl Walter saw he grew   1240
  So pale, and lay so low,
Away his brace of swords he threw,
  And raised his fainting foe.

Then rang the list with shouts of joy,
  Loud and more loud they grew,   1245
And many a bonnet to the sky
  And many a coif they threw.

The tear stood in the father's eye,—
  He wiped his aged brow,—
"Give me thy hand, my gallant boy,   1250
  I knew thee not till now.

My liege, my king, this is my son
  Whom I present to thee;
Nor would I change Wat Hamilton
  For any lad I see!"—   1255

"Welcome, my friend and warrior old;
  This gallant son of thine
Is much too good for baron bold,
  He must be son of mine!

For he shall wed my daughter dear,   1260
  The flower of fair Scotland;

The badge of honour he shall wear,
    And sit at my right hand.

And he shall have the lands of Kyle,
    And royal bounds of Clyde;   1265
And he shall have all Arran's isle
    To dower his royal bride."

The princess smiled, the princess flushed,
    O, but her heart was fain;
And ay her cheek of beauty blushed   1270
    Like rose-bud in the rain.

From this the Hamiltons of Clyde
    Their royal lineage draw;
And thus was won the fairest bride
    That Scotland ever saw!   1275

When ceased the lay, the plaudits rung,
Not for the bard, or song he sung;
But every eye with pleasure shone,
And cast its smiles on one alone,—
That one was princely Hamilton!   1280
And well the gallant chief approved
The bard who sung of sire beloved,
And pleased were all the court to see
The minstrel hailed so courteously.

    Again is every courtier's gaze   1285
Speaking suspense, and deep amaze;
The bard was stately, dark, and stern,—
'Twas Drummond, from the moors of Ern.
Tall was his frame, his fore-head high,
Still and mysterious was his eye;   1290
His look was like a winter day,
When storms and winds have sunk away.

    Well versed was he in holy lore;
In cloistered dome the cowl he wore;

But wearied with the eternal strain   1295
Of formal breviats, cold and vain,
He wooed, in depth of Highland dale,
The silver spring, and mountain gale.

  In gray Glen-Ample's forest deep,
Hid from the rains and tempest's sweep,   1300
In bosom of an aged wood
His solitary cottage stood.
Its walls were bastioned, dark, and dern,
Dark was its roof of filmot fern,
And dark the vista down the linn,   1305
But all was love and peace within.
Religion, man's first friend and best,
Was in that home a constant guest:
There, sweetly, every morn and even,
Warm orisons were poured to heaven: 1310
And every cliff Glen-Ample knew,
And green wood on her banks that grew,
In answer to his bounding string,
Had learned the hymns of heaven to sing;
With many a song of mystic lore,   1315
Rude as when sung in days of yore.

  His were the snowy flocks, that strayed
Adown Glen-Airtney's forest glade;
And his the goat, and chesnut hind,
Where proud Ben-Vorlich cleaves the wind: 1320
There oft, when suns of summer shone,
The bard would sit, and muse alone,
Of innocence, expelled by man;
Of nature's fair and wonderous plan;
Of the eternal throne sublime;   1325
Of visions seen in antient time,
Till his rapt soul would leave her home
In visionary worlds to roam.
Then would the mists that wandered bye
Seem hovering spirits to his eye: 1330
Then would the breeze's whistling sweep,
Soft lulling in the cavern deep,
Seem to the enthusiast's dreaming ear
The words of spirits whispering near.

Loathed his firm soul, the measured chime   1335
And florid films of modern rhyme;
No other lays became his tongue
But those his rude fore-fathers sung.
And when by wandering minstrel warned,
The mandate of his Queen he learned,   1340
So much he prized the ancient strain,
High hopes had he the prize to gain.
With modest, yet majestic mien,
He tuned his harp of solemn strain:
O list the tale, ye fair and young,   1345
A lay so strange was never sung!

Kilmeny

THE THIRTEENTH BARD'S SONG

Bonnye Kilmeny gede up the glen;
But it walsna to meite Duneira's men,
Nor the rozy munke of the isle to see,
For Kilmeny was pure as pure culde be.   1350
It was only to heire the yorline syng,
And pu the blew kress-flouir runde the spryng;
To pu the hyp and the hyndberrye,
And the nytt that hang fra the hesil tree;
For Kilmeny was pure as pure culde be.   1355
But lang may her minny luke ouir the wa,
And lang may scho seike in the greinwood schaw;
Lang the lairde of Duneira bleme,
And lang, lang greite or Kilmeny come heme.

Quhan mony lang day had comit and fledde,   1360
Quhan grief grew caulm, and hope was deade,
Quhan mes for Kilmeny's soul had beine sung,
Quhan the bedis-man had prayit, and the deide-bell rung;
Lete, lete in ane glomyn, quhan all was still,
Quhan the freenge was reid on the wastlin hill,   1365
The wud was sere, the moon i'the wene,
The reike of the cot hang ouir the playne,
Like ane littil wee cludde in the worild its lene;
Quhan the ingil lowit with ane eiry leme,
Lete, lete in the glomyn, Kilmeny came heme!   1370

"Kilmeny, Kilmeny, quhair haif ye beine?
Lang haif we socht beth holt and deine;
By lynn, by furde, and greinwudde tree,
Yet ye ir helsome and fayir to see.
Quhair gat ye that joup of the lille scheine?   1375
That bonny snoode of the byrk se greine?
And these rosis, the fayrist that ever war seine?
Kilmeny, Kilmeny, quhair haif ye beine?"—

Kilmeny luckit up with ane lovelye grace,
But ne smyle was seine on Kilmeny's face;   1380
Als still was her luke, and als still was her ee,
Als the stilnesse that lay on the emerant lee,
Or the myst that sleips on ane waveless sea.
For Kilmeny had beine scho kend nocht quhair,
And Kilmeny had seine quhat scho culde not declayre;   1385
Kilmeny had beine quhair the cocke nevir crew,
Quhair the rayne nevir fell, and the wynd nevir blue.
But it seemit as the herpe of the skye had rung,
And the ayries of heauin playit runde her tung,
Quhan scho spak of the luvlye formis scho had
          seine,   1390
And ane land quhair synn had nevir beine;
Ane land of love, and ane land of lychte,
Withoutten sonne, or mone, or nychte:
Where the ryver swait ane lyving streime,
And the lychte ane pure and cludlesse beime: 1395
The land of veizion it wald seime,
And still ane everlestyng dreime.

In yond grein wudde there is a waike,
And in that waike there is a wene,
     And in that wene there is a maike,   1400
That nouther hes flesch, blude, nor bene;
And dune in yond greinwudde he walkis his lene.

In that greine wene Kilmeny lay,
Her bosom happit with flouris gay;
But the ayre was soft, and the silens deipe,   1405
And bonny Kilmeny fell sunde asleipe.
Scho kend ne mair, nor openit her ee,
Till wekit by the hymis of ane farr cuntrye.

Scho wekit on ane cuche of the sylk se slim,
All stryppit with the barris of the raynbowis rim;   1410
And luvlye beingis runde war ryfe,
Quha erst had travellit mortyl lyfe;
And ay they smilet, and gan to speire,
"What spyrit hes brochte this mortyl heire?"

"Lang haif I raikit the worild wide,"   1415
Ane meike and reverent fere replyit;
"Beth nycht and day I haif watchit the fayre,
Eident a thousande eiris and mayre.
Yes, I haif watchit ouir ilk degree,
Quhairevir blumis femenitye;   1420
And sinless virgin, free of stain
In mind and body, faund I nane.
Nevir, sen the banquhet of tyme,
Fand I vyrgin in her pryme,
Quhill anis this bonny maydin I saw   1425
As spotless as the mornyng snaw:
Full twentye eiris scho has levit as fre
As the spirits that sojurn this countrye.
I haif brochte her away fra the snairis of men,
That synn or dethe scho nevir may ken."   1430

They claspit her weste and handis fair,
They kissit her cheik, and they kembit her hayir,
And runde cam ilka blumyng fere,
Sayn, "Bonny Kilmeny, yer welcome here!
Wemyng are freit of the littand scorne: 1435
O, blest be the day Kilmeny was born!
Now shall the land of the spiritis see,
Now shall it ken quhat ane womyn may be!
Mony long eir, in sorrow and pain,
Mony long eir thro' the worild we haif gane,   1440
Comyshonit to watch fayir womynkinde,
For its they quha nurice the imortyl minde.
We haif watchit their stepis as the dawnyng shone,
And deipe in the greinwud walkis alone,
By lille bouir, and silken bedde,   1445
The vewless teiris haif ouir them shedde;
Haif suthit their ardent myndis to sleep,
Or left the cuche of luife to weip.

We haif sein! we haif sein! but the tyme mene come,
And the angelis will blush at the day of doom!   1450

O, wald the fayrest of mortyl kynde
Ay keipe thilke holye troths in mynde,
That kyndred spyritis ilk motion see,
Quha watch their wayis with ankshes ee,
And griefe for the guilt of humainitye!   1455
Och, sweit to hevin the maydenis prayer,
And the siche that hevis ane bosom se fayir!
And deire to hevin the wordis of truthe,
And the prayze of vertu fra beautyis muthe!
And deire to the viewles formis of ayir,   1460
The mynde that kythis as the body fayir!

O, bonnye Kilmeny! fre fra stayne,
Gin evir ye seike the worild agayne,
That worild of synn, of sorrow, and feire,
O, tell of the joyis that are wayting heire!   1465
And tell of the sygnis ye shall shortlye see;
Of the tymes that are now, and the tymes that shall be."

They liftit Kilmeny, they ledde her away,
And scho walkit in the lychte of ane sonles day:
The skye was ane dome of kristel brichte,   1470
The fountyn of veezion, and fountyn of lichte:
The emerant feildes war of dazzling glow,
And the flouris of everlestyng blow.
Than deipe in the streime her body they layde,
That her yudith and beautye mocht nevir fede;   1475
And they smylit on hevin, quhan they saw her lye
In the streime of lyfe that wanderit bye.
And scho herde ane songe, scho herde it sung,
Scho kend nochte quhair; but se sweitlye it rung,
It fell on her eare lyke ane dreime of the morne: 1480
"O! blist be the daye Kilmeny was born!
Now shall the land of the spyritis see,
Now shall it ken quhat ane womyn may be!
The sun that shynis on the worild se brychte,
Ane borrowit gleide fra the fountaine of lychte;   1485
And the moone that sleikis the skye se dun,
Lyke ane gouden bow, or ane beimles sun,

Shall skulk awaye, and be seine ne mayir,
And the angelis shall miss them travelling the ayr.
But lang, lang aftir bethe nychte and day,   1490
Quhan the sun and the worild haif elyit awaye;
Quhan the synnir hes gene to his wesum doome,
Kilmeny shall smyle in eternal bloome!"

They soofit her awaye to ane mountyn greine,
To see quhat mortyl nevir had seine;   1495
And they seted her hiche on ane purpil swerde,
And bade her heide quhat scho saw and herde;
And note the chaingis the spyritis wrochte,
For now scho leevit in the land of thochte.
Scho lukit, and scho saw ne sone nor skyis,   1500
But ane kristel dome of a thusend dyis.
Scho luckit, and scho saw ne land arychte,
But ane endles whirle of glory and lychte.
And radiant beingis went and came
Far swifter than wynde, or the lynkit flame.   1505
Scho haide her ene fra the daiziling view;
Scho lukit agayn, and the schene was new.

Scho saw ane sun on a simmer skye,
And cludis of amber sailing bye;
Ane lovlye land anethe her laye.   1510
And that land had lekis and mountaynis graye;
And that land had vallies and horye pylis,
And merlit seas, and a thusande ylis.
Scho saw the korne waif on the vaile;
Scho saw the deire rin down the daile;   1515
And mony a mortyl toyling sore,
And scho thochte scho had seine the land before.

Scho saw ane ledy sit on a throne,
The fayrest that evir the sun shone on!
Ane lyon lickit her hand of mylke,   1520
And scho held him in ane leish of sylk;
And ane leifu mayden stude at her knee,
With ane sylver wand, and meltyng ee.
But ther cam ane leman out of the west,
To woo the ledy that he luvit best;   1525
And he sent ane boy her herte to prove,

And scho took him in, and scho callit him love;
But quhan to her breist he gan to cling,
Scho dreit the payne of the serpentis sting.

   Than ane gruff untowyrd gysart came, 1530
And he hundit the lyon on his dame;
And the leifu mayde with the meltyng eye,
Scho droppit ane tear, and passit bye;
And scho saw quhill the queen fra the lyon fled,
Quhill the bonniest flouir in the worild lay deide. 1535
Ane koffin was set on a distant playne,
And scho saw the reide blude fall like rayne:
Then bonny Kilmeny's herte grew saire,
And scho turnit away, and dochte luke ne maire.

   Then the gruff grim keryl girnit amain, 1540
And they trampit him downe, but he rase againe;
And he baitit the lyon to diedis of weir,
Quhill he lepit the blude to the kyngdome deire.
But the lyon grew straung, and dainger-prief,
Quhan crownit with the rose and the claiver leife; 1545
Then he lauchit at the keryl, and chesit him away
To feide with the deire on the mountayn gray:
He goulit at the keryl, and he geckit at hevin,
But his merk was set, and his erilis given.
Kilmeny a while her ene withdrewe; 1550
Scho lukit agene, and the schene was new.

   Scho saw arunde her, fayir wanfurlit,
Ane haf of all the glowing worild,
Quhair oceanis rowit, and ryveris ran,
To bunde the aymis of sinful man. 1555
Scho saw ane pepil, ferse and fell,
Burst fra their bundis like feindis of hell;
The lille grew, and the egil flew,
And scho herkit on her revining crew.
The wedos wailit, and the reid blude ran, 1560
And scho thretinit ane end to the race of man:
Scho nevir lenit, nor stoode in awe,
Quhill claught by the lyonis deadly paw.
Och! then the egil swinkit for lyfe,
And brainzelit up ane mortyl stryfe; 1565

But flew scho north, or flew scho suthe,
Scho met with the goul of the lyonis muthe.

With ane mootit wing, and wefu mene,
The egil sochte her eiry agene;
But lang may scho cour in the bloody este,   1570
And lang, lang sleik her oundit breste,
Afore scho sey ane other flychte,
To play with the norlan lyonis mychte.

To sing of the sychtis Kilmeny saw,
Se far surpassing naturis law,   1575
The syngeris voyse wald synk away,
And the stryng of his herpe wald cese to play.
But scho saw quhill the sorrouis of man war bye,
And all was lufe and hermonye;
Quhill the sternis of hevin fell lownly away,   1580
Lyke the flekis of snaw on a winter day.

Then Kilmeny beggit agene to see
The freindis scho had left in her ayn countrye,
To tell of the plesse quhair scho had been,
And the wonderis that lay in the land unseen;   1585
To warn the living maydenis fayir,
The luvit of hevin, the spiritis care,
That all quhase myndis unmelit remaine
Shall blume in beauty quhan tyme is gene.

With distant museke, soft and deipe,   1590
They lullit Kilmeny sunde asleepe;
And quhan scho wekinit, scho lay her lene,
All happit with flouris, in the greinwud wene.
Quhan sevin lang yeiris had cumit and fledde;
Quhan greif was calm, and hope was dede;   1595
Quhan scairse was rememberit Kilmeny's neme,
Lete, lete in a gloamyn Kilmeny cam heme!

And O, her beauty was fayir to see,
But still and steedfast was her ee!
Her seymar was the lille flouir,   1600
And her cheik the moss-rose in the shouir;

And her voyse lyke the distant melodye,
That floatis alang the silver sea.
But scho luvit to raike the lenely glen,
And keepit away fra the hauntis of men;   1605
Her holy hymis unherde to syng,
To suke the flouris, and drynk the spryng.
But quhairevir her pecefu form appeirit,
The wylde besties of the hill war cheirit;
The ouf playit lythely runde the feilde,   1610
The lordlye byson lowit and kneilit;
The dun deire wooit with manyr bland,
And courit aneath her lille hand.
And quhan at evin the woodlandis rung,
Quhan hymis of other worildis scho sung,   1615
In extacye of sweite devotion,
Och, then the glen was all in motion.
The wylde bestis of the foreste came,
Brak fra their buchtis and faldis the tame,
And govit by, charmit and amaizit;   1620
Even the dull cattil crunit and gazit,
And waulit about in ankshuse payne
For some the misterye to explayne.
The bizerd cam with the thrystle-coke;
The korbye left hir houf in the roke;   1625
The black-burd alang with the egil flew;
The hynde cam trippyng ouir the dew;
The ouf and the kydd their raike began,
And the tod, and the lam, and the leurit ran;
The hauke and the herne attour them hung,   1630
And the merl and the maives forehooit their yung;
And all in ane pecefu ryng war hurlit:
It was lyke ane eve in a sinlesse worild!

    Quhan a munthe and a day had comit and gene,
Kilmeny sochte the greinwud wene;   1635
There layde her doune on the levis se greine,
But Kilmeny on yirth was nevir mayre seine.
But och, the wordis that fell fra her muthe,
War wordis of wonder, and wordis of truthe!
But all the land was in fiere and dreide,   1640
For they kendna whether scho was lyving or deide.
It walsna her heme, and scho culdna remayne;

Scho left this worild of sorrow and paine,
And returnit to the land of thochte againe.

He ceased; and all with kind concern   1645
Blest in their hearts the bard of Ern.

By that the chill and piercing air,
The pallid hue of ladies fair,
The hidden yawn, and drumbly eye,
Loudly announced the morning nigh.   1650
Beckoned the Queen with courteous smile,
And breathless silence gazed the while:—

"I hold it best, my lords," she said,
"For knight, for dame, and lovely maid,
At wassail, wake, or revel hall,   1655
To part before the senses pall.
Sweet though the draught of pleasure be,
Why should we drain it to the lee?
Though here the minstrel's fancy play,
Light as the breeze of summer-day;   1660
Though there in solemn cadence flow,
Smooth as the night-wind o'er the snow;
Now bound away with rolling sweep,
Like tempest o'er the raving deep;
High on the morning's golden screen,   1665
Or casemate of the rainbow lean;—
Such beauties were in vain prolonged,
The soul is cloyed, the minstrel wronged.

"Loud is the morning-blast, and chill,
The snow-drift speeds along the hill;   1670
Let ladies of the storm beware,
And lords of ladies take a care;
From lanes and alleys guard them well,
Where lurking ghost or sprite may dwell;
But most avoid the dazzling flare,   1675
And spirit of the morning air;
Hide from their eyes that hideous form,
The ruthless angel of the storm.

I wish, for every gallant's sake,
That none may rue our royal wake: 1680
I wish what most his heart approves,
And every lady what she loves,—
Sweet be her sleep on bed of down,
And pleasing be her dreams till noon.
And when you hear the bugle's strain,   1685
I hope to see you all again."—

   Whether the Queen to fear inclined,
Or spoke to chear the minstrel's mind,
Certes, she spoke with meaning leer,
And ladies smiled her words to hear.   1690
Yet, though the dawn of morning shone,
No lady from that night-wake gone,
Not even the Queen, durst sleep alone.
And scarce had Sleep, with throb and sigh,
O'er breast of snow, and moistened eye,   1695
Outspread his shadowy canopy,
When every fervid female mind,
Or sailed with witches on the wind,
Drank, unobserved, the potent wine,
Or floated on the foamy brine.   1700
Some strove the land of thought to win,
Impelled by hope, withstood by sin;
And some with angry spirit stood
By lonely stream, or pathless wood.
And oft was heard the broken sigh,   1705
The half-formed prayer, and smothered cry;
So much the minds of old and young
Were moved by what the minstrels sung.
What Lady Gordon did or said
Could not be learned from lady's maid,   1710
And Huntley swore and shook his head.
But she and all her buskined train
Appeared not at the wake again.

END OF NIGHT THE SECOND

The Queen's Wake

Night the Third

The
Queen's Wake

NIGHT THE THIRD

THE storm had ceased to shroud the hill;
The morning's breath was pure and chill;
And when the sun rose from the main,
No eye the glory could sustain.
The icicles so dazzling bright; 5
The spreading wold so smooth and white;
The cloudless sky, the air so sheen,
That roes on Pentland's top were seen;
And Grampian mountains, frowning high,
Seemed froze amid the northern sky. 10
The frame was braced, the mind set free
To feat, or brisk hilarity.

The sun, far on his southern throne,
Glowed in stern majesty alone:
'Twas like the loved, the toilsome day, 15
That dawns on mountains west away,
When the furred Indian hunter hastes
Far up his Appalachian wastes,
To range the savage haunts, and dare
In his dark home the sullen bear. 20
And ere that noonday-sun had shone
Right on the banks of Duddingston,
Heavens! what a scene of noise and glee,
And busy brisk anxiety!
There age and youth their pastime take 25
On the smooth ice that chained the lake.
The Highland chief, the Border knight,
In waving plumes, and baldricks bright,
Join in the bloodless friendly war,
The sounding-stone to hurl afar. 30
The hair-breadth aim, the plaudits due,
The rap, the shout, the ardour grew,
Till drowsy day her curtain drew.

The youth, on cramps of polished steel,
Joined in the race, the curve, the wheel;   35
With arms outstretched, and foot aside,
Like lightning o'er the lake they glide;
And eastward far their impulse keep,
Like angels journeying o'er the deep.

When night her spangled flag unfurled   40
Wide o'er a wan and sheeted world,
In keen debate homeward they hie,
For well they knew the wake was nigh.

By mountain sheer, and column tall,
How solemn was that evening fall!   45
The air was calm, the stars were bright,
The hoar frost flightered down the night;
But oft the list'ning groups stood still,
For spirits talked along the hill.
The fairy tribes had gone to won   50
In southland climes beneath the sun;
By shady woods, and waters sheen,
And vales of everlasting green,
To sing of Scotia's woodlands wild,
Where human face had never smiled.   55
The ghost had left the haunted yew,
The wayward bogle fled the clough,
The darksome pool of crisp and foam
Was now no more the kelpie's home:
But polar spirits sure had spread   60
O'er hills which native fays had fled;
For all along from cliff and tree,
On Arthur's hill, and Salisbury,
Came voices floating down the air
From viewless shades that lingered there: 65
The words were fraught with mystery;
Voices of men they could not be.
Youths turned their faces to the sky,
With beating heart, and bended eye;
Old chieftains walked with hastened tread,   70
Loath that their hearts should bow to dread.
They feared the spirits of the hill
To sinful Scotland boded ill.

Orion up his baldrick drew,
The evening star was still in view, 75
Scarce had the Pleiades cleared the main,
Or Charles reyoked his golden wain,
When from the palace turrets rang
The bugle's note with warning clang;
Each tower, each spire, in music spake, 80
"Haste, nobles, to Queen Mary's wake."
The blooming maid ran to bedight,
In spangled lace, and robe of white,
That graceful emblem of her youth,
Of guileless heart, and maiden truth. 85
The matron decked her candid frame
In moony broach, and silk of flame;
And every Earl and Baron bold
Sparkled in clasp and loop of gold.
'Twas the last night of hope and fear, 90
That bards could sing, or Sovereign hear;
And just ere rose the Christmas sun,
The envied prize was lost and won.

The bard that night who foremost came
Was not enrolled, nor known his name; 95
A youth he was of manly mold,
Gentle as lamb, as lion bold;
But his fair face, and forehead high,
Glowed with intrusive modesty.

'Twas said by bank of southland stream 100
Glided his youth in soothing dream;
The harp he loved, and wont to stray
Far to the wilds and woods away,
And sing to brooks that gurgled bye
Of maiden's form and maiden's eye; 105
That, when this dream of youth was past,
Deep in the shade his harp he cast;
In busy life his cares beguiled,
His heart was true, and fortune smiled.
But when the royal wake began, 110
Joyful he came the foremost man,
To see the matchless bard approved,
And list the strains he once had loved.

Two nights had passed—the bards had sung,—
Queen Mary's harp from ceiling hung,   115
On which was graved her lovely mold,
Beset with crowns and flowers of gold;
And many a gem of dazzling dye
Glowed on that prize to minstrel's eye.

The youth had heard each minstrel's strain,   120
And, fearing northern bard would gain,
To try his youthful skill was moved,
Not for himself, but friends he loved.

Mary Scott

THE FOURTEENTH BARD'S SONG

Lord Pringle's steed neighs in the stall,
    His panoply is irksome grown,   125
His plumed helm hangs in the hall,
    His broad claymore is berry brown.

No more his bugle's evening peal
    Bids vassal arm and yeoman ride,
To drive the deer of Otterdale,   130
    Or foray on the Border side.

Instead of whoop and battle knell,
    Of warrior's song, and revel free,
Is heard the lute's alluring swell
    Within the halls of Torwoodlee.   135

Sick lies his heart without relief;
    Tis love that breeds the warrior's woe,
For daughter of a froward chief,
    A freebooter, his mortal foe.

But O, that maiden's form of grace,   140
    And eye of love, to him were dear!
The smile that dimpled on her face
    Was deadlier than the Border spear.

That form was not the poplar's stem,
   That smile the dawning's purple line;   145
Nor was that eye the dazzling gem
   That glows adown the Indian mine.

But would you praise the poplar pale,
   Or morn in wreath of roses drest;
The fairest flower that woos the vale,   150
   Or down that clothes the solan's breast;

A thousand times beyond, above,
   What rapt enthusiast ever saw;
Compare them to that mould of love,–
   Young Mary Scott of Tushilaw!   155

The war-flame glows on Ettrick pen,
   Bounds forth the foray swift as wind,
And Tushilaw and all his men
   Have left their homes afar behind.

O lady, lady, learn thy creed,   160
   And mark the watch-dog's boist'rous din!
The abbot comes with book and bead,
   O haste and let the father in!

And, lady, mark his locks so gray,
   His beard so long, and colour wan;   165
O he has mourned for many a day,
   And sorrowed o'er the sins of man!

And yet so stately is his mien,
   His step so firm, and breast so bold;
His brawny leg and form I ween   170
   Are wonderous for a man so old.

Short was his greeting, short and low,
   His blessing short as prayer could be;
But oft he sighed, and boded woe,
   And spoke of sin and misery.   175

To shrift, to shrift, now ladies all,
   Your prayers and Ave Marias learn;

Haste, trembling, to the vesper hall,
 For ah! the priest is dark and stern.

Short was the task of lady old,   180
 Short as confession well could be;
The abbot's orisons were cold,
 His absolutions frank and free.

Go, Mary Scott, thy spirit meek
 Lay open to the searcher's eye;   185
And let the tear bedew thy cheek,
 Thy sins are of a crimson dye.

For many a lover thou hast slain,
 And many yet lies sick for thee,—
Young Gilmanscleuch and Deloraine,   190
 And Pringle, lord of Torwoodlee.

Tell every wish thy bosom near,
 No other sin, dear maid, hast thou;
And well the abbot loves to hear
 Thy plights of love and simple vow.   195

"Why stays my Mary Scott so long?
 What guilt can youth and beauty wail?
Of fervent thought, and passion strong,
 Heavens! what a sickening tedious tale!"

O lady cease; the maiden's mind,   200
 Though pure as morning's cloudless beam,
A crime in every wish can find,
 In noontide glance, and midnight dream.

To woman's heart when fair and free,
 Her sins seem great and manifold;   205
When sunk in guilt and misery,
 No crime can then her soul behold.

'Tis sweet to see the opening flower
 Spread its fair bosom to the sun;
'Tis sweet to hear in vernal bower   210
 The thrush's earliest hymn begun:

But sweeter far the prayer that wrings
   The tear from maiden's beaming eye;
And sweeter far the hymn she sings
   In grateful holy ecstacy.   215

The mass was said, but cold and dry
   That mass to heaven the father sent;
With book, and bead, and rosary,
   The abbot to his chamber went.

The watch-dog rests with folded eye   220
   Beneath the portal's gray festoon;
The wildered Ettrick wanders bye,
   Loud murmuring to the careless moon.

The warder lists with hope and dread
   Far distant shout of fray begun;   225
The cricket tunes his tiny reed,
   And harps behind the embers dun.

Why does the warder bend his head,
   And silent stand the casement near?
The cricket stops his little reed,   230
   The sound of gentle step to hear.

O many a wight from Border brake
   Has reaved the drowsy warden round;
And many a daughter lain awake,
   When parents trowed them sleeping sound.   235

The abbot's bed is well down spread,
   The abbot's bed is soft and fair,
The abbot's bed is cold as lead—
   For why—the abbot is not there.

Was that the blast of bugle, borne   240
   Far on the night-wind, wavering shrill?
'Tis nothing but the shepherd's horn
   That keeps the watch on Cacra hill.

What means the warder's answering note?
   The moon is west, 'tis near the day;   245

I thought I heard the warriors shout,
    'Tis time the abbot were away!

The bittern mounts the morning air,
    And rings the sky with quavering croon;
The watch-dog sallies from his lair,   250
    And bays the wind and setting moon.

'Tis not the breeze, nor bittern's wail,
    Has rouzed the guarder from his den;
Along the bank, in belt and mail,
    Comes Tushilaw and all his men.   255

The abbot, from his casement, saw
    The Forest chieftain's proud array;
He heard the voice of Tushilaw—
    The abbot's heart grew cold as clay!

"Haste, maidens, call my lady fair,   260
    That room may for my warriors be;
And bid my daughter come and share
    The cup of joy with them and me.

Say we have fought and won the fray,
    Have lowered our haughty foeman's pride;   265
And we have driven the richest prey
    That ever lowed by Ettrick side."

To hear a tale of vanquished foes
    His lady came right cheerfully;
And Mary Scott, like morning rose,   270
    Stood blushing at her father's knee.

Fast flowed the warrior's ruthless tale,
    And ay the red cup past between;
But Mary Scott grew lily pale,
    And trembled like the aspin green.   275

"Now lady give me welcome cheer,
    Queen of the Border thou shalt be;
For I have brought thee gold and gear,
    And humbled haughty Torwoodlee.

I beat his yeomen in the glen,   280
   I loosed his horses from the stall,
I slew the blood-hound in his den,
   And sought the chief through tower and hall.

'Tis said in hamlet mean and dark
   Nightly he lies with leman dear;   285
O, I would give ten thousand mark,
   To see his head upon my spear!

Go, maidens, every mat be spread
   On heather, haum, or roegrass heap,
And make for me the scarlet bed,   290
   For I have need of rest and sleep."

"Nay, my good lord, make other choice,
   In that you cannot rest to day;
For there in peaceful slumber lies
   A holy abbot, old and gray."   295

The chieftain's cheek to crimson grew,
   Dropt from his hand the rosy wine—
"An abbot! curse the canting crew!
   An abbot sleep in couch of mine!

Now, lady, as my soul shall thrive,   300
   I'd rather trust my child and thee,
With my two greatest foes alive,
   The king of Scots and Torwoodlee.

The lazy hoard of Melrose vale
   Has brought my life, my all to stake: 305
O, lady! I have heard a tale,
   The thought o't makes my heart to ache!

Go, warriors, hale the villain forth,
   Bring not his loathful form to me;
The gate stands open to the north,   310
   The rope hangs o'er the gallows tree.

There shall the burning breeze of noon
   Rock the old sensual sluggard blind;

There let him swing, till sun and moon
    Have three times left the world behind."   315

O abbot, abbot, say thy prayers,
    With orisons load every breath;
The Forest trooper's on the stairs,
    To drag thee to a shameful death.

O abbot, abbot, quit thy bed,   320
    Ill armed art thou to meet the strife;
Haste, don thy beard, and quoif thy head,
    And guard the door for death or life.

Thy arm is firm, thy heart is stout,
    Yet thou canst neither fight nor flee;   325
But beauty stands thy guard without,
    Yes, beauty weeps and pleads for thee.

Proud, ruthless man, by vengeance driven,
    Regardless hears a brother plead;
Regardless sees the brand of heaven   330
    Red quivering o'er his guilty head:

But once let woman's soothing tongue
    Implore his help or clemency,
Around him let her arms be flung,
    Or at his feet her bended knee;   335

The world's a shadow! vengeance sleeps!
    The child of reason stands revealed—
When beauty pleads, when woman weeps,
    He is not man who scorns to yield.

Stern Tushilaw is gone to sleep,   340
    Laughing at woman's dread of sin;
But first he bade his warriors keep
    All robbers out, and abbots in.

The abbot from his casement high
    Looked out to see the peep of day;   345
The scene that met the abbot's eye
    Filled him with wonder and dismay.

'Twas not the dews of dawning mild,
    The mountain's hues of silver gray,
Nor yet the Ettrick's windings wild,   350
    By belted holm and bosky brae;

Nor moorland Rankleburn, that raved
    By covert, clough, and greenwood shaw;
Nor dappled flag of day, that waved
    In streamers pale from Gilmans-law: 355

But many a doubted ox there lay
    At rest upon the castle lea;
And there he saw his gallant gray,
    And all the steeds of Torwoodlee.

"Beshrew the wont!" the abbot said,   360
    "The charge runs high for lodging here;
The guard is deep, the path way-laid,
    My homilies shall cost me dear.

Come well, come woe, with dauntless core
    I'll kneel, and con my breviary;   365
If Tushilaw is versed in lore,
    'Twill be an awkward game with me."

Now Tushilaw he waked and slept,
    And dreamed and thought till noontide hour;
But ay this query upmost kept,   370
    "What seeks the abbot in my tower?"

Stern Tushilaw came down the stair
    With doubtful and indignant eye,
And found the holy man at prayer,
    With book, and cross, and rosary.   375

"To book, to book, thou reaver red,
    Of absolution thou hast need;
The sword of heaven hangs o'er thy head,
    Death is thy doom, and hell thy meed!"

"I'll take my chance, thou priest of sin,   380
    Thy absolutions I disdain;

But I will noose thy bearded chin,
  If thus thou talkest to me again.

Declare thy business, and thy name,
  Or short the route to thee is given?"–   385
"The abbot I of Coldinghame,
  My errand is the cause of heaven."–

"That shalt thou prove ere we two part;
  Some robber thou, or royal spy:
But, villain, I will search thy heart,   390
  And chain thee in the deep to lie!

"Hence with thy rubbish, hest and ban,
  Whinyards to keep the weak in awe;
The scorn of heaven, the shame of man–
  No books nor beads for Tushilaw!"–   395

"Oh! lost to mercy, faith, and love!
  Thy bolts and chains are nought to me;
I'll call an angel from above,
  That soon will set the pris'ner free."–

Bold Tushilaw, o'er strone and steep,   400
  Pursues the roe and dusky deer;
The abbot lies in dungeon deep,
  The maidens wail, the matrons fear.

The sweetest flower on Ettrick shaw
  Bends its fair form o'er grated keep;   405
Young Mary Scott of Tushilaw
  Sleeps but to sigh, and wakes to weep.

Bold Tushilaw, with horn and hound,
  Pursues the deer o'er holt and lea;
And rides and rules the Border round,   410
  From Philiphaugh to Gilnockye.

His page rode down by Melrose fair,
  His page rode down by Coldinghame;
But not a priest was missing there,
  Nor abbot, friar, nor monk of name.   415

The evening came; it was the last
  The abbot in this world should see;
The bonds are firm, the bolts are fast,
  No angel comes to set him free.

Yes, at the stillest hour of night   420
  Softly unfolds the iron door;
Beamed through the gloom unwonted light,
  That light a beauteous angel bore.

Fair was the form that o'er him hung,
  And fair the hands that set him free;   425
The trembling whispers of her tongue
  Softer than seraph's melody.

The abbot's soul was all on flame,
  Wild transport through his bosom ran;
For never angel's airy frame   430
  Was half so sweet to mortal man!

Why walks young Mary Scott so late,
  In veil and cloak of cramasye?
The porter opens wide the gate,
  His bonnet moves, and bends his knee.   435

Long may the wondering porter wait,
  Before the lady form return;
"Speed, abbot speed, nor halt nor bate,
  Nor look thou back to Rankleburn!"

The day arrives, the ladies plead   440
  In vain for yon mysterious wight;
For Tushilaw his doom decreed,
  Were he an abbot, lord, or knight.

The chieftain called his warriors stout,
  And ranged them round the gallows tree,   445
Then bade them bring the abbot out,
  The fate of fraud that all might see.

The men return of sense bereft,
  Faulter their tongues, their eye-balls glare;

The door was locked, the fetters left—   450
  All close! the abbot was not there!

The wondering warriors bow to God,
  And matins to the Virgin hum;
But Tushilaw he gloomed and strode,
  And walked into the castle dumb.   455

But to the Virgin's sacred name
  The vow was paid in many a cell;
And many a rich oblation came,
  For that amazing miracle.

Lord Pringle walked his glens alone,   460
  Nor flock nor lowing herd he saw;
But even the king upon the throne
  Quaked at the name of Tushilaw.

Lord Pringle's heart was all on flame,
  Nor peace nor joy his bosom knew;   465
'Twas for the kindest, sweetest dame,
  That ever brushed the Forest dew.

Gone is one month with smile and sigh,
  With dream by night and wish by day;
A second came with moistened eye;   470
  Another came and past away.

Why is the flower of yonder pile
  Bending its stem to court decay,
And Mary Scott's benignant smile
  Like sun-beam in a winter day?   475

Sometimes her colour's like the rose,
  Sometimes 'tis like the lily pale;
The flower that in the forest grows
  Is fallen before the summer gale.

A mother's fostering breast is warm,   480
  And dark her doubts of love I ween;
For why—she felt its early harm—
  A mother's eye is sharp and keen!

'Tis done! the woman stands revealed!
　　Stern Tushilaw is waked to see;   485
The bearded priest so well concealed,
　　Was Pringle, lord of Torwoodlee!

Oh never was the thunder's jar,
　　The red tornado's wasting wing,
Nor all the elemental war,   490
　　Like fury of the Border king.

He laughed aloud—his faulchion eyed—
　　A laugh of burning vengeance borne!—
"Does thus the coward trow," he cried,
　　"To hold his conqueror's power to scorn!   495

Thinks Tushilaw of maids or wives,
　　Or such a thing as Torwoodlee!
Had Mary Scott a thousand lives,
　　These lives were all too few for me!

Ere midnight, in the secret cave,   500
　　This sword shall pierce her bosom's core,
Though I go childless to my grave,
　　And rue the deed for evermore!

O had I lulled the imp to rest
　　When first she lisped her name to me,   505
Or pierced her little guileless breast
　　When smiling on her nurse's knee!"

"Just is your vengeance, my good lord,
　　'Tis just and right our daughter die;
Far sharper than a foeman's sword   510
　　Is family shame and injury.

But trust the ruthless deed to me;
　　I have a vial potent good;
Unmeet that all the Scotts should see
　　A daughter's corse embalmed in blood!   515

Unmeet her gallant kinsmen know
　　The guilt of one so fair and young;

No cup should to her mem'ry flow,
　　No requiem o'er her grave be sung.

My potent draught has erst proved true   520
　　Beneath my own and husband's eye;
Trust me, ere falls the morning dew,
　　In dreamless sleep shall Mary lie!"–

"Even go thy way, thy words are true,
　　I knew thy dauntless soul before;   525
But list–if thou deceivest me too,
　　Thou hast a head! I say no more."–

Stern Tushilaw strode o'er the ley,
　　And, wondering, by the twilight saw
A crystal tear drop from his eye,   530
　　The first e'er shed by Tushilaw!

O grievous are the bonds of steel,
　　And blasted hope 'tis hard to prove;
More grievous far it is to feel
　　Ingratitude from those we love.   535

"What brings my lady mother here,
　　Pale as the morning shower and cold?
In her dark eye why stands the tear?
　　Why in her hand a cup of gold?"–

"My Mary, thou art ill at rest,   540
　　Fervid and feverish is thy blood;
Still yearns o'er thee thy mother's breast,
　　Take this, my child, 'tis for thy good!"–

O sad, sad was young Mary's plight!
　　She took the cup–no word she spake: 545
She had even wished that very night
　　To sleep, and never more to wake.

She took the cup–she drank it dry,
　　Then pillowed soft her beauteous head,
And calmly watched her mother's eye;   550
　　But O that eye was hard to read!

Her moistened eyes, so mild and meek,
   Soon sunk their auburn fringe beneath;
The ringlets on her damask cheek
   Heaved gentler with her stealing breath!   555

She turned her face unto the wall,
   Her colour changed to pallid clay;
Long ere the dews began to fall,
   The flower of Ettrick lifeless lay!

Why underneath her winding sheet   560
   Does broidered silk her form enfold?
Why is cold Mary's buskined feet
   All laced with belts and bands of gold?

"What boots to me these robes so gay?
   To wear them now no child have I!   565
They should have graced her bridal day,
   Now they must in the church-yard lie!

I thought to see my daughter ride,
   In golden gear and cramasye,
To Mary's fane, the loveliest bride   570
   Ere to the Virgin bent the knee.

Now I may by her funeral wain
   Ride silent o'er the mountain gray:
Her revel hall, the gloomy fane;
   Her bridal bed, the cheerless clay!"–   575

Why that rich snood with plume and lace
   Round Mary's lifeless temples drawn?
Why is the napkin o'er her face,
   A fragment of the lily lawn?

"My Mary has another home;   580
   And far, far though her journey be,
When she to Paradise shall come,
   Then will my child remember me!"

O many a flower was round her spread,
   And many a pearl and diamond bright,   585

And many a window round her head
  Shed on her form a bootless light!

Lord Pringle sat on Maygill brae,
  Pondering on war and vengeance meet;
The Cadan toiled in narrow way,   590
  The Tweed rolled far beneath his feet.

Not Tweed, by gulf and whirlpool mazed,
  Through dark wood-glen, by him was seen;
For still his thought-set eye was raised
  To Ettrick mountains, wild and green.   595

Sullen he sat, unstaid, unblest,
  He thought of battle, broil, and blood;
He never crossed, he never wist
  Till by his side a Palmer stood.

"Haste, my good lord, this letter read,   600
  Ill bodes it listless thus to be;
Upon a die I've set my head,
  And brought this letter far to thee."—

Lord Pringle looked the letter on,
  His face grew pale as winter sky;   605
But, ere the half of it was done,
  The tear of joy stood in his eye.

A purse he to the Palmer threw,
  Mounted the cleft of aged tree,
Three times aloud his bugle blew,   610
  And hasted home to Torwoodlee.

'Twas scarcely past the hour of noon
  When first the foray whoop began;
And, in the wan light of the moon,
  Through March and Teviotdale it ran.   615

Far to the south it spread away,
  Startled the hind by fold and tree;
And ay the watchword of the fray
  Was, "Ride for Ker and Torwoodlee!"

When next the day began to fade,   620
   The warriors round their chieftains range;
And many a solemn vow they made,
   And many an oath of fell revenge.

The Pringles' plumes indignant dance—
   It was a gallant sight to see;   625
And many a Ker, with sword and lance,
   Stood rank and file on Torwoodlee.

As they fared up yon craigy glen,
   Where Tweed sweeps round the Thorny-hill,
Old Gideon Murray and his men   630
   The foray joined with right good will.

They hasted up by Plora side,
   And north above Mount-Benger turn,
And loathly forced with them to ride
   Black Douglas of the Craigy-burn.   635

When they came nigh Saint Mary's lake
   The day-sky glimmered on the dew;
They hid their horses in the brake,
   And lurked in heath and braken clough.

The lake one purple valley lay,   640
   Where tints of glowing light were seen;
The ganza waved his cuneal way,
   With yellow oar, and quoif of green.

The dark cock bayed above the coomb,
   Throned mid the wavy fringe of gold,   645
Unwreathed from dawning's fairy loom,
   In many a soft vermilion fold.

The tiny skiffs of silver mist
   Lingered along the slumbering vale;
Belled the gray stag with fervid breast   650
   High on the moors of Meggat-dale.

There hid in clough and hollow den,
   Gazing around the still sublime,

There lay Lord Pringle and his men
    On beds of heath, and moorland thyme.   655

That morning found rough Tushilaw
    In all the father's guise appear;
An end of all his hopes he saw
    Shrouded in Mary's gilded bier.

No eye could trace without concern   660
    The suffering warrior's troubled look;
The throbs that heaved his bosom stern,
    No ear could bear, no heart could brook.

"Woe be to thee, thou wicked dame!
    My Mary's prayers and accents mild   665
Might well have rendered vengeance lame—
    This hand could ne'er have slain my child!

But thou, in frenzied fatal hour,
    Reft the sweet life thou gavest away,
And crushed to earth the fairest flower   670
    That ever breathed the breeze of day.

My all is lost, my hope is fled,
    The sword shall ne'er be drawn for me;
Unblest, unhonoured my gray head—
    My child! would I had died for thee!"—   675

The bell tolls o'er a new made grave;
    The lengthened funeral train is seen
Stemming the Yarrow's silver wave,
    And darkening Dryhope holms so green.

When nigh the virgin's fane they drew,   680
    Just by the verge of holy ground,
The Kers and Pringles left the clough,
    And hemmed the wondering Scotts around.

Vassal and peasant seized with dread,
    Sped off, and looked not once behind;   685
And all who came for wine and bread,
    Fled like the chaff before the wind.

But all the Scotts together flew,–
   For every Scott of name was there,–
In sullen mood their weapons drew, 690
   And back to back for fight prepare.

Rough was the onset–boast, nor threat,
   Nor word, was heard from friend or foe;
At once began the work of fate,
   With perilous thrust, and deadly blow. 695

O but the Harden lads were true,
   And bore them bravely in the broil!
The doughty laird of wild Buccleugh
   Raged like a lion in the toil.

Young Raeburn tilted gallantly; 700
   But Ralph of Gilmanscleuch was slain,
Philip and Hugh of Baillilee,
   And William laird of Deloraine.

But Francis, Lord of Thirlestane,
   To all the gallant name a soil, 705
While blood of kinsmen fell like rain,
   Crept underneath a braken coil.

Old Tushilaw, with sword in hand,
   And heart to fiercest woes a prey,
Seemed courting every foeman's brand, 710
   And fought in hottest of the fray.

In vain the gallant kinsmen stood
   Wedged in a firm and bristled ring;
Their funeral weeds are bathed in blood,
   No corslets round their bosoms cling. 715

Against the lance and helmed file
   Their courage, might, and skill were vain;
Short was the conflict, short the while
   Ere all the Scotts were bound or slain.

When first the hostile band upsprung, 720
   The body in the church was laid,

Where vows were made, and requiems sung,
    By matron, monk, and weeping maid.

Lord Pringle came—before his eye
    The monks and maidens kneeled in fear;   725
But Lady Tushilaw stood bye,
    And pointed to her Mary's bier!

"Thou lord of guile, and malice keen,
    What boots this doleful work to thee!
Could Scotland such a pair have seen   730
    As Mary Scott and Torwoodlee?"—

Lord Pringle came, no word he spake,
    Nor owned the pangs his bosom knew;
But his full heart was like to break
    In every throb his bosom drew.   735

"O I had weened with fondest heart—
    Woe to the guileful friend who lied!—
This day should join us ne'er to part,
    This day that I should win my bride!

But I will see that face so meek,   740
    Cold, pale, and lifeless though it be;
And I will kiss that comely cheek,
    Once sweeter than the rose to me."—

With trembling hand he raised the lid,
    Sweet was the perfume round that flew;   745
For there were strewed the roses red,
    And every flower the Forest knew.

He drew the fair lawn from her face,
    'Twas decked with many a costly wreath;
And still it wore a soothing grace   750
    Even in the chill abodes of death.

And ay he prest the cheek so white,
    And ay he kissed the lips beloved,
Till pitying maidens wept outright,
    And even the frigid monks were moved.   755

Why starts Lord Pringle to his knee?
Why bend his eyes with watchful strain?
The maidens shriek his mien to see;
The startled priests inquire in vain!

Was that a sob, an earthly sigh,   760
That heaved the flowers so lightly shed?
'Twas but the wind that wandered bye,
And kissed the bosom of the dead!

Are these the glowing tints of life
O'er Mary's cheek that come and fly?   765
Ah, no! the red flowers round are rife,
The rosebud flings its softened dye.

Why grows the gazer's sight so dim?
Stay, dear illusion, still beguile!
Thou art worth crowns and worlds to him—   770
Last, dear illusion, last a while!

Short was thy sway, frenzied and short,
For ever fell the veil on thee;
Thy startling form of fears the sport,
Vanished in sweet reality!   775

'Tis past! and darkly stands revealed
A mother's cares and purpose deep:
That kiss, the last adieu that sealed,
Waked Mary from her death-like sleep!

Slowly she raised her form of grace,   780
Her eyes no ray conceptive flung;
And O, her mild, her languid face,
Was like a flower too early sprung!

"O I lie sick and weary here,
My heart is bound in moveless chain;   785
Another cup, my mother dear,
I cannot sleep though I would fain!"—

She drank the wine with calm delay,
She drank the wine with pause and sigh:

Slowly, as wakes the dawning day,   790
  Dawned long lost thought in Mary's eye.

She looked at pall, she looked at bier,
  At altar, shrine, and rosary;
She saw her lady mother near,
  And at her side brave Torwoodlee!   795

'Twas all a dream, nor boded good,
  A phantom of the fevered brain!
She laid her down in moaning mood,
  To soothe her woes in sleep again.

Needs not to paint that joyful hour,   800
  The nuptial vow, the bridal glee,
How Mary Scott, the Forest flower,
  Was borne a bride to Torwoodlee.

Needs not to say, how warriors prayed
  When Mary glided from the dome;   805
They thought the Virgin's holy shade
  In likeness of the dead had come.

Diamond and ruby rayed her waist,
  And twinkled round her brow so fair;
She wore more gold upon her breast   810
  Than would have bought the hills of Yair.

A foot so light, a form so meet,
  Ne'er trode Saint Mary's lonely lea;
A bride so gay, a face so sweet,
  The Yarrow braes shall never see.   815

Old Tushilaw deigned not to smile,
  No grateful word his tongue could say,
He took one kiss, blest her the while,
  Wiped his dark eye, and turned away.

The Scotts were freed, and peace restored;   820
  Each Scott, each Ker, each Pringle swore,
Swore by his name, and by his sword,
  To be firm friends for evermore.

Lord Pringle's hills were stocked anew,
   Drove after drove came nightly free;   825
But many a Border baron knew
   Whence came the dower to Torwoodlee.

———————

   Scarce had the closing measure rung,
When from the ring the minstrel sprung,
And his gilt harp, of flowery frame,   830
Left ready for the next that came.
Loud were the plaudits,—all the fair
Their eyes turned to the royal chair:
They looked again,—no bard was there!
But whisper, smile, and question ran,   835
Around the ring anent the man;
While all the nobles of the south
Lauded the generous stranger youth.

   The next was bred on southern shore,
Beneath the mists of Lammermore;   840
And long, by Nith and crystal Tweed,
Had taught the Border youth to read.
The strains of Greece, the bard of Troy,
Were all his theme, and all his joy.

   Well toned his voice of wars to sing;   845
His hair was dark as raven's wing;
His eye an intellectual lance,
No heart could bear its searching glance:
But every bard to him was dear;
His heart was kind, his soul sincere.   850

   When first of royal wake he heard,
Forthwith it chained his sole regard:
It was his thought, his hourly theme,
His morning prayer, his midnight dream.
Knights, dames, and squires of each degree,   855
He deemed as fond of songs as he,
And talked of them continually.
But when he heard the Highland strain,

Scarce could his breast his soul contain;
'Twas all unequalled, and would make   860
Immortal bards! immortal wake!
About Dunedin streets he ran,
Each knight he met, each maid, each man,
In field, in alley, tower, or hall,
The wake was first, the wake was all.   865

Alike to him the south or north,
So high he held the minstrel worth,
So high his ardent mind was wrought,
Once of himself he scarcely thought.
Dear to his heart the strain sublime,   870
The strain admired in ancient time;
And, of his minstrel honours proud,
He strung his harp too high, too loud.

King Edward's Dream

THE FIFTEENTH BARD'S SONG

The heath-cock had whirred at the break of the morn,
The moon of her tassels of silver was shorn,   875
When hoary king Edward lay tossing in ire,
His blood in a ferment, his bosom on fire;
His battle files, stretched o'er the valley, were still
As Eden's pine forests that darkened the hill.

He slept—but his visions were loathly and grim: 880
How quivered his lip! and how quaked every limb!
His dull moving eye showed how troubled his rest,
And deep were the throbs of his labouring breast.

He saw the Scot's banner red streaming on high;
The fierce Scottish warriors determined and nigh;   885
Their columns of steel, and bright gleaming before,
The lance, the broad target, and Highland claymore.
And, lo! at their head, in stern glory appeared,
That hero of heroes so hated and feared;
'Twas the exile of Rachrin that led the array,   890

And Wallace's spirit was pointing the way:
His eye was a torch, beaming ruin and wrath,
And graved on his helmet was—*Vengeance or Death!*

   In far Ethiopia's desert domain,
Where whirlwinds new mountains up-pile on the plain,   895
Their crested brown billows, fierce curling on high,
O'ershadow the sun, and are tossed to the sky;
But, meeting each other, they burst and recoil,
Mix, thunder, and sink, with a reeling turmoil:
As dreadful the onset that Edward beheld,   900
As fast his brave legions were heaped on the field.

   The plaided blue Highlander, swift as the wind,
Spread terror before him, and ruin behind.
Thick clouds of blood-vapour brood over the slain,
And Pembroke and Howard are stretched on the plain.   905

   The chieftain he hated, all covered with blood,
Still nearer and nearer approached where he stood;
He could not retreat, and no succour was near—
"Die, scorpion!" he cried, and pursued his career.
The king felt the iron retreat from the wound,   910
No hand to uphold him, he sunk on the ground:
His spirit escaped on the wings of the wind,
Left terror, confusion, and carnage behind,
Till on the green Pentland he thought he sat lone,
And pondered on troubles and times that were gone.   915

   He looked over meadow, broad river, and downe,
From Ochel's fair mountains to Lammermore brown;
He still found his heart and desires were the same;
He wished to leave Scotland nor sceptre nor name.

   He thought, as he lay on the green mountain thyme,   920
A spirit approached him in manner sublime.
At first she appeared like a streamer of light,
But still as she neared she was formed to his sight.
Her robe was the blue silken veil of the sky,
The drop of the amethyst deepened its dye;   925
Her crown was a helmet, emblazoned with pearl;
Her mantle the sunbeam, her bracelets the beryl;

Her hands and her feet like the bright burning levin;
Her face was the face of an angel from heaven:
Around her the winds and the echoes grew still,   930
And rainbows were formed in the cloud of the hill.

    Like music that floats o'er the soft heaving deep,
When twilight has lulled all the breezes asleep,
The wild fairy airs in our forests that rung,
Or hymn of the sky by a seraph when sung;   935
So sweet were the tones on his fancy that broke,
When the guardian of Scotland's proud mountains thus
        spoke:—

    "What boots, mighty Edward, thy victories won:
'Tis over; thy sand of existence is run;
Thy laurels are faded, dispersed in the blast;   940
Thy soul from the bar of Omnipotence cast,
To wander bewildered o'er mountain and plain,
O'er lands thou hast steeped with the blood of the slain.

    I heard of thy guerdon, I heard it on high:
Thou'rt doomed on those mountains to linger and lie,   945
The mark of the tempest, the sport of the wind,
The tempest of conscience, the storm of the mind,
Till people thou'st hated, and sworn to subdue,
Triumphant from bondage shall burst in thy view,
Their sceptre and liberty bravely regain,   950
And climb to renown over mountains of slain.

    I thought (and I joined my endeavours to thine,)
The time was arrived when the two should combine;
For 'tis known that they will 'mong the hosts of the sky,
And we thought that blest æra of concord was nigh.   955
But ages unborn yet shall flit on the wing,
And Scotland to England ere then give a king;
A father to monarchs, whose flourishing sway
The ocean and ends of the earth shall obey.

    See yon little hamlet o'ershadowed with smoke,   960
See yon hoary battlement throned on the rock,
Even there shall a city in splendour break forth,
The haughty Dunedin, the queen of the north;

There learning shall flourish, and liberty smile,
The awe of the world, and the pride of the isle.   965

But thy lonely spirit shall roam in dismay,
And weep o'er thy labours so soon to decay.
In yon western plain, where thy power overthrew
The bulwarks of Caledon, valiant and few;
Where beamed the red faulchion of ravage and wrath;   970
Where tyranny, horsed on the dragons of death,
Rode ruthless through blood of the honoured and just.
When Græme and brave Stuart lay bleeding in dust,
The wailings of liberty pierced the sky;
Th' Everlasting, in pity, averted his eye!   975

Even there shall the flower of thy nations combined,
Proud England, green Erin, and Normandy joined,
Exulting in numbers, and dreadful array,
Led on by Carnarvon, to Scotland away,
As thick as the snow-flakes that pour from the pole,   980
Or silver-maned waves on the ocean that roll.
A handful of heroes, all desperate driven,
Impelled by the might and the vengeance of heaven;
By them shall his legions be all overborne,
And melt from the field like the mist of the morn.   985
The Thistle shall rear her rough front to the sky,
And the Rose and the Shamrock at Carron shall die.

How couldst thou imagine those spirits of flame
Would stoop to oppression, to slavery, and shame!
Ah! never; the lion may couch to thy sway,   990
The mighty leviathan bend and obey;
But the Scots, round their king and broad banner unfurled,
Their mountains will keep against thee and the world."

King Edward awoke with a groan and a start,
The vision was vanished, but not from his heart!   995
His courage was high, but his vigour was gone;
He cursed the Scotch nation, and bade them lead on.
His legions moved on like a cloud of the west;
But fierce was the fever that boiled in his breast
On sand of the Solway they rested his bed,   1000
Where the soul of the king and the warrior fled!

He heard not the sound of the evening curfew;
But the whisper that died on his tongue, was—"subdue!"

The bard had sung so bold and high,
While patriot fire flashed from his eye,   1005
That ere King Edward won to rest,
Or sheet was spread above his breast,
The harp-strings jarred in wild mistone;
The minstrel throbbed, his voice was gone.
Upon his harp he leaned his head,   1010
And softly from the ring was led.

The next was from a western vale,
Where Nith winds slowly down the dale;
Where play the waves o'er golden grain,
Like mimic billows of the main.   1015
Of the old elm his harp was made,
That bent o'er Cluden's loneliest shade:
No gilded sculpture round her flamed,
For his own hand that harp had framed,
In stolen hours, when labour done,   1020
He strayed to view the parting sun.
O when the toy to him so fair,
Began to form beneath his care,
How danced his youthful heart with joy!
How constant grew the dear employ!   1025
The sun would chamber in the Ken;
The red star rise o'er Locherben;
The solemn moon, in sickly hue,
Waked from her eastern couch of dew,
Would half way gain the vault on high,   1030
Bathe in the Nith, slow stealing bye,
And still the bard his task would ply.

When his first notes, from covert grey,
Arrested maiden on her way;
When ceased the reaper's evening tale,   1035
And paused the shepherd of the dale,—
Bootless all higher worldly bliss,

To crown our minstrel's happiness!
What all the joys by fortune given,
To cloyless song, the gift of heaven?   1040

    That harp could make the matron stare,
Bristle the peasant's hoary hair,
Make patriot-breasts with ardour glow,
And warrior pant to meet the foe;
And long by Nith the maidens young   1045
Shall chaunt the strains their minstrel sung:
At ewe-bught, or at evening fold,
When resting on the daisied wold,
Combing their locks of waving gold,
Oft the fair group enrapt, shall name   1050
Their lost, their darling Cunninghame:
His was a song beloved in youth,—
A tale of weir—a tale of truth.

Dumlanrig

THE SIXTEENTH BARD'S SONG

Who's he stands at Dumlanrig's gate?
Who raps so loud, and raps so late?   1055
Nor warder's threat, nor porter's growl,
Question, nor watch-dog's angry howl,
He once regards, but rap and call,
Thundering alternate, shake the wall.
The captive, stretched in dungeon deep,   1060
Waked from his painful visioned sleep;
His meagre form from pavement raised,
And listened to the sounds amazed:
Both bayle and keep rang with the din,
And Douglas heard the noise within.   1065

    "Ho! rise, Dumlanrig! all's at stake!
Ho! rise, Dumlanrig! Douglas, wake!—
Blow, warder—blow thy warning shrill,
Light up the beacon on the hill,
For round thee reaves thy ruthless foe.—   1070
Arise, Dumlanrig! Douglas, ho!"

His fur-cloak round him Douglas threw,
And to the crennel eager flew.
"What news? what news? thou stalwart groom,
Who thus, in midnight's deepest gloom,   1075
Bring'st to my gate the loud alarm
Of foray wide, and country harm?
What are thy dangers? what thy fears?
Say out thy message, Douglas hears."

"Haste, Douglas! Douglas, arm with speed,   1080
And mount thy fleetest battle steed;
For Lennox, with the southern host,
Whom thou hast baulked and curbed the most,
Like locusts from the Solway blown,
Are spread upon thy mountains brown;   1085
Broke from their camp in search of prey,
They drive thy flocks and herds away;
Roused by revenge, and hunger keen,
They've swept the hills of fair Dalveen;
Nor left thee bullock, goat, or steer,   1090
On all the holms of Durisdeer.

"One troop came to my father's hall;
They burnt our tower,—they took our all.
My dear, my only sister May,
By force the ruffians bore away;   1095
Nor kid, nor lamb, bleats in the glen,
Around all lonely Locherben!

"My twenty men, I have no moe,
Eager to cross the roaming foe,
Well armed with hawberk and broad sword,   1100
Keep ward at Cample's rugged ford.
Before they bear their prey across,
Some Southrons shall their helmets lose,
If not the heads those helmets shield,
O, haste thee, Douglas, to the field!"   1105
With that his horse around he drew,
And down the path like lightning flew.

"Arm," cried the Douglas, "one and all!"
And vanished from the echoing wall.

"Arm!" was the word; along it ran   1110
Through manor, bayle, and barbican;
And clank and clatter burst at once
From every loop of hall and sconce.
With whoop of groom, and warder's call,
And prancing steeds, 'twas hurry all.   1115

   At first, like thunder's distant tone,
The rattling din came rolling on,
Echoed Dumlanrig woods around;
Louder and louder swelled the sound,
Till like the sheeted flame of wonder,   1120
That rends the shoals of heaven asunder.

   When first the word, "to arms!" was given,
Glowed all the eastern porch of heaven;
A wreathy cloud of orient brown,
Had heralded the rising moon,   1125
Whose verge was like a silver bow,
Bending o'er Ganna's lofty brow;
And ere above the mountain blue
Her wasted orb was rolled in view,
A thousand men, in armour sheen,   1130
Stood ranked upon Dumlanrig green.

   The Nith they stemmed in firm array;
For Cample-ford they bent their way.
Than Douglas and his men that night,
Never saw yeoman nobler sight;   1135
Mounted on tall curvetting steed,
He rode undaunted at their head;
His shadow on the water still,
Like giant on a moving hill.
The ghastly bull's-head scowled on high,   1140
Emblem of death to foeman's eye;
And bloody hearts on streamers pale,
Waved wildly in the midnight gale.

   O, haste thee, Douglas! haste and ride!
Thy kinsmen's corpses stem the tide!   1145
What red, what dauntless youth is he,
Who stands in Cample to the knee?

Whose arm of steel, and weapon good,
Still dyes the stream with Southern blood,
While round him fall his faithful men?   1150
'Tis Morison of Locherben.

O, haste thee, Douglas, to the fray,
Ere won be that important way!
The Southron's countless prey, within
The dreadful coils of Crighup linn,   1155
No passage from the moor can find,—
The wood below, the gulf behind:
One ford there is, and one alone,
And in that ford stands Morison.
Who passes there, or man or beast,   1160
Must make their passage o'er his breast,
And over heaps of mangled dead,
That dam red Cample from its bed.
His sister's cries his soul alarm,
And add new vigour to his arm.   1165
His twenty men are waned to ten.
O, haste to dauntless Locherben!

The Southrons, baulked, impatient turn,
And crowd once more the fatal bourn.
All desperate grew the work of death,   1170
No yielding but with yielding breath;
Even still lay every death-struck man,
For footing to the furious van.
The little band was seized with dread,
Behind their rampart of the dead: 1175
Power from their arms began to fly,
And hope within their breasts to die,
When loud they heard the cheering word
Of—"Douglas! Douglas!" cross the ford:
Then turned the Southron swift as wind,   1180
For fierce the battle raged behind.

O, stay, brave Morison! O, stay!
Guard but that pass till break of day;
Thy flocks, thy sister to retrieve,
That task to doughty Douglas leave: 1185
Let not thine ardour all betray,—
Thy might is spent—brave warrior, stay.

O, for the lyre of heaven, that rung
When Linden's lofty hymn was sung!
Or his, who from the height beheld   1190
The reeling strife of Flodden field!
Then far on wing of genius borne
Should ring the wonders of that morn:
Morn!–ah! how many a warrior bold,
That morn was never to behold!   1195
When rival rank to rank drew nigh,
When eye was fixed on foeman's eye,
When lowered was lance, and bent was bow,
And faulchion clenched to strike the blow,
No breath was heard, nor clank of mail,   1200
Each face with rage grew deadly pale.
Trembled the moon's reluctant ray;
The breeze of heaven sunk soft away.

So furious was that onset's shock,
Destruction's gates at once unlock: 1205
'Twas like the earthquake's hollow groan,
When towers and towns are overthrown:
'Twas like the river's midnight crush,
When snows dissolve, and torrents rush;
When fields of ice, in rude array,   1210
Obstruct its own resistless way:
'Twas like the whirlwind's rending sweep:
'Twas like the tempest of the deep,
Where Corrybraken's surges driven,
Meet, mount, and lash the breast of heaven.   1215

'Twas foot to foot, and brand to brand;
Oft hilt to hilt, and hand to hand;
Oft gallant foemen, woe to tell,
Dead in each other's bosoms fell!
The horsemen met with might and main,   1220
Then reeled, and wheeled, and met again.
A thousand spears on hawberks bang;
A thousand swords on helmets clang.
Where might was with the feebler blent,
Still there the line of battle bent;   1225
As oft recoiled from flank assail,
While blows fell thick as rattling hail.

Nature stood mute that fateful hour,
All save the ranks on Cample moor,
And mountain goats that left their den,   1230
And bleating fled to Garroch glen.

Dumlanrig, ay in battle keen,
The foremost in the broil was seen:
Woe to the warrior dared withstand
The progress of his deadly brand!   1235
He sat so firm, he reined so well,
Whole ranks before his charger fell.
A valiant youth kept by his side,
With crest and armour crimson-dyed;
Charged still with him the yielding foe,   1240
And seconded his every blow.
The Douglas wondered whence he came,
And asked his lineage and his name.
'Twas he who kept the narrow way,
Who raised at first the battle fray,   1245
And roused Dumlanrig and his men,–
Brave Morison of Locherben.

"My chief," he said, "forgive my fear
For one than life to me more dear;
But late I heard my sister cry,   1250
'Dumlanrig, now thy weapon ply.'
Her guard waits in yon hollow lea,
Beneath the shade of spreading tree."

Dumlanrig's eye with ardour shone;
"Follow!" he cried, and spurred him on.   1255
A close gazoon the horsemen made,
Douglas and Morison the head,
And through the ranks impetuous bore,
By dint of lance and broad claymore,
Mid shouts, and groans of parting life,   1260
For hard and doubtful was the strife.
Behind a knight, firm belted on,
They found the fair May Morison.
But why, through all Dumlanrig's train,
Search her bright eyes, and search in vain?   1265
A stranger mounts her on his steed;

Brave Morison, where art thou fled?
The drivers for their booty feared,
And, soon as Cample-ford was cleared,
To work they fell, and forced away   1270
Across the stream their mighty prey.
The bleating flocks in terror ran
Across the bloody breast of man;
Even the dull cattle gazed with dread,
And, lowing, foundered o'er the dead.   1275

   The Southrons still the fight maintain;
Though broke, they closed and fought again,
Till shouting drivers gave the word,
That all the flocks had cleared the ford;
Then to that pass the bands retire,   1280
And safely braved Dumlanrig's ire.
Rashly he tried, and tried in vain,
That steep, that fatal path to gain;
Madly prolonged th' unequal fray,
And lost his men, and lost the day.   1285
Amid the battle's fiercest shock,
Three spears were on his bosom broke,
Then forced in flight to seek remede.
Had it not been his noble steed,
That swift away his master bore,   1290
He ne'er had seen Dumlanrig more.

   The day-beam, from his moonlight sleep,
O'er Queensberry began to peep;
Kneeled drowsy on the mountain fern,
At length rose tiptoe on the cairn,   1295
Embracing, in his bosom pale,
The stars, the moon, and shadowy dale.
Then what a scene appal'd the view,
On Cample moor, as dawning grew!
Along the purple heather spread,   1300
Lay mixed the dying and the dead;
Stern foemen there from quarrel cease,
Who ne'er before had met in peace.
Two kinsmen good the Douglas lost,
And full three hundred of his host;   1305
With one by him lamented most,

The flower of all the Nithsdale men,
Young Morison of Locherben.

The Southrons did no foot pursue,
Nor seek the conflict to renew.   1310
They knew not at the rising sun
What mischief they'd to Douglas done,
But to the south pursued their way,
Glad to escape with such a prey.

Brave Douglas, where thy pride of weir?   1315
How stinted in thy bold career!
Woe, that the Lowther eagle's look
Should shrink before the Lowland rook!
Woe, that the lordly lion's paw
Of ravening wolves should sink in awe!   1320
But doubly woe, the purple heart
Should tarnished from the field depart!

Was it the loss of kinsmen dear,
Or crusted scratch of Southern spear?
Was it thy dumb, thy sullen host,   1325
Thy glory by misconduct lost?
Or thy proud bosom, swelling high,
Made the round tear roll in thine eye?
Ah! no; thy heart was doomed to prove
The sharper pang of slighted love.   1330

What vision lingers on the heath,
Flitting across the field of death?
Its gliding motion, smooth and still
As vapour on the twilight hill,
Or the last ray of falling even   1335
Shed through the parting clouds of heaven?

Is it a sprite that roams forlorn?
Or angel from the bowers of morn,
Come down a tear of heaven to shed,
In pity o'er the valiant dead?   1340
No vain, no fleeting phantom this!
No vision from the bowers of bliss!
Its radiant eye, and stately tread,

Bespeak some beauteous mountain maid;
No rose of Eden's bosom meek,   1345
Could match that maiden's moistened cheek;
No drifted wreath of morning snow,
The whiteness of her lofty brow;
Nor gem of India's purest dye,
The lustre of her eagle eye.   1350

  When beauty, Eden's bowers within,
First stretched the arm to deeds of sin;
When passion burned, and prudence slept,
The pitying angels bent and wept.
But tears more soft were never shed,   1355
No, not when angels bowed the head,
A sigh more mild did never breathe
O'er human nature whelmed in death,
Nor woe and dignity combine
In face so lovely, so benign,   1360
As Douglas saw that dismal hour,
Bent o'er a corse on Cample moor.
A lady o'er her shield, her trust,
A brave, an only brother's dust.

  What heart of man unmoved can lie,   1365
When plays the smile in beauty's eye?
Or when a form of grace and love
To music's notes can lightly move?
Yes; there are hearts unmoved can see
The smile, the ring, the revelry;   1370
But heart of warrior ne'er could bear
The beam of beauty's crystal tear.
Well was that morn the maxim proved,–
The Douglas saw, the Douglas loved.

  "O, cease thy tears, my lovely May,   1375
Sweet floweret of the banks of Ae,
His soul thou never canst recal;
He fell as warrior wont to fall.
Deep, deep the loss we both bewail:
But that deep loss to countervail,   .   1380
Far as the day-flight of the hern,
From Locherben to green Glencairn,

From where the Shinnel torrents pour
To the lone vales of Crawford-moor,
The fairy links of Tweed and Lyne,   1385
All, all the Douglas has, is thine,
And Douglas too; whate'er betide,
Straight thou shalt be Dumlanrig's bride."

"What! mighty chief, a bride to thee!
No, by yon heaven's High Majesty,   1390
Sooner I'll beg, forlorn and poor,
Bent at thy meanest vassal's door,
Than look thy splendid halls within,
Thou deer wrapt in a lion's skin.

"Here lies the kindest, bravest man;   1395
There lie thy kinsmen, pale and wan;
What boots thy boasted mountains green?
Nor flock, nor herd, can there be seen;
All driven before thy vaunting foe
To ruthless slaughter, bleat and low,   1400
Whilst thou,–shame on thy dastard head!–
A wooing com'st amidst the dead.

"O, that this feeble maiden hand
Could bend the bow, or wield the brand!
If yeomen mustered in my hall,   1405
Or trooped obsequious at my call,
My country's honour I'd restore,
And shame thy face for evermore.
Go, first thy flocks and herds regain;
Revenge thy friends in battle slain;   1410
Thy wounded honour heal; that done,
Douglas may ask May Morison."

Dumlanrig's blood to's bosom rushed,
His manly cheek like crimson blushed.
He called three yeomen to his side: 1415
"Haste, gallant warriors, haste and ride,
Warn Lindsay on the banks of Daur,
The fierce M'Turk and Lochinvaur:
Tell them that Lennox flies amain;
That Maxwell and Glencairn are ta'en;   1420

Kilpatrick with the spoiler rides;
The Johnston flies, and Jardine hides:
That I alone am left to fight,
For country's cause and sovereign's right.
My friends are fallen,—my warriors toiled,— 1425
My towns are burnt,—my vassals spoiled:
Yet say—before to-morrow's sun
With amber tips the mountain dun,
Either that host of ruthless thieves
I'll scatter like the forest leaves, 1430
Or my wrung heart shall cease to play,
And my right hand the sword to sway.
At Blackwood I'll their coming bide:
Haste, gallant warriors, haste and ride."

He spoke:—each yeoman bent his eye, 1435
And forward stooped in act to fly;
No plea was urged, no short demur;
Each heel was turned to strike the spur.

As ever ye saw the red deer's brood,
From covert sprung, traverse the wood; 1440
Or heath-fowl beat the mountain wind,
And leave the fowler fixt behind;
As ever ye saw three arrows spring
At once from yew-bow's twanging string,—
So flew the messengers of death, 1445
And lessening, vanished on the heath.

The Douglas bade his troops with speed
Prepare due honours for the dead,
And meet well armed at evening still
On the green cone of Blackford-hill. 1450
There came M'Turk to aid the war,
With troops from Shinnel glens and Scaur;
Fierce Gordon with the clans of Ken,
And Lindsay with his Crawford men;
Old Morton, too, forlorn and gray, 1455
Whose son had fallen at break of day.

If troops on earth may e'er withstand
An onset made by Scottish brand,

Then lawless rapine sways the throng,
And conscience whispers—"this is wrong:"   1460
But should a foe, whate'er his might,
To Scotia's dust dispute our right,
Or dare on native mountain claim
The poorest atom boasts our name,
Though high that warrior's banners soar,   1465
Let him beware the broad claymore.

Scotland! thy honours long have stood,
Though rudely cropt, though rolled in blood,
Yet, bathed in warm and purple dew,
More glorious o'er the ruin grew.   1470
Long flourish thy paternal line;
Arabia's lineage stoops to thine.

Dumlanrig found his foes secure,
Stretched on the ridge of Locher-moor.
The hum that wandered from their host,   1475
Far on the midnight breeze was lost.
No deafening drum, no bugle's swell,
No watch-word past from centinel,
No slight vibration stirred the air
To warn the Scot a foe was there,   1480
Save bleat of flocks that wandered slow,
And oxen's deep and sullen low.

What horrors o'er the warrior hang!
What vultures watch his soul to fang!
What toils! what snares!—he hies him on   1485
Where lightnings flash, and thunders groan;
Where havock strikes whole legions low,
And death's red billows murmuring flow;
Yet still he fumes and flounders on,
Till crushed the moth—its mem'ry gone!   1490

Why should the bard, who loves to mourn
His maiden's scorn by mountain bourn,
Or pour his wild harp's fairy tone
From sounding cliff or green-wood lone,
Of slaughtered foemen proudly tell,   1495
On deeds of death and horror dwell?

Dread was Dumlanrig's martial ire,
Fierce on the foe he rushed like fire.
Lindsay of Crauford, known to fame,
That night first gained a hero's name.   1500
M'Turk stood deep in Southron gore,
And legions down before him bore;
And Gordon, with his Galloway crew,
O'er floundering ranks resistless flew.
Short was the strife!—they fled as fast   1505
As chaff before the northern blast.

Dumlanrig's flocks were not a few,
And well their worth Dumlanrig knew;
But ne'er so proud was he before
Of his broad bounds, and countless store,   1510
As when they strung up Nithsdale plain,
Well guarded to their hills again.
With Douglas' name the green-woods rung,
As battle-songs his warriors sung.
The banners streamed in double row,   1515
The heart above, the rose below.
His visage glowed, his pulse beat high,
And gladness sparkled in his eye:
For why, he knew the lovely May,
Who in Kilpatrick's castle lay,   1520
With joy his proud return would view,
And her impetuous censure rue.

Well judged he:—Why should haughty chief
Intrude himself on lady's grief,
As if his right, as nought but he   1525
Were worthy her anxiety.
No, warrior: keep thy distance due;
Beauty is proud and jealous too.
If fair and young thy maiden be,
Know she knew that ere told by thee.   1530
Be kind, be gentle, heave the sigh,
And blush before her piercing eye;
For though thou'rt noble, brave, and young,
If rough thy mien and rude thy tongue,
Though proudly towers thy trophied pile,   1535
Hope not for beauty's yielding smile.

Oh! well it suits the brave and high,
Gentle to prove in lady's eye.

Dumlanrig found his lovely flower
Fair as the sun-beam o'er the shower,   1540
Gentle as zephyr of the plain,
Sweet as the rose-bud after rain:
Gone all her scorn and maiden pride,
She blushed Dumlanrig's lovely bride.

James of Dumlanrig, though thy name   1545
Scarce vibrates in the ear of fame,
But for thy might and valour keen,
That gallant house had never been.

Blest be thy mem'ry, gallant man,
Oft flashed thy broad sword in the van;   1550
When stern rebellion reared the brand,
And stained the laurels of our land,
No knight, unshaken, stood like thee
In right of injured majesty:
Ev'n yet, o'er thy forgotten bier,   1555
A minstrel drops the burning tear,
And strikes his wild harp's boldest string,
Thy honours on the breeze to fling,
That mountains once thine own may know
From whom the Queensberry honours flow.   1560

Fair be thy mem'ry, gallant knight!
So true in love, so brave in fight!
Though o'er thy children's princely urn
The sculpture towers, and seraphs mourn,
O'er thy green grave shall wave the yew,   1565
And heaven distil its earliest dew.

———————

When ceased the bard's protracted song,
Circled a smile the fair among;
The song was free, and soft its fall,
So soothing, yet so bold withal,   1570

They loved it well, yet, sooth to say,
Too long, too varied was the lay.

'Twas now the witching time of night,
When reason strays, and forms that fright
Are shadowed on the palsied sight;   1575
When fancy moulds upon the mind
Light visions on the passing wind,
And wooes, with faultering tongue and sigh,
The shades o'er memory's wilds that fly;
And much the circle longed to hear   1580
Of gliding ghost, or gifted seer,
That in that still and solemn hour
Might stretch imagination's power,
And restless fancy revel free
In painful, pleasing luxury.   1585
Just as the battle tale was done,
The watchman called the hour of one.

Lucky the hour for him who came,
Lucky the wish of every dame,
The bard who rose at herald's call   1590
Was wont to sing in Highland hall,
Where the wild chieftain of M'Lean
Upheld his dark Hebridian reign;
Where floated crane and clamorous gull
Above the misty shores of Mull;   1595
And evermore the billows rave
Round many a saint and sovereign's grave.
There round Columba's ruins gray
The shades of monks are wont to stray,
And slender forms of nuns, that weep   1600
In moonlight by the murmuring deep,
O'er early loves and passions crost,
And being's end for ever lost.
No earthly form their names to save,
No stem to flourish o'er their grave,   1605
No blood of theirs beyond the shrine
To nurse the human soul divine,
Still cherish youth by time unworn,
And flow in ages yet unborn.
While mind, surviving evermore,   1610
Unbodied seeks that lonely shore.

In that wild land our minstrel bred,
From youth a life of song had led,
Wandering each shore and upland dull
With Allan Bawn, the bard of Mull,   1615
To sing the deeds of old Fingal,
In every cot and Highland hall.

Well knew he every ghost that came
To visit fair Hebridian dame,
Was that of monk or abbot gone,   1620
Who once, in cell of pictured stone,
Of woman thought, and her alone.

Well knew he every female shade
To westland chief that visit paid
In morning pale, or evening dun,   1625
Was that of fair lamenting nun,
Who once, in cloistered home forlorn,
Languished for joys in youth forsworn;
And oft himself had seen them glide
At dawning from his own bed-side.   1630

Forth stepped he with uncourtly bow,
The heron plume waved o'er his brow,
His garb was blent with varied shade,
And round him flowed his Highland plaid.
But woe to Southland dame and knight   1635
In minstrel's tale who took delight.
Though known the air, the song he sung
Was in the barbarous Highland tongue:
But tartaned chiefs in raptures hear
The strains, the words, to them so dear.   1640

Thus run the bold portentous lay,
As near as Southern tongue can say.

The Abbot M'Kinnon

THE SEVENTEENTH BARD'S SONG

M'Kinnon's tall mast salutes the day,
And beckons the breeze in Iona bay;
Plays lightly up in the morning sky,   1645
And nods to the green wave rolling bye;
The anchor upheaves, the sails unfurl,
The pennons of silk in the breezes curl;
But not one monk on holy ground
Knows whither the Abbot M'Kinnon is bound.   1650

Well could that bark o'er the ocean glide,
Though monks and friars alone must guide;
For never man of other degree
On board that sacred ship might be.
On deck M'Kinnon walked soft and slow;   1655
The haulers sung from the gilded prow;
The helmsman turned his brow to the sky,
Upraised his cowl, and upraised his eye,
And away shot the bark, on the wing of the wind,
Over billow and bay like an image of mind.   1660

Aloft on the turret the monks appear,
To see where the bark of their abbot would bear;
They saw her sweep from Iona bay,
And turn her prow to the north away,
Still lessen to view in the hazy screen,   1665
And vanish amid the islands green.
Then they turned their eyes to the female dome,
And thought of the nuns till the abbot came home.

Three times the night with aspect dull
Came stealing over the moors of Mull;   1670
Three times the sea-gull left the deep,
To doze on the knob of the dizzy steep,
By the sound of the ocean lull'd to sleep;
And still the watch-lights sailors see
On the top of the spire, and the top of Dun-ye;   1675
And the laugh rings through the sacred dome,
For still the abbot is not come home.

But the wolf that nightly swam the sound,
From Ross's rude impervious bound,
On the ravenous burrowing race to feed,   1680
That loved to haunt the home of the dead,
To him Saint Columb had left in trust,
To guard the bones of the royal and just,
Of saints and of kings the sacred dust:
The savage was scared from his charnel of death,   1685
And swam to his home in hunger and wrath,
For he momently saw, through the night so dun,
The cowering monk, and the veiled nun,
Whispering, sighing, and stealing away
By cross dark alley, and portal gray.   1690
O, wise was the founder, and well said he,
"Where there are women mischief must be."

No more the watch-fires gleam to the blast,
M'Kinnon and friends arrive at last.
A stranger youth to the isle they brought,   1695
Modest of mien and deep of thought,
In costly sacred robes bedight,
And he lodged with the abbot by day and by night.

His breast was graceful, and round withal,
His leg was taper, his foot was small,   1700
And his tread so light that it flung no sound
On listening ear or vault around.
His eye was the morning's brightest ray,
And his neck like the swan's in Iona bay;
His teeth the ivory polished new,   1705
And his lip like the morel when glossed with dew,
While under his cowl's embroidered fold
Were seen the curls of waving gold.
This comely youth, of beauty so bright,
Abode with the abbot by day and by night.   1710

When arm in arm they walked the isle,
Young friars would beckon, and monks would smile;
But sires, in dread of sins unshriven,
Would shake their heads and look up to heaven,
Afraid the frown of the saint to see,   1715
Who reared their temple amid the sea,

And pledged his soul to guard the dome,
Till virtue should fly her western home.
But now a stranger of hidden degree,
Too fair, too gentle a man to be, 1720
This stranger of beauty and step so light
Abode with the abbot by day and by night.

The months and the days flew lightly bye,
The monks were kind and the nuns were shy;
But the gray haired sires, in trembling mood, 1725
Kneel'd at the altar and kissed the rood.

M'Kinnon he dreamed that the saint of the isle
Stood by his side, and with courteous smile
Bade him arise from his guilty sleep,
And pay his respects to the God of the deep, 1730
In temple that north in the main appeared,
Which fire from bowels of ocean had seared,
Which the giant builders of heaven had reared,
To rival in grandeur the stately pile
Himself had upreared in Iona's isle; 1735
For round them rose the mountains of sand,
The fishes had left the coasts of the land,
And so high ran the waves of the angry sea,
They had drizzled the cross on the top of Dun-ye.
The cycle was closed, and the period run, 1740
He had vowed to the sea, he had vowed to the sun,
If in that time rose trouble or pain,
Their homage to pay to the God of the main.
Then he bade him haste and the rites prepare,
Named all the monks should with him fare, 1745
And promised again to see him there.

M'Kinnon awoke from his visioned sleep,
He opened his casement and looked on the deep;
He looked to the mountains, he looked to the shore,
The vision amazed him and troubled him sore, 1750
He never had heard of the rite before;
But all was so plain, he thought meet to obey,
He durst not decline, and he would not delay.

Uprose the abbot, uprose the morn,
Uprose the sun from the Bens of Lorn; 1755

And the bark her course to the northward framed,
With all on board whom the saint had named.

The clouds were journeying east the sky,
The wind was low and the swell was high,
And the glossy sea was heaving bright   1760
Like ridges and hills of liquid light;
While far on her lubric bosom were seen
The magic dyes of purple and green.

How joyed the bark her sides to lave!
She leaned to the lee, and she girdled the wave;   1765
Aloft on the stayless verge she hung,
Light on the steep wave veered and swung,
And the crests of the billows before her flung.
Loud murmured the ocean with gulp and with growl,
The seal swam aloof and the dark sea fowl;   1770
The pye-duck sought the depth of the main,
And rose in the wheel of her wake again;
And behind her, far to the southward, shone
A pathway of snow on the waste alone.

But now the dreadful strand they gain,   1775
Where rose the sacred dome of the main;
Oft had they seen the place before,
And kept aloof from the dismal shore,
But now it rose before their prow,
And what they beheld they did not know.   1780
The tall grey forms, in close-set file,
Upholding the roof of that holy pile;
The sheets of foam and the clouds of spray,
And the groans that rushed from the portals grey,
Appalled their hearts and drove them away.   1785

They wheeled their bark to the east around,
And moored in basin, by rocks imbound;
Then awed to silence, they trode the strand
Where furnaced pillars in order stand,
All framed of the liquid burning levin,   1790
And bent like the bow that spans the heaven,
Or upright ranged in horrid array,
With purfle of green o'er the darksome gray.

Their path was on wonderous pavement of old,
Its blocks all cast in some giant mould, 1795
Fair hewn and grooved by no mortal hand,
With countermure guarded by sea and by land.
The watcher Bushella frowned over their way,
Enrobed in the sea-baize, and hooded with grey;
The warder that stands by that dome of the deep, 1800
With spray-shower and rainbow, the entrance to keep.
But when they drew nigh to the chancel of ocean,
And saw her waves rush to their raving devotion,
Astounded and awed to the antes they clung,
And listened the hymns in her temple she sung. 1805
The song of the cliff, when the winter winds blow,
The thunder of heaven, the earthquake below,
Conjoined like the voice of a maiden would be,
Compared with the anthem there sung by the sea.

The solemn rows in that darksome den, 1810
Were dimly seen like the forms of men,
Like giant monks in ages agone,
Whom the God of the ocean had seared to stone,
And bound in his temple for ever to lean,
In sackcloth of grey and visors of green, 1815
An everlasting worship to keep,
And the big salt tears eternally weep.

So rapid the motion, the whirl and the boil,
So loud was the tumult, so fierce the turmoil,
Appalled from those portals of terror they turn, 1820
On pillar of marble their incense to burn.
Around the holy flame they pray,
Then turning their faces all west away,
On angel pavement each bent his knee,
And sung this hymn to the God of the sea. 1825

The Monks' Hymn

Thou, who makest the ocean to flow,
Thou, who walkest the channels below;
To thee, to thee, this incense we heap,
Thou, who knowest not slumber nor sleep,
Great spirit that movest on the face of the deep! 1830

To thee, to thee, we sing to thee,
God of the western wind, God of the sea.

To thee, who gatherest with thy right hand
The little fishes around our land;
To thee, who breathest in the bellied sail,   1835
Rul'st the shark and the rolling whale,
Fling'st the sinner to downward grave,
Light'st the gleam on the mane of the wave,
Bid'st the billows thy reign deform,
Laugh'st in the whirlwind, sing'st in the storm,   1840
Or risest like mountain amid the sea
Where mountain was never and never will be,
And rear'st thy proud and thy pale chaperoon
Mid walks of the angels and ways of the moon;
To thee, to thee, this wine we pour,   1845
God of the western wind, God of the shower.

To thee, who bid'st those mountains of brine
Softly sink in the fair moonshine,
And spread'st thy couch of silver light,
To lure to thy bosom the queen of the night,   1850
Who weavest the cloud of the ocean dew,
And the mist that sleeps on her breast so blue;
When the murmurs die at the base of the hill,
And the shadows lie rocked and slumbering still,
And the Solan's young, and the lines of foam,   1855
Are scarcely heaved on thy peaceful home,
We pour this oil and this wine to thee,
God of the western wind, God of the sea!
"Greater yet must the offering be."

The monks gazed round, the abbot grew wan,   1860
For the closing notes were not sung by man,
They came from the rock, or they came from the air,
From voice they knew not, and knew not where;
But it sung with a mournful melody,
"Greater yet must the offering be."   1865

In holy dread they past away,
And they walked the ridge of that isle so grey,

And saw the white waves toil and fret,
An hundred fathoms below their feet;
They looked to the countless isles that lie,   1870
From Barra to Mull, and from Jura to Skye;
They looked to heaven, they looked to the main,
They looked at all with a silent pain,
As on places they were not to see again.

A little bay lies hid from sight,   1875
O'erhung by cliffs of dreadful height;
When they drew nigh that airy steep,
They heard a voice rise from the deep,
And that voice was sweet as voice could be,
And they feared it came from the maid of the sea.   1880

M'Kinnon lay stretched on the verge of the hill,
And peeped from the height on the bay so still;
And he saw her sit on a weedy stone,
Laving her fair breast, and singing alone;
And aye she sank the wave within,   1885
Till it gurgled around her lovely chin,
Then combed her locks of the pale sea-green,
And ay this song was heard between.

The Mermaid's Song

Matilda of Skye
Alone may lie,   1890
And list to the wind that whistles by:
Sad may she be,
For deep in the sea,
Deep, deep, deep in the sea!
This night her lover shall sleep with me.   1895
She may turn and hide
From the spirits that glide,
And the ghost that stands at her bed-side;
But never a kiss the vow shall seal,
Nor warm embrace her bosom feel;   1900
For far, far down in the floors below,
Moist as this rock-weed, cold as the snow,
With the eel, and the clam, and the pearl of the deep,
On soft sea-flowers her lover shall sleep,

And long and sound shall his slumber be   1905
In the coral bowers of the deep with me.

   The trembling sun, far, far away,
Shall pour on his couch a softened ray,
And his mantle shall wave in the flowing tide,
And the little fishes shall turn aside;   1910
But the waves and the tides of the sea shall cease,
Ere wakes her love from his bed of peace.
No home!—no kiss!—No, never! never!
His couch is spread for ever and ever.

   The abbot arose in dumb dismay,   1915
They turned and fled from the height away,
For dark and portentous was the day.
When they came in view of their rocking sail,
They saw an old man who sat on the wale;
His beard was long, and silver grey,   1920
Like the rime that falls at the break of day;
His locks like wool, and his colour wan,
And he scarcely looked like an earthly man.

   They asked his errand, they asked his name,
Whereunto bound, and whence he came;   1925
But a sullen thoughtful silence he kept,
And turned his face to the sea and wept.
Some gave him welcome, and some gave him scorn,
But the abbot stood pale, with terror o'erborne;
He tried to be jocund, but trembled the more,   1930
For he thought he had seen the face before.

   Away went the ship with her canvass all spread,
So glad to escape from that island of dread;
And skimmed the blue wave like a streamer of light,
Till fell the dim veil 'twixt the day and the night.   1935

   Then the old man arose and stood up on the prow,
And fixed his dim eyes on the ocean below;
And they heard him saying, "Oh, woe is me!
But great as the sin must the sacrifice be."

Oh, mild was his eye, and his manner sublime,   1940
When he looked unto heaven, and said—"Now is the
    time."
He looked to the weather, he looked to the lee,
He looked as for something he dreaded to see,
Then stretched his pale hand, and pointed his eye
To a gleam on the verge of the eastern sky.   1945

    The monks soon beheld, on the lofty Ben-More,
A sight which they never had seen before,
A belt of blue lightning around it was driven,
And its crown was encircled by morion of heaven,
And they heard a herald that loud did cry,   1950
"Prepare the way for the Abbot of I!"

    Then a sound arose, they knew not where,
It came from the sea, or it came from the air,
'Twas louder than tempest that ever blew,
And the sea-fowls screamed, and in terror flew;   1955
Some ran to the cords, some kneeled at the shrine,
But all the wild elements seemed to combine;
'Twas just but one moment of stir and commotion,
And down went the ship like a bird of the ocean.

    This moment she sailed all stately and fair,   1960
The next nor ship nor shadow was there,
But a boil that arose from the deep below,
A mounting gurgling column of snow;
It sunk away with a murmuring moan,
The sea is calm, and the sinners are gone.   1965

END OF NIGHT THE THIRD

Conclusion

Conclusion

FRIEND of the bard! peace to thy heart,
Long hast thou acted generous part,
Long has thy courteous heart in pain
Attended to a feeble strain,
While oft abashed has sunk thine eye,—   5
Thy task is done, the Wake is bye.

  I saw thy fear, I knew it just;
'Twas not for minstrels long in dust,
But for the fond and ventrous swain
Who dared to wake their notes again;   10
Yet oft thine eye has spoke delight,
I marked it well, and blest the sight:
No sour disdain, nor manner cold,
Noted contempt for tales of old;
Oft hast thou at the fancies smiled,   15
And marvelled at the legends wild.
Thy task is o'er; peace to thy heart!
For thou hast acted generous part.

  'Tis said that thirty bards appeared,
That thirty names were registered,   20
With whom were titled chiefs combined,
But some are lost, and some declined.
Woe's me, that all my mountain lore
Has been unfit to rescue more!
And that my guideless rustic skill   25
Has told those ancient tales so ill.

  The prize harp still hung on the wall;
The bards were warned to leave the hall,
Till courtiers gave the judgment true,
To whom the splendid prize was due.   30
What curious wight will pass with me,
The anxious motley group to see;
List their remarks of right and wrong,
Of skilful hand and faulty song,
And drink one glass the bards among?   35

There sit the men—behold them there,
Made maidens quake and courtiers stare,
Whose names shall future ages tell;
What do they seem? behold them well.
A simpler race you shall not see,   40
Awkward and vain as men can be;
Light as the fumes of fervid wine,
Or foam-bells floating on the brine,
The gossamers in air that sail,
Or down that dances in the gale.   45

Each spoke of others fame and skill
With high applause, but jealous will.
Each song, each strain, he erst had known,
And all had faults except his own:
Plaudits were mixed with meaning jeers,   50
For all had hopes, and all had fears.

A herald rose the court among,
And named each bard, and named his song:
Rizzio was named from royal chair—
"Rizzio!" re-echoed many a fair.   55
Each song had some that song approved,
And voices gave for bard beloved.
The first division called and done,
Gardyn stood highest just by one.

Queen Mary reddened, wroth was she   60
Her favourite thus outdone to see,
Reproved her squire in high disdain,
And caused him call the votes again.
Strange though it seem, the truth I say,
Feature of that unyielding day,   65
Her favourite's voters counted o'er,
Were found much fewer than before.
Glistened her eyes with pungent dew;
She found with whom she had to do.

Again the royal gallery rung   70
With names of those who second sung,
When, spite of haughty Highland blood,
The bard of Ettrick upmost stood.

The rest were named who sung so late,
And after long and keen debate,   75
The specious nobles of the south
Carried the nameless stranger youth;
Though Highland wrath was at the full,
Contending for the bard of Mull.

Then did the worst dispute begin,   80
Which of the *three* the prize should win.
'Twas party all—not minstrel worth,
But honour of the south and north;
And nought was heard throughout the court,
But taunt, and sneer, and keen retort.   85
High run the words, and fierce the fume,
And from beneath each nodding plume
Red look was cast that vengeance said,
And palm on broad-sword's hilt was laid,
While Lowland jeer, and Highland mood,   90
Threatened to end the Wake in blood.

Rose from his seat the Lord of Mar,
Serene in counsel as in war.
"For shame," said he, "contendents all!
This outrage done in royal hall,   95
Is to our country foul disgrace.
What! mock our Sovereign to her face!
Whose generous heart and taste refined,
Alike to bard and courtier kind,
This high repast for all designed.   100
For shame! your party strife suspend,
And list the counsel of a friend.

"Unmeet it is for you or me
To lessen one of all the three,
Each excellent in his degree;   105
But taste, as sapient sages tell,
Varies with climes in which we dwell.

"Fair emblem of the Border dale,
Is cadence soft and simple tale;
While stern romantic Highland clime,   110
Still nourishes the rude sublime.

"If Border ear may taste the worth
Of the wild pathos of the north,
Or that sublimed by Ossian's lay,
By forest dark and mountain gray,   115
By clouds which frowning cliffs deform,
By roaring flood and raving storm,
Enjoy the smooth, the fairy tale,
Or evening song of Teviotdale;
Then trow you may the tides adjourn,   120
And Nature from her path-way turn;
The wild-duck drive to mountain tree,
The capperkayle to swim the sea,
The heath-cock to the shelvy shore,
The partridge to the mountain hoar,   125
And bring the red-eyed ptarmigan
To dwell by the abodes of man.

"To end this strife, unruled and vain,
Let all the three be called again;
Their skill alternately be tried,   130
And let the Queen alone decide.
Then hushed be jeer and answer proud,"–
He said, and all consenting, bowed.

When word was brought to bard's retreat,
The group were all in dire debate;   135
The Border youth (that stranger wight)
Had quarrelled with the clans outright;
Had placed their merits out of ken,
Deriding both the songs and men.
'Tis said–but few the charge believes,–   140
He branded them as fools and thieves.
Certes that war and woe had been,
For gleaming dirks unsheathed were seen,
For Highland minstrels ill could brook
His taunting word and haughty look.   145

The youth was chaffed, and with disdain
Refused to touch his harp again;
Said he desired no more renown
Than keep those Highland boasters down;
Now he had seen them quite outdone,   150

The south had two, the north but one;
But should they bear the prize away,
For that he should not, would not play;
He cared for no such guerdon mean,
Nor for the harp, nor for the Queen.   155

   His claim withdrawn, the victors twain
Repaired to prove their skill again.

   The song that tuneful Gardyn sung
Is still admired by old and young,
And long shall be at evening fold,   160
While songs are sung or tales are told.
Of stolen delights began the song,
Of love the Carron woods among,
Of lady borne from Carron side
To Barnard towers and halls of pride,   165
Of jealous lord and doubtful bride,
And ended with Gilmorice' doom
Cut off in manhood's early bloom.
Soft rung the closing notes and slow,
And every heart was steeped in woe.   170

   The harp of Ettrick rung again,
Her bard, intent on fairy strain,
And fairy freak by moonlight shaw,
Sung young Tam Lean of Carterha'.

   Queen Mary's harp on high that hung,   175
And every tone responsive rung,
With gems and gold that dazzling shone,
That harp is to the Highlands gone.
Gardyn is crowned with garlands gay,
And bears the envied prize away.   180
Long, long that harp, the hills among,
Resounded Ossian's mounting song;
Waked slumbering lyres from every tree
Adown the banks of Don and Dee,
At length was borne, by beauteous bride,   185
To woo the airs on Garry side.

   When full two hundred years had fled,
And all the northern bards were dead,

That costly harp, of wonderous mould,
Defaced of all its gems and gold,   190
With that which Gardyn erst did play,
Back to Dunedin found its way.

  As Mary's hand the victor crowned,
And twined the wreath his temples round,
Loud were the shouts of Highland chief–   195
The Lowlanders were dumb with grief;
And the poor bard of Ettrick stood
Like statue pale, in moveless mood;
Like ghost, which oft his eyes had seen
At gloaming in his glens so green.   200
Queen Mary saw the minstrel's pain,
And bade from bootless grief refrain.

  She said a boon to him should fall
Worth all the harps in royal hall;
Of Scottish song a countless store,   205
Precious remains of minstrel lore,
And cottage, by a silver rill,
Should all reward his rustic skill:
Did other gift his bosom claim,
He needed but that gift to name.   210

  "O, my fair Queen," the minstrel said,
With faultering voice and hanging head,
"Your cottage keep, and minstrel lore,–
Grant me a harp, I ask no more.
From thy own hand a lyre I crave,   215
That boon alone my heart can save."

  "Well hast thou asked; and be it known,
I have a harp of old renown
Hath many an ardent wight beguiled,
'Twas framed by wizard of the wild,   220
And will not yield one measure bland
Beneath a skilless stranger hand;
But once her powers by progress found,
O there is magic in the sound.

  "When worldly woes oppress thy heart,   225
And thou and all must share a part,

Should scorn be cast from maiden's eye,
Should friendship fail, or fortune fly;
Steal with thy harp to lonely brake,
Her wild, her soothing numbers wake,   230
And soon corroding cares shall cease,
And passion's host be lulled to peace;
Angels a gilded screen shall cast,
That cheers the future, veils the past.

"That harp will make the elves of eve   235
Their dwelling in the moon-beam leave,
And ope thine eyes by haunted tree
Their glittering tiny forms to see.
The flitting shades that woo the glen
'Twill shape to forms of living men,   240
To forms on earth no more you see,
Who once were loved, and aye will be;
And holiest converse you may prove
Of things below and things above."

"That is, that is the harp for me!"   245
Said the rapt bard in ecstacy;
"This soothing, this exhaustless store,
Grant me, my Queen, I ask no more."

O, when the weeping minstrel laid
The relic in his old grey plaid,   250
When Holyrood he left behind
To gain his hills of mist and wind,
Never was hero of renown,
Or monarch prouder of his crown.
He tript the vale, he climbed the coomb,   255
The mountain breeze began to boom;
Ay when the magic chords it rung,
He raised his voice and blithely sung.
"Hush, my wild harp, thy notes forbear;
No blooming maids nor elves are here: 260
Forbear a while that witching tone,
Thou must not, canst not sing alone.
When Summer flings her watchet screen
At eve o'er Ettrick woods so green,
Thy notes shall many a heart beguile;   265

Young beauty's eye shall o'er thee smile,
And fairies trip it merrily
Around my royal harp and me."

  Long has that harp of magic tone
To all the minstrel world been known: 270
Who has not heard her witching lays,
Of Ettrick banks and Yarrow braes?
But that sweet bard, who sung and played
Of many a feat and Border raid,
Of many a knight and lovely maid,   275
When forced to leave his harp behind,
Did all her tuneful chords unwind;
And many ages past and came
Ere man so well could tune the same.

  Bangour the daring task essayed,   280
Not half the chords his fingers played;
Yet even then some thrilling lays
Bespoke the harp of ancient days.

  Redoubted Ramsay's peasant skill
Flung some strained notes along the hill;   285
His was some lyre from lady's hall,
And not the mountain harp at all.

  Langhorne arrived from Southern dale,
And chimed his notes on Yarrow vale,
They would not, could not, touch the heart;   290
His was the modish lyre of art.

  Sweet rung the harp to Logan's hand:
Then Leyden came from Border land,
With dauntless heart and ardour high,
And wild impatience in his eye.   295
Though false his tones at times might be,
Though wild notes marred the symphony
Between, the glowing measure stole
That spoke the bard's inspired soul.
Sad were those strains, when hymn'd afar,   300
On the green vales of Malabar:
O'er seas beneath the golden morn,

They travelled, on the monsoon borne,
Thrilling the heart of Indian maid,
Beneath the wild banana's shade.–   305
Leyden, a shepherd wails thy fate,
And Scotland knows her loss too late!

The day arrived–blest be the day,
Walter the abbot came that way!–
The sacred relic met his view–   310
Ah! well the pledge of heaven he knew!
He screwed the chords, he tried a strain;
'Twas wild–he tuned and tried again,
Then poured the numbers bold and free,
The simple magic melody.   315

The land was charmed to list his lays;
It knew the harp of ancient days.
The Border chiefs, that long had been
In sepulchres unhearsed and green,
Passed from their mouldy vaults away,   320
In armour red, and stern array,
And by their moonlight halls were seen,
In visor, helm, and habergeon.
Even fairies sought our land again,
So powerful was the magic strain.   325

Blest be his generous heart for ay!
He told me where the relic lay;
Pointed my way with ready will,
Afar on Ettrick's wildest hill;
Watched my first notes with curious eye,   330
And wondered at my minstrelsy:
He little weened, a parent's tongue
Such strains had o'er my cradle sung.

But when, to native feelings true,
I struck upon a chord was new;   335
When by myself I 'gan to play,
He tried to wile my harp away.
Just when her notes began with skill,
To sound beneath the southern hill,
And twine around my bosom's core,   340

How could we part for evermore?
'Twas kindness all, I cannot blame,
For bootless is the minstrel flame;
But sure, a bard might well have known
Another's feelings by his own!   345

  Of change enamoured, woe the while!
He left our mountains, left the isle;
And far to other kingdoms bore
The Caledonian harp of yore;
But, to the hand that framed her true,   350
Only by force one strain she threw.
That harp he never more shall see,
Unless 'mong Scotland's hills with me.

Now, my loved harp, a while farewell;
  I leave thee on the old gray thorn;   355
The evening dews will mar thy swell,
  That waked to joy the cheerful morn.

Farewell, sweet soother of my woe.
  Chill blows the blast around my head;
And louder yet that blast may blow,   360
  When down this weary vale I've sped.

The wreath lies on Saint Mary's shore;
  The mountain sounds are harsh and loud;
The lofty brows of stern Clokmore
  Are visored with the moving cloud.   365

But Winter's deadly hues shall fade
  On moorland bald and mountain shaw,
And soon the rainbow's lovely shade
  Sleep on the breast of Bowerhope Law;

Then will the glowing suns of spring,   370
  The genial shower and stealing dew,
Wake every forest bird to sing,
  And every mountain flower renew.

But not the rainbow's ample ring,
  That spans the glen and mountain gray,   375
Though fanned by western breeze's wing,
  And sunned by summer's glowing ray,

To man decayed, can ever more
  Renew the age of love and glee!
Can ever second spring restore   380
  To my old mountain harp and me!

But when the hue of softened green
  Spreads over hill and lonely lea,
And lowly primrose opes unseen
  Her virgin bosom to the bee: 385

When hawthorns breathe their odours far,
  And carols hail the year's return,
And daisy spreads her silver star
  Unheeded by the mountain burn;

Then will I seek the aged thorn,   390
  The haunted wild and fairy ring,
Where oft thy erring numbers born
  Have taught the wandering winds to sing.

END OF THE QUEEN'S WAKE

Notes

Notes

Note I.

Those wakes, now played by minstrels poor,
At midnight's darkest, chillest hour,
Those humble wakes, now scorned by all,
Were first begun in courtly hall.–Page 9.

In former days, the term *wake* was only used to distinguish the festive meeting which took place on the evening previous to the dedication of any particular church or chapel. The company sat up all the night, and, in England, amused themselves in various ways, as their inclinations were by habit or study directed. In Scotland, however, which was always the land of music and of song, music and song were the principal–often the only amusements of the wake. These songs were generally of a sacred or serious nature, and were chaunted to the old simple melodies of the country. *The Bush aboon Traquair, The Broom of Cowdenknows, John come kiss me now,* and many others, are still extant, set to the Psalms of David, and other spiritual songs, the Psalms being turned into a rude metre corresponding to the various measures of the tunes.

The difference in the application of the term which exists in the two sister kingdoms, sufficiently explains the consequences of the wakes in either. In England they have given rise to many fairs and festivals of long standing; and, from that origin, every fair or festival is denominated a *wake*. In Scotland the term is not used to distinguish any thing either subsistent or relative, save those serenades played by itinerant and nameless minstrels in the streets and squares of Edinburgh, which are inhabited by the great and wealthy, after midnight, about the time of the Christmas holydays. These seem to be the only remainder of the ancient wakes now in Scotland, and their effect upon a mind that delights in music is soothing and delicious beyond all previous conception. A person who can relish the concord of sweet sounds, gradually recalled from sleep by the music of the wakes, of which he had no previous anticipation, never fails of being deprived, for a considerable time, of all recollection, what condition, what place, or what world he is in. The minstrels who, in the reign of the Stuarts, enjoyed privileges which were even denied to the principal nobility, were, by degrees, driven from the tables of the great to the second, and afterwards to the common hall, that their music and songs might be heard, while they themselves were unseen. From the common hall they were obliged to retire to the porch or court; and so low has the characters of the minstrels descended, that the performers of the Christmas wakes are wholly unknown to the most part of those whom they serenade. They seem to be despised, but enjoy some small privileges, in order to keep up a name of high and ancient origin.

Note II.

There rode the lords of France and Spain,
Of England, Flanders, and Lorrain,
While serried thousands round them stood,
From shore of Leith to Holyrood.–P. 11.

Hollingshed describes Queen Mary's landing in Scotland, with her early misfortunes and accomplishments, after this manner: "She arrived at Leith the 20th of August, in the year of our Lord 1561, where she was honourably received by the Earl of Argyle, the Lord Erskine, the Prior of St Andrews, and the burgesses of Edinburgh, and conveyed to the Abbie of Holie-rood-house, for (as saith Buchannan) when some had spread abroad her landing in Scotland, the nobility and others assembled out of all parts of the realme, as it were to a common spectacle.

"This did they, partly to congratulate her return, and partly to shew the dutie which they alwais bear unto her (when she was absent,) either to have thanks therefore, or to prevent the slanders of the enemies: wherefore not a few, by these beginnings of her reign, did gesse what would follow, although, in those so variable notions of the minds of the people, every one was very desirous to see their Queen offered unto them, (unlooked for,) after so many haps of both fortunes as had befallen her. For, when she was but six days old, she lost her father among the cruel tempests of battle, and was, with great diligence, brought up by her mother, (being a chosen and worthy person), but yet left as a prize to others, by reason of civil sedition in Scotland, and of outward wars with other nations, being further led abroad to all the dangers of frowning fortune, before she could know what evil did mean.

"For leaving her own country, she was nourished as a banished person, and hardly preserved in life from the weapons of her enemies, and violence of the seas. After which fortune began to flatter her, in that she honoured her with a worthy marriage, which, in truth, was rather a shadow of joie to this queen, than any comfort at all. For, shortly after the same, all things were turned to sorrow, by the death of her new young husband, and of her old and grieved mother, by loss of her new kingdom, and by the doubtful possession of her old heritable realme. But as for these things she was both pitied and praised, so was she also for gifts of nature as much beloved and favoured, in that beneficial nature (or rather good God) had indued her with a beautiful face, a well composed body, an excellent wit, a mild nature, and good behaviour, which she had artificially furthered by courtly education and affable demeanor. Whereby, at the first sight, she wan unto her the hearts of most, and confirmed the love of her faithful subjects."–*Holl.* p. 314. Arbroath Ed.

With regard to the music, which so deeply engaged her attention, we have different accounts by contemporaries, and those at complete variance with one another. Knox says, "Fyres of joy were set furth at night, and a companie of maist honest men, with instruments of musick, gave ther salutation at hir chalmer windo: the melodie, as sche alledged, lyked her weill, and sche willed the sam to be continued sum nychts eftir with grit dilligence." But Dufresnoy, who was one of the party who accompanied the Queen, gives a very different account of these Scottish minstrels. "We landed at Leith," says he, "and went from thence to Edinburgh, which is but a short league distant. The Queen went there on horseback, and the lords and ladies who accompanied her upon the little wretched hackneys of the country, as wretchedly capparisoned; at sight of which the Queen began to weep, and to compare them with the pomp and superb palfreys of France. But there was no remedy but patience. What was worst of all, being arrived at Edinburgh, and retired to rest in the Abbey (which is really a fine building, and not at all partaking of the rudeness of that country), there came under her window a crew of five or six hundred scoundrels from the city, who gave her a serenade with wretched violins and little rebecks, of which there are enough in that country, and began to sing Psalms so miserably mistimed and mistuned, that nothing could be worse. Alas! what music! and what a night's rest!"

The Frenchman has had no taste for Scottish music—such another concert is certainly not in record.

Note III.

Ah! Kennedy, vengeance hangs over thine head!
Escape to thy native Glengarry forlorn.–P. 32.

The Clan Kennedy was only in the present age finally expelled from Glen-Garry, and forced to scatter over this and other countries. Its character among the Highlanders, is that of the most savage and irreclaimable tribe that ever infested the mountains of the north.

Note IV.

The Witch of Fife.–P. 40.

It may suffice to mention once for all, that the catastrophe of this tale, as well as the principal events related in the tales of *Old David* and *M'Gregor*, are all founded on popular traditions. So is also the romantic story of Kilmeny's disappearance and revisiting her friends, after being seven years in Fairyland. The tradition bears some resemblance to the old ballads of Tam Lean and Thomas of Erceldon; and it is not improbable that all the three may have drawn their origin from the same ancient romance.

Note V.

Glen-Avin.–P. 57.

There are many scenes among the Grampian deserts which amaze the traveller who ventures to explore them; and in the most pathless wastes the most striking landscapes are often concealed. Glen-Avin ex-

ceeds them all in what may be termed stern and solemn grandeur. It is
indeed a sublime solitude, in which the principal feature is deformity;
yet that deformity is mixed with lines of wild beauty, such as an exten-
sive lake, with its islets and bays, the straggling trees, and the spots of
shaded green; and altogether it is such a scene as man has rarely looked
upon. I spent a summer day in visiting it. The hills were clear of mist,
yet the heavens were extremely dark—the effect upon the scene ex-
ceeded all description. My mind, during the whole day, experienced the
same sort of sensation as if I had been in a dream; and on returning
from the excursion, I did not wonder at the superstition of the neigh-
bouring inhabitants, who believe it to be the summer haunt of innumer-
able tribes of fairies, and many other spirits, some of whom seem to be
the most fantastic, and to behave in the most eccentric manner, of any I
ever before heard of. Though the glen is upwards of twenty miles in
length, and of prodigious extent, it contains no human habitation. It lies
in the west corner of Banffshire, in the very middle of the Grampian
hills.

Note VI.
Oft had that seer at dawn of morn
Beheld the fahm glide o'er the fell.—P. 58.

Fahm is a little ugly monster, who frequents the summits of the moun-
tains around Glen-Avin, and no other place in the world that I know of.
My guide, D. M'Queen, declared that he had himself seen him, and, by
his description, Fahm appears to be no native of this world, but an
occasional visitant, whose intentions are evil and dangerous. He is only
seen about the break of day, and on the highest verge of the mountain.
His head is twice as large as his whole body beside; and if any living
creature cross the track over which he has passed before the sun shine
upon it, certain death is the consequence. The head of that person or
animal instantly begins to swell, grows to an immense size, and finally
bursts. Such a disease is really incident to sheep on those heights, and in
several parts of the kingdom, where the grounds are elevated to a great
height above the sea; but in no place save Glen-Avin is Fahm blamed for it.

Note VII.
Even far on Yarrow's fairy dale,
The shepherd paused in dumb dismay,
And passing shrieks adown the vale,
Lured many a pitying hind away.—P. 60.

It was reckoned a curious and unaccountable circumstance, that, dur-
ing the time of a great fall of snow by night, a cry, as of a person who
had lost his way in the storm, was heard along the vale of Ettrick from
its head to its foot. What was the people's astonishment, when it was
authenticated, that upwards of twenty parties had all been out with
torches, lanthorns, &c. at the same hour of the night, calling and search-

ing after some unknown person, whom they believed perishing in the snow, and that none of them had discovered any such person—the word spread; the circumstances were magnified—and the consternation became general. The people believed that a whole horde of evil spirits had been abroad in the valley, endeavouring to lure them abroad to their destruction—there was no man sure of his life!—prayers and thanksgivings were offered up to heaven in every hamlet, and resolutions unanimously formed, that no man perishing in the snow should ever be looked after again as long as the world stood.

When the astonishment had somewhat subsided by exhausting itself, and the tale of horror spread too wide ever to be recalled, a lad, without the smallest reference to the phenomenon, chanced to mention, that on the night of the storm, when he was out on the hill turning his sheep to some shelter, a flock of swans passed over his head toward the western sea, which was a sure signal of severe weather; and that at intervals they were always shouting and answering one another, in an extraordinary, and rather fearsome manner.—It was an unfortunate discovery, and marred the harmony of many an evening's conversation! In whatever cot the circumstance was mentioned, the old shepherds rose and went out—the younkers, who had listened to the prayers with reverence and fear, bit their lips—the matrons plied away at their wheels in silence—it was singular that none of them should have known the voice of a swan from that of the devil!—they were very angry with the lad, and regarded him as a sort of blasphemer.

Note VIII.
See yon lone cairn so gray with age,
Above the base of proud Cairn-Gorm.—P. 61.

I only saw this old cairn at a distance; but the narrative which my guide gave me of the old man's loss was very affecting. He had gone to the forest in November to look after some goats that were missing, when a dreadful storm came suddenly on, the effects of which were felt throughout the kingdom. It was well enough known that he was lost in the forest, but the snow being so deep, it was judged impossible to find the body, and no one looked after it. It was not discovered until the harvest following, when it was found accidentally by a shepherd. The plaid and clothes which were uppermost not being decayed, it appeared like the body of a man lying entire; but when he began to move them, the dry bones rattled together, and the bare white scull was lying in the bonnet.

Note IX.
Old David.—P. 63.

I remember hearing a very old man, named David Laidlaw, who lived somewhere in the neighbourhood of Hawick, relate many of the adventures of this old moss-trooper, his great progenitor, and the first who ever bore the name. He described him as a great champion–a man quite invincible, and quoted several verses of a ballad relating to him, which I never heard either before or since. I remember only one of them.

> There was ane banna of barley meal
> Cam duntin dune by Davy's sheil,
> But out cam Davy and his lads,
> And dang the banna a' in blads.

He explained how this "bannock of barley meal" meant a rich booty, which the old hero captured from a band of marauders. He lived at Garwell in Eskdale-moor.

Lochy-Law, where the principal scene of this tale is laid, is a hill on the lands of Shorthope in the wilds of Ettrick. The Fairy Slack is up in the middle of the hill, a very curious ravine, and would be much more so when overshadowed with wood. The Back-burn which joins the Ettrick immediately below this hill, has been haunted time immemorial, both by the fairies, and the ghost of a wandering minstrel who was cruelly murdered there, and who sleeps in a lone grave a small distance from the ford.

Note X.
And fears of witch and fairy raid,
Have like a morning dream decayed.–P. 72.

The fairies have now totally disappeared, and it is a pity they should; for they seem to have been the most delightful little spirits that ever haunted the Scottish dells. There are only very few now remaining alive who have ever seen them; and when they did, it was on Hallow-evenings while they were young, when the gospel was not very rife in the country. But, strange as it may appear, with the witches it is far otherwise. Never, in the most superstitious ages, was the existence of witches, or the influence of their diabolical power, more firmly believed in, than by the inhabitants of the mountains of Ettrick Forest at the present day. Many precautions and charms are used to avert this influence, and scarcely does a summer elapse in which there are not some of the most gross incantations practised, in order to free flocks and herds from the blasting power of these old hags. There are two farmers still living, who will both make oath that they have wounded several old wives with shot as they were traversing the air in the shapes of moor-fowl and partridges.–A very singular amusement that for old wives!–I heard one of these *gentlemen* relate, with the utmost seriousness, and as a matter he did not wish to be generally known, that one morning, going out a fowling, he sprung a pair of moor-fowl in a place where it was not customary for moor-fowl to stay–he fired at the hen–wounded her, and eyed her until she alighted beyond an old dike–when he went to the spot, his astonishment may be well conceived, when he found *Nell* —, picking the hail out of her limbs! He was extremely vexed that he had not shot the cock, for he was almost certain he was no other than *Wattie Grieve!!!*

The tales and anecdotes of celebrated witches that are still related in the country, are extremely whimsical and diverting. The following is a *well-authenticated one.* A number of gentlemen were one day met for a chace on the lands of Newhouse and Kirkhope–their greyhounds were numerous and keen, but not a hare could they raise. At length a boy came to them, who offered to start a hare to them, if they would give him a guinea, and the black greyhound to hold. The demand was singular, but it was peremptory, and on other conditions he would not comply. The guerdon was accordingly paid–the hare was started, and the sport afforded by the chace was excellent–the greyhounds were all baffled, and began to give up one by one, when one of the party came slily behind the boy and cut the leish in which he held the black dog–away he flew to join the chace.–The boy losing all recollection, ran, bawling out with great vociferation, "Huy, mither, rin!! Hay, rin ye auld witch, if ever ye ran i' yer life!! Rin, mither, rin!!" The black dog came fast up with her, and was just beginning to *mouth her,* when she sprung in at the window of a little cottage and escaped. The riders soon came to the place, and entered the cot in search of the hare; but lo! there was no living creature there but the old woman lying panting in a bed, so breathless that she could not speak a word!!!

But the best old witch tale that remains, is that which is related of the celebrated Michael Scott, Master of Oakwad. Mr Walter Scott has preserved it, but so altered from the original way, that it is not easy to recognize it. The old people tell it as follows: There was one of Mr Michael's tenants who had a wife that was the most notable witch of the age. So extraordinary were her powers, that the country people began to put them in competition with those of the Master, and say, that in *some cantrips* she surpassed him. Michael could ill brook such insinuations; for there is always jealousy between great characters, and went over one day with his dogs on pretence of hunting, but in reality with an intent of exercising some of his infernal power in the chastisement of Lucky — (I have the best reason in the world for concealing her reputed name.) He found her alone in the field weeding lint; and desired her, in a friendly manner, to show him some of her powerful art. She was very angry with him, and denied that she had any supernatural skill. He, however, continuing to press her, she told him sharply to let her alone, else she would make him repent the day he troubled her. How she perceived the virtues of Michael's wand is not known, but in a moment she snatched it from his hand, and gave him three lashes with it. The knight was momently changed to a hare, when the malicious and inveterate hag cried out, laughing, "Shu, Michael, rin or dee!" and baited all his own dogs upon him. He was extremely hard hunted, and was obliged to swim the river, and take shelter in the sewer of his own castle from the fury of his pursuers, where he got leisure to change himself again to a man.

Michael being extremely chagrined at having been thus outwitted, studied a deadly revenge; and going over afterwards to hunt, he sent his man to Fauldshope to borrow some bread from Lucky — to give to his dogs, for that he had neglected to feed them before he came from home. If she gave him the bread, he was to thank her and come away; but if she refused it, he gave him a line written in red characters, which he was to lodge above the lintel as he came out. The servant found her baking of bread, as his master assured him he would, and delivered his message. She received him most ungraciously, and absolutely refused to give him any bread, alleging, as an excuse, that she had not as much as would serve her own reapers to dinner. The man said no more, but lodged the line as directed, and returned to his master. The powerful spell had the desired effect; Lucky — instantly threw off her clothes, and danced round and round the fire like one quite mad, singing the while with great glee,

> "Master Michael Scott's man
> Cam seekin bread an' gat nane."

The dinner hour arrived, but the reapers looked in vain for their dame, who was wont to bring it to them to the field. The goodman sent home a servant girl to assist her, but neither did she return. At length he ordered them to go and take their dinner at home, for he suspected his spouse had taken some of her *tirravies*. All of them went inadvertently into the house, and, as soon as they passed beneath the mighty charm, were seized with the same mania, and followed the example of their mistress. The goodman, who had tarried behind, setting some shocks of corn, came home last; and hearing the noise ere ever he came near the house, he did not venture to go in, but peeped in at the window. There he beheld all his people dancing naked round and round the fire, and singing, "Master Michael Scott's man," with the most frantic wildness. His wife was by that time quite exhausted, and the rest were half trailing her around. She could only now and then pronounce a syllable of the song, which she did with a kind of scream, yet seemed as intent on the sport as ever.

The goodman mounted his horse, and rode with all speed to the Master, to enquire what he had done to his people which had put them all mad. Michael bade him take down the note from the lintel and burn it, which he did, and all the people returned to their senses. Poor Lucky — died overnight, and Michael remained unmatched and alone in all the arts of enchantment and necromancy.

Note XI.
The Spectre's Cradle Song.—P. 76.

I mentioned formerly that the tale of M'Gregor is founded on a popular Highland tradition—so also is this Song of the Spectre in the introduction to it, which to me, at least, gives it a peculiar interest. As I was once travelling up Glen-Dochart, attended by Donald Fisher, a shepherd of that country, he pointed out to me some curious green dens, by the side of the large rivulet which descends from the back of Ben More, the name of which, in the Gaelic language, signifies *the abode of the fairies.* A native of that country, who is still living, happening to be benighted there one summer evening, without knowing that the place was haunted, wrapped himself in his plaid, and lay down to sleep till the morning. About midnight he was awaked by the most enchanting music; and on listening, he heard it to be the voice of a woman singing to her child. She sung the verses twice over, so that next morning he had several of them by heart. Fisher had heard them often recited in Gaelic, and he said they were wild beyond human conception. He remembered only a few lines, which were to the same purport with the Spirit's Song here inserted, namely, that she (the singer) had brought her babe from the regions below to be cooled by the breeze of the world, and that they would soon be obliged to part, for the child was going to heaven, and she was to remain for a season in purgatory. I had not before heard any thing so truly romantic.

Note XII.
That the pine, which for ages had shed a bright halo,
Afar round the mountains of Highland Glen-Falo,
Should wither and fall ere the turn of yon moon,
Smit through by the canker of hated Colquhoon.—P. 79.

The pine was the standard, and is still the crest of the M'Gregors; and it is well known that the proscription of that clan was occasioned by a slaughter of the Colquhoons, who were its constant and inveterate enemies. That bloody business let loose the vengeance of the country upon them, which had nearly extirpated the name. The Campbells and the Grahams arose and hunted them down like wild beasts, until a M'Gregor could no more be found.

Note XIII.
Earl Walter.—P. 82.

This ballad is founded on a well known historical fact. Hollingshed mentions it slightly in the following words. "A Frenchman named Sir Anthony Darcie, knight, called afterwards *Le Sir de la Bawtie,* came through England into Scotland, to seek feats of arms. And coming to the king the four and twentie of September, the Lord Hamilton fought with him right valiantly, and so as neither of them lost any piece of honour."

Note XIV.
From this the Hamiltons of Clyde,
Their royal lineage draw.—P. 90.

The Princess Margaret of Scotland was married to the Lord Hamilton when only sixteen years of age, who received the earldom of Arran as her dowry. Hollingshed says, "Of this marriage, those of the house of Hamilton are descended, and are nearest of blood to the crown of Scotland, as they pretend; for (as saith Lesleus, *lib.* viii, p. 316.) if the line of the Stewards fail, the crown is to come to them."

Note XV.
Kilmeny.—P. 92.

Beside the old tradition on which this ballad is founded, there are some modern incidents of a similar nature, which cannot well be accounted for, yet are as well attested as any occurrence that has taken place in the present age. The relation may be amusing to some readers.

A man in the parish of Traquair, and county of Peebles, was busied one day casting turf in a large open field opposite to the mansion-house—the spot is well known, and still pointed out as rather unsafe; his daughter, a child seven years of age, was playing beside him, and amusing him with her prattle. Chancing to ask a question at her, he was astonished at receiving no answer, and, looking behind him, he perceived that his child was not there. He always averred that, as far as he could remember, she had been talking to him about half a minute before; he was certain it was not above a whole one at most. It was in vain that he ran searching all about like one distracted, calling her name;—no trace of her remained. He went home in a state of mind that may be better conceived than expressed, and raised the people of the parish, who searched for her several days with the same success. Every pool in the river, every bush and den on the mountains around was searched in vain. It was remarked that the father never much encouraged the search, being thoroughly persuaded that she was carried away by some invisible being, else she could not have vanished so suddenly. As a last resource, he applied to the minister of Inverlethen, a neighbouring divine of exemplary piety and zeal in religious matters, who enjoined him to cause prayers be offered to God for her in seven Christian churches, next Sabbath, at the same instant of time; "and then," said he, "if she is dead, God will forgive our sin in praying for the dead, as we do it through ignorance; and if she is still alive, I will answer for it, that all the devils in hell shall be unable to keep her." The injunction was punctually attended to. She was remembered in the prayers of all the neighbouring congregations, next Sunday, at the same hour, and never were there such prayers for fervour heard before. There was one divine in particular, Mr Davidson, who prayed in such a manner that all the hearers trembled. As the old divine foreboded, so it fell out. On that very day, and within an hour of the time on which these prayers were offered, the girl was found, in the Plora wood, sitting, picking the bark from a tree. She could give no perfect account of the circumstances which had befallen to her, but she said she did not want plenty of meat, for that her mother came and fed her with milk and bread several times a day, and sung her to sleep at night. Her skin had acquired a blueish cast, which wore gradually off in the course of a few weeks. Her name was Salton,—she lived to be the mother of a family.

Another circumstance, though it happened still later, is not less remarkable. A shepherd of Tushilaw, in the parish of Ettrick, whose name was Walter Dalgliesh, went out to the heights of that farm, one Sabbath morning, to herd the young sheep for his son, and let him to church. He took his own dinner along with him, and his son's breakfast. When the sermons were over, the lad went straight home, and did not return to his father. Night came, but nothing of the old shepherd appeared. When it grew very late his dog came home—seemed terrified, and refused to take any meat. The family were ill at ease during the night, especially as they never had known his dog leave him before; and early next morning the lad arose and went to the height to look after his father and his flock. He found his sheep all scattered, and his father's dinner unbroken, lying on the same spot where they had parted the day before. At the distance of 20 yards from the spot, the plaid which the old man wore was lying as if it had been flung from him, and a little farther on, in the same direction, his bonnet was found, but nothing of himself. The country people, as on all such occasions, rose in great numbers, and searched for him many days. My father, and several old men still alive, were of the party. He could not be found or heard of, neither dead nor alive, and at length they gave up all thoughts of ever seeing him more.

On the 20th day after his disappearance, a shepherd's wife, at a place called Berry-bush, came in as the family was sitting down to dinner, and said, that if it were possible to believe that Walter Dalgleish was still in existence, she would say yonder was he coming down the hill. They all ran out to watch the phenomena, and as the person approached nigher, they perceived that it was actually he, walking without his plaid and his bonnet. The place where he was first descried is not a mile distant from that where he was last seen. When he came into the house, he shook hands with them all—asked for his family, and spoke as if he had been absent for years, and as if convinced something had befallen them. As they perceived something singular in his looks and manner, they unfortunately forbore asking him any questions at first, but desired him to sit and share their dinner. This he readily complied with, and began to sup some broth with seeming eagerness. He had only taken one or two spoonfuls when he suddenly stopped, a kind of rattling noise was heard in his breast, and he sunk back in a faint. They put him to bed, and from that time forth he never spoke another word that any person could make sense of. He was removed to his own home, where he lingered a few weeks, and then died. What befel him remains to this day a mystery, and for ever must.

Note XVI.
But oft the listening groups stood still,
For spirits talked along the hill.–P. 106.

The echoes of evening, which are occasioned by the voices or mirth of different parties not aware of each other, have a curious and striking effect. I have known some country people terrified almost out of their senses at hearing voices and laughter among cliffs, where they knew it impossible for human being to reach. Some of the echoes around Edinburgh are extremely grand; what would they then be were the hills covered with wood? I have witnessed nothing more romantic than from a situation behind the Pleasance, where all the noises of the city are completely hushed, to hear the notes of the drum, trumpet, and bugle, poured from the cliffs of Salisbury, and the viewless cannons thundering from the rock. The effect is truly sublime.

Note XVII.
Mary Scott.–P. 108.

This ballad is founded on the old song of *The grey Goss Hawk*. The catastrophe is the same, and happens at the same place, namely, in St Mary's churchyard. The castle of Tushilaw, where the chief scene of the tale is laid, stood on a shelve of the hill which overlooks the junction of the rivers Ettrick and Rankleburn. It is a singular situation, and seems to have been chosen for the extensive prospect of the valley which it commands both to the east and west. It was the finest old baronial castle of which the Forest can boast, but the upper arches and turrets fell in, of late years, with a crash that alarmed the whole neighbourhood. It is now a huge heap of ruins. Its last inhabitant was Adam Scott, who was long denominated in the south the *King of the Border*, but the courtiers called him the *King of Thieves*. King James V. acted upon the same principle with these powerful chiefs, most of whom disregarded his authority, as Bonaparte has done with the sovereigns of Europe. He always managed matters so as to take each of them single-handed—made a rapid and secret march—overthrew one or two of them, and then returned directly home till matters were ripe for taking the advantage of some other. He marched on one day from Edinburgh to Meggatdale, accompanied by a chosen body of horsemen, surprised Peres Cockburn, a bold and capricious outlaw who tyrannized over those parts, hanged him over his own gate, sacked and burnt his castle of Henderland, and divided his lands between two of his principal followers, Sir James Stuart and the Lord Hume. From Henderland he marched across the mountains by a wild unfrequented path, still called *the King's Road*, and appeared before the gates of Tushilaw about sun-rise. Scott was completely taken by surprise; he, however, rushed to arms with his few friends who were present, and, after a desperate but unequal conflict, King James overcame him, plundered his castle of riches and stores to a prodigious amount, hanged the old Border king over a huge tree which is still growing in the corner of the castle yard, and over which he himself had hanged many a one, carried his head with him in triumph to Edinburgh, and placed it on a pole over one of the ports. There was a long and deadly feud between the Scotts and the Kers in those days; the Pringles, Murrays, and others around, always joined with the latter, in order to keep down the too powerful Scotts, who were not noted as the best of neighbours.

Note XVIII.
King Edward's dream.–P. 130.

The scene of this ballad is on the banks of the Eden in Cumberland, a day's march back from Burgh, on the sands of Solway, where King Edward I. died, in the midst of an expedition against the Scots, in which he had solemnly sworn to extirpate them as a nation.

Note XIX.
Dumlanrig.–P. 135.

This ballad relates to a well-known historical fact, of which tradition has preserved an accurate and feasible detail. The battles took place two or three years subsequent to the death of King James V. I have heard that it is succinctly related by some historian, but I have forgot who it is. Hollingshed gives a long bungling account of the matter, but places the one battle a year before the other; whereas it does not appear that Lennox made two excursions into Nithsdale, at the head of the English forces, or fought two bloody battles with the laird of Dumlanrig on the same ground, as the historian would insinuate. He says, that Dumlanrig, after pursuing them cautiously for some time, was overthrown in attempting to cross a ford of the river too rashly, that he lost two of his principal kinsmen, and 200 of his followers, had several spears broken upon his body, and escaped only by the goodness of his horse. The battle which took place next night, he relates as having happened next year; but it must be visible to every reader that he is speaking of the same incidents in the annals of both years. In the second engagement he acknowledges that Dumlanrig defeated the English horse, which he attributes to a desertion from the latter, but that, after pursuing them as far as Dalswinton, they were joined by the foot, and retrieved the day. The account given of the battles by Lesleus and Fran. Thin seems to have been so different, that they have misled the chronologer; the names of the towns and villages appearing to him so different, whereas a local knowledge of the country would have convinced him that both accounts related to the same engagements.

Note XX.
M'Kinnon the Abbot–P. 151.

To describe the astonishing scenes to which this romantic tale relates, Icolmkill and Staffa, so well known to the curious, would only be multiplying pages to no purpose.

Note XXI.
O, wise was the founder, and well said he,
"Where there are women mischief must be!"–P. 152.

St Columba placed the nuns in an island at a little distance from I, as the natives call Iona. He would not suffer either a cow or a woman to set foot on it; "for where there are cows," said he, "there must be women; and where there are women, there must be mischief."

Note XXII.
The harp of Ettrick rung again.–P. 167.

That some notable bard flourished in Ettrick Forest in that age, is evident from the numerous ballads and songs which relate to places in that country, and incidents that happened there. Many of these are of a very superior cast. *Outlaw Murray, Young Tam Lean Of Carterhaugh, Jamie Telfer i' the fair Dodhead, The dowy Downs of Yarrow,* and many others are of the number. Dumbar, in his lament for the bards, merely mentions him by the title of *Etrick*; more of him we know not.

Note XXIII.
Gardyn is crowned with garlands gay,
And bears the envied prize away.–P. 167.

Queen Mary's harp, of most curious workmanship, was found in the house of Lude, on the banks of the Garry in Athol, as was the old Caledonian harp. They were both brought to that house by a bride, which the chieftain of Lude married from the family of Gardyn of Banchory, (now Garden of Troup.) It was defaced of all its gems, and Queen Mary's portrait, set in gold, during the last rebellion. See Gunn *on the Harp.*

Note XXIV.
Bangour the daring task essayed.–P. 170.

Alluding to his popular ballad beginning, *Busk ye, busk ye, my bonny bonny bride."*

Note XXV.
Redoubted Ramsay.–P. 170.

Alluding to his song of *Ettrick Banks,* in the *Tea-Table Miscellany.*

Note XXVI.
Langhorne arrived, &c.–P. 170.

Alluding to his poem of *Genius and Valour,* or *Yarrow Banks,* and *Groves of Endermay.*

Note XXVII.
Sweet rung the harp to Logan's hand.–P. 170.

Alluding to his beautiful song, *The Braes of Yarrow.*

THE END

Marie Queen of Scots

*Sketched by Sir John Medina, from a Picture in the
Royal Cabinet at Versailles.*

Etched by W. & D. Lizars.

THE

QUEEN'S WAKE:

A

Legendary Poem.

By JAMES HOGG.

Be mine to read the visions old,
Which thy awakening Bards have told;
And whilst they meet my tranced view,
Hold each strange tale devoutly true.

COLLINS.

FIFTH EDITION.

EDINBURGH;

WILLIAM BLACKWOOD, PRINCE'S-STREET:

AND JOHN MURRAY, ALBEMARLE-STREET, LONDON.

1819.

TO

Her Royal Highness

PRINCESS CHARLOTTE OF WALES,

A SHEPHERD

AMONG

THE MOUNTAINS OF SCOTLAND,

DEDICATES

THIS POEM.

ELTRIVE, *May* 1811.

Introduction

Introduction

Now burst, ye Winter clouds that lower,
Fling from your folds the piercing shower;
Sing to the tower and leafless tree,
Ye cold winds of adversity;
Your blights, your chilling influence shed,   5
On wareless heart, and houseless head,
Your ruth or fury I disdain,
I've found my Mountain Lyre again.

Come to my heart, my only stay!
Companion of a happier day!   10
Thou gift of Heaven, thou pledge of good,
Harp of the mountain and the wood!
I little thought, when first I tried
Thy notes by lone Saint Mary's side,
When in a deep untrodden den,   15
I found thee in the braken glen,
I little thought that idle toy
Should e'er become my only joy!

A maiden's youthful smiles had wove
Around my heart the toils of love,   20
When first thy magic wires I rung,
And on the breeze thy numbers flung.
The fervid tear played in mine eye;
I trembled, wept, and wondered why.
Sweet was the thrilling ecstacy: 25
I know not if 'twas love or thee.

Weened not my heart, when youth had flown
Friendship would fade, or fortune frown;
When pleasure, love, and mirth were past,
That thou should'st prove my all at last!   30
Jeered by conceit and lordly pride,
I flung my soothing harp aside;
With wayward fortune strove a while;
Wrecked in a world of self and guile.

Again I sought the braken hill;   35
Again sat musing by the rill;
My wild sensations all were gone,
And only thou wert left alone.
Long hast thou in the moorland lain,
Now welcome to my heart again.   40

The russet weed of mountain gray
No more shall round thy border play;
No more the brake-flowers, o'er thee piled,
Shall mar thy tones and measures wild.
Harp of the Forest, thou shalt be   45
Fair as the bud on forest tree!
Sweet be thy strains, as those that swell
In Ettrick's green and fairy dell;
Soft as the breeze of falling even,
And purer than the dews of heaven.   50

Of minstrel honours, now no more;
Of bards, who sung in days of yore;
Of gallant chiefs, in courtly guise;
Of ladies' smiles, of ladies' eyes;
Of royal feast and obsequies;   55
When Caledon, with look severe,
Saw Beauty's hand her sceptre bear,–
By cliff and haunted wild I'll sing,
Responsive to thy dulcet string.

When wanes the circling year away,   60
When scarcely smiles the doubtful day,
Fair daughter of Dunedin, say,
Hast thou not heard, at midnight deep,
Soft music on thy slumbers creep?
At such a time, if careless thrown   65
Thy slender form on couch of down,
Hast thou not felt, to nature true,
The tear steal from thine eye so blue?
If then thy guiltless bosom strove
In blissful dreams of conscious love,   70
And even shrunk from proffer bland
Of lover's visionary hand,
On such ecstatic dream when brake

The music of the midnight Wake,
Hast thou not weened thyself on high, 75
List'ning to angels' melody,
'Scaped from a world of cares away,
To dream of love and bliss for aye?

The dream dispelled, the music gone,
Hast thou not, sighing, all alone, 80
Proffered thy vows to Heaven, and then
Blest the sweet Wake, and slept again?

Then list, ye maidens, to my lay,
Though old the tale, and past the day;
Those Wakes, now played by minstrels poor, 85
At midnight's darkest, chillest hour,
Those humble Wakes, now scorned by all,
Were first begun in courtly hall,
When royal MARY, blithe of mood,
Kept holiday at Holyrood. 90

Scotland, involved in factious broils,
Groaned deep beneath her woes and toils,
And looked o'er meadow, dale, and lea,
For many a day her Queen to see;
Hoping that then her woes would cease, 95
And all her vallies smile in peace.
The Spring was past, the Summer gone;
Still vacant stood the Scottish throne:
But scarce had Autumn's mellow hand
Waved her rich banner o'er the land, 100
When rang the shouts, from tower and tree,
That Scotland's Queen was on the sea.
Swift spread the news o'er down and dale,
Swift as the lively autumn gale;
Away, away, it echoed still, 105
O'er many a moor and Highland hill,
Till rang each glen and verdant plain,
From Cheviot to the northern main.

Each bard attuned the loyal lay,
And for Dunedin hied away; 110
Each harp was strung in woodland bower,

In praise of beauty's bonniest flower.
The chiefs forsook their ladies fair;
The priest his beads and books of prayer;
The farmer left his harvest day,   115
The shepherd all his flocks to stray;
The forester forsook the wood,
And hasted on to Holyrood.

After a youth, by woes o'ercast,
After a thousand sorrows past,   120
The lovely Mary once again
Set foot upon her native plain;
Kneeled on the pier with modest grace,
And turned to heaven her beauteous face.
'Twas then the caps in air were blended,   125
A thousand thousand shouts ascended;
Shivered the breeze around the throng;
Gray barrier cliffs the peals prolong;
And every tongue gave thanks to Heaven,
That Mary to their hopes was given.   130

Her comely form and graceful mien,
Bespoke the Lady and the Queen;
The woes of one so fair and young,
Moved every heart and every tongue.
Driven from her home, a helpless child,   135
To brave the winds and billows wild;
An exile bred in realms afar,
Amid commotion, broil, and war.
In one short year her hopes all crossed,—
A parent, husband, kingdom lost!   140
And all ere eighteen years had shed
Their honours o'er her royal head.
For such a Queen, the Stuarts' heir,
A Queen so courteous, young, and fair,
Who would not every foe defy!   145
Who would not stand! who would not die!

Light on her airy steed she sprung,
Around with golden tassels hung,
No chieftain there rode half so free,
Or half so light and gracefully.   150

How sweet to see her ringlets pale
Wide waving in the southland gale,
Which through the broom-wood blossoms flew,
To fan her cheeks of rosy hue!
Whene'er it heaved her bosom's screen,   155
What beauties in her form were seen!
And when her courser's mane it swung,
A thousand silver bells were rung.
A sight so fair, on Scottish plain,
A Scot shall never see again.   160

When Mary turned her wondering eyes
On rocks that seemed to prop the skies;
On palace, park, and battled pile;
On lake, on river, sea, and isle;
O'er woods and meadows bathed in dew,   165
To distant mountains wild and blue;
She thought the isle that gave her birth,
The sweetest, wildest land on earth.

Slowly she ambled on her way
Amid her lords and ladies gay.   170
Priest, abbot, layman, all were there,
And Presbyter with look severe.
There rode the lords of France and Spain,
Of England, Flanders, and Lorraine,
While serried thousands round them stood,   175
From shore of Leith to Holyrood.

Though Mary's heart was light as air
To find a home so wild and fair;
To see a gathered nation by,
And rays of joy from every eye;   180
Though frequent shouts the welkin broke,
Though courtiers bowed and ladies spoke,
An absent look they oft could trace
Deep settled on her comely face.
Was it the thought, that all alone   185
She must support a rocking throne?
That Caledonia's rugged land
Might scorn a Lady's weak command,
And the Red Lion's haughty eye
Scowl at a maiden's feet to lie?   190

No; 'twas the notes of Scottish song,
Soft pealing from the countless throng.
So mellowed came the distant swell,
That on her ravished ear it fell
Like dew of heaven, at evening close,   195
On forest flower or woodland rose.
For Mary's heart, to nature true,
The powers of song and music knew:
But all the choral measures bland,
Of anthems sung in southern land,   200
Appeared an useless pile of art,
Unfit to sway or melt the heart,
Compared with that which floated by,–
Her simple native melody.

As she drew nigh the Abbey stile,   205
She halted, reined, and bent the while:
She heard the Caledonian lyre
Pour forth its notes of runic fire;
But scarcely caught the ravished Queen,
The minstrel's song that flowed between;   210
Entranced upon the strain she hung,
'Twas thus the gray-haired minstrel sung.–

The Song

"O! Lady dear, fair is thy noon,
But man is like the inconstant moon:
Last night she smiled o'er lawn and lea;   215
That moon will change, and so will he.

"Thy time, dear Lady, 's a passing shower;
Thy beauty is but a fading flower;
Watch thy young bosom, and maiden eye,
For the shower must fall, and the flow'ret die."–   220

What ails my Queen? said good Argyle,
Why fades upon her cheek the smile?
Say, rears your steed too fierce and high?
Or sits your golden seat awry?

Ah! no, my Lord! this noble steed, 225
Of Rouen's calm and generous breed,
Has borne me over hill and plain,
Swift as the dun-deer of the Seine.
But such a wild and simple lay,
Poured from the harp of minstrel gray, 230
My every sense away it stole,
And swayed a while my raptured soul.
O! say, my Lord (for you must know
What strains along your vallies flow,
And all the hoards of Highland lore), 235
Was ever song so sweet before?—

Replied the Earl, as round he flung,—
Feeble the strain that minstrel sung!
My royal Dame, if once you heard
The Scottish lay from Highland bard, 240
Then might you say, in raptures meet,
No song was ever half so sweet!

It nerves the arm of warrior wight
To deeds of more than mortal might;
'Twill make the maid, in all her charms, 245
Fall weeping in her lover's arms;
'Twill charm the mermaid from the deep;
Make mountain oaks to bend and weep;
Thrill every heart with horrors dire,
And shape the breeze to forms of fire. 250

When poured from greenwood-bower at even,
'Twill draw the spirits down from heaven;
And all the fays that haunt the wood,
To dance around in frantic mood,
And tune their mimic harps so boon 255
Beneath the cliff and midnight moon.
Ah! yes, my Queen! if once you heard
The Scottish lay from Highland bard,
Then might you say in raptures meet,
No song was ever half so sweet.— 260

Queen Mary lighted in the court;
Queen Mary joined the evening's sport;

Yet though at table all were seen,
To wonder at her air and mien;
Though courtiers fawned and ladies sung,   265
Still in her ear the accents rung,–
"*Watch thy young bosom, and maiden eye,*
"*For the shower must fall, and the flowret die.*"
These words prophetic seemed to be,
Foreboding wo and misery;   270
And much she wished to prove ere long,
The wonderous powers of Scottish song.

When next to ride the Queen was bound,
To view the city's ample round,
On high amid the gathered crowd,   275
A herald thus proclaim'd aloud:–

"Peace, peace to Scotland's wasted vales,
To her dark heaths and Highland dales;
To her brave sons of warlike mood,
To all her daughters fair and good;   280
Peace o'er her ruined vales shall pour,
Like beam of heaven behind the shower.
Let every harp and echo ring;
Let maidens smile and poets sing;
For love and peace entwined shall sleep,   285
Calm as the moon-beam on the deep;
By waving wood and wandering rill,
On purple heath and Highland hill.

"The soul of warrior stern to charm,
And bigotry and rage disarm,   290
Our Queen commands, that every bard
Due honours have, and high regard.
If, to his song of rolling fire,
He join the Caledonian lyre,
And skill in legendary lore,   295
Still higher shall his honours soar.
For all the arts beneath the heaven,
That man has found, or God has given,
None draws the soul so sweet away,
As music's melting mystic lay;   300
Slight emblem of the bliss above,
It soothes the spirit all to love.

"To cherish this attractive art,
To lull the passions, mend the heart,
And break the moping zealot's chains,   305
Hear what our lovely Queen ordains.

"Each Caledonian bard must seek
Her courtly halls on Christmas week,
That then the Royal Wake may be
Cheered by their thrilling minstrelsy.   310
No ribaldry the Queen must hear,
No song unmeet for maiden's ear,
No jest, nor adulation bland,
But legends of our native land;
And he whom most the court regards,   315
High be his honours and rewards.
Let every Scottish bard give ear,
Let every Scottish bard appear;
He then before the court must stand,
In native garb, with harp in hand.   320
At home no minstrel dare to tarry:
High the behest.—God save Queen Mary!"

Little recked they, that idle throng,
Of music's power or minstrel's song;
But crowding their young Queen around,   325
Whose stately courser pawed the ground,
Her beauty more their wonder swayed,
Than all the noisy herald said;
Judging the proffer all in sport,
An idle whim of idle court.   330
But many a bard preferred his prayer;
For many a Scottish bard was there.
Quaked each fond heart with raptures strong,
Each thought upon his harp and song;
And turning home without delay,   335
Coned his wild strain by mountain gray.

Each glen was sought for tales of old,
Of luckless love, of warrior bold,
Of ravished maid, or stolen child
By freakish fairy of the wild;   340
Of sheeted ghost, that had revealed

Dark deeds of guilt from man concealed;
Of boding dreams, of wandering spright,
Of dead-lights glimmering through the night;
Yea, every tale of ruth or weir,   345
Could waken pity, love, or fear,
Were decked anew, with anxious pain,
And sung to native airs again.

Alas! those lays of fire once more
Are wrecked 'mid heaps of mouldering lore!   350
And feeble he who dares presume
That heavenly Wake-light to relume.
But, grieved the legendary lay
Should perish from our land for aye,
While sings the lark above the wold,   355
And all his flocks rest in the fold,
Fondly he strikes, beside the pen,
The harp of Yarrow's braken glen.

December came; his aspect stern
Glared deadly o'er the mountain cairn;   360
A polar sheet was round him flung,
And ice-spears at his girdle hung;
O'er frigid field, and drifted cone,
He strode undaunted and alone;
Or, throned amid the Grampians gray,   365
Kept thaws and suns of heaven at bay.

Not stern December's fierce control
Could quench the flame of minstrel's soul:
Little recked they, our bards of old,
Of Autumn's showers, or Winter's cold.   370
Sound slept they on the nighted hill,
Lulled by the winds or babbling rill:
Curtained within the Winter cloud;
The heath their couch, the sky their shroud.
Yet their's the strains that touch the heart,   375
Bold, rapid, wild, and void of art.

Unlike the bards, whose milky lays
Delight in these degenerate days:
Their crystal spring, and heather brown,
Is changed to wine and couch of down;   380

Effeminate as lady gay,—
Such as the bard, so is his lay!

But then was seen, from every vale,
Through drifting snows and rattling hail,
Each Caledonian minstrel true,   385
Dressed in his plaid and bonnet blue,
With harp across his shoulders slung,
And music murmuring round his tongue,
Forcing his way, in raptures high,
To Holyrood his skill to try.   390

Ah! when at home the songs they raised,
When gaping rustics stood and gazed,
Each bard believed, with ready will,
Unmatched his song, unmatched his skill!
But when the royal halls appeared,   395
Each aspect changed, each bosom feared;
And when in court of Holyrood
Filed harps and bards around him stood,
His eye emitted cheerless ray,
His hope, his spirit sunk away: 400
There stood the minstrel, but his mind
Seemed left in native glen behind.

Unknown to men of sordid heart,
What joys the poet's hopes impart;
Unknown, how his high soul is torn   405
By cold neglect, or canting scorn:
That meteor torch of mental light,
A breath can quench, or kindle bright.
Oft has that mind, which braved serene
The shafts of poverty and pain,   410
The Summer toil, the Winter blast,
Fallen victim to a frown at last.
Easy the boon he asks of thee;
O! spare his heart in courtesy!

There rolled each bard his anxious eye,   415
Or strode his adversary by.
No cause was there for names to scan,
Each minstrel's plaid bespoke his clan;

And the blunt borderer's plain array,
The bonnet broad and blanket gray.   420
Bard sought of bard a look to steal;
Eyes measured each from head to heel.
Much wonder rose, that men so famed,
Men save with rapture never named,
Looked only so,–they could not tell,–   425
Like other men, and scarce so well.
Though keen the blast, and long the way,
When twilight closed that dubious day,
When round the table all were set,
Small heart had they to talk or eat;   430
Red look askance, blunt whisper low,
Awkward remark, uncourtly bow,
Were all that past in that bright throng,
That group of genuine sons of song.

One did the honours of the board,   435
Who seemed a courtier or a lord.
Strange his array and speech withal,
Gael deemed him southern–southern, Gael.
Courteous his mien, his accents weak,
Lady in manner as in make;   440
Yet round the board a whisper ran,
That that same gay and simpering man
A minstrel was of wonderous fame,
Who from a distant region came,
To bear the prize beyond the sea   445
To the green shores of Italy.

The wine was served, and, sooth to say,
Insensibly it stole away.
Thrice did they drain the allotted store,
And wondering skinkers dun for more;   450
Which vanished swifter than the first,–
Little weened they the poets' thirst.

Still as that ruddy juice they drained,
The eyes were cleared, the speech regained;
And latent sparks of fancy glowed,   455
Till one abundant torrent flowed
Of wit, of humour, social glee,
Wild music, mirth, and revelry.

Just when a jest had thrilled the crowd,
Just when the laugh was long and loud, 460
Entered a squire with summons smart;–
That was the knell that pierced the heart!–
"The court awaits;" he bowed–was gone,–
Our bards sat changed to busts of stone.
As ever ye heard the green-wood dell, 465
On morn of June one warbled swell,
If burst the thunder from on high,
How hushed the woodland melody!
Even so our bards shrunk at the view
Of what they wished, and what they knew. 470

Their numbers given, the lots were cast,
To fix the names of first and last;
Then to the dazzling hall were led,
Poor minstrels less alive than dead.

There such a scene entranced the view, 475
As heart of poet never knew.
'Twas not the flash of golden gear,
Nor blaze of silver chandelier;
Not Scotland's chiefs of noble air,
Nor dazzling rows of ladies fair; 480
'Twas one enthroned the rest above,–
Sure 'twas the Queen of grace and love!
Taper the form, and fair the breast
Yon radiant golden zones invest,
Where the vexed rubies blench in death, 485
Beneath yon lips and balmy breath.
Coronal gems of every dye,
Look dim above yon beaming eye:
Yon cheeks outvie the dawning's glow,
Red shadowed on a wreath of snow. 490

Oft the rapt bard had thought alone,
Of charms by mankind never known,
Of virgins, pure as opening day,
Or bosom of the flower of May:
Oft dreamed of beings free from stain, 495
Of maidens of the emerald main,
Of fairy dames in grove at even,

Of angels in the walks of heaven:
But, nor in earth, the sea, nor sky,
In fairy dream, nor fancy's eye,   500
Vision his soul had ever seen
Like MARY STUART, Scotland's Queen.

The Queen's Wake

Night the First

The

Queen's Wake

NIGHT THE FIRST

HUSHED was the Court—the courtiers gazed—
Each eye was bent, each soul amazed,
To see that group of genuine worth,
Those far-famed minstrels of the north.
So motley wild their garments seemed;   5
Their eyes, where tints of madness gleamed,
Fired with impatience every breast,
And expectation stood confest.

Short was the pause; the stranger youth,
The gaudy minstrel of the south,   10
Whose glossy eye and lady form
Had never braved the northern storm,
Stepped lightly forth,—kneeled three times low,—
And then, with many a smile and bow,
Mounted the form amid the ring,   15
And rung his harp's responsive string.
Though true the chords, and mellow-toned,
Long, long he twisted, long he coned;
Well pleased to hear his name they knew;
"'Tis Rizzio!" round in whispers flew.   20

Valet with Parma's knight he came,
An angler in the tides of fame;
And oft had tried, with anxious pain,
Respect of Scotland's Queen to gain.
Too well his eye, with searching art,   25
Perceived her fond, her wareless heart;
And though unskilled in Scottish song,
Her notice he had wooed so long;
With pain by night, and care by day,
He framed this fervid, flowery lay.—   30

Malcolm of Lorn

THE FIRST BARD'S SONG

I.

Came ye by Ora's verdant steep,
  That smiles the restless ocean over?
Heard ye a suffering maiden weep?
  Heard ye her name a faithful lover?
Saw ye an aged matron stand   35
O'er yon green grave above the strand,
Bent like the trunk of withered tree,
Or yon old thorn that sips the sea?
Fixed her dim eye, her face as pale
  As the mists that o'er her flew: 40
Her joy is fled like the flower of the vale,
  Her hope like the morning dew!
That matron was lately as proud of her stay,
As the mightiest monarch of sceptre or sway:
O list to the tale! 'tis a tale of soft sorrow,   45
Of Malcolm of Lorn, and young Ann of Glen-Ora.

II.

The sun is sweet at early morn,
  Just blushing from the ocean's bosom;
The rose that decks the woodland thorn
  Is fairest in its opening blossom;   50
Sweeter than opening rose in dew,
Than vernal flowers of richest hue,
Than fragrant birch or weeping willow,
Than red sun resting on the billow;
Sweeter than aught to mortals given   55
  The heart and soul to prove;
Sweeter than aught beneath the heaven,
  The joys of early love!
Never did maiden, and manly youth,
Love with such fervor, and love with such truth;   60
Or pleasures and virtues alternately borrow,
As Malcolm of Lorn, and fair Ann of Glen-Ora.

III.

The day is come, the dreaded day,
  Must part two loving hearts for ever;

The ship lies rocking in the bay,   65
   The boat comes rippling up the river:
O happy has the gloaming's eye
   In green Glen-Ora's bosom seen them!
But soon shall lands and nations lie,
   And angry oceans roll between them.   70
Yes, they must part, for ever part,
Chill falls the truth on either heart;
For honour, titles, wealth, and state,
In distant lands her sire await.
The maid must with her sire away,   75
   She cannot stay behind;
Strait to the south the pennons play,
   And steady is the wind.
Shall Malcolm relinquish the home of his youth,
And sail with his love to the lands of the south?   80
Ah, no! for his father is gone to the tomb:
One parent survives in her desolate home!
No child but her Malcolm to cheer her lone way:
Break not her fond heart, gentle Malcolm, O, stay!

IV.

The boat impatient leans ashore,   85
   Her prow sleeps on a sandy pillow;
The rower leans upon his oar,
   Already bent to brush the billow.
O! Malcolm, view yon melting eyes,
   With tears yon stainless roses steeping!   90
O! Malcolm, list thy mother's sighs;
   She's leaning o'er her staff and weeping!
Thy Anna's heart is bound to thine,
And must that gentle heart repine!
Quick from the shore the boat must fly;   95
Her soul is speaking through her eye;
Think of thy joys in Ora's shade;
   From Anna canst thou sever?
Think of the vows thou often hast made,
   To love the dear maiden for ever.   100
And canst thou forego such beauty and youth,
Such maiden honour and spotless truth?
Forbid it!–He yields; to the boat he draws nigh.
Haste, Malcolm, aboard, and revert not thine eye.

V.

That trembling voice, in murmurs weak,   105
   Comes not to blast the hopes before thee;
For pity, Malcolm, turn, and take
   A last farewell of her that bore thee.
She says no word to mar thy bliss;
A last embrace, a parting kiss,   110
Her love deserves;—then be thou gone;
A mother's joys are thine alone.
Friendship may fade, and fortune prove
   Deceitful to thy heart;
But never can a mother's love   115
   From her own offspring part.
That tender form, now bent and gray,
Shall quickly sink to her native clay;
Then who shall watch her parting breath,
And shed a tear o'er her couch of death?   120
Who follow the dust to its long long home,
And lay that head in an honoured tomb?

VI.

Oft hast thou, to her bosom prest,
   For many a day about been borne;
Oft hushed and cradled on her breast,   125
   And canst thou leave that breast forlorn?
O'er all thy ails her heart has bled;
Oft has she watched beside thy bed;
Oft prayed for thee in dell at even,
Beneath the pitying stars of heaven.   130
Ah! Malcolm, ne'er was parent yet
   So tender, so benign!
Never was maid so loved, so sweet,
   Nor soul so rent as thine!
He looked to the boat,—slow she heaved from the
   shore;   135
He saw his loved Anna all speechless implore:
But, grasped by a cold and a trembling hand,
He clung to his parent, and sunk on the strand.

VII.

The boat across the tide flew fast,
   And left a silver curve behind;   140
Loud sung the sailor from the mast,

Spreading his sails before the wind.
The stately ship, adown the bay,
  A corslet framed of heaving snow,
And flurred on high the slender spray,   145
  Till rainbows gleamed around her prow.
How strained was Malcolm's watery eye,
Yon fleeting vision to descry!
But, ah! her virgin form so fair,
Soon vanished in the liquid air.   150
Away to Ora's headland steep
  The youth retired the while,
And saw th' unpitying vessel sweep
  Around yon Highland isle.
His heart and his mind with that vessel had gone;   155
His sorrow was deep, and despairing his moan,
When, lifting his eyes from the green heaving deep,
He prayed the Almighty his Anna to keep.

VIII.

High o'er the crested cliffs of Lorn
  The curlew coned her wild bravura;   160
The sun, in pall of purple borne,
  Was hastening down the steeps of Jura.
The glowing ocean heaved her breast,
  Her wandering lover's glances under;
And shewed his radiant form, imprest   165
  Deep in a wavy world of wonder.
Not all the ocean's dyes at even,
Though varied as the bow of heaven;
The countless isles so dusky blue,
Nor medley of the gray curlew,   170
Could light on Malcolm's spirit shed;
  Their glory all was gone!
For his joy was fled, his hope was dead,
  And his heart forsaken and lone.
The sea-bird sought her roofless nest,   175
To warm her brood with her downy breast;
And near her home, on the margin dun,
A mother weeps o'er her duteous son.

IX.

One little boat alone is seen
  On all the lovely dappled main,   180

That softly sinks the waves between,
  Then vaults their heaving breasts again;
With snowy sail, and rower's sweep,
  Across the tide she seems to fly.
Why bears she on yon headland steep,   185
  Where neither house nor home is nigh?
Is that a vision from the deep
That springs ashore and scales the steep,
Nor ever stays its ardent haste
Till sunk upon young Malcolm's breast!   190
O! spare that breast so lowly laid,
  So fraught with deepest sorrow!
It is his own, his darling maid,
  Young Anna of Glen-Ora!–
"My Malcolm! part we ne'er again!   195
My father saw thy bosom's pain;
Pitied my grief from thee to sever;
Now I, and Glen-Ora, am thine for ever!"–

                    X.

That blaze of joy, through clouds of woe,
  Too fierce upon his heart did fall.   200
For, ah! the shaft had left the bow,
  Which power of man could not recall!
No word of love could Malcolm speak;
  No raptured kiss his lips impart;
No tear bedewed his shivering cheek,   205
  To ease the grasp that held his heart.
His arms essayed one kind embrace–
  Will they enclose her? never! never!
A smile set softly on his face,
  But ah! the eye was set for ever!   210
'Twas more than broken heart could brook!
How throbs that breast!–How still that look!
One shiver more! All! all is o'er!–
As melts the wave on level shore;
As fades the dye of falling even,   215
Far on the silver verge of heaven;
As on thy ear, the minstrel's lay,–
So died the comely youth away."

The strain died soft in note of woe,
Nor breath nor whisper 'gan to flow   220
From courtly circle; all as still
As midnight on the lonely hill.
So well that foreign minstrel's strain
Had mimicked passion, woe, and pain,
Seemed even the chilly hand of death   225
Stealing away his mellow breath.
So sighed—so stopp'd—so died his lay,—
His spirit too seemed fled for aye.

    'Tis true, the gay attentive throng
Admired, but loved not much, his song;   230
Admired his wonderous voice and skill,
His harp that thrilled or wept at will.
But that affected gaudy rhyme,
The querulous keys and changing chime,
Scarce could the Highland chieftain brook: 235
Disdain seemed kindling in his look,
That song so vapid, artful, terse,
Should e'er compete with Scottish verse.

    But she, the fairest of the fair,
Who sat enthroned in gilded chair,   240
Well skilled in foreign minstrelsy
And artful airs of Italy,
Listened his song, with raptures wild,
And on the happy minstrel smiled.
Soon did the wily stranger's eye   245
The notice most he wished espy,
Then poured his numbers bold and free,
Fired by the grace of majesty;
And when his last notes died away,
When sunk in well-feigned death he lay,   250
When round the crowd began to ring,
Thinking his spirit on the wing,—
First of the dames she came along,
Wept, sighed, and marvelled 'mid the throng.
And when they raised him, it was said   255
The beauteous Sovereign deigned her aid;
And in her hands, so soft and warm,
Upheld the minstrel's hand and arm.

Then oped his eye with rapture fired;
He smiled, and, bowing oft, retired;   260
Pleased he so soon had realized,
What more than gold or fame he prized.

Next in the list was Gardyn's name:
No sooner called than forth he came.
Stately he strode, nor bow made he,   265
Nor even a look of courtesy.
The simpering cringe, and fawning look,
Of him who late the lists forsook,
Roused his proud heart, and fired his eye,
That glowed with native dignity.   270

Full sixty years the bard had seen,
Yet still his manly form and mien,
His garb of ancient Caledon,
Where lines of silk and scarlet shone,
And golden garters 'neath his knee,   275
Announced no man of mean degree.

Upon his harp, of wonderous frame,
Was carved his lineage and his name.
There stood the cross that name above,
Fair emblem of Almighty love;   280
Beneath rose an embossment proud,—
A rose beneath a thistle bowed.

Lightly upon the form he sprung,
And his bold harp impetuous rung.
Not one by one the chords he tried,   285
But brushed them o'er from side to side,
With either hand, so rapid, loud,
Shook were the halls of Holyrood.
Then in a mellow tone, and strong,
He poured this wild and dreadful song.—   290

𝔜𝔬𝔲𝔫𝔤 𝔎𝔢𝔫𝔫𝔢𝔡𝔶

THE SECOND BARD'S SONG

I.

When the gusts of October had rifled the thorn,
   Had dappled the woodland, and umbered the plain,
In den of the mountain was Kennedy born:
   There hushed by the tempest, baptized with the rain.
His cradle, a mat that swung light on the oak;   295
His couch, the sear mountain-fern, spread on the rock;
The white knobs of ice from the chilled nipple hung,
And loud winter-torrents his lullaby sung.

II.

Unheeded he shivered, unheeded he cried;
   Soon died on the breeze of the forest his moan.   300
To his wailings, the weary wood-echo replied;
   His watcher, the wondering redbreast alone.
Oft gazed his young eye on the whirl of the storm,
And all the wild shades that the desert deform;
From cleft in the correi, which thunders had riven,   305
It oped on the pale fleeting billows of heaven.

III.

The nursling of misery, young Kennedy learned
   His hunger, his thirst, and his passions to feed:
With pity for others his heart never yearned,–
   Their pain was his pleasure,–their sorrow his meed.   310
His eye was the eagle's, the twilight his hue;
His stature like pine of the hill where he grew;
His soul was the neal-fire, inhaled from his den,
And never knew fear, save for ghost of the glen.

IV.

His father a chief, for barbarity known,   315
   Proscribed, and by gallant Macdougal expelled;
Where rolls the dark Teith through the valley of Down,
   The conqueror's menial he toiled in the field.
His master he loved not, obeyed with a scowl,
Scarce smothered his hate, and his rancour of soul;   320
When challenged, his eye and his colour would change,
His proud bosom nursing and planning revenge.

V.

Matilda, ah! woe that the wild rose's dye,
  Shed over thy maiden cheek, caused thee to rue!
O! why was the sphere of thy love-rolling eye   325
  Inlaid with the diamond, and dipt in the dew?
Thy father's sole daughter; his hope, and his care;
The child of his age, and the child of his prayer;
And thine was the heart that was gentle and kind,
And light as the feather, that sports in the wind.   330

VI.

To her home from the Lowlands, Matilda returned;
  All fair was her form, and untainted her mind.
Young Kennedy saw her, his appetite burned
  As fierce as the moor-flame impelled by the wind.
Was it love? No; the ray his dark soul never knew,   335
That spark which eternity burns to renew.
'Twas the flash of desire, kindled fierce by revenge,
Which savages feel the brown desert that range.

VII.

Sweet woman! too well is thy tenderness known;
  Too often deep sorrow succeeds thy love-smile;   340
Too oft, in a moment, thy peace overthrown,—
  Fair butt of delusion, of passion, and guile!
What heart will not bleed for Matilda so gay,
To art and to long perseverance a prey?
Why sings yon scared blackbird in sorrowful mood?   345
Why blushes the daisy deep in the green-wood?

VIII.

Sweet woman! with virtue, thou'rt lofty, thou'rt free;
  Yield that, thou'rt a slave, and the mark of disdain:
No blossom of spring is beleaguered like thee,
  Though brushed by the lightning, the wind, and the rain. 350
Matilda is fallen! With tears in her eye,
She seeks her destroyer; but only can sigh.
Matilda has fallen, and sorrow her doom,—
The flower of the valley is nipt in the bloom.

IX.

Ah! Kennedy, vengeance hangs over thine head!   355
  Escape to thy native Glengary forlorn.

Why art thou at midnight away from thy bed?
Why quakes thy big heart at the break of the morn?
Why chatters yon Magpie on gable so loud?
Why flits yon light vision in gossamer shroud?　　　360
How came yon white doves from the window to fly,
And hover on weariless wing to the sky?

X.

Yon Pie is the prophet of terror and death:
　　O'er Abel's green arbour that omen was given.
Yon pale boding phantom, a messenger wraith;　　　365
　　Yon doves two fair angels commissioned of Heaven.
The sun is in state, and the reapers in motion;
Why were they not called to their morning devotion?
Why slumbers Macdougal so long in his bed?
Ah! pale on his couch the old chieftain lies dead!　　　370

XI.

Though grateful the hope to the death-bed that flies,
　　That lovers and friends o'er our ashes will weep;
The soul, when released from her lingering ties,
　　In secret may see if their sorrows are deep.
Who wept for the worthy Macdougal?—Not one!　　　375
His darling Matilda, who, two months agone,
Would have mourned for her father in sorrow extreme,
Indulged in a painful delectable dream.

XII.

But, why do the matrons, while dressing the dead,
　　Sit silent, and look as if something they knew?　　　380
Why gaze on the features? Why move they the head,
　　And point at the bosom so dappled and blue?
Say, was there foul play?—Then, why sleeps the red thunder?
Ah! hold, for Suspicion stands silent with wonder.
The body's entomb'd, and the green turf laid over,—　　　385
Matilda is wed to her dark Highland lover.

XIII.

Yes, the new moon that stooped over green Aberfoyle,
　　And shed her light dews on a father's new grave,
Beheld, in her wane, the gay wedding turmoil,
　　And lighted the bride to her chamber at eve:　　　390
Blue, blue was the heaven; and, o'er the wide scene,

A vapoury silver veil floated serene,
A fairy perspective, that bore from the eye
Wood, mountain, and meadow, in distance to lie.

XIV.

The scene was so still, it was all like a vision;   395
   The lamp of the moon seemed as fading for ever.
'Twas awfully soft, without shade or elision;
   And nothing was heard but the rush of the river.
But why won't the bride-maidens walk on the lea,
Nor lovers steal out to the sycamore tree?   400
Why turn to the hall with those looks of confusion?
There's nothing abroad!–'tis a dream!–a delusion!

XV.

But why do the horses snort over their food,
   And cling to the manger in seeming dismay?
What scares the old owlet afar to the wood?   405
   Why screams the blue heron, as hastening away?
Say, why is the dog hid so deep in his cover?
Each window barred up, and the curtain drawn over;
Each white maiden bosom still heaving so high,
And fixed on another each fear-speaking eye?   410

XVI.

'Tis all an illusion! the lamp let us trim!
   Come, rouse thee, old minstrel, to strains of renown;
The old cup is empty, fill round to the brim,
   And drink the young pair to their chamber just gone.
Ha! why is the cup from the lip ta'en away?   415
Why fix'd every form like a statue of clay?
Say, whence is that outcry of horrid despair?
Haste, fly to the marriage bed-chamber, 'tis there.

XVII.

O! haste thee, Strath-Allan, Glen-Ogle, away,
   These outcries betoken wild horror and woe;   420
The dull ear of midnight is stunned with dismay;
   Glen-Ogle! Strath-Allan! fly swift as the roe.
'Mid darkness and death, on eternity's brim,
You stood with Macdonald and Archbald the grim;
Then why do you hesitate? why do you stand   425
With claymore unsheathed, and red taper in hand?

XVIII.

The tumult is o'er; not a murmur nor groan;
    What footsteps so madly pace through the saloon?
'Tis Kennedy, naked and ghastly alone,
    Who hies him away by the light of the moon.   430
All prostrate and bleeding, Matilda they found,
The threshold her pillow, her couch the cold ground;
Her features distorted, her colour the clay,
Her feelings, her voice, and her reason away.

XIX.

Ere morn they returned; but how well had they never!   435
    They brought with them horror too deep to sustain;
Returned but to chasten, and vanish for ever,
    To harrow the bosom and fever the brain.
List, list to her tale, youth, levity, beauty;–
O! sweet is the path of devotion and duty!–   440
When pleasure smiles sweetest, dread danger and death,
And think of Matilda, the flower of the Teith.

XX.

The Bride's Tale

"I had just laid me down, but no word could I pray!
    I had pillowed my head, and drawn up the bed-cover;
I thought of the grave where my loved father lay,   445
    So damp and so cold, with the grass growing over.
I look'd to my husband; but just as he came
To enter my couch, it seemed all in a flame,
A ghastly refulgence as bright as day-noon,
Though shut was the chamber from eye of the moon.   450

XXI.

"Bestower of being! in pity, O! hide
    That sight from the eye of my spirit for ever;
That page from the volume of memory divide,
    Or memory and being eternally sever!
My father approached; our bed-curtains he drew;   455
Ah! well the gray locks and pale features I knew.
I saw his fixt eye-balls indignantly glow;
Yet still in that look there was pity and woe.

XXII.

"O! hide thee, my daughter, he eagerly cried;
  O haste from the bed of that parricide lover!   460
Embrace not thy husband, unfortunate bride,
  Thy red cup of misery already runs over.
He strangled thy father! thy guilt paved the way;
Thy heart yet is blameless, O fly while you may!
Thy portion of life must calamity leaven;   465
But fly while there's hope of forgiveness from Heaven.

XXIII.

"And thou, fell destroyer of virtue and life!
  O! well may'st thou quake at thy terrible doom;
For body or soul, with barbarity rife,
  On earth is no refuge, in heaven no room.   470
Fly whither thou wilt, I will follow thee still,
To dens of the forest, or mists of the hill;
The task I'm assigned, which I'll never forego,
But chace thee from earth to thy dwelling below.

XXIV.

"The cave shall not cover, the cloud shall not hide thee;   475
  At noon I will wither thy sight with my frown;
In gloom of the night, I will lay me beside thee,
  And pierce with this weapon thy bosom of stone.
Fast fled the despoiler with howlings most dire,
Fast followed the spirit with rapier of fire;   480
Away, and away, through the silent saloon,
And away, and away, by the light of the moon.

XXV.

"To follow I tried, but sunk down at the door,
  Alas! from that trance that I ever awoke!
How wanders my mind! I shall see him no more,   485
  Till God shall yon gates everlasting unlock.
My poor brow is open, 'tis burning with pain,
O kiss it, sweet vision! O kiss it again!
Now give me thine hand; I will fly! I will fly!
Away, on the morn's dappled wing, to the sky."   490

XXVI.

The Conclusion

O! shepherd of Braco, look well to thy flock,
  The piles of Glen-Ardochy murmur and jar;
The rook and the raven converse from the rock,
  The beasts of the forest are howling afar.
Shrill pipes the goss-hawk his dire tidings to tell,   495
The gray mountain-falcon accords with his yell;
Aloft on bold pinion the eagle is borne,
To ring the alarm at the gates of the morn.

XXVII.

Ah! shepherd, thy kids wander safe in the wood,
  Thy lambs feed in peace on Ben-Ardochy's brow;   500
Then why is the hoary cliff sheeted with blood?
  And what the poor carcase lies mangled below?
Oh hie thee away to thy hut at the fountain,
And dig a lone grave on the top of yon mountain;
But fly it for ever when falls the gray gloaming,   505
For there a grim phantom still naked is roaming.

———————————

Gardyn with stately step withdrew,
While plaudits round the circle flew.

  Woe that the bard, whose thrilling song
Has poured from age to age along,   510
Should perish from the lists of fame,
And lose his only boon—a name.
Yet many a song of wonderous power,
Well known in cot and green-wood bower,
Wherever swells the shepherd's reed   515
On Yarrow's banks and braes of Tweed;
Yes, many a song of olden time,
Of rude array, and air sublime,
Though long on time's dark whirlpool tossed,
The song is saved, the bard is lost.   520

  Yet have I weened, when these I sung
On Ettrick banks, while mind was young;

When on the eve their strains I threw,
And youths and maidens round me drew;
Or chaunted in the lonely glen,   525
Far from the haunts and eyes of men;
Yes, I have weened, with fondest sigh,
The spirit of the bard was nigh:
Swung by the breeze on braken pile,
Or hovering o'er me with a smile.   530
Would fancy still her dreams combine,
That spirit, too, might breathe on mine;
Well pleased to see her songs the joy
Of that poor lonely shepherd boy.

'Tis said, and I believe the tale,   535
That many rhymes which still prevail,
Of genuine ardour, bold and free,
Were aye admired, and aye will be,
Had never been, or shortly stood,
But for that Wake at Holyrood.   540
Certes that many a bard of name,
Who there appeared and strove for fame,
No record names, nor minstrel's tongue;
Not even are known the lays they sung.

The fifth was from a western shore,   545
Where rolls the dark and sullen Orr.
Of peasant make, and doubtful mien,
Affecting airs of proud disdain;
Wide curled his raven locks and high,
Dark was his visage, dark his eye,   550
That glanced around on dames and men
Like falcons on the cliffs of Ken.
Some ruffian mendicant, whose wit
Presumed at much, for all unfit.
No one could read the character,   555
If *knave* or *genius* writ was there;
But all supposed, from mien and frame,
From Erin he an exile came.

With hollow voice, and harp ill strung,
Some bungling parody he sung,   560
Well known to maid and matron gray,

Through all the glens of Galloway;
For often had he conned it there,
With simpering and affected air.
Listened the Court, with sidelong bend,   565
In wonder how the strain would end.
But long ere that it grew so plain,
They scarce from hooting could refrain;
And each to others 'gan to say,
"What good can come from Galloway?"   570

   Woe for the *man* so indiscreet!
For bard would be a name unmeet
For self-sufficient sordid elf,
Whom none admires but he himself.
Unheard by him the scorner's tongue,   575
For still he capered and he sung,
With many an awkward gape the while,
And many a dark delighted smile,
Till round the throne the murmurs ran,
Till ladies blushed behind the fan;   580
And when the rustic ceased to sing,
A hiss of scorn ran round the ring.
Dark grinned the fool around the form,
With blood-shot eye, and face of storm;
Sprung from his seat, with awkward leap,   585
And muttered curses dark and deep.

   The sixth, too, from that country he,
Where heath-cocks bay o'er western Dee;
Where Summer spreads her purple screen
O'er moors where greensward ne'er was seen;   590
Nor shade, o'er all the prospect stern,
Save crusted rock, or warrior's cairn.

   Gentle his form, his manners meet,
His harp was soft, his voice was sweet;
He sung Lochryan's hapless maid,   595
In bloom of youth by love betrayed:
Turned from her lover's bower at last,
To brave the chilly midnight blast;
And bitterer far, the pangs to prove,
Of ruined fame, and slighted love;   600

A tender babe, her arms within,
Sobbing and "shivering at the chin."
No lady's cheek in court was dry,
So softly poured the melody.

The eighth was from the Leven coast: 605
The rest who sung that night are lost.

Mounted the bard of Fife on high,
Bushy his beard, and wild his eye:
His cheek was furrowed by the gale,
And his thin locks were long and pale.   610
Full hardly passed he through the throng,
Dragging on crutches, slow along,
His feeble and unhealthy frame,
And kindness welcomed as he came.
His unpresuming aspect mild,   615
Calm and benignant as a child,
Yet spoke to all that viewed him nigh,
That more was there than met the eye.
Some wizard of the shore he seemed,
Who through the scenes of life had dreamed,   620
Of spells that vital life benumb,
Of formless spirits wandering dumb,
Where aspins in the moon-beam quake,
By mouldering pile, or mountain lake.

He deemed that fays and spectres wan   625
Held converse with the thoughts of man;
In dreams their future fates foretold,
And spread the death-flame on the wold;
Or flagged at eve each restless wing,
In dells their vesper hymns to sing.   630

Such was our bard, such were his lays:
And long by green Benarty's base,
His wild wood notes, from ivy cave,
Had waked the dawning from the wave.
At evening fall, in lonesome dale,   635
He kept strange converse with the gale;
Held worldly pomp in high derision,
And wandered in a world of vision.

Of mountain ash his harp was framed,
The brazen chords all trembling flamed, 640
As in a rugged northern tongue,
This mad unearthly song he sung.

The Witch of Fife

THE EIGHTH BARD'S SONG

"Quhare haif ye been, ye ill womyne,
    These three lang nightis fra hame?
Quhat garris the sweit drap fra yer brow, 645
    Like clotis of the saut sea faem?

"It fearis me muckil ye haif seen
    Quhat good man never knew;
It fearis me muckil ye haif been
    Quhare the gray cock never crew. 650

"But the spell may crack, and the brydel breck,
    Then sherpe yer werde will be;
Ye had better sleipe in yer bed at hame,
    Wi' yer deire littil bairnis and me."—

'Sit dune, sit dune, my leil auld man, 655
    Sit dune, and listin to me;
I'll gar the hayre stand on yer crown,
    And the cauld sweit blind yer e'e.

'But tell nae wordis, my gude auld man,
    Tell never word again; 660
Or deire shall be yer courtisye,
    And driche and sair yer pain.

'The first leet night, quhan the new moon set,
    Quhan all was douffe and mirk,
We saddled ouir naigis wi' the moon-fern leif, 665
    And rode fra Kilmerrin kirk.

'Some horses ware of the brume-cow framit,
    And some of the greine bay tree;

But mine was made of ane humloke schaw,
    And a stout stallion was he.   670

'We raide the tod doune on the hill,
    The martin on the law;
And we huntyd the hoolet out of brethe,
    And forcit him doune to fa.'–

"Quhat guid was that, ye ill womyne?   675
    Quhat guid was that to thee?
Ye wald better haif been in yer bed at hame,
    Wi' yer deire littil bairnis and me."–

'And aye we raide, and se merrily we raide,
    Throw the merkist gloffis of the night;   680
And we swam the floode, and we darnit the woode,
    Till we cam to the Lommond height.

'And quhen we cam to the Lommond height,
    Se lythlye we lychtid doune;
And we drank fra the hornis that never grew,   685
    The beer that was never browin.

'Then up there raise ane wee wee man,
    Franethe the moss-gray stane;
His fece was wan like the collifloure,
    For he nouthir had blude nor bane.   690

'He set ane reid-pipe till his muthe,
    And he playit se bonnilye,
Till the gray curlew, and the black-cock, flew
    To listen his melodye.

'It rang se sweet through the grein Lommond,   695
    That the nycht-winde lowner blew;
And it soupit alang the Loch Leven,
    And wakinit the white sea-mew.

'It rang se sweet through the grein Lommond,
    Se sweitly butt and se shill,   700
That the wezilis laup out of their mouldy holis,
    And dancit on the mydnycht hill.

'The corby craw cam gledgin near,
    The ern gede veeryng bye;
And the troutis laup out of the Leven Loch,   705
    Charmit with the melodye.

'And aye we dancit on the grein Lommond,
    Till the dawn on the ocean grew:
Ne wonder I was a weary wycht
    Quhan I cam hame to you.'–   710

"Quhat guid, quhat guid, my weird weird wyfe,
    Quhat guid was that to thee?
Ye wald better haif bein in yer bed at hame,
    Wi' yer deire littil bairnis and me."

'The second nycht, quhan the new moon set,   715
    O'er the roaryng sea we flew;
The cockle-shell our trusty bark,
    Our sailis of the grein sea-rue.

'And the bauld windis blew, and the fire-flauchtis flew,
    And the sea ran to the skie;   720
And the thunner it growlit, and the sea-dogs howlit,
    As we gaed scouryng bye.

'And aye we mountit the sea-green hillis,
    Quhill we brushit thro' the cludis of the hevin;
Than sousit dounright like the stern-shot light,   725
    Fra the liftis blue casement driven.

'But our taickil stood, and our bark was good,
    And se pang was our pearily prowe;
Quhan we culdna speil the brow of the wavis,
    We needilit them throu belowe.   730

'As fast as the hail, as fast as the gale,
    As fast as the midnycht leme,
We borit the breiste of the burstyng swale,
    Or fluffit i' the flotyng faem.

'And quhan to the Norraway shore we wan,   735
    We muntyd our steedis of the wynd,

And we splashit the floode, and we darnit the woode,
    And we left the shouir behynde.

'Fleet is the roe on the grein Lommond,
    And swift is the couryng grew;   740
The rein-deer dun can eithly run,
    Quhan the houndis and the hornis pursue.

'But nowther the roe, nor the rein-deir dun,
    The hinde nor the couryng grew,
Culd fly owr muntaine, muir, and dale,   745
    As owr braw steedis they flew.

'The dales war deep, and the Doffrinis steep,
    And we rase to the skyis e'e-bree;
Quhite, quhite was ouir rode, that was never trode,
    Owr the snawis of eternity!   750

'And quhan we cam to the Lapland lone,
    The fairies war all in array;
For all the genii of the north
    War keepyng their holeday.

'The warlock men and the weird wemyng,   755
    And the fays of the wood and the steep,
And the phantom hunteris all war there,
    And the mermaidis of the deep.

'And they washit us all with the witch-water,
    Distillit fra the moorland dew,   760
Quhill our beauty blumit like the Lapland rose,
    That wylde in the foreste grew.'—

"Ye lee, ye lee, ye ill womyne,
    Se loud as I heir ye lee!
For the warst-faurd wyfe on the shoris of Fyfe   765
    Is cumlye comparet wi' thee."—

'Then the mer-maidis sang and the woodlandis rang,
    Se sweetly swellit the quire;
On every cliff a herpe they hang,
    On every tree a lyre.   770

Witch of Fife

'And aye they sang, and the woodlandis rang,
    And we drank, and we drank se deep;
Then soft in the armis of the warlock men,
    We laid us dune to sleep.'–

"Away, away, ye ill womyne,   775
    An ill deide met ye dee!
Quhan ye hae pruvit se false to yer God,
    Ye can never pruve trew to me."–

'And there we lernit fra the fairy foke,
    And fra our master true,   780
The wordis that can beire us throu the air,
    And lokkis and baris undo.

'Last nycht we met at Maisry's cot;
    Richt weil the wordis we knew;
And we set a foot on the black cruik-shell,   785
    And out at the lum we flew.

'And we flew owr hill, and we flew owr dale,
    And we flew owr firth and sea,
Until we cam to merry Carlisle,
    Quhar we lightit on the lea.   790

'We gaed to the vault beyound the towir,
    Quhar we enterit free as ayr;
And we drank, and we drank of the bishopis wine
    Quhill we culde drynk ne mair.'–

"Gin that be trew, my gude auld wyfe,   795
    Whilk thou hast tauld to me,
Betide my death, betide my lyfe,
    I'll beire thee companye.

"Neist tyme ye gaung to merry Carlisle
    To drynk of the blude-reid wine,   800
Beshrew my heart, I'll fly with thee,
    If the diel should fly behynde."

'Ah! little do ye ken, my silly auld man,
    The daingeris we maun dree;

Last nichte we drank of the bishopis wyne,   805
   Quhill near near taen war we.

'Afore we wan to the sandy ford,
   The gor-cockis nichering flew;
The lofty crest of Ettrick Pen
   Was wavit about with blew,   810
And, flichtering throu the air, we fand
   The chill chill mornyng dew.

'As we flew owr the hillis of Braid,
   The sun rase fair and clear;
There gurly James, and his baronis braw,   815
   War out to hunt the deere.

'Their bowis they drew, their arrowis flew,
   And peircit the ayr with speede,
Quhill purpil fell the mornyng dew
   With witch-blude rank and reide.   820

'Littil do ye ken, my silly auld man,
   The dangeris we maun dree;
Ne wonder I am a weary wycht
   Quhan I come hame to thee.'–

"But tell me the *word*, my gude auld wyfe,   825
   Come tell it me speedilye:
For I lang to drink of the gude reide wyne,
   And to wyng the ayr with thee.

"Yer hellish horse I wilna ryde,
   Nor sail the seas in the wynd;   830
But I can flee as well as thee,
   And I'll drynk quhile ye be blynd."–

'O fy! O fy! my leil auld man,
   That word I darena tell;
It wald turn this warld all upside down,   835
   And make it warse than hell.

'For all the lasses in the land
   Wald munt the wynd and fly;

And the men wald doff their doublets syde,
 And after them wald ply.'–   840

But the auld gudeman was ane cunnyng auld man,
 And ane cunnyng auld man was he;
And he watchit, and he watchit for mony a nychte,
 The witches' flychte to see.

Ane nychte he darnit in Maisry's cot;   845
 The fearless haggs came in;
And he heard the word of awsome weird,
 And he saw their deedis of synn.

Then ane by ane, they said that word,
 As fast to the fire they drew;   850
Then set a foot on the black cruik-shell,
 And out at the lum they flew.

The auld gudeman cam fra his hole
 With feire and muckil dreide,
But yet he culdna think to rue,   855
 For the wyne came in his head.

He set his foot in the black cruik-shell,
 With ane fixit and ane wawlyng e'e;
And he said the word that I darena say,
 And out at the lum flew he.   860

The witches skalit the moon-beam pale;
 Deep groanit the trembling wynde;
But they never wist till our auld gudeman
 Was hoveryng them behynde.

They flew to the vaultis of merry Carlisle, 865
 Quhair they enterit free as ayr;
And they drank and they drank of the bishopis wyne
 Quhill they culde drynk ne mair.

The auld gudeman he grew se crouse,
 He dancit on the mouldy ground,   870
And he sang the bonniest sangs of Fife,
 And he tuzzlit the kerlyngs round.

And aye he peircit the tither butt,
  And he suckit, and he suckit se lang,
Quhill his e'en they closit, and his voice grew low,   875
  And his tongue wald hardly gang.

The kerlyngs drank of the bishopis wyne
  Quhill they scentit the mornyng wynde;
Then clove again the yeilding ayr,
  And left the auld man behynde.   880

And aye he slepit on the damp damp floor,
  He slepit and he snorit amain;
He never dreamit he was far fra hame,
  Or that the auld wyvis war gane.

And aye he slepit on the damp damp floor,   885
  Quhill past the mid-day highte,
Quhan wakenit by five rough Englishmen,
  That trailit him to the lychte.

"Now quha are ye, ye silly auld man,
  That sleepis se sound and se weil?   890
Or how gat ye into the bishopis vault
  Throu lokkis and barris of steel?"

The auld gudeman he tryit to speak,
  But ane word he culdna fynde;
He tryit to think, but his head whirlit round,   895
  And ane thing he culdna mynde:–
"I cam fra Fyfe," the auld man cryit,
  "And I cam on the midnight wynde."

They nickit the auld man, and they prickit the auld man,
  And they yerkit his limbis with twine,   900
Quhill the reide blude ran in his hose and shoon,
  But some cryit it was wyne.

They lickit the auld man, and they prickit the auld man,
  And they tyit him till ane stone;
And they set ane bele-fire him about,   905
  To burn him skin and bone.

"O wae to me!" said the puir auld man,
   "That ever I saw the day!
And wae be to all the ill wemyng
   That lead puir men astray!   910

"Let nevir ane auld man after this
   To lawless greide inclyne;
Let nevir ane auld man after this
   Rin post to the deil for wyne."

The reike flew up in the auld manis face,   915
   And choukit him bitterlye;
And the lowe cam up with ane angry blese,
   And it syngit his auld breek-nee.

He lukit to the land fra whence he came,
   For lukis he culde get ne mae;   920
And he thochte of his deire littil bairnis at hame,
   And O the auld man was wae!

But they turnit their facis to the sun,
   With gloffe and wonderous glair,
For they saw ane thing beth lairge and dun,   925
   Comin swaipin down the aire.

That burd it cam fra the landis o' Fife,
   And it cam rycht tymeouslye,
For quha was it but the auld manis wife,
   Just comit his dethe to see.   930

Scho pat ane reide cap on his heide,
   And the auld gudeman lookit fain,
Then whisperit ane word intil his lug,
   And tovit to the aire again.

The auld gudeman he gae ane bob   935
   I' the mids o' the burnyng lowe;
And the sheklis that band him to the ring,
   They fell fra his armis like towe.

He drew his breath, and he said the word,
   And he said it with muckle glee,   940

Then set his fit on the burnyng pile,
   And away to the aire flew he.

Till aince he cleirit the swirlyng reike,
   He lukit beth ferit and sad;
But whan he wan to the lycht blue aire,   945
   He lauchit as he'd been mad.

His armis war spred, and his heide was hiche,
   And his feite stack out behynde;
And the laibies of the auld manis cote
   War wauffyng in the wynde.   950

And aye he neicherit, and aye he flew,
   For he thochte the ploy se raire;
It was like the voice of the gainder blue,
   Whan he flees throu the aire.

He lukit back to the Carlisle men   955
   As he borit the norlan sky;
He noddit his heide, and gae ane girn,
   But he nevir said gude-bye.

They vanisht far i' the liftis blue wale,
   Ne maire the English saw,   960
But the auld manis lauche cam on the gale,
   With a lang and a loud gaffa.

May everilke man in the land of Fife
   Read what the drinkeris dree;
And nevir curse his puir auld wife,   965
   Rychte wicked altho scho be.

   When ceased the minstrel's crazy song,
His heedful glance embraced the throng,
And found the smile of free delight
Dimpling the cheeks of ladies bright.   970
Ah! never yet was bard unmoved,
When beauty smiled or birth approved!

For though his song he holds at nought—
"An idle strain! a passing thought!"
Child of the soul! 'tis held more dear   975
Than aught by mortals valued here.

When Leven's bard the Court had viewed,
His eye, his vigour, was renewed.
No, not the evening's closing eye,
Veiled in the rainbow's deepest dye,   980
By summer breezes lulled to rest,
Cradled on Leven's silver breast,
Or slumbering on the distant sea,
Imparted sweeter ecstacy.

Nor even the angel of the night,   985
Kindling his holy sphere of light,
Afar upon the heaving deep,
To light a world of peaceful sleep,
Though in her beam night-spirits glanced,
And lovely fays in circles danced,   990
Or rank by rank rode lightly bye,
Was sweeter to our minstrel's eye.

Unheard the bird of morning crew;
Unheard the breeze of Ocean blew;
The night unweened had passed away,   995
And dawning ushered in the day.
The Queen's young maids, of cherub hue,
Aside the silken curtains drew,
And lo the Night, in still profound,
In fleece of heaven had clothed the ground;   1000
And still her furs, so light and fair,
Floated along the morning air.
Low stooped the pine amid the wood,
And the tall cliffs of Salsbury stood
Like marble columns bent and riven,   1005
Propping a pale and frowning heaven.

The Queen bent from her gilded chair,
And waved her hand with graceful air:—
"Break up the court, my lords; away,

And use the day as best you may,   1010
In sleep, in love, or wassail cheer;
The day is dark, the evening near,
Say, will you grace my halls the while,
And in the dance the day beguile?
Break up the court, my lords; away,   1015
And use the day as best you may.
Give order that my minstrels true
Have royal fare and honours due;
And warned by evening's bugle shrill,
We meet to judge their minstrel skill."—   1020

　　Whether that Royal Wake gave birth
To days of sleep and nights of mirth,
Which kings and courtiers still approve,
Which sages blame, and ladies love,
Imports not;—but our courtly throng   1025
(That chapel Wake being kept so long)
Slept out the lowering short-lived days,
And heard by night their native lays,
Till fell the eve of Christmas good,
The dedication of the rood.   1030

　　Ah me! at routs and revels gay,
Reproach of this unthrifty day,
Though none amongst the dames or men
Rank higher than a citizen,
In chair or chariot all are borne,   1035
Closed from the piercing eye of morn;
But then, though dawning blasts were keen,
Scotland's high dames you might have seen,
Ere from the banquet hall they rose,
Shift their laced shoes and silken hose;   1040
Their broidered kirtles round them throw,
And wade their way through wreaths of snow,
Leaning on Lord or lover's arm,
Cheerful and reckless of all harm.
Vanished those hardy times outright;   1045
So is our ancient Scottish might.

　　Sweet be her home, admired her charms,
Bliss to her couch in lover's arms,

I bid in every minstrel's name,
I bid to every lovely dame,   1050
That ever gave one hour away
To cheer the bard or list his lay!

  To all who love the raptures high
Of Scottish song and minstrelsy,
Till next the night, in sable shroud,   1055
Shall wrap the halls of Holyrood,
That rival minstrels' songs I borrow—
I bid a hearty kind good-morrow.

END OF NIGHT THE FIRST

The Queen's Wake

Night the Second

The
Queen's Wake

SCARCE fled the dawning's dubious gray,
So transient was that dismal day.
The lurid vapours, dense and stern,
Unpierced save by the crusted cairn,
In tenfold shroud the heavens deform;   5
While far within the brooding storm,
Travelled the sun in lonely blue,
And noontide wore a twilight hue.

   The sprites that through the welkin wing,
That light and shade alternate bring,   10
That wrap the eve in dusky veil,
And weave the morning's purple rail;
From pendent clouds of deepest grain,
Shed that dull twilight o'er the main.
Each spire, each tower, and cliff sublime, 15
Were hooded in the wreathy rime;
And all, ere fell the murk of even,
Were lost within the folds of heaven.
It seemed as if the welkin's breast
Had bowed upon the world to rest;   20
As heaven and earth to close began,
And seal the destiny of man.

   The supper bell at Court had rung;
The mass was said, the vesper sung;
In true devotion's sweetest mood,   25
Beauty had kneeled before the rood;
But all was done in secret guise,
Close from the zealot's searching eyes.

   Then burst the bugle's lordly peal
Along the earth's incumbent veil;   30
Swam on the cloud and lingering shower,
To festive hall and lady's bower;

And found its way, with rapid boom,
To rocks far curtained in the gloom,
And waked their viewless bugle's strain,   35
That sung the softened notes again.

    Upsprung the maid from her love-dream;
The matron from her silken seam;
The abbot from his holy shrine;
The chiefs and warriors from their wine: 40
For aye the bugle seemed to say,
"The Wake's begun! away, away!"

    Fast poured they in, all fair and boon,
Till crowded was the grand saloon;
And scarce was left a little ring,   45
In which the rival bards might sing.
First in the list that night to play,
Was Farquhar, from the hills of Spey:
A gay and comely youth was he,
And seemed of noble pedigree.   50
Well known to him Loch-Avin's shore,
And all the dens of dark Glen-More;
Where oft, amid his roving clan,
His shaft had pierced the ptarmigan;
And oft the dun-deer's velvet side   55
That winged shaft had ruthless dyed,
Had struck the heath-cock whirring high,
And brought the eagle from the sky;
And he had dragged the scaly brood
From every Highland lake and flood.   60

    Amid those scenes the youth was bred,
Where Nature's eye is stern and dread;
'Mid forests dark, and caverns wild,
And mountains above mountains piled,
Whose hoary summits, tempest-riven,   65
Uprear eternal snows to heaven.
In Cumbria's dells he too had staid,
Raving like one in trance that's laid,
Of things which Nature gave not birth;
Of heavenly damsels born of earth;   70
Of pestilence and charnel den;

Of ships, and seas, and souls of men.
A moonstruck youth, by all confest,
The dreamer of the watery West.
His locks were fair as sunny sky;   75
His cheek was ruddy, bright his eye;
His speech was like the music's voice
Mixed with the cataract's swaying noise;
His harp strings sounded wild and deep,
With lulling swell and lordly sweep.   80

  Aloof from battle's fierce alarms,
Prone his young mind to music's charms.
The cliffs and woods of dark Glen-More
He taught to chant in mystic lore;
For well he weened, by tarn and hill,   85
Kind viewless spirits wandered still;
And fondly trowed the groups to spy,
Listening his cliff-born melody.
On Leven's bard with scorn he looked,
His homely song he scarcely brooked;   90
But proudly mounting on the form,
Thus sung *The Spirit of the Storm.*

Glen-Avin

THE NINTH BARD'S SONG

Beyond the grizly cliffs, which guard
  The infant rills of Highland Dee,
Where hunter's horn was never heard,   95
  Nor bugle of the forest bee;

'Mid wastes that dern and dreary lie,
  One mountain rears his mighty form,
Disturbs the moon in passing bye,
  And smiles above the thunder storm.   100

There Avin spreads her ample deep,
  To mirror cliffs that brush the wain;
Whose frigid eyes eternal weep,
  In summer suns and Autumn rain.

There matin hymn was never sung;   105
    Nor vesper, save the plover's wail;
But mountain eagles breed their young,
    And aërial spirits ride the gale.

An hoary sage once lingered there,
    Intent to prove some mystic scene;   110
Though cavern deep, and forest sere,
    Had whooped November's boisterous reign.

That noontide fell so stern and still,
    The breath of nature seemed away;
The distant sigh of mountain rill   115
    Alone disturbed that solemn day.

Oft had that seer, at break of morn,
    Beheld the fahm glide o'er the fell;
And 'neath the new moon's silver horn,
    The fairies dancing in the dell.   120

Had seen the spirits of the Glen,
    In every form that Ossian knew;
And wailings heard for living men,
    Were never more the light to view.

But, ah! that dull foreboding day,   125
    He saw what mortal could not bear;
A sight that scared the erne away,
    And drove the wild deer from his lair.

Firm in his magic ring he stood,
    When, lo! aloft on gray Cairn-Gorm,   130
A form appeared that chilled his blood,–
    The giant Spirit of the Storm.

His face was like the spectre wan,
    Slow gliding from the midnight isle;
His stature, on the mighty plan   135
    Of smoke-tower o'er the burning pile.

Red, red and grizly were his eyes;
    His cap the moon-cloud's silver gray;

His staff the writhed snake, that lies
   Pale, bending o'er the milky-way.   140

He cried, "Away! begone, begone!
   Half-naked, hoary, feeble form!
How darest thou seek my realms alone,
   And brave the Angel of the Storm?"—

"And who art thou," the seer replied,   145
   "That bear'st destruction on thy brow?
Whose eye no mortal can abide;
   Dread mountain Spirit! what art thou?"

"Within this desert, dank and lone,
   Since rolled the world a shoreless sea,   150
I've held my elemental throne,
   The terror of thy race and thee.

"I wrap the sun of heaven in blood,
   Veiling his orient beams of light;
And hide the moon in sable shroud,   155
   Far in the alcove of the night.

"I ride the red bolt's rapid wing,
   High on the sweeping whirlwind sail,
And list to hear my tempests sing
   Around Glen-Avin's ample wale.   160

"These everlasting hills are riven;
   Their reverend heads are bald and gray;
The Greenland waves salute the heaven,
   And quench the burning stars with spray.

"Who was it reared those whelming waves?   165
   Who scalped the brows of old Cairn-Gorm?
And scooped these ever-yawning caves?
   'Twas I, the Spirit of the Storm.

"And hence shalt thou, for evermore,
   Be doomed to ride the blast with me;   170
To shriek, amid the tempest's roar,
   By fountain, ford, and forest tree."

The wizard cowered him to the earth,
   And orisons of dread began:
"Hence, Spirit of infernal birth!   175
   Thou enemy of God and man!"

He waved his sceptre north away,
   The arctic ring was rift asunder;
And through the heaven, the startling bray
   Burst louder than the loudest thunder.   180

The feathery clouds, condensed and curled,
   In columns swept the quaking glen;
Destruction down the dale was hurled,
   O'er bleating flocks and wondering men.

The Grampians groaned beneath the storm;   185
   New mountains o'er the correis lean'd;
Ben-Nevis shook his shaggy form,
   And wondered what his Sovereign mean'd.

Even far on Yarrow's fairy dale,
   The shepherd paused in dumb dismay;   190
There passing shrieks adown the vale
   Lured many a pitying hind away.

The Lowthers felt the tyrant's wrath;
   Proud Hartfell quaked beneath his brand;
And Cheviot heard the cries of death,   195
   Guarding his loved Northumberland.

But, O! as fell that fateful night,
   What horrors Avin wilds deform,
And choke the ghastly lingering light!
   There whirled the vortex of the storm.   200

Ere morn the wind grew deadly still,
   And dawning in the air updrew
From many a shelve and shining hill,
   Her folding robe of fairy blue.

Then, what a smooth and wonderous scene   205
   Hung o'er Loch-Avin's lonely breast!

Not top of tallest pine was seen,
   On which the dazzled eye could rest.

But mitred cliff, and crested fell,
   In lucid curls her brows adorn,   210
Aloft the radiant crescents swell,
   All pure as robes by angels worn.

Sound sleeps our seer, far from the day,
   Beneath yon sleek and wreathed cone!
His spirit steals, unmissed, away,   215
   And dreams across the desert lone.

Sound sleeps our seer! the tempests rave,
   And cold sheets o'er his bosom fling;
The moldwarp digs his mossy grave;
   His requiem Avin eagles sing.   220

Why howls the fox above yon wreath,
   That mocks the blazing Summer sun?
Why croaks the sable bird of death,
   As hovering o'er yon desert dun?

When circling years have past away,   225
   And Summer blooms in Avin glen,
Why stands yon peasant in dismay,
   Still gazing o'er the bloated den?

Green grows the grass! the bones are white!
   Not bones of mountain stag they seem!   230
There hooted once the owl by night,
   Above the dead-light's lambent beam!

See yon lone cairn, so gray with age,
   Above the base of proud Cairn-Gorm:
There lies the dust of Avin's sage,   235
   Who raised the Spirit of the Storm.

Yet still at eve, or midnight drear,
   When Wintry winds begin to sweep,
When passing shrieks assail thine ear,
   Or murmurs by the mountain steep;   240

When from the dark and sedgy dells
  Came eldrich cries of wildered men,
Or wind-harp at thy window swells,—
  Beware the sprite of Avin-Glen!

———————

  Young Farquhar ceased, and, rising slow,   245
Doffed his plumed bonnet, wiped his brow,
And flushed with conscious dignity,
Cast o'er the crowd his falcon eye,
And found them all in silence deep,
As listening for the tempest's sweep.   250
So well his tale of Avin's seer
Suited the rigour of the year;
So high his strain, so bold his lyre,
So fraught with rays of Celtic fire,
They almost weened each hum that past   255
The spirit of the northern blast.

  The next was named,—the very sound
Excited merriment around.
But when the bard himself appeared,
The ladies smiled, the courtiers sneered;   260
For such a simple air and mien
Before a court had never been.
A clown he was, bred in the wild,
And late from native moors exiled,
In hopes his mellow mountain strain   265
High favour from the great would gain.
Poor wight! he never weened how hard
For poverty to earn regard!
Dejection o'er his visage ran,
His coat was bare, his colour wan,   270
His forest doublet darned and torn,
His shepherd plaid all rent and worn;
Yet dear the symbols to his eye,
Memorials of a time gone bye.

  The bard on Ettrick's mountains green   275
In Nature's bosom nursed had been,
And oft had marked in forest lone

Her beauties on her mountain throne;
Had seen her deck the wild-wood tree,
And star with snowy gems the lea;   280
In loveliest colours paint the plain,
And sow the moor with purple grain;
By golden mead and mountain sheer,
Had viewed the Ettrick waving clear,
Where shadowy flocks of purest snow   285
Seemed grazing in a world below.

Instead of Ocean's billowy pride,
Where monsters play and navies ride,
Oft had he viewed, as morning rose,
The bosom of the lonely Lowes,   290
Plowed far by many a downy keel,
Of wild-duck and of vagrant teal.
Oft thrilled his heart at close of even,
To see the dappled vales of heaven,
With many a mountain, moor, and tree,   295
Asleep upon the St Mary;
The pilot swan majestic wind,
With all his cygnet fleet behind,
So softly sail, and swiftly row,
With sable oar and silken prow.   300
Instead of war's unhallowed form,
His eye had seen the thunder-storm
Descend within the mountain's brim,
And shroud him in its chambers grim;
Then from its bowels burst amain   305
The sheeted flame and sounding rain,
And by the bolts in thunder borne,
The heaven's own breast and mountain torn;
The wild roe from the forest driven;
The oaks of ages peeled and riven;   310
Impending oceans whirl and boil,
Convulsed by Nature's grand turmoil.

Instead of arms or golden crest,
His harp with mimic flowers was drest:
Around, in graceful streamers, fell   315
The briar-rose and the heather bell;
And there, his learning deep to prove,

Naturæ Donum graved above.
When o'er her mellow notes he ran,
And his wild mountain chant began,   320
Then first was noted in his eye,
A gleam of native energy.

Old David

THE TENTH BARD'S SONG

Old David rose ere it was day,
And climbed old Wonfell's wizard brae;
Looked round, with visage grim and sour,   325
O'er Ettrick woods and Eskdale-moor.
An outlaw from the south he came,
And Ludlow was his father's name;
His native land had used him ill,
And Scotland bore him no good-will.   330

As fixed he stood, in sullen scorn,
Regardless of the streaks of morn,
Old David spied, on Wonfell cone,
A fairy band come riding on.
A lovelier troop was never seen;   335
Their steeds were white, their doublets green,
Their faces shone like opening morn,
And bloomed like roses on the thorn.
At every flowing mane was hung
A silver bell that lightly rung;   340
That sound, borne on the breeze away,
Oft set the mountaineer to pray.

Old David crept close in the heath,
Scarce moved a limb, scarce drew a breath;
But as the tinkling sound came nigh,   345
Old David's heart beat wonderous high.
He thought of riding on the wind;
Of leaving hawk and hern behind;
Of sailing lightly o'er the sea,
In mussel shell, to Germany;   350
Of revel raids by dale and down;
Of lighting torches at the moon;

Or through the sounding spheres to sing,
Borne on the fiery meteor's wing;
Of dancing 'neath the moonlight sky;   355
Of sleeping in the dew-cup's eye.
And then he thought—O! dread to tell!—
Of tithes the fairies paid to hell!

    David turned up a reverend eye,
And fixed it on the morning sky;   360
He knew a mighty one lived there,
That sometimes heard a warrior's prayer—
No word, save one, could David say;
Old David had not learned to pray.

    Scarce will a Scotsman yet regard   365
What David saw, and what he heard.
He heard their horses snort and tread,
And every word the rider said;
While green portmanteaus, long and low,
Lay bended o'er each saddle bow.   370
A lovely maiden rode between,
Whom David judged the Fairy Queen;
But strange! he heard her moans resound,
And saw her feet with fetters bound.

    Fast spur they on through bush and brake;   375
To Ettrick woods their course they take.
Old David followed still in view,
Till near the Lochilaw they drew;
There in a deep and wonderous dell,
Where wandering sun-beam never fell,   380
Where noon-tide breezes never blew,
From flowers to drink the morning dew;
There, underneath the sylvan shade,
The fairies' spacious bower was made.
Its rampart was the tangling sloe,   385
The bending briar, and misletoe;
And o'er its roof, the crooked oak
Waved wildly from the frowning rock.

    This wonderous bower, this haunted dell,
The forest shepherd shunned as hell!   390

When sound of fairies' silver horn
Came on the evening breezes borne,
Homeward he fled, nor made a stand,
Thinking the spirits hard at hand.
But when he heard the eldrich swell   395
Of giggling laugh and bridle bell,
Or saw the riders troop along,
His orisons were loud and strong.
His household fare he yielded free
To this mysterious company,   400
The fairest maid his cot within
Resigned with awe and little din;
True he might weep, but nothing say,
For none durst say the fairies nay.

Old David hasted home that night,   405
A wondering and a wearied wight.
Seven sons he had, alert and keen,
Had all in Border battles been;
Had wielded brand, and bent the bow,
For those who sought their overthrow.   410
Their hearts were true, their arms were strong,
Their faulchions keen, their arrows long;
The race of fairies they denied—
No fairies kept the English side.

Our yeomen on their armour threw,   415
Their brands of steel and bows of yew,
Long arrows at their backs they sling,
Fledged from the Snowdon eagle's wing,
And boun' away brisk as the wind,
The sire before, the sons behind.   420

That evening fell so sweetly still,
So mild on lonely moor and hill,
The little genii of the fell
Forsook the purple heather-bell,
And all their dripping beds of dew,   425
In wind-flower, thyme, and violet blue;
Aloft their viewless looms they heave,
And dew-webs round the helmets weave.
The waning moon her lustre threw

Pale round her throne of softened blue;   430
Her circuit, round the southland sky,
Was languid, low, and quickly bye;
Leaning on cloud so faint and fair,
And cradled on the golden air;
Modest and pale as maiden bride,   435
She sunk upon the trembling tide.

   What late in daylight proved a jest,
Was now the doubt of every breast.
That fairies *were*, was not disputed;
But *what* they were was greatly doubted.   440
Each argument was guarded well,
With "if," and "should," and "who can tell."

   "Sure He that made majestic man,
And framed the world's stupendous plan;
Who placed on high the steady pole,   445
And sowed the stars that round it roll;
And made that sky, so large and blue–
Could surely make a fairy too."

   The sooth to say, each valiant core
Knew feelings never felt before.   450
Oft had they darned the midnight brake,
Fearless of aught save bog and lake;
But now the nod of sapling fir,
The heath-cock's loud exulting whirr,
The cry of hern from sedgy pool,   455
Or airy bleeter's rolling howl,
Came fraught with more dismaying dread
Than warder's horn, or warrior's tread.

   Just as the gloom of midnight fell,
They reached the fairies' lonely dell.   460
O heavens! that dell was dark as death!
Perhaps the pit-fall yawned beneath!
Perhaps that lane that winded low,
Led to a nether world of woe!
But stern necessity's control,   465
Resistless sways the human soul.

The bows are bent, the tinders smoke
With fire by sword struck from the rock.
Old David held the torch before;
His right hand heaved a dread claymore,   470
Whose Rippon edge he meant to try
On the first fairy met his eye.
Above his head his brand was raised;
Above his head the taper blazed;
A sterner or a ghastlier sight,   475
Ne'er entered bower at dead of night.
Below each lifted arm was seen
The barbed point of arrow keen,
Which waited but the twang of bow
To fly like lightning on the foe.   480
Slow move they on, with steady eye,
Resolved to conquer or to die.

At length they spied a massive door,
Deep in a nook, unseen before;
And by it slept, on wicker chair,   485
A sprite of dreadful form and air.
His grizly beard flowed round his throat,
Like shaggy hair of mountain goat;
His open jaws and visage grim,
His half-shut eye so deadly dim,   490
Made David's blood to's bosom rush,
And his gray hair his helmet brush.
He squared, and made his faulchion wheel
Around his back from head to heel;
Then, rising tiptoe, struck amain,   495
Down fell the sleeper's head in twain;
And springing blood, in veil of smoke,
Whizzed high against the bending oak.

"By heaven!" said George, with jocund air,
"Father, if all the fairies there   500
Are of the same materials made,
Let them beware the Rippon blade!"
A ghastly smile was seen to play
O'er David's visage, stern and gray;
He hoped, and feared; but ne'er till then   505
Knew whether he fought with sprites or men.

The massy door they next unlock,
That oped to hall beneath the rock,
In which new wonders met the eye:
The room was ample, rude, and high,   510
The arches caverned, dark, and torn,
On Nature's rifted columns borne;
Of moulding rude the embrazure,
And all the wild entablature;
And far o'er roof and architrave,   515
The ivy's ringlets bend and wave.
In each abrupt recess was seen
A couch of heath and rushes green;
While every alcove's sombre hue,
Was gemm'd with drops of midnight dew.   520

Why stand our heroes still as death,
Nor muscle move, nor heave a breath?
See how the sire his torch has lowered,
And bends recumbent o'er his sword!
The arcubalister has thrown   525
His threatening, thirsty arrows down!
Struck in one moment, all the band
Entranced like moveless statues stand!
Enchantment sure arrests the spear,
And stints the warrior's bold career!   530

List, list, what mellow angel-sound
Distils from yonder gloom profound!
'Tis not the note of gathering shell,
Of fairy horn, nor silver bell!
No, 'tis the lute's mellifluous swell,   535
Mixed with a maiden's voice so clear,
The flitting bats flock round to hear!

So wildly o'er the vault it rung,
That song, if in the green-wood sung,
Would draw the fays of wood and plain   540
To kiss the lips that poured the strain.
The lofty pine would listening lean;
The wild birch wave her tresses green;
And larks, that rose the dawn to greet,
Drop lifeless at the singer's feet.   545

The air was old, the measure slow,
The words were plain, but words of woe.

Soft died the strain; the warriors stand,
Nor rested lance, nor lifted brand,
But listening bend, in hopes again   550
To hear that sweetly plaintive strain.
'Tis gone! and each uplifts his eye,
As waked from dream of ecstacy.

Why stoops young Owen's gilded crest?
Why heave those groans from Owen's breast?   555
While kinsmen's eyes in raptures speak,
Why steals the tear o'er Owen's cheek?
That melting song, that song of pain,
Was sung to Owen's favourite strain;
The words were new, but that sweet lay   560
Had Owen heard in happier day.

Fast press they on; in close-set row,
Winded the lab'rinth far and low,
Till, in the cave's extremest bound,
Arrayed in sea-green silk, they found   565
Five beauteous dames, all fair and young;
And she, who late so sweetly sung,
Sat leaning o'er a silver lute,
Pale with despair, with terror mute.

When back her auburn locks she threw,   570
And raised her eyes so lovely blue,
'Twas like the woodland rose in dew!
That look was soft as morning flower,
And mild as sun-beam through the shower.
Old David gazed, and weened the while,   575
He saw a suffering angel smile;
Weened he had heard a seraph sing,
And sounds of a celestial string.
But when young Owen met her view,
She shrieked, and to his bosom flew: 580
For, oft before, in Moodlaw bowers,
They two had passed the evening hours.
She was the loveliest mountain maid,

That e'er by grove or riv'let strayed;
Old Raeburn's child, the fairest flower 585
That ever bloomed in Eskdale-moor.
'Twas she the Sire that morn had seen,
And judged to be the Fairy Queen;
'Twas she who framed the artless lay,
That stopt the warriors on their way. 590

Close to her lover's breast she clung,
And round his neck enraptured hung:—
"O my dear Owen! haste and tell,
What caused you dare this lonely dell,
And seek your maid, at midnight still, 595
Deep in the bowels of the hill?
Here in this dark and drear abode,
By all deserted but my God,
Must I have reft the life he gave,
Or lived in shame a villain's slave. 600
I was, at midnight's murkest hour,
Stole from my father's stately tower,
And never thought again to view
The sun or sky's ethereal blue;
But since the first of Border-men 605
Has found me in this dismal den,
I to his arms for shelter fly,
With him to live, or with him die."

How glowed brave Owen's manly face,
While in that lady's kind embrace! 610
Warm tears of joy his utterance staid;
"O, my loved Ann!" was all he said.
Though well they loved, her high estate
Caused Owen aye aloof to wait;
And watch her bower, beside the rill, 615
When twilight rocked the breezes still,
And waked the music of the grove
To hymn the vesper song of love.
Then underneath the green-wood bough,
Oft had they breathed the tender vow. 620

With Ann of Raeburn here they found
The flowers of all the Border round;

From whom the strangest tale they hear,
That e'er astounded warrior's ear.
'Twould make even Superstition blush,   625
And all her tales of spirits hush.

  That night the spoilers ranged the vale,
By Dryhope towers, and Meggat-dale.
Ah! little trowed the fraudful train,
They ne'er should see their wealth again!   630
Their lemans, and their mighty store,
For which they nightly toils had bore,
Full twenty Autumn moons and more!
They little deemed, when morning dawned,
To meet the deadly Rippon brand;   635
And only find, at their return,
In their loved cave an early urn.
Ill suits it simple bard to tell
Of bloody work that there befel.
He lists not deeds of death to sing,   640
Of splintered spear, and twanging string,
Of piercing arrow's purpled wing,
How faulchions flash, and helmets ring.
Not one of all that prowling band,
So long the terror of the land,   645
Not one escaped their deeds to tell;
All in the winding lab'rinth fell.
The spoil was from the cave conveyed,
Where in a heap the dead were laid;
The outer cave our yeomen fill,   650
And left them in the hollow hill.

  But still that dell, and bourn beneath,
The forest shepherd dreads as death.
Not there at evening dares he stray,
Though love impatient points the way;   655
Though throbs his heart the maid to see,
That's waiting by the trysting tree.

  Even the old Sire, so reverend gray,
Ere turns the scale of night and day,
Oft breathes the short and ardent prayer,   660
That Heaven may guard his footsteps there;

His eyes, meantime, so dim with dread,
Scarce ken the turf his foot must tread.
For still 'tis told, and still believed,
That there the spirits were deceived,   665
And maidens from their grasp retrieved:
That this they still preserve in mind,
And watch, when sighs the midnight wind,
To wreck their rage on humankind.

    Old David, for this doughty raid,   670
Was keeper of the forest made;
A trooper he of gallant fame,
And first of all the Laidlaw name.

    E'er since, in Ettrick's glens so green,
Spirits, though there, are seldom seen;   675
And fears of elf, and fairy raid,
Have like a morning dream decayed.
The bare-foot maid, of rosy hue,
Dares from the heath-flower brush the dew,
To meet her love in moon-light still,   680
By flowery den or tinkling rill;
And well dares she till midnight stay,
Among the coils of fragrant hay.

    True, some weak shepherds, gone astray,
As fell the dusk of Hallow-day,   685
Have heard the tinkling sound aloof,
And gentle tread of horse's hoof;
And flying swifter than the wind,
Left all their scattered flocks behind.

    True, when the evening tales are told,   690
When winter nights are dark and cold,
The boy dares not to barn repair
Alone, to say his evening prayer;
Nor dare the maiden ope the door,
Unless her lover walk before;   695
Then well can counterfeit the fright,
If star-beam on the water light;
And to his breast in terror cling,
For "such a dread and dangerous thing!"

O, Ettrick! shelter of my youth!   700
Thou sweetest glen of all the south!
Thy fairy tales, and songs of yore,
Shall never fire my bosom more.
Thy winding glades, and mountains wild,
The scenes that pleased me when a child,   705
Each verdant vale, and flowery lea,
Still in my midnight dreams I see;
And waking oft, I sigh for thee;
Thy hapless bard, though forced to roam
Afar from thee without a home,   710
Still there his glowing breast shall turn,
Till thy green bosom fold his urn.
Then, underneath thy mountain stone,
Shall sleep unnoticed and unknown.

When ceased the shepherd's simple lay,   715
With careless mien he lounged away.
No bow he deigned, nor anxious looked
How the gay throng their minstrel brooked.
No doubt within his bosom grew,
That to his skill the prize was due.   720
Well might he hope, for while he sung,
Louder and louder plaudits rung;
And when he ceased his numbers wild,
Fair Royalty approved and smiled.
Long had the bard, with hopes elate,   725
Sung to the low, the gay, the great;
And once had dared, at flatterer's call,
To tune his harp in Branxholm hall;
But nor his notes of soothing sound,
Nor zealous word of bard renowned,   730
Might those persuade, that worth could be
Inherent in such mean degree.
But when the smile of Sovereign fair
Attested genuine nature there,
Throbbed high with rapture every breast,   735
And all his merit stood confest.

Different the next the herald named;
Warrior he was, in battle maimed,
When Lennox, on the downs of Kyle,
O'erthrew Maconnel and Argyle.   740
Unable more the sword to wield
With dark Clan-Alpine in the field,
Or rouse the dun deer from her den
With fierce Macfarlane and his men;
He strove to earn a minstrel name,   745
And fondly nursed the sacred flame.
Warm was his heart, and bold his strain;
Wild fancies in his moody brain
Gambolled, unbridled, and unbound,
Lured by a shade, decoyed by sound.   750

In tender age, when mind was free,
As standing by his nurse's knee,
He heard a tale, so passing strange,
Of injured spirit's cool revenge,
It chilled his heart with blasting dread,   755
Which never more that bosom fled.
When passion's flush had fled his eye,
And gray hairs told that youth was bye,
Still quaked his heart at bush or stone,
As wandering in the gloom alone.   760

Where foxes roam, and eagles rave,
And dark woods round Ben-Lomond wave,
Once on a night, a night of dread!
He held convention with the dead;
Brought warnings to the house of death,   765
And tidings from a world beneath.

Loud blew the blast—the evening came,
The way was long, the minstrel lame;
The mountain's side was dern with oak,
Darkened with pine, and ribbed with rock;   770
Blue billows round its base were driven,
Its top was steeped in waves of heaven.
The wood, the wind, the billow's moan,
All spoke in language of their own,
But too well to our minstrel known.   775

Wearied, bewildered, in amaze,
Hymning in heart the Virgin's praise,
A cross he framed, of birchen bough,
And 'neath that cross he laid him low;
Hid by the heath, and Highland plaid,   780
His old harp in his bosom laid.
O! when the winds that wandered by,
Sung on her breast their lullaby,
How thrilled the tones his bosom through,
And deeper, holier, poured his vow!   785

No sleep was his—he raised his eye,
To note if dangerous place was nigh.
There columned rocks, abrupt and rude,
Hung o'er his gateless solitude:
The muffled sloe, and tangling brier,   790
Precluded freak or entrance here;
But yonder oped a little path,
O'ershadowed, deep, and dark as death.
Trembling, he groped around his lair
For mountain ash, but none was there.   795
Teeming with forms, his terror grew;
Heedful he watched, for well he knew,
That in that dark and devious dell,
Some lingering ghost or sprite must dwell:
So as he trowed, so it befel.   800

The stars were wrapt in curtain gray,
The blast of midnight died away;
'Twas just the hour of solemn dread,
When walk the spirits of the dead.
Rustled the leaves with gentle motion,   805
Groaned his chilled soul in deep devotion.
The lake-fowl's wake was heard no more;
The wave forgot to brush the shore;
Hushed was the bleat, on moor and hill;
The wandering clouds of heaven stood still.   810

What heart could bear, what eye could meet,
The spirits in their lone retreat!
Rustled again the darksome dell;

Straight on the minstrel's vision fell
A trembling and unwonted light,   815
That showed the phantoms to his sight.

    Came first a slender female form,
Pale as the moon in Winter storm;
A babe of sweet simplicity
Clung to her breast as pale as she,   820
And aye she sung its lullaby.
That cradle-song of the phantom's child,
O! but it was soothing, holy, and wild!
But, O! that song can ill be sung,
By Lowland bard, or Lowland tongue.   825

The Spectre's Cradle-Song

    Hush, my bonny babe! hush, and be still!
Thy mother's arms shall shield thee from ill.
Far have I borne thee, in sorrow and pain,
To drink the breeze of the world again.
The dew shall moisten thy brow so meek,   830
And the breeze of midnight fan thy cheek,
And soon shall we rest in the bow of the hill;
Hush, my bonny babe: hush, and be still!
For thee have I travailed, in weakness and woe,
The world above and the world below.   835
My heart was soft, and it fell in the snare;
Thy father was cruel, but thou wert fair.
I sinned, I sorrowed, I died for thee;
Smile, my bonny babe! smile on me!

    See yon thick clouds of murky hue;   840
Yon star that peeps from its window blue;
Above yon clouds, that wander far,
Away, above yon little star,
There's a home of peace that shall soon be thine,
And there shalt thou see thy Father and mine.   845
The flowers of the world shall bud and decay,
The trees of the forest be weeded away;
But there shalt *thou* bloom for ever and aye.
The time will come, I shall follow thee;

But long, long hence that time shall be;   850
O weep not thou for thy mother's ill;
Hush, my bonny babe! hush, and be still!

Slow moved she on with dignity,
Nor bush, nor brake, nor rock, nor tree,
Her footsteps staid—o'er cliff so bold,   855
Where scarce the roe her foot could hold,
Stately she wandered, firm and free,
Singing her softened lullaby.

Three naked phantoms next came on;
They beckoned low, past, and were gone.   860
Then came a troop of sheeted dead,
With shade of chieftain at their head.
And with our bard, in brake forlorn,
Held converse till the break of morn.
Their ghostly rites, their looks, their mould,   865
Or words to man, he never told;
But much he learned of mystery,
Of that was past, and that should be.
Thenceforth he troubles oft divined,
And scarcely held his perfect mind;   870
Yet still the song, admired when young,
He loved, and that in Court he sung.

The Fate of Macgregor

THE ELEVENTH BARD'S SONG

"Macgregor, Macgregor, remember our foemen;
The moon rises broad from the brow of Ben-Lomond;
The clans are impatient, and chide thy delay;   875
Arise! let us bound to Glen-Lyon away."—

Stern scowled the Macgregor, then silent and sullen,
He turned his red eye to the braes of Strathfillan;
"Go, Malcolm, to sleep, let the clans be dismissed;
The Campbells this night for Macgregor must rest."—   880

"Macgregor, Macgregor, our scouts have been flying,
Three days, round the hills of M'Nab and Glen-Lyon;
Of riding and running such tidings they bear,
We must meet them at home else they'll quickly be here."—

"The Campbell may come, as his promises bind him,   885
And haughty M'Nab, with his giants behind him;
This night I am bound to relinquish the fray,
And do what it freezes my vitals to say.
Forgive me, dear brother, this horror of mind;
Thou knowest in the strife I was never behind,   890
Nor ever receded a foot from the van,
Or blenched at the ire or the prowess of man.
But I've sworn by the cross, by my God, and by all!
An oath which I cannot, and dare not recall—
Ere the shadows of midnight fall east from the pile,   895
To meet with a spirit this night in Glen-Gyle.

Last night, in my chamber, all thoughtful and lone,
I called to remembrance some deeds I had done,
When entered a lady, with visage so wan,
And looks, such as never were fastened on man.   900
I knew her, O brother! I knew her too well!
Of that once fair dame such a tale I could tell,
As would thrill thy bold heart; but how long she remained,
So racked was my spirit, my bosom so pained,
I knew not—but ages seemed short to the while.   905
Though proffer the Highlands, nay, all the green isle,
With length of existence no man can enjoy,
The same to endure, the dread proffer I'd fly!
The thrice-threatened pangs of last night to forego,
Macgregor would dive to the mansions below.   910
Despairing and mad, to futurity blind,
The present to shun, and some respite to find,
I swore, ere the shadow fell east from the pile,
To meet her alone by the brook of Glen-Gyle.

She told me, and turned my chilled heart to a stone,   915
The glory and name of Macgregor was gone:
That the pine, which for ages had shed a bright halo,
Afar on the mountains of Highland Glen-Falo,
Should wither and fall ere the turn of yon moon,
Smit through by the canker of hated Colquhoun: 920

That a feast on Macgregors each day should be common,
For years, to the eagles of Lennox and Lomond.

A parting embrace, in one moment, she gave:
Her breath was a furnace, her bosom the grave!
Then flitting elusive, she said, with a frown,   925
"The mighty Macgregor shall yet be my own!"–

"Macgregor, thy fancies are wild as the wind;
The dreams of the night have disordered thy mind.
Come, buckle thy panoply–march to the field–
See, brother, how hacked are thy helmet and shield!   930
Ay, that was M'Nab, in the height of his pride,
When the lions of Dochart stood firm by his side.
This night the proud chief his presumption shall rue;
Rise, brother, these chinks in his heart-blood will glue:
Thy fantasies frightful shall flit on the wing,   935
When loud with thy bugle Glen-Lyon shall ring."–

Like glimpse of the moon through the storm of the night,
Macgregor's red eye shed one sparkle of light:
It faded–it darkened–he shuddered–he sighed–
"No! not for the universe!" low he replied.   940

Away went Macgregor, but went not alone;
To watch the dread rendezvous, Malcolm has gone.
They oared the broad Lomond, so still and serene,
And deep in her bosom, how awful the scene!
O'er mountains inverted the blue waters curled,   945
And rocked them on skies of a far nether world.

All silent they went, for the time was approaching;
The moon the blue zenith already was touching;
No foot was abroad on the forest or hill,
No sound but the lullaby sung by the rill;   950
Young Malcolm at distance, couched, trembling the while–
Macgregor stood lone by the brook of Glen-Gyle.

Few minutes had passed, ere they spied on the stream,
A skiff sailing light, where a lady did seem;
Her sail was the web of the gossamer's loom,   955
The glow-worm her wakelight, the rainbow her boom;
A dim rayless beam was her prow and her mast,

Like wold-fire, at midnight, that glares on the waste.
Though rough was the river with rock and cascade,
No torrent, no rock, her velocity staid; 960
She wimpled the water to weather and lee,
And heaved as if borne on the waves of the sea.
Mute Nature was roused in the bounds of the glen;
The wild deer of Gairtney abandoned his den,
Fled panting away, over river and isle, 965
Nor once turned his eye to the brook of Glen-Gyle.

The fox fled in terror; the eagle awoke,
As slumbering he dozed on the shelve of the rock;
Astonished, to hide in the moon-beam he flew,
And screwed the night-heaven till lost in the blue. 970

Young Malcolm beheld the pale lady approach,
The chieftain salute her, and shrink from her touch.
He saw the Macgregor kneel down on the plain,
As begging for something he could not obtain;
She raised him indignant, derided his stay, 975
Then bore him on board, set her sail, and away.

Though fast the red bark down the river did glide,
Yet faster ran Malcolm adown by its side;
"Macgregor! Macgregor!" he bitterly cried;
"Macgregor! Macgregor!" the echoes replied. 980
He struck at the lady, but, strange though it seem,
His sword only fell on the rocks and the stream;
But the groans from the boat, that ascended amain,
Were groans from a bosom in horror and pain.—
They reached the dark lake, and bore lightly away; 985
Macgregor is vanished for ever and aye!

———————

Abrupt as glance of morning sun,
The bard of Lomond's lay is done.
Loves not the swain, from path of dew,
At morn the golden orb to view, 990
Rise broad and yellow from the main,
While scarce a shadow lines the plain;
Well knows he then the gathering cloud

Shall all his noontide glories shroud.
Like smile of morn before the rain,   995
Appeared the minstrel's mounting strain.
As easy inexperienced hind,
Who sees not coming rains and wind,
The beacon of the dawning hour,
Nor notes the blink before the shower,   1000
Astonished, 'mid his open grain,
Sees round him pour the sudden rain—
So looked the still attentive throng,
When closed at once Macfarlane's song.

Time was it—when he 'gan to tell   1005
Of spectre stern, and barge of hell;
Loud, and more loud, the minstrel sung;
Loud, and more loud, the chords he rung;
Wild grew his looks, for well he knew
The scene was dread, the tale was true;   1010
And ere Loch-Ketturine's wave was won,
Faultered his voice, his breath was done.
He raised his brown hand to his brow,
To veil his eye's enraptured glow;
Flung back his locks of silver gray,   1015
Lifted his crutch, and limped away.

The Bard of Clyde stepped next in view;
Tall was his form, his harp was new;
Brightened his dark eye as he sung;
A stammer fluttered on his tongue;   1020
A captain in the wars was he,
And sprung of noble pedigree.

Earl Walter

THE TWELFTH BARD'S SONG

"What makes Earl Walter pace the wood
    In the wan light of the moon?
Why altered is Earl Walter's mood   1025
    So strangely, and so soon?"—

"It is his lot to fight a knight
  Whom man could never tame,
To-morrow, in his Sovereign's sight,
  Or bear perpetual shame."—   1030

"Go warn the Clyde, go warn the Ayr,
  Go warn them suddenly,
If none will fight for Earl Walter,
  Some one may fight for me."—

"Now hold your tongue, my daughter dear,   1035
  Now hold your tongue for shame!
For never shall my son Walter
  Disgrace his father's name.

"Shall ladies tell, and minstrels sing,
  How lord of Scottish blood,   1040
By proxy fought before his king?
  No, never! by the rood!"—

Earl Walter rose ere it was day,
  For battle made him boun';
Earl Walter mounted his bonny gray,   1045
  And rode to Stirling town.

Old Hamilton from the tower came down,
  "Go saddle a steed for me,
And I'll away to Stirling town,
  This deadly bout to see.   1050

"Mine eye is dim, my locks are gray,
  My cheek is furred and wan;
Ah, me! but I have seen the day
  I feared not single man!

"Bring me my steed," said Hamilton;   1055
  "Darcie his vaunts may rue;
Whoever slays my only son
  Must fight the father too.

"Whoever fights my noble son
  May foin the best he can;   1060

Whoever braves Wat Hamilton,
   Shall know he braves a man."—

And there was riding in belt and brand,
   And running o'er holt and lea!
For all the lords of fair Scotland   1065
   Came there the fight to see.

And squire, and groom, and baron bold,
   Trooping in thousands came,
And many a hind, and warrior old,
   And many a lovely dame.   1070

When good Earl Walter rode the ring,
   Upon his mettled gray,
There was none so ready as our good king
   To bid that Earl good day.

For one so gallant and so young,   1075
   Oh, many a heart beat high;
And no fair eye in all the throng,
   Nor rosy cheek, was dry.

But up then spoke the king's daughter,
   Fair Margaret was her name,—   1080
"If we should lose brave Earl Walter,
   My sire is sore to blame.

"Forbid the fight, my liege, I pray,
   Upon my bended knee."—
"Daughter, I'm loth to say you nay;   1085
   It cannot, must not be."—

"Proclaim it round," the princess cried,
   "Proclaim it suddenly;
If none will fight for Earl Walter,
   Some one may fight for me.   1090

"In Douglas-dale I have a tower,
   With many a holm and hill,
I'll give them all, and ten times more,
   To him will Darcie kill."—

But up then spoke old Hamilton,   1095
   And doffed his bonnet blue;
In his sunk eye the tear-drop shone,
   And his gray locks o'er it flew:–

"Cease, cease, thou lovely royal maid,
   Small cause hast thou for pain;   1100
Wat Hamilton shall have no aid
   'Gainst lord of France or Spain.

"I love my boy; but should he fly,
   Or other for him fight,
Heaven grant that first his parent's eye   1105
   May set in endless night!"–

Young Margaret blushed, her weeping staid,
   And quietly looked on:
Now Margaret was the fairest maid
   On whom the daylight shone.   1110

Her eye was like the star of love,
   That blinks across the evening dun;
The locks that waved that eye above,
   Like light clouds curling round the sun.

When Darcie entered in the ring,   1115
   A shudder round the circle flew:
Like men who from a serpent spring,
   They startled at the view.

His look so fierce, his crest so high,
   His belts and bands of gold,   1120
And the glances of his charger's eye
   Were dreadful to behold.

But when he saw Earl Walter's face,
   So rosy and so young,
He frowned, and sneered with haughty grace,   1125
   And round disdainful flung.

"What! dost thou turn my skill to sport,
   And break thy jests on me?

Thinkst thou I sought the Scottish court,
   To play with boys like thee?   1130

"Fond youth go home and learn to ride;
   For pity get thee gone;
Tilt with the girls and boys of Clyde,
   And boast of what thou'st done.

"If Darcie's spear but touch thy breast,   1135
   It flies thy body through;
If Darcie's sword come o'er thy crest,
   It cleaves thy heart in two."

"I came not here to vaunt, Darcie;
   I came not here to scold;   1140
It ill befits a knight like thee
   Such proud discourse to hold.

"To-morrow boast, amid the throng,
   Of deeds which thou hast done;
To-day restrain thy saucy tongue;   1145
   Rude blusterer, come on!"

Rip went the spurs in either steed,
   To different posts they sprung;
Quivered each spear o'er charger's head;
   Forward each warrior hung.   1150

The horn blew once—the horn blew twice—
   Oh! many a heart beat high!
'Twas silence all!—the horn blew thrice—
   Dazzled was every eye.

Hast thou not seen, from heaven, in ire,   1155
   The eagle swift descend?
Hast thou not seen the sheeted fire
   The lowering darkness rend?

Not faster glides the eagle gray
   Adown the yielding wind;   1160
Not faster bears the bolt away,
   Leaving the storm behind;

Than flew the warriors on their way,
  With full suspended breath;
Than flew the warriors on their way   1165
  Across the field of death.

So fierce the shock, so loud the clang,
  The gleams of fire were seen;
The rocks and towers of Stirling rang,
  And the red blood fell between.   1170

Earl Walter's gray was borne aside,
  Lord Darcie's black held on.
"Oh! ever alack," fair Margaret cried,
  "The brave Earl Walter's gone!"
"Oh! ever alack," the king replied,   1175
  "That ever the deed was done!"–

Earl Walter's broken corslet doffed,
  He turned with lightened eye;
His glancing spear he raised aloft,
  And seemed to threat the sky.   1180

Lord Darcie's spear aimed at his breast,
  He parried dext'rously;
Then caught him rudely by the wrist,
  Saying, "Warrior, come with me!"–

Lord Darcie drew, Lord Darcie threw;   1185
  But threw and drew in vain;
Lord Darcie drew, Lord Darcie threw,
  And spurred his black amain.

Down came Lord Darcie, casque and brand
  Loud rattled on the clay;   1190
Down came Earl Walter, hand in hand,
  And head to head they lay.

Lord Darcie's steed turned to his lord,
  And trembling stood behind;
But off Earl Walter's dapple scoured   1195
  Far fleeter than the wind;
Nor stop, nor stay, nor gate, nor ford,
  Could make her look behind.

O'er holt, o'er hill, o'er slope and slack,
   She sought her native stall;   1200
She liked not Darcie's doughty black,
   Nor Darcie's spear at all.

"Even go thy ways," Earl Walter cried,
   "Since better may not be;
I'll trust my life with weapon tried,   1205
   But never again with thee.

"Rise up, Lord Darcie, sey thy brand,
   And fling thy mail away;
For foot to foot, and hand to hand,
   We'll now decide the day."–   1210

So said, so done; their helms they flung,
   Their doublets linked and sheen;
And hawberk, armlet, cuirass, rung
   Promiscuous on the green.

"Now, Darcie! now thy dreaded name,   1215
   That oft has chilled a foe,
Thy hard-earned honours, and thy fame,
   Depend on every blow.

"Sharp be thine eye, and firm thy hand;
   Thy heart unmoved remain;   1220
For never was the Scottish brand
   Upreared, and reared in vain."–

"Now do thy best, young Hamilton,
   Rewarded shalt thou be;
Thy king, thy country, and thy kin,   1225
   All, all depend on thee!

"Thy father's heart yearns for his son,
   The ladies' cheeks grow wan;
Wat Hamilton! Wat Hamilton!
   Now prove thyself a man!"   1230

What makes Lord Darcie shift and dance
   So fast around the plain?

What makes Lord Darcie strike and lance,
   As passion fired his brain?

"Lay on, lay on," said Hamilton;   1235
   "Thou bear'st thee boist'rously;
If thou shouldst pelt till day be done,
   Thy weapon I defy."

What makes Lord Darcie shift and wear
   So fast around the plain?   1240
Why is Lord Darcie's hollands fair
   All stripped with crimson grain?–

The first blow that Earl Walter made
   He clove his whiskered chin,
"Beshrew thy heart," Lord Darcie said,   1245
   "Ye sharply do begin!"

The next blow that Earl Walter made,
   Quite through the gare it ran.
"Now, by my faith," Lord Darcie said,
   "That's stricken like a man."   1250

The third blow that Earl Walter made,
   It pierced his lordly side.
"Now, by my troth," Lord Darcie said,
   "Thy marks are ill to bide."

Lord Darcie's sword he forced a-hight,   1255
   And tripped him on the plain.
"O, ever alack," then cried the knight,
   "I ne'er shall rise again!"

When good Earl Walter saw he grew
   So pale, and lay so low,   1260
Away his brace of swords he threw,
   And raised his fainting foe.

Then rang the list with shouts of joy,
   Loud and more loud they grew,
And many a bonnet to the sky   1265
   And many a coif they threw.

The tear stood in the father's eye,—
  He wiped his aged brow,—
"Give me thy hand, my gallant boy!
  I knew thee not till now.   1270

"My liege, my king, this is my son
  Whom I present to thee;
Nor would I change Wat Hamilton
  For all the lads I see!"—

"Welcome, my friend and warrior old!   1275
  This gallant son of thine
Is much too good for baron bold,
  He must be son of mine!

"For he shall wed my daughter dear,
  The flower of fair Scotland;   1280
The badge of honour he shall wear,
  And sit at my right hand.

"And he shall have the lands of Kyle,
  And royal bounds of Clyde;
And he shall have all Arran's isle   1285
  To dower his royal bride."

The princess smiled, and sore was flushed,
  O, but her heart was fain!
And aye her cheek of beauty blushed
  Like rose-bud in the rain.   1290

From this the Hamiltons of Clyde
  Their royal lineage draw;
And thus was won the fairest bride
  That Scotland ever saw!

When ceased the lay, the plaudits rung,   1295
Not for the bard, or song he sung;
But every eye with pleasure shone,
And cast its smiles on one alone,—
That one was princely Hamilton!

And well the gallant chief approved   1300
The bard who sung of sire beloved,
And pleased were all the court to see
The minstrel hailed so courteously.

   Again is every courtier's gaze
Speaking suspense, and deep amaze;   1305
The bard was stately, dark and stern,—
'Twas Drummond from the moors of Ern.
Tall was his frame, his forehead high,
Still and mysterious was his eye;
His look was like a winter day,   1310
When storms and winds have sunk away.

   Well versed was he in holy lore;
In cloistered dome the cowl he wore;
But, wearied with the eternal strain
Of formal breviats, cold and vain,   1315
He wooed, in depth of Highland dale,
The silver spring and mountain gale.

   In gray Glen-Ample's forest deep,
Hid from the rains and tempest's sweep,
In bosom of an aged wood   1320
His solitary cottage stood.
Its walls were bastioned, dark, and dern,
Dark was its roof of filmot fern,
And dark the vista down the linn,
But all was love and peace within.   1325
Religion, man's first friend and best,
Was in that home a constant guest;
There, sweetly, every morn and even,
Warm orisons were poured to Heaven:
And every cliff Glen-Ample knew,   1330
And green wood on her banks that grew,
In answer to his bounding string,
Had learned the hymns of Heaven to sing;
With many a song of mystic lore,
Rude as when sung in days of yore.   1335

   His were the snowy flocks, that strayed
Adown Glen-Airtney's forest glade;

And his the goat, and chesnut hind,
Where proud Ben-Vorlich cleaves the wind:
There oft, when suns of summer shone,   1340
The bard would sit, and muse alone,
Of innocence, expelled by man;
Of nature's fair and wonderous plan;
Of the eternal throne sublime,
Of visions seen in ancient time,   1345
Till his rapt soul would leave her home
In visionary worlds to roam.
Then would the mists that wandered bye
Seem hovering spirits to his eye:
Then would the breeze's whistling sweep,   1350
Soft lulling in the cavern deep,
Seem to the enthusiast's dreaming ear
The words of spirits whispered near.

    Loathed his firm soul the measured chime
And florid films of modern rhyme;   1355
No other lays became his tongue
But those his rude forefathers sung.
And when, by wandering minstrel warned,
The mandate of his queen he learned,
So much he prized the ancient strain,   1360
High hopes had he the prize to gain.
With modest, yet majestic mien,
He tuned his harp of solemn strain:
O list the tale, ye fair and young,
A lay so strange was never sung!   1365

Kilmeny

THE THIRTEENTH BARD'S SONG

    Bonny Kilmeny gaed up the glen;
But it wasna to meet Duneira's men,
Nor the rosy monk of the isle to see,
For Kilmeny was pure as pure could be.
It was only to hear the Yorlin sing,   1370
And pu' the cress-flower round the spring;
The scarlet hypp and the hindberrye,

And the nut that hang frae the hazel tree;
For Kilmeny was pure as pure could be.
But lang may her minny look o'er the wa', 1375
And lang may she seek i' the green-wood shaw;
Lang the laird of Duneira blame,
And lang, lang greet or Kilmeny come hame!

When many a day had come and fled,
When grief grew calm, and hope was dead, 1380
When mess for Kilmeny's soul had been sung,
When the bedes-man had prayed, and the dead-bell rung,
Late, late in a gloamin when all was still,
When the fringe was red on the westlin hill,
The wood was sere, the moon i' the wane, 1385
The reek o' the cot hung over the plain,
Like a little wee cloud in the world its lane;
When the ingle lowed with an eiry leme,
Late, late in the gloamin Kilmeny came hame!

"Kilmeny, Kilmeny, where have you been? 1390
Lang hae we sought baith holt and den;
By linn, by ford, and green-wood tree,
Yet you are halesome and fair to see.
Where gat you that joup o' the lilly scheen?
That bonny snood of the birk sae green? 1395
And these roses, the fairest that ever were seen?
Kilmeny, Kilmeny, where have you been?"

Kilmeny looked up with a lovely grace,
But nae smile was seen on Kilmeny's face;
As still was her look, and as still was her ee, 1400
As the stillness that lay on the emerant lea,
Or the mist that sleeps on a waveless sea.
For Kilmeny had been she knew not where,
And Kilmeny had seen what she could not declare;
Kilmeny had been where the cock never crew, 1405
Where the rain never fell, and the wind never blew,
But it seemed as the harp of the sky had rung,
And the airs of heaven played round her tongue,
When she spake of the lovely forms she had seen,
And a land where sin had never been; 1410
A land of love, and a land of light,
Withouten sun, or moon, or night:
Where the river swa'd a living stream,

And the light a pure celestial beam:
The land of vision it would seem,   1415
A still, an everlasting dream.

 In yon green-wood there is a waik,
And in that waik there is a wene,
 And in that wene there is a maike,
That neither has flesh, blood, nor bane;   1420
 And down in yon green-wood he walks his lane.

 In that green wene Kilmeny lay,
Her bosom happed wi' the flowerits gay;
But the air was soft and the silence deep,
And bonny Kilmeny fell sound asleep.   1425
She kend nae mair, nor opened her ee,
Till waked by the hymns of a far countrye.

 She 'wakened on couch of the silk sae slim,
All striped wi' the bars of the rainbow's rim;
And lovely beings round were rife,   1430
Who erst had travelled mortal life;
And aye they smiled, and 'gan to speer,
"What spirit has brought this mortal here?"—

 "Lang have I journeyed the world wide,"
A meek and reverend fere replied;   1435
"Baith night and day I have watched the fair,
Eident a thousand years and mair.
Yes, I have watched o'er ilk degree,
Wherever blooms femenitye;
But sinless virgin, free of stain   1440
In mind and body, fand I nane.
Never, since the banquet of time,
Found I a virgin in her prime,
Till late this bonny maiden I saw
As spotless as the morning snaw: 1445
Full twenty years she has lived as free
As the spirits that sojourn this countrye.
I have brought her away frae the snares of men,
That sin or death she never may ken."—

 They clasped her waiste and her hands sae fair,   1450
They kissed her cheek, and they kemed her hair,
And round came many a blooming fere,
Saying, "Bonny Kilmeny, ye're welcome here!

Women are freed of the littand scorn:
O, blessed be the day Kilmeny was born!   1455
Now shall the land of the spirits see,
Now shall it ken what a woman may be!
Many a lang year in sorrow and pain,
Many a lang year through the world we've gane,
Commissioned to watch fair womankind,   1460
For its they who nurice th' immortal mind.
We have watched their steps as the dawning shone,
And deep in the green-wood walks alone;
By lilly bower and silken bed,
The viewless tears have o'er them shed;   1465
Have soothed their ardent minds to sleep,
Or left the couch of love to weep.
We have seen! we have seen! but the time must come,
And the angels will weep at the day of doom!

    "O, would the fairest of mortal kind   1470
Aye keep the holy truths in mind,
That kindred spirits their motions see,
Who watch their ways with anxious ee,
And grieve for the guilt of humanitye!
O, sweet to Heaven the maiden's prayer,   1475
And the sigh that heaves a bosom sae fair!
And dear to Heaven the words of truth,
And the praise of virtue frae beauty's mouth!
And dear to the viewless forms of air,
The minds that kyth as the body fair!   1480

    "O, bonny Kilmeny! free frae stain,
If ever you seek the world again,
That world of sin, of sorrow and fear,
O, tell of the joys that are waiting here;
And tell of the signs you shall shortly see;   1485
Of the times that are now, and the times that shall be."–

    They lifted Kilmeny, they led her away,
And she walked in the light of a sunless day:
The sky was a dome of crystal bright,
The fountain of vision, and fountain of light: 1490
The emerald fields were of dazzling glow,
And the flowers of everlasting blow.
Then deep in the stream her body they laid,
That her youth and beauty never might fade;

And they smiled on heaven, when they saw her lie   1495
In the stream of life that wandered bye.
And she heard a song, she heard it sung,
She kend not where; but sae sweetly it rung,
It fell on her ear like a dream of the morn:
"O! blest be the day Kilmeny was born!   1500
Now shall the land of the spirits see,
Now shall it ken what a woman may be!
The sun that shines on the world sae bright,
A borrowed gleid frae the fountain of light;
And the moon that sleeks the sky sae dun,   1505
Like a gouden bow, or a beamless sun,
Shall wear away, and be seen nae mair,
And the angels shall miss them travelling the air.
But lang, lang after baith night and day,
When the sun and the world have elyed away;   1510
When the sinner has gane to his waesome doom,
Kilmeny shall smile in eternal bloom!"—

   They bore her away she wist not how,
For she felt not arm nor rest below;
But so swift they wained her through the light,   1515
'Twas like the motion of sound or sight;
They seemed to split the gales of air,
And yet nor gale nor breeze was there.
Unnumbered groves below them grew,
They came, they past, and backward flew,   1520
Like floods of blossoms gliding on,
In moment seen, in moment gone.
O, never vales to mortal view
Appeared like those o'er which they flew!
That land to human spirits given,   1525
The lowermost vales of the storied heaven;
From thence they can view the world below,
And heaven's blue gates with sapphires glow,
More glory yet unmeet to know.

   They bore her far to a mountain green,   1530
To see what mortal never had seen;
And they seated her high on a purple sward,
And bade her heed what she saw and heard,
And note the changes the spirits wrought,
For now she lived in the land of thought.   1535

She looked, and she saw nor sun nor skies,
But a crystal dome of a thousand dies.
She looked, and she saw nae land aright,
But an endless whirl of glory and light.
And radiant beings went and came   1540
Far swifter than wind, or the linked flame.
She hid her een frae the dazzling view;
She looked again and the scene was new.

   She saw a sun on a summer sky,
And clouds of amber sailing bye;   1545
A lovely land beneath her lay,
And that land had glens and mountains gray;
And that land had vallies and hoary piles,
And marled seas, and a thousand isles;
Its fields were speckled, its forests green,   1550
And its lakes were all of the dazzling sheen,
Like magic mirrors, where slumbering lay
The sun and the sky and the cloudlet gray;
Which heaved and trembled and gently swung,
On every shore they seemed to be hung;   1555
For there they were seen on their downward plain
A thousand times and a thousand again;
In winding lake and placid firth,
Little peaceful heavens in the bosom of earth.

   Kilmeny sighed and seemed to grieve,   1560
For she found her heart to that land did cleave;
She saw the corn wave on the vale,
She saw the deer run down the dale;
She saw the plaid and the broad claymore,
And the brows that the badge of freedom bore;   1565
And she thought she had seen the land before.

   She saw a lady sit on a throne,
The fairest that ever the sun shone on!
A lion licked her hand of milk,
And she held him in a leish of silk;   1570
And a leifu' maiden stood at her knee,
With a silver wand and melting ee;
Her sovereign shield till love stole in,
And poisoned all the fount within.

   Then a gruff untoward bedeman came,   1575

And hundit the lion on his dame:
And the guardian maid wi' the dauntless ee,
She dropped a tear, and left her knee;
And she saw till the queen frae the lion fled,
Till the bonniest flower of the world lay dead.   1580
A coffin was set on a distant plain,
And she saw the red blood fall like rain:
Then bonny Kilmeny's heart grew sair,
And she turned away, and could look nae mair.

    Then the gruff grim carle girned amain,   1585
And they trampled him down, but he rose again;
And he baited the lion to deeds of weir,
Till he lapped the blood to the kingdom dear;
And weening his head was danger-preef,
When crowned with the rose and clover leaf,   1590
He gowled at the carle, and chased him away
To feed wi' the deer on the mountain gray.
He gowled at the carle, and he gecked at heaven,
But his mark was set, and his arles given.
Kilmeny a while her een withdrew;   1595
She looked again, and the scene was new.

    She saw below her fair unfurled
One half of all the glowing world,
Where oceans rolled, and rivers ran,
To bound the aims of sinful man.   1600
She saw a people, fierce and fell,
Burst frae their bounds like fiends of hell;
There lilies grew, and the eagle flew,
And she herked on her ravening crew,
Till the cities and towers were wrapt in a blaze,   1605
And the thunder it roared o'er the lands and the seas.
The widows they wailed, and the red blood ran,
And she threatened an end to the race of man:
She never lened, nor stood in awe,
Till claught by the lion's deadly paw.   1610
Oh! then the eagle swinked for life,
And brainzelled up a mortal strife;
But flew she north, or flew she south,
She met wi' the gowl of the lion's mouth.

    With a mooted wing and waefu' maen,   1615
The eagle sought her eiry again;

But lang may she cour in her bloody nest,
And lang, lang sleek her wounded breast,
Before she sey another flight,
To play wi' the norland lion's might.   1620

   But to sing the sights Kilmeny saw,
So far surpassing nature's law,
The singer's voice wad sink away,
And the string of his harp wad cease to play.
But she saw till the sorrows of man were bye,   1625
And all was love and harmony;
Till the stars of heaven fell calmly away,
Like the flakes of snaw on a winter day.

   Then Kilmeny begged again to see
The friends she had left in her own country,   1630
To tell of the place where she had been,
And the glories that lay in the land unseen;
To warn the living maidens fair,
The loved of Heaven, the spirits' care,
That all whose minds unmeled remain   1635
Shall bloom in beauty when time is gane.

   With distant music, soft and deep,
They lulled Kilmeny sound asleep;
And when she awakened, she lay her lane,
All happed with flowers in the green-wood wene.   1640
When seven lang years had come and fled;
When grief was calm, and hope was dead;
When scarce was remembered Kilmeny's name,
Late, late in a gloamin Kilmeny came hame!
And O, her beauty was fair to see,   1645
But still and stedfast was her ee!
Such beauty bard may never declare,
For there was no pride nor passion there;
And the soft desire of maidens een
In that mild face could never be seen.   1650
Her seymar was the lilly flower,
And her cheek the moss-rose in the shower;
And her voice like the distant melodye,
That floats along the twilight sea.
But she loved to raike the lanely glen,   1655
And keeped afar frae the haunts of men;
Her holy hymns unheard to sing,

To suck the flowers, and drink the spring.
But wherever her peaceful form appeared,
The wild beasts of the hill were cheered;   1660
The wolf played blythly round the field,
The lordly byson lowed and kneeled;
The dun deer wooed with manner bland,
And cowered aneath her lilly hand.
And when at even the woodlands rung,   1665
When hymns of other worlds she sung,
In ecstacy of sweet devotion,
O, then the glen was all in motion.
The wild beasts of the forest came,
Broke from their bughts and faulds the tame,   1670
And goved around, charmed and amazed;
Even the dull cattle crooned and gazed,
And murmured and looked with anxious pain
For something the mystery to explain.
The buzzard came with the throstle-cock;   1675
The corby left her houf in the rock;
The blackbird alang wi' the eagle flew;
The hind came tripping o'er the dew;
The wolf and the kid their raike began,
And the tod, and the lamb, and the leveret ran;   1680
The hawk and the hern attour them hung,
And the merl and the mavis forhooyed their young;
And all in a peaceful ring were hurled:
It was like an eve in a sinless world!

When a month and a day had come and gane,   1685
Kilmeny sought the greenwood wene;
There laid her down on the leaves sae green,
And Kilmeny on earth was never mair seen.
But O, the words that fell from her mouth,
Were words of wonder, and words of truth!   1690
But all the land were in fear and dread,
For they kendna whether she was living or dead.
It wasna her hame, and she couldna remain;
She left this world of sorrow and pain,
And returned to the land of thought again.   1695

He ceased; and all with kind concern
Blest in their hearts the bard of Ern.

By that the chill and piercing air,
The pallid hue of ladies fair,
The hidden yawn, and drumbly eye,   1700
Loudly announced the morning nigh.
Beckoned the Queen with courteous smile,
And breathless silence gazed the while:—

"I hold it best, my lords," she said,
"For knight, for dame, and lovely maid,   1705
At wassail, wake, or revel hall,
To part before the senses pall.
Sweet though the draught of pleasure be,
Why should we drain it to the lee?
Though here the minstrel's fancy play,   1710
Light as the breeze of summer-day;
Though there in solemn cadence flow,
Smooth as the night-wind o'er the snow;
Now bound away with rolling sweep,
Like tempest o'er the raving deep;   1715
High on the morning's golden screen,
Or casemate of the rainbow lean;—
Such beauties were in vain prolonged,
The soul is cloyed, the minstrel wronged.

"Loud is the morning-blast and chill,   1720
The snow-drift speeds along the hill;
Let ladies of the storm beware,
And knights of ladies take a care;
From lanes and alleys guard them well,
Where lurking ghost or sprite may dwell;   1725
But most avoid the dazzling flare,
And spirit of the morning air;
Hide from their eyes that hideous form,
The ruthless angel of the storm.
I wish, for every gallant's sake,   1730
That none may rue our Royal Wake:
I wish what most his heart approves,
And every lady what she loves,—
Sweet be her sleep on bed of down,

And pleasing be her dreams till noon.　　　　1735
And when you hear the bugle's strain,
I hope to see you all again."—

Whether the Queen to fear inclined,
Or spoke to cheer the minstrel's mind,
Certes, she spoke with meaning leer,　　　　1740
And ladies smiled her words to hear.
Yet, though the dawn of morning shone,
No lady from that night-wake gone,
Not even the Queen durst sleep alone.
And scarce had Sleep, with throb and sigh,　　　　1745
O'er breast of snow, and moistened eye,
Outspread his shadowy canopy,
When every fervid female mind,
Or sailed with witches on the wind,
In Carlisle drank the potent wine,　　　　1750
Or floated on the foamy brine.
Some strove the land of thought to win,
Impelled by hope, withstood by sin;
And some with angry spirit stood
By lonely stream, or pathless wood.　　　　1755
And oft was heard the broken sigh,
The half-formed prayer, and smothered cry;
So much the minds of old and young
Were moved by what the minstrels sung.
What Lady Gordon did or said　　　　1760
Could not be learned from lady's maid,
And Huntly swore and shook his head.
But she and all her buskined train
Appeared not at the Wake again.

END OF NIGHT THE SECOND

The Queen's Wake

Night the Third

The

Queen's Wake

THE storm had ceased to shroud the hill;
The morning's breath was pure and chill;
And when the sun rose from the main,
No eye the glory could sustain.
The icicles so dazzling bright;   5
The spreading wold so smooth and white;
The cloudless sky, the air so sheen,
That roes on Pentland's top were seen;
And Grampian mountains, frowning high,
Seemed froze amid the northern sky.   10
The frame was braced, the mind set free
To feat, or brisk hilarity.

    The sun, far on his southern throne,
Glowed in stern majesty alone:
'Twas like the loved, the toilsome day,   15
That dawns on mountains west away,
When the furred Indian hunter hastes
Far up his Appalachian wastes,
To range the savage haunts, and dare
In his dark home the sullen bear.   20
And ere that noonday-sun had shone
Right on the banks of Duddingston,
Heavens! what a scene of noise and glee,
And busy brisk anxiety!
There age and youth their pastime take   25
On the smooth ice that chains the lake.
The Highland chief, the Border knight,
In waving plumes, and baldricks bright,
Join in the bloodless friendly war,
The sounding-stone to hurl afar.   30
The hair-breadth aim, the plaudits due,
The rap, the shout, the ardour grew,
Till drowsy day her curtain drew.

The youth, on cramps of polished steel,
Joined in the race, the curve, the wheel;   35
With arms outstretched, and foot aside,
Like lightning o'er the lake they glide;
And eastward far their impulse keep,
Like angels journeying o'er the deep.

When night her spangled flag unfurled   40
Wide o'er a wan and sheeted world,
In keen debate homeward they hie,
For well they knew the Wake was nigh.

By mountain sheer, and column tall,
How solemn was that evening fall!   45
The air was calm, the stars were bright,
The hoar frost flightered down the night;
But oft the list'ning groups stood still,
For spirits talked along the hill.
The fairy tribes had gone to won   50
In southland climes beneath the sun;
By shady woods, and waters sheen,
And vales of everlasting green,
To sing of Scotia's woodlands wild,
Where human face had never smiled.   55
The ghost had left the haunted yew,
The wayward bogle fled the clough,
The darksome pool of crisp and foam
Was now no more the kelpies' home:
But polar spirits sure had spread   60
O'er hills which native fays had fled;
For all along, from cliff and tree,
On Arthur's hill, and Salisbury,
Came voices floating down the air
From viewless shades that lingered there: 65
The words were fraught with mystery;
Voices of men they could not be.
Youths turned their faces to the sky,
With beating heart, and bended eye;
Old chieftains walked with hastened tread,   70
Loath that their hearts should bow to dread.
They feared the spirits of the hill
To sinful Scotland boded ill.

Orion up his baldrick drew,
The evening star was still in view,   75
Scarce had the Pleiades cleared the main,
Or Charles reyoked his golden wain,
When from the palace-turrets rang
The bugle's note with warning clang;
Each tower, each spire, in music spake,   80
"Haste, nobles, to Queen Mary's Wake."
The blooming maid ran to bedight,
In spangled lace, and robe of white,
That graceful emblem of her youth,
Of guileless heart, and maiden truth.   85
The matron decked her candid frame
In moony broach, and silk of flame;
And every Earl and Baron bold
Sparkled in clasp and loop of gold.
'Twas the last night of hope and fear,   90
That bards could sing, or Sovereign hear;
And just ere rose the Christmas sun,
The envied prize was lost and won.

The bard that night who foremost came
Was not enrolled, nor known his name;   95
A youth he was of manly mold,
Gentle as lamb, as lion bold;
But his fair face, and forehead high,
Glowed with intrusive modesty.

'Twas said by bank of southland stream   100
Glided his youth in soothing dream;
The harp he loved, and wont to stray
Far to the wilds and woods away,
And sing to brooks that gurgled bye
Of maiden's form and maiden's eye;   105
That, when this dream of youth was past,
Deep in the shade his harp he cast;
In busy life his cares beguiled,
His heart was true, and fortune smiled.
But when the Royal Wake began,   110
Joyful he came the foremost man,
To see the matchless bard approved,
And list the strains he once had loved.

Two nights had passed, the bards had sung–
Queen Mary's harp from ceiling hung,   115
On which was graved her lovely mold,
Beset with crowns and flowers of gold;
And many a gem of dazzling dye
Glowed on that prize to minstrel's eye.

The youth had heard each minstrel's strain,   120
And, fearing northern bard would gain,
To try his youthful skill was moved,
Not for himself, but friends he loved.

Mary Scott

THE FOURTEENTH BARD'S SONG

Lord Pringle's steed neighs in the stall,
    His panoply is irksome grown,   125
His plumed helm hangs in the hall,
    His broad claymore is berry brown.

No more his bugle's evening peal
    Bids vassal arm and yeoman ride,
To drive the deer of Otterdale,   130
    Or foray on the Border side.

Instead of whoop and battle knell,
    Of warrior's song, and revel free,
Is heard the lute's voluptuous swell
    Within the halls of Torwoodlee.   135

Sick lies his heart without relief;
    'Tis love that breeds the warrior's woe,
For daughter of a froward chief,
    A freebooter, his mortal foe.

But O, that maiden's form of grace,   140
    And eye of love, to him were dear!
The smile that dimpled on her face
    Was deadlier than the Border spear.

That form was not the poplar's stem,
 That smile the dawning's purple line; 145
Nor was that eye the dazzling gem
 That glows adown the Indian mine.

But would you praise the poplar pale,
 Or morn in wreath of roses drest;
The fairest flower that woos the vale, 150
 Or down that clothes the solan's breast;

A thousand times beyond, above,
 What rapt enthusiast ever saw;
Compare them to that mould of love—
 Young Mary Scott of Tushilaw! 155

The war-flame glows on Ettrick pen,
 Bounds forth the foray swift as wind,
And Tushilaw and all his men
 Have left their homes afar behind.

O lady, lady, learn thy creed, 160
 And mark the watch-dog's boist'rous din;
The abbot comes with book and bead,
 O haste and let the father in!

And, lady, mark his locks so gray,
 His beard so long, and colour wan; 165
O he has mourned for many a day,
 And sorrowed o'er the sins of man!

And yet so stately is his mien,
 His step so firm, and breast so bold;
His brawny leg and form, I ween, 170
 Are wonderous for a man so old.

Short was his greeting, short and low,
 His blessing short as prayer could be;
But oft he sighed, and boded woe,
 And spoke of sin and misery. 175

To shrift, to shrift, now ladies all,
 Your prayers and Ave Marias learn;

Haste, trembling, to the vesper hall,
     For ah! the priest is dark and stern.

Short was the task of lady old,   180
     Short as confession well could be;
The abbot's orisons were cold,
     His absolutions frank and free.

Go, Mary Scott, thy spirit meek
     Lay open to the searcher's eye;   185
And let the tear bedew thy cheek,
     Thy sins are of a crimson dye.

For many a lover thou hast slain,
     And many yet lies sick for thee—
Young Gilmanscleuch and Deloraine,   190
     And Pringle, lord of Torwoodlee.

Tell every wish thy bosom near,
     No other sin, dear maid, hast thou;
And well the abbot loves to hear
     Thy plights of love and simple vow.   195

"Why stays my Mary Scott so long?
     What guilt can youth and beauty wail?
Of fervent thought and passion strong,
     Heavens! what a sickening tedious tale!"

O lady, cease; the maiden's mind,   200
     Though pure as morning's cloudless beam,
A crime in every wish can find,
     In noontide glance, and midnight dream.

To woman's heart when fair and free,
     Her sins seem great and manifold;   205
When sunk in guilt and misery,
     No crime can then her soul behold.

'Tis sweet to see the opening flower
     Spread its fair bosom to the sun;
'Tis sweet to hear in vernal bower   210
     The thrush's earliest hymn begun:

But sweeter far the prayer that wrings
   The tear from maiden's beaming eye;
And sweeter far the hymn she sings
   In grateful holy ecstacy.   215

The mass was said, but cold and dry
   That mass to Heaven the father sent;
With book, and bead, and rosary,
   The abbot to his chamber went.

The watch-dog rests with folded eye   220
   Beneath the portal's gray festoon;
The wildered Ettrick wanders bye,
   Loud murmuring to the careless moon.

The warder lists with hope and dread
   Far distant shout of fray begun;   225
The cricket tunes his tiny reed,
   And harps behind the embers dun.

Why does the warder bend his head,
   And silent stand the casement near?
The cricket stops his little reed,   230
   The sound of gentle step to hear.

O many a wight from Border brake
   Has reaved the drowsy warden round;
And many a daughter lain awake,
   When parents trowed them sleeping sound.   235

The abbot's bed is well down spread,
   The abbot's bed is soft and fair,
The abbot's bed is cold as lead—
   For why?—the abbot is not there.

Was that the blast of bugle, borne   240
   Far on the night-wind, wavering shrill?
'Tis nothing but the shepherd's horn
   That keeps the watch on Cacra hill.

What means the warder's answering note?
   The moon is west, 'tis near the day;   245

I thought I heard the warrior's shout,
   'Tis time the abbot were away!

The bittern mounts the morning air;
   And rings the sky with quavering croon;
The watch-dog sallies from his lair,   250
   And bays the wind and setting moon.

'Tis not the breeze, nor bittern's wail,
   Has roused the guarder from his den;
Along the bank, in belt and mail,
   Comes Tushilaw and all his men.   255

The abbot, from his casement, saw
   The forest chieftain's proud array;
He heard the voice of Tushilaw—
   The abbot's heart grew cold as clay!

"Haste, maidens, call my lady fair,   260
   That room may for my warriors be;
And bid my daughter come and share
   The cup of joy with them and me.

"Say we have fought and won the fray,
   Have lowered our haughty foeman's pride;   265
And we have driven the richest prey
   That ever lowed by Ettrick side."—

To hear a tale of vanquished foes
   His lady came right cheerfully;
And Mary Scott, like morning rose,   270
   Stood blushing at her father's knee.

Fast flowed the warrior's ruthless tale,
   And aye the red cup passed between;
But Mary Scott grew lily pale,
   And trembled like the aspin green.   275

"Now, lady, give me welcome cheer,
   Queen of the border thou shalt be;
For I have brought thee gold and gear,
   And humbled haughty Torwoodlee.

"I beat his yeomen in the glen,   280
   I loosed his horses from the stall,
I slew the blood-hound in his den,
   And sought the chief through tower and hall.

"'Tis said in hamlet mean and dark
   Nightly he lies with leman dear;   285
O, I would give ten thousand mark,
   To see his head upon my spear!

"Go, maidens, every mat be spread
   On heather, haum, or roegrass heap,
And make for me the scarlet bed,   290
   For I have need of rest and sleep."—

"Nay, my good lord, make other choice,
   In that you cannot rest to-day;
For there in peaceful slumber lies
   A holy abbot, old and gray."   295

The chieftain's cheek to crimson grew,
   Dropt from his hand the rosy wine—
"An abbot! curse the canting crew!
   An abbot sleep in couch of mine!

"Now, lady, as my soul shall thrive,   300
   I'd rather trust my child and thee
With my two greatest foes alive,
   The king of Scots and Torwoodlee.

"The lazy hoard of Melrose vale
   Has brought my life, my all to stake: 305
O, lady! I have heard a tale,
   The thought o't makes my heart to ache!

"Go, warriors, hale the villain forth,
   Bring not his loathful form to me;
The gate stands open to the north,   310
   The rope hangs o'er the gallows tree.

"There shall the burning breeze of noon
   Rock the old sensual sluggard blind;

There let him swing, till sun and moon
  Have three times left the world behind."–   315

O abbot, abbot, say thy prayers,
  With orisons load every breath;
The forest trooper's on the stairs,
  To drag thee to a shameful death.

O abbot, abbot, quit thy bed,   320
  Ill armed art thou to meet the strife;
Haste, don thy beard, and quoif thy head,
  And guard the door for death or life.

Thy arm is firm, thy heart is stout,
  Yet thou canst neither fight nor flee;   325
But beauty stands thy guard without,
  Yes, beauty weeps and pleads for thee.

Proud, ruthless man, by vengeance driven,
  Regardless hears a brother plead;
Regardless sees the brand of Heaven   330
  Red quivering o'er his guilty head:

But once let woman's soothing tongue
  Implore his help or clemency,
Around him let her arms be flung,
  Or at his feet her bended knee;   335

The world's a shadow! vengeance sleeps!
  The child of reason stands revealed–
When beauty pleads, when woman weeps,
  He is not man who scorns to yield.

Stern Tushilaw is gone to sleep,   340
  Laughing at woman's dread of sin;
But first he bade his warriors keep
  All robbers out, and abbots in.

The abbot from his casement high
  Looked out to see the peep of day;   345
The scene that met the abbot's eye
  Filled him with wonder and dismay.

'Twas not the dews of dawning mild,
   The mountain's hues of silver gray,
Nor yet the Ettrick's windings wild,   350
   By belted holm and bosky brae;

Nor moorland Rankleburn, that raved
   By covert, clough, and greenwood shaw;
Nor dappled flag of day, that waved
   In streamers pale from Gilmans-law: 355

But many a doubted ox there lay
   At rest upon the castle lea;
And there he saw his gallant gray,
   And all the steeds of Torwoodlee.

"Beshrew the wont!" the abbot said,   360
   "The charge runs high for lodging here;
The guard is deep, the path way-laid,
   My homilies shall cost me dear.

"Come well, come woe, with dauntless core
   I'll kneel, and con my breviary;   365
If Tushilaw is versed in lore,
   'Twill be an awkward game with me."–

Now Tushilaw he waked and slept,
   And dreamed and thought till noontide hour;
But aye this query upmost kept,   370
   "What seeks the abbot in my tower?"

Stern Tushilaw came down the stair
   With doubtful and indignant eye,
And found the holy man at prayer,
   With book, and cross, and rosary.   375

"To book, to book, thou reaver red,
   Of absolution thou hast need;
The sword of Heaven hangs o'er thy head,
   Death is thy doom and hell thy meed!"–

"I'll take my chance, thou priest of sin,   380
   Thy absolutions I disdain;

But I will noose thy bearded chin,
   If thus thou talkest to me again.

"Declare thy business and thy name,
   Or short the route to thee is given!"–   385
"The abbot I of Coldinghame,
   My errand is the cause of Heaven."–

"That shalt thou prove ere we two part;
   Some robber thou, or royal spy:
But, villain, I will search thy heart,   390
   And chain thee in the deep to lie!

"Hence with thy rubbish, hest and ban,
   Whinyards to keep the weak in awe;
The scorn of Heaven, the shame of man–
   No books nor beads for Tushilaw!"   395

"Oh! lost to mercy, faith, and love!
   Thy bolts and chains are nought to me;
I'll call an angel from above,
   That soon will set the pris'ner free."–

Bold Tushilaw, o'er strone and steep,   400
   Pursues the roe and dusky deer;
The abbot lies in dungeon deep,
   The maidens wail, the matrons fear.

The sweetest flower on Ettrick shaw
   Bends its fair form o'er grated keep;   405
Young Mary Scott of Tushilaw
   Sleeps but to sigh, and wakes to weep.

Bold Tushilaw, with horn and hound,
   Pursues the deer o'er holt and lea;
And rides and rules the Border round,   410
   From Philiphaugh to Gilnockye.

His page rode down by Melrose fair,
   His page rode down by Coldinghame;
But not a priest was missing there,
   Nor abbot, friar, nor monk of name.   415

The evening came; it was the last
  The abbot in this world should see;
The bonds are firm, the bolts are fast,
  No angel comes to set him free.

Yes, at the stillest hour of night   420
  Softly unfolds the iron door;
Beamed through the gloom unwonted light,
  That light a beauteous angel bore.

Fair was the form that o'er him hung,
  And fair the hands that set him free;   425
The trembling whispers of her tongue
  Softer than seraph's melody.

The abbot's soul was all on flame,
  Wild transport through his bosom ran;
For never angel's airy frame   430
  Was half so sweet to mortal man!

Why walks young Mary Scott so late,
  In veil and cloak of cramasye?
The porter opens wide the gate,
  His bonnet moves, and bends his knee.   435

Long may the wondering porter wait,
  Before the lady form return;
"Speed, abbot, speed, nor halt nor bate,
  Nor look thou back to Rankleburn!"

The day arrives, the ladies plead   440
  In vain for yon mysterious wight;
For Tushilaw his doom decreed,
  Were he an abbot, lord, or knight.

The chieftain called his warriors stout,
  And ranged them round the gallows tree,   445
Then bade them bring the abbot out,
  The fate of fraud that all might see.

The men return of sense bereft,
  Faulter their tongues, their eye-balls glare;

The door was locked, the fetters left—   450
   All close! the abbot was not there!

The wondering warriors bow to God,
   And matins to the Virgin hum;
But Tushilaw he gloomed and strode,
   And walked into the castle dumb.   455

But to the Virgin's sacred name
   The vow was paid in many a cell;
And many a rich oblation came,
   For that amazing miracle.

Lord Pringle walked his glens alone,   460
   Nor flock nor lowing herd he saw;
But even the king upon the throne
   Quaked at the name of Tushilaw.

Lord Pringle's heart was all on flame,
   Nor peace nor joy his bosom knew,   465
'Twas for the kindest, sweetest dame,
   That ever brushed the Forest dew.

Gone is one month with smile and sigh,
   With dream by night and wish by day;
A second came with moistened eye;   470
   Another came and passed away.

Why is the flower of yonder pile
   Bending its stem to court decay,
And Mary Scott's benignant smile
   Like sun-beam in a winter day?   475

Sometimes her colour's like the rose,
   Sometimes 'tis like the lily pale;
The flower that in the forest grows
   Is fallen before the summer gale.

A mother's fostering breast is warm,   480
   And dark her doubts of love I ween:
For why?—she felt its early harm—
   A mother's eye is sharp and keen!

'Tis done! the woman stands revealed!
   Stern Tushilaw is waked to see;   485
The bearded priest so well concealed,
   Was Pringle, lord of Torwoodlee!

Oh never was the thunder's jar,
   The red tornado's wasting wing,
Nor all the elemental war,   490
   Like fury of the Border king.

He laughed aloud–his faulchion eyed–
   A laugh of burning vengeance born!–
"Does thus the coward trow," he cried,
   "To hold his conqueror's power to scorn!   495

"Thinks Tushilaw of maids or wives,
   Or such a thing as Torwoodlee!
Had Mary Scott a thousand lives,
   These lives were all too few for me!

"Ere midnight, in the secret cave,   500
   This sword shall pierce her bosom's core,
Though I go childless to my grave,
   And rue the deed for evermore!

"O had I lulled the imp to rest
   When first she lisped her name to me,   505
Or pierced her little guileless breast
   When smiling on her nurse's knee!"–

"Just is your vengeance, my good lord,
   'Tis just and meet our daughter die;
For sharper than a foeman's sword   510
   Is family shame and injury.

"But trust the ruthless deed to me;
   I have a vial potent, good;
Unmeet that all the Scotts should see
   A daughter's corse embalmed in blood!   515

"Unmeet her gallant kinsmen know
   The guilt of one so fair and young;

No cup should to her mem'ry flow,
   No requiem o'er her grave be sung.

"My potent draught has erst proved true   520
   Beneath my own and husband's eye;
Trust me, ere falls the morning dew,
   In dreamless sleep shall Mary lie!"—

"Even go thy way, thy words are true,
   I knew thy dauntless soul before;   525
But list—if thou deceivest me too,
   Thou hast a head! I say no more."—

Stern Tushilaw strode o'er the ley,
   And, wondering, by the twilight saw
A crystal tear drop from his eye,   530
   The first e'er shed by Tushilaw!

O grievous are the bonds of steel,
   And blasted hope 'tis hard to prove;
More grievous far it is to feel
   Ingratitude from those we love.   535

"What brings my lady mother here,
   Pale as the morning shower and cold?
In her dark eye why stands the tear?
   Why in her hand a cup of gold?"—

"My Mary, thou art ill at rest,   540
   Fervid and feverish is thy blood;
Still yearns o'er thee thy mother's breast,
   Take this, my child, 'tis for thy good!"—

O sad, sad was young Mary's plight!
   She took the cup—no word she spake: 545
She had even wished that very night
   To sleep, and never more to wake.

She took the cup—she drank it dry,
   Then pillowed soft her beauteous head,
And calmly watched her mother's eye;   550
   But O that eye was hard to read!

Her moistened eyes, so mild and meek,
  Soon sunk their auburn fringe beneath;
The ringlets on her damask cheek
  Heaved gentler with her stealing breath!   555

She turned her face unto the wall,
  Her colour changed to pallid clay;
Long ere the dews began to fall,
  The flower of Ettrick lifeless lay!

Why underneath her winding sheet   560
  Does broidered silk her form enfold?
Why is cold Mary's buskined feet
  All laced with belts and bands of gold?

"What boots to me these robes so gay?
  To wear them now no child have I!   565
They should have graced her bridal day,
  Now they must in the church-yard lie!

"I thought to see my daughter ride,
  In golden gear and cramasye,
To Mary's fane, the loveliest bride   570
  E'er to the Virgin bent the knee.

"Now I may by her funeral wain
  Ride silent o'er the mountain gray:
Her revel hall, the gloomy fane;
  Her bridal bed, the cheerless clay!"   575

Why that rich snood with plume and lace
  Round Mary's lifeless temples drawn?
Why is the napkin o'er her face,
  A fragment of the lily lawn?

"My Mary has another home;   580
  And far, far though her journey be,
When she to Paradise shall come,
  Then will my child remember me!"–

O many a flower was round her spread,
  And many a pearl and diamond bright,   585

And many a window round her head
  Shed on her form a bootless light!

Lord Pringle sat on Maygill brae,
  Pondering on war and vengeance meet;
The Cadan toiled in narrow way,   590
  The Tweed rolled far beneath his feet.

Not Tweed, by gulf and whirlpool mazed,
  Through dark wood-glen, by him was seen;
For still his thought-set eye was raised
  To Ettrick mountains, wild and green.   595

Sullen he sat, unstaid, unblest,
  He thought of battle, broil, and blood;
He never crossed, he never wist
  Till by his side a Palmer stood.

"Haste, my good lord, this letter read,   600
  Ill bodes it listless thus to be;
Upon a die I've set my head,
  And brought this letter far to thee."—

Lord Pringle looked the letter on,
  His face grew pale as winter sky;   605
But, ere the half of it was done,
  The tear of joy stood in his eye.

A purse he to the Palmer threw,
  Mounted the cleft of aged tree,
Three times aloud his bugle blew,   610
  And hasted home to Torwoodlee.

'Twas scarcely past the hour of noon
  When first the foray whoop began;
And, in the wan light of the moon,
  Through March and Teviotdale it ran.   615

Far to the south it spread away,
  Startled the hind by fold and tree;
And aye the watch-word of the fray
  Was, "Ride for Ker and Torwoodlee!"

When next the day began to fade, 620
    The warriors round their chieftains range;
And many a solemn vow they made,
    And many an oath of fell revenge.

The Pringles' plumes indignant dance—
    It was a gallant sight to see; 625
And many a Ker, with sword and lance,
    Stood rank and file on Torwoodlee.

As they fared up yon craigy glen,
    Where Tweed sweeps round the Thorny-hill,
Old Gideon Murray and his men 630
    The foray joined with right good-will.

They hasted up by Plora side,
    And north above Mount-Benger turn,
And lothly forced with them to ride
    Black Douglas of the Craigy-burn. 635

When they came nigh Saint Mary's lake
    The day-sky glimmered on the dew;
They hid their horses in the brake,
    And lurked in heath and braken clough.

The lake one purple valley lay, 640
    Where tints of glowing light were seen;
The ganza waved his cuneal way,
    With yellow oar and quoif of green.

The dark cock bayed above the coomb,
    Throned mid the wavy fringe of gold, 645
Unwreathed from dawning's fairy loom,
    In many a soft vermilion fold.

The tiny skiffs of silver mist
    Lingered along the slumbering vale;
Belled the gray stag with fervid breast 650
    High on the moors of Meggat-dale.

There hid in clough and hollow den,
    Gazing around the still sublime,

There lay Lord Pringle and his men
   On beds of heath and moorland thyme.   655

That morning found rough Tushilaw
   In all the father's guise appear;
An end of all his hopes he saw
   Shrouded in Mary's gilded bier.

No eye could trace without concern   660
   The suffering warrior's troubled look;
The throbs that heaved his bosom stern,
   No ear could bear, no heart could brook.

"Woe be to thee, thou wicked dame!
   My Mary's prayers and accents mild   665
Might well have rendered vengeance lame—
   This hand could ne'er have slain my child!

"But thou, in frenzied fatal hour,
   Reft the sweet life thou gavest away,
And crushed to earth the fairest flower   670
   That ever breathed the breeze of day.

"My all is lost, my hope is fled,
   The sword shall ne'er be drawn for me;
Unblest, unhonoured my gray head—
   My child! would I had died for thee!"—   675

The bell tolls o'er a new-made grave;
   The lengthened funeral train is seen
Stemming the Yarrow's silver wave,
   And darkening Dryhope holms so green.

When nigh the virgin's fane they drew,   680
   Just by the verge of holy ground,
The Kers and Pringles left the clough,
   And hemmed the wondering Scotts around.

Vassal and peasant, seized with dread,
   Sped off, and looked not once behind;   685
And all who came for wine and bread,
   Fled like the chaff before the wind.

But all the Scotts together flew,—
   For every Scott of name was there,—
In sullen mood their weapons drew,   690
   And back to back for fight prepare.

Rough was the onset—boast, nor threat,
   Nor word, was heard from friend or foe;
At once began the work of fate,
   With perilous thrust and deadly blow.   695

O but the Harden lads were true,
   And bore them bravely in the broil!
The doughty laird of wild Buccleugh
   Raged like a lion in the toil.

His sword on bassenet was broke,   700
   The blood was streaming to his heel,
But soon to ward the fatal stroke
   Up rattled twenty blades of steel.

Young Raeburn tilted gallantly;
   But Ralph of Gilmanscleugh was slain,   705
Philip and Hugh of Baillilee,
   And William laird of Deloraine.

Red Will of Thirlestane came on,
   With his long sword and sullen eye;
Jealous of ancient honours won,   710
   Woe to the wight that came him nigh!

He was the last the ranks to break,
   And, flying, fought full desperately;
At length within his feudal lake
   He stood, and fought unto the knee.   715

Wild looked he round from side to side;
   No friendly skiff was there that day!
For why? the knight in bootless pride,
   Had driven them from the wave away.

Sore did he rue the stern decree!   720
   Red rolled the billow from the west;

And fishes swam indignantly
  Deep o'er the hero's boardly breast.

When loud has roared the wintry storm,
  Till winds have ceased, and rains are gone,   725
There oft the shepherd's trembling form
  Stands gazing o'er gigantic bone,

Pondering of Time's unstaying tide;
  Of ancient chiefs by kinsmen slain;
Of feudal rights, and feudal pride,   730
  And reckless Will of Thirlestane.

But long shall Ettrick rue the strife
  That reft her brave and generous son,
Who ne'er in all his restless life
  Did unbecoming thing—but one.   735

Old Tushilaw, with sword in hand,
  And heart to fiercest woes a prey,
Seemed courting every foeman's brand,
  And fought in hottest of the fray.

In vain the gallant kinsmen stood   740
  Wedged in a firm and bristled ring;
Their funeral weeds are bathed in blood,
  No corslets round their bosoms cling.

Against the lance and helmed file
  Their courage, might, and skill were vain;   745
Short was the conflict, short the while
  Ere all the Scotts were bound or slain.

When first the hostile band upsprung,
  The body in the church was laid,
Where vows were made, and requiems sung,   750
  By matron, monk, and weeping maid.

Lord Pringle came—before his eye
  The monks and maidens kneeled in fear;
But Lady Tushilaw stood bye,
  And pointed to her Mary's bier!   755

"Thou lord of guile and malice keen,
   What boots this doleful work to thee!
Could Scotland such a pair have seen
   As Mary Scott and Torwoodlee?"–

Lord Pringle came, no word he spake,   760
   Nor owned the pangs his bosom knew;
But his full heart was like to break
   In every throb his bosom drew.

"O I had weened with fondest heart–
   Woe to the guileful friend who lied!–   765
This day should join us ne'er to part,
   This day that I should win my bride!

"But I will see that face so meek,
   Cold, pale, and lifeless though it be;
And I will kiss that comely cheek,   770
   Once sweeter than the rose to me."–

With trembling hand he raised the lid,
   Sweet was the perfume round that flew;
For there were strewed the roses red,
   And every flower the Forest knew.   775

He drew the fair lawn from her face,
   'Twas decked with many a costly wreath;
And still it wore a soothing grace
   Even in the chill abodes of death.

And aye he prest the cheek so white,   780
   And aye he kissed the lips beloved,
Till pitying maidens wept outright,
   And even the frigid monks were moved.

Why starts Lord Pringle to his knee?
   Why bend his eyes with watchful strain?   785
The maidens shriek his mien to see;
   The startled priests inquire in vain!

Was that a sob, an earthly sigh,
   That heaved the flowers so lightly shed?

'Twas but the wind that wandered bye,   790
    And kissed the bosom of the dead!

Are these the glowing tints of life
    O'er Mary's cheek that come and fly?
Ah, no! the red flowers round are rife,
    The rosebud flings its softened dye.   795

Why grows the gazer's sight so dim;
    Stay, dear illusion, still beguile!
Thou art worth crowns and worlds to him—
    Last, dear illusion, last awhile!

Short was thy sway, frenzied and short,   800
    For ever fell the veil on thee;
Thy startling form of fears the sport,
    Vanished in sweet reality!

'Tis past! and darkly stand revealed
    A mother's cares and purpose deep: 805
That kiss, the last adieu that sealed,
    Waked Mary from her death-like sleep!

Slowly she raised her form of grace,
    Her eyes no ray conceptive flung;
And O, her mild, her languid face,   810
    Was like a flower too early sprung!

"O I lie sick and weary here,
    My heart is bound in moveless chain;
Another cup, my mother dear,
    I cannot sleep though I would fain!"—   815

She drank the wine with calm delay,
    She drank the wine with pause and sigh:
Slowly, as wakes the dawning day,
    Dawned long-lost thought in Mary's eye.

She looked at pall, she looked at bier,   820
    At altar, shrine, and rosary;
She saw her lady mother near,
    And at her side brave Torwoodlee!

'Twas all a dream, nor boded good,
    A phantom of the fevered brain!   825
She laid her down in moaning mood,
    To sooth her woes in sleep again.

Needs not to paint that joyful hour,
    The nuptial vow, the bridal glee,
How Mary Scott, the Forest flower,   830
    Was borne a bride to Torwoodlee.

Needs not to say, how warriors prayed
    When Mary glided from the dome;
They thought the Virgin's holy shade
    In likeness of the dead had come.   835

Diamond and ruby rayed her waist,
    And twinkled round her brow so fair;
She wore more gold upon her breast
    Than would have bought the hills of Yair.

A foot so light, a form so meet,   840
    Ne'er trode Saint Mary's lonely lea;
A bride so gay, a face so sweet,
    The Yarrow braes shall never see.

Old Tushilaw deigned not to smile,
    No grateful word his tongue could say,   845
He took one kiss, blest her the while,
    Wiped his dark eye, and turned away.

The Scotts were freed, and peace restored;
    Each Scott, each Ker, each Pringle swore,
Swore by his name, and by his sword,   850
    To be firm friends for evermore.

Lord Pringle's hills were stocked anew,
    Drove after drove came nightly free;
But many a Border Baron knew
    Whence came the dower to Torwoodlee.   855

Scarce had the closing measure rung,
When from the ring the minstrel sprung,
O'er foot of maid, and cane of man,
Three times he foundered as he ran,
And his gilt harp, of flowery frame,   860
Left ready for the next that came.
Loud were the plaudits,—all the fair
Their eyes turned to the royal chair:
They looked again,—no bard was there!
But whisper, smile, and question ran,   865
Around the ring anent the man;
While all the nobles of the south
Lauded the generous stranger youth.

The next was bred on southern shore,
Beneath the mists of Lammermore;   870
And long, by Nith and crystal Tweed,
Had taught the Border youth to read.
The strains of Greece, the bard of Troy,
Were all his theme, and all his joy.

Well toned his voice of wars to sing;   875
His hair was dark as raven's wing;
His eye an intellectual lance;
No heart could bear its searching glance:
But every bard to him was dear;
His heart was kind, his soul sincere.   880

When first of Royal Wake he heard,
Forthwith it chained his sole regard:
It was his thought, his hourly theme,
His morning prayer, his midnight dream.
Knights, dames, and squires of each degree,   885
He deemed as fond of songs as he,
And talked of them continually.
But when he heard the Highland strain,
Scarce could his breast his soul contain;
'Twas all unequalled, and would make   890
Immortal Bards! immortal Wake!
About Dunedin streets he ran,
Each knight he met, each maid, each man,

In field, in alley, tower, or hall,
The Wake was first, the Wake was all.   895

   Alike to him the south or north,
So high he held the minstrel worth,
So high his ardent mind was wrought,
Once of himself he scarcely thought.
Dear to his heart the strain sublime,   900
The strain admired in ancient time;
And of his minstrel honours proud,
He strung his harp too high, too loud.

King Edward's Dream

THE FIFTEENTH BARD'S SONG

The heath-cock had whirred at the break of the morn,
The moon of her tassels of silver was shorn,   905
When hoary King Edward lay tossing in ire,
His blood in a ferment, his bosom on fire;
His battle-files, stretched o'er the valley, were still
As Eden's pine forests that darkened the hill.

   He slept—but his visions were loathly and grim: 910
How quivered his lip! and how quaked every limb!
His dull moving eye showed how troubled his rest,
And deep were the throbs of his labouring breast.

   He saw the Scot's banner red streaming on high;
The fierce Scottish warriors determined and nigh;   915
Their columns of steel, and, bright gleaming before,
The lance, the broad target, and Highland claymore.
And, lo! at their head, in stern glory appeared
That hero of heroes so hated and feared;
'Twas the exile of Rachrin that led the array,   920
And Wallace's spirit was pointing the way:
His eye was a torch, beaming ruin and wrath,
And graved on his helmet was—*Vengeance or Death!*

   In far Ethiopia's desert domain,
Where whirlwinds new mountains up-pile on the plain,   925

Their crested brown billows, fierce curling on high,
O'ershadow the sun, and are tossed to the sky;
But, meeting each other, they burst and recoil,
Mix, thunder, and sink, with a reeling turmoil:
As dreadful the onset that Edward beheld,   930
As fast his brave legions were heaped on the field.

    The plaided blue Highlander, swift as the wind,
Spread terror before him, and ruin behind.
Thick clouds of blood-vapour brood over the slain,
And Pembroke and Howard are stretched on the plain.   935

    The chieftain he hated, all covered with blood,
Still nearer and nearer approached where he stood;
He could not retreat, and no succour was near—
"Die, scorpion!" he cried, and pursued his career.
The king felt the iron retreat from the wound,   940
No hand to uphold him, he sunk on the ground:
His spirit escaped on the wings of the wind,
Left terror, confusion, and carnage behind,
Till on the green Pentland he thought he sat lone,
And pondered on troubles and times that were gone.   945

    He looked over meadow, broad river, and downe,
From Ochel's fair mountains to Lammermore brown;
He still found his heart and desires were the same;
He wished to leave Scotland nor sceptre nor name.

    He thought, as he lay on the green mountain thyme,   950
A spirit approached him in manner sublime.
At first she appeared like a streamer of light,
But still as she neared she was formed to his sight.
Her robe was the blue silken veil of the sky,
The drop of the amethyst deepened its dye;   955
Her crown was a helmet, emblazoned with pearl;
Her mantle the sunbeam, her bracelets the beryl;
Her hands and her feet like the bright burning levin;
Her face was the face of an angel from heaven:
Around her the winds and the echoes grew still,   960
And rainbows were formed in the cloud of the hill.

Like music that floats o'er the soft heaving deep,
When twilight has lulled all the breezes asleep,
The wild fairy airs in our forests that rung,
Or hymn of the sky by a seraph when sung;   965
So sweet were the tones on the fancy that broke,
When the Guardian of Scotland's proud mountains thus
    spoke:–

"What boots, mighty Edward, thy victories won?
'Tis over; thy sand of existence is run;
Thy laurels are faded, dispersed in the blast;   970
Thy soul from the bar of Omnipotence cast,
To wander bewildered o'er mountain and plain,
O'er lands thou hast steeped with the blood of the slain.

"I heard of thy guerdon, I heard it on high:
Thou'rt doomed on these mountains to linger and lie,   975
The mark of the tempest, the sport of the wind,
The tempest of conscience, the storm of the mind,
Till people thou'st hated, and sworn to subdue,
Triumphant from bondage shall burst in thy view,
Their sceptre and liberty bravely regain,   980
And climb to renown over mountains of slain.

"I thought (and I joined my endeavours to thine,)
The time was arrived when the two should combine;
For 'tis known that they will 'mong the hosts of the sky,
And we thought that blest æra of concord was nigh.   985
But ages unborn yet shall flit on the wing,
And Scotland to England ere then give a king;
A father to monarchs, whose flourishing sway
The ocean and ends of the earth shall obey.

"See yon little hamlet o'ershadowed with smoke,   990
See yon hoary battlement throned on the rock,
Even there shall a city in splendour break forth,
The haughty Dunedin, the Queen of the North;
There learning shall flourish, and liberty smile,
The awe of the world, and the pride of the isle.   995

"But thy lonely spirit shall roam in dismay;
And weep o'er thy labours so soon to decay.

In yon western plain, where thy power overthrew
The bulwarks of Caledon, valiant and few;
Where beamed the red faulchion of ravage and wrath;   1000
Where tyranny, horsed on the dragons of death,
Rode ruthless through blood of the honoured and just.
When Græme and brave Stuart lay bleeding in dust,
The wailings of liberty pierced the sky;
Th' Eternal, in pity, averted his eye!   1005

"Even there shall the power of thy nations combined,
Proud England, green Erin, and Normandy joined,
Exulting in numbers, and dreadful array,
Led on by Carnarvon, to Scotland away,
As thick as the snow-flakes that pour from the pole,   1010
Or silver-maned waves on the ocean that roll.
A handful of heroes, all desperate driven,
Impelled by the might and the vengeance of Heaven;
By them shall his legions be all overborne,
And melt from the field like the mist of the morn.   1015
The Thistle shall rear her rough front to the sky,
And the Rose and the Shamrock at Carron shall die.

"How couldst thou imagine those spirits of flame
Would stoop to oppression, to slavery, and shame!
Ah! never; the lion may couch to thy sway,   1020
The mighty leviathan bend and obey;
But the Scots, round their king and broad banner unfurled,
Their mountains will keep against thee and the world."

King Edward awoke with a groan and a start,
The vision was vanished, but not from his heart!   1025
His courage was high, but his vigour was gone;
He cursed the Scotch nation, and bade them lead on.
His legions moved on like a cloud of the west;
But fierce was the fever that boiled in his breast.
On sand of the Solway they rested his bed,   1030
Where the soul of the king and the warrior fled;
He heard not the sound of the evening curfew;
But the whisper that died on his tongue was—"Subdue!"

The bard had sung so bold and high,
While patriot fire flashed from his eye,   1035
That ere King Edward won to rest,
Or sheet was spread above his breast,
The harp-strings jarred in wild mistone;
The minstrel throbbed, his voice was gone.
Upon his harp he leaned his head,   1040
And softly from the ring was led.

The next was from a western vale,
Where Nith winds slowly down the dale;
Where play the waves o'er golden grain,
Like mimic billows of the main.   1045
Of the old elm his harp was made,
That bent o'er Cluden's loneliest shade:
No gilded sculpture round her flamed,
For his own hand that harp had framed,
In stolen hours, when, labour done,   1050
He strayed to view the parting sun.
O when the toy to him so fair,
Began to form beneath his care,
How danced his youthful heart with joy!
How constant grew the dear employ!   1055
The sun would chamber in the Ken;
The red star rise o'er Locherben;
The solemn moon, in sickly hue,
Waked from her eastern couch of dew,
Would half way gain the vault on high,   1060
Bathe in the Nith, slow stealing by,
And still the bard his task would ply.

When his first notes, from covert gray,
Arrested maiden on her way;
When ceased the reaper's evening tale,   1065
And paused the shepherd of the dale,—
Bootless all higher worldly bliss,
To crown our minstrel's happiness!
What all the joys by fortune given,
To cloyless song, the gift of Heaven?   1070

That harp could make the matron stare,
Bristle the peasant's hoary hair,

Make patriot-breasts with ardour glow,
And warrior pant to meet the foe;
And long by Nith the maidens young   1075
Shall chant the strains their minstrel sung;
At ewe-bught, or at evening fold,
When resting on the daisied wold,
Combing their locks of waving gold,
Oft the fair group enrapt, shall name   1080
Their lost, their darling Cunninghame;
His was a song beloved in youth,—
A tale of weir—a tale of truth.

Dumlanrig

THE SIXTEENTH BARD'S SONG

Who's he that at Dumlanrig's gate
Hollas so loud, and raps so late?   1085
Nor warder's threat, nor porter's growl,
Question, nor watch-dog's angry howl,
He once regards, but rap and call,
Thundering alternate shake the wall.
The captive, stretched in dungeon deep,   1090
Waked from his painful visioned sleep;
His meagre form from pavement raised,
And listened to the sounds amazed:
Both bayle and keep rang with the din,
And Douglas heard the noise within.   1095

    "Ho! rise, Dumlanrig! all's at stake!
Ho! rise, Dumlanrig! Douglas, wake!—
Blow, warder—blow thy warning shrill,
Light up the beacon on the hill,
For round thee reaves thy ruthless foe.—   1100
Arise, Dumlanrig! Douglas, ho!"—

    His fur-cloak round him Douglas threw,
And to the crennel eager flew.
"What news? what news? thou stalwart groom,
Who thus, in midnight's deepest gloom,   1105
Bring'st to my gate the loud alarm
Of foray wide and country harm?

What are thy dangers? what thy fears?
Say out thy message, Douglas hears."

"Haste, Douglas! Douglas, arm with speed,　1110
And mount thy fleetest battle steed;
For Lennox, with the southern host,
Whom thou hast baulked and curbed the most,
Like locusts from the Solway blown,
Are spread upon thy mountains brown;　1115
Broke from their camp in search of prey,
They drive thy flocks and herds away;
Roused by revenge, and hunger keen,
They've swept the hills of fair Dalveen;
Nor left thee bullock, goat, or steer,　1120
On all the holms of Durisdeer.

"One troop came to my father's hall;
They burnt our tower,—they took our all.
My dear, my only sister May,
By force the ruffians bore away;　1125
Nor kid, nor lamb, bleats in the glen,
Around all lonely Locherben!

"My twenty men, I have no moe,
Eager to cross the roaming foe,
Well armed with hauberk and broad sword,　1130
Keep ward at Cample's rugged ford.
Before they bear their prey across,
Some Southrons shall their helmets lose,
If not the heads those helmets shield,—
O, haste thee, Douglas, to the field!"—　1135
With that his horse around he drew,
And down the path like lightning flew.

"Arm," cried the Douglas, "one and all!"
And vanished from the echoing wall.
"Arm!" was the word; along it ran　1140
Through manor, bayle, and barbican;
And clank and clatter burst at once
From every loop of hall and sconce.
With whoop of groom, and warder's call,
And prancing steeds, 'twas hurry all.　1145

At first, like thunder's distant tone,
The rattling din came rolling on,
Echoed Dumlanrig woods around;
Louder and louder swelled the sound,
Till like the sheeted flame of wonder,   1150
That rends the shoals of heaven asunder.

When first the word, "To arms!" was given,
Glowed all the eastern porch of heaven;
A wreathy cloud of orient brown,
Had heralded the rising moon,   1155
Whose verge was like a silver bow,
Bending o'er Ganna's lofty brow;
And ere above the mountain blue
Her wasted orb was rolled in view,
A thousand men, in armour sheen,   1160
Stood ranked upon Dumlanrig green.

The Nith they stemmed in firm array;
For Cample-ford they bent their way.
Than Douglas and his men that night,
Never saw yeomen nobler sight;   1165
Mounted on tall curvetting steed,
He rode undaunted at their head;
His shadow on the water still,
Like giant on a moving hill.
The ghastly bull's-head scowled on high,   1170
Emblem of death to foemen's eye;
And bloody hearts on streamers pale,
Waved wildly in the midnight gale.

O, haste thee, Douglas! haste and ride!
Thy kinsmen's corpses stem the tide!   1175
What red, what dauntless youth is he,
Who stands in Cample to the knee;
Whose arm of steel, and weapon good,
Still dyes the stream with Southern blood,
While round him fall his faithful men?   1180
'Tis Morison of Locherben.

O, haste thee, Douglas, to the fray,
Ere won be that important way!

The Southron's countless prey, within
The dreadful coils of Crighup linn,   1185
No passage from the moor can find,–
The wood below, the gulf behind:
One pass there is, and one alone,
And in that pass stands Morison.
Who crosses there, or man or beast,   1190
Must make their passage o'er his breast,
And over heaps of mangled dead,
That dam red Cample from its bed.
His sister's cries his soul alarm,
And add new vigour to his arm.   1195
His twenty men are waned to ten.
O, haste to dauntless Locherben!

The Southrons, baulked, impatient turn,
And crowd once more the fatal bourn.
All desperate grew the work of death,   1200
No yielding but with yielding breath;
Even still lay every death-struck man,
For footing to the furious van.
The little band was seized with dread,
Behind their rampart of the dead: 1205
Power from their arms began to fly,
And hope within their breasts to die,
When loud they heard the cheering word
Of–"Douglas! Douglas!" cross the ford;
Then turned the Southron swift as wind,   1210
For fierce the battle raged behind.

O, stay, brave Morison! O, stay!
Guard but that pass till break of day;
Thy flocks, thy sister to retrieve,
That task to doughty Douglas leave: 1215
Let not thine ardour all betray,–
Thy might is spent–brave warrior, stay.

O, for the lyre of heaven, that rung
When Linden's lofty hymn was sung;
Or his, who from the height beheld   1220
The reeling strife of Flodden field!
Then far on wing of genius borne
Should ring the wonders of that morn:

Morn!–ah! how many a warrior bold
That morn was never to behold!   1225
When rival rank to rank drew nigh,
When eye was fixed on foeman's eye,
When lowered was lance, and bent was bow,
And faulchion clenched to strike the blow,
No breath was heard, nor clank of mail,   1230
Each face with rage grew deadly pale.
Trembled the moon's reluctant ray;
The breeze of heaven sunk soft away.

So furious was that onset's shock,
Destruction's gates at once unlock: 1235
'Twas like the earthquake's hollow groan,
When towers and towns are overthrown:
'Twas like the river's midnight crush,
When snows dissolve, and torrents rush;
When fields of ice, in rude array,   1240
Obstruct its own resistless way:
'Twas like the whirlwind's rending sweep:
'Twas like the tempest of the deep,
Where Corrybraken's surges driven,
Meet, mount, and lash the breast of heaven.   1245

'Twas foot to foot, and brand to brand;
Oft hilt to hilt, and hand to hand;
Oft gallant foemen, woe to tell,
Dead in each other's bosoms fell!
The horsemen met with might and main,   1250
Then reeled, and wheeled, and met again.
A thousand spears on hawberks bang;
A thousand swords on helmets clang.
Where might was with the feebler blent,
Still there the line of battle bent;   1255
As oft recoiled from flank assail,
While blows fell thick as rattling hail.
Nature stood mute that fateful hour,
All save the ranks on Cample-moor,
And mountain goats that left their den,   1260
And bleating fled to Garroch glen.

Dumlanrig, aye in battle keen,
The foremost in the broil was seen:

Woe to the warrior dared withstand
The progress of his deadly brand!   1265
He sat so firm, he reined so well,
Whole ranks before his charger fell.
A valiant youth kept by his side,
With crest and armour crimson-dyed;
Charged still with him the yielding foe,   1270
And seconded his every blow.
The Douglas wondered whence he came,
And asked his lineage and his name.
'Twas he who kept the narrow way,
Who raised at first the battle-fray,   1275
And roused Dumlanrig and his men,—
Brave Morison of Locherben.

   "My chief," he said, "forgive my fear
For one than life to me more dear;
But late I heard my sister cry,   1280
'Dumlanrig, now thy weapon ply.'—
Her guard waits in yon hollow lea,
Beneath the shade of spreading tree."—

   Dumlanrig's eye with ardour shone;
"Follow!" he cried, and spurred him on.   1285
A close gazoon the horsemen made,
Douglas and Morison the head,
And through the ranks impetuous bore,
By dint of lance and broad claymore,
Mid shouts, and groans of parting life,   1290
For hard and doubtful was the strife.
Behind a knight, firm belted on,
They found the fair May Morison.
But why, through all Dumlanrig's train,
Search her bright eyes, and search in vain?   1295
A stranger mounts her on his steed;
Brave Morison, where art thou fled?
The drivers for their booty feared,
And, soon as Cample-ford was cleared,
To work they fell, and forced away   1300
Across the stream their mighty prey.
The bleating flocks in terror ran
Across the bloody breast of man;

Even the dull cattle gazed with dread,
And, lowing, foundered o'er the dead.   1305

   The Southrons still the fight maintain;
Though broke, they closed and fought again,
Till shouting drivers gave the word,
That all the flocks had cleared the ford;
Then to that pass the bands retire,   1310
And safely braved Dumlanrig's ire.
Rashly he tried, and tried in vain,
That steep, that fatal path to gain;
Madly prolonged th' unequal fray,
And lost his men, and lost the day.   1315
Amid the battle's fiercest shock,
Three spears were on his bosom broke,
Then forced in flight to seek remede.
Had it not been his noble steed,
That swift away his master bore,   1320
He ne'er had seen Dumlanrig more.

   The day-beam, from his moonlight sleep,
O'er Queensberry began to peep,
Kneeled drowsy on the mountain fern,
At length rose tiptoe on the cairn,   1325
Embracing, in his bosom pale,
The stars, the moon, and shadowy dale.
Then what a scene appalled the view,
On Cample-moor, as dawning grew!
Along the purple heather spread,   1330
Lay mixed the dying and the dead;
Stern foemen there from quarrel cease,
Who ne'er before had met in peace.
Two kinsmen good the Douglas lost,
And full three hundred of his host;   1335
With one by him lamented most,
The flower of all the Nithsdale men,
Young Morison of Locherben.

   The Southrons did no foot pursue,
Nor seek the conflict to renew.   1340
They knew not at the rising sun
What mischief they'd to Douglas done,

But to the south pursued their way,
Glad to escape with such a prey.

   Brave Douglas, where thy pride of weir? 1345
How stinted in thy bold career!
Woe, that the Lowther eagle's look
Should shrink before the Lowland rook!
Woe, that the lordly lion's paw
Of ravening wolves should sink in awe! 1350
But doubly woe, the purple heart
Should tarnished from the field depart!

   Was it the loss of kinsmen dear,
Or crusted scratch of Southron spear?
Was it thy dumb thy sullen host, 1355
Thy glory by misconduct lost?
Or thy proud bosom, swelling high,
Made the round tear roll in thine eye?
Ah! no; thy heart was doomed to prove
The sharper pang of slighted love. 1360

   What vision lingers on the heath,
Flitting across the field of death;
Its gliding motion, smooth and still
As vapour on the twilight hill,
Or the last ray of falling even 1365
Shed through the parting clouds of heaven?

   Is it a sprite that roams forlorn?
Or angel from the bowers of morn,
Come down a tear of heaven to shed,
In pity o'er the valiant dead? 1370
No vain, no fleeting phantom this!
No vision from the bowers of bliss!
Its radiant eye, and stately tread,
Bespeak some beauteous mountain maid;
No rose of Eden's bosom meek, 1375
Could match that maiden's moistened cheek;
No drifted wreath of morning snow,
The whiteness of her lofty brow;
Nor gem of India's purest dye,
The lustre of her eagle eye. 1380

When beauty, Eden's bowers within,
First stretched the arm to deeds of sin;
When passion burned, and prudence slept,
The pitying angels bent and wept.
But tears more soft were never shed,   1385
No, not when angels bowed the head,
A sigh more mild did never breathe
O'er human nature whelmed in death,
Nor woe and dignity combine
In face so lovely, so benign,   1390
As Douglas saw that dismal hour,
Bent o'er a corse on Cample-moor;
A lady o'er her shield, her trust,
A brave, an only brother's dust.

What heart of man unmoved can lie,   1395
When plays the smile in beauty's eye?
Or when a form of grace and love
To music's notes can lightly move?
Yes: there are hearts unmoved can see
The smile, the ring, the revelry;   1400
But heart of warrior ne'er could bear
The beam of beauty's crystal tear.
Well was that morn the maxim proved—
The Douglas saw, the Douglas loved.

"O, cease thy tears, my lovely May,   1405
Sweet floweret of the banks of Ae,
His soul thou never canst recall;
He fell as warrior wont to fall.
Deep, deep the loss we both bewail:
But that deep loss to countervail,   1410
Far as the day-flight of the hern,
From Locherben to green Glencairn,
From where the Shinnel torrents pour
To the lone vales of Crawford-moor,
The fairy links of Tweed and Lyne,   1415
All, all the Douglas has, is thine,
And Douglas too; whate'er betide,
Straight thou shalt be Dumlanrig's bride."—

"What! mighty chief, a bride to thee!
No, by yon heaven's High Majesty,   1420

Sooner I'll beg, forlorn and poor,
Bent at thy meanest vassal's door,
Than look thy splendid halls within,
Thou deer, wrapt in a lion's skin!

"Here lies thy bravest knight in death; 1425
Thy kinsmen strew the purple heath;
What boots thy boasted mountains green?
Nor flock, nor herd, can there be seen;
All driven before thy vaunting foe
To ruthless slaughter, bleat and low, 1430
Whilst thou—shame on thy dastard head!–
A wooing com'st amid the dead.

"O, that this feeble maiden hand
Could bend the bow, or wield the brand!
If yeomen mustered in my hall, 1435
Or trooped obsequious at my call,
My country's honour I'd restore,
And shame thy face for evermore.
Go, first thy flocks and herds regain;
Revenge thy friends in battle slain; 1440
Thy wounded honour heal; that done,
Douglas may ask May Morison."

Dumlanrig's blood to's bosom rushed,
His manly cheek like crimson blushed.
He called three yeomen to his side: 1445
"Haste, gallant warriors, haste and ride!
Warn Lindsay on the banks of Daur,
The fierce M'Turk and Lochinvaur;
Tell them that Lennox flies amain;
That Maxwell and Glencairn are ta'en; 1450
Kilpatrick with the spoiler rides;
The Johnston flies, and Jardine hides:
That I alone am left to fight,
For country's cause and sovereign's right.
My friends are fallen—my warriors toiled— 1455
My towns are burnt—my vassals spoiled:
Yet say—before to-morrow's sun
With amber tips the mountain dun,
Either that host of ruthless thieves

I'll scatter like the forest leaves,   1460
Or my wrung heart shall cease to play,
And my right hand the sword to sway.
At Blackwood I'll their coming bide:
Haste, gallant warriors, haste and ride!"—

He spoke:—each yeoman bent his eye,   1465
And forward stooped in act to fly;
No plea was urged, no short demur;
Each heel was turned to strike the spur.

As ever ye saw the red deer's brood,
From covert sprung, traverse the wood;   1470
Or heath-fowl beat the mountain wind,
And leave the fowler fixt behind;
As ever ye saw three arrows spring
At once from yew-bow's twanging string—
So flew the messengers of death,   1475
And, lessening, vanished on the heath.

The Douglas bade his troops with speed
Prepare due honours for the dead,
And meet well armed at evening still
On the green cone of Blackford-hill.   1480
There came M'Turk to aid the war,
With troops from Shinnel glens and Scaur;
Fierce Gordon with the clans of Ken,
And Lindsay with his Crawford men;
Old Morton, too, forlorn and gray,   1485
Whose son had fallen at break of day.

If troops on earth may e'er withstand
An onset made by Scottish brand,
Then lawless rapine sways the throng,
And conscience whispers—"This is wrong:"   1490
But should a foe, whate'er his might,
To Scotia's soil dispute her right,
Or dare on native mountain claim
The poorest atom boasts her name,
Though high that warrior's banners soar,   1495
Let him beware the broad claymore.

Scotland! thy honours long have stood,
Though rudely cropt, though rolled in blood,
Yet, bathed in warm and purple dew,
More glorious o'er the ruin grew.   1500
Long flourished thy paternal line;
Arabia's lineage stoops to thine.

Dumlanrig found his foes secure,
Stretched on the ridge of Locher-moor.
The hum that wandered from their host,   1505
Far on the midnight breeze was lost.
No deafening drum, no bugle's swell,
No watch-word past from centinel,
No slight vibration stirred the air
To warn the Scot a foe was there,   1510
Save bleat of flocks that wandered slow,
And oxen's deep and sullen low.

What horrors o'er the warrior hang!
What vultures watch his soul to fang!
What toils! what snares!—he hies him on   1515
Where lightnings flash, and thunders groan;
Where havock strikes whole legions low,
And death's red billows murmuring flow;
Yet still he fumes and flounders on,
Till crushed the moth—its mem'ry gone!   1520

Why should the bard, who loves to mourn
His maiden's scorn by mountain bourn,
Or pour his wild harp's fairy tone
From sounding cliff or green-wood lone,
Of slaughtered foemen proudly tell,   1525
On deeds of death and horror dwell?

Dread was Dumlanrig's martial ire,
Fierce on the foe he rushed like fire.
Lindsay of Crawford, known to fame,
That night first gained a hero's name.   1530
The brave M'Turk of Stenhouse stood
Bathed to the knees in Southron blood;
A bold and generous chief was he,
And come of ancient pedigree;

And Gordon with his Galloway crew,   1535
O'er floundering ranks resistless flew.
Short was the strife!—they fled as fast
As chaff before the northern blast.

Dumlanrig's flocks were not a few,
And well their worth Dumlanrig knew;   1540
But ne'er so proud was he before
Of his broad bounds and countless store,
As when they strung up Nithsdale plain,
Well guarded to their hills again.
With Douglas' name the green-woods rung,   1545
As battle-songs his warriors sung.
The banners streamed in double row,
The heart above, the rose below.
His visage glowed, his pulse beat high,
And gladness sparkled in his eye: 1550
For why, he knew the lovely May,
Who in Kilpatrick's castle lay,
With joy his proud return would view,
And her impetuous censure rue.

Well judged he:—Why should haughty chief   1555
Intrude himself on lady's grief,
As if his right, as nought but he
Were worthy her anxiety.
No, warrior: keep thy distance due;
Beauty is proud and jealous too.   1560
If fair and young thy maiden be,
Know she knew that ere told by thee.
Be kind, be gentle, heave the sigh,
And blush before her piercing eye;
For though thou'rt noble, brave, and young,   1565
If rough thy mien and rude thy tongue,
Though proudly towers thy trophied pile,
Hope not for beauty's yielding smile.
Oh! well it suits the brave and high,
Gentle to prove in lady's eye.   1570

Dumlanrig found his lovely flower
Fair as the sun-beam o'er the shower,
Gentle as zephyr of the plain,

Sweet as the rose-bud after rain:
Gone all her scorn and maiden pride,   1575
She blushed Dumlanrig's lovely bride.

   James of Dumlanrig, though thy name
Scarce vibrates in the ear of fame,
But for thy might and valour keen,
That gallant house had never been.   1580

   Blest be thy mem'ry, gallant man!
Oft flashed thy broad sword in the van
When stern rebellion reared the brand,
And stained the laurels of our land,
No knight unshaken stood like thee   1585
In right of injured majesty:
Ev'n yet, o'er thy forgotten bier,
A minstrel drops the burning tear,
And strikes his wild harp's boldest string,
Thy honours on the breeze to fling,   1590
That mountains once thine own may know
From whom the Queensberry honours flow.

   Fair be thy mem'ry, gallant knight!
So true in love, so brave in fight!
Though o'er thy children's princely urn   1595
The sculpture towers, and seraphs mourn,
O'er thy green grave shall wave the yew,
And heaven distil its earliest dew.

When ceased the bard's protracted song,
Circled a smile the fair among;   1600
The song was free, and soft its fall,
So soothing, yet so bold withal,
They loved it well, yet, sooth to say,
Too long, too varied was the lay.

   'Twas now the witching time of night,   1605
When reason strays, and forms that fright
Are shadowed on the palsied sight;

When fancy moulds upon the mind
Light visions on the passing wind,
And woos, with faultering tongue and sigh,   1610
The shades o'er memory's wilds that fly;
And much the circle longed to hear
Of gliding ghost, or gifted seer,
That in that still and solemn hour
Might stretch imagination's power,   1615
And restless fancy revel free
In painful, pleasing luxury.
Just as the battle-tale was done,
The watchman called the hour of one.

    Lucky the hour for him who came,   1620
Lucky the wish of every dame,
The bard who rose at herald's call
Was wont to sing in Highland hall,
Where the wild chieftain of M'Lean
Upheld his dark Hebridian reign;   1625
Where floated crane and clamorous gull
Above the misty shores of Mull;
And evermore the billows rave
Round many a saint and sovereign's grave.
There round Columba's ruins gray   1630
The shades of monks are wont to stray,
And slender forms of nuns, that weep
In moonlight by the murmuring deep,
O'er early loves and passions crost,
And being's end for ever lost.   1635
No earthly form their names to save,
No stem to flourish o'er their grave,
No blood of theirs beyond the shrine
To nurse the human soul divine,
Still cherish youth by time unworn,   1640
And flow in ages yet unborn.
While mind, surviving evermore,
Unbodied seeks that lonely shore.

    In that wild land our minstrel bred,
From youth a life of song had led,   1645
Wandering each shore and upland dull
With Allan Bawn, the bard of Mull,

To sing the deeds of old Fingal,
In every cot and Highland hall.

  Well knew he every ghost that came   1650
To visit fair Hebridian dame,
Was that of monk or abbot gone,
Who once, in cell of pictured stone,
Of woman thought, and her alone.

  Well knew he every female shade   1655
To westland chief that visit paid
In morning pale, or evening dun,
Was that of fair lamenting nun,
Who once, in cloistered home forlorn,
Languished for joys in youth forsworn;   1660
And oft himself had seen them glide
At dawning from his own bed-side.

  Forth stepped he with uncourtly bow,
The heron plume waved o'er his brow,
His garb was blent with varied shade,   1665
And round him flowed his Highland plaid.
But woe to Southland dame and knight
In minstrel's tale who took delight.
Though known the air, the song he sung
Was in the barbarous Highland tongue: 1670
But tartaned chiefs in raptures hear
The strains, the words, to them so dear.

  Thus run the bold portentous lay,
As near as Southern tongue can say.

The Abbot M'Kinnon

THE SEVENTEENTH BARD'S SONG

  M'Kinnon's tall mast salutes the day,   1675
And beckons the breeze in Iona bay;
Plays lightly up in the morning sky,
And nods to the green wave rolling bye;

The anchor upheaves, the sails unfurl,
The pennons of silk in the breezes curl;   1680
But not one monk on holy ground
Knows whither the Abbot M'Kinnon is bound.

Well could that bark o'er the ocean glide,
Though monks and friars alone must guide;
For never man of other degree   1685
On board that sacred ship might be.
On deck M'Kinnon walked soft and slow;
The haulers sung from the gilded prow;
The helmsman turned his brow to the sky,
Upraised his cowl, and upraised his eye,   1690
And away shot the bark on the wing of the wind,
Over billow and bay like an image of mind.

Aloft on the turret the monks appear,
To see where the bark of their abbot would bear;
They saw her sweep from Iona bay,   1695
And turn her prow to the north away,
Still lessen to view in the hazy screen,
And vanish amid the islands green.
Then they turned their eyes to the female dome,
And thought of the nuns till the abbot came home.   1700

Three times the night with aspect dull
Came stealing o'er the moors of Mull;
Three times the sea-gull left the deep,
To doze on the knob of the dizzy steep,
By the sound of the ocean lull'd to sleep;   1705
And still the watch-lights sailors see
On the top of the spire, and the top of Dun-ye;
And the laugh rings through the sacred dome,
For still the abbot is not come home.

But the wolf that nightly swam the sound,   1710
From Ross's rude impervious bound,
On the ravenous burrowing race to feed,
That loved to haunt the home of the dead,
To him Saint Columb had left in trust,
To guard the bones of the royal and just,   1715
Of saints and of kings the sacred dust;

The savage was scared from his charnel of death,
And swam to his home in hunger and wrath,
For he momently saw, through the night so dun,
The cowering monk, and the veiled nun,   1720
Whispering, sighing, and stealing away
By cross dark alley, and portal gray.
O, wise was the founder, and well said he,
"Where there are women mischief must be."

No more the watch-fires gleam to the blast,   1725
M'Kinnon and friends arrive at last.
A stranger youth to the isle they brought,
Modest of mien and deep of thought,
In costly sacred robes bedight,
And he lodged with the abbot by day and by night.   1730

His breast was graceful, and round withal,
His leg was taper, his foot was small,
And his tread so light that it flung no sound
On listening ear or vault around.
His eye was the morning's brightest ray,   1735
And his neck like the swan's in Iona bay;
His teeth the ivory polished new,
And his lip like the morel when glossed with dew,
While under his cowl's embroidered fold
Were seen the curls of waving gold.   1740
This comely youth, of beauty so bright,
Abode with the abbot by day and by night.

When arm in arm they walked the isle,
Young friars would beckon, and monks would smile;
But sires, in dread of sins unshriven,   1745
Would shake their heads and look up to heaven,
Afraid the frown of the saint to see,
Who reared their temple amid the sea,
And pledged his soul to guard the dome,
Till virtue should fly her western home.   1750
But now a stranger of hidden degree,
Too fair, too gentle, a man to be,
This stranger of beauty and step so light
Abode with the abbot by day and by night.

The months and the days flew lightly bye,   1755
The monks were kind and the nuns were shy;
But the gray-haired sires, in trembling mood,
Kneel'd at the altar and kissed the rood.

M'Kinnon he dreamed that the saint of the isle
Stood by his side, and with courteous smile   1760
Bade him arise from his guilty sleep,
And pay his respects to the God of the deep,
In temple that north in the main appeared,
Which fire from bowels of ocean had seared,
Which the giant builders of heaven had reared,   1765
To rival in grandeur the stately pile
Himself had upreared in Iona's isle;
For round them rose the mountains of sand,
The fishes had left the coasts of the land,
And so high ran the waves of the angry sea,   1770
They had drizzled the cross on the top of Dun-ye.
The cycle was closed, and the period run,
He had vowed to the sea, he had vowed to the sun,
If in that time rose trouble or pain,
Their homage to pay to the God of the main.   1775
Then he bade him haste and the rites prepare,
Named all the monks should with him fare,
And promised again to see him there.

M'Kinnon awoke from his visioned sleep,
He opened his casement and looked on the deep;   1780
He looked to the mountains, he looked to the shore,
The vision amazed him and troubled him sore,
He never had heard of the rite before;
But all was so plain, he thought meet to obey,
He durst not decline, and he would not delay.   1785

Uprose the abbot, uprose the morn,
Uprose the sun from the Bens of Lorn;
And the bark her course to the northward framed,
With all on board whom the saint had named.

The clouds were journeying east the sky,   1790
The wind was low and the swell was high,
And the glossy sea was heaving bright

Like ridges and hills of liquid light;
While far on her lubric bosom were seen
The magic dyes of purple and green.   1795

How joyed the bark her sides to lave!
She leaned to the lee, and she girdled the wave;
Aloft on the stayless verge she hung,
Light on the steep wave veered and swung,
And the crests of the billows before her flung.   1800
Loud murmured the ocean with downward growl,
The seal swam aloof and the dark sea fowl;
The pye-duck sought the depth of the main,
And rose in the wheel of her wake again;
And behind her, far to the southward, shone   1805
A pathway of snow on the waste alone.

But now the dreadful strand they gain,
Where rose the sacred dome of the main;
Oft had they seen the place before,
And kept aloof from the dismal shore,   1810
But now it rose before their prow,
And what they beheld they did not know.
The tall gray forms, in close-set file,
Upholding the roof of that holy pile;
The sheets of foam and the clouds of spray,   1815
And the groans that rushed from the portals gray,
Appalled their hearts, and drove them away.

They wheeled their bark to the east around,
And moored in basin, by rocks imbound;
Then, awed to silence, they trode the strand   1820
Where furnaced pillars in order stand,
All framed of the liquid burning levin,
And bent like the bow that spans the heaven,
Or upright ranged in horrid array,
With purfle of green o'er the darksome gray.   1825

Their path was on wonderous pavement of old,
Its blocks all cast in some giant mould,
Fair hewn and grooved by no mortal hand,
With countermure guarded by sea and by land.
The watcher Bushella frowned over their way,   1830

Enrobed in the sea-baize, and hooded with gray;
The warder that stands by that dome of the deep,
With spray-shower and rainbow, the entrance to keep.
But when they drew nigh to the chancel of Ocean,
And saw her waves rush to their raving devotion,   1835
Astounded and awed to the antes they clung,
And listened the hymns in her temple she sung.
The song of the cliff, when the winter winds blow,
The thunder of heaven, the earthquake below,
Conjoined, like the voice of a maiden would be,   1840
Compared with the anthem there sung by the sea.

The solemn rows in that darksome den,
Were dimly seen like the forms of men,
Like giant monks in ages agone,
Whom the God of the ocean had seared to stone,   1845
And bound in his temple for ever to lean,
In sackcloth of gray and visors of green,
An everlasting worship to keep,
And the big salt tears eternally weep.

So rapid the motion, the whirl and the boil,   1850
So loud was the tumult, so fierce the turmoil,
Appalled from those portals of terror they turn,
On pillar of marble their incense to burn.
Around the holy flame they pray,
Then turning their faces all west away,   1855
On angel pavement each bent his knee,
And sung this hymn to the God of the sea.

The Monks' Hymn

Thou, who makest the ocean to flow,
Thou, who walkest the channels below;
To thee, to thee, this incense we heap,   1860
Thou, who knowest not slumber nor sleep,
Great Spirit that movest on the face of the deep!
To thee, to thee, we sing to thee,
God of the western wind, God of the sea.

To thee, who bring'st with thy right hand   1865
The little fishes around our land;

To thee, who breathest in the bosom'd sail,
Rul'st the shark and the rolling whale,
Fling'st the sinner to downward grave,
Light'st the gleam on the mane of the wave, 1870
Bid'st the billows thy reign deform,
Laugh'st in the whirlwind, sing'st in the storm;
Or risest like mountain amid the sea,
Where mountain was never, and never will be
And rear'st thy proud and thy pale chaperoon 1875
'Mid walks of the angels and ways of the moon.
To thee, to thee, this wine we pour,
God of the western wind, God of the shower.

To thee, who bid'st those mountains of brine
Softly sink in the fair moonshine, 1880
And spread'st thy couch of silver light,
To lure to thy bosom the queen of the night,
Who weavest the cloud of the ocean dew,
And the mist that sleeps on her breast so blue;
When the murmurs die at the base of the hill, 1885
And the shadows lie rocked and slumbering still,
And the Solan's young, and the lines of foam,
Are scarcely heaved on thy peaceful home,
We pour this oil and this wine to thee,
God of the western wind, God of the sea!— 1890
"Greater yet must the offering be."

———————————

The monks gazed round, the abbot grew wan,
For the closing notes were not sung by man.
They came from the rock, or they came from the air,
From voice they knew not, and knew not where; 1895
But it sung with a mournful melody,
"Greater yet must the offering be."

In holy dread they past away,
And they walked the ridge of that isle so gray,
And saw the white waves toil and fret, 1900
An hundred fathoms below their feet;
They looked to the countless isles that lie,
From Barra to Mull, and from Jura to Skye;

They looked to heaven, they looked to the main,
They looked at all with a silent pain,   1905
As on places they were not to see again.

   A little bay lies hid from sight,
O'erhung by cliffs of dreadful height;
When they drew nigh that airy steep,
They heard a voice rise from the deep,   1910
And that voice was sweet as voice could be,
And they feared it came from the Maid of the Sea.

   M'Kinnon lay stretched on the verge of the hill,
And peeped from the height on the bay so still;
And he saw her sit on a weedy stone,   1915
Laving her fair breast, and singing alone;
And aye she sank the wave within,
Till it gurgled around her lovely chin,
Then combed her locks of the pale sea-green,
And aye this song was heard between.   1920

The Mermaid's Song

    Matilda of Skye
    Alone may lie,
And list to the wind that whistles by:
    Sad may she be,
    For deep in the sea,   1925
  Deep, deep, deep in the sea,
This night her lover shall sleep with me.
    She may turn and hide
    From the spirits that glide,
And the ghost that stands at her bed-side: 1930
But never a kiss the vow shall seal,
Nor warm embrace her bosom feel;
For far, far down in the floors below,
Moist as this rock-weed, cold as the snow,
With the eel, and the clam, and the pearl of the deep,
On soft sea-flowers her lover shall sleep,
And long and sound shall his slumber be
In the coral bowers of the deep with me.

   The trembling sun, far, far away,
Shall pour on his couch a softened ray,   1940

And his mantle shall wave in the flowing tide,
And the little fishes shall turn aside;
But the waves and the tides of the sea shall cease,
Ere wakes her love from his bed of peace.
No home!—no kiss!—No, never! never!   1945
His couch is spread for ever and ever.

The abbot arose in dumb dismay,
They turned and fled from the height away,
For dark and portentous was the day.
When they came in view of their rocking sail,   1950
They saw an old man who sat on the wale;
His beard was long, and silver grey,
Like the rime that falls at the break of day;
His locks like wool, and his colour wan,
And he scarcely looked like an earthly man.   1955

They asked his errand, they asked his name,
Whereunto bound, and whence he came;
But a sullen thoughtful silence he kept,
And turned his face to the sea and wept.
Some gave him welcome, and some gave him scorn, 1960
But the abbot stood pale, with terror o'erborne;
He tried to be jocund, but trembled the more,
For he thought he had seen the face before.

Away went the ship with her canvass all spread,
So glad to escape from that island of dread;   1965
And skimmed the blue wave like a streamer of light,
Till fell the dim veil 'twixt the day and the night.

Then the old man arose and stood up on the prow,
And fixed his dim eyes on the ocean below;
And they heard him saying, "Oh, woe is me!   1970
But great as the sin must the sacrifice be."
Oh, mild was his eye, and his manner sublime,
When he looked unto Heaven, and said—"Now is the
      time."
He looked to the weather, he looked to the lee,
He looked as for something he dreaded to see,   1975

Then stretched his pale hand, and pointed his eye
To a gleam on the verge of the eastern sky.

The monks soon beheld, on the lofty Ben-More,
A sight which they never had seen before,
A belt of blue lightning around it was driven,   1980
And its crown was encircled by morion of heaven;
And they heard a herald that loud did cry,
"Prepare the way for the Abbot of I!"

Then a sound arose, they knew not where,
It came from the sea, or it came from the air,   1985
'Twas louder than tempest that ever blew,
And the sea-fowls screamed, and in terror flew;
Some ran to the cords, some kneeled at the shrine,
But all the wild elements seemed to combine;
'Twas just but one moment of stir and commotion,   1990
And down went the ship like a bird of the ocean.

This moment she sailed all stately and fair,
The next nor ship nor shadow was there,
But a boil that arose from the deep below,
A mounting gurgling column of snow;   1995
It sunk away with a murmuring moan,
The sea is calm, and the sinners are gone.

END OF NIGHT THE THIRD

Conclusion

Conclusion

FRIEND of the bard! peace to thy heart,
Long hast thou acted generous part,
Long hast thou courteously in pain
Attended to a feeble strain,
While oft abashed has sunk thine eye,—   5
Thy task is done, the Wake is bye.

   I saw thy fear, I knew it just;
'Twas not for minstrels long in dust,
But for the fond and venturous swain
Who dared to wake their notes again;   10
Yet oft thine eye has spoke delight,
I marked it well, and blest the sight:
No sour disdain, nor manner cold,
Noted contempt for tales of old;
Oft hast thou at the fancies smiled,   15
And marvelled at the legends wild.
Thy task is o'er; peace to thy heart!
For thou hast acted generous part.

   'Tis said that thirty bards appeared,
That thirty names were registered,   20
With whom were titled chiefs combined,
But some are lost, and some declined.
Woe's me, that all my mountain lore
Has been unfit to rescue more!
And that my guideless rustic skill   25
Has told those ancient tales so ill.

   The prize harp still hung on the wall;
The bards were warned to leave the hall,
Till courtiers gave the judgment true,
To whom the splendid prize was due.   30
What curious wight will pass with me,
The anxious motley group to see;
List their remarks of right and wrong,
Of skilful hand and faulty song,
And drink one glass the bards among?   35

There sit the men—behold them there,
Made maidens quake and courtiers stare,
Whose names shall future ages tell;
What do they seem? behold them well.
A simpler race you shall not see,   40
Awkward and vain as men can be:
Light as the fumes of fervid wine,
Or foam-bells floating on the brine,
The gossamers in air that sail,
Or down that dances in the gale.   45

Each spoke of others fame and skill
With high applause, but jealous will.
Each song, each strain, he erst had known,
And all had faults except his own:
Plaudits were mixed with meaning jeers,   50
For all had hopes, and all had fears.

A herald rose the court among,
And named each bard and named his song;
Rizzio was named from royal chair—
"Rizzio!" re-echoed many a fair.   55
Each song had some that song approved,
And voices gave for bard beloved.
The first division called and done,
Gardyn stood highest just by one.
No merits can the courtier sway,   60
'Twas then, it seems, as at this day.

Queen Mary reddened, wroth was she
Her favourite thus outdone to see,
Reproved her squire in high disdain,
And caused him call the votes again.   65
Strange though it seem, the truth I say,
Feature of that unyielding day,
Her favourite's voters counted o'er,
Were found much fewer than before.
Glistened her eyes with pungent dew: 70
She found with whom she had to do.

Again the royal gallery rung
With names of those who second sung,

When, spite of haughty Highland blood,
The Bard of Ettrick upmost stood.   75

The rest were named who sung so late,
And after long and keen debate,
The specious nobles of the south
Carried the nameless stranger youth;
Though Highland wrath was at the full,   80
Contending for the Bard of Mull.

Then did the worst dispute begin,
Which of the *three* the prize should win.
'Twas party all—not minstrel worth,
But honour of the south and north;   85
And nought was heard throughout the court,
But taunt, and sneer, and keen retort.
High run the words, and fierce the fume,
And from beneath each nodding plume
Red look was cast that vengeance said,   90
And palm on broad-sword's hilt was laid,
While Lowland jeer, and Highland mood,
Threatened to end the Wake in blood.

Rose from his seat the Lord of Mar,
Serene in counsel as in war.   95
"For shame," said he, "contendants all!
This outrage done in royal hall,
Is to our country foul disgrace.
What! mock our Sovereign to her face!
Whose generous heart and taste refined,   100
Alike to bard and courtier kind,
This high repast for all designed.
For shame! your party strife suspend,
And list the counsel of a friend.

"Unmeet it is for you or me   105
To lessen one of all the three,
Each excellent in his degree;
But taste, as sapient sages tell,
Varies with climes in which we dwell.

"Fair emblem of the Border dale,   110
Is cadence soft and simple tale;

While stern romantic Highland clime,
Still nourishes the rude sublime.

"If Border ear may taste the worth
Of the wild pathos of the north,   115
Or that sublimed by Ossian's lay,
By forest dark and mountain gray,
By clouds which frowning cliffs deform,
By roaring flood and raving storm,
Enjoy the smooth, the fairy tale,   120
Or evening song of Teviotdale;
Then trow you may the tides adjourn,
And nature from her path-way turn;
The wild-duck drive to mountain tree,
The capperkayle to swim the sea,   125
The heath-cock to the shelvy shore,
The partridge to the mountain hoar,
And bring the red-eyed ptarmigan
To dwell by the abodes of man.

"To end this strife, unruled and vain,   130
Let all the three be called again;
Their skill alternately be tried,
And let the Queen alone decide.
Then hushed be jeer and answer proud,"–
He said, and all, consenting, bowed.   135

When word was brought to bard's retreat,
The group were all in dire debate;
The Border youth (that stranger wight)
Had quarrelled with the clans outright;
Had placed their merits out of ken,   140
Deriding both the songs and men.
'Tis said–but few the charge believes–
He branded them as fools and thieves.
Certes that war and woe had been,
For gleaming dirks unsheathed were seen,   145
For Highland minstrels ill could brook
His taunting word and haughty look.

The youth was chafed, and with disdain
Refused to touch his harp again;

Drawn and Engraved by Daniel Somerville 1807.

QUEEN MARY'S HARP.

Said he desired no more renown   150
Than keep those Highland boasters down;
Now he had seen them quite outdone,
The south had two, the north but one;
But should they bear the prize away,
For that he should not, would not play;   155
He cared for no such guerdon mean,
Nor for the harp, nor for the Queen.

His claim withdrawn, the victors twain
Repaired to prove their skill again.

The song that tuneful Gardyn sung   160
Is still admired by old and young,
And long shall be at evening fold,
While songs are sung or tales are told.
Of stolen delights began the song,
Of love the Carron woods among,   165
Of lady borne from Carron side
To Barnard towers and halls of pride,
Of jealous lord and doubtful bride,
And ended with Gilmorice' doom
Cut off in manhood's early bloom.   170
Soft rung the closing notes and slow,
And every heart was steeped in woe.

The harp of Ettrick rung again,
Her bard, intent on fairy strain,
And fairy freak by moonlight shaw,   175
Sung young Tam Lean of Carterha'.

Queen Mary's harp on high that hung,
And every tone responsive rung,
With gems and gold that dazzling shone,
That harp is to the Highlands gone,   180
Gardyn is crowned with garlands gay,
And bears the envied prize away.
Long, long that harp, the hills among,
Resounded Ossian's warrior song;
Waked slumbering lyres from every tree   185
Adown the banks of Don and Dee,
At length was borne, by beauteous bride,
To woo the airs on Garry side.

When full two hundred years had fled,
And all the northern bards were dead,   190
That costly harp, of wonderous mould,
Defaced of all its gems and gold,
With that which Gardyn erst did play,
Back to Dunedin found its way.

As Mary's hand the victor crowned,   195
And twined the wreath his temples round,
Loud were the shouts of Highland chief–
The Lowlanders were dumb with grief;
And the poor Bard of Ettrick stood
Like statue pale, in moveless mood;   200
Like ghost, which oft his eyes had seen
At gloaming in his glens so green.
Queen Mary saw the minstrel's pain,
And bade from bootless grief refrain.

She said a boon to him should fall   205
Worth all the harps in royal hall;
Of Scottish song a countless store,
Precious remains of minstrel lore,
And cottage, by a silver rill,
Should all reward his rustic skill: 210
Did other gift his bosom claim,
He needed but that gift to name.

"O, my fair Queen," the minstrel said,
With faultering voice and hanging head,
"Your cottage keep, and minstrel lore–   215
Grant me a harp, I ask no more.
From thy own hand a lyre I crave,
That boon alone my heart can save."

"Well hast thou asked; and be it known,
I have a harp of old renown   220
Hath many an ardent wight beguiled;
'Twas framed by wizard of the wild,
And will not yield one measure bland
Beneath a skilless stranger hand;
But once her powers by progress found,   225
O there is magic in the sound!

"When worldly woes oppress thy heart—
And thou and all must share a part—
Should scorn be cast from maiden's eye,
Should friendship fail, or fortune fly,   230
Steal with thy harp to lonely brake,
Her wild, her soothing numbers wake,
And soon corroding cares shall cease,
And passion's host be lulled to peace;
Angels a gilded screen shall cast,   235
That cheers the future, veils the past.

"That harp will make the elves of eve
Their dwelling in the moon-beam leave,
And ope thine eyes by haunted tree
Their glittering tiny forms to see.   240
The flitting shades that woo the glen
'Twill shape to forms of living men,
To forms on earth no more you see,
Who once were loved, and aye will be;
And holiest converse you may prove   245
Of things below and things above."

"That is, that is the harp for me!"
Said the rapt bard in ecstacy;
"This soothing, this exhaustless store,
Grant me, my Queen, I ask no more."   250

O, when the weeping minstrel laid
The relic in his old gray plaid,
When Holyrood he left behind
To gain his hills of mist and wind,
Never was hero of renown,   255
Or monarch prouder of his crown.
He tript the vale, he climbed the coomb,
The mountain breeze began to boom;
Aye when the magic chords it rung,
He raised his voice and blithely sung.   260
"Hush, my wild harp, thy notes forbear;
No blooming maids nor elves are here:
Forbear a while that witching tone,
Thou must not, canst not sing alone.
When Summer flings her watchet screen   265

At eve o'er Ettrick woods so green,
Thy notes shall many a heart beguile;
Young Beauty's eye shall o'er thee smile,
And fairies trip it merrily
Around my royal harp and me."   270

Long has that harp of magic tone
To all the minstrel world been known:
Who has not heard her witching lays,
Of Ettrick banks and Yarrow braes?
But that sweet bard, who sung and played   275
Of many a feat and Border raid,
Of many a knight and lovely maid,
When forced to leave his harp behind,
Did all her tuneful chords unwind;
And many ages past and came   280
Ere man so well could tune the same.

Bangour the daring task essayed,
Not half the chords his fingers played;
Yet even then some thrilling lays
Bespoke the harp of ancient days.   285

Redoubted Ramsay's peasant skill
Flung some strained notes along the hill;
His was some lyre from lady's hall,
And not the mountain harp at all.

Langhorn arrived from Southern dale,   290
And chimed his notes on Yarrow vale,
They would not, could not, touch the heart;
His was the modish lyre of art.

Sweet rung the harp to Logan's hand:
Then Leyden came from Border land,   295
With dauntless heart and ardour high,
And wild impatience in his eye.
Though false his tones at times might be,
Though wild notes marred the symphony
Between, the glowing measure stole   300
That spoke the bard's inspired soul.
Sad were those strains, when hymned afar,

On the green vales of Malabar:
O'er seas beneath the golden morn,
They travelled on the monsoon borne, 305
Thrilling the heart of Indian maid,
Beneath the wild banana's shade.—
Leyden! a shepherd wails thy fate,
And Scotland knows her loss too late.

The day arrived—blest be the day, 310
Walter the Abbot came that way!—
The sacred relic met his view—
Ah! well the pledge of Heaven he knew!
He screwed the chords, he tried a strain;
'Twas wild—he tuned and tried again, 315
Then poured the numbers bold and free,
The ancient magic melody.

The land was charmed to list his lays;
It knew the harp of ancient days.
The Border chiefs, that long had been 320
In sepulchres unhearsed and green,
Passed from their mouldy vaults away,
In armour red and stern array,
And by their moonlight halls were seen,
In visor, helm, and habergeon. 325
Even fairies sought our land again,
So powerful was the magic strain.

Blest be his generous heart for aye!
He told me where the relic lay;
Pointed my way with ready will, 330
Afar on Ettrick's wildest hill;
Watched my first notes with curious eye,
And wondered at my minstrelsy:
He little weened a parent's tongue
Such strains had o'er my cradle sung. 335

O could the bard I loved so long,
Reprove my fond aspiring song!
Or could his tongue of candour say,
That I should throw my harp away!
Just when her notes began with skill, 340

To sound beneath the southern hill,
And twine around my bosom's core,
How could we part for evermore!
'Twas kindness all, I cannot blame,
For bootless is the minstrel flame;   345
But sure a bard might well have known
Another's feelings by his own!

   Of change enamoured, woe the while!
He left our mountains, left the isle;
And far to other kingdoms bore   350
The Caledonian harp of yore;
But, to the hand that framed her true,
Only by force one strain she threw.
That harp he never more shall see,
Unless 'mong Scotland's hills with me.   355

Now, my loved Harp, a while farewell;
   I leave thee on the old gray thorn;
The evening dews will mar thy swell,
   That waked to joy the cheerful morn.

Farewell, sweet soother of my woe!   360
   Chill blows the blast around my head;
And louder yet that blast may blow,
   When down this weary vale I've sped.

The wreath lies on Saint Mary's shore;
   The mountain sounds are harsh and loud;   365
The lofty brows of stern Clokmore
   Are visored with the moving cloud.

But Winter's deadly hues shall fade
   On moorland bald and mountain shaw,
And soon the rainbow's lovely shade   370
   Sleep on the breast of Bowerhope Law;

Then will the glowing suns of spring,
   The genial shower and stealing dew,
Wake every forest bird to sing,
   And every mountain flower renew.   375

But not the rainbow's ample ring,
   That spans the glen and mountain grey,
Though fanned by western breeze's wing,
   And sunned by summer's glowing ray,

To man decayed, can ever more   380
   Renew the age of love and glee!
Can ever second spring restore
   To my old mountain Harp and me!

But when the hue of softened green
   Spreads over hill and lonely lea,   385
And lowly primrose opes unseen
   Her virgin bosom to the bee;

When hawthorns breathe their odours far,
   And carols hail the year's return;
And daisy spreads her silver star   390
   Unheeded by the mountain burn;

Then will I seek the aged thorn,
   The haunted wild and fairy ring,
Where oft thy erring numbers borne
   Have taught the wandering winds to sing.   395

END OF THE QUEEN'S WAKE

Notes

Notes

NOTE I.

Those wakes, now played by minstrels poor,
At midnight's darkest, chillest hour,
Those humble wakes, now scorned by all,
Were first begun in courtly hall.–Page 201.

In former days, the term *Wake* was only used to distinguish the festive meeting which took place on the evening previous to the dedication of any particular church or chapel. The company sat up all the night, and, in England, amused themselves in various ways, as their inclinations were by habit or study directed. In Scotland, however, which was always the land of music and of song, music and song were the principal, often the only, amusements of the Wake. These songs were generally of a sacred or serious nature, and were chanted to the old simple melodies of the country. *The Bush aboon Traquair, The Broom of Cowdenknows, John come kiss me now*, and many others, are still extant, set to the Psalms of David, and other spiritual songs, the Psalms being turned into a rude metre corresponding to the various measures of the tunes.

The difference in the application of the term which exists in the two sister kingdoms, sufficiently explains the consequences of the wakes in either. In England they have given rise to many fairs and festivals of long standing; and, from that origin, every fair or festival is denominated a *wake*. In Scotland the term is not used to distinguish any thing either subsistent or relative, save those serenades played by itinerant and nameless minstrels in the streets and squares of Edinburgh, which are inhabited by the great and wealthy, after midnight, about the time of the Christmas holidays. These seem to be the only remainder of the ancient wakes now in Scotland, and their effect upon a mind that delights in music is soothing and delicious beyond all previous conception. A person who can relish the concord of sweet sounds, gradually recalled from sleep by the music of the wakes, of which he had no previous anticipation, never fails of being deprived, for a considerable time, of all recollection, what condition, what place, or what world he is in. The minstrels who, in the reign of the Stuarts, enjoyed privileges which were even denied to the principal nobility, were, by degrees, driven from the tables of the great to the second, and afterwards to the common hall, that their music and songs might be heard, while they themselves were unseen. From the common hall they were obliged to retire to the porch or court; and so low has the characters of the minstrels descended, that the performers of the Christmas wakes are wholly unknown to the most part of those whom they serenade. They seem to be despised, but enjoy some small privileges, in order to keep up a name of high and ancient origin.

NOTE II.

There rode the lords of France and Spain,
Of England, Flanders, and Lorraine,
While serried thousands round them stood,
From shore of Leith to Holyrood.–P. 203.

Hollingshed describes Queen Mary's landing in Scotland, with her early misfortunes and accomplishments, after this manner: "She arrived at Leith the 20th of August, in the year of our Lord 1561, where she was honourably received by the Earl of Argyle, the Lord Erskine, the Prior of St Andrew's, and the burgesses of Edinburgh, and conveyed to the Abbie of Holie-rood-house, for (as saith Buchanan) when some had spread abroad her landing in Scotland, the nobility and others assembled out of all parts of the realme, as it were to a common spectacle.

"This did they, partly to congratulate her return, and partly to shew the dutie which they alwais bear unto her (when she was absent), either to have thanks therefore, or to prevent the slanders of the enemies: wherefore not a few, by these beginnings of her reign, did gesse what would follow, although, in those so variable notions of the minds of the people, every one was very desirous to see their Queen offered unto them (unlooked for), after so many haps of both fortunes as had befallen her. For, when she was but six days old, she lost her father among the cruel tempests of battle, and was, with great diligence, brought up by her mother (being a chosen and worthy person), but yet left as a prize to others, by reason of civil sedition in Scotland, and of outward wars with other nations, being further led abroad to all the dangers of frowning fortune, before she could know what evil did mean.

"For leaving her own country, she was nourished as a banished person, and hardly preserved in life from the weapons of her enemies, and violence of the seas. After which fortune began to flatter her, in that she honoured her with a worthy marriage, which, in truth, was rather a shadow of joie to this queen, than any comfort at all. For, shortly after the same, all things were turned to sorrow, by the death of her new young husband, and of her old and grieved mother, by loss of her new kingdom, and by the doubtful possession of her old heritable realme. But as for these things she was both pitied and praised, so was she also for gifts of nature as much beloved and favoured, in that beneficial nature (or rather good God) had indued her with a beautiful face, a well composed body, an excellent wit, a mild nature, and good behaviour, which she had artificially furthered by courtly education, and affable demeanor. Whereby, at the first sight, she wan unto her the hearts of most, and confirmed the love of her faithful subjects."–*Holl.* p. 314. Arbroath Ed.

With regard to the music, which so deeply engaged her attention, we have different accounts by contemporaries, and those at complete variance with one another. Knox says, "Fyres of joy were set furth at night, and a companie of maist honest men, with instruments of musick, gave ther salutation at hir chalmer windo: the melodie, as sche alledged, lyked her weill, and sche willed the sam to be continued sum nychts efter with grit diligence." But Dufresnoy, who was one of the party who accompanied the Queen, gives a very different account of these Scotish minstrels. "We landed at Leith," says he, "and went from thence to Edinburgh, which is but a short league distant. The Queen went there on horseback, and the lords and ladies who accompanied her upon the little wretched hackneys of the country, as wretchedly capparisoned; at sight of which the Queen began to weep, and to compare them with the pomp and superb palfreys of France. But there was no remedy but patience. What was worst of all, being arrived at Edinburgh, and retired to rest in the Abbey (which is really a fine building, and not at all partaking of the rudeness of that country), there came under her window a crew of five or six hundred scoundrels from the city, who gave her a serenade with wretched violins and little rebecks, of which there are enough in that country, and began to sing Psalms so miserably mistimed and mistuned, that nothing could be worse. Alas! what music! and what a night's rest!"

This Frenchman has had no taste for Scotish music—such another concert is certainly not in record.

NOTE III.
Ah! Kennedy, vengeance hangs over thine head!
Escape to thy native Glengary forlorn.–P. 224.

The Clan Kennedy was only in the present age finally expelled from Glen-Gary, and forced to scatter over this and other countries. Its character among the Highlanders is that of the most savage and irreclaimable tribe that ever infested the mountains of the north.

NOTE IV.
The Witch of Fife.–P. 233.

It may suffice to mention, once for all, that the catastrophe of this tale, as well as the principal events related in the tales of *Old David* and *M'Gregor*, are all founded on popular traditions. So is also the romantic story of Kilmeny's disappearance and revisiting her friends, after being seven years in Fairyland. The tradition bears some resemblance to the old ballads of Tam Lean and Thomas of Erceldon; and it is not improbable that all the three may have drawn their origin from the same ancient romance.

NOTE V.
Glen-Avin.–P. 253.

There are many scenes among the Grampian deserts which amaze the traveller who ventures to explore them; and in the most pathless wastes the most striking landscapes are often concealed. Glen-Avin exceeds them all in what may be termed stern and solemn grandeur. It is

indeed a sublime solitude, in which the principal feature is deformity;
yet that deformity is mixed with lines of wild beauty, such as an exten-
sive lake, with its islets and bays, the straggling trees, and the spots of
shaded green; and, altogether, it is such a scene as man has rarely looked
upon. I spent a summer day in visiting it. The hills were clear of mist,
yet the heavens were extremely dark—the effect upon the scene ex-
ceeded all description. My mind, during the whole day, experienced the
same sort of sensation as if I had been in a dream; and on returning
from the excursion, I did not wonder at the superstition of the neigh-
bouring inhabitants, who believe it to be the summer haunt of innumer-
able tribes of fairies, and many other spirits, some of whom seem to be
the most fantastic, and to behave in the most eccentric manner, of any I
ever before heard of. Though the glen is upwards of twenty miles in
length, and of prodigious extent, it contains no human habitation. It lies
in the west corner of Banffshire, in the very middle of the Grampian
hills.

NOTE VI.
Oft had that seer, at break of morn,
Beheld the fahm glide o'er the fell.—P. 254.

Fahm is a little ugly monster, who frequents the summits of the moun-
tains around Glen-Avin, and no other place in the world that I know of.
My guide, D. M'Queen, declared that he had himself seen him; and, by
his description, Fahm appears to be no native of this world, but an
occasional visitant, whose intentions are evil and dangerous. He is only
seen about the break of day, and on the highest verge of the mountain.
His head is twice as large as his whole body beside; and if any living
creature cross the track over which he has passed before the sun shine
upon it, certain death is the consequence. The head of that person or
animal instantly begins to swell, grows to an immense size, and finally
bursts. Such a disease is really incident to sheep on those heights, and in
several parts of the kingdom, where the grounds are elevated to a great
height above the sea; but in no place save Glen-Avin is Fahm blamed for it.

NOTE VII.
Even far on Yarrow's fairy dale,
The shepherd paused in dumb dismay,
There passing shrieks adown the vale
Lured many a pitying hind away.—P. 256.

It was reckoned a curious and unaccountable circumstance, that, dur-
ing the time of a great fall of snow by night, a cry, as of a person who
had lost his way in the storm, was heard along the vale of Ettrick from
its head to its foot. What was the people's astonishment, when it was
authenticated, that upwards of twenty parties had all been out with
torches, lanthorns, &c. at the same hour of the night, calling and search-
ing after some unknown person, whom they believed perishing in the

snow, and that none of them had discovered any such person—the word spread; the circumstances were magnified—and the consternation became general. The people believed that a whole horde of evil spirits had been abroad in the valley, endeavouring to lure them abroad to their destruction—there was no man sure of his life!—prayers and thanksgivings were offered up to Heaven in every hamlet, and resolutions unanimously formed, that no man perishing in the snow should ever be looked after again as long as the world stood.

When the astonishment had somewhat subsided by exhausting itself, and the tale of horror spread too wide ever to be recalled, a lad, without the smallest reference to the phenomenon, chanced to mention, that on the night of the storm, when he was out on the hill turning his sheep to some shelter, a flock of swans passed over his head toward the western sea, which was a sure signal of severe weather; and that at intervals they were always shouting and answering one another, in an extraordinary, and rather fearsome manner.—It was an unfortunate discovery, and marred the harmony of many an evening's conversation! In whatever cot the circumstance was mentioned, the old shepherds rose and went out—the younkers, who had listened to the prayers with reverence and fear, bit their lips—the matrons plied away at their wheels in silence—it was singular that none of them should have known the voice of a swan from that of the devil!—they were very angry with the lad, and regarded him as a sort of blasphemer.

Note VIII.
See yon lone cairn, so gray with age,
Above the base of proud Cairn-Gorm.—P. 257.

I only saw this old cairn at a distance; but the narrative which my guide gave me of the old man's loss was very affecting. He had gone to the forest in November to look after some goats that were missing, when a dreadful storm came suddenly on, the effects of which were felt throughout the kingdom. It was well enough known that he was lost in the forest, but the snow being so deep, it was judged impossible to find the body, and no one looked after it. It was not discovered until the harvest following, when it was found accidentally by a shepherd. The plaid and clothes which were uppermost not being decayed, it appeared like the body of a man lying entire; but when he began to move them, the dry bones rattled together, and the bare white scull was lying in the bonnet.

Note IX.
Old David.—P. 260.

I remember hearing a very old man, named David Laidlaw, who lived somewhere in the neighbourhood of Hawick, relate many of the adventures of this old moss-trooper, his great progenitor, and the first who ever bore the name. He described him as a great champion—a man quite invincible, and quoted several verses of a ballad relating to him, which I never heard either before or since. I remember only one of them:

> There was ane banna of barley meal
> Cam duntin dune by Davy's sheil,
> But out cam Davy and his lads,
> And dang the banna a' in blads.

He explained how this "bannock of barley meal" meant a rich booty, which the old hero captured from a band of marauders. He lived at Garwell in Eskdale-moor.

Lochy-Law, where the principal scene of this tale is laid, is a hill on the lands of Shorthope in the wilds of Ettrick. The Fairy Slack is up in the middle of the hill, a very curious ravine, and would be much more so when overshadowed with wood. The Back-burn which joins the Ettrick immediately below this hill, has been haunted time immemorial, both by the fairies, and the ghost of a wandering minstrel who was cruelly murdered there, and who sleeps in a lone grave a small distance from the ford.

NOTE X.

And fears of elf, and fairy raid,
Have like a morning dream decayed.—P. 269.

The fairies have now totally disappeared, and it is a pity they should; for they seem to have been the most delightful little spirits that ever haunted the Scotish dells. There are only very few now remaining alive who have ever seen them; and when they did, it was on Hallow-evenings while they were young, when the gospel was not very rife in the country. But, strange as it may appear, with the witches it is far otherwise. Never, in the most superstitious ages, was the existence of witches, or the influence of their diabolical power, more firmly believed in, than by the inhabitants of the mountains of Ettrick Forest at the present day. Many precautions and charms are used to avert this influence, and scarcely does a summer elapse in which there are not some of the most gross incantations practised, in order to free flocks and herds from the blasting power of these old hags. There are two farmers still living, who will both make oath that they have wounded several old wives with shot as they were traversing the air in the shapes of moor-fowl and partridges. A very singular amusement that for old wives!—I heard one of these *gentlemen* relate, with the utmost seriousness, and as a matter he did not wish to be generally known, that one morning, going out a fowling, he sprung a pair of moor-fowl in a place where it was not customary for moor-fowl to stay—he fired at the hen—wounded her, and eyed her until she alighted beyond an old dyke—when he went to the spot, his astonishment may be well conceived, when he found Nell —

picking the hail out of her limbs! He was extremely vexed that he had not shot the cock, for he was almost certain he was no other than *Wattie Grieve!!!*

The tales and anecdotes of celebrated witches, that are still related in the country, are extremely whimsical and diverting. The following is a *well-authenticated one.* A number of gentlemen were one day met for a chase on the lands of Newhouse and Kirkhope—their greyhounds were numerous and keen, but not a hare could they raise. At length a boy came to them, who offered to start a hare to them, if they would give him a guinea, and the black greyhound to hold. The demand was singular, but it was peremptory, and on other conditions he would not comply. The guerdon was accordingly paid—the hare was started, and the sport afforded by the chase was excellent—the greyhounds were all baffled, and began to give up one by one, when one of the party came slily behind the boy, and cut the leish in which he held the black dog—away he flew to join the chase.—The boy, losing all recollection, ran, bawling out with great vociferation, "Huy, mither, rin!! Hay, rin, ye auld witch, if ever ye ran i' yer life!! Rin, mither, rin!!" The black dog came fast up with her, and was just beginning to *mouth her*, when she sprung in at the window of a little cottage and escaped. The riders soon came to the place, and entered the cot in search of the hare; but, lo! there was no living creature there but the old woman lying panting in a bed, so breathless that she could not speak a word!!!

But the best old witch tale that remains, is that which is related of the celebrated Michael Scott, Master of Oakwad. Mr Walter Scott has preserved it, but so altered from the original way, that it is not easy to recognize it. The old people tell it as follows: There was one of Mr Michael's tenants who had a wife that was the most notable witch of the age. So extraordinary were her powers, that the country people began to put them in competition with those of the Master, and say, that in some *cantrips* she surpassed him. Michael could ill brook such insinuations; for there is always jealousy between great characters, and went over one day with his dogs on pretence of hunting, but in reality with an intent of exercising some of his infernal power in the chastisement of Lucky — (I have the best reason in the world for concealing her reputed name). He found her alone in the field weeding lint; and desired her, in a friendly manner, to show him some of her powerful art. She was very angry with him, and denied that she had any supernatural skill. He, however, continuing to press her, she told him sharply to let her alone, else she would make him repent the day he troubled her. How she perceived the virtues of Michael's wand is not known, but in a moment she snatched it from his hand, and gave him three lashes with it. The knight was momently changed to a hare, when the malicious and inveterate hag cried out, laughing, "Shu, Michael, rin or dee!" and baited all his own dogs upon him. He was extremely hard hunted, and was obliged to swim the river, and take shelter in the sewer of his own castle from the fury of his pursuers, where he got leisure to change himself again to a man.

Michael being extremely chagrined at having been thus outwitted, studied a deadly revenge; and going over afterwards to hunt, he sent his man to Fauldshope to borrow some bread from Lucky — to give to his dogs, for that he had neglected to feed them before he came from home. If she gave him the bread, he was to thank her and come away; but if she refused it, he gave him a line written in red characters, which he was to lodge above the lintel as he came out. The servant found her baking of bread, as his master assured him he would, and delivered his message. She received him most ungraciously, and absolutely refused to give him any bread, alleging, as an excuse, that she had not as much as would serve her own reapers to dinner. The man said no more, but lodged the line as directed, and returned to his master. The powerful spell had the desired effect; Lucky — instantly threw off her clothes, and danced round and round the fire like one quite mad, singing the while with great glee,

> "Master Michael Scott's man
> Cam seekin bread an' gat nane."

The dinner hour arrived, but the reapers looked in vain for their dame, who was wont to bring it to them to the field. The goodman sent home a servant girl to assist her, but neither did she return. At length he ordered them to go and take their dinner at home, for he suspected his spouse had taken some of her *tirravies*. All of them went inadvertently into the house, and, as soon as they passed beneath the mighty charm, were seized with the same mania, and followed the example of their mistress. The goodman, who had tarried behind, setting some shocks of corn, came home last; and hearing the noise ere ever he came near the house, he did not venture to go in, but peeped in at the window. There he beheld all his people dancing naked round and round the fire, and singing, "Master Michael Scott's man," with the most frantic wildness. His wife was by that time quite exhausted, and the rest were half trailing her around. She could only now and then pronounce a syllable of the song, which she did with a kind of scream, yet seemed as intent on the sport as ever.

The goodman mounted his horse, and rode with all speed to the Master, to inquire what he had done to his people which had put them all mad. Michael bade him take down the note from the lintel and burn it, which he did, and all the people returned to their senses. Poor Lucky — died overnight, and Michael remained unmatched and alone in all the arts of enchantment and necromancy.

Note XI.
The Spectre's Cradle Song.–P. 273.

I mentioned formerly that the tale of M'Gregor is founded on a popular Highland tradition—so also is this Song of the Spectre in the introduction to it, which, to me at least, gives it a peculiar interest. As I was once travelling up Glen-Dochart, attended by Donald Fisher, a shepherd of that country, he pointed out to me some curious green dens, by the side of the large rivulet which descends from the back of Ben More, the name of which, in the Gaelic language, signifies *the abode of the fairies*. A native of that country, who is still living, happening to be benighted there one summer evening, without knowing that the place was haunted, wrapped himself in his plaid, and lay down to sleep till the morning. About midnight he was awaked by the most enchanting music; and on listening, he heard it to be the voice of a woman singing to her child. She sung the verses twice over, so that next morning he had several of them by heart. Fisher had heard them often recited in Gaelic, and he said they were wild beyond human conception. He remembered only a few lines, which were to the same purport with the Spirit's Song here inserted, namely, that she (the singer) had brought her babe from the regions below to be cooled by the breeze of the world, and that they would soon be obliged to part, for the child was going to heaven, and she was to remain for a season in purgatory. I had not before heard any thing so truly romantic.

NOTE XII.

That the pine, which for ages had shed a bright halo,
Afar on the mountains of Highland Glen-Falo,
Should wither and fall ere the turn of yon moon,
Smit through by the canker of hated Colquhoun.—P. 275.

The pine was the standard, and is still the crest of the M'Gregors; and it is well known that the proscription of that clan was occasioned by a slaughter of the Colquhouns, who were its constant and inveterate enemies. That bloody business let loose the vengeance of the country upon them, which had nearly extirpated the name. The Campbells and the Grahams arose and hunted them down like wild beasts, until a M'Gregor could no more be found.

Note XIII.
Earl Walter.—P. 278.

This ballad is founded on a well-known historical fact. Hollingshed mentions it slightly in the following words: "A Frenchman named Sir Anthony Darcie, knight, called afterwards *Le Sir de la Bawtie*, came through England into Scotland, to seek feats of arms. And coming to the king the four and twentie of September, the Lord Hamilton fought with him right valiantly, and so as neither of them lost any piece of honour."

NOTE XIV.
From this the Hamiltons of Clyde,
Their royal lineage draw.—P. 286.

The Princess Margaret of Scotland was married to the Lord Hamil-

ton when only sixteen years of age, who received the earldom of Arran
as her dowry. Hollingshed says, "Of this marriage, those of the house of
Hamilton are descended, and are nearest of blood to the crown of
Scotland, as they pretend; for (as saith Lesleus, lib. viii, p. 316,) if the
line of the Stewards fail, the crown is to come to them."

NOTE XV.
Kilmeny.–P. 288.

Beside the old tradition on which this ballad is founded, there are
some modern incidents of a similar nature, which cannot well be ac-
counted for, yet are as well attested as any occurrence that has taken
place in the present age. The relation may be amusing to some readers.

A man in the parish of Traquair, and county of Peebles, was busied
one day casting turf in a large open field opposite to the mansion-house–
the spot is well known, and still pointed out as rather unsafe; his daugh-
ter, a child seven years of age, was playing beside him, and amusing him
with her prattle. Chancing to ask a question at her, he was surprised at
receiving no answer, and, looking behind him, he perceived that his
child was not there. He always averred that, as far as he could remem-
ber, she had been talking to him about half a minute before; he was
certain it was not above a whole one at most. It was in vain that he ran
searching all about like one distracted, calling her name;–no trace of her
remained. He went home in a state of mind that may be better con-
ceived than expressed, and raised the people of the parish, who searched
for her several days with the same success. Every pool in the river,
every bush and den on the mountains around was searched in vain. It
was remarked that the father never much encouraged the search, being
thoroughly persuaded that she was carried away by some invisible be-
ing, else she could not have vanished so suddenly. As a last resource, he
applied to the minister of Inverlethen, a neighbouring divine of exem-
plary piety and zeal in religious matters, who enjoined him to cause
prayers be offered to God for her in seven Christian churches, next
Sabbath, at the same instant of time; "and then," said he, "if she is dead,
God will forgive our sin in praying for the dead, as we do it through
ignorance; and if she is still alive, I will answer for it, that all the devils in
hell shall be unable to keep her." The injunction was punctually attended
to. She was remembered in the prayers of all the neighbouring congre-
gations, next Sunday, at the same hour, and never were there such
prayers for fervour heard before. There was one divine in particular,
Mr Davidson, who prayed in such a manner that all the hearers trem-
bled. As the old divine foreboded, so it fell out. On that very day, and
within an hour of the time on which these prayers were offered, the girl
was found, in the Plora wood, sitting, picking the bark from a tree. She
could give no perfect account of the circumstances which had befallen to
her, but she said she did not want plenty of meat, for that her mother
came and fed her with milk and bread several times a-day, and sung her

to sleep at night. Her skin had acquired a bluish cast, which wore gradually off in the course of a few weeks. Her name was Jane Brown, she lived to a very advanced age, and was known to many still alive. Every circumstance of this story is truth, if the father's report of the suddenness of her disappearance may be relied on.

Another circumstance, though it happened still later, is not less remarkable. A shepherd of Tushilaw, in the parish of Ettrick, whose name was Walter Dalgleish, went out to the heights of that farm, one Sabbath morning, to herd the young sheep for his son, and let him to church. He took his own dinner along with him, and his son's breakfast. When the sermons were over, the lad went straight home, and did not return to his father. Night came, but nothing of the old shepherd appeared. When it grew very late his dog came home—seemed terrified, and refused to take any meat. The family were ill at ease during the night, especially as they never had known his dog leave him before; and early next morning the lad arose and went to the height to look after his father and his flock. He found his sheep all scattered, and his father's dinner unbroken, lying on the same spot where they had parted the day before. At the distance of 20 yards from the spot, the plaid which the old man wore was lying as if it had been flung from him, and a little farther on, in the same direction, his bonnet was found, but nothing of himself. The country people, as on all such occasions, rose in great numbers, and searched for him many days. My father, and several old men still alive, were of the party. He could not be found or heard of, neither dead nor alive, and at length they gave up all thoughts of ever seeing him more.

On the 20th day after his disappearance, a shepherd's wife, at a place called Berry-bush, came in as the family was sitting down to dinner, and said, that if it were possible to believe that Walter Dalgleish was still in existence, she would say yonder was he coming down the hill. They all ran out to watch the phenomenon, and as the person approached nigher, they perceived that it was actually he, walking without his plaid and his bonnet. The place where he was first descried is not a mile distant from that where he was last seen, and there is neither brake, hag, nor bush. When he came into the house, he shook hands with them all—asked for his family, and spoke as if he had been absent for years, and as if convinced something had befallen them. As they perceived something singular in his looks and manner, they unfortunately forebore asking him any questions at first, but desired him to sit and share their dinner. This he readily complied with, and began to sup some broth with seeming eagerness. He had only taken one or two spoonfuls when he suddenly stopped, a kind of rattling noise was heard in his breast, and he sunk back in a faint. They put him to bed, and from that time forth, he never spoke another word that any person could make sense of. He was removed to his own home, where he lingered a few weeks, and then died. What befel him remains to this day a mystery, and for ever must.

NOTE XVI.

But oft the list'ning groups stood still,
For spirits talked along the hill.–P. 302.

The echoes of evening, which are occasioned by the voices or mirth
of different parties not aware of each other, have a curious and striking
effect. I have known some country people terrified almost out of their
senses at hearing voices and laughter among cliffs, where they knew it
impossible for human being to reach. Some of the echoes around Edin-
burgh are extremely grand; what would they then be were the hills
covered with wood? I have witnessed nothing more romantic than from
a situation behind the Pleasance, where all the noises of the city are
completely hushed, to hear the notes of the drum, trumpet, and bugle,
poured from the cliffs of Salisbury, and the viewless cannons thundering
from the rock. The effect is truly sublime.

NOTE XVII.

Mary Scott.–P. 304.

This ballad is founded on the old song of *The Grey Goss Hawk*. The
catastrophe is the same, and happens at the same place, namely, in St
Mary's church-yard. The castle of Tushilaw, where the chief scene of the
tale is laid, stood on a shelve of the hill which overlooks the junction of
the rivers Ettrick and Rankleburn. It is a singular situation, and seems to
have been chosen for the extensive prospect of the valley which it com-
mands both to the east and west. It was the finest old baronial castle of
which the Forest can boast, but the upper arches and turrets fell in, of
late years, with a crash that alarmed the whole neighbourhood. It is now
a huge heap of ruins. Its last inhabitant was Adam Scott, who was long
denominated in the south the *King of the Border*, but the courtiers called
him the *King of Thieves*. King James V. acted upon the same principle
with these powerful chiefs, most of whom disregarded his authority, as
Bonaparte did with the sovereigns of Europe. He always managed mat-
ters so as to take each of them single-handed—made a rapid and secret
march—overthrew one or two of them, and then returned directly home
till matters were ripe for taking the advantage of some other. He marched
on one day from Edinburgh to Meggatdale, accompanied by a chosen
body of horsemen, surprised Peres Cockburn, a bold and capricious
outlaw who tyrannized over those parts, hanged him over his own gate,
sacked and burnt his castle of Henderland, and divided his lands be-
tween two of his principal followers, Sir James Stuart and the Lord
Hume. From Henderland he marched across the mountains by a wild
unfrequented path, still called *the King's Road*, and appeared before the
gates of Tushilaw about sun-rise. Scott was completely taken by sur-
prise; he, however, rushed to arms with his few friends who were present,
and, after a desperate but unequal conflict, King James overcame him,
plundered his castle of riches and stores to a prodigious amount, hanged

the old Border King over a huge tree which is still growing in the corner of the castle-yard, and over which he himself had hanged many a one, carried his head with him in triumph to Edinburgh, and placed it on a pole over one of the ports. There was a long and deadly feud between the Scotts and the Kers in those days; the Pringles, Murrays, and others around, always joined with the latter, in order to keep down the too powerful Scotts, who were not noted as the best of neighbours.

Note XVIII.
King Edward's dream.—P. 327.

The scene of this ballad is on the banks of the Eden in Cumberland, a day's march back from Burgh, on the sands of Solway, where King Edward I. died, in the midst of an expedition against the Scots, in which he had solemnly sworn to extirpate them as a nation.

Note XIX.
Dumlanrig.—P. 332.

This ballad relates to a well-known historical fact, of which tradition has preserved an accurate and feasible detail. The battles took place two or three years subsequent to the death of King James V. I have heard that it is succinctly related by some historian, but I have forgot who it is. Hollingshed gives a long bungling account of the matter, but places the one battle a year before the other; whereas it does not appear that Lennox made two excursions into Nithsdale, at the head of the English forces, or fought two bloody battles with the laird of Dumlanrig on the same ground, as the historian would insinuate. He says, that Dumlanrig, after pursuing them cautiously for some time, was overthrown in attempting to cross a ford of the river too rashly; that he lost two of his principal kinsmen, and 200 of his followers; had several spears broken upon his body, and escaped only by the goodness of his horse. The battle which took place next night, he relates as having happened next year; but it must be visible to every reader that he is speaking of the same incidents in the annals of both years. In the second engagement he acknowledges that Dumlanrig defeated the English horse, which he attributes to a desertion from the latter, but that, after pursuing them as far as Dalswinton, they were joined by the foot, and retrieved the day. The account given of the battles, by Lesleus and Fran. Thin, seems to have been so different, that they have misled the chronologer; the names of the towns and villages appearing to him so different, whereas a local knowledge of the country would have convinced him that both accounts related to the same engagement.

Note XX.
M'Kinnon, the Abbot—P. 347.

To describe the astonishing scenes to which this romantic tale relates, Icolmkill and Staffa, so well known to the curious, would only be multiplying pages to no purpose. By the Temple of the ocean is meant the Isle of Staffa, and by its chancel the cave of Fingal.

NOTE XXI.

O, wise was the founder, and well said he,
"Where there are women mischief must be!"—P. 349.

St Columba placed the nuns in an island at a little distance from I, as the natives call Iona. He would not suffer either a cow or a woman to set foot on it; "for where there are cows," said he, "there must be women; and where there are women, there must be mischief."

NOTE XXII.

The Harp of Ettrick rung again.—P. 365.

That some notable bard flourished in Ettrick Forest in that age is evident, from the numerous ballads and songs which relate to places in that country, and incidents that happened there. Many of these are of a very superior cast. *Outlaw Murray, Young Tam Lean of Carterhaugh, Jamie Telfer i' the fair Dodhead, The dowy Downs of Yarrow,* and many others, are of the number. Dunbar, in his Lament for the Bards, merely mentions him by the title of *Ettrick;* more of him we know not.

NOTE XXIII.

Gardyn is crowned with garlands gay,
And bears the envied prize away.—P. 365.

Queen Mary's harp, of most curious workmanship, was found in the house of Lude, on the banks of the Garry in Athol, as was the old Caledonian harp. They were both brought to that house by a bride, which the chieftain of Lude married from the family of Gardyn of Banchory (now Garden of Troup). It was defaced of all its ornaments, and Queen Mary's portrait, set in gold and jewels, during the time of the last rebellion. How it came into the possession of that family is not known, at least traditions vary considerably regarding the incident. But there is every reason to suppose, that it was given in consequence of some musical excellency in one or other of the Gardyns; for it may scarcely be deemed, that the royal donor would confer so rich and so curious an instrument on one who could make no use of it. So far does the tale correspond with truth, and there is, besides, a farther coincidence of which I was not previously aware. I find, that Queen Mary actually gave a grand treat at Holyrood-house at the very time specified in the Poem, where great proficiency was displayed both in music and dancing.

NOTE XXIV.

Coomb—is a Scots Lowland term, and used to distinguish all such hills as are scooped out on one side in form of a crescent. The bosom of the

hill, or that portion which lies within the lunated verge, is always de-
nominated *the coomb.*

Note XXV.

Shaw—is likewise a Lowland term, and denotes the snout, or brow of
a hill; but the part so denominated is always understood to be of a
particular form, broad at the base, and contracted to a point above.
Each of these terms conveys to the mind a strong picture of the place so
designed. Both are very common.

Note XXVI.

Law—signifies a detached hill of any description, but more generally
such as are of a round or conical form. It seems to bear the same
acceptation in the Lowlands of Scotland, as *Ben* does in the Highlands.
The term is supposed to have had its derivation from the circumstance
of the ancient inhabitants of the country distributing the *law* on the tops
of such hills; and where no one of that form was nigh, artificial mounds
were raised in the neighbourhood of towns for that purpose. Hence
they were originally called *Law-hills;* but, by a natural and easy contrac-
tion, the *laws* and the *hills* of the country came to signify the same thing.
A little affinity may still be traced;—both were effective in impeding the
progress of an hostile invader; while the hardy native surmounted both
without difficulty, and without concern.

Note XXVII.

Glen—is a term common to every part of Scotland alike, and invari-
ably denotes the whole course of a mountain stream, with all the hills
and vallies on each side to the first summit. It is an indefinite term, and
describes no particular size, or local appearance of a river, or the scenery
contiguous to it, farther than that it is one, and inclined to be narrow
and confined between the hills; these glens being from one to thirty
miles in length, and proportionably dissimilar in other respects. By a
Glen, however, is generally to be understood a branch of a greater river.
The course of the great river is denominated the *Strath*, as Strath-Tay,
Strath-Spey, &c.; and the lesser rivers, which communicate with these,
are the *Glens.* There may be a few exceptions from this general rule, but
they are of no avail as affecting the acceptation of the term whenever it
is used as descriptive.

Note XXVIII.

Strone.—(Only once used.)—*A Strone* is that hill which terminates the
range. It is a Highland term, but common in the middle districts of
Scotland.

Note XXIX.

Ben—is likewise a Highland term, and denotes a mountain of a pyramidal form, which stands unconnected with others.

Note XXX.

Dale—is the course of a Lowland river, with its adjacent hills and vallies. It conveys the same meaning as Strath does in the Highlands.

Note XXXI.

Wale—(only once used)—is a Hebridean term, and signifies the verge or brim of the mountain. It is supposed to be modern, and used only in those maritime districts, as having a reference to the gunnel, or wale, of a ship or boat.

Note XXXII.

Cory, or *Correi*—is a northern term, and is invariably descriptive of a green hollow part of the mountain, from which a rivulet descends.

Note XXXIII.

If there is any other word or term peculiar to Scotland, I am not aware of it. The Songs of the two bards, indeed, who affect to imitate the ancient manner, abound with old Scotch words and terms, which, it is presumed, the rythm, the tenor of the verse, and the narrative, will illustrate, though they may not be found in any glossary of that language. These are, indeed, generally so notoriously deficient and absurd, that it is painful for any one conversant in the genuine old provincial dialect to look into them.

Ignorant, however, as I am of every dialect save my mother tongue, I imagine that I understand so much of the English language as to perceive that its muscular strength consists in the energy of its primitive stem—in the trunk from which all its foliage hath sprung, and around which its exuberant tendrils are all entwined and interwoven—I mean the remains of the ancient Teutonic. On the strength of this conceived principle, which may haply be erroneous, I have laid it down as a maxim, that the greater number of these old words and terms that can be introduced with propriety into our language, the better. To this my casual innovations must be attributed. The authority of Grahame and Scott has of late rendered a few of these old terms legitimate. If I had been as much master of the standard language as they, I would have introduced ten times more.

NOTE XXXIV.

THE following Poem was inserted by the Publisher of the Second Edition, as illustrative of some of the Songs in the Work. It was written and sent to him by B. BARTON, Esq. Woodbridge, Suffolk.

SHEPHERD of Ettrick! as of yore
　　To humble swains the Seraphs sung,
Again, though now unseen, they pour
　　Their hallow'd strains from mortal tongue.

For O! celestial are the tones
　　The minstrel strikes to Malcolm's sorrow;
When Jura, echoing back his moans,
　　Claims the lost maiden of Glen-ora.

Soft dies the strain; the cords now ring,
　　Swept by a more impetuous hand;
Indignant Gardyn strikes the string,
　　And terror chills the listening band.

Now from the cliffs of old Cairn-gorm,
　　Dark gathering clouds the tempest bring;
He comes, the Spirit of the Storm!
　　And at the rustling of his wing,

The harp's wild notes, now high, now low,
　　In varying cadence swell or fall,
Like wintry winds in wild Glencoe,
　　Or ruined Bothwell's roofless hall.

A wilder strain is wafted near
　　As from the regions of the sky;
And where's the mortal that can hear
　　Unmoved the Spectre's lullaby?

To weave the due reward of praise
　　For every rival bard were vain;
Nor suits an humble poet's lays,
　　Who loves, yet fears a loftier strain.

Yet must I pause upon the tale
　　Of that strange bark for Staffa bound;
Proudly she greets the morning gale,
　　Proudly she sails from holy ground.

O, never yet has ship that traced
  The pathless bosom of the main,
Been with such magic numbers graced,
  Or honoured with so sweet a strain.

But who, that sees the morning rise
  Serenely bright, can tell the hour
When the rough tempest of the skies
  Shall next display its awful power?

And who, that sees the floating bark
  Sail forth obedient to the gale,
Foresees the impending horrors dark,
  That swell the terror of the tale?

Nor can I pass in silence by
  That favoured maiden's wondrous doom,
Who, 'neath a self-illumined sky,
  Saw fields and flowers in endless bloom.

O Heaven-taught Shepherd! when or where
  Was that ethereal legend wrought?
What urged thee thus a flight to dare
  Through realms by former bards unsought?

Say, hast thou, like Kilmeny, been
  Transported to the land of thought;
And thence, by minstrel vision keen,
  The fire of inspiration caught?

It must be so: in cottage lone,
  To dreams of poesy resigned,
From Ettrick's banks thy soul has flown,
  And earth-born follies left behind.

Then through those scenes Kilmeny saw,
  In trance ecstatic hast thou roved,
And witnessed, but with holy awe,
  What mortal fancy never proved.

O Shepherd! since 'tis thine to boast
  The fascinating powers of song,
Far, far above the countless host,
  Who swell the Muses' suppliant throng,

The GIFT OF GOD distrust no more,
  His inspiration be thy guide;
Be heard thy harp from shore to shore,
  Thy song's reward thy country's pride.

WOODBRIDGE, *April* 21, 1813.

THE END

Appendix
Advertisements for *The Queen's Wake*

As discussed in the present edition's Introduction (pp. xlix–l), the publisher
George Goldie inserted the following 'Advertisement' in the second edition of
The Queen's Wake (1813):

> THE *Publisher having been favoured with letters from gentlemen in various parts
> of the United Kingdom respecting the Author of the* QUEEN'S WAKE, *and most
> of them expressing doubts of his being a Scotch Shepherd; he takes this opportunity
> of assuring the Public, that* THE QUEEN'S WAKE *is really and truly the produc-
> tion of* JAMES HOGG, *a* common shepherd, *bred among the mountains of
> Ettrick Forest, who went to service when only seven years of age; and since that
> period has never received any education whatever. Upon the consistency of this
> statement, with the merits of the following Work, it does not become him to make any
> observation; all he wishes to say is, that it is* strictly true, *which he states upon the
> best of all possible authority—his own knowledge.*
>
> *Upon answering one of the letters above alluded to, he received another, with the
> following verses inclosed, which he takes the liberty to insert, judging, that their
> intrinsic merit, as well as the allusions to the different ballads which they contain,
> render them a suitable accompaniment to the present edition of the Work.*

In the second, third, and fourth editions of *The Queen's Wake* this 'Advertise-
ment' served to introduce Bernard Barton's 'Stanzas Addressed to The Ettrick
Shepherd on the Publication of *The Queen's Wake*'. In the fifth edition (1819)
Barton's poem was printed in Hogg's final Note. In the present edition it
appears in Hogg's final Note in the 1819 version of the text, and it is dis-
cussed in the final note of the 'Editor's Notes'.

Walter Scott drafted another advertisement for *The Queen's Wake* when a
subscription edition was being planned in 1817 (see the present edition's In-
troduction, pp. lxviii–lxix). His draft survives at the National Library of Scot-
land (MS 30921), and is endorsed 'Prospectus | of | Subscription for | Quarto
Edition | of | Queen's Wake | Drawn up by Mr Scott | Saturday Morning | 24
May 1817'. The draft has the following heading: 'For the Benefit of the Au-
thor | The Queens Wake | A Legendary poem | By James Hogg | Ornamented
with Engravings | Price To Subscribers two guineas'. In the transcription below
deletions by Scott are enclosed in angle brackets <thus>.

> The present work is undertaken by the friends of the ingenious author
> with the purpose of rendering whatever profit may arise from the
> publication directly available to his benefit. It is unnecessary to dwell
> on the various circumstances which in the present state of literature
> render even such works as the Queens Wake which have enjoyed a

<considerable> distinguished share of the public favour less advantageous to the authors fortune than to his reputation. Nor is there any occasion to state any special reasons why in the present case the friends of an author whose merit has raised him from the humble situation of a shepherd to no low rank in British literature are desirous to add solid emolument to his barren laurels. But they are bound in justice to the booksellers to state that this measure has the warm concurrence of those with whose interest it might most seem to interfere & that the gentlemen of the trade have liberally promised their disinterested efforts in favour of the present undertaking

In making this appeal to the public the friends of the author give an opportunity to the admirers of living genius <to come forward> (and they may add of modest worth) to step forward in its behalf. The great stain upon our age has been the neglect of one self-elevated genius whose circumstances were not greatly different from those of Mr Hogg, and such a stigma is sufficient for one generation The present proposal affords an opportunity of averting it which it can scarce be doubted will meet a general & favourable reception

Scott's draft provided the basis of an advertisement printed in the *Edinburgh Evening Courant* of 26 May 1817. Presumably the changes in the printed version were made by William Blackwood, as publisher of the proposed subscription edition. At all events, the printed advertisement reads as follows:

FOR THE BENEFIT OF THE AUTHOR.

To be published by subscription.

ELEGANTLY PRINTED IN QUARTO, ORNAMENTED
WITH ENGRAVINGS FROM DESIGNS BY SCOTTISH ARTISTS,

THE QUEEN'S WAKE.

A Legendary Poem.

BY JAMES HOGG,

THE FIFTH EDITION.

Price to Subscribers Two Guineas, to be paid on delivery.

———————

THE present work is undertaken by the friends of the author, for the purpose of rendering whatever profit may arise from the publication directly available to his benefit. It is unnecessary to dwell on the peculiarity of Mr Hogg's situation, occasioned by the misfortunes of his

first publisher, which deprived him of the advantages he would other-
wise have derived from the merited success of this work. Nor is there
occasion to state any special reasons why, in the present case, the
friends of an author, whose merit has raised him from the humble
situation of a shepherd to no low rank in British literature, are desir-
ous to add solid emolument to his barren laurels. But they are bound
in justice to his booksellers to state, that this measure has their warm
concurrence, though it might seem to interfere with their interests, and
that the gentlemen of the trade have liberally promised their disinter-
ested efforts in favour of the present undertaking.

In making this appeal to the public, the friends of the author give an
opportunity to the admirers of living genius, and, they may add, of
modest worth, to step forward in its behalf. The great stain upon our
age, has been the neglect of one self-elevated genius, whose circum-
stances were not greatly different from those of Mr Hogg, and such a
stigma is sufficient for one generation. The present proposal affords
an opportunity of averting it, which, it can scarce be doubted, will meet
with a general and favourable reception.

Subscribers' names will be received by the author, and his friends;
as well as by his publishers, Mr BLACKWOOD, No. 17. Prince's Street,
Edinburgh; and Mr MURRAY, Albemarle Street, London; to whom
gentlemen, wishing to interest themselves in this undertaking, may
apply for subscription papers.

As we have seen in the present edition's Introduction (p. lxix), subscrip-
tions for the projected edition came in slowly, and it was decided to scale
down the project. A printed subscription paper for *The Queen's Wake* survives
at the National Library of Scotland (MS 4937, fol. 82). In this document the
word 'Quarto' has been changed to 'Royal Octavo', and 'Two Guineas' has
been changed to 'One Guinea'. The statement that the subscription edition is
to be 'ornamented with engravings from designs by Scottish artists' has been
scored out, and the following note in Scott's hand is added underneath:

The original intention of those interesting themselves in this publica-
tion was that it should be adorned with engravings from designs by
Scottish artists and having been so advertized the design has met with
<the> liberal encouragement from the public. It has been found how-
ever that the considerable expence attending the execution of engrav-
ings while it must necessarily occasion an high price being put on the
work would also considerably interfere with the authors profit which
has been already announced. The frontispiece representing (from the
Witch of Fife) a dance of Scottish witches with the fairies of Lapland is
therefore the only embellishment proposed. It is the gift of an amateur
friendly to that genius of which he himself professes no common share
the traits of whose pencil are marked by a mingled wildness gaiety and
humour happily adapted to a subject so singular
In consequence of dropping the idea of other embellishments the

Subscription price of the work is reduced from two to one guinea which the friends of the author trust may extend the subscription more widely and much more than compensate any diminution of direct emolument on single copies.

This change of <intention> the mode of publication being necessarily to be explained as well to the subscribers as to the public gives the friends <M^r> of the Ettricke Shepherd another opportunity of urging his well-merited claim to the protection and patronage of his country. He has now been frequently before the public seldom without applause and never with reproach. His efforts have been dedicated to the peculiar service of Caledonia. He has described her mountains and glens, embodied her <traditions> legends, cherished and <encouraged> preserved her decaying traditions, celebrated her heroes, and animated her public spirit. To him we <will owe> & our posterity will owe not only that much relative to Scotland has been preserved but that it has been rendered worthy of preservation and will pass down to future generations with an interest which <they> the simple legends did not in themselves possess. Above all the "Shepherd's reed" has been uniformly tuned in the cause of religion virtue moral truth & patriotic feeling. It were a disgrace to national feelings which have seldom been addressed in vain should the present appeal remain <unheard> unheeded and those who have the honor to bring it before the public confidently hope that the sum of their efforts may be to <secure> place on a permanent footing the humble independence of one who as an author and as a man merits alike their support and patronage.

The subscription edition of *The Queen's Wake* was published in 1819 as the 'fifth' edition, and a 'sixth' edition was produced at the same time for the trade. An advertisement for the sixth edition of *The Queen's Wake* appeared in the *Edinburgh Evening Courant* for 1 July 1819, and contains a line about Hogg's novel *The Brownie of Bodsbeck* (1818). There then follows a note about the subscription edition:

> *** The Author's edition of the QUEEN'S WAKE, in royal octavo, with plates, price One Guinea to subscribers, is now ready for delivery.
>
> Such of the Author's Friends as have not already sent in their names, will do so without loss of time, there being only 100 copies unsubscribed for, and on the first of August the price of the remaining copies will be raised to one guinea and a half.

Two separately printed but undated lists of subscribers' names have been inserted at the back of one of the copies of the fifth edition held by Stirling University Library (Res MAS 810.Q8, copy 2): both lists are headed 'Subscription Edition | of the | Queen's Wake'. The first runs to 8 printed pages, and is introduced as follows:

> The Author's Edition of The QUEEN'S WAKE, in royal octavo, with

plates, price ONE GUINEA, will be delivered to the Subscribers in a few days.

The following Gentlemen have subscribed to MR HOGG'S friends in Edinburgh; but Gentlemen whose names happen to be omitted will be so good as give them in to the AUTHOR, or to MR BLACKWOOD.

The list itself includes just under 200 names, but some of those listed have subscribed for multiple copies: for example 'Archibald Constable, Esq. Edinburgh, 10 copies'; 'John Murray, Esq. London, 25 copies'; Walter Scott, Esq. 20 copies'. Pasted in at the front of this Stirling copy of the fifth edition of *The Queen's Wake* is Hogg's printed and signed receipt ('N° 227', dated '1st June 1819') for the subscription of 'Mʳ Shaw Writer Cupar Fife', whose name is duly recorded in the printed list of subscribers.

The second list in this copy of *The Queen's Wake* runs to 4 printed pages. It announces that the subscription edition 'is now ready for delivery to the Subscribers', and continues:

As this Edition will belong solely to the Subscribers, and will not be printed again in the same style of elegance, it is hoped that such of the Author's Friends as have not already sent in their Names will do so without loss of time, there being only 100 Copies unsubscribed for.

The following have subscribed since the publication of the former List.

About 65 additional names are recorded.

For further details regarding the subscription copies of the fifth edition of *The Queen's Wake*, see the Blackwood Papers in the National Library of Scotland at MS 30002, fols 32–33, and also Hogg's letter to Blackwood of 10 December 1819 in Gillian Hughes's forthcoming S/SC edition of Hogg's *Letters*. (The original letter is in the National Library of Scotland at MS 4004, fols 160–61.)

I am most grateful to Dr Gillian Hughes for providing me with the manuscript transcriptions which form the basis of this Appendix.

Note on the Texts

For reasons that are set out in its Introduction, the present edition prints two versions of *The Queen's Wake*: that of the first edition of 1813, and that of the fifth edition of 1819. The processes of revision that produced the differences between these two versions are discussed in the Introduction, and significant individual differences are recorded and discussed in the Editor's Notes. This Note on the Texts focuses on the present edition's choice of copy-text for the 1813 and for the 1819 versions of Hogg's poem, and on the emendations that have been made to the two copy-texts.

The 1813 Version

The first edition of *The Queen's* Wake was published by George Goldie in 1813, but neither printer's copy nor proofs for this edition appear to have survived. However, four pages of manuscript in Hogg's hand, containing most of the text of 'Earl Walter' (the Twelfth Bard's song), survive in the James Fraser Gluck manuscript collection at the Buffalo & Erie County Public Library, New York State. It appears that this manuscript was presented to Bernard Barton by Woodthorpe Collett (a graduate of Cambridge University), and it is accompanied by a letter to Barton of 13 July 1831 in which Collett writes: 'The enclosed paper was given me by a friend at College in 1820, who had it from Thomas Moore with a statement that it came into his hands among other writings from James Hogg'. In its wording, this manuscript is very close to the first edition of *The Queen's Wake*, but shows some significant differences from the third and fifth editions. It carries no indication (such as printer's marks) to suggest that it may once have formed part of the printer's copy for the first edition. It may be Hogg had this manuscript in hand as a draft before beginning work on *The Queen's Wake*, or it may be that he transcribed it (perhaps from the first edition, and perhaps in response to a request from a collector of autograph material) after the publication of the poem. At all events, the few differences in wording between the manuscript of 'Earl Walter' and the first edition are all explicable as examples of the kind of minor variation that tends to occur when a text is being transcribed. For example, the first edition has 'girls and boys of Clyde,' (*1813*, Night the Second, l. 1114), while the manuscript has 'boys & girls of Clyde'.

Likewise, a manuscript of 'Glen-Avin' (the Ninth Bard's song) survives at the National Library of Scotland as MS 912, fols 16–17. The text in this manuscript differs significantly from the published texts, and may represent an earlier version of the poem which Hogg revised for *The Queen's Wake* (cf. Introduction, p. xxv). It is hoped that the manuscript 'Glen-Avin' will be included in a future S/SC volume devoted to Hogg's uncollected poems.

In the absence of printer's copy or proofs, the first edition is the natural choice for the copy-text for the 1813 version of *The Queen's Wake*. In the present edition the emendations that are listed below have been made to this copy-text, in order to correct what appear to be clear errors by the printer of the first edition. In this list the emended version is given first, with a reference to the present edition. The original reading of the first edition then follows.

26, l. 125 cradled] craddled
31, l. 316 Macdougal] Macdougald [See ll. 369 and 375, and later editions.]
33, l. 380 look as if] look as of
34, l. 399 won't] wont
59, l. 168 men.] man. [Has to rhyme with 'glen'.]
69, l. 519 mellifluous] melliflous
70, l. 576 hung:—] sung:—
74, l. 732 brain] brain;
82, *heading* TWELFTH BARD'S] ELEVENTH BARD'S
83, l. 1036 steed,"] stead,"
85, l. 1093 dun;] dim; [Has to rhyme with 'sun'.]
86, l. 1129 posts they sprung;] posts sprung; [Scansion.]
88, l. 1212 What] "What
88, l. 1216 "Lay on,] Lay on,
88, l. 1219 defy."] defy.
88, l. 1223 grain?—] grain?"—
96, l. 1490 But] Bnt
106, l. 48 list'ning] listning
114, l. 339 yield.] yield."
115, l. 379 meed!"] meed!
115, l. 380 "I'll] I'll
116, l. 392 "Hence] Hence
121, l. 583 me!"] me!
123, l. 632 Plora] Ploro [See Editor's Notes 123, ll. 632–35: *o* and *a* are often difficult to distinguish in Hogg's hand.]
138, l. 1168 The Southrons, baulked,] The Southron's baulked,
140, l. 1266 steed;] stead;
141, l. 1289 steed,] stead,
178 (d) accounts by contemporaries,] accounts by cotemporaries,
187 (b) take any meat.] take any meat
187 (d) seeming eagerness.] seeming eagernes.

The 1819 Version

Hogg prepared printer's copy for the fifth edition of *The Queen's Wake* (1819) by marking up a set of sheets that had been printed for the revised third edition of 1814. The resulting document survives at the National Library of Scotland as MS 20440, and the fifth edition was carefully prepared from this document by the Edinburgh printers Oliver & Boyd. In *A Critique of Modern Textual Criticism* (University of Chicago Press, 1983), Jerome McGann has argued persuasively that when an author's work begins its passage to publication, it normally undergoes 'a series of interventions which some textual critics see as a process of contamination, but which may equally well be seen as a process of training the poem for its appearances in the world' (p. 51). The training of the 1819 version of *The Queen's Wake* for its appearances in the world was done carefully and competently, and (in line with the thrust of McGann's argument) the fifth edition has therefore been chosen as the present edition's copy-text. However, the following emendations have been made to this copy-text, in order to correct what appear to be errors by the printer. In preparing these emendations, the evidence provided by NLS MS 20440 has been taken into account. For further discussion of the revisions made by Hogg in NLS MS 20440, see the Introduction (pp. lxxi–lxxiv), and the section of the Editor's Notes devoted to the 1819 version of *The Queen's Wake*.

In the list of emendations below, the emended version is given first, with page and line number referring to the present edition. The original reading of the fifth edition then follows.

206, l. 302 soothes] sooths
231, l. 590 moors] moor's
254, l. 116 day.] day,
255, l. 149 lone,] long, [Has to rhyme with 'throne'.]
256, l. 195 heard] heart
257, l. 236 Storm.] Storm,
258, l. 275 mountains] mountain
261, l. 373 resound,] resound.
273, l. 830 meek,] meek.
274, l. 854 nor rock,] or rock,
278, l. 994 shroud.] shroud,
284, l. 1231 What] "What
285, l. 1238 defy."] defy.
285, l. 1239 What] "What
285, l. 1242 grain?–] grain?"–
298, l. 1744 Queen] queen
304, l. 132 whoop] hoop
312, l. 392 "Hence] Hence
314, l. 453 the Virgin] the virgin [The lower-case *v* comes in via the third edition.]
317, l. 552 eyes,] eye,
323, l. 775 Forest] forest
328, l. 929 turmoil:] turmoil.
345, l. 1606 fright] fright,
349, l. 1737 new,] knew,
352, l. 1834 Ocean,] ocean, [Unusually, Hogg's revision in NLS MS 20440 (to a capital letter) was missed by the printer.]
354, l. 1921 Matilda] Maltilda
369, l. 325 visor,] visor

Editor's Notes

In the Notes that follow, references to the present edition's 1813 and 1819 texts of *The Queen's Wake* include page and line numbers. References to Hogg's Notes include a letter enclosed in brackets: (a) indicates that the passage found is in the first quarter of the page, while (b) refers to the second quarter, (c) to the third quarter, and (d) to the fourth quarter. Where it seems useful to discuss the meaning of particular phrases, this is done in the Notes: single words are dealt with in the Glossary. Quotations from the Bible are from the King James version, the translation most familiar to Hogg and his contemporaries. For references to plays by Shakespeare, the edition used has been *The Complete Works: Compact Edition*, ed. by Stanley Wells and Gary Taylor (Oxford: Clarendon Press, 1988). For references to other volumes of the Stirling / South Carolina Edition the editor's name is given after the title, with the abbreviation 'S/SC' and date of first publication following in parentheses. References to Sir Walter Scott's fiction are to the Edinburgh Edition of the Waverley Novels (EEWN). Mention is also frequently made of Scott's famous and influential collection of traditional ballads, *Minstrelsy of the Scottish Border* (1802–03). The first edition of the *Minstrelsy* was published in two volumes (Kelso: printed by James Ballantyne for Cadell and Davies, London; and sold by Manners and Miller, and Constable, Edinburgh, 1802). An additional third volume was included in the second edition (Edinburgh: printed by James Ballantyne for Longman and Rees, London; and sold by Manners and Miller, and Constable, Edinburgh, 1803). In the Notes below, the National Library of Scotland is abbreviated as NLS and the title of the periodical *Studies in Hogg and his World* is abbreviated as *SHW*. The Notes are greatly indebted to standard works such as *The Dictionary of National Biography* (cited as *DNB*), *The Oxford English Dictionary* (cited as *OED*), and *The Scottish National Dictionary* (cited as *SND*). References to 'Child' are to the ballad numbers in *The English and Scottish Popular Ballads*, ed. by Francis James Child, 5 vols (Boston: Houghton Mifflin, 1882–98). References to 'Kinsley' are to the poem numbers in *The Poems and Songs of Robert Burns*, ed. by James Kinsley, 3 vols (Oxford: Clarendon Press, 1968). Preparation of the Notes below has been greatly assisted by consultation of R. A. Houston and W. W. J. Knox, *The New Penguin History of Scotland* (London: Allen Lane, 2001); Michael Lynch, *Scotland: A New History* (London: Pimlico, 1992); and *The Oxford Companion to Scottish History*, ed. by Michael Lynch (Oxford: Oxford University Press, 2001). Two books frequently quoted in the Editorial Notes are referred to by the following abbreviations:

Groome: *Ordnance Gazetteer of Scotland: A Survey of Scottish Topography*, ed. by Francis H. Groome, 6 vols (Edinburgh: Jack, 1882–85) (Quotations from Groome in the Notes below are from the entries for the various places under discussion.)

Holinshed: Raphael Holinshed, *The Scottish Chronicle; or, A Complete History and Description of Scotland*, 2 vols (Arbroath: J. Findlay, 1805)

The 1813 Version of *The Queen's Wake*

1 **(Titlepage)** the epigraph is altered from ll. 8–12 of the Antistrophe of 'Ode to Fear' in William Collins, *Odes on Several Descriptive and Allegoric Subjects* (London: A. Millar, 1747), p. 8. The original passage reads:

> Dark Pow'r, with shudd'ring meek submitted Thought
> Be mine, to read the Visions old,
> Which thy awak'ning Bards have told:
> And lest thou meet my blasted View,
> Hold each strange Tale devoutly true.

3 **(Dedication)** Princess Charlotte of Wales (1796–1817), the only child of the Prince Regent (later George IV), was in her late teens when *The Queen's Wake* was first published in 1813. As Mary, Queen of Scots was likewise in her late teens when she returned to Scotland in 1561, Hogg's dedication of his poem seems apt. Princess Charlotte angered her father by breaking off her engagement to William, Prince of Orange in 1814. She married Prince Leopold of Saxe-Coburg in 1816, and died in childbirth in 1817. In 'Memoir of the Author's Life' Hogg writes of *The Queen's Wake*:

> As it related to the amusements of a young queen, I thought I could dedicate it to no one so appropriately as to her royal and beautiful descendant, the Princess Charlotte; which I did. By the advice of some friends, I got a large paper copy bound up in an elegant antique style, which cost three guineas, and sent it as a present to her Royal Highness, directing it to the care of Dr. Fisher, bishop of Salisbury, and requesting him to present it to his royal pupil. His lordship was neither at the pains to acknowledge the receipt of the work or of my letter, nor, I dare say, to deliver it as directed. The dedication I have never had the heart to cancel, even now when she is no more, and I have let the original date remain. (Hogg, *Altrive Tales*, ed. by Gillian Hughes (S/SC, 2003), p. 34: for the 'original date', see the note on 195 (Dedication), below.)

Introduction

Hogg makes use of a variety of verse forms in *The Queen's Wake*. Here, as in other parts of the linking narrative, he follows a long tradition by using iambic tetrameter couplets for narrative verse. In Scottish poetry this tradition can be traced back as far as John Barbour's fourteenth-century poem *The Bruce*, and in the early 1810s it was currently active in (for example) Walter Scott's best-selling verse narratives.

7, l. 8 **I've found my Mountain Lyre again** Hogg here declares that in *The Queen's Wake* of 1813 he is resuming his poetic career by reconnecting with the oral tradition of his native Ettrick, on which he had drawn while writing the ballads and songs of *The Mountain Bard* (1807).

7, l. 14 **by lone Saint Mary's side** St Mary's Loch, at the head of the Yarrow Valley, lies at the heart of Hogg's native district of Ettrick Forest. A medieval church dedicated to the Blessed Virgin Mary stood on the hillside above St Mary's Loch. This church features in Hogg's short story 'Mary Burnet' in *The Shepherd's Calendar*, and forms the subject of his poem 'St Mary of the Lows', which was included in *A Queer Book*. It appears that in

Hogg's day St Mary's church was ruinous, but its graveyard was still in use: see Hogg, *A Queer Book*, ed. by P. D. Garside (S/SC, 1995), pp. 254–55.

7, l. 33 With wayward fortune strove a while after achieving a modest success with *The Mountain Bard* in 1807, Hogg tried unsuccessfully to establish himself as a farmer in Dumfriesshire. Since 1810 he had been attempting (with little success) to establish himself as a professional man of letters in Edinburgh. *The Queen's Wake* (1813) was not quite the last throw of the dice for Hogg, but he badly needed a success with this poem in his struggle with wayward fortune.

8, l. 45 Harp of the Forest another indication that Hogg proposes to reconnect with the oral tradition of his native Ettrick Forest.

8, l. 48 Ettrick's green and fairy dell Hogg's maternal grandfather Will Laidlaw of Phaup was reputed to be the last man in Ettrick Forest 'who heard, saw, and conversed with the fairies': see Hogg, *The Shepherd's Calendar*, ed. by Douglas S. Mack (S/SC, 1995), p. 107.

8, l. 62 Fair daughter of Dunedin *Dunedin* is the Gaelic name for Edinburgh. In Hogg's epic poem *Queen Hynde* (1824) the narrative voice frequently addresses the 'Maid of Dunedin' as a typical representative of modern readers of poetry.

9, l. 85 Those wakes, now played by minstrels poor see Hogg's Note I, p. 177 above. *OED* indicates that Hogg uses *wake* idiosyncratically: 'used by Hogg for: A serenade, nocturnal song'.

9, l. 90 Holyrood the Palace of Holyroodhouse in Edinburgh has its origins in an Augustinian monastery founded in 1128 by David I, King of Scots, but by the time of James IV (grandfather of Mary, Queen of Scots) the royal palace at Holyrood had come to eclipse the monastery in size and importance, and the Palace of Holyroodhouse was to play a central role in the dramatic events of Mary's reign. In the twenty-first century Holyrood is still very much an active royal palace, being the official residence in Scotland of the British monarch. The new Scottish Parliament building is currently (2004) under construction at Holyrood, adjacent to the palace. Ian Gow writes: 'The Abbey of Holyrood probably took its name from its most precious relic, a fragment of the True Cross, which had been brought to Scotland by King David I's mother, St Margaret. In later medieval legend, the King founded his abbey on the spot where, while out hunting, he had a vision of a beautiful stag with a cross or "rood" between its antlers. The symbol of the abbey, and its successor the palace, is therefore a stag's head with the horns framing a cross' (Ian Gow, *The Palace of Holyroodhouse: Official Guidebook* (London: Royal Collection Enterprises, 2002), p. 10).

9, l. 91 Scotland, involved in factious broils Mary returned to Scotland in 1561 to take up personal rule (as the Catholic Queen of a newly Protestant country) at a time of turbulence with regard to the Scottish Reformation of 1560: see the present edition's Introduction, pp. xxxviii–xlviii above.

9, l. 99 scarce had Autumn's mellow hand the Queen arrived by sea at Leith (Edinburgh's port) on 19 August 1561. Working from Holinshed, Hogg gives the date as 20 August in Note II (p. 178 above).

9, l. 108 From Cheviot to the northern main Scotland's southern boundary is marked by the Cheviot Hills, and its northern boundary is marked by the ocean.

10, l. 140 A parent, husband, kingdom lost! Mary had reigned briefly as Queen Consort of France, from the accidental death of her father-in-law Henry II in July 1559 until the sudden death (from an ear infection) of her young husband, François II, in December 1560. Mary's mother Mary of Guise-Lorraine, widow of James V, had been Regent of Scotland, but died in Edinburgh Castle on 11 June 1560.

11, l. 158 A thousand silver bells were rung echoes descriptions in traditional ballads of the Fairy Queen as she rides on horseback, as for example in the second stanza of 'Thomas Rymer' (Child 37A): 'At ilka tett of her horse's mane | Hung fifty silver bells and nine'. The opening section of Book Sixth of Hogg's epic poem *Queen Hynde* invokes 'my loved muse, my Fairy Queen', and speaks of 'the bells of her palfrey's flowing mane' (*Queen Hynde*, ed. by Suzanne Gilbert and Douglas S. Mack (S/SC, 1998), p. 180). In this passage Hogg also refers to Edmund Spenser's *The Faerie Queen*, a poem which celebrates Queen Mary's cousin and rival, Queen Elizabeth of England.

11, l. 162 On rocks that seemed to prop the skies Holyrood is situated below the spectacular Salisbury Crags, which rise to 574 feet, and which feature prominently in Hogg's most famous novel, *The Private Memoirs and Confessions of a Justified Sinner* (1824).

11, l. 172 Presbyter with look severe a pointer to the coming conflicts of Mary's reign. The (Presbyterian) Church of Scotland of Hogg's day sympathised with Reformers such as John Knox in their opposition to the Catholic Mary, Queen of Scots.

11, l. 173 There rode the lords of France and Spain see Hogg's Note II, and the commentary in the Editor's Notes on 178–79 Note II.

11, l. 189 the Red Lion's haughty eye the *SND* (under *lion*) records that the red lion rampant was adopted as the royal emblem of Scotland by William the Lion (1165–1214).

12, ll. 191–92 the notes of Scottish song, | Soft pealing from the countless throng significantly, the Queen's heart, 'to nature true' (l. 197), responds warmly to the 'simple native melody' (l. 204) of 'the Caledonian lyre' (l. 207). This crucial incident looks forward to the Caledonian harp which the Queen will award to the Bard of Ettrick: see this edition's Introduction, pp. xxv–xxxiii.

12, ll. 213–20 "O! Lady dear [...] flowret die."– Gillian Hughes has noted an advertisement in the *Edinburgh Evening Courant* for 1 July 1813, which records under 'New Music' that 'O Lady Dear' (described as 'A Song from *The Queen's Wake*') is 'this day published' by Penson, Robertson of Edinburgh, as 'the first of a series from that work'. Hogg reprinted the song in *Songs by the Ettrick Shepherd* (Edinburgh: Blackwood; London: Cadell, 1831), where he noted that 'it was set to music on a single sheet by Mr Monzanni' (p. 288). However, no copy of an early song sheet of 'O! Lady Dear' is known to the present writer.

12, l. 221 good Argyle from someone, like Hogg, who was in sympathy with Mary, Queen of Scots and who was knowledgeable about the events of her reign, the 'good' here may carry a hint of irony. Mary's return to Scotland had been immediately preceded by the 'Wars of the Congregation' of 1559–60, waged by the Protestant 'Lords of the Congregation of Christ' (one of whom was the Earl of Argyll) against the Catholic Church and

forces loyal to the Queen Regent, Mary of Guise-Lorraine (mother of
Mary, Queen of Scots). Between the death of Mary of Guise-Lorraine in
June 1560 and the return of Mary, Queen of Scots in August 1561, the
Scottish Parliament (encouraged by the Lords of the Congregation) passed
the legislation that brought in the Scottish Reformation. The Wars of the
Congregation had been triggered in May 1559 when a sermon against
'idolatry', preached in Perth by the fiery Reformer John Knox, provoked
an iconoclastic riot. The Earls (later Dukes) of Argyll were Highlanders,
chiefs of the powerful Clan Campbell. They consistently supported the
Protestant and Presbyterian cause, and they were to remain troublesome
opponents of the Stuarts over several generations. Earls and Dukes of
Argyll appear elsewhere in Hogg's writings as (often morally ambiguous)
champions of the Protestant cause: see for example 'Some Remarkable
Passages in the Life of an Edinburgh Baillie' in *Tales of the Wars of Montrose*
(1835) and 'The Adventures of Captain John Lochy' in *Altrive Tales* (1832).
The long conflict between the Argyll dynasty and the Stuarts is resonantly
present in Scott's *Redgauntlet* (1824), in which the narrative reaches its memo-
rable climax when a member of the Argyll / Campbell dynasty faces down
a final (fictional) attempt in the 1760s to restore the Stuarts to the British
throne. Similarly, in Scott's novel *The Heart of Mid-Lothian* (1818) a benign
Duke of Argyll operates confidently and effectively in the 1730s, at the
heart of the power-structures of a Hanoverian Britain from which the de-
posed Stuarts have been exiled. The mention of 'good Argyle' at this point
in *The Queen's Wake* subliminally confirms the Song's hint that many trou-
bles lie ahead for Mary personally and for the Stuarts as a dynasty.

13, ll. 226–28 **Rouen's calm and generous breed, [...] the dun-deer of
the Seine** writing in 1812 in a Britain at war with Napoleonic France,
Hogg's sympathetic portrait of Mary nevertheless stresses her French back-
ground.

13, l. 238 **Feeble the strain that minstrel sung!** as a Highland aristocrat, the
Earl of Argyll rejects the song that came from the Lowland crowd, and
instead exalts the Highland tradition of poetry. In doing so, he sets out
what will prove to be the battle lines of the forthcoming contest of Queen
Mary's wake: see the present edition's Introduction, pp. xxxiv–xxxviii.

13, l. 240 **The Scottish lay from Highland bard** the attitudes of Hogg's
contemporaries towards Highland poetry were deeply influenced by the
famous *Ossian* poems of James Macpherson (1736–96): see the present
edition's Introduction, pp. xxxii–xxxiii.

13, l. 248 **Make mountain oaks to bend and weep** this calls to mind the
Greek legendary hero Orpheus, whose entrancing music made even trees
and rocks bend to listen.

14, l. 275 **"Peace, peace to Scotland's wasted vales** the reference here is to
the Wars of the Congregation of 1559–60: see note on p. 12, l. 221.

15, l. 306 **on Easter week** this connects the celebration at Queen Mary's
wake of Scotland's now neglected poetic traditions with the possibilities of
new life and resurrection associated with Easter. It also connects the wake
with the old Catholic world of medieval Scotland, rather than with the
modern Presbyterian world of Hogg's period, in which the celebration of
Easter (and Christmas) would still have been regarded by many as suspi-
ciously 'papist'. However, later in the poem it appears that Queen Mary's

wake takes place during the Christmas festivities, rather than at Easter: see, for example, p. 50, l. 955 and p. 107, l. 92.

16, l. 356 The harp of Yarrow's braken glen for much of his adult life Hogg lived in the Yarrow Valley in his native Ettrick Forest, and he died in his Yarrow home. Yarrow features in many of the best-known old oral traditional ballads, and its resulting poetic resonance is recorded in Wordsworth's 'Yarrow Unvisited', 'Yarrow Visited', and 'Yarrow Revisited'. The former poem relates to Wordsworth's 1803 tour of Scotland, and was first published in *Poems, in Two Volumes* (1807). However, Wordsworth first visited Yarrow (in Hogg's company) in 1814, and 'Yarrow Visited' was published in *Poems*, 2 vols (1815). In his 'Extempore Effusion Upon the Death of James Hogg' (1835) Wordsworth writes: 'When first, descending from the moorlands, | I saw the Stream of Yarrow glide | Across a bare and open valley, | The Ettrick Shepherd was my guide'.

16, l. 363 the Grampians the major mountain range of Highland Scotland. For further details see note on 60, ll. 169–71.

17, l. 384 plaid and bonnet blue traditional items of male Scottish dress. A *plaid* is a blanket-like garment: Highlanders wore multi-coloured tartan plaids, while the plaids of Border shepherds like Hogg were a plain grey check. A *blue bonnet* was a flat-topped round cap, without a snout. The term was often associated with a Scotsman as the wearer of such a cap, and especially with Scottish Covenanters and Presbyterians, and with marauders (*SND*).

18, ll. 443–44 To bear the prize [...] | To [...] Italy this echoes the expressions of regret, characteristic of eighteenth-century Scottish poetry, about the ousting of traditional Scottish songs by fashionable Italian music: see for example Robert Fergusson's 'Elegy, On the Death of Scots Music' and John Skinner's 'Tullochgorum'. Such sentiments are also expressed in Hogg's Preface in his book of songs *The Forest Minstrel* (1810). However, Hogg's lines here also point to David Rizzio, one of the most notorious members of Queen Mary's court circle: see note on 23, l. 20.

Night the First

23, l. 20 Rizzio the appearance at the wake of Queen Mary's influential Italian secretary, David Rizzio or Riccio (1533?–1566) is another reminder of troubles ahead. Mary married her cousin Lord Darnley in 1565, but in 1566 Darnley and a group of Protestant assassins murdered Rizzio in the Queen's private apartments at Holyrood. The murder took place while the Queen was six months pregnant, but her child (the future James VI of Scotland and I of England) was born safely in due course. David Rizzio was born *c.* 1533 near Turin, the son of a musician, from whom he received a good musical education. Having spent time in the service of the Archbishop of Turin, and later of the Duke of Savoy, he accompanied the Marquis of Moretto (ambassador of the Duke of Savoy) to Scotland in the autumn of 1561. Queen Mary 'being at this time in need of a bass singer to complete the quartette in her private chapel, Riccio was recommended to her by the marquis, and, giving special satisfaction, was retained in the queen's service as "valet de chambre"' (*DNB*).

Malcolm of Lorn

For Rizzio's song, the rhythm and rhyme-scheme become more elaborate,

showy, and irregular: iambic and anapestic rhythms alternate, there is fre-
quent use of feminine rhyme, and in each stanza quatrains alternate with
runs of couplets. Rizzio's stanza form can be seen as a flashy variant of
traditional 'rhyme royal', in which each stanza consists of a quatrain dove-
tailed with two couplets in the pattern *ababbcc*. In accordance with what the
Queen has in mind for the wake, Rizzio produces a song that tells a Scot-
tish story. He also contrives to pay a compliment to the Earl of Argyll,
chief of the Clan Campbell (see note on 12, l. 221), by placing the events
of the tale in Lorn, a district of the Western Highlands that forms part of
the territory of Clan Campbell. Since before Hogg's day, the eldest son of
the Duke of Argyll has been given the title of Marquis of Lorn.

24, ll. 31, 46 Ora's verdant steep [...] Ann of Glen-Ora it may be that
Rizzio's 'Ora' is an echo of the name of Ossian's famous 'Falls of Lora',
which are traditionally identified with tidal rapids near the mouth of Loch
Etive in Lorn. If 'Ora' is indeed merely an echo of 'Falls of Lora', then
Rizzio (appropriately enough) does not seem to share the secure and de-
tailed grasp of the geography of Scotland shown by the Scottish competi-
tors at the wake.

24, l. 41 Her joy is fled like the flower of the vale Rizzio returns to the
theme and imagery of the Song that moved the Queen in the Introduction.

27, l. 162 the steeps of Jura one of the largest of the Western Isles, Jura lies
to the south of Lorn. Its landscape includes two hills ('the Paps of Jura'),
said to take the form of a woman's breasts.

30, l. 263 Next in the list was Gardyn's name Hogg's poem has two prize
harps, based on two old Scottish harps which in Hogg's day were in the
possession of the Robertson family 'in the house of Lude, in the Highlands
of Perthshire': these two harps are now (2004) preserved in the National
Museum of Scotland, in Edinburgh, and they are discussed in the present
edition's Introduction, pp. xxviii–xxix. One of these harps, the aristocratic
'Harp of Queen Mary', had been presented by Mary, Queen of Scots to
'Miss Beatrix Gardyn, daughter of Mr Gardyn of Banchory'. The Second
Bard of *The Queen's Wake* is doubtless called Gardyn in reference to the link
between the 'Harp of Queen Mary' and the Gardyns of Banchory.

30, l. 282 A rose beneath a thistle bowed the rose is the emblem of Eng-
land, and the thistle is the emblem of Scotland. In line with Katie Trumpener's
thesis in *Bardic Nationalism*, Gardyn has a harp that associates him with an
aristocratic Scottish bardic tradition devoted to resisting the assimilation of
Scottish culture to English norms (see the present edition's Introduction, p.
xxvii).

Young Kennedy

As is the case in 'Malcolm of Lorn', the stanzas of 'Young Kennedy' are
numbered and consist of quatrains followed by sets of couplets. However,
in Gardyn's song this pattern is much more disciplined than in Rizzio's, as
Gardyn's stanzas regularly have a single quatrain followed by two couplets.
'Young Kennedy' owes a debt to the Gothic poems in *Tales of Wonder; Written
and Collected by M. G. Lewis*, 2 vols (London: J. Bell, 1801), a celebrated
collection which includes Scott's Gothic poems 'Glenfinlas' and 'The Wild
Huntsmen' as well as Burns's 'Tam o' Shanter' and traditional ballads of
the supernatural such as 'Tam Lin' and 'Sweet William's Ghost' (Child 39
and 77). For 'Young Kennedy', Hogg seems to have 'Glenfinlas' particularly

in mind—like 'Young Kennedy', Scott's poem is a tale of seduction and supernatural death set in 'the Highlands of Perthshire' (*Tales of Wonder*, I, 122). Hogg mentions 'Glenfinlas' in the final paragraph of the first letter (addressed to Scott) of 'A Journey Through the Western Highlands and Islands of Scotland on the months of May, June, July, and August. A.D. 1803' (Stirling University Library, MS 25 box 1 (2), notebook 1 fol. 11– notebook 3 fol. 4 (notebook 1 fols 14–15):

> At Kilmahogg, a paltry village about a mile beyond Callender, I parted with Macmillan; and crossing the Teith, turned to the left: you may guess that I was glad at getting safely past from this village, for its name signifies, *the burial place of Hogg*. [...] I proceeded several miles without meeting with any thing remarkable. I went quite out of my road to see Glenfinlas, merely because it was the scene of a poem in which I delighted; but could see nothing more than in other glen's; the hills were covered with mist down to the middle, yet I saw enough to convince me that it was an excellent sheep range.

31, l. 293 Kennedy 'Ulric Kennedy went from Carrick at an early period and settled in Lochaber, from whom and his followers are descended the Mac Ulrics of that country, who put themselves under the leading of the Camerons. They were accounted rather a lawless race, and a song composed by one of this clan, when in prison for cattle-stealing, is very popular in the Highlands' (James Logan, *McIan's Costumes of the Clans of Scotland* (Glasgow: Bryce, 1899), pp. 260–61): cf. note on 32, l. 356.

31, l. 316 Proscribed, and by gallant Macdougal expelled perhaps intended to suggest the MacDonells or Macdonnells of Glengarry, without explicitly linking that famous Highland family with the Gothic horrors of 'Young Kennedy': see note on 32, l. 356.

31, l. 317 Where rolls the dark Teith through the valley of Down the Teith, a major tributary of the Forth, rises in the Highlands. It features prominently in Scott's 'Glenfinlas' (see headnote on 'Young Kennedy', above), and is probably introduced in 'Young Kennedy' for that reason. The Perthshire village of Doune ('Down') lies near the Highland / Lowland border, to the west of Stirling. Doune Castle (which is associated with 'The Bonny Earl of Murray', Child 181) overlooks the Teith, and dates from the late fourteenth century. It has been a possession of Stuarts throughout its history. The Perthshire location of Gardyn's 'Young Kennedy' helps to connect this bard and his song with Queen Mary's Harp, the House of Lude in 'the Highlands of Perthshire', and the Gardyns of Banchory (see note on 30, l. 263).

32, l. 354 The flower of the valley is nipt in the bloom! like Rizzio, Gardyn provides a variation on the theme and imagery of the Song ('O! Lady dear') in the Introduction.

32, l. 356 thy native Glengary there is a Glengarry in western Inverness-shire, of which Groome records (under 'Glengarry'): 'From the beginning of the 16th century Glengarry was held by the Macdonnells, the last of whose chiefs, Col. Alexander Ranaldson Macdonnell, maintained to the day of his death (1828) the style of living of his ancestors, and is deemed the prototype of Fergus Mac Ivor in *Waverley*'. This Glengarry is in the vicinity of Lochaber: see note on 31, l. 293. However, there may also be a reference here to the Perthshire Glengarry (see Groome under 'Garry'), as

Hogg's Note XXIII locates Queen Mary's Harp 'in the house of Lude, on the banks of the Garry in Athol'. Lude lies a little to the north of the Perthshire village of Blair Atholl, which is on the River Garry in the Highland district of Atholl. Nearby is Blair Castle, seat of the Dukes of Atholl, members of the Murray family.

33, ll. 359–61 yon magpie [...] yon white doves traditionally, the magpie (a member of the crow family) is regarded as a bird of ill omen, while doves are emblematic of the Holy Spirit. This connects with Hogg's story 'Tibby Johnston's Wraith', which draws on the traditional belief that crows will come to take away the souls of recently-deceased persons destined for hell, while doves will collect those destined for heaven: see Hogg, *Winter Evening Tales*, ed. by Ian Duncan (S/SC, 2002), p. 505.

33, l. 364 Abel's green arbour Genesis 4 records that Abel, 'a keeper of sheep' and the second son of Adam and Eve, became the world's first murder victim when killed by his older brother Cain, 'a tiller of the ground'.

33, l. 365 a messenger wraith 'when a wraith is seen before death, that is a spirit sent to conduct the dying person to its new dwelling [...] Now, when the wraith appears after death, that's the soul o' the deceased, that gets liberty to appear to the ane of a' its acquaintances that is the soonest to follow it; and it does that just afore it leaves this world for the last time; and that's the true doctrine o' wraiths' (Hogg, 'Tibby Johnston's Wraith', in *Winter Evening Tales*, ed. by Ian Duncan (S/SC, 2002), p. 505). In his 'Memoir of the Author's Life' Hogg records that his own wraith was seen during a serious illness, but he nevertheless recovered: see *Altrive Tales*, ed. by Gillian Hughes (S/SC, 2003), p. 20.

33, l. 368 Why were they not called to their morning devotion? the head of the family would normally be expected to call the household together for morning and evening prayers.

33, l. 387 Aberfoyle the clachan (village) of Aberfoyle lies about thirteen miles west of Doune. It features in Scott's *Rob Roy* (published December 1817).

34, l. 419 Strath-Allan, Glen-Ogle an example of the Scottish practice of referring to landowners by the names of their estates. Strathallan, in Perthshire, is the valley of the Allan Water, and forms a natural route in a north-easterly direction from the vicinity of Doune. Glen Ogle ('the valley of dread'), also in Perthshire, lies about twelve miles to the north-west of Doune, and forms part of the natural route from Doune towards the north and west.

34, l. 424 You stood with Macdonald and Archbald the grim two of the major Scottish aristocrats of the later fourteenth century: Archibald the Grim, third Earl of Douglas (d. 1400), was an extremely powerful figure in southern Scotland, while John Macdonald, Lord of the Isles and Earl of Ross (d. 1388) held sway in the Islands and Central Highlands. For a survey of the inter-connections and rivalry between their families, see Ranald Nicholson, *Scotland: The Later Middle Ages*, The Edinburgh History of Scotland, 2 (Edinburgh: Mercat Press, 1974; repr. 1997).

37, l. 491 shepherd of Braco the village of Braco is in Strathallan (see note on 34, l. 419). It appears that Young Kennedy is heading in the direction of the Perthshire Glengarry: see note on 32, l. 356.

37, l. 492 The piles of Glen-Ardochy massive earthworks, the remains of a

Roman fort, are situated at Ardoch near Braco.

37, l. 504 dig a lone grave on the top of yon mountain for the practice of burying suicides on hilltops, see Peter Garside's note '171(a) customary in the south of Scotland', in Hogg, *The Private Memoirs and Confessions of a Justified Sinner*, ed. by P. D. Garside (S/SC, 2001), pp. 252–53.

37, ll. 521–22 when these I sung | On Ettrick banks we have had a song from Italy and a song from the Highlands, but in this section of the linking narrative the focus moves to the Lowlands, and Hogg here presents himself as a product and inheritor of the old Lowland tradition of oral poetry to be found in the Borders 'On Yarrow's banks and braes of Tweed' (l. 516).

38, l. 545 The fifth was from a western shore the present writer owns a copy of the fifth edition (1819) of *The Queen's Wake* presented by Hogg to his nephew James Gray (see Alan Grant, 'A Presentation Copy of *The Queen's Wake*', *Newsletter of the James Hogg Society*, 8 (1989), 21–22). In manuscript annotations in this copy, Hogg gives the name of the modern Scottish poets on whom the descriptions of some of the Bards of *The Queen's Wake* are based, and the name given for the fifth bard is 'Mr John Morison'. This is presumably John Morrison (1782–1853), surveyor and artist, and a native of Kirkcudbrightshire in Galloway. Morrison, who undertook a survey of Scott's Abbotsford estate in 1819–20, describes visiting Hogg during Hogg's Dumfriesshire years (1805–09) in 'Random Reminiscences of Sir Walter Scott, of the Ettrick Shepherd, of Sir Henry Raeburn, &c., &c.— No. 1', *Tait's Edinburgh Magazine*, 10 (September 1843), 569–78 (pp. 573–74). It appears that, before the publication of *Marmion* (1808), Scott read over breakfast 'the two middle cantos' of his poem to Hogg, Morrison, and John Grieve (three 'great enthusiasts' for poetry): see Hogg, *Anecdotes of Scott*, ed. by Jill Rubenstein (S/SC, 1999), pp. 24–25, 54–55, 104. Hogg also mentions Morrison in the section of his 'Reminiscences of Former Days' devoted to Allan Cunningham: see Hogg, *Altrive Tales*, ed. by Gillian Hughes, (S/SC, 2003), p. 71. According to *The Bards of Galloway: A Collection of Poems, Songs, Ballads &c. by Natives of Galloway*, ed. by Malcolm M. Harper (Dalbeattie: Thomas Fraser, 1889), Morrison studied painting under Nasmyth of Edinburgh; he published a small volume of *Poems* in 1832; and he was 'famed for his pointed satiric remarks' (p. 253). There is a note about Morrison in *The Letters of Sir Walter Scott*, ed. H. J. C. Grierson, 12 vols (London: Constable: 1932–37), VI, 456–57. In her forthcoming S/SC edition of Hogg's *Letters*, and in her forthcoming biography of Hogg, Gillian Hughes will discuss evidence that suggests that in 1809 Hogg and Morrison may have been rival lovers of Margaret Beattie while Hogg was farming at Locherben in Dumfriesshire, and that later in the 1810s Hogg was irritated by the flattering behaviour of Morrison towards his bride-to-be, Margaret Phillips. See also the present edition's Introduction, p. xv.

38, ll. 546, 552, 560 Orr [...] Ken [...] Galloway the geographical references in the description of the fifth bard indicate that he comes from Galloway, the extreme south-western corner of Scotland: Urr ('Orr') and Ken are rivers of Galloway.

38, l. 558 "Fair Margaret" a reference to the traditional oral ballad 'Fair Margaret and Sweet William' (Child 74). There may also be a reference to Hogg's lover Margaret Beattie: see note on 38, l. 545.

39, l. 573 The sixth 'The Revd William Gillespie', according to Hogg's anno-
tated copy. William Gillespie (1776–1825) was minister of Kells in Gallo-
way, where his father John (a friend of Burns) had been his predecessor. In
1805 William Gillespie published *The Progress of Refinement: An Allegorical
Poem, with Other Poems*, and he was also a contributor to Hogg's periodical
The Spy: see *The Spy*, ed. by Gillian Hughes (S/SC, 2000), pp. 561–62.

39, l. 574 western Dee the Dee is a river of Kirkcudbrightshire, in Galloway,
and part of its course lies in the parish of Kells (see note on 39, l. 573). This
river is not to be confused with the river Dee which rises in the Cairngorm
Mountains and enters the sea at Aberdeen in north-east Scotland (see note
on 57, l. 78).

39, l. 575 Where Summer spreads her purple screen when the heather
blooms on the moors.

39, l. 581 Lochryan's hapless maid the reference is to the traditional oral
ballad 'The Lass of Roch Royal' (Child 76), published by Scott as 'The Lass
of Lochroyan' in the second volume of *Minstrelsy of the Scottish Border* (1802–
03). Loch Ryan is a large arm of the sea on the western coast of Galloway.

39, l. 588 "shivering at the chin." I am indebted to Janette Currie for point-
ing out to me that Hogg is here quoting from the traditional oral ballad
'The Mother's Malison, or, Clyde's Water' (see Child 216 C, stanza 14).
Child notes that 'the passage [...] in which the mother, pretending to be her
daughter, repels the lover, and the daughter, who has dreamed that her
lover had come and had been refused admittance, is told by her mother
that this had actually happened, and sets off in pursuit of her lover, seems
to have been adopted from "The Lass of Roch Royal", No. 76' (see note
on 39, l. 581 above).

39, ll. 591–93 The eighth was from the Leven coast [...] bard of Fife Loch
Leven is a large freshwater loch in eastern Scotland, lying in the small
county of Kinross but immediately adjacent to the county of Fife, home of
this bard. (Fife lies to the north of Edinburgh, across the estuary of the
River Forth.) This mention of Loch Leven is another veiled reference to
troubles to come for Queen Mary. In 1566 Rizzio had been murdered, in
the presence of the pregnant Queen, by a group including her husband
Darnley (see note on 23, l. 20). Darnley was himself murdered in February
1567. The Earl of Bothwell was widely suspected, and Mary lost much
support when she married Bothwell in May 1567. A coalition of Catholic
and Protestant nobles confronted the Queen in June 1567. As a result
Bothwell was exiled, and Mary was imprisoned in Lochleven Castle for the
best part of a year. Early in her imprisonment here, in July 1567, she was
forced to abdicate, after which her infant son was crowned without delay at
Stirling as James VI. Being situated on an island in a large loch, Lochleven
Castle was a secure prison. Nevertheless, Mary managed to escape in May
1568 with the help of Willie Douglas, who looked after the castle's boats.
The Queen quickly raised a large army, but she was defeated at the battle
of Langside. She then fled to England to seek shelter from her cousin
Queen Elizabeth, but what she in fact found in England was imprisonment
and eventual execution.

40, l. 610 Benarty's this hill lies immediately to the south of Loch Leven.

40, l. 611 wild wood notes echoes Milton, 'L' Allegro': 'Then to the well-trod
stage anon, | If Jonson's learned sock be on, | Or sweetest Shakespeare

fancy's child | Warble his native wood-notes wild' (ll. 131–34). The Eighth
Bard is being associated with the inspired natural spontaneity of Shake-
speare, as opposed to the more laboured learning of Ben Jonson. Burns
used the motto 'wood notes wild' on his seal.

40, l. 617 Of mountain ash his harp was framed the mountain ash or
rowan was believed to provide protection against witchcraft and the super-
natural.

The Witch of Fife

This song is sung by a Bard who 'Held worldly pomp in high derision' (l.
615), and exhibits its credentials as a poem of the people by using the
'ballad stanza'–that is, a four-line stanza which alternates four-beat and
three-beat lines. As well as being used in the traditional oral ballads with
which Hogg grew up, it is also used in famous Romantic-era ballad imita-
tions such as Coleridge's 'The Rime of the Ancient Mariner'. Interestingly,
the central female characters of the previous two songs of Night the First
are victims of male inadequacy or ferocity, but in the Eighth Bard's de-
motic and subversive song the Witch is Queen of the Revels in Lapland
and Carlisle, and is very much in control of her own destiny. In this song it
is not the Witch but her greedy and drunken husband who emerges as
victim when he is burned 'skin and bone' (l. 884). For Hogg's traditional
sources for 'The Witch of Fife' see his Note IV (p. 179), and the note below
on p. 179, Note IV.

41, l. 644 Kilmerrin kirk Kilmaron Hill lies about two miles north-west of
the town of Cupar in Fife. James Wilkie writes: 'Another interesting, if
somewhat mysterious, Irish saint is S. Ronan, identified by Skene with the
Abbot of Kingarth in Bute. [...] The lands of Kilmaron, near Cupar, "the
church of my own Ron," after the affectionate Celtic fashion, still tell of the
chapel that stood there, and the ruins of which could be traced less than a
century and a half ago': see Wilkie's *The History of Fife from the Earliest Times
to the Nineteenth Century* (Edinburgh: Blackwood, 1924), p. 64.

41, l. 660 to the Lommond height the Lomond Hills (East Lomond, West
Lomond, and Bishop Hill) lie immediately to the east of Loch Leven,
partly in Kinross and partly in Fife (see note on 39, ll. 591–93). According
to local tradition, 'Carlin Maggie' was 'the head of a coven of witches whose
favourite meeting place was the gorge cleft between the West Lomond and
the Bishop Hill': see James Wilkie, *Bygone Fife North of the Lomonds* (Edin-
burgh: Moray Press, 1938), pp. 10–11. For West Lomond as a scene of
diabolic supernatural activity in another Hogg text, see *The Private Memoirs
and Confessions of a Justified Sinner*, ed. by P. D. Garside (S/SC, 2001), p. 137.

43, l. 725 the Doffrinis steep the Dovre Fjeld mountain range in Norway.

43, l. 729 Lapland a possible echo of *Paradise Lost*. In Book II of Milton's
poem, Satan encounters his progeny Sin and Death at the gates of Hell as
he sets out to subvert the newly-created Earth, in which Adam and Eve are
still relishing the joys of Eden. The figure of Sin is being tormented by hell-
hounds, her own progeny. These hell-hounds are compared to the beings
who 'follow the Night-hag', when

> riding through the air she comes
> Lured with the smell of infant blood, to dance
> With Lapland witches.   (ll. 662–65)

44, ll. 747–48 On every cliff a herpe they hang, | On every tree a lyre this points to the Eolian harp, a stringed instrument that produces a musical sound when the wind passes over the strings. For the Romantics, the Eolian harp was a symbol of poetic inspiration, and in *Queen Hynde* (1824) Hogg goes out of his way to associate his own poetry ('an uncouth harp of olden key') with the natural (as opposed to artificial) poetry of the Eolian harp: see *Queen Hynde*, ed. by Suzanne Gilbert and Douglas S. Mack (S/SC, 1998), p. xl. The Eolian harp is likewise evoked elsewhere in *The Queen's Wake*: see for example Night the Second *1813* ll. 765–69, and Conclusion *1813* ll. 390–93. There is also an echo here of the opening of Psalm 137: 'By the rivers of Babylon, there we sat down, yea, we wept, when we remembered Zion. We hanged our harps upon the willows in the midst thereof'.

44, l. 758 our master true the Devil.

45, l. 785 the sandy ford suggests the landscape of the Solway Firth, which lies to the north of Carlisle and which marks part of the boundary between Scotland and England.

45, l. 787 Ettrick Pen a mountain at the head of the Ettrick Valley, adjacent to Phaup, the home of Hogg's grandfather Will Laidlaw (see note on 8, l. 48). Hogg associates Ettrick Pen with witchcraft in his poem 'The Wyffe of Ezdel-more': see *A Queer Book*, ed. by P. D. Garside (S/SC, 1995), pp. 1–28 and 226–30.

45, l. 791 the hillis of Braid the Braid Hills lie immediately to the south of Edinburgh.

45, l. 793 gurly James Scotland had seven Stuart kings called James, so this is in a sense a generic figure. However, a specific reference may be intended to James IV, grandfather of Mary, Queen of Scots. In 'Mary Burnet' Hogg writes that in the reign of James IV 'fairies, brownies, and witches, were at the rifest in Scotland': see *The Shepherd's Calendar*, ed. by Douglas S. Mack (S/SC, 1995), p. 212.

49, l. 930 the tall cliffs of Salsbury stood for the Salisbury Crags, see note on 11, l. 162.

50, l. 952 That chapel wake presumably an indication that the wake is held in the large public space provided by the chapel (abbey church) which stands adjacent to the palace at Holyrood, and in which Mary's marriages to Darnley and to Bothwell took place. This building was also used for the Scottish coronation of Charles I in 1633, but it is now ruinous.

50, l. 956 The dedication of the rood possibly a reference to the naming of Holyrood (see note on 9, l. 90). However, it appears that Hogg originally envisaged Queen Mary's wake as taking place at Easter, but later changed to Christmas: see note on 15, l. 306. I am indebted to Gillian Hughes for a suggestion that this line may therefore be a survival of a reference to the Catholic tradition of veneration of the cross (*rood*) on Good Friday.

50, l. 957 routs and revels gay in the lines that follow, the festivities of Hogg's Edinburgh are contrasted with those of the 1560s. *OED* defines *rout* (9) as 'a fashionable gathering or assembly, a large evening party or reception, much in vogue in the eighteenth and early nineteenth centuries'.

50–51, ll. 973–78 Sweet be her home, [...] list his lay! I am grateful to Gillian Hughes for pointing out to me that these five lines show a marked resemblance to the first four lines of a twelve-line poem that Hogg has inscribed (in pencil) on the leaf facing the half-title, in a copy (now in the

Fales Library & Special Collections, New York University) of the sixth edition (1807; first edition 1805) of Scott's *The Lay of the Last Minstrel*. Hogg's manuscript poem thanks the woman who lent him this book, apparently during his Dumfriesshire years (1805–1809). The half-title of the Fales volume carries on its fly-leaf the ink inscription 'To Mrs Thomson | from her attached friend L. C. | 10th May 1808.–'. The existence of this manuscript poem tends to confirm Hogg's suggestion in 'Memoir of the Author's Life' that, while writing *The Queen's Wake* in 1812, he was able to draw on a body of verse he had already composed: see the present edition's Introduction, p. xxv.

Night the Second

55, ll. 24–28 The mass was said, [...] Close from the zealot's searching eyes here, as elsewhere in *The Queen's Wake*, Hogg shows an unexpected tendency to sympathise with Mary's Catholicism against Knox's reforming zeal: see the present edition's Introduction, pp. xxxviii–xlviii.

56, l. 48 Farquhar, from the hills of Spey the entry for the Farquharsons in James Logan, *McIan's Costumes of the Clans of Scotland* (Glasgow: Bryce, 1899) begins as follows (see pp. 46–47):

> This is a division of the great Clan Chattan, and they are derived by their family historians and current traditions from Shah of Rothiemurchus in Strathspey, who was lineally descended from the ancient Thanes of Fife. [...] Fearchar, son of Shah, lived in the reigns of Robert II. and III., and married a daughter of Patrick Mac Dhoncha', ancestor of the Robertsons of Lude, by whom he left a son Donald, who likewise married a Robertson, of the Calveen family. [...] from Fearchar the clan receives the appellation Mac'earchar or Farquharson.

Rothiemurchus lies in the upper valley of the river Spey, below the Cairngorm Mountains that will provide the setting for this bard's song. Clearly, 'Farquhar, from the hills of Spey' is a representative of the ancient and aristocratic Highland bardic tradition symbolised by the Harp of Queen Mary.

56, l. 51 Loch Avin's shore Loch Avon is situated in wild and remote country in the Cairngorm Mountains, near the mountains of Cairn Gorm and Ben MacDui. It lies about five miles to the south of Rothiemurchus (see note on 56, l. 48).

56, l. 52 dark Glen-More is immediately adjacent to Rothiemurchus (see note on 56, l. 48).

Glen-Avin

Glen Avon, the valley of the River Avon, runs eastward from Loch Avon in the Cairngorm Mountains, and in his Note V (pp. 179–80) Hogg writes that it exceeds all other parts of the Highlands 'in what may be termed stern and solemn grandeur'. For details of a visit Hogg made to Glen Avon in 1802 see his Note V and the note below on 179–80, Note V.

57, l. 78 The infant rills of Highland Dee this river Dee rises near Ben MacDui in the Cairngorm mountains and enters the sea at Aberdeen in north-east Scotland: see note on 39, l. 574.

57, l. 82 One mountain rears his mighty form Ben MacDui is the highest mountain in the area, and the second highest mountain in Scotland after Ben Nevis.

57, l. 86 the wain a group of seven bright stars in the constellation Ursa Major is commonly called Charles's Wain, or the Plough.

58, l. 102 the fahm a mis-rendering of Gaelic *famh*. Glen Avon lies in the Banffshire parish of Kirkmichael, and confirmation of Hogg's account of beliefs about this creature (see his Note VI, p. 180) is to be found in the Rev. John Grant's entry for this parish in Sir John Sinclair, *The Statistical Account of Scotland*, 21 vols (Edinburgh: Creech, 1791–99), XII, 425–74 (p. 449). Likewise, in a discussion of 'Head-Ill' in *The Shepherd's Guide: Being a Practical Treatise on the Diseases of Sheep* (Edinburgh: Constable; London: Murray, 1807), Hogg writes (pp. 114–15):

> But on the mountains around Cairn-Gorm and Lochavin, its attacks are so visible on those sheep that feed on the tops of the hills, that the natives, in their usual superstitious way, ascribe it to a præternatural, and very singular cause. They say, that a most deformed little monster inhabits the very tops of these mountains, whom they call *Phaam*: that it is very seldom seen; but whenever it is seen, it is early on the morning, immediately after the break of day; that his head is larger than his whole body; that his intents are evil and dangerous; that he is no earthly creature; and if any living man, or animal, come near the place where he has been, before the sun shine upon it, the head of that man, or animal, will immediately swell, and bring on its death in great pain; and that his baneful influences are often very severely felt amongst their flocks.

Hogg goes on to speculate that the head-ill is 'occasioned by some poisonous herbage that grows on these heights; for surely no reptile can chuse them for their residence' (p. 115). In his account of his 1802 Highland journey, Hogg records that his guide in Glen Avon 'told me likewise of a little deformed monster, whose head was larger than its whole body, which was sometimes seen on the tops of these mountains very early in the morning, of so banefull a nature, that it was certain death to come near it, or even to touch the ground where it had passed, unless the sun had first shone upon it': see 'The Unpublished Conclusion of James Hogg's 1802 Highland Journey', ed. by H. B. de Groot, *SHW*, 6 (1995), 55–66 (p. 56).

58, l. 106 Ossian For Hogg's contemporaries, mention of Highland poetry would immediately have called to mind the *Ossian* poems of James Macpherson (1736–96). These were allegedly translations of third-century Gaelic epics by the blind warrior-bard Ossian, but were vigorously denounced as fakes and forgeries by no less a figure than Dr Samuel Johnson. Nevertheless, Macpherson's *Ossian* poems were profoundly influential, and their many enthusiastic admirers included Napoleon. While they are not, as claimed, literal translations of third-century epics, Macpherson's *Ossian* texts nevertheless draw heavily on genuine Gaelic traditions and poems, and in them can be traced some of the first stirrings of European Romanticism. Macpherson grew up in Badenoch, which forms part of the valley of the Spey a little above Rothiemurchus: see note on 56, l. 48. In his entry on Kirkmichael in *The Statistical Account of Scotland* (see note on 58, l. 102), the Rev. John Grant writes of Glen Avon:

In the Gaelic, the vernacular idiom, it is called Strath-ath-fhin, from "Strath," a dale, "ath," a ford, and "Fin," the hero Fingal, so highly celebrated in the Poems of Ossian. It is generally written Strath-avan, avan being the appellative for a river; but the former etymon approaches much nearer to the provincial pronunciation. (pp. 425–26)

In his account of his 1802 Highland journey (see note on 58, l. 102) Hogg writes: 'This river, which in the gaelic they pronounce Adh-fion, the inhabitants say, received its name from the unfortunate circumstance of Fingal losing his consort there, who was drowned in crossing that impetous stream' (*SHW*, 6 (1995), p. 55). For a valuable discussion of Hogg and Macpherson see Valentina Bold, 'The Mountain Bard: James Hogg and Macpherson's Ossian', *SHW*, 9 (1998), 32–44.

59–61, ll. 149–204 Who was it reared [...] Avin eagles sing. Hogg quotes these lines (omitting ll. 153–60) in 'Storms' (1819): see Hogg, *The Shepherd's Calendar*, ed. by Douglas S. Mack (S/SC, 1995), pp. 19–21. In 'Storms', Hogg recounts his experiences as a shepherd during the great snow-storm that disrupted the meeting of his 'literary society' in 1794: see the present edition's Introduction, p. xxi.

60, ll. 169–71 The Grampians [...] Ben-Nevis the Grampians are the mountains that form the boundary between Highland and Lowland Scotland, and the Cairngorm Mountains form part of the central Grampians. Ben Nevis, the highest mountain in Britain, is situated in the Grampians near Fort William, and lies to the west of the Cairngorms.

60, ll. 173–80 Yarrow's fairy dale [...] Lowthers [...] Hartfell [...] Cheviot [...] Northumberland see Hogg's Note VII (pp. 180–81). Here the focus shifts south, to the border region between Scotland and England. Yarrow is a river of Ettrick Forest, and during the 1790s Hogg worked as a shepherd in the Yarrow valley. The Lowthers are a range of hills in southern Scotland, partly in Lanarkshire and partly in Dumfriesshire. Hartfell is a mountain near Moffat in Dumfriesshire. Northumberland is the county that occupies the extreme north-eastern corner of England.

61, l. 217 See yon lone cairn see Hogg's Note VIII (p. 181).

62, l. 238 fraught with rays of Celtic fire this reminder that 'Glen-Avin' exemplifies the poetry of the Celtic Highlands sets up a contrast with the next poem, which exemplifies the very different poetic tradition of the Borders.

62, l. 248 And late from native moors exiled needless to say, the Bard of Ettrick is a portrait of Hogg himself, and is recorded as such in Hogg's annotated copy. Most of *The Queen's Wake* was written in 1812, and as recently as 1810 Hogg had come to Edinburgh to try to establish himself as a professional writer, a move undertaken because he could not obtain work as a shepherd in his native Ettrick: see Introduction, p. xv.

62, l. 266 sow the moor with purple grain much of Ettrick is moorland, which in late summer and early autumn is covered with beautiful but unproductive purple heather flowers. Much of the moorland of Ettrick Forest was (and is) the property of the Dukes of Buccleuch, and in his 'Reminiscences of Former Days' Hogg quotes an old rhyme: 'Had heather-bells been corn of the best, | The Buccleuch mill would have had a noble grist'. See Hogg, *Altrive Tales*, ed. by Gillian Hughes (S/SC, 2003), pp. 62, 250.

62, l. 274 the lonely Lowes the Loch of the Lowes, which is adjacent to St

Mary's Loch at the head of the Yarrow valley, was one of Hogg's favourite places in his native Ettrick Forest. A large Victorian statue of Hogg over-looks the narrow spit of land which separates the two lochs. Tibbie Shiel's Inn (a frequent Hogg haunt) is situated here.

63, ll. 280–81 the Saint Mary. | The pilot swan another reference to St Mary's Loch, and an echo of Wordsworth's 'Yarrow Unvisited' (composed 1803, published 1807): 'Let [...] | The Swan on still St Mary's Lake | Float double, Swan and Shadow!'. Likewise, the feast in Canto Sixth of Scott's *Lay of the Last Minstrel* (1805) consists in part of 'cygnet from St Mary's wave' (stanza VI).

63, l. 302 *Naturæ Donum* this Latin phrase means 'the gift of nature', and it seems clear that Hogg (as a self-educated writer) felt that it expressed the character of his own poetic talent. When he sealed his letters, Hogg (as a kind of signature) was in the habit of impressing the sealing wax with the words 'Naturæ Donum', and the image of a harp entwined with wild flow-ers. He also used these words and that image on his book labels. In what is clearly a deeply-felt passage at the end of Book 1 of *Queen Hynde* (1824), Hogg associates his poetry with Nature rather than Art, and compares it to the wild flowers of the moors rather than the cultivated flowers of a gar-den.

Old David

See Hogg's Note IX, pp. 181–82. This song, sung by the bard who repre-sents Hogg himself (see note on 62, l. 248), adopts the metrical pattern of the linking narrative of *The Queen's Wake*.

63, ll. 308–10 Wonfell's wizard brae [...] Ettrick woods and Eskdale-moor Wind Fell stands above Ettrick Head, the source of the River Ettrick. From this hill views open up of the Ettrick valley (to the north-east) and the adjacent district of Eskdalemuir (to the south-east). Peter Garside has pointed out that in Hogg's poem 'The Wyffe of Ezdel-more', the witch of Eskdalemuir 'has her den in the region of the hill streams which flow into the White Esk from high points such as Ettrick Pen and Phawhope Hill': see Hogg, *A Queer Book*, ed. by P. D. Garside (S/SC, 1995), p. 226. Wind Fell is one of these 'high points' (although it is not specifically named by Garside). As we have seen (note on 8, l. 48), Hogg's maternal grandfather Will Laidlaw of the nearby Phaup (Phawhope) was reputed to be the last man in Ettrick Forest 'who heard, saw, and conversed with the fairies'. For further details of Will's encounters with the fairies, see Hogg, *The Shepherd's Calendar*, ed. by Douglas S. Mack (S/SC, 1995), pp. 107–11.

64, l. 311 from the south i.e. from England.

64, l. 312 Ludlow was his father's name Ludlow, a town in the English county of Shropshire, lies near the border with Wales. As Hogg explains in Note IX (pp. 181–82), the Old David of this poem was 'the first who ever bore the name' of Laidlaw. Hogg's maternal grandfather was Will Laidlaw of Phaup (see note on 8, l. 48). The song of the Bard of Ettrick, that is to say, celebrates the exploits of Old David Laidlaw, the progenitor of Hogg's mother's family.

64, l. 320 their doublets green fairies traditionally wear green: see, for ex-ample, 'Thomas Rymer' (Child 37).

64, l. 324 A silver bell cf. note on 11, l. 158.

64, l. 342 tithes the fairies paid to hell! cf. 'Tam Lin' (Child 39A), stanzas 23–24.

65, l. 362 Lochilaw for this fairy-haunted hill in Ettrick, see Hogg's Note IX, pp. 181–82 (p. 182). It stands above the south bank of the Ettrick, just downstream from Phawhope Hill, and it appears on modern maps as Lochy Law.

66, l. 391 Seven sons he had in popular tradition seven and three are numbers of mystical significance.

66, ll. 401–02 Long arrows [...] Snowdon eagle's wing these reminders that Old David is 'from the south' (l. 311) associate him with both England and Wales. The longbow, famously, was a particularly effective weapon in English hands in medieval warfare. Eagles are birds of the mountains, and Snowdon (in Wales) is the highest mountain in either England or Wales (cf. note on 64, l. 312).

66, l. 407 The little genii of the fell the small size of these beings does not necessarily suggest that they are fairies. F. Marian McNeill writes:

> The fairies of Celtic tradition bear no resemblance to the gossamer-winged flower-sprites of the modern child's picture-books. They are of nearly normal stature, and their mode of life corresponds closely with human life; in fact, they differ from human beings only in their supernatural knowledge and power.

See McNeill, *The Silver Bough*, 4 vols (Glasgow: MacLellan, 1957–68), I, 100.

67, l. 429 the steady pole the pole-star, in the Little Bear, keeps steady at the north pole of the heavens.

67, l. 455 Rippon edge spurs made at Ripon (formerly written as *Rippon*) in Yorkshire were famed for their high quality and sharpness.

70, ll. 565–70 in Moodlaw bowers [...] Old Raeburn's child [...] Eskdale-moor the Moodlaw Burn and the Rae Burn are adjacent tributaries of the White Esk in Eskdalemuir, near Garwald Water. I am grateful to Gillian Hughes for informing me that James Brydon, tenant of Moodlaw farm on the Moodlaw Burn, was awarded a five-guinea premium by the Highland Society in 1832 'for the best pen of five Gimmers of the same breed' (see the *Edinburgh Evening Courant* for 31 January 1833). A *gimmer* is a female sheep between its first and second shearing.

71, l. 612 By Dryhope towers, and Meggat-dale this points to a raid in nearby Yarrow. Megget Water flows out of its mountainous valley into St Mary's Loch, while Yarrow Water flows out of St Mary's Loch near Dryhope Tower.

72, l. 657 first of all the Laidlaw name see note on 64, l. 312.

72, ll. 660–61 And fears of elf, and fairy raid, | Have like a morning dream decayed see Hogg's Note X (pp. 182–84). In 'Old David', as in his novel *The Brownie of Bodsbeck* (1818), Hogg exuberantly evokes the sense of the supernatural that was strongly present in Ettrick oral tradition, but then provides a rational explanation for the apparently supernatural events of his narrative. The present writer has argued that *The Brownie of Bodsbeck*, although revised and published in the later 1810s, may well have been originally drafted in the early 1810s: see Hogg, *The Brownie of Bodsbeck*, ed. by Douglas S. Mack (Edinburgh: Scottish Academic Press, 1976), pp. xiii–xvii. If this argument is accepted, it may be that Hogg in the early 1810s (being still comparatively inexperienced as a writer) felt a need to cover his back by distancing himself from the allegedly naïve superstitions of his native tradition (which he nevertheless relished). On this view, it was only later that he became self-confident enough to generate the dark ambiguities of texts such as *The Private Memoirs and Confessions of a Justified Sinner* (1824), texts in which the supernatural remains disturbingly present as a possibility that cannot be entirely dismissed.

73, l. 669 **the dusk of Hallow-day** a reference to the traditional belief that supernatural beings manifest themselves at Halloween, the eve of Hallowmas (All Saints Day). One of Will o' Phaup's encounters with the fairies took place at 'All-hallow-eve': see Hogg, *The Shepherd's Calendar*, ed. by Douglas S. Mack (S/SC, 1995), p. 108.

74, ll. 711–12 **And once had dared, at flatterer's call, | To tune his harp in Branxholm hall** this sets up an implied comparison between the bard of Ettrick and the minstrel of Scott's long narrative poem *The Lay of the Last Minstrel* (1805): see the present edition's Introduction, pp. xxxv–xxxvii.

74, ll. 723–24 **When Lennox, on the downs of Kyle, | O'erthrew Maconnel and Argyle** 'Lennox' is Matthew Stewart, Earl of Lennox (1516–71), a prominent figure during the reign of Mary, Queen of Scots, and father of Lord Darnley, Mary's second husband (see notes on 23, l. 20 and 39, ll. 591–93). On the death of James V in 1542, Lennox and James Hamilton, second Earl of Arran had contending claims to be regarded as next in line of succession after the dead King's infant daughter Mary, and the resulting power struggle between Lennox and Arran was complicated by Mary's significance in the power struggle between England and France (see the present edition's Introduction, pp. xxxviii–xxxix). In pursuit of his own family interest and in an attempt to overthrow Arran, Lennox gave his allegiance to Henry VIII of England, who in 1544 appointed him Lieutenant for the north of England and the south of Scotland. Lennox then came from England to his family's power base at Dumbarton Castle, which stands on the Clyde about 5 miles south of the southern end of Loch Lomond. Failing to rally support there, he retreated to England with his men, inflicting damage as he went. Holinshed (II, 224) writes of this incident as follows:

> the earl of *Lennox* with 500 men landed in another part of *Argile*, and remaining on land a whole day together, burnt, spoiled, and wasted the countrie: the earl of *Argile* with 2000 men giving the looking on, and not once offering the skirmish, so that the earl of *Lennox* with his soldiers retired to his ships without incounter.
>
> After this they invaded the *Isle* of *Kinter*, where *James MacKonnel* dwelled, burnt many places in that countrie, took and carried away great booties of cattle and other goods. All the coasts of *Kile*, *Carrike*, and *Coningham*, and likewise of *Galloway* remained in continuall fear, so that oftentimes their beacons were fired, and manie of the noblemen constrained to come to the earl of *Lennox*, suing to him for assurance. In these exploits the earl had with him *Walter MacFerlane* of *Tirbat* [...].

Tarbet lies on the western shore of Loch Lomond, in MacFarlane territory.

74, l. 726 **dark Clan-Alpine** Scott discusses this clan in his Introduction to the Magnum Opus edition of his novel *Rob Roy*: 'The sept of MacGregor claimed a descent from Gregor, or Gregorius, third son, it is said, of Alpin King of Scots, who flourished about 787. Hence their original patronymic is MacAlpine, and they are usually termed the Clan Alpine.' (See Scott, *Rob Roy*, ed. by Ian Duncan (Oxford: Oxford University Press, 1998), p. 6.) 'Clan-Alpine' is the wild Highland clan that features prominently in Scott's long narrative poem *The Lady of the Lake* (1810), the lake in question being Loch Katrine (see note on 75, l. 746).

74, l. 728 fierce Macfarlane the west side of the northern part of Loch Lomond is the territory of the MacFarlanes.

75, l. 746 Ben-Lomond a Highland mountain of western Scotland, not to be confused with the Lomond Hills which lie in the Lowland counties of Kinross and Fife in eastern Scotland (see note on 41, l. 660). Ben Lomond is situated about 25 miles to the north-west of Glasgow, on the eastern shore of Loch Lomond near the Highland / Lowland border. It lies about eight miles to the south-west of Loch Katrine and the Trossachs, scene of Scott's poem *The Lady of the Lake*.

76, l. 779 For mountain ash see note on 40, l. 617 for the traditional belief that the rowan or mountain ash could give protection against witchcraft and the supernatural.

76–77, ll. 810–35 The Spectre's Cradle-Song for Hogg's account of the background to this lyric, see his Note XI, pp. 184–85. Revised versions of 'The Spectre's Cradle Song', 'O! Lady Dear' (see note on 12, ll. 213–20), and 'The Monks' Hymn' (see note on 155–56, ll. 1826–59) were included in *Songs by the Ettrick Shepherd* (Edinburgh: Blackwood; London: Cadell, 1831), pp. 288–93 'as pieces that might be successfully set to music' (p. 291). However, no early sheet publication of these songs has been traced.

Macgregor

The eleventh bard's song is reprinted from no. 40 (for 1 June 1811) of Hogg's periodical *The Spy*, where it appears as 'Macgregor.—A Highland Tale' (see *The Spy*, ed. by Gillian Hughes (S/SC, 2000), pp. 402–05). The remainder of no 40 of *The Spy* is devoted to the first of two letters to 'The Spy' by 'Malise', in which Hogg pokes fun at the current wild enthusiasm for Scott's Highland poem *The Lady of the Lake* (1810). (These 'Malise' letters were reprinted in Hogg's *Winter Evening Tales* (1820) as 'Highland Adventures': see *Winter Evening Tales*, ed. Ian Duncan (S/SC, 2002), pp. 107–18.) Hogg's admiration for *The Lady of the Lake* is evident in the 'Malise' letters, but in them he also suggests that to some extent Scott's poem tends to go over the top and lose its grip on reality. Seen in its context in *The Spy*, 'Macgregor' (with its emotional extravagance and its driving, irregular anapestic rhythm) is a 'Highland Tale' that is deliberately extravagant as Hogg devotes a number of his periodical to an affectionate sending up of Scott's Highland poem. Seen in its new context in *The Queen's Wake*, 'Macgregor' stands in marked and telling contrast to the more sober way in which similar material is presented in 'Old David', the song sung by the previous bard, who is no less a person than the Bard of Ettrick himself.

78, l. 856 Macgregor in discussing this clan in his Introduction to *Rob Roy* (see note on 74, l. 726), Scott writes:

They are accounted one of the most ancient clans in the Highlands, [...] and occupied at one period very extensive possessions in

Perthshire and Argyleshire, which they imprudently continued to hold by the *coire a glaive*, that is, the right of the sword. Their neighbours, the Earls of Argyle [cf. note on 12, l. 221] and Breadalbane, in the meanwhile, managed to have the lands occupied by the MacGregors engrossed in those charters which they easily obtained from the Crown; and thus constituted a legal right in their own favour, without much regard to its justice. As opportunity occurred of annoying or extirpating their neighbours, they gradually extended their own domains, by usurping, under the pretext of such royal grants, those of their more uncivilized neighbours. A Sir Duncan Campbell of Lochow [...] is said to have been peculiarly successful in those acts of spoilation upon the clan MacGregor. [...] In an Act of Privy Council at Stirling, 22d September, 1563, in the reign of Queen Mary, commission is granted to the most powerful nobles, and chiefs of the clans, to pursue the clan Gregor with fire and sword. (Scott, *Rob Roy*, ed. by Ian Duncan (Oxford: Oxford University Press, 1998), pp. 6–7.)

78, l. 857 Ben-Lomond this points to the heartland of the MacGregor territory, which centred on the area between Loch Katrine and the eastern shore of the northern part of Loch Lomond. Cf. note on 75, l. 746.

78, l. 859 Glen-Lyon lies about 20 miles north of Loch Katrine, in the territory of the Campbells, enemies of the MacGregors (see note on 78, l. 856).

78, l. 861 Strathfillan Strath Fillan, part of the territory of the McNabs, lies about eight miles to the north of the northern end of Loch Katrine (see note on 75, l. 746).

78, l. 863 Campbells see note on 78, l. 856.

78, l. 865 the hills of M'Nab the mountainous country around Strath Fillan.

78, l. 869 M'Nab, with his giants behind him in Malise's letter in no 40 of *The Spy* Hogg mentions Francis MacNab (1734–1816), 16th Chief of MacNab, a man of gigantic height. Hogg ate breakfast with him at Callander (near the Trossachs) during his 1803 Highland journey: see Hogg, *The Spy*, ed. by Gillian Hughes (S/SC, 2000), pp. 397, 616; and Hogg, *Winter Evening Tales*, ed. by Ian Duncan (S/SC, 2002), pp. 107, 558.

78, l. 879 Glen-Gyle lies to the north-west of the northern end of Loch Katrine, into which Glengyle Water flows. This part of Loch Katrine lies about 3 miles to the east of the upper part of Loch Lomond, and Glengyle Water ('the brook of Glen-Gyle', l. 897) rises less than a mile from the eastern shore of Loch Lomond.

79, ll. 900–03 That the pine [...] hated Colquhoun see Hogg's Note XII, p. 185. The MacGregors were at feud with the Colquhouns of Luss, whose territory was adjacent to the south-western part of Loch Lomond. Peter Garside has argued convincingly that Hogg based aspects of the Colwan family in *Confessions of a Justified Sinner* on the Colquhouns of Luss: see Hogg, *The Private Memoirs and Confessions of a Justified Sinner*, ed. by P. D. Garside (S/SC, 2001), pp. xxviii, 212.

79, l. 901 Glen-Falo presumably Glen Falloch, which lies immediately to the north of Loch Lomond: the River Falloch flows through Glen Falloch, and enters Loch Lomond at its northern end. The northernmost part of the MacGregor territory around Loch Lomond included part of Glen Falloch.

79, l. 905 Lennox the district that encircles the southern portion of Loch Lomond.

79, l. 915 the lions of Dochart Glen Dochart lies in McNab territory, adjacent to Strath Fillan (see note on 78, l. 861).

79, l. 917 will glue at this point *The Spy* has 'we'll glue', but all editions of *The Queen's Wake* have 'will glue'.

80, l. 926 They oared the broad Lomond they row up Loch Lomond in order to land near the head of Glen Gyle (see note on 78, l. 879).

80, l. 947 the wild deer of Gairtney Loch Katrine lies in Strath Gartney.

82, l. 994 ere Loch Ketturine's wave was won the 'barge of hell' sails down Glengyle Water into Loch Katrine, 'the dark lake' (l. 968): see notes on 78, l. 879 and 80, l. 926.

82, l. 1000 The Bard of Clyde the Clyde is the major river of the western Lowlands.

82, l. 1003 But plain his garb, and plain his lay an indication that with the Bard of Clyde we return to the demotic Lowland tradition. This line from *The Queen's Wake* was quoted on the titlepage of William Nicholson's *Tales in Verse and Miscellaneous Poems* (Edinburgh, 1814). Nicholson (1783–1849) was a Galloway pedlar and poet, and the 'Advertisement' to his 1814 publication expresses his gratitude to 'the celebrated Mr Hogg, for his generous and unwearied attention, since the Author came to Edinburgh, where he was almost friendless and unknown'.

Earl Walter

In the Bard of Clyde's song we return to the stanza pattern of the traditional Scottish ballads, which confirms that the Bard of Clyde operates within the demotic oral poetic tradition of Lowland Scotland. Nevertheless, 'Earl Walter' focuses on aristocrats. In doing so, it follows the example of some traditional ballads, such as 'The Bonny Earl of Murray' (Child 181) and 'Child Maurice' (Child 83). Likewise, Hogg's own modern ballad imitation 'Gilmanscleuch' from *The Mountain Bard* (1807) focuses on the aristocratic Scott family. For understandable reasons, 'Gilmanscleuch' was one of Walter Scott's favourites among Hogg's ballad imitations, but Hogg himself told Scott 'It is least my favourite of all the ballads' (see 'Two Versions of "Gilmanscleuch"', ed. by Suzanne Gilbert, *SHW*, 9 (1998), 92–128 (pp. 93, 97). At all events, 'Earl Walter' has much in common with Hogg's *Mountain Bard* ballad imitations, and with 'Gilmanscleuch' in particular, and it may be that 'Earl Walter' was one of the poems Hogg had to hand when he began work on *The Queen's Wake* in 1812 (see the present edition's Introduction, p. xxv). A manuscript of the first forty-seven stanzas of 'Earl Walter', apparently in Hogg's hand, survives in the Buffalo and Erie County Public Library, Buffalo, New York. This manuscript is discussed in the present edition's Note on the Texts (pp. 399–401). In 'Earl Walter', Hogg conflates two crucial incidents in the rise to power of the aristocratic Hamilton family: see Hogg's Notes XIII–XIV (pp. 185–86), and Editor's Notes on 185 Note XIII and 185–86 Note XIV.

82, l. 1012 the Ayr like the Clyde, an important river of the western Lowlands. The Ayr enters the Clyde's estuary at the town of Ayr.

83, l. 1027 rode to Stirling town one of the major palaces of the Scottish monarchs was situated within the fortifications of Stirling Castle.

83, l. 1028 Old Hamilton from the tower came down in a note to his imitation ballad 'Cadyow Castle' Scott writes: 'The ruins of Cadyow, or

Cadzow castle, the ancient baronial residence of the family of Hamilton, are situated upon the precipitous banks of the river Evan, about two miles above its junction with the Clyde. It was dismantled, in the conclusion of the civil wars, during the reign of the unfortunate Mary, to whose cause the house of Hamilton devoted themselves with a generous zeal, which occasioned their temporary obscurity, and, very nearly, their total ruin' (see Scott, *Minstrelsy of the Scottish Border*, 2nd ed., 3 vols (Edinburgh, 1803), III, 380. Scott's poem begins (p. 386) 'When princely Hamilton's abode | Ennobled Cadyow's Gothic towers'.

83, l. 1037 Darcie see Hogg's Note XIII (p. 185) and Editor's Notes, 185 Note XIII.

84, ll. 1060–61 the king's daughter, | Fair Margaret was her name Princess Mary (not Margaret), daughter of James II and sister of James III, seems to be intended: see Hogg's Note XIV (pp. 185–86) and Editor's Notes 185–86 Note XIV.

84, l. 1072 Douglas-dale the valley of Douglas Water lies to the north of the Lowther Hills, and Douglas Water joins the Clyde near the small town of Lanark. This valley is the heartland of the powerful Douglas family.

90, l. 1264 Kyle a district of Ayrshire in south-west Scotland. Robert Burns, as his song ('There was a Lad', Kinsley 140) famously says, was a lad who was born in Kyle.

90, l. 1266 Arran's isle the large island of Arran lies in the Firth of Clyde, and faces the Ayrshire coast. See also the note on 185–86 Note XIV.

90, l. 1288 Drummond, from the moors of Ern Loch Earn is a substantial freshwater lake in the territory of the Drummond family, and is situated some 15 miles north-west from Loch Katrine, in the Highlands but near the Lowland border. About 1490 James IV (Queen Mary's grandfather) granted permission to John 1st Lord Drummond to build a stronghold on the site (some 10 miles south-west of Loch Earn) where the magnificent Drummond Castle now stands. The 4th Lord Drummond was created 1st Earl of Perth in 1605 by Queen Mary's son James VI and I. Almost a century later James Drummond (1648–1716), 4th Earl of Perth, was created 1st Duke of Perth by Queen Mary's great-grandson, the deposed and exiled James VII and II. John Drummond (1649–1714), brother of the 1st Duke of Perth, was likewise created the Jacobite Duke of Melfort. James Drummond (1675–1720), 2nd Duke of Perth, commanded the Jacobite cavalry at Sheriffmuir in 1715, while James Drummond (1713–47), 3rd Duke of Perth, commanded the Jacobite left wing at Culloden in 1746. All these Jacobite Dukes were Roman Catholics. The Drummond estates were attainted in 1746, but were restored in 1785 by Act of Parliament to a descendant of the 1st Duke of Melfort, who was duly created Baron Perth of Stobhall. Lord Perth was succeeded in 1800 by his daughter Clementina Drummond (1786–1865). In short, 'Drummond from the moors of Ern' is not a portrait of an individual, but he represents and embodies an old, aristocratic, Catholic, and Jacobite family. Indeed, members of this family appear elsewhere in Hogg's writings. In *The Private Memoirs and Confessions of a Justified Sinner* (1824), George Colwan's group of Jacobite friends includes Thomas Drummond, 'second son to a John, Duke of Melfort, who lived abroad with the royal family of the Stuarts' (S/SC edition, ed. by P. D. Garside (2001), p. 38: see also p. 63). In his edition of the *Justified Sinner* (p.

226), Peter Garside agrees with David Groves in seeing 'strong similarities between the Thomas Drummond of this novel and a similarly-named character in Hogg's "The Adventures of Captain John Lochy", published in his *Altrive Tales* (London, 1832)'. Gillian Hughes suggests that the Lieutenant Drummond of *Altrive Tales* ('a great party man, and an adherent of the banished Stuarts') may be based on 'Edward Drummond (1690–1760), son to the Earl of Perth by his third wife, Mary': see *Altrive Tales*, ed. by Gillian Hughes (S/SC, 2003), pp. 89, 261–62.

90–91, ll. 1293–98 Well versed was he in holy lore [...] mountain gale in the portrait of the thirteenth bard, the Catholic piety of the Drummonds is blended with Ossianic elements. Interestingly, this aristocratic religious mystic and poet is depicted as a shepherd (see l. 1317). The Ettrick Shepherd appears to be claiming kinship with the aristocratic Drummond—and, by implication, he is perhaps claiming kinship (beyond Drummond) with David, the shepherd-poet-king of the Old Testament.

91, ll. 1299–320 Glen-Ample's forest deep [...] Glen-Airtney's forest [...] Ben-Vorlich locations near Loch Earn. Ben Vorlich is a mountain to the south of the loch; Glen Ample lies to the west of Ben Vorlich, stretching south from the loch's western end; and Glen Artney lies to the east of Ben Vorlich.

Kilmeny

Hogg uses his 'ancient style' for the language of this poem: see the present edition's Introduction, pp. xlii–xliii. The couplets of 'Kilmeny', like the couplets of Coleridge's 'Christabel' and Scott's *Lay of the Last Minstrel*, are in 'sprung rhythm' (to use Hopkins's phrase). For a discussion of the innovative metre of 'Christabel' and the *Lay*, see John Sutherland, *The Life of Walter Scott: A Critical Biography* (Oxford: Blackwell, 1995), pp. 100–02. In his Note IV (see p. 179), Hogg links 'Kilmeny' to 'the old ballads of Tam Lean and Thomas of Erceldon'. For these famous ballads of fairy abduction, see Child 39 ('Tam Lin') and Child 37 ('Thomas Rymer'). In his Note XV (see pp. 186–87) Hogg gives an account of 'some modern incidents of a similar nature', drawn from his own territory in the Borders. Night the Second thus reaches its climax in a poem that is shown to connect not only with the Highland tradition of Drummond, its aristocratic bard, but also with the popular tradition of the ballads of the Borders.

92, l. 1348 Duneira's men Dunira lies about 3 miles to the east of the eastern end of Loch Earn.

93, l. 1376 snoode of the byrk se greine the birch tree as headwear for those returned from the dead also appears in the traditional ballad 'The Wife of Usher's Well' (Child 79A), stanzas 5–6:

> It fell about the Martinmass,
>   When nights are lang and mirk,
> The carlin wife's three sons came hame,
>   And their hats were o the birk.
>
> It neither grew in syke nor ditch,
>   Nor yet in ony sheugh;
> But at the gates o Paradise,
>   That birk grew fair eneugh.

93, ll. 1398–402 In yond grein wudde [...] walkis his lene for a discussion of this difficult passage and its connection with the old oral ballad tradition, see the present edition's Introduction, pp. xliii–xliv.

95, l. 1474 deipe in the streime her body they layde this points to the rebirth to a new life associated with the sacrament of baptism: cf. the account of the baptism of Jesus in the river Jordan in Mark 1. 9–11. 'The Witch of Fife' ll. 737–40 offers an echo of this passage in 'Kilmeny', and presents a contrasting parallel.

95, l. 1477 the streime of lyfe echoes Revelation 22. 1–8.

96, l. 1494 They soofit her awaye to ane mountyn greine a possible echo of Books XI and XII of Milton's *Paradise Lost*: see the present edition's Introduction, pp. xliv–xlv.

96, l. 1510 Ane lovlye land Scotland.

96, l. 1518 ane ledy sit on a throne Mary, Queen of Scots.

96, l. 1520 Ane lyon the lion of Scotland: see note on 11, l. 189.

96–97, ll. 1522–29 ane leifu mayden [...] the payne of the serpentis sting quoting this passage under 'LEEFU 3', the *SND* glosses *leifu* as 'full of love, lovely', but adds that here 'the word may be intended as a variant of LEAL, chaste'. At all events, the 'leifu mayden' seems to be Mary's guardian angel, and this figure's tearful departure (ll. 1532–33) signifies Queen Mary's loss of innocence, her Fall: cf. 'serpentis sting'. Connections between 'Kilmeny' and Milton's *Paradise Lost* are discussed in the present edition's Introduction, pp. xliv–xlv.

96, l. 1524 ane leman out of the west this points to Darnley (one of the Lennox Stuarts of the west of Scotland), but there may also be a reference to Mary's third husband the Earl of Bothwell (Bothwell is likewise in the west): see notes on 23, l. 20 and 39, ll. 591–93.

96, l. 1526 he sent ane boy her herte to prove Cupid, the Roman boy-god of love.

97, l. 1530 ane gruff untowyrd gysart John Knox, who led the Protestant opposition to Mary.

97, ll. 1534–37 quhill the queen fra the lyon fled, [...] reide blude fall like rayne summarises Queen Mary's flight into England after the Battle of Langside, and her subsequent execution: cf. note on 39, ll. 591–93. The 'lyon', being the royal emblem of Scotland (see note on 11, l. 189), can represent either the people or the monarch.

97, ll. 1540–49 the gruff grim keryl [...] his erilis given these lines point to the continuing conflicts with Knox's successors experienced by Queen Mary's descendants James VI & I, Charles I, Charles II, and James VII & II. It is recorded that James VI will be strengthened in this struggle when, on the death of Queen Elizabeth of England, he inherits the English throne and is 'crownit with the rose [emblem of England] and the claiver leife [emblem of Ireland]'. However, James VII & II will get his comeuppance ('erilis') for persecuting Knox's successors the Covenanters, whom he had chased away 'To feide with the deire on the mountayn gray'. (James VII was deposed in the 'Glorious Revolution' of 1688–89.)

97, ll. 1556–57 ane pepil, [...] Burst fra their bundis Kilmeny's vision of the future now comes up to date, and focuses on the French Revolution and the Napoleonic Wars.

97, l. 1558 The lille [...] the egil the lily and the eagle are emblems of France. The 'eagle' had a particular resonance in 1812 when Hogg was writing *The Queen's Wake*, as the regiments of the armies of Napoleonic Imperial France were currently carrying their 'eagles' or standards into a series of crucial battles. However, both the lily (l. 1600) and the eagle (l. 1626) are drawn into the vision of ultimate peace and harmony of 'Kilmeny', ll. 1590–1633.

97, l. 1563 the lyonis deadly paw the lion is now the emblem of the new state, Britain, founded in 1707 by the Treaty of Union between England and Scotland. In 1813 this description of the triumph of the lion over the eagle would tend to boost morale in a Britain currently engaged in a long war with France. Final victory in this war did not come until 1815, at the Battle of Waterloo.

99, ll. 1608–33 But quhairevir [...] a sinlesse worold for a discussion of this passage, see the present edition's Introduction, p. xliv.

101, l. 1689 she spoke with meaning leer this connects with the theme of lost innocence, suggested in 'Kilmeny'.

101, ll. 1709–11 Lady Gordon [...] Huntley this passage, placed prominently at the end of Night the Second, points to tensions among the great aristocratic houses of Scotland as they compete for the power that will flow from the favour of the newly-returned Queen. 'Lady Gordon' is Anne, daughter of James Hamilton (*d.* 1575), second Earl of Arran, a man of Protestant sympathies, who would have had a strong claim to the throne if Mary were to die ('Earl Walter' in *The Queen's Wake* explains the basis of the Hamilton claim). At the time of Queen Mary's return from France in 1561, Hamilton's daughter Anne was married to George, Lord Gordon, heir to George, fourth Earl of Huntley (1514–62), a man of Catholic sympathies. Lady Gordon's father, who hoped that his eldest son would marry the Queen, was nevertheless ill at ease (fearing plots) on her return from France, and note was taken at the time of his absence from some of the festivities held to welcome Mary back to Scotland (*DNB*). In Hogg's poem, Lady Gordon's father-in-law, the fourth Earl of Huntley, is annoyed because his daughter-in-law's absence will hinder his plans to gain the Queen's favour. In context, the final lines of Night the Second suggest that the young Queen (even as she enjoys her Wake) is enmeshed in a threatening world of aristocratic rivalry, plotting, and power politics.

101, l. 1712 her buskined train speaking to Oberon, Titania describes Hippolyta as 'the bouncing Amazon, | Your buskined mistress and your warrior love' (Shakespeare, *A Midsummer Night's Dream*, II. 1. 70–71).

Night the Third

104, l. 8 Pentland's top the Pentland Hills lie to the south of Edinburgh.

105–06, ll. 22–37 the banks of Duddingston [...] o'er the lake they glide Duddingston Loch, situated in Edinburgh to the south-east of Arthur's Seat and immediately adjacent to Holyrood Park, was much used in Hogg's day for ice-skating and for the Scottish winter sport of curling (which involves throwing stones along the ice towards a target area). For Hogg's own exploits as a curler on Duddingston Loch, see the Appendix on 'James Hogg and Winter Sports' in David Groves, *James Hogg and the St Ronan's Border Club* (Dollar: Mack, 1987), pp. 41–44.

106, ll. 60–61 But polar spirits sure had spread | O'er hills which native fays had fled as Night the Third opens, Hogg envisages a sunlit winter Edinburgh poised between the old world of medieval Catholic Scotland,

and the modern world of Protestantism and the Enlightenment. The old native Scottish fairies, bogles, and kelpies have departed as modernity advances, but at this particular moment as the Wake approaches its climax, the old world briefly reasserts itself and 'polar spirits' (one thinks of 'The Ancient Mariner') animate the lively but threatening winter scene.

107, l. 74 Orion up his baldrick drew Orion is a large and brilliant constellation figured as a hunter with belt ('baldrick') and sword.

107, l. 75 The evening star the planet Venus.

107, l. 76 the Pleiades a cluster of stars visible to the naked eye made up of at least seven stars, and given the common name of 'the Seven Sisters'.

107, l. 77 Or Charles reyoked his golden wain seven prominent stars within the constellation Ursa Major, commonly called Charles's Wain, or the Plough.

107, l. 94 The bard that night who foremost came Hogg's annotated copy identifies this bard as his old Ettrick friend 'Mr. John Grieve', who by the early 1810s had become a prosperous Edinburgh hatter. The present edition's Introduction (pp. xiv, xxv) discusses Grieve's importance to Hogg at the time when *The Queen's Wake* was being written. Gillian Hughes gives a valuable account of Grieve in her edition of Hogg, *Altrive Tales* (S/SC, 2003), pp. 221, 228.

Mary Scott

Grieve's song (see note on 107, l. 94), appropriately, is set in Ettrick Forest and has deep roots in Ettrick oral tradition. In his Note XVII (pp. 188–89) Hogg writes that 'Mary Scott' is 'founded on the old song of *The grey Goss Hawk*', and some of the central narrative features of Hogg's poem are indeed based on the old ballad (Child 96) that had appeared in Scott's *Minstrelsy of the Scottish Border* (1802–03) under the title 'The Gay Goss Hawk'. However, in the *Minstrelsy* the hawk's feathers are twice described as 'gray', which lends some support to Hogg's title. It may be that, in calling this ballad '*The grey Goss Hawk*', Hogg is signalling that he is not dependent on the *Minstrelsy*, but has his own independent access to oral tradition. 'Mary Scott' is written in quatrains that evoke the traditional ballad stanza.

108, l. 130 Otterdale carries a suggestion of the ballad 'The Battle of Otterburn' (Child 161). Otterburn is in Redesdale in Northumberland.

108, l. 135 Torwoodlee is situated on Gala Water just upstream from the town of Galashiels, and Gala Water joins the Tweed (from the north) just below Galashiels. Torwoodlee lies just under two miles north-east of the village of Clovenfords (see note on 122, ll. 588–91). Groome records: 'Held by his ancestors since 1509, Torwoodlee now belongs to James Thomas Pringle, Esq. (b. 1832; suc. 1859)'.

109, l. 155 Tushilaw is situated about 17 miles south-west of Torwoodlee. In his Note XVII (pp. 188–89) Hogg accurately records that Tushilaw 'overlooks the junction of the rivers Ettrick and Rankleburn'.

109, l. 156 Ettrick pen a mountain at the head of the Ettrick valley, about 9 miles upstream from Tushilaw.

110, l. 190 Young Gilmanscleuch and Deloraine members of the Scott clan, with bases in the Ettrick valley. Gilmanscleuch and Deloraine lie about three or four miles downstream from Tushilaw, with Gilmanscleuch being to the north of the river, and Deloraine to the south. The Scotts of

Gilmanscleuch are the subject of Hogg's poem 'Gilmanscleuch' in *The Mountain Bard* (1807): see Suzanne Gilbert, 'Two Versions of "Gilmanscleuch"', *SHW*, 9 (1998), 92–128. William of Deloraine is one of the prominent Scotts in Walter Scott's poem *The Lay of the Last Minstrel* (1805).

111, l. 243 Cacra hill is on the south side of Ettrick Water, opposite Tushilaw. Grieve's Ettrick home was at Cacrabank, under Cacra Hill.

112, l. 277 Queen of the Border as Hogg points out in his Note XVII (pp. 188–89), Adam Scott of Tushilaw 'was long denominated in the south the *King of the Border*'.

113, l. 303 The king of Scots James V, who executed Adam Scott of Tushilaw in 1530: see Jamie Cameron, *James V: The Personal Rule 1528–1542* (East Linton: Tuckwell Press, 1998), p. 75.

113, l. 304 The lazy hoard of Melrose vale the monks of Melrose Abbey (which features prominently in *The Lay of the Last Minstrel*). Melrose is on the Tweed, a little downstream from Galashiels.

115, l. 355 Gilmans-law a hill above Gilmanscleuch, to the east of Tushielaw.

116, l. 386 Coldinghame there was a medieval priory at Coldingham on the Berwickshire coast.

116, ll. 398–99 I'll call an angel from above, | That soon will set the pris'ner free echoes St Peter's rescue from prison by an angel (Acts 12. 1–11).

116, l. 411 From Philiphaugh to Gilnockye in effect, the Ettrick Valley and Eskdale, adjacent valleys that for Hogg represented the heartland of the Scottish Borders. Philiphaugh lies at the confluence of Ettrick and Yarrow, near Selkirk, and was the scene of a notable battle in 1645: see 'The Battle of Philiphaugh' (Child 202) and Hogg's story 'Wat Pringle o' the Yair' in *Tales of the Wars of Montrose*, ed. by Gillian Hughes (S/SC, 1996), pp. 191–222. Gilnockie Tower was situated on the River Esk to the south of Langholm, near the English Border. Groome records that 'the Border peel-tower of Gilnockie stood on a small promontory, washed on three sides by the river Esk, so steep and rocky as to be scarcely accessible except on the land side, and defended there by a deep ditch. It gave designation to Johnie Armstrong, the Border freebooter of ballad fame'. In the traditional ballad 'Johnie Armstrong' (Child 169), Johnie is 'Laird of Gilnockie' (see the first stanza of Child 169C, a version reprinted by Child from Allan Ramsay's *The Ever Green*). Armstrong was executed by James V in 1529 or 1530, during the king's efforts to gain control of the lawless Borders.

117, l. 433 cloak of cramasye in traditional oral culture, cramasye (crimson) suggests female sexual freedom, as in the old song 'Waly, Waly, Gin Love be Bonny': 'When we came in by Glasgow town, | We were a comely sight to see; | My love was cled in the black velvet, | And I my sell in cramasie'. (See the introductory note to Child 204 'Jamie Douglas', in which the old song is reprinted from Allan Ramsay's *Tea-Table Miscellany*.)

121, l. 570 Mary's fane St Mary's church (long gone) and churchyard (still surviving), above St Mary's Loch in the Yarrow valley. As Hogg records in his Note XVII (p. 188–89), this was the site of the 'catastrophe' of Child 96, 'The Gay Goshawk'. St Mary's churchyard was clearly a location resonantly significant for Hogg with regard to the Border past: see his poem 'St Mary of the Lows' and his short story 'Mary Burnet' (*A Queer Book*, ed. by P. D. Garside (S/SC. 1995), pp. 153–56; and *The Shepherd's Calendar*, ed. by

Douglas S. Mack (S/SC, 1995), pp. 200–22).

122, ll. 588–91 Maygill brae [...] The Cadan [...] The Tweed Meigle (Maygill?) overlooks Caddon Water, near the village of Clovenfords (see note on 108, l. 135). Clovenfords lies about a mile upstream from the point at which Caddon Water joins the Tweed. Abbotsford, Walter Scott's home, is situated on the Tweed near the town of Galashiels, and Caddon Water joins the Tweed about five miles upstream from Abbotsford. Ettrick Water joins the Tweed (from the south) about halfway between Caddon Water and Abbotsford. The confluence of Ettrick Water and Yarrow Water is about four miles upstream from Ettrick's confluence with the Tweed near the town of Selkirk.

122–23, ll. 615–27 March and Teviotdale [...] rank and file on Torwoodlee an anti-Scott coalition assembles from various parts of the Scottish Borders: see Hogg's Note XVII (pp. 188–89).

123, ll. 629–30 Tweed sweeps round the Thorny-hill [...] Gideon Murray the anti-Scott coalition, having travelled from Torwoodlee down Caddon Water to the Tweed, turn upstream and soon come to Thornylee Craigs and Elibank. Juden (Gideon) Murray of Elibank features as an enemy of the Scotts in Hogg's poem 'The Fray of Elibank' in *The Mountain Bard* (1807).

123, ll. 632–35 Plora [...] Mount-Benger [...] Black Douglas of the Craigy-burn as they head for the Yarrow valley, St Mary's Loch, and St Mary's church (cf. note on 121, l. 570), the anti-Scott group move a little further up the Tweed, then turn into the valley of the Plora Burn, which enters the Tweed opposite the small town of Walkerburn. This route takes them south towards Yarrow, which in due course they approach via the northern slopes of Mountbenger Law. From here, St Mary's church lies about five miles to the south-west. Approximately midway between the church and Mountbenger Law is Blackhouse, the farm at which Hogg worked as a shepherd during the 1790s. Blackhouse stands at the junction of Craighope Burn and the Douglas Burn, and at Blackhouse there is an old tower, described by Hogg as 'that ruinous habitation of The Black Douglasses' (see 'Storms' in *The Shepherd's Calendar* (S/SC, 1995), 1–21 (p. 6). This presumably is where the group collects 'Black Douglas of the Craigy-burn [i.e. Craighope Burn?]'. However, Craigieburn actually lies on Moffat Water about 18 miles south-west from Mountbenger Law (that is to say about 15 miles beyond St Mary's Church)—which means that the anti-Scott group could only reach Craigieburn by a long detour. Craigieburn appears in its real location in Hogg's poem 'Mess John' (from *The Mountain Bard*), in which the Episcopal priest of St Mary's church uses sorcery to entice 'the lass of Craigyburn' to his home, where he rapes her. 'Mess John' is based on what appears to have been a well-known Ettrick traditional tale—a tale that also feeds into Hogg's novel *The Brownie of Bodsbeck* and his short story 'Mary Burnet': see note on 121, l. 570. No doubt Hogg wished to insert a reminder of this traditional tale into his *Queen's Wake* story of St Mary's church.

123, l. 651 Meggat-dale Megget Water flows into St Mary's Loch a little to the west of St Mary's churchyard.

124, l. 679 Dryhope Yarrow Water flows from the eastern end of St Mary's loch, at Dryhope.

125, l. 689–704 For every Scott of name was there [...] Thirlestane these lines offer a roll call of the names of the main branches of the Scott family in the Scottish Borders.

125, ll. 704–07 But Francis, Lord of Thirlestane [...] a braken coil the 'Lord of Thirlestane' in 1813 was Francis, seventh Baron Napier (1758–1823), Lord Lieutenant of Selkirkshire, and a descendant of the Scotts of Thirlestane. Hogg's slim volume of *Scottish Pastorals* (Edinburgh: John Taylor, 1801) caused trouble for its author because of an indiscreet mention of Lord Napier's name in connection with controversy over a radical Kelso newspaper: see Hogg *Scottish Pastorals*, ed. by Elaine Petrie (Stirling: Stirling University Press, 1988), pp. xi, 8, 46–47. The lines on 'Francis, Lord of Thirlestane' in the 1813 version of *The Queen's Wake* are replaced by a longer passage on 'Red Will of Thirlestane' in the 1819 version, in which Hogg gives vent to his feelings with regard to a quarrel with Lord Napier's son, Captain William Napier: see note on 321–22, ll. 708–35.

129, l. 839 The next was bred on southern shore Hogg's annotated copy (see note on 38, l. 545) records that the fifteenth bard is 'The Revd James Gray | Afterwards my brother in law | J. H.'. James Gray was born (1770) in Duns, a Berwickshire market town situated immediately to the south of the Lammermuir Hills. Duns is in the south-eastern corner of Scotland, and lies about seven miles north of the Tweed (which here forms the border with England). An excellent Greek and Latin scholar and a man of passionately-held radical political views, Gray taught from 1794 till 1801 at the high school of Dumfries, an important town in south-west Scotland, situated on the River Nith. During his Dumfries years Gray became the intimate friend of Robert Burns and taught the poet's sons. He also married Mary Phillips, sister of Margaret Phillips who later became Hogg's wife. In a valuable account of Hogg's warm friendship with Gray, Gillian Hughes records that Hogg 'arranged with the firm of Longman for the anonymous publication in 1814 of Gray's *Cona; or, the Vale of Clwyd*': see Hogg, *The Spy*, ed. by Gillian Hughes (S/SC, 2000), pp. 562–63 (p. 563). Gray's first wife (Mary Phillips) died on 9 November 1806 after the birth of her eighth child, and Gray subsequently married Mary Peacock in 1808. In 1801 Gray became classics master of the High School at Edinburgh, but in 1820 his application to become rector of that school was unsuccessful. After becoming rector of the academy at Belfast in 1820, Gray took holy orders and in 1826 went to India as chaplain in the East India company's service. He died in India in 1830.

King Edward's Dream

The fifteenth bard's song was originally one of Hogg's contributions to his own periodical *The Spy*, where it appeared in no 20 (for 12 January 1811): see *The Spy*, ed. by Gillian Hughes (S/SC, 2000), pp. 209–12. Like the eleventh bard's song 'Macgregor' (also reprinted from *The Spy*), 'King Edward's Dream' is an emotionally highly charged poem written in a driving anapestic rhythm. As Hogg's Note XVIII (p. 189) explains, 'King Edward's Dream' is set shortly before the death in 1307 at Burgh-by-Sands of Edward I of England ('the Hammer of the Scots') as he prepared to invade Scotland. (Robert Bruce had been crowned as Robert I, King of Scots, in 1306.) Hogg's poem echoes the mood of Burns's famous song

'Robert Bruce's March to Bannockburn' (Kinsley 425), which begins 'SCOTS, wha hae wi' WALLACE bled, | Scots, wham BRUCE has aften led'. William Wallace and Robert Bruce were, of course, leaders of popular Scottish resistance to King Edward's ambition to conquer Scotland. Significantly, however, Burns's rousing call to arms in defence of 'liberty' was written in 1793, at a time when the French Revolution had established a new republic that seemed set to achieve its ambition to export its principles of Liberty, Fraternity, and Equality to the furthest corners of Europe, including Scotland. 'Robert Bruce's March' celebrates 'liberty' by focusing on Bruce's crucial defeat of an invading English army at Bannockburn in 1314, but it is also consciously concerned with 'liberty' in the context of current events in France: see J. De Lancey Ferguson, *The Letters of Robert Burns*, 2nd edn, ed. by G. Ross Roy, 2 vols (Oxford: Clarendon Press, 1985), II, 235–36. For a discussion of the radical political background to 'Robert Bruce's March' see Liam McIlvanney, *Burns the Radical*, (East Linton: Tuckwell, 2002), pp. 212–13. In a letter to John Ballantyne [January 1815] Hogg objects to Scott's recently-published poem *The Lord of the Isles*, in which Robert Bruce figures: 'I likewise expected some finer bursts of feeling with regard to Scottish independence–the coaxing apology to England is below any Scot to have uttered' (Fales Library & Special Collections, New York University, Fales MSS 89.20). 'King Edward's Dream' is Hogg's own poem, and it reflects the radical flavour of his periodical *The Spy*, in which it first appeared. However, it also very aptly reflects James Gray's radical politics and his sympathy with Burns (see note on 129, l. 839).

130, l. 879 Eden's pine forests that is, the River Eden, in Cumberland, which flows into the Solway Firth near Burgh-by-Sands: see Hogg's Note XVIII (p. 189) and the introductory note above on 'King Edward's Dream'.

130, l. 890 the exile of Rachrin John Barbour's fourteenth-century poem *The Bruce* records that Robert I (Bruce) had to retreat to the Irish island of Rathlin ('Rauchryne') during the period between his coronation in 1306 and the death of Edward I of England in 1307: see Barbour, *The Bruce*, ed. by A. A. M. Duncan (Edinburgh: Canongate, 1997), pp. 144–51, 166–67.

131, l. 891 Wallace's spirit William Wallace (*c.* 1270–1305), younger son of a Clydesdale laird, led Scottish popular resistance to Edward I of England, and in later centuries became a symbol of the defence of Scottish liberty against English aggression. Wallace was captured by the forces of England's King Edward I in 1304, and after a show trial in Westminster Hall in 1305 he was dragged on a hurdle to Smithfield, where 'he was hanged, cut down while still alive, and butchered; his head was set above London bridge and parts of his dismembered body were sent north for display' (Ranald Nicholson, *Scotland: The Later Middle Ages*, The Edinburgh History of Scotland, 2 (Edinburgh: Mercat Press, 1974; repr. 1997), p. 68).

131, l. 905 Pembroke and Howard two powerful aristocratic English families prominent in the medieval wars between England and Scotland. Thus Aymer de Valence, Earl of Pembroke, was an early military opponent of Robert I, and Thomas Howard, Earl of Surrey and Duke of Norfolk, defeated James IV at Flodden in 1513 in a battle that had disastrous consequences for Scotland.

131, ll. 914–17 green Pentland [...] Ochel's fair mountains to Lammermore brown from the Pentland Hills to the south of Edinburgh there are panoramic views north-west to the Ochil Hills and east to the Lammermuir Hills.

132, ll. 948–50 Till people thou'st hated [...] liberty bravely regain while pointing to the decisive victory at Bannockburn in 1314 won by a Scottish army led by Robert I over Edward II's invading English army, these lines in Hogg's poem are also particularly reminiscent of the radical spirit of Burns's 'Robert Bruce's March to Bannockburn', discussed in the introductory note on 'King Edward's Dream', above.

132, ll. 952–59 I thought [...] ends of the earth shall obey in this verse paragraph Scotland's guardian angel looks forward to the Imperial Britain that will result from the Union between England and Scotland. The assertion that Imperial Britain will eventually rule the ends of the earth was an encouraging one in 1813, when the Napoleonic Wars saw Britain locked in conflict with Imperial France. Indeed, Wallace and Bruce as defenders of liberty against the tyrant Edward I are invoked by implication in support of a Britain threatened with invasion by the tyrant Napoleon. Burns expresses similar sentiments about Britain and its war with France in his song 'The Dumfries Volunteers' (Kinsley 484). Significantly, the guardian angel in Hogg's poem indicates that the Union will not result from English conquest of Scotland, but will develop after James VI, King of Scots (son of Mary, Queen of Scots) inherits the English throne.

132, l. 960 yon little hamlet o'ershadowed with smoke Edinburgh was nicknamed 'Auld Reekie', because the smoke from its many chimneys was visible at a great distance.

133, ll. 968–75 In yon western plain [...] averted his eye Scotland's guardian angel makes King Edward look west from the Pentlands along the extensive valley of the River Forth to the site of his victory at Falkirk over Wallace in 1298. Book XI of Blind Harry's fifteenth-century poem *Wallace* includes laments for the deaths at Falkirk of 'Schyr Iohn the Graym' and Sir John Stewart: see *Hary's Wallace*, ed. by Matthew P. McDiarmid, Scottish Text Society, Fourth Series, 4–5, 2 vols (Edinburgh: Scottish Text Society, 1968–69), II, 41–77.

133, ll. 976–87 Even there [...] at Carron shall die in the same 'western plain' (see previous note) Edward I is made to see the site of the comprehensive Scottish victory in 1314 at Bannockburn near Stirling against King Edward II and his allies. At Bannockburn the English army, although heavily outnumbering the Scots, was routed and driven back towards the River Carron and Falkirk. The thistle is the emblem of Scotland, the rose is the emblem of England, and the shamrock is the emblem of Ireland. According to Barbour, the English army at Bannockburn included 'off Irland a great menge' (*The Bruce*, ed. Duncan, p. 409).

133, l. 979 led on by Carnarvon Edward I's heir, Edward of Caernarfon, who would become Edward II on his father's death.

133, l. 1000 On sand of the Solway King Edward died within sight of Scotland at Burgh-by-Sands, which is adjacent to the Solway Firth.

134–35, ll. 1012–51 The next was from a western vale [...] their darling Cunninghame in his annotated copy of the fifth edition of *The Queen's Wake* (see note on 38, l. 545), Hogg indicates that the sixteenth bard is a portrait of Allan Cunningham (1784–1842). Allan grew up in Nithsdale at Dalswinton, about a mile from Ellisland farm, and his father was on friendly terms with Burns during Burns's years at Ellisland (1788–91). Allan had literary ambitions from an early age, but when he was ten years old he was apprenticed to his older brother James, a stonemason at Dalswinton. R. H. Cromek's *Remains of Nithsdale and Galloway Song* (London: Cadell and Davies, 1810) in fact largely consists of material composed by Allan Cunningham, who moved to London in 1810, finding employment there from 1814 till 1840 with the sculptor Francis Chantrey. Cunningham remained active as a writer 'in stolen hours, when labour done' (l. 1020) while working for Chantrey, and his output is impressive both in quality and quantity. See the present edition's Introduction, pp. lvi–lvii for an account of Hogg's first meeting with Allan Cunningham. In *East Galloway Sketches* (Castle Douglas: Adam Rae, 1901), Alexander Trotter asserts (p. 196) that 'the Bard of Nith and Clouden' in *The Queen's Wake* 'is Thomas Mouncey [Cunningham], not Allan as is generally supposed'. Hogg certainly admired the poetry of Allan's older brother Thomas Mouncey (see the present edition's Introduction, p. lvii), and Thomas Mouncey Cunningham contributed songs to Hogg's *The Forest Minstrel* (1810). Nevertheless, the 'general supposition' that the Bard of Nith is Allan Cunningham is supported by Hogg's note in the annotated copy. It is of course possible that Hogg had Thomas Mouncey in mind for the first edition of 1813, but had Allan in mind for the fifth edition of 1819. However, the 1813 and 1819 descriptions of the Bard of Nith are virtually identical.

134, l. 1017 Cluden's loneliest shade the Cluden joins the Nith at Lincluden, one and a half miles north of Dumfries. 'It figures in our pastoral poetry as "lonely Cluden's hermit stream"' (Groome).

134, l. 1026 The sun would chamber in the Ken Loch Ken, the River Ken, and the Glenkens district of Galloway lie to the west of Nithsdale.

134, l. 1027 The red star the planet Mars, named after the god of war.

134, l. 1027 Locherben lies in the foothills of the Lowthers, about 6 miles to the east of Drumlanrig in Upper Nithsdale (see note on 135, l. 1065), and Hogg leased this farm and the farm of Corfardin from 1807 till 1809. Furthermore, Locherben is near Queensberry Hill, where Hogg first met Allan Cunningham (see the present edition's Introduction, pp. lvi–lvii). Appropriately, Locherben is an important setting in 'Dumlanrig', the sixteenth bard's song.

Dumlanrig

Drumlanrig (here, as at some other points in *The Queen's Wake*, a place name is slightly altered) is situated 17 miles north-west of Dumfries. The subject-matter of 'Dumlanrig' looks back to traditional ballads of Border warfare such as 'The Battle of Otterburn' (Child 161) and 'Kinmont Willie' (Child 186). As the notes below suggest, Hogg loosely bases the narrative of 'Dumlanrig' on events that took place early in the reign of Mary, Queen of Scots.

135, l. 1065 And Douglas heard the noise within 'The barony of Drumlanrig belonged to the Douglases as early at least as 1356, and for four centuries passed from father to son with only a single break (1578), and then from grandsire to grandson. In 1388 James, second earl of Douglas, conferred it on the elder of his two natural sons, Sir William de Douglas, first Baron of Drumlanrig, whose namesake and ninth descendant was created Viscount of Drumlanrig in 1628 and Earl of Queensberry in 1633. William, third Earl (1637–95) was created Duke of Queensberry and Earl of Drumlanrig in 1684; and Charles, third Duke (1698–1778), was succeeded by his first cousin, William, third Earl of March and Ruglen (1725–1810). "Old Q.," that spoiler of woods and patron of the turf, the "degenerate Douglas" of Wordsworth's indignant sonnet, was in turn succeeded by Henry, third Duke of Buccleuch, great-grandson of the second Duke of Queensberry' (quoted from the entry for *Drumlanrig Castle* in Groome). The recent death of 'Old Q' in 1810 meant that the Douglases of Drumlanrig retained a current resonance when Hogg was writing *The Queen's Wake*. Equally, for Hogg's Scottish readers mention of the Douglas family would immediately call to mind 'the Good' Sir James Douglas (1286?–1330), a man remembered with affection in Scottish folk tradition, along with Wallace and Bruce, as one of the heroes of the Wars of Independence. Both in Hogg's poem and in the historical record, the 'James of Dumlanrig' (l. 1545) who opposed Lennox was, like his namesake the Good Sir James, a focus for Scottish resistance to English incursions in the south-west.

136, l. 1082 Lennox, with the southern host following his incursion into Scotland in the English interest in 1544 (see note on 74, ll. 723–24), the Earl of Lennox also led English incursions into south-west Scotland in 1547 and 1548. These incursions are discussed by Holinshed (II, 240–46): see also the article in the *DNB* on Matthew Stewart, Earl of Lennox (1516–71). For the poetic purposes of 'Dumlanrig' Hogg conflates the incursions of 1547 and 1548, and makes the outcome much more favourable to the Scots than it in fact was. He then proceeds in his Note XIX (p. 189) to muddy the waters with regard to the historical accuracy of his poem.

136, l. 1084 Solway marks the western part of the border between Scotland and England.

136, ll. 1089–91 Dalveen [...] Durisdeer Dalveen is 'a wild pass (1200 feet) over the Lowther Mountains, from the head-streams of Powtrail Water in Crawford parish, Lanarkshire, to those of Carron Water in Durisdeer, Dumfriesshire' (Groome). Drumlanrig is in Durisdeer parish.

136, l. 1097 Locherben see note on 134, l. 1027.

136, l. 1101 Cample's rugged ford Cample Water flows into the Nith near Thornhill, at a point which is a couple of miles further south than Drumlanrig and Locherben.

137, l. 1127 Ganna's lofty brow Gana Hill, one of the highest of the Lowthers, lies near the head of Daer Water, about six miles to the east of Drumlanrig.

137, l. 1140–41 The ghastly bull's-head scowled on high, | Emblem of death to foeman's eye a reference to an attempt by Chancellor Crichton to curb the power of the Douglases during the minority of James II. When Archibald, fifth earl of Douglas, died in 1439 he was succeeded by his son William, who was then in his early teens. William and his brother David accepted an invitation to dine in Edinburgh Castle on 24 November 1440. 'At the close of the dinner Chancellor Crichton placed a bull's head on the table, "quhilk was ane signe and taikin of condemnatour to the death". The two Douglas brothers were seized and put through a rigmarole of a trial before being beheaded on the castle hill' (Ranald Nicholson, *Scotland: The Later Middle Ages*, The Edinburgh History of Scotland, 2 (Edinburgh: Mercat Press, 1974; repr. 1997), p. 330). Thereafter a bull's head could be interpreted as a 'sign and token' of a Douglas out for revenge.

137, l. 1142 bloody hearts a Douglas family emblem, referring back to the Wars of Independence. Robert I was buried at Dunfermline, but his heart was removed before burial and the Good Sir James Douglas (see note on 135, l. 1065), in accordance with the King's dying wish, set out on a pilgrimage to the Holy Land carrying the dead King's heart. However, Sir James was killed on the way, fighting against the Moors at Andalusia. Robert I's heart was returned to Scotland, and was buried at the high altar of Melrose Abbey.

138, l. 1151 Morison of Locherben the resonance of the Border name of Morison, or Morrison, is indicated by a character in Scott's short story 'The Two Drovers' who declares: 'I am Hugh Morrison from Glenae, come of the Manly Morrisons of auld langsyne' (see Scott, *Chronicles of the Canongate*, ed. by Claire Lamont (Edinburgh: Edinburgh University Press, 2000), p. 128). It will be remembered that a later farmer of Locherben was one James Hogg (see note on 134, l. 1027), and this of course lends further resonance to the situation.

138, l. 1155 Crighup linn Crichope Linn is a waterfall on the Hope Burn near its junction with Cample Water (see note on 136, l. 1101). The Hope Burn flows down to Crichope Linn from Threip Moor.

139, ll. 1188–89 O, for the lyre of heaven [...] Linden's lofty hymn the church of Lindean, near the Selkirkshire town of Galashiels, 'disused since 1586', was the place 'where the body of William Douglas, the Knight of Liddesdale, lay during the night after his assassination (1353)' (Groome, under *Lindean*). According to the *DNB*, this Sir William Douglas 'was the eldest lawful son of Sir James Douglas of Lothian, though he has been called by many the natural son of the "Good" Sir James'. The death of Sir William featured in 'The Knight of Liddesdale', a ballad (Child 160) of which only a fragment survives. *The Mountain Bard* (1807) includes 'The Death of Douglas, Lord of Liddisdale', which is Hogg's attempt to reconstruct and recreate this ancient ballad.

139, ll. 1190–91 Or his, who from the height beheld | The reeling strife of Flodden Field a reference to Scott's *Marmion* (1808), which culminates in a memorable account of the Battle of Flodden Field (1513). At this battle James IV, King of Scots, having led a Scottish invasion of England, was heavily defeated and lost his life. Scott narrates the battle from the point of view of three of his characters: 'Blount and Fitz-Eustace rested still | With Lady Clare upon the hill' (stanza XXVI, Canto Sixth).

139, l. 1214 Corrybraken's surges Corryvreckan, the famous whirlpool off the northern tip of the island of Jura.

140, l. 1231 Garroch glen if the goats fled up the Hope Burn (see note on 138, 1155) they would come first to Threip Moor and then to Locherben, which stands in the glen of Garroch Water.

141, l. 1293 Queensberry see note on 134, l. 1027.

142, l. 1317 the Lowther eagle's look the Lowther Hills lie immediately to the east of Upper Nithsdale and Drumlanrig.

142, l. 1321 the purple heart see note on 137, l. 1142.

143, l. 1376 Sweet floweret of the banks of Ae Garroch Water flows into Capel Water a little below Locherben, and Capel Water then flows into the Water of Ae.

143–44, ll. 1382–85 Glencairn [...] Shinnel [...] Crawford-moor [...] Tweed and Lyne as he outlines the extent of his domains, Douglas points to Glencairn, a parish on the western border of Nithsdale which includes the village of Moniaive; to Shinnel Water, a small river of Tynron parish, Upper Nithsdale; to Crawford-moor, which lies to the north of Drumlanrig, across the Lowther Hills; and to the River Tweed and Lyne Water, which rise to the north-east of Drumlanrig, beyond the Lowthers.

144, l. 1417 Lindsay on the banks of Daur Daer Water lies north-east of Drumlanrig, in the Lowther Hills, and flows north towards the village of Crawford. David Lindsay, tenth Earl of Crawford (d. 1574) was a supporter of Mary, Queen of Scots.

144, l. 1418 The fierce M'Turk [...] Lochinvaur 'Dumlanrig' is set in the part of Scotland in which Hogg lived during his Dumfriesshire years (1805–09), and here we appear to have an oblique reference to James M'Turk, a friend from those years. M'Turk was a farmer at Stenhouse in Tynron parish (see *1819*, l. 1531), near Hogg's farm of Corfardin (see note on 134, l. 1027), and when Hogg had to give up Corfardin because of the death of his flock in the winter of 1808, he went to live with M'Turk at Stenhouse for three months, before establishing himself at Locherben. The confluence of Shinnel and Scaur Waters is in Tynron parish, and in 'Dumlanrig', M'Turk comes to the assistance of Douglas 'with troops from Shinnel glens and Scaur' (*1813*, l. 1452). The real-life James M'Turk was an important subscriber to *The Queen's Wake*, and when the poem was published at the end of January 1813 Hogg invited his eldest son, Robert M'Turk, to a celebratory dinner at John Grieve's house in Edinburgh. I am grateful to Gillian Hughes for providing me with the above information on James M'Turk: Dr Hughes is currently writing a biography of Hogg for publication by the Edinburgh University Press. A literary allusion follows the personal allusion to M'Turk: 'Young Lochinvar', Scott's famous song of Border derring-do, had appeared in Canto V of *Marmion* (1808). Groome records that *Lochinvar* is a lake in Kircudbrightshire in Galloway which 'contains an islet, with vestiges of the ancient baronial fortalice of the Gordons, Knights of Lochinvar, ancestors of the Viscounts Kenmure, and one of them the theme of Lady Heron's song in *Marmion*, "Young Lochinvar"'.

144–45, ll. 1420–22 Maxwell [...] Glencairn [...] Kilpatrick [...] Johnston [...] Jardine Hogg takes these names from the account in Holinshed (II, 241–43: see note on 136, l. 1082).

145, l. 1433 Blackwood on the Nith, about 9 miles south of Drumlanrig.

145, l. 1450 Blackford-hill not identified.

145, ll. 1451–52 M'Turk [...] With troops from Shinnel glens and Scaur see note on 144, l. 1418.

145, l. 1453 Gordon with the clans of Ken see notes on 134, l. 1026 and 144, l. 1418.

145, l. 1454 Lindsay with his Crawford men see note on 144, l. 1417.

145, l. 1455 Morton Morton Castle, situated about 2 miles east of Drumlanrig, was owned by the branch of the Douglases who became Earls of Morton.

146, l. 1472 Arabia's lineage stoops to thine according to Holinshed (I, 36), 'The Scotishmen, according to the manner of other nations, esteeming it a glorie to fetch their beginning of great anciencie, say that their originall descent came from the Greeks and Egyptians'. Gathelus, 'the sonne of Cecrops, who builded the citie of Athens', married the daughter of Pharao Orus: 'Here you must understand, that Pharaos daughter which Gathelus thus maried, was called Scota, of whome such as came of the posteritie of that nation were afterwards, and are at this present day called *Scoti*, that is to say Scotishmen, and the land where they inhabit *Scotia*, that is to say, Scotland'.

146, l. 1474 Locher-moor perhaps Lochar Moss, which lies to the south-east of Dumfries, between the town and the Solway, and thus on the route to England from Nithsdale.

148, ll. 1545–60 James of Dumlanrig [...] From whom the Queensberry honours flow a characteristically mischievous piece of Hogg chutzpah lurks not far below the surface here. In 'Dumlanrig' the admirable 'young Morison' is Hogg's predecessor as farmer of Locherben, and Hogg clearly identifies with him. May Morison marries James of Dumlanrig, ancestor of the ducal houses of Queensberry and Buccleuch. It would appear that the honours of these houses flow from being descended, as it were, from Hogg's sister.

149, ll. 1592–95 chieftain of M'Lean [...] misty shores of Mull the first three bards of Night the Third having been portraits of friends of Hogg from southern Scotland, we now return to the Highlands for the final competitor. Mull is one of the largest islands of the Inner Hebrides, and Castle Duart, stronghold of the chiefs of the Clan MacLean, is on the eastern coast of Mull.

149, ll. 1597–98 many a saint and sovereign's grave [...] Columba's ruins the focus now shifts to Iona, the small island off the west coast of Mull on which St Columba (in Gaelic, Colum Cille) founded a monastery in 563. Monastic life continued in Iona in various forms for around a thousand years, but came to an end during the reign of Mary, Queen of Scots as a result of the Reformation of 1560. The monastic buildings became ruinous, and were visited in this condition by Johnson and Boswell in 1773. Columba was regarded with particular veneration in medieval Scotland: for example, his 'relic-shrine, the *Brecchennach* or Monymusk reliquary, was carried before the victorious Scottish army at Bannockburn' (*Oxford Companion*, p. 103). This veneration helps to explain why a royal burial-ground (the Reilig Odhráin) was established on Columba's island. Part of the action of Hogg's epic poem *Queen Hynde* (1824) takes place on Iona, and Columba is one of the poem's major characters.

149, l. 1600 slender forms of nuns a nunnery, for Augustinian nuns, was founded on Iona about 1200.

150, l. 1615 Allan Bawn, the bard of Mull another Highland 'bard of Mull' features in Hogg's epic poem *Queen Hynde*, ed. Suzanne Gilbert and Douglas S. Mack (S/SC, 1998), p. 29.

150, l. 1616 Fingal one of the heroes of James Macpherson's *Ossian* poems, which are discussed in the present edition's Introduction (pp. xxxii–xxxiii).

The Abbot M'Kinnon

As with 'Kilmeny', Hogg here uses couplets in a 'sprung rhythm' reminiscent of Coleridge's 'Christabel' and Scott's *Lay of the Last Minstrel*. For a discussion of John Mackinnon, the last Abbot of Iona, and of 'The Abbot M'Kinnon', see the present edition's Introduction, pp. xlvi–xlvii.

151, l. 1675 Dun-ye the summit of the hill of Dun I is the highest point on Iona.

152, l. 1679 Ross's rude impervious bound the Sound of Iona separates Columba's island from the rugged peninsula known as the Ross of Mull.

152, l. 1680 the ravenous burrowing race rabbits.

152, l. 1692 "Where there are women mischief must be." 'A Gaelic proverb attached itself to Colum Cille at some point and stuck there: "Far am bi bò bi bean agus far am bi bean bi buaireadh; Where there is a cow there is a woman and where there is a woman there is mischief". The eminent good sense of the first phrase is usually overlooked. Milking and tending cattle have for a very long time been traditionally female occupations in the Highlands. The saying has been taken to mean that the saint banished both species to the conveniently named Eilean nam Ban—the island of women—close to the Ross of Mull coast' (E. Mairi MacArthur, *Columba's Island: Iona from Past to Present* (Edinburgh: Edinburgh University Press, 1995), p. 24). See also Hogg's Note XXI (p. 190).

153, ll. 1731–32 In temple that north in the main appeared, | Which fire from bowels of ocean had seared the island of Staffa, formed by volcanic action, lies to the north of Iona. 'Three strands combine to make Fingal's Cave on Staffa perhaps the best known of all caves. Its structure is unique. Nowhere else is there a sea-cave formed completely in hexagonally-jointed basalt. To this distinctiveness, drama and intense interest are imparted by the size, the sounds, the colours, and the remarkable symmetry of this 227-foot cavern; and by Nature's gift of fractured columns forming a crude walkway just above high-water level, allowing exploring visitors to go far inside' (Alastair de Watteville, *The Island of Staffa* (Romsey: Romsey Fine Art, 1993), p. 14). There is evidence which suggests that Hogg visited Staffa at some point after 1804 and before 1815: see H. B. de Groot, 'Scott, Hogg, and the Album in the Inn on Ulva', *SHW*, 14 (2003), 93–99 (p. 97).

153, ll. 1734–35 the stately pile | Himself had upreared in Iona's isle the present Iona Abbey dates mainly from the fifteenth century. However, it occupies the site of Columba's monastery. Oddly, from within Fingal's Cave, the restricted view out of the narrow entrance includes, in the distance, Iona Abbey.

153, l. 1755 Uprose the sun from the Bens of Lorn the mountains ('Bens') of the mainland district of Lorn lie to the east of Iona, beyond Mull.

154, ll. 1781–93 The tall grey forms [...] green o'er the darksome gray in this passage the monks, approaching Staffa from the south, see Fingal's Cave, which is at the southern tip of the island. Awed, they veer to the east to find a landing-place. Hogg's description of the scene is accurate. For example, some of Staffa's basalt columns are indeed bent (l. 1791), because of the weight of volcanic debris that fell on them before they cooled.

155, l. 1794 on wonderous pavement of old the cave is approached along a causeway formed by snapped-off basalt columns, the sea being immediately on the left and the base of a cliff being immediately on the right.

155, l. 1798 The watcher Bushella in the sea off the causeway mentioned in the previous note, and close to the shore, is an islet called in Gaelic *Am Buachaille*, 'the Shepherd'. The islet consists entirely of basalt columns.

155, l. 1809 the anthem there sung by the sea the sound of the sea in

Fingal's cave inspired Mendelssohn's well-known 'Hebrides' overture.

155–56, ll. 1826–59 The Monks' Hymn Hogg included a revised version of this song under the title 'Hymn to the God of the Sea' in *Songs by the Ettrick Shepherd* (Edinburgh: Blackwood; London: Cadell, 1831), pp. 291–93. See also notes on 12, ll. 213–20 and 76–77, ll. 810–35.

157, ll. 1870–71 the countless isles that lie, | From Barra to Mull, and from Jura to Skye from Staffa, Barra lies to the west, Mull to the east, Jura to the south, and Skye to the north. There are many islands within sight of Staffa.

159, l. 1951 the Abbot of I 'The old Gaelic names for the island [Iona] are Hii, Ia or simply I, the last still in use, and often it came to be called Icolmkill, the isle of Colum of the Church, because of Columba's association with it' (Ian Findlay, *Columba* (Edinburgh: Chambers, 1992), p. 111).

Conclusion

165, l. 77 the nameless stranger youth i.e. the fourteenth bard, John Grieve.

165, l. 92 the Lord of Mar John Erskine, Earl of Mar (*d.* 1572) was a prominent figure during the reign of Mary, Queen of Scots. After the Regent Lennox was assassinated in 1571 'he was quickly succeeded by the more conciliatory figure of the Earl of Mar' (Michael Lynch, *Scotland: A New History* (London: Pimlico, 1992), p. 220). The Earl of Mar was a supporter of Mary during the early part of her reign, but turned against the Queen after the murder of Darnley and her marriage to Bothwell.

166, l. 119 Teviotdale one of the valleys of the Scottish Borders, Teviotdale lies to the south of the Ettrick valley, and runs parallel with it.

167, l. 167 Gilmorice' doom for his second song Gardyn sings the traditional ballad 'Child Maurice' (Child 83): the details mentioned in Hogg's narrative closely match Child 83 version F, 'Gil Morrice'. In this version the opening line 'Gil Morrice was an erles son' introduces a tale of aristocratic lust and murder.

167, l. 174 Tam Lean of Carterha' the bard of Ettrick is clearly a member of Hogg's 'mountain and fairy school' (see Introduction, p. xxxv). He sings the traditional ballad 'Tam Lin' (Child 39), in which Janet rescues her lover Tam Lin of Carterhaugh from the power of the Fairy Queen. Carterhaugh is in the Ettrick valley, near the junction of Ettrick and Yarrow.

167, l. 184 Don and Dee rivers of north-east Scotland that rise in the Highlands and enter the sea at Aberdeen. For the Dee, see note on 57, l. 78.

167–68, ll. 185–92 borne, by beauteous bride [...] Back to Dunedin found its way Hogg refers here to the real 'harp of Queen Mary': see Hogg's Note XXIII (p. 190) and the present edition's Introduction, pp. xxviii–xxix.

170, ll. 271–72 her witching lays, | Of Ettrick banks and Yarrow braes cf. Hogg's Note XXII (p. 190).

170, ll. 280–92 Bangour [...] Logan's hand Hogg mentions the following poets who have attempted to play the harp of Ettrick: William Hamilton of Bangour (1704–54); Allan Ramsay (1686–1758); John Langhorne (1735–79); and John Logan (1748–88). For further details see Hogg's Notes XXIV–XXVII (p. 190), and the corresponding Editor's Notes, below.

170–71, ll. 293–307 Then Leyden came from Border land [...] Scotland knows her loss too late John Leyden (1775–1811), poet, physician, and linguist, cut a memorable figure as a student training for the ministry at Edinburgh University: 'The rustic yet undaunted manner, the humble dress, the high harsh tone of his voice, joined to the broad provincial accent of Teviotdale, discomposed on this first occasion the gravity of the professor, and totally routed that of the students. But it was soon perceived that these uncouth attributes were joined to qualities which commanded respect and admiration. [...] and to those among the students who did not admit literary proficiency as a shelter for the ridicule due since the days of Juvenal to the scholar's worn coat and unfashionable demeanour, Leyden was in no respect averse from showing strong reasons adapted to their comprehension, and affecting their personal safety, for keeping their mirth within decent bounds' (Robert Chambers, *A Biographical Dictionary of Eminent Scotsmen*, 4 vols (Glasgow: Blackie, 1835) III, 419). Leyden helped Scott collect material for the first two volumes of *Minstrelsy of the Scottish Border* (1802). Having obtained a medical qualification at St Andrews, in 1803 Leyden went to India, where he served in a variety of medical and other posts, and studied the languages and literature of the sub-continent. In 1811 he accompanied Lord Minto to Java, where he died in that year.

170, l. 301 Malabar a district of India.

171, l. 309 Walter the abbot Walter Scott. *The Queen's Wake* was written in 1812, and Scott moved to his new home at Abbotsford in May 1812.

171, ll. 312–15 he tried a strain; | 'Twas wild [...] simple magic melody Scott's poetic career got off to something of a false start when translations of Gothic poems by Bürger (1796) and Goethe (1799) were followed by a contribution to M. G. Lewis's *Tales of Wonder* (1801). After editing *Minstrelsy of the Scottish Border*, a collection of traditional ballads (3 vols, 1802–03), Scott found success with *The Lay of the Last Minstrel* (1805), his own recreation of the 'simple magic melody' of the old Border minstrelsy.

171, l. 322 their moonlight halls moonlight features strongly in *The Lay of the Last Minstrel*: thus the first Canto ends with a moonlight journey, and the second Canto begins with Scott's famous lines on Melrose by moonlight.

171, l. 324 fairies sought our land again Gilpin Horner, the goblin page, features prominently in *The Lay of the Last Minstrel*.

171, ll. 332–33 He little weened, a parent's tongue | Such strains had o'er my cradle sung in effect Hogg is here claiming to be able to operate within a popular oral tradition that Scott can only observe as an outsider.

171–72, ll. 334–45 But when, to native feelings true [...] Another's feelings by his own this passage is discussed in the present edition's Introduction, pp. lvii–lviii.

172, ll. 347–49 He left our mountains [...] The Caledonian harp of yore writing in 1812, Hogg in these lines presents Scott's poetic career since *The Lay of the Last Minstrel* (1805) as a disappointing departure from the old minstrelsy of the Scottish Border, that is to say from the old oral ballads that Hogg associates with 'the Caledonian harp of yore'. The *Lay* was followed first by *Marmion* (1808), which has an English hero; then by *The Lady of the Lake* (1810), which is largely set in the Highlands. During 1812, when Hogg was writing *The Queen's Wake*, Scott was writing *Rokeby* (1813). This book-length poem is set in the north of England–a fact that in 1812 was no doubt known in the small gossipy world of literary Edinburgh, to which both Hogg and Scott belonged. Scott's career as an anonymous novelist did not begin until *Waverley* (1814).

172, l. 351 Only by force one strain she threw the harp under discussion here is the harp of the old minstrelsy of the Scottish Border, re-tuned and played by Scott to magnificent effect in *The Lay of the Last Minstrel*. Enamoured of change, however, Scott has left the Border mountains (ll. 346–47) for other interests and other harps (see previous note). *Marmion* may have an English hero, but it is about the Battle of Flodden Field, a powerfully resonant event for Ettrick Forest. This, then, is still a performance on the old harp, albeit a forced one, as Scott's interests are already beginning to wander elsewhere–and when we come to *The Lady of the Lake* and *Rokeby* Scott has abandoned the old harp in favour of new instruments. Indeed, to use the terminology of *The Queen's Wake*, one might think of *The Lady of the Lake* as a product of the Harp of Queen Mary as opposed to the Caledonian Harp.

172, l. 362 Saint Mary's shore *The Queen's Wake* ends where it began, on the banks of St Mary's Loch at the heart of Hogg's native district: see note on 7, l. 14.

172, l. 364 Clokmore Clockmore is the highest of the hills that overlook the valley of Megget Water. This river flows into St Mary's Loch opposite Bowerhope Law.

172, l. 369 Bowerhope Law this hill dominates the south-eastern side of St Mary's Loch.

Hogg's Notes

In page references to Hogg's Notes, (a) indicates the first quarter of the page, (b) the second quarter, (c) the third quarter, and (d) the final quarter. The Notes to *The Queen's Wake* follow the precedent provided by Scott's long narrative poems, and Hogg's Notes at times seem to aim to echo the scholarly and learned tone of Scott's Notes.

177 Note I According to the *OED* Hogg's definition of *wake* is unique: 'Used by Hogg for a serenade, nocturnal song'. The *SND* concurs: 'Only in Hogg: a serenade, a midnight concert of song or instrumental music'. Perhaps, however, Hogg's use of the word is not entirely eccentric. In its usual senses, *wake* carries connotations of death and mourning as well as of celebration, and it may be that Hogg intended Queen Mary's 'Wake' to convey a sense of something valuable that has been lost, that is to be both mourned and celebrated, and that needs (if possible) to be resurrected.

177(b) the Psalms being turned into a rude metre Hogg eloquently expresses his affection for the Scottish metrical Psalms in 'A Letter from Yarrow. The Scottish Psalmody Defended', *Edinburgh Literary Journal*, 13 March 1830, pp. 162–63.

177(d) The minstrels who, in the reign of the Stuarts, enjoyed privileges Hogg here echoes Scott's view as expressed in *The Lay of the Last Minstrel*: see the present edition's Introduction, pp. xxxvi.

178–79 Note II Hogg's quotations here are accurate in substance but inaccurate in detail. His sources are Holinshed, and John Knox, *The History of the Reformation of Religion within the Realm of Scotland* (Edinburgh, 1790), Book IV p. 263. The Dufresnoy reference has not been traced.

179 Note III see notes on 31, l. 293 and 32, l. 356.

179 Note IV Hogg writes here that 'The Witch of Fife', 'Old David', 'Macgregor', and 'Kilmeny' are all 'founded on popular traditions'. The 'popular tradition' on which 'The Witch of Fife' is founded was also familiar to Burns, who describes it in a letter to Captain Francis Grose (? June 1790). In this letter Burns gives an account of the two witch stories relating to Alloway Kirk on which he based his 'Tam o' Shanter' (Kinsley 321), the best-known of all the poems of the Scottish Lowland popular tradition. Burns then adds: 'The last relation I shall give, though equally true, is not so well identified as the two former, with regard to the scene: but as the best authorities give it for Aloway, I shall relate it'. According to Burns, a young shepherd boy, when passing the Kirk late on a summer evening, 'fell in with a crew of men and women, who were busy pulling stems of the plant ragwort. He observed that as each person pulled a ragwort, he or she got astride of it and called out, "Up horsie!" on which the ragwort flew off, like Pegasus, through the air with its rider'. Burns goes on to say that the boy did likewise, and flew with the others to 'a merchant's wine cellar in Bordeaux, where, without saying by your leave, they quaffed away at the best the cellar could afford, until the morning'. The 'poor shepherd lad', very drunk, fell asleep and was left behind by the others, to be discovered in the cellar next day. 'Somebody that understood Scotch, asking him what he was, he said he was such-a-one's herd in Aloway; and by some means or other getting home again, he lived long to tell the world the wondrous tale': see *The Letters of Robert Burns*, ed. by J. De Lancy Ferguson, 2nd edn, rev. by G. Ross Roy, 2 vols (Oxford: Clarendon Press: 1985), II, 29–31 (p. 31). For further information, see Barbara Bloedé, 'The Witchcraft Tradition in Hogg's Tales and Verse', *SHW*, 1 (1990), 91–102 (pp. 98–101). See also Thomas Davidson, *Rowan Tree and Red Thread: A Scottish Witchcraft Miscellany* (Edinburgh: Oliver and Boyd, 1949), p. 85 for a variant that locates this story at Yarrowford in the Yarrow valley, rather than Alloway. 'The Witch of Fife' can be seen as a tribute to Burns, being written very much in the spirit of 'Tam o' Shanter'. In his 'Memoir of the Author's Life' Hogg records that 'Tam o' Shanter' was his favourite poem (*Altrive Tales*, ed. by Gillian Hughes (S/SC, 2003), pp. 17–18).

179(d) the old ballads of Tam Lean and Thomas of Erceldon for these famous ballads of fairy abduction, see Child 39 ('Tam Lin') and Child 37 ('Thomas Rymer').

179–80 Note V Hogg visited Glen Avon in 1802: see 'The Unpublished Conclusion of James Hogg's 1802 Highland Journey', ed. by H. B. de Groot, *SHW*, 6 (1995), 55–66 (pp. 55–57). Hogg here writes: 'I never saw a scene that I took more pleasure in contemplating [...] it hath a gloomy sublimity peculiar to itself, the viewing of which fills the mind with still solemnity' (p. 56).

180 Note VI see note on 58, l. 102.

182(b) He lived at Garwell in Eskdale-moor in *The Three Perils of Woman* (1823) Hogg situates Bellsburnfoot, home of the archetypal Border farmer Daniel Bell, in the vicinity of Garwald Water in Eskdalemuir. After rising on the slopes of Ettrick Pen (a mountain that overlooks both the Ettrick valley and Eskdalemuir), Garwald Water joins the White Esk at Garwaldwaterfoot. Hogg seems to have regarded this area as the Border heartland: see the paperback edition of *The Three Perils of Woman*, ed. by

Antony Hasler and Douglas S. Mack (Edinburgh: Edinburgh University Press, 2002), pp. 422–26.

182(d) There are two farmers still living, who will both make oath that they have wounded several old wives with shot as they were traversing the air in the shapes of moor-fowl and partridges in discussing the context of Hogg's 'The Wyffe of Ezdel-more' (a poem of witchcraft, set in Eskdalemuir), Peter Garside mentions this note in *The Queen's Wake* and suggests that the farmers concerned may have been James Glendinning and Thomas Beattie: see Hogg, *A Queer Book*, ed. by P. D. Garside (S/SC, 1995), pp. 227–28. Garside goes on to mention that the transformation of lovers into moor-fowl 'features in Hogg's prose story, "The Hunt of Eildon" (see *The Brownie of Bodsbeck; and other Tales* (1818), vol. II, pp. 334–38)'.

183(a) the lands of Newhouse and Kirkhope lie in the Ettrick valley, just upstream from the village of Ettrickbridge.

183(c) Mr Walter Scott has preserved it, but so altered [...]. The old people tell it as follows here as elsewhere Hogg boldly asserts that he has a more direct relationship than Scott with the old Border oral tradition that produced the ballads recorded in Scott's *Minstrelsy of the Scottish Border* (1802–03). Scott's version of this traditional story appears in his notes to his poem *The Lay of the Last Minstrel* (1805):

> Upon another occasion, the magician, having studied so long in the mountains that he became faint for want of food, sent his servant to procure some from the nearest farm-house. The attendant received a churlish denial from the farmer. Michael commanded him to return to this rustic Nabal, and lay before him his cap, or bonnet, repeating these words,
>
> > Maister Michael Scott's man
> > Sought meat, and gat nane.
>
> When this was done and said, the enchanted bonnet became suddenly inflated, and began to run round the house with great speed, pursued by the farmer, his wife, his servants, and the reapers, who were on the neighbouring *har'st rigg*. No one had the power to resist the fascination, or refrain from joining in pursuit of the bonnet, until they were totally exhausted with their ludicrous exercise. A similar charm occurs in *Houn de Bourdeaux*, and in the ingenious Oriental tale, called the *Caliph Vathek*. (Scott, *The Lay of the Last Minstrel* (London: Longman; Edinburgh: Constable, 1805), p. 239.)

Scott here, as elsewhere in his notes on *The Lay of the Last Minstrel*, adopts the tone of a detached investigator as he records the beliefs of the people he describes as 'the Scottish peasants' (p. 212) and 'the Scottish vulgar' (p. 213). Here we have Scott as a gentlemanly heir of the Enlightenment, collecting and recording evidence about the superstitions of the peasantry. Hogg, on the other hand, seems to lay claim to a more intimate connection with the old oral popular traditions of the Borders: 'The old people tell it as follows'. John Stagg's *The Cumbrian Minstrel*, 2 vols (Manchester: T. Wilkinson, 1821) has a version of the traditional story that is similar to Hogg's version, while differing from it in detail (I, 7–8).

185(a) Glen-Dochart [...] Ben More Glen Dochart lies immediately to the west of Loch Tay and about ten miles north of Loch Katrine: cf. note on

79, l. 915. Ben More lies immediately to the south of the western end of Glen Dochart.

185 Note XII cf. notes on 74, l. 726, on 78, l. 856, and on 79, ll. 900–03.

185 Note XIII Hogg quotes from Holinshed II, 126. This 'Lord Hamilton' is James Hamilton, second Baron Hamilton and first Earl of Arran (1477?– 1529), only son of Sir James Hamilton of Cadzow, first Baron Hamilton (*d.* 1479), by his second wife, the Princess Mary, daughter of James II. The *DNB* records that the second Baron Hamilton

> was a proficient in all the knightly accomplishments of the time, and one of the chief performers at the famous tournaments of the court of James IV. At the tournament held in honour of the king's marriage, Hamilton fought in the barriers with the famous French knight, Anthony D'Arcy de la Bastie. Though neither was victorious, the king was so pleased with the carriage of Lord Hamilton, as well as with his magnificent retinue, that on 11 Aug. he granted him a patent creating him Earl of Arran.

James Hamilton (*d.* 1575), second Earl of Arran and son of the first Earl, was a prominent figure in the reign of Mary, Queen of Scots: see notes on 74, ll. 723–24 and 101, ll. 1709–11.

185–186 Note XIV Hogg quotes from Holinshed II, 103. In creating 'Earl Walter', Hogg conflates and re-imagines two separate events in the rise of the Hamilton family to power: the tournament exploits of the second Baron Hamilton in the reign of James IV (see previous note), and the royal marriage of the first Baron Hamilton in the reign of James III. The *DNB* records that the first Baron Hamilton

> became one of the most trusted friends and counsellors of James III, and after the forfeiture of Thomas Boyd, earl of Arran, in 1469, he married Boyd's widow, the Princess Mary Stewart, daughter of James II. [...] By this marriage with the king's sister the house of Hamilton gained a great position, and became the nearest family to the throne.

186(b) the parish of Traquair this Peeblesshire parish contains the hamlet of Traquair and the mansion-house of Traquair. This mansion-house, said to be the oldest continuously-inhabited house in Scotland, stands in the Quair valley on the opposite bank of the Tweed from Innerleithen.

186(c) the minister of Inverlethen the town of Innerleithen lies on the Tweed between Peebles and Galashiels, and was widely identified as the 'St Ronan's Well' of Scott's novel of that name (1824). Gilbert Hutcheson was minister of Innerleithen from 1727 until his death in 1754, and his successor was Stephen Oliver, in office from 1755 till 1776 (see Hew Scott, *Fasti Ecclesiæ Scoticanæ*, 7 vols (Edinburgh: Oliver and Boyd, 1915–28), I, 274–75).

186(d) Mr Davidson probably Alexander Davidson, who was minister of Traquair from 1744 until his death in 1759 (*Fasti Ecclesiæ Scoticanæ*, I, 294).

186(d) the Plora wood Plora Craig and Plora Rig lie about two miles to the east of the mansion-house of Traquair.

187(a) Tushilaw see note on 109, l. 155.

187(c) Berry-bush lies in the hills between the Ettrick and Yarrow valleys, about two miles north-west of Tushilaw.

188(b) the Pleasance [...] the cliffs of Salisbury [...] the rock the Pleasance is a street in the Old Town of Edinburgh; for 'the cliffs of Salisbury' see the note on 11, l. 162; and 'the rock' is the massive Castle Rock, on which Edinburgh Castle is built.

188(d) Henderland lies in Meggetdale, a little under a mile from the point at which Megget Water flows into St Mary's Loch.

189 Note XIX see note on 136, l. 1082.

189 Note XX see note on 159, l. 1951.

190 Note XXI see notes on 152, l. 1692 and 159, l. 1951.

190 Note XXII the ballads Hogg mentions all have a setting in Ettrick Forest. They are 'The Outlaw Murray' (Child 305); 'Tam Lin' (Child 39); 'Jamie Telfer of the Fair Dodhead' (Child 190); and 'The Braes o Yarrow' (Child 214). These four ballads all appear in Scott's *Minstrelsy of the Scottish Border* (1802–03). In a letter to Scott of 30 June [1802?], Hogg writes: 'I am surprised to find that the songs in your collection differ so widely from my mother's. ... "Jamie Telfer" differs in many particulars' (quoted from Child, IV, 518). William Dunbar's famous poem 'I that in heill was and gladnes' (the familiar title 'Lament for the Makars' goes back no further than the eighteenth century) does not contain a reference to a bard of Ettrick in all its versions, but the Bannatyne Manuscript and Maitland Folio Manuscript texts do mention 'Ettrik' in stanza 14: see *The Poems of William Dunbar*, ed. by Priscilla Bawcutt, 2 vols (Glasgow: ASLS, 1998), I, 96 and II, 335. I am grateful to Meiko O'Halloran for sending me the following extract from her forthcoming thesis: 'The poem is thought to have been written shortly after the death of "Stobo", alias John Reid, in July 1505. Sir David Dalrymple of Hailes coined the title "Lament for the Deth of the Makkaris" in his collection, *Ancient Scottish Poems* (1770), a response to Allan Ramsay's *The Ever Green*. It seems likely that Hogg was familiar with Lord Hailes's volume as he is one of the few editors who prints "Ettrik" in the text. Ramsay, like recent editors James Kinsley and Priscilla Bawcutt, reads "Ettrik" as a mistake in the manuscript for "And eik"'.

190 Note XXIII in the first edition a final gathering begins after 'by a bride, which the' in the second sentence of this note. The final gathering contains only the remainder of Note XXIII and Notes XXIV–XXVII (all brief), and it would have been printed along with the first edition's preliminaries (titlepage, dedication, etc.). As the present edition's Introduction explains (pp. xlix–l), the second edition of *The Queen's Wake* was a re-issue of sheets of the first edition with new preliminaries. In this situation the final gathering could also be reprinted, and this gave Hogg an opportunity to add some new material at the end of his Notes. He duly did so, and the new material was carried through to the 1819 version of *The Queen's Wake* (see below). However the first edition's Notes XXIV–XXVII were omitted in the process, and are now reprinted for the first time. Readers of *The Queen's Wake* have tended to lose sight of these illuminating Notes as a result of their omission from the second edition onwards.

190 Note XXIV this Note and the three which follow combine to indicate that Hogg is not attempting in this part of *The Queen's Wake* to outline a national Scottish poetic tradition, but is providing a list of poets who have attempted to play the harp of Ettrick by writing about Ettrick Forest and its rivers of Yarrow and Ettrick. William Hamilton of Bangour (1704–54), a Jacobite who fought in the rising of 1745–46, was the author of 'The Braes of Yarrow', which Wordsworth mentions in a headnote to 'Yarrow Unvisited' (composed 1803, published 1807) as 'the exquisite Ballad of Hamilton, beginning "Busk ye, busk ye, my bonny Bride"'. According to James Paterson, this ballad by Hamilton is 'supposed to have been suggested by "The Dowie Dens of Yarrow," a more ancient ballad, published for the first time in Scott's Border Minstrelsy' (see *The Poems and Songs of William Hamilton of Bangour*, ed. by James Paterson (Edinburgh: Stevenson, 1850), p. 11). The 'more ancient ballad' in question is Child 214 'The Braes o Yarrow', called 'The Dowie Dens of Yarrow' in Scott's *Minstrelsy*. In his introductory note on this ballad, Child records that Scott's version in the *Minstrelsy* is based on material supplied by Hogg from Ettrick tradition.

190 Note XXV Allan Ramsay (1686–1758) was a man of Jacobite sympathies, and his song collection *The Tea-Table Miscellany* (1723–37) contained work by Ramsay himself and by others, as well as traditional songs. It includes 'Ettrick Banks', which begins: 'On Ettrick banks, in a summer's night, | At glowming when the sheep drave hame'. *The Tea-Table Miscellany* does not give clear attributions of authorship, but 'Ettrick Banks' seems to be a traditional song rather than the work of Ramsay himself: see *Scottish Song: A Selection*, ed. by Mary Carlyle Aitken (London: Macmillan, 1874), pp. 193–94.

190 Note XXVI John Langhorne (1735–79), an English clergyman and poet, was author of 'Genius and Valour: A Pastoral Poem Written in Honour of a Sister Kingdom' (1763), in which it is said that Scotland's wild scenes 'Oft led her faeries to the Shepherd's lay, | By Yarrow's banks, or groves of Endermay'. The poem later comments on the religious conflicts of the seventeenth century: 'Nor longer vocal with the Shepherd's lay | Were Yarrow's banks, or groves of Endermay'. Presumably 'Endermay' is Invermay, which Groome describes as 'a seat of Lord Clinton in Forteviot parish, SE Perthshire [...]. "The Birks of Invermay" are the theme of a well known lyric by David Mallet, and seem to have been sung by earlier poets'. David Mallet or Malloch (1705?–1765), was born near Crieff in Perthshire. He contributed to Ramsay's *Tea-Table Miscellany*, but like his friend James Thomson (author of *The Seasons*), he made his career in London rather than Scotland.

190 Note XXVII John Logan (1748–88), a Scottish clergyman and poet, was author of a song entitled 'The Braes of Yarrow', and he also wrote some of the well-known metrical paraphrases of Biblical passages used in the worship of the Church of Scotland.

The 1819 Version of *The Queen's Wake*

The notes below should be read in conjunction with the above notes on the 1813 version of Hogg's poem, to which cross references are given. Additional material is provided at points where the text of the fifth edition's 1819 version of *The Queen's Wake* differs significantly from the 1813 version. In revising his poem for the 1819 version, Hogg marked up a disbound set of the sheets printed for the third edition: see Introduction, pp. lxxi–lxxv, and the notes below. When an 1819 reading made its first appearance in either the second or third edition, this is also noted below.

192 (Portrait of Queen Mary) for Meiko O'Halloran's discussion of this portrait, see pp. lxxxix–xcv of the present edition.

193 (Titlepage) see note on **1 (Titlepage)**.

195 (Dedication) see note on **3 (Dedication)**. The dedication is undated in all the pre-1819 editions, but in the fifth and sixth editions 'ELTRIVE, *May* 1811' is added. No doubt this change was made in 1819 because Princess Charlotte had died in 1817. However, there appears to have been a muddle in implementing the change: May 1811 seems too early a date for the dedication of a poem first published in 1813, and Hogg did not receive the farm of Eltrive (aka Altrive Lake) until 1815. The Dedication is missing from NLS MS 20440.

Introduction

199, l. 8 *to* 210, ll. 445–46 for the 1819 Introduction, see also the notes on the 1813 version, at **7, l. 8 *to* 18, ll. 443–44** above.

206, ll. 269–70 These words [...] wo and misery these two lines were added in the fifth edition.

206, l. 274 the city's ample round changed in the fifth edition from 'the lands and city round'.

207, l. 308 Christmas week changed in the fifth edition from 'Easter week': see note on 15, l. 306.

207, l. 323 idle throng changed in the fifth edition from 'countless throng'. This alteration, like those recorded in the three previous notes, occurs in a part of the text now missing from NLS MS 20440.

211, l. 469 shrunk changed in the fifth edition from 'sunk': from Hogg's marking in NLS MS 20440.

Night the First

215, l. 20 for the 1819 opening linking narrative for Night the First, see also the note on the 1813 version, at **23, l. 20**, above.

Malcolm of Lorn

216, ll. 31, 46 *to* 222, l. 282 for the 1819 'Malcolm of Lorn' and the subsequent linking narrative, see also the notes on the 1813 version at **24, ll. 31, 46 *to* 30, l. 282**, above.

219, l. 149 virgin form changed in the fifth edition from 'lessening form': from NLS MS 20440.

220, l. 212 How still changed in the fifth edition from 'How glazed': from NLS MS 20440.

Young Kennedy

223, l. 293 *to* 233, l. 639 for the 1819 'Young Kennedy' and the subsequent linking narrative, see also the notes on the 1813 version at **31, l. 293 *to* 40, l. 617**, above.

226, ll. 417–18 these lines are re-cast in the fifth edition, by way of Hogg's markings in NLS MS 20440: cf. 34, ll. 417–18.

227, ll. 445–48 these lines are re-cast in the fifth edition, based on Hogg's changes in NLS MS 20440: cf. 35, ll. 445–48.

230–31, ll. 545–86 The fifth [...] curses dark and deep the fifth bard appears to be a portrait of John Morrison (1782–1853), a native of Kirkcudbrightshire in Galloway: see note on 38, l. 545. This description, already unfavourable in the earlier editions, becomes noticeably harsher in the fifth edition (following Hogg's revisions in NLS MS 20440). In part, this is because of the addition of lines 553–54 and 569–80. *1819* introduces revisions as well as additions, however: for example *1813* has 'With hollow voice, and harp well strung, | "Fair Margaret" was the song he sung' (ll. 557–58), but *1819* has 'With hollow voice, and harp ill strung, | Some bungling parody he sung' (ll. 559–60). It appears that Morrison objected aggressively to his portrait in the first edition, and in response Hogg made the description still harsher in the fifth edition. In a letter to Scott of 3 April 1813 Hogg writes: 'A gentleman who deems himself libelled at in the Wake has sent a long poem to Edin. to be printed *in quarto* which he denominates *The Hoggiad* or *A Supplement to the Queen's Wake* It is the most abusive thing I ever saw but has otherwise some merit' (NLS, MS 3884, fols 122–23). Unfortunately *The Hoggiad* (which sounds interesting) does not seem to have been published.

231, l. 570 "What good can come from Galloway?" an echo of John 1. 46: 'And Nathaniel said unto him, Can there any good thing come out of Nazareth?' Writing of Hogg's poem 'The Grousome Caryl', Peter Garside remarks: 'mock-derogatory comments against Galloway are something of a running joke in Hogg. Compare, e.g., "Tam Craik's Tale" in *The Three Perils of Man* (1822): "The only rational hope concerning it is, that, as it is a sort of butt-end of the creation, it will perhaps sink in the ocean, and mankind will be rid of it" (vol. II, p. 319)': see Hogg, *A Queer Book*, ed. by P. D. Garside, (S/SC, 1995), p. 247.

232–33, ll. 605–42 The eighth [...] mad unearthly song he sung various changes in the fifth edition (deriving from Hogg's markings in NLS MS 20440) convert the description of the eighth bard into a portrait of William Tennant (1784–1848), an identification confirmed by Hogg's annotated copy. These changes include the addition of *1819*'s ll. 611–18, and the conversion of the eighth bard from a 'wizard of the wild' (*1813*, l. 597) to a 'wizard of the shore' (*1819*, l. 619). Born lame, and noted for his good nature, Tennant found fame through his poem *Anster Fair* (1812), which is set in his birthplace, the Fife seaport of Anstruther. Later in life this largely self-taught man became Professor of Oriental Languages at the University of St Andrews.

The Witch of Fife

233, l. 666 *to* 246–47, ll. 1047–52 for 'The Witch of Fife' of 1819 and the subsequent linking narrative, see also the notes on the 1813 version at **41, l. 644 *to* 50–51, ll. 973–78**, above.

237 (Witch of Fife) for Meiko O'Halloran's discussion of this illustration, see pp. xcv–xcvii of the present edition.

242, l. 906–244, l. 966 following a suggestion from Scott, Hogg revised the ending to 'The Witch of Fife' for the third edition of *The Queen's Wake* (1814), and the revised ending was carried over into the fifth edition (1819): see the present edition's Introduction, pp. liii–liv, lxxi. In the original version, the old man is 'burnit [...] skin and bone', and the following two stanzas conclude the narrative by drawing a 'Tam o' Shanter'-like mock moral (*1813*, ll. 884–92). In the revised version, however, the old man's captors merely *prepare* to 'burn him skin and bone'; the sentiments of the next two stanzas are now put into the mouth of the old man himself; and 52 new lines of narrative are then added, to enable the old man to make his escape (*1819*, ll. 906–966).

Night the Second

251, ll. 24–28 *to* 252, l. 52 for the 1819 opening linking narrative for Night the Second, see also the notes on the 1813 version at **55, ll. 24–28 *to* 56, l. 52**, above.

251, l. 6 brooding storm substituted in the fifth edition for 'moving storm': from Hogg's marking in NLS MS 20440.

252–53, ll. 59–60, 67–80 these lines, added to the fifth edition by way of NLS MS 20440, convert the portrait of the ninth bard into a likeness of John Wilson (1785–1854), Professor of Moral Philosophy in the University of Edinburgh and the 'Christopher North' of *Blackwood's Edinburgh Magazine*. This identification is confirmed by Hogg's note in his annotated copy. Hogg's portrait of Wilson seems to have been softened at the proof stage: instead of the fifth edition's ll. 79–80, NLS MS 20440 has: 'But his affections were not true, | Nor friendship's holy ties he knew'. Wilson was remarkable for his athletic and sporting prowess, and for a certain grandiloquent emotional extravagance in his poetry: *The City of the Plague* (1816) does indeed focus on 'pestilence and charnel den', while *The Isle of Palms* (1812) is much concerned with voyages, shipwreck, and moonlight. Wilson was a Lowlander, originally from Paisley in the west of Scotland, but he had a house at Elleray in the Lake District ('Cumbria's dells').

Glen-Avin

253, l. 94 *to* 260, l. 318 for the 1819 'Glen-Avin' and the subsequent linking narrative, see also the notes on the 1813 version at **57, l. 78 *to* 63, l. 302**, above.

255, l. 143 seek my realms changed in the fifth edition from 'hold my realms': from Hogg's revision in NLS MS 20440.

256, l. 191 There passing changed in the fifth edition from 'And passing': from Hogg's revision in NLS MS 20440.

Old David

260, ll. 324–26 *to* 272, l. 795 for the 1819 'Old David' and the subsequent linking narrative, see the notes on the 1813 version at **63, ll. 308–10 *to* 76, l. 779**, above.

The Spectre's Cradle-Song

274, ll. 851–52 O weep not thou for thy mother's ill; | Hush, my bonny babe! hush, and be still! changed in the fifth edition from the single line 'Smile now, my bonny babe! smile on me!': from NLS MS 20440.

274, l. 856 Where scarce the roe her foot changed in the fifth edition from 'Where not the wren its foot': from NLS MS 20440.

The Fate of Macgregor

274, l. 873 *to* 278, l. 1022 for 'The Fate of Macgregor' of 1819 and the subsequent linking narrative, see also the notes on the 1813 version at **78, l. 856 *to* 82, l. 1003**, above. In 1813, the title of this song was simply 'Macgregor', but was changed in NLS MS 20440.

277, l. 968 dozed on changed in the fifth edition from 'dozed in': from NLS MS 20440.

278, ll. 1017–22 The Bard of Clyde [...] noble pedigree these lines were substantially re-cast in the fifth edition by way of NLS MS 20440 (cf. *1813*, ll. 1000–03) to produce a new portrait. Hogg's annotated copy identifies *1819*'s 'Bard of Clyde' as 'Capt Tom Hamilton', that is to say Thomas Hamilton (1789–1842), who was born and brought up in Glasgow, and who served as a Captain in an infantry regiment during the Peninsular War. Retiring on half pay about 1818, he quickly established himself as one of the leading writers of *Blackwood's Edinburgh Magazine*. His novel *The Youth and Manhood of Cyril Thornton* was published by Blackwood in 1827. The *DNB* records that Thomas Hamilton 'was the second son of William Hamilton (1758–1790) [q.v.], professor of anatomy and botany, Glasgow, and was younger brother of Sir William Hamilton (1788–1856) [q.v.], the metaphysician'. Thomas Hamilton's older brother established a claim to a baronetcy in 1816.

Earl Walter

279, l. 1031 *to* 287–88, ll. 1318–39 for the 1819 'Earl Walter' and the subsequent linking narrative, see also the notes on the 1813 version at **82, l. 1012 *to* 91, ll. 1299–320**, above. In the 1819 version, the Bard of Clyde is no longer the demotic figure of the earlier editions: see note on 82, l. 1003. In addition to the changes for the fifth edition, there were a few small changes to 'Earl Walter' in the third edition.

279, l. 1027 "It is his lot to fight changed in the fifth edition from '"Ah! he is fallen to fight' (*1813*, l. 1008): from Hogg's revision in NLS MS 20440.

279, l. 1054 I feared not single changed in the third edition from 'I feared no single' (*1813*, l. 1035). This change was carried forward to the fifth edition.

281, l. 1106 endless night changed in the third edition from 'starless night' (*1813*, l. 1087). This change was carried forward to the fifth edition.

282, ll. 1143–45 amid the throng, [...] restrain thy saucy tongue changed in the third edition from 'amid the rout, [...] beware thy saucy snout' (*1813*, ll. 1124–26). This change was carried forward to the fifth edition.

285, l. 1244 whiskered changed in the fifth edition from 'bearded' (*1813*, l. 1225): from Hogg's revision in NLS MS 20440.

285, l. 1252 pierced changed in the fifth edition from 'scooped' (*1813*, l. 1233): from Hogg's revision in NLS MS 20440.

286, l. 1274 all the lads I see changed in the third edition from 'any lad I see' (*1813*, l. 1255). This change was carried forward to the fifth edition.

286, l. 1287 and sore was flushed changed in the fifth edition from 'the princess flushed' (*1813*, l. 1268): from Hogg's revision in NLS MS 20440.

288, l. 1353 spirits whispered changed in the fifth edition from 'spirits whispering' (*1813*, l. 1334): from Hogg's revision in NLS MS 20440.

Kilmeny

288, l. 1367 *to* 298, l. 1763 for the 1819 'Kilmeny' and the subsequent linking narrative, see also the notes on the 1813 version at **92, l. 1348 *to* 101, l. 1712**, above. In the first edition 'Kilmeny' had appeared in Hogg's 'ancient style', but it is converted into modern literary Scots in the third and subsequent editions. In addition, some lines were added post-1813, while other lines were removed: see notes below.

292, ll. 1513–29 They bore her away [...] unmeet to know these lines were added in the third edition and carried forward to the fifth edition.

293, ll. 1550–61 Its fields were speckled [...] to that land did cleave these lines were added in the third edition and carried forward to the fifth edition.

293, ll. 1573–74 Her sovereign shield [...] all the fount within these lines appear in the third edition and are carried forward to the fifth edition. They replace ll. 1524–29 in the first edition:

> But ther cam ane leman out of the west,
> To woo the ledy that he luvit best;
> And he sent ane boy her herte to prove,
> And scho took him in, and scho callit him love;
> But quhan to her breist he gan to cling,
> Scho dreit the payne of the serpentis sting.

293, l. 1575 bedeman in the third and subsequent editions, this word replaces the first edition's 'gysart' (*1813*, l. 1530).

294, l. 1589 And weening his head was danger-preef in the third and subsequent editions, this line replaces the first edition's 'But the lyon grew straung, and dainger-prief' (*1813*, l. 1544).

294, ll. 1605–06 Till the cities [...] the lands and the seas these lines were added in the third edition, and were carried forward into the fifth edition.

295, ll. 1647–50 Such beauty [...] could never be seen these lines were added in the third edition, and were carried forward into the fifth edition.

295, l. 1654 twilight sea in the third and subsequent editions, this word replaces the first edition's 'silver' (*1813*, l. 1603).

296, l. 1673 And murmured and looked with anxious pain in the third and subsequent editions, this line replaces the first edition's 'And waulit about in ankshuse payne' (*1813*, l. 1622).

297, l. 1723 knights changed in the fifth edition from 'lords' (*1813*, l. 1672): from Hogg's revision in NLS MS 20440.

298, l. 1750 In Carlisle drank the changed in the fifth edition from 'Drank, unobserved, the' (*1813*, l. 1699): from NLS MS 20440.

Night the Third

301, l. 8 to 303, l. 94 for the 1819 opening linking narrative of Night the Third, see also the notes on the 1813 version at **104, l. 8 to 107, l. 94**, above.

301, l. 26 chains changed in the fifth edition from 'chained' (*1813*, l. 26): from Hogg's revision in NLS MS 20440.

Mary Scott

304, l. 130 to 326, l. 869 for the 1819 'Mary Scott' and the subsequent linking narrative, see also the notes on the 1813 version at **108, l. 130 to 129, l. 839**, above.

304, l. 134 voluptuous in the third and subsequent editions, this word replaces the first edition's 'alluring' (*1813*, l. 134).

308, l. 249 quavering in NLS MS 20440 Hogg sometimes (as here) restores an *1813* reading that had been lost in the third edition because of a printer's error. The third edition has 'quivering' at this point.

315, l. 493 born changed in the fifth edition from 'borne': from Hogg's revision in NLS MS 20440.

315, l. 509 just and meet changed in the fifth edition from 'just and right' (*1813*, l. 509): from Hogg's revision in NLS MS 20440.

315, l. 510 For in the third and subsequent editions, this word replaces the first edition's 'Far' (*1813*, l. 510).

321, ll. 700–703 His sword on bassenet [...] blades of steel these lines were added in the fifth edition: from Hogg's revision in NLS MS 20440.

321–22, ll. 708–35 Red Will of Thirlestane [...] unbecoming thing–but one in the fifth edition these lines replaced a single stanza that had appeared in the earlier editions: 'But Francis, Lord of Thirlestane, | To all the gallant name a soil, | While blood of kinsmen fell like rain, | Crept underneath a braken coil' (*1813*, ll. 704–07). On 8 March 1818 Hogg wrote about this revised passage to William John Napier (1786–1834), who had served as a Captain in the Royal Navy during the Napoleonic Wars, and who was the eldest son of Francis seventh Baron Napier. The Napier family owned land in Ettrick through their descent from the Scotts of Thirlestane, and in 1816 Captain Napier settled in Ettrick for some years, where he devoted himself to sheep-farming, road-building, and other rural affairs. Indeed, he wrote *A Treatise on Practical Store-Farming as Applicable to the Mountainous Region of Etterick Forest* (Edinburgh: Waugh and Innes, 1822). He succeeded as eighth Baron Napier in 1823 by the death of his father, and in 1824 resumed his naval career.

Hogg, whose earlier quarrel with Francis seventh Baron Napier is reflected in the 1813 version of the poem (see note on 125, ll. 704–07), was also in dispute with Captain Napier. According to James Russell's *Reminiscences of Yarrow* (Edinburgh: Blackwood, 1886), pp. 100–02, Lord Napier had right of property in the shore-lines of St Mary's Loch and the adjacent Loch of the Lowes, and Russell mentions an 'unwarranted attack by the Ettrick Shepherd, in the "Queen's Wake" on Lord Napier, for the removal of a boathouse erected without leave'. Russell goes on to record that Napier wrote on the margin of his copy of the poem: 'I suppose this is a return for my not acceding to his request that I would debar all others, and grant the proprietorship solely to him'. Another version of this dispute appears in the last part of Henry Scott Riddell's 'James Hogg, the Ettrick Shepherd', *Hogg's Weekly Instructor*, 21 August 1847, pp. 403–09 (p. 408): 'When the late Lord Napier destroyed from off the banks of St Mary the boat and boat house which Mr Ballantyne of Tinnis had put upon it, and which was ever free to Hogg and his friends, the poet and his lordship corresponded by letter on the subject, and the matter was somewhat made up; nevertheless, nine or ten verses were inserted in the ballad of Mary Scott [...]'. The dispute over the Boathouse seems to have taken place at some point between 1816 and early 1818. Although the two men came to be on friendly terms, this incident clearly continued to rankle on both sides, and in his *Songs by the Ettrick Shepherd* (Edinburgh: Blackwood; London, Cadell, 1831), p. 224 Hogg wrote: 'Lord Napier never did so cruel a thing, not even on the high seas, as the interdicting of me from sailing on that beloved lake, which if I have not rendered classical, has not been my blame. But the credit will be his own,– that is some comfort'. In his letter to Napier of 8 March 1818 Hogg writes:

> In revising the Queen's Wake for this new and splendid edition which Mr. Scott has set on foot I came to an odious reflection on some one of your ancestors which had quite escaped my memory. [...] Of course

the moment that my eye came on it I blotted it out, but in its place I could not refrain having a joke upon you for though I regard you as a most noble fellow I cannot help thinking there is something peculiar in your character. The verses at present run thus but as they will not go through the press for more than a month I have plenty of time to revise or alter them   (NLS, MS 786, fols 55–56)

Hogg's letter goes on to give a somewhat different version of what was eventually published as ll. 708–35 in the 1819 *Queen's Wake* (see the text of this letter in the forthcoming S/SC edition of Hogg's *Letters*, edited by Gillian Hughes). These lines, as they appear in the 1819 *Queen's Wake*, derive from Hogg's markings in NLS MS 20440. His revision of this passage is discussed in the present edition's Introduction, pp. lxxii–lxxiii. I am particularly grateful to Gillian Hughes for her assistance with this note.

326, ll. 858–59 O'er foot of maid [...] as he ran these lines were added in the fifth edition: from Hogg's revision in NLS MS 20440.

King Edward's Dream

327, l. 909 *to* 331, l. 1057 for the 1819 'King Edward's Dream' and the subsequent linking narrative, see also the notes on the 1813 version at **130, l. 879 *to* 134, l. 1027**, above.

329, l. 966 the fancy this reading was introduced by the third edition. The first edition, like *The Spy*, has 'his fancy' (*1813*, l. 936).

330, l. 1005 Eternal changed in the fifth edition from 'Everlasting' (*1813*, l. 975): from Hogg's revision in NLS MS 20440.

330, l. 1006 the power this reading was introduced by the third edition. The first edition, like *The Spy*, has 'the flower' (*1813*, l. 976).

Dumlanrig

332, l. 1095 *to* 347, l. 1648 for the 1819 'Dumlanrig' and the subsequent linking narrative, see also the notes on the 1813 version at **135, l. 1065 *to* 150, l. 1616**, above.

332, ll. 1084–85 Who's he that at [...] Hollas so loud, and changed in the fifth edition from 'Who's he stands at [...] Who raps so loud, and' (*1813*, ll. 1054–55): from Hogg's revision in NLS MS 20440.

335, ll. 1188–90 One pass [...] in that pass [...] Who crosses changed in the fifth edition from 'One ford [...] in that ford [...] Who passes' (*1813*, ll. 1158–60): from Hogg's revision in NLS MS 20440.

341, ll. 1425–26 "Here lies thy bravest knight in death; | Thy kinsmen strew the purple heath changed in the fifth edition from 'Here lies the kindest, bravest man; | There lie thy kinsmen, pale and wan' (*1813*, ll. 1395–96): from Hogg's revision in NLS MS 20440.

341, l. 1432 amid changed in the fifth edition from 'amidst' (*1813*, l. 1402): from Hogg's revision in NLS MS 20440.

342, ll. 1492–94 To Scotia's soil dispute her right, [...] boasts her name changed in the fifth edition from 'To Scotia's dust dispute our right, [...] boasts our name' (*1813*, ll. 1462–64): from Hogg's revision in NLS MS 20440.

343, l. 1501 flourished in the third and subsequent editions, this word replaces the first edition's 'flourish' (*1813*, l. 1471).

343, ll. 1531–34 The brave M'Turk of Stenhouse [...] ancient pedigree in the fifth edition these four lines replace 'M'Turk stood deep in Southron gore, | And legions down before him bore' (*1813*, ll. 1501–02): from Hogg's revision in NLS MS 20440. For 'Stenhouse', see note on 144, l. 1418.

The Abbot M'Kinnon

348, l. 1707 to 356, l. 1983 for 'The Abbot M'Kinnon' of 1819, see also the notes on the 1813 version at **151, l. 1675 to 159, l. 1951**, above.

351, l. 1801 with downward growl changed in the fifth edition (in response to Hogg's marking in NLS 20440) from the first edition's 'with gulp and with growl' (*1813*, l. 1769); the third edition has 'with gulph and with growl'.

352–53, ll. 1865–67 bring'st [...] bosom'd changed in the fifth edition from 'gatherest [...] bellied' (*1813*, ll. 1833–35): from Hogg's revision in NLS MS 20440.

Conclusion

361, l. 79 to 370, l. 371 for the 1819 Conclusion, see also the notes on the 1813 version at **165, l. 77 to 172, l. 369**, above.

359, l. 3 Long hast thou courteously in pain in the third and subsequent editions, this line replaces the first edition's 'Long has thy courteous heart in pain' (*1813*, l. 3).

360, ll. 60–61 No merits can [...] as at this day these lines were added in the fifth edition: from Hogg's revision in NLS MS 20440.

364 (Queen Mary's Harp) for Meiko O'Halloran's discussion of this illustrative plate, see pp. xcviii–c of the present edition.

365, l. 184 Ossian's warrior song changed in the fifth edition from 'Ossian's mounting song' (*1813*, l. 182): from Hogg's revision in NLS MS 20440. The third edition has 'Ossian's mountain song'.

369, l. 317 The ancient magic melody changed in the fifth edition from the first edition's 'The simple magic melody' (*1813*, l. 315): from Hogg's revision in NLS MS 20440.

369, ll. 336–39 O could the bard [...] That I should throw my harp away! Hogg re-cast these lines in the third edition, and the revised version was carried forward to the fifth and subsequent editions: see *1813* ll. 334–37, and the present edition's Introduction, pp. lvii–lix.

Hogg's Notes

375 to 388 for comment on Hogg's Notes, see also the notes on **177 to 190**, above.

377(b) This Frenchman has had no taste for Scotish music changed in the fifth edition (in response to Hogg's marking in NLS MS 20440) from the first edition's 'The Frenchman has had no taste for Scotish music'

384(b) he was surprised at receiving no answer the third edition substituted 'surprised' for 'astonished' here, and the change was carried forward to subsequent editions.

385(a) Her name was Jane Brown, she lived [...] may be relied on substituted in the fifth edition for 'Her name was Salton,–she lived to be the mother of a family': from Hogg's revision in NLS MS 20440.

385(c) and there is neither brake, hag, nor bush added in the fifth edition: from Hogg's revision in NLS MS 20440.

386(c) as Bonaparte did substituted in the fifth edition for 'as Bonaparte has done': a telling little reminder that the Napoleonic Wars were in full swing in 1813 when the first edition of *The Queen's Wake* was published, but were over when the fifth edition appeared in 1819.

387(d) the same engagement substituted in the fifth edition for 'the same engagements': from Hogg's revision in NLS MS 20440.

388(a) By the Temple of the ocean is meant the Isle of Staffa, and by its chancel the cave of Fingal added in the fifth edition: from Hogg's revision in NLS MS 20440.

388 Note XXIII this note was revised and extended in the second edition, and the changes were carried forward to subsequent editions.

388–90 Note XXIV [...] Note XXXIII in the second edition these Notes replaced the last four Notes of the first edition, and this change was carried forward to subsequent editions.

390(d) Grahame the Scottish poet John Grahame (1765–1811), best known for *The Sabbath* (1804) and *The Birds of Scotland* (1806). His writings exhibit a deeply-felt sympathy with the Covenanters. For a discussion by Hogg of Grahame's poetry see *The Spy*, ed. by Gillian Hughes (S/SC, 2000), pp. 44–46.

391–93 Note XXXIV in June 1813, George Goldie sought to build on the success of the first edition (January 1813) of *The Queen's Wake* by issuing a second edition which consisted of the remaining copies of the first edition, with replacement pages at the beginning and end (see the present edition's Introduction, pp. xlviii–l). The replacement pages contain new material, including an 'Advertisement' by Goldie, reprinted in the present edition's Appendix. This 'Advertisement' sets out to highlight the extraordinary fact that *The Queen's Wake* was the work of a largely self-taught former farm labourer, and it reinforces this point by introducing laudatory 'Stanzas Addressed to The Ettrick Shepherd on the publication of The Queen's Wake', a poem by the Suffolk poet and merchant Bernard Barton. An earlier version of Barton's poem had been published in the *Edinburgh Evening Courant* for 29 April 1813: for further information see the first volume of Gillian Hughes's forthcoming S/SC edition of Hogg's *Letters* (letters to Barton of 14 May and 7 June 1813, and editorial commentary). Goldie's 'Advertisement' and Barton's 'Stanzas' were retained in the third (1814) and fourth (1815) editions of Hogg's poem, but by 1818, when the fifth edition was being prepared, the moment of these documents of 1813 was felt to have passed. Hogg wrote to William Blackwood as follows on 12 October 1818:

> I do not like to throw out Mr Barton's verses altogether as he requested that they might be continued in every edition and I believe I promised in a letter that they should. They look however extremely clumsy as they are. How do you think it would do to give a short abstract of my literary life in the subscription edition and contrive to throw them into it? (NLS, MS 4003, fols 99–100)

In the event, Barton's 'Stanzas' were included in the fifth edition's Notes as Note XXXIV.

Glossary

The glossary is intended as a convenient guide to terms in *The Queen's Wake* that may be puzzling—for example because they are obsolete, because they are used in an unfamiliar way, or (as with *gazoon* and *wake*) because they are used in a way that is unique to Hogg. 'The Witch of Fife' and 'Kilmeny' are written in Hogg's 'ancient style'—a combination of archaism, English, and Scots—and this presents the reader with an added challenge. As a general guide words ending *is* are in the plural form; the letter *y* represents *i* or *e*; and words ending *it* represent the past-tense verb ending *ed*. Hogg glossed some of the 'Scotticisms' in the poem, and these words are listed below with a reference to Hogg's Note. Explanations of phrases, expressions, and idioms of more than one word may be found in the Editor's Notes. For further study of Hogg's use of Scots, see *The Concise Scots Dictionary*, ed. by Mairi Robinson (Aberdeen: Aberdeen University Press, 1985), and *The Scottish National Dictionary*, ed. by William Grant and David Murison, 10 vols (Edinburgh: Scottish National Dictionary Association, 1931–76). For discussions of Hogg's 'ancient style' see *A Queer Book*, ed. by P. D. Garside (S/SC, 1995), pp. xv–xvi, and P. D. Garside, 'Notes on Editing James Hogg's "Ringan and May"', *The Bibliotheck*, 16 (1989), 40–53. The present glossary is much indebted to *The Oxford English Dictionary*.

abash: to confound, disconcert

absolution: remission or forgiveness of sins declared by ecclesiastical authority

a-hight: on high

alack: exclamation of regret or surprise

alang: along

als: as

amain: vehemently, violently, at full speed

ane: a; one

anent: in respect of or with reference to; concerning

anethe: beneath

anis: once

ankshes: anxious

antes: an architectural term, concerning the angles or junction of walls

architrave: an architectural term, the lowest division of the entablature, consisting of the main beam that rests immediately upon the abacus on the capital of a column

arcubalister: a cross-bow-man

arles: money paid as a token of engagement of services

armlet: a piece of armour for the arm

arms: heraldic insignia

artless: natural; sincere, guileless

arychte: aright

aspin: the aspen tree; (fig.) quivering or shaking

assail: to assault, attack

attour: over

attuned: brought into musical accord; made harmonious

auld: old

ay, aye: continually, ever, always; yes

ayries: airy or of air; shadowy, insubstantial

bairnis: children

baitit: persecuted or harassed

baldrick: a richly ornamented

leather belt or girdle worn
pendent across the chest and
used to support a sword, bugle
etc.

ban: a formal ecclesiastical denuncia-
tion; to curse

bane: bone

banna, bannock unleavened bread
made from barley or pease
meal

bar: a tribunal

barbican: a loophole in the wall of a
castle through which missiles
might be discharged

bard: a minstrel-poet

bark: a small sailing vessel

basin: a dock

bastioned: fortified

bate: lessen in force or intensity; to
mitigate, diminish

bauld: bold

baulked: foiled, checked, thwarted

bayle: circuits of walls or defences
that surround the keep

be: are

beads: the rosary

bedeman: one who prays for the soul
or spiritual welfare of another

bedight: dress; arrayed

bedis-man: see *bedeman*

befel: fell out in the course of events,
happened

behest: an injunction, command; a
vow or promise

bein: been

beire: to carry; to take along as a
companion

bele-fire: a roaring fire; a bonfire

bell: the cry of a stag or buck at
rutting time

belled: cried (of a stag or buck at
rutting time)

bellied: made large and full; blown
or puffed out

ben: see Hogg's Note XXIX, p. 390

benighted: overtaken by darkness
before reaching one's final
destination

benignant: gracious; kindly manner

beryl: a transparent precious stone
of a yellowish green colour

beshrew: to invoke a curse on

bespoke, bespeak: indicated, the
outward expression of

beth(e): both

betide: to happen

bewail: to lament loudly

bier: a movable stand on which a
corpse is placed before burial;
sepulchre, tomb

birchen: made of birch wood

bittern: a large stocky bird of the
heron family

bizerd: [buzzard], a large bird of prey
of the falcon family

black-cock: the male of the black
grouse

blads: fragments; pieces

bland: pleasing to the senses;
soothing; (of persons) gentle;
unstimulating

blasted: blighted

bleeter: the snipe, known for its
distinctive bleating sound in
flight

bleme: blame

blench: [archaic form of blanch]
become pale

blenched: avoided, shirked; flinched
from

blent: mingled

blight: a malignant influence; to
wither hopes or prospects

bloated: withered, dried up

blow: to bloom

blude: blood

blue heron: the night heron (now
rare)

boardly: burly

boil: a state of agitation

boom: a beam; a long wooden spar
that extends a sail on a sailing
vessel

boon: well, good; a request; a favour
or gift

bootless: unprofitable, useless

boots: advantage, good, profit

booty: spoil or plunder taken in war or by force

borit: made holes, bored through

bosky: covered with bushes or under-wood

boun': to prepare, make ready

bourn: [burn] a small stream

bower: a place closed over with branches of trees or plants; a shady recess

brace: a pair, two

brae: a steep slope; a hillside

brainzelled, brainzelit: created a commotion

brak: broke out

brake: the bracken or fern; a clump of bushes or brushwood; broke out, started up

brake-flowers: the spore-bearing fronds of the *osmunda* or royal fern have a flower-like appearance; general term for wild flowers, or wild roses

braken: see *brake*

braken coil: see *coil*

brand: a sword, weapon

braw: fine, splendid

brawny: muscular

bray: a loud cry; shriek

brazen: brass

breek-nee: the knee of the breeches leg

brek: to break

brethe: breath

breviary: the book containing the 'Divine Office' of the Roman Catholic church that is recited daily by those in office

breviate: the daily portion to be read in the breviary

briar: a prickly thorn bush; a wild rose bush

brier: see *briar*

bristled: tightly formed; stood shoulder to shoulder

broad sword: a cutting sword with a broad blade

brochte: brought

broidered: ornamented with needle-work, often inlaid with precious gems

broil: to contend in a confused struggle or irregular fight

brooked: endured, tolerated; found agreeable

broom-wood blossom: a shrub (*Sarothamnus or Cytisus Scoparious*) bearing large yellow flowers

brume-cow: a branch of broom

brydel: a bridle

buchtis, bughts: sheepfolds

bulwarks: defenders

bunde: to bind

burgess: a magistrate, or member of civic governing body

burn: a brook, stream

buskin: a shoe or half boot

buskined: lofty

byrk: the birch tree

byson: a species of wild ox

cairn: a pile of stones raised as a memorial stone or marker; (fig.) mountain top (see Hogg's Note VIII, pp. 181, 379)

cam: came

canker: spite; malignancy

canting: using affected language

cantrips: a spell or charm of necromancy or witchcraft; a witch's trick

capparisoned: decked, ornamented

capperkayle: (capercaillie) the wood grouse

carle: a man; a man of the common people, (Scots) a fellow, especially one possessing the qualities of sturdiness or strength

casemate: an embrazure, see below

casement: a casement window; the window frame

casque: a piece of armour to cover the head; a helmet

cauld: cold

caulm: calm

celestial: of a heavenly nature

certes: certain

chaffed: vexed, angered, disturbed

chair: a light vehicle drawn by one horse; a chaise

chalmer: a chamber

chancel: a temple

chaperoon: a kind of hood or hooded cloak

charnel: a burial place or cemetery

chaunt: to chant

chaunted: played musical pipes

cherub: (fig.) a beautiful and innocent child or young woman

chief, chieftain: the head of a clan or feudal community

clan: a family or group bearing a common name united under a chief

claught: seized with claws; struck a heavy blow

claymore: a two-edged broad-sword

clough: a narrow valley or glen

cloyed: gratified beyond desire; satiated

cloyless: that which cannot cloy

clown: a rustic or peasant; without refinement or culture; ill-bred

cludis: the clouds

coif: a close-fitting skull cap of iron or steel worn under the helmet; generally, a skull-cap

coil: a haycock

collifloure: a cauliflower

comyshonit: commissioned

comit: came

con: to study or learn by repetition; to commit to memory

cone: (fig.) a mountain top

coned: began

confession: acknowledgement of sin or sinfulness

confest: revealed, open to recognition

coomb: see Hogg's Note XXIV, pp. 388–89

corby craw: the raven

cords: the rigging of a sailing ship

coronal: relating to a crown or coronation

correi: see Hogg's Note XXXII, p. 390

corse: a corpse

corslet: a tight-fitting garment for the body; a piece of defensive body armour

cot: a cottage

cote: a coat

counterfeit: to pretend; to feign

countermure: the outer wall of defences

countervail: compensate

courser: a swift horse; a stallion

courtisye: 'courtesy', Scots legal term for the liferent conferred on a widower from his dead wife's property

cour: to cower

courying: [coursing] racing

covert: a hiding place; a place that gives shelter to wild animals or game; a thicket

cowl: a hooded garment worn by monks

craigy: craggy; steep or rugged

cramasye: crimson; crimson cloth

cramps: skates

creed: summary of the Christian doctrine; confession of faith

crennel: a battlement

crew: a large gathering

croon: a loud, bell-like deep sound; to make such a sound

crouse: merry; spirited

cruik-shell: a hook for suspending a pot, etc, over a fire

crunit: see *croon*

cuche: a sofa

cuirass: body-armour comprised of a back plate and breast plate buckled together

culd(e): could

culdna: could not

cuneal: wedge-shaped

curfew: the ringing of a bell as a signal to extinguish all fires and lights

curlew: a very large wading bird with

long down-curved bill, the upperparts are brownish-grey

curvetting: leaping or frisking

dainger-prief: [danger-proof] invincible

dale: see Hogg's Note XXX, p. 390

dang: knocked, struck with heavy blows

dapple: a horse with a mottled coat

darnit, darned: threaded in and out; to move in a zig-zag motion

dastard: a coward

dead-lights: phosphorescence seen hovering over an unburied corpse or in graveyards

death-flame: a dead-light

dee: to die

degree: rank or station

deid-bell: a bell tolled at death; a passing bell

deide: death

deil: the devil

deine: a cave; a narrow valley, usually covered with trees; also a dell

dell: a deep, natural hollow or vale covered with trees or foliage

den: see *deine*

dern: dark, sombre, solitary, desolate; hidden, concealed

despoiler: one who strips another of their possessions by violence

dike: a ditch; a boundary wall of stones or turf

din: a disturbance; a loud noise

dirk: a Highlander's dagger

dochte: unable, unwilling

doff: take off a piece of clothing

doublet: a close-fitting body garment worn by men; body armour

douffe: dull

doughty: valiant, brave, stout

doune: down

dounright: right or straight down

dower: dowry

drap: to drop

dreide: to dread

dreit: dreaded

dressing: preparing

dree: to endure, suffer

driche: severe

drumbly: muddled, confused

dulcet: pleasing to hear; gentle, soothing

dun: a dull or dingy brown colour; a hill; to beat, to thump

dune: down

duntin: falling heavily; thudding

dye: colour or hue

dyne: down

e'e: the eye

ee-bree: the eyebrow

eident: assiduous; conscientious

eiris: years

eithly : easily

elate: raised

eldrich: weird, ghostly, unearthly

elyit, elyed: [*ely,* to disappear] vanished gradually

emblazoned: beautifully adorned

embrazure: architectural term, a slanting or bevelling of the sides of an opening to a wall for a window or door, so that the inside profile of the window is larger than that of the outside

emerant: emerald (fig.)

ene: the eyes

entablature: architectural term, part above the column, including the architrave, the frieze and the cornice

erilis: see *arles*

ern, erne: the eagle

erste: formerly; at first

essayed: tried, attempted

este: a nest

everilke: every

ewe-bught: a small inner sheepfold for milking ewes

extirpated: rendered extinct; destroyed utterly

fa': to fall

faem: foam

fahm: a small, mole-like animal (see Hogg's Note VI, pp. 180, 378)

fain: glad; happy

falcon: small bird of prey

faldis: [folds] enclosures for penning cattle or sheep

fane: [archaic form of fain] pleasure; a temple

faulchion: a curved broad sword

fauld: fold

faulds: see *faldis*

fa(u)nd: found

fay: a fairy

fece: the face

feire: to fear

fell: strong

femenitye: femininity

fere: a companion; a dwarf

ferit: afraid

ferment: to agitate, stir up

fervid: intensely passionate

festoon: an architectural carving or moulding in the form of a chain or garland of flowers, leaves, etc.

filmot: the colour of a dead or faded leaf

fire flauchtis: flashes of lightning

firth: a wide inlet of the sea, an estuary

fit: foot

flank: the extreme left or right side of an army

flee: to fly

flichtering: flying awkwardly

flightered: flickered, glimmered

films: layers

flowret, floweret: a small flower

fluffit: fluttered, flapped

flurred: flew up

foemen: enemies in war, adversaries

foin: to thrust at with a pointed weapon

foke: folk

fold: see *faldis*

foray: a hostile raid

forehooit, forhooyed: abandoned

fowler: a hunter of wild birds or game for sport or food

fra(e): from

frame: the body; disposition or countenance

framit: framed; made

framed: see *framit*

franethe: from below or underneath

fraudful: treacherous

fray: an attack, a skirmish

fre: free

freak, freakish: a trick; capricious humour or whim

freebooter: one who goes about in search of plunder

freenge: a fringe

froward: perverse, ungovernable, self-willed

furth: forth; outside, out of doors

gaed: went

Gael: a Highlander

gainder: a gander

gan: began

gane: gone

ganza: a diving bird

gar, garris: to cause or make something be done

garb: official or distinctive dress

gare: that part of the body close to which is the gusset of a shirt

gat: got

gaudy: gay, dashing

gaung: go

gazoon: a tightly formed wedge-shaped body of men

gear: equipment; possessions, property, money

gecked, geckit: a gesture of derision; mocked, derided

gede: went

gene: gone

genii: demons or spirits of good or evil intent in human affairs

genius: inherent ability; having intelligence

gin: if

girdle: a belt; (fig.) the waist

girnit: screwed up (the face) or gnashed (the teeth) in rage or disapproval

glair: Scots form of glare

gledgin: leering

gleide: a spark, glimmer of fire or light

glen: see Hogg's Note XXVII, p. 389

gloffis: frights; shivering or shuddering from shock

glomyn: [gloaming] evening twilight, dusk

gossamer: a fine filmy substance, made from cobwebs, that is seen floating in the air in calm weather

goss-hawk: a large, short-winged hawk

gor-cock(is): the red grouse cock

gouden: golden

goul: to yell or cry bitterly or threateningly

govit, goved: wandered aimlessly

gowl, gowled: see *goul*

graved: engraved

gray: old, ancient

greensward: grassland; pasture

greide: greed

greine: green

greite: [greet] to cry, weep, lament

grew: a greyhound

gude: good

gudeman: the head of the household

guerdon: to give as a reward; a recompense

guid: good

guile: cunning, deceit, treachery

guise: behaviour, conduct

gurly: surly, cross, ill-humoured

gysart: a factious, hot-headed man (from 'Guise', a faction in 16th-century France)

habergeon: a sleeveless coat or jacket of mail or armour

hackneys: horses of middle size for ordinary riding

hags, haggs: ill-tempered, violent women; dirty, slovenly women

haide: hid

haif: have

hale: to violently draw or pull

halesome: wholesome, sound, healthful

happit: covered, surrounded, enfolded

haps: shortened form of *happenings*, events

hauberk: a long coat made of chain mail

haulers: (fig.) oarsmen

haum: the stems or stocks of various plants left after harvesting, used for thatching

havock: destructive devastation

hawberk: see *hauberk*

heath-cock: the black grouse cock

heide: the head

heir: hear

helm: a helmet

helsome: see *halesome*

heme: a home

heritable: capable of being inherited

herkit: harkened, or listened to

herkit, herked: urged on with encouraging cries

hern: a heron

herte: heart

hesil: hazel

hest: vow; bidding, command

hevis: heaves

hie: to hasten, to go quickly

hind, hinde, hynde: a farm hand; a female of the red deer

hindberrye: a wild raspberry

hoar frost: frost that covers objects with white

hoary: ancient; (of people) having white or grey hair

holeday: holiday, holy day

hollands: clothing made from coarse linen cloth

holm: a stretch of low-lying land by a river

holt: a wood; a copse

homilies: preaching
hoolet: the owl
houf: a favourite haunt or resting-place; shelter
humlo(c)ke: the common hemlock plant, such as cow parsley
hundit: hounded; driven out with dogs or by violence
huntyd: hunted
hurlit: thrown together
hyndberrye: see *hindberrye*

ilk: every
ill: evil, wicked; badly
ingil: fire on an open hearth
intil: into
ir: are
i' the: in the

jocund: mirthful, merry, cheerful
joup: a woman's bodice, jacket or gown

keep: the central tower of a medieval castle, the last and strongest defence
kelpie: a water demon
kembit, kemed: combed
ken: know; have knowledge or understanding
kendna: negative form of ken
kerlyngs: witches; women
keryl: see *carle*
kirk: a church; in pre-Reformation Scotland, refers to the Roman Catholic Church
kirtles: garments to protect the clothes such as a cloak, or outer petticoat
knave: a servant, a menial
korbye: a raven; a corbie crow
kress-flour: a flower of the cress plant
kythis, kyth: shows one or itself

laibies: the flaps or skirt of a man's coat
lambent: a flame that plays lightly upon or glides over a surface without heating or burning it; shining with a soft clear light and without fierce heat
lang: long
lanthorn: archaic form of lantern, often made from horn
latent: hidden, concealed; present but not exhibited
lauche: to laugh; laughter
lauchit: laughed
laup: leaped
lave: to wash against, to flow along or past
laving: washing
law: see Hogg's Note XXVI, p. 389
lawn: fine linen, resembling cambric
lay: short lyric or narrative poem intended to be sung
layman: a man who is not a cleric
lea: grass land; meadow
leaven: alter by modifying or tempering
lee: wine sediment; the last drop; to tell lies; the leeward side, away from the wind; see also *lea*
leet-night: appointed or nominated night
leif: a leaf
leifu: full of love, lovely; chaste
leil(e): loyal, faithful
leman: lover or sweetheart; paramour; unlawful mistress or illicit lover
leme: [loom] the indistinct appearance of something seen through a haze or at great distance; a haze or fog
lene: alone, solitary
lened, lenit: sojourned, remained
lepit: lapped
lete: late
leurit: [leveret] a young hare
leviathan: a real or imaginary aquatic animal of enormous size
levin: lightning; any bright light or flame
levis: leaves

ley: archaic form of lea
lickit: thrashed, chastised
liege: the superior to whom one owes feudal allegiance or service
liftis: the sky's
lightit: alighted
lille: lily
lineage: ancestry
links: a stretch of open undulating sandy ground, often near the sea shore
linn: a waterfall; precipice or ravine
list: give ear; be attentive
littand: staining
loathly: repulsively, with loathing; hideous, horrible
lokks: locks
lone: loan, common pastureland, or green
lore: religious doctrine; a body of knowledge; (poetically) that which is spoken
lothly: see *loathly*
lowe: a flame, the reddest part of a fire
lowit: glowed; lowed
lowner: became calm; calmly
lownly: softly, quietly
lubric: smooth; unsteady, unsettled
lufe, luife: love
lum: chimney
lute: a stringed musical instrument struck with the fingers
lychte: light
lynkit: swift
lynn: see *linn*
lyre: a harp-like stringed instrument
lythlye: lightly
lychtid: alighted, dismounted

mae: more
maen: to moan
maike: an image; a form, resemblance
mail: armour made of chain-mail
maives: [mavis] the song thrush
margin: (fig.) a beach or shore
marled: streaked

martin: a bird of the swallow family
mass: the celebration of the Eucharist; the rite or form of liturgy used in the (pre-Reformation) celebration of the Eucharist
massy: solid and weighty
matins: morning prayers
maun, mene: must
mayre: more
mazed: wound or circled around in a winding motion
mead: poetic form of meadow
meed: reward or recompense
mendicant: a beggar
mene: to moan; see also *maun*
merk: a sum of money equal to two thirds of a pound
merkist: dark, gloomy, murky, darkest
merl: a blackbird or merlin (a small falcon)
merlit: see *marled*
mes: see *mass*
met: may
mettled: full of mettle, natural spirit, vigour
mien: carriage or manner of a person, expressive of character or mood
milky: effeminate, weakly amiable
minny: affectionate name for a mother
minstrelsy: minstrel poetry
mirk: see *merkist*
mistone: discord
mocht: might
modish: according to the mode or prevailing fashion; fashionable
moe: poetic form of more
moldwarp: the mole
mony: many
moony: moon-shaped
moor-flame: will o' the wisp
moorfowl: the red grouse

mootit: almost soundless, whispering
morel: a morello cherry
morion: black smoky quartz

moss-gray: (fig.) ancient

moss-rose: a garden variety of the cabbage rose

moss-trooper: a border freebooter; marauder; border cattle reaver (thief)

motley: a cloth of mixed colour, a mixture

mould: the form or shape of a person's body; pattern, model

mouldering: crumbling into fragments; decaying

mountain ash: the aspen

muckil: a great deal, much

muir: a moor

munt: to mount

murk: twilight

muthe: the mouth

mynde: to recollect, remember

nae: no

naigis: [nags] small riding horses

naked: unembodied (ghostly)

ne: no

neal-fire: annealed, toughened with fire

needlit: moved like a needle rapidly through, or in and out

neicherit, nichering: sniggered, sniggering

neist: next

nocht: not

norlan: northern

nouther, nowther: neither

nurice: nourish

nytt: a nut

oblation: an offering of thanks

obsequies: funeral rites or ceremonies

obsequious: dutiful, obedient

onset: to set upon, attack, assault

orient: a region of the heavens where the sun and other heavenly bodies rise

orisons: prayers; harangue, oral address

ouf: the wolf

ouir: our; over

oundit: wounded

owlet: the owl

owr: our; over

palfreys: saddle-horses for ladies

pall: a beam; a cloth of black, purple, or white velvet, spread over a coffin or tomb

palmer: a pilgrim or itinerant monk who travelled from shrine to shrine, under a vow of perpetual poverty; a pilgrim

palsied: paralysed; trembling

pang: tightly packed or formed

panoply: a complete suit of armour worn by a soldier of ancient or medieval times

partridge: a game bird

pat: put

peeled: with bark removed

pelt: keep hammering or striking

pen: shortened form of sheep-pen

pendent: hanging or floating

pennons: the long pointed streamers of a ship; pennants

pie: poetic variant of magpie

pile: a small castle, tower, or stronghold; a peel on the Scottish Border; a large mass

pinion: wings as of a bird

pit-fall: the opening to the underworld place of evil spirits and lost souls; hell, or some part of it

plaid: a rectangular length of coarse woollen cloth, often worn as an outer garment (often in tartan); a shawl

plover: a bird of the lapwing family (*Charadriidae*)

plume: an ornament symbolising dignity, consisting of a large bunch of feathers usually of a black colour in funeral processions

ply: to strive

poesy: poetry

pole: the north or south pole; the pole star

portentous: foreboding

portmanteaus: cases or bags for carrying clothing and other items when travelling

post: at great speed

prickit: pierced

proffer: a proposal; to offer or present oneself

progenitor: an ancestor, forefather

proscribed, proscription: published or posted the name of a person as condemned; denounced as dangerous

proxy: act as a substitute

ptarmigan: a mountain-dwelling grouse, it has red markings around the eye socket

pu: to pull

puir: poor

pungent: (fig.) keenly painful or distressing

purfle: a decorative border

purgatory: a place or state in which souls after death are purified from venial sins

pye-duck: a duck with pied or different coloured plumage

quha: who

quha(i)re, quhair: where

quhairever: wherever

quhan: when

quhase: whose

quhat: what

quhen: when

quhile, quhill: until

quhite: white

quoif: see *coif*

raide: rode

raik, raike: to journey, stroll, rove; to wander through; to make one's way

rail: a mantle or cloak

rampart: a defensive mound

rank: diseased

rapier: a long pointed, two-edged sword

rapine: acts of violent robbery or pillage

rase: rose [up]

rayed: encircled

reave: to commit plunder, robbery or pillage; to carry off (persons)

reaver: a robber or plunderer

rebeck: a medieval three-stringed instrument, an early form of fiddle

recked: cared, heeded, regarded

reed: a reed made into a musical pipe

reft: past participle of reave; to take

refulgence: radiance

reide: red

reide-pipe: a reed-pipe

reike: smoke from a chimney

relume: to rekindle, re-light

remede: redress

rent: torn, split

requiem: a special mass, said or sung for the dead

richt: right

rill: a stream, a rivulet

rime: hoar-frost; a frosty haze or mist

rin: to run

rock-weed: sea weed

rode: a track, a path

roe: a small species of deer

roegrass: pasture-land

roke: a rookery

rood: the cross (as a symbol of Christianity)

rosary: a string of beads carried on the person and used to assist the memory in the recital of a series of prayers

rout: see the note on 50, l. 957 in the Editor's Notes

runde: round

rune: a Scandinavian letter or character having mysterious or magical powers attributed to it

runic: (of poetry) belonging to ancient Scandinavia or the north

russet: reddish-brown colour
ruth: mischief, calamity, ruin

sair(e): sore
sallies: suddenly starts into activity
saloon: a large and lofty apartment
  used as the principal reception
  room in a great house or palace
saut: salt
schaw: see Hogg's Note XXV on
  shaw, p. 389
scheine: sheen
schene: scene
scho: she
sconce: a screen or shelter (of stone
  or wood) for concealment or
  defence
scourying: scurrying
se: so
sea-baize: [archaic] a fine cloth or
  covering of a greenish colour
seam: a woman's sewing or needle-
  work
sea-mew: the common gull
sea-rue: shrub of the genus *Ruta*
seer: one to whom divine revelations
  are made in visions
sen: since
seraph: an angel of the highest of the
  nine orders; serene or blissful
sere: withered
serried: in close order
sey: attempt (something difficult)
seymar: a robe or loose light gar-
  ment for women; an undergar-
  ment, chemise
shaw: see *schaw*
sheeted: wrapped in a sheet, or
  winding-sheet (of the dead and
  ghosts); (fig.) spread out like a
  sheet
sherpe: sharp
shill: shrill
shiel: a shepherd's summer hut; a
  small house or shelter
shoris: shores
shouir: shore; a shower of rain
shrift: to shrive, to make one's

confession
shroud: a covering, protection
shulde: should
siche: to sigh
simmer: summer
skiff: a small sea-going boat
skinkers: drinkers
slack: a hollow, often between hills
sleik: smooth; gloss
sloe: the blackthorn
sluggard: one who is lazy, a sloth
snawis: snows
snood, snoode: a ribbon for tying the
  hair, worn by young unmarried
  women as a sign of virginity
sochte: sought
solan: a gannet, a large white sea
  bird with black-tipped wings
sooth: truth
soofit: [souched] whizzed or whirred
  through the air
soupit: swept
sousit: fell down heavily
southern: a Lowlander
specious: lacking in sincerity
speer: ask questions, inquire
speil: to climb: clamber up
speire: see *speer*
spectre: a phantom or ghost of
  terrifying nature
spoilers: plunderers, robbers, those
  who pillage
spright, sprite: a supernatural being;
  goblin, fairy, etc.
staff: a walking stick
stane: a stone
stayless: ceaseless
steed: a stallion; a spirited horse
sternis: the stars
stern-shot: a shooting star
strand: the coast, shore; landing
  place by the side of navigable
  water
strone: see Hogg's Note XVIII,
  p. 389
sunde: sound
suthe: south
suthit: soothed

swain: a shepherd
swait: swayed; held dominion over
swaipin: sweeping
swale: swell
sweit: to sweat
swerde: sward
swinked, swinkit: struggled hard or
    intensely
sylvan: that which belongs to or
    pertains to the wood

taen: taken
taper: (of persons) slender; a light
target: a shield
tarn: a small mountain lake having
    no significant tributaries
tartaned: dressed in tartan
teal: the smallest European freshwa-
    ter duck
than: then
thilke: those; these
throstle-coke: a male song-thrush
throw: through
thrystle-cock: a male song-thrush
thunner: thunder
till: to
tilted: encountered or combated
tirravies: fits of rage or bad temper;
    tantrums
tithe: pay a levy or tax amounting to
    one tenth of the annual income
tither: the other one
tod: a fox
tovit: rose in the air, spiralled
    upwards; moved at speed
towe: a cord made from flax or
    hemp fibres
transport: to carry away with
    strength of emotion; to put in
    ecstasy
troths: truths
trow: to believe, to think, to sup-
    pose, to imagine
tuzzlit: pulled or knocked about,
    handled roughly (especially of
    women); dishevelled
tyme: time

umbered: stained dark brown
unblest: miserable, wretched
unmelit: [unmelled] virginal; pure
unshriven: unconfessed
unstaid: unsettled
unweened: unnoticed, unheeded

vaile: a valley
van: the foremost division of a
    military force when advancing
    into battle
vassal: in the feudal system, one
    who holds land from a superior
    under condition of allegiance; a
    subordinate, subject
vaunts: boasting; bragging
veixion: a vision
ventrous: adventurous
verdant: a green hue or colour;
    green with vegetation
vermilion: a bright red or scarlet
    colour
vernal: of spring-time
vesper: evening prayers or devo-
    tions; evensong
vertu: virtue
vewless: invisible
viewless: see *vewless*
visor: the front part of a helmet
vitals: the internal energy, or guiding
    spirit necessary to maintain life

wa: a wall
wae: sad
waif: to wave
waike: a walk; a pasture for cattle
wain: [constellation of] the plough
wained: carried or conveyed in a
    carriage or such like
wake, Wake: a serenade, or nocturnal
    song (see Hogg's Note I,
    pp. 177, 375); a vigil
wald: would
wale: see Hogg's Note, XXXI,
    p. 390
walsna: was not
wan: dismal; fearful; pallid; (won)
    reached, gained

wane: to decrease; dwindle

wanfurlit: unfurled

war, ware: were

ward: to guard, to defend, to protect (from)

warder: a soldier or other set to guard an entrance, watchman on a tower

ware: were

wareless: unwary, incautious, imprudent

warlock: a male witch; an evil person

warse: worse

warst-faurd: ugliest

wassail: spiced wine; revelling; carol singing; carousing

watchet: the colour of light blue

watch-lights: night-lights; lights carried by a watch-man

wauffyng: flapping, waving in the air

waulit: rolled the eyes wildly

wawlyng: see *waulit*

wedows: widows

weeded: carried off, removed by death

ween: think, surmise, suppose; to expect, anticipate

wefu: woeful

weil: well

weir: war

weird: strange, uncanny

wekit, wekinit: wakened

welkin: the arch or vault of heaven; the sky; the firmament

wemyng: women

wene: a dwelling-place; habitation: see also *wane*

werde: word

wesoum: full of woe

weste: the waist

westlin: western

wezilis: weasels

whilk: which

whinyards: short swords

wi': with

wight: a person

wilna: will not

wind-flower: the wood anemone

wind-harp: the Eolian (of the wind) harp, a Romantic symbol of poetic inspiration

wires: metallic strings

wist: past tense of 'wit', to know

witching: enchanting

wold: a piece of open country, or rolling uplands

wold-fire: see *dead lights*; will o' the wisp

womyne: a woman; women

won: to dwell, to live

wont: the habit of doing something

wraith: an apparition of a living person usually taken as an omen of death; a ghost, the apparition of a dead person

wrocht: wrought

wroth: stirred to wrath, made angry

wud: a wood

wycht: see *wight*

yeomen: faithful attendants, usually of a superior rank

yer: your

yerkit: bound tightly; beat, whipped, struck

yew-bow: a bow made from the heavy, elastic wood of the yew tree, the twigs are regarded as emblems of grief

yirth: the earth; of the world

ylis: isles

yond: that, those

yorline: the yellowhammer

younkers: children, youngsters

yudith: a youth

zephyr: a soft, mild gentle westerly wind or breeze

zones: encircling bands, belts, or stripes of colour; girdles